CHIN P'ING MEI

CHIN P'ING MEI

The Adventurous History of
Hsi Men and his Six Wives

With an Introduction by Arthur Waley

A PERIGEE BOOK

Perigee Books
are published by
G. P. Putnam's Sons
200 Madison Avenue
New York, New York 10016

Library of Congress Cataloging in Publication Data

Hsiao-hsiao-sheng.
Chin P'ing Mei.

Translation of: Chin P'ing Mei tz'u hua.
Attributed to Hsiao-hsiao-sheng. Cf. The classic
Chinese novel / C.T. Hsia. 1968.
Reprint. Originally published: New York: G. P. Putnam's Sons, 1940
I. Miall, Bernard, 1876-   . II. Title.
PL2698.H730513   1982   895.1'34   82-5261
ISBN 0-399-50657-8   AACR2

First Perigee printing, 1982

PRINTED IN THE UNITED STATES OF AMERICA

CONTENTS

v

vii

INTRODUCTION: *The Legend of the* "*Chin P'ing Mei*"

THE following, pieced together from various sources, is the legend of how the *Chin P'ing Mei* came to be written: in the middle of the sixteenth century A.D. a humble official named Wang Yü happened to be the owner of a very important picture,[1] the *Going Up River* by Chang Tse-tuan of the Sung dynasty. It was important not only as a work of art but also as a historical document, for it portrayed the splendors of K'ai-feng Fu, the Northern Sung capital, previous to its destruction in A.D. 1127 by the Kin Tartars. The picture was coveted by a wicked and tyrannical official named Yen Sung,[2] who made every effort to secure it. For a long time Wang Yü held out; but the wicked Yen Sung having finally become all-powerful in the Government was able to threaten Wang with the complete ruin of himself and his family, and at last Wang saw no alternative but to consent.

To show off his new acquisition Yen Sung gave a banquet to which he invited the celebrated statesman and writer Tang Shun-chih.[3] To his host's astonishment the distinguished guest showed very little interest in the picture, and when pressed for an opinion, declared that it was a copy. That a person of literary and political eminence could be mistaken on a point of connoisseurship was, according to the ideas of the day, out of the question. Henceforward Yen Sung's only thought was how he could best revenge himself on Wang Yü, who, he felt certain, had kept the original picture, sending in its place a worthless copy. Yen had not long to wait for his opportunity. In 1550 the Tartar chieftain Amda broke through the defenses of the Chihli frontier at a point for the protection of which

[1] See *Notes*, page xx

ix

Wang Yü was responsible. Yen impeached him, and Wang Yü was executed.

This, however, was only the beginning of a vendetta. Yen Sung died in 1568. But meanwhile Wang Yü's son Wang Shih-cheng [4] had begun to make his mark as a man of great literary attainments and determined character. His one regret was that the death of Yen Sung had deprived him of the chance of directly avenging his father's impeachment. But Yen Sung's son, Yen Shih-fan, execrated in Chinese legend as the paragon of treachery and corruption, had been partly responsible for the impeachment of Wang Yü, and it was against Yen Shih-fan that the vendetta of the Wang family was now directed. Many are the stories of Yen's miraculous escapes from the assassins whom the filial Wang Shih-cheng hired to avenge his father's death. But Yen was strongly and ingeniously guarded; as indeed he needed to be, for he had many hereditary enemies. Famous among Yen's means of self-protection was a writing-brush which when held near the lamp (as though to trim the hairs) emitted a deadly projectile.

One day at a public occasion of some kind Yen Shih-fan and Wang Shih-cheng found themselves standing side by side. "Are you writing anything now?" Yen asked him, in order to make conversation. In reality he took no interest in the Confucian studies of Wang Shih-cheng, but was known to be an avid reader of love stories. Suddenly a plan came into Wang Shih-cheng's head. Close to where they were standing was a metal vase, with a spray of plum-blossom in it. "Yes," he answered. "I have just finished a novel called *Chin P'ing Mei (Metal Vase Plum-blossom)*."

Wang Shih-cheng went home and casting about for a subject found in the twenty-second chapter of the famous novel *Shui Hu Chuan* a starting-point for the book to the production of which he was now committed.

Wang Shih-cheng was a great Confucian scholar, and consequently (according to popular belief in China) there was no literary feat of which he was not capable. In a few weeks he had written the *Chin P'ing Mei,* a novel of some 1,600 pages, weaving into it (in the portrayal of Hsi Men Ch'ing, the hero of the book) a pitiless satire on the private life of his enemy Yen Shih-fan. That Hsi Men Ch'ing stood for Yen Shih-fan was a fact that no one could fail to recognize. For Hsi-men means Western Gate and Shi-fan's other name was Tung-lou, which means Eastern Tower. Moreover (so the legend asserts) Shih-fan's "nursery-name" was Ch'ing.

But Wang Shih-cheng was not content merely to hurt his enemy's feelings. At the corner of each page he rubbed in a grain or two of deadly poison. The paper on which Chinese books were at that time written was very thin. The pages were apt to stick together, and the reader would generally wet a finger in his mouth in order to turn over rapidly without tearing the page.

The book arrived, with Wang's compliments. The poison worked slowly enough to let Yen read to the last page the story of his own degraded existence. Then he fell dead.

When Yen was lying in state, a mysterious stranger, enveloped in a huge cloak, arrived at the house, saying that he had once been an intimate friend of the deceased and wished to see the corpse before the coffin was sealed. He was admitted, and left alone in the room. For some minutes a noise of bitter wailing, sufficient to convince the household of the mourner's genuine distress, proceeded from the closed room. Then with bowed head and the great cloak wrapped about him, the stranger hurried from the house. When, however, the workmen came to seal up the coffin, they found that the corpse had been mutilated; the right arm had been severed and removed. The mysterious stranger was, of course, Wang Shih-cheng who, not content with merely causing his enemy's death, felt that his duty was not done till he had added to murder the final outrage of mutilation.

Such is the popular legend concerning the authorship and intention of the *Chin P'ing Mei.*

I will now turn to what we actually know from contemporary evidence about the origin and early history of the book.

The Facts about the "Chin P'ing Mei"

Till a few years ago mystery surrounded the date and authorship of all the more important early Chinese novels. Tradition placed the *Romance of the Three Kingdoms* and the *Hsi Yu Chi (Travels to the West)* in the thirteenth century. The great bandit story *Shui Hu Chuan* was placed in the fourteenth or fifteenth century. Thanks to the researches of scholars such as Hu Shih and Lu Hsün, we now know that the *Romance of the Three Kingdoms* did not reach its present form till the seventeenth century. The *Travels to the West* was written by Wu Ch'eng-en, who died in 1582. The *Shui Hu Chuan* reached a form approximating to its present one about 1500; the text we usually read is some sixty years later.

In each case the facts turned out to be very different from the current tradition. I have just recounted the popular legend concerning the origin of the *Chin P'ing Mei*. What are the facts? Unfortunately this book has not been subjected to the same sort of scientific inquiry as has elucidated the origin of the other important novels. A certain amount of material has indeed been collected; but no effort has been made to sift it. I can only here offer a very imperfect and fragmentary attempt to fill this gap.

The first mention of the book is by Yüan Hung-tao, who lived from 1568 to 1610. In his *Rules for Wine-drinkers,*[5] composed about 1595-1600, Hung gives a list of books that should be studied by the Complete Drinker. Among novels, he should on no account neglect the *Shui Hu Chuan* and the *Chin P'ing Mei*. A drinker who has not these at his fingers' ends is a mere soaker and no true drinking companion.

The next reference is in the *Ku Ch'ü Tsa Yen*[6] of Shen Te-fu, who lived from 1578 to 1642. "Yüan Hung-tao," says Shen Te-fu, "in his *Rules for Drinkers* ranks the *Chin P'ing Mei* with the *Shui Hu Chuan,* regarding them both as unacknowledged classics. This made me regret that I had never seen it. In the year Ping Wu [1606] I met Yüan Hung-tao in the Capital [Peking] and asked him whether he had ever seen a complete copy. He said he had seen several chapters, which had surprised and delighted him; but that the only complete copy now in existence was owned by Li Yen-po of Ma-ch'eng,[7] also known as Liu Ch'eng-hsi. Liu's copy had been obtained through his wife, whose relative Hsü Wen-cheng[8] had allowed a copy to be made.

"Three years later when [Yüan Hung-tao's younger brother] Hsiao-hsiu came up to the Capital for his examinations[9] he was carrying this book in his own hand. He lent it me to have it copied, and I was able to bring it back [to Soochow]. My Soochow friend Feng Yu-lung[10] was astonished and delighted by the book. He egged me on to sell it to a printer, pointing out that I should get a big price. And Ma Chung-lang, who at the time had a position in the Customs Service at Soochow, also tried to persuade me that if I were willing to let a printer have the work, I need never again be short of cash.

"I replied that a book of this kind was bound to get printed in the end. Indeed once it was published it would have so huge a circulation as definitely to lower the moral tone of the community. It would be awkward for me if when I came at last before the Tribunal of Yama, King of Death, he were to ask whether I had any hand in starting this general downfall. It would prove a poor bargain if, as a result of my share in the work, I found myself cast into the pits of Hell.

"Ma Chung-lang could only agree with me, and in consequence I locked the book safely away.

"But not long afterwards [the book was printed and] the whole of Soochow was littered with it. But the copy from which the printer worked lacked chapters LIII to LVII. They were looked for everywhere, but could not be found, and in the end they were supplied by the ingenuity of a hack. Unfortunately his style was of the roughest and clumsiest, and at times he even introduced expressions in Soochow dialect. Thus the continuity of the work was destroyed and the thread of the narrative completely interrupted. A single glance is sufficient to show that these chapters are not genuine.[11]

"It is said that the book was written by a well-known scholar of the Chia-ching period [1522-66], and that it contains lampoons on contemporary characters. Thus Ts'ai Ching and his son are said to be Yen Sung and Yen Shih-fan; Liu Ling-so is T'ao Chung-wen; Chu Mien is Lu Ping, and so on. I was also told by Yüan Hung-tao. . . ." The passage then discusses a sequel to the *Chin P'ing Mei,* called *Yü Chiao Li,* which is, however, quite a different work from the one familiar to European readers in Julien's translation.

As regards the supposed attacks on real persons, it may be said at once that the later legend which regards Hsi Men Ch'ing, the hero of the book, as the character through whom some contemporary person was satirized has much more to be said for it than the theory here put forward by Shen Te-fu. Ts'ai Ching, Lin Ling-so, and Chu Mien play an extremely small part in the book, and though, true to their character in Chinese historical legend, they figure as villains, they are portrayed in so generalized and summary a way and are so seldom mentioned, that they can scarcely have been intended as vehicles for personal satire. We see that, as author of the book, Shen Te-fu mentions "a well-known scholar of the Chia Ching period." By far the best-known scholar of the period was Wang Shih-cheng; and just as in our own Middle Ages "a well-known wizard" will certainly turn sooner or later into Merlin himself, or "a famous captain" into Alexander, so this "well-known scholar" was exceedingly likely to turn into Wang Shih-cheng.

The "Chin P'ing Mei" and the Censorship

We have seen that the first printed edition of the book was made at Soochow a little after 1609. At that time there was no legislation against "licentious fiction," under which heading the book came subsequently to be regarded. The Ming Code contains no injunction against such fiction, chiefly no doubt because until well into the Ming dynasty fiction had not advanced beyond a very elementary stage. But Confucianism was, especially since the Sung dynasty, a Puritanical and ascetic creed, teaching that man's only spiritual concern should be the restoration of his Natural State *(hsing-ming),* the primal beauty of which is marred by every stirring of the appetites or emotions. Now Confucianism, with whatever impatience it may at various periods have been regarded at Court, was always during the period in question the official creed of the bureaucracy; and the fact that at the time when the *Chin P'ing Mei* was written and for a hundred years afterwards licentious novels were permitted, does not mean that the Government during this period took a lenient view of this sort of fiction or indeed of fiction in general. It merely means that during the close of the Ming dynasty.the popular development of the novel was too new a thing to attract the attention of the Government.

When the Manchus conquered China in the middle of the seventeenth century the Government had its hands full in censuring patriotic, anti-Manchu literature. Some recent authors speak of an edict against indecent literature in 1652. Personally I can find no trace of it, and am inclined to think that legislation against "baleful words" *(yao-yen,* pretended omens foretelling the fall of the dynasty, and the like) has been mistaken for legislation against love stories. But in 1687 a certain Liu K'ai in a "mixed petition" demanded among other things that improper novels should be forbidden. The demand was accorded and an edict issued *(Ta Ch'ing Sheng Hsün* XXV, f. 22 recto): "It is certain that licentious novels are likely to have a bad effect on my people, depraving their morals and poisoning their minds. It must likewise be mentioned that demonic teaching by Buddhist and Taoist priests has also an unsettling and pernicious effect. . . . Both [i.e., immoral novels and "black-magic"] should be rigidly suppressed."

So far as I know, no copy of the first edition (c.1610) of the *Chin P'ing Mei* survives; an edition with preface dated 1617 was discovered some years ago, and has been reprinted in a limited edition.

But the *Chin P'ing Mei* was one of the three or four most popular novels. The world was unwilling to exist without it. In 1695 a Soochow publisher reprinted the work, providing it with an elaborate series of preliminaries and a marginal gloss the object of which was to prove that the book is to be regarded as a monument of China's most admired virtue—Filial Piety, its composition having been the means by which a dutiful son compassed the death of his father's murderer.

A preface was provided in which a person using the pseudonym Hsieh I (that this is not a real name is made clear in the preface itself) suggests that the work is either by Wang Shih-cheng or was written (at his instigation) by a pupil. In the preliminaries by "Chang Ch'u-p'o" (this too is no doubt a pseudonym) as well as in the marginal glosses, particularly in the last chapter, the book is held up to admiration as a work of pious vendetta. All this assumes the existence of the legend I have related above, and it seems then that this legend grew up during the course of the seventeenth century. Presently I will consider what probability there is that the novel emanated either from Wang Shih-cheng or from someone in his milieu. For the moment it will be convenient to trace a little further the history of the book itself.

Despite the Emperor K'ang Hsi's edict of 1687 the *Chin P'ing Mei* continued to be read and admired. In 1708 it was translated into Manchu. There is even a legend [12] that the translation was made by a brother of the Emperor whose edict we have cited. In 1753, however, the translation of novels into Manchu was entirely forbidden,[13] the Emperor Ch'ien Lung considering that the young Manchu nobility was better employed in studying history and the Confucian Classics.

Meanwhile, as regards the general public, the attitude of the Government became more and more severe. In 1725 a special clause [14] was added to the Code of the Manchu dynasty in which obscene fiction was again forbidden, very heavy penalties being incurred by those (whether author, publisher or bookseller) who infringed the clause. Officials were to be degraded; military men to receive a hundred lashes of the bastinado and be banished three thousand leagues. Booksellers were to receive a hundred lashes and be exiled for three years. People merely caught buying or reading such works were to receive a hundred lashes, without exile.

This law remained in force till the fall of the Manchu dynasty in 1912.

Europeans have often spoken as though there existed in China something equivalent to the Roman Catholic Index. This is not accurate. But since very early times (certainly from the sixth century onwards) there was a strict political and religious censorship. This must always have necessitated the circulation among magistrates, and later (when these came into existence) among booksellers, of lists of condemned works. This was certainly the case with apocryphal Buddhist literature, and many of these lists still survive. The book censorship during the Manchu dynasty was principally directed against Irredentist (i.e., anti-Manchu) literature, and lists were circulated to booksellers and magistrates in connection with this restriction. In the second half of the eighteenth century a grand quest for anti-dynastic literature was inaugurated, the results of which were embodied in a series of catalogues.[15] The last of these (1789) also contains a list of "indecent" books; but to say, as Western writers have done, that the *Chin P'ing Mei* was "placed on the Index" soon after its (i.e., the *Chin P'ing Mei's*) appearance, is doubly misleading, for at the time when it was written there was no law against love literature and for two hundred years afterwards nothing resembling an Index.

The result of the Edict of 1687 and the law of 1725 was that henceforward the book was sold surreptitiously. Subsequent editions continued to bear the date 1695 and the imprint of the Crane in the Swamp Hall. Possessors of copies with this imprint must therefore not jump to the conclusion that they have the original 1695 edition. In some cases the typography of such copies makes it clear that they are not older than the nineteenth century. Of these copies with the date 1695 some are illustrated, some are not. It has not been ascertained whether the illustrated edition is the earlier.

The Milieu which produced the "Chin P'ing Mei"

The literary world in the second half of the sixteenth century was divided into two camps. The traditionalist party, headed by Wang Shih-cheng, maintained that nothing worthy of serious attention had been written since the middle of the eighth century. For the more popular forms of literature, the *Tz'u* (Songs without Music) of the Sung dynasty, the *Ch'ü* (Dramatic Lyrics) of the Mongol period, and for the colloquial novels of their day they showed no understanding. Their opponents, who are often called the Kung-an School, from the name of the place where Yüan Hung-tao was born, believed on the other hand that literature must maintain a connection with real life. Hung-tao belongs to a slightly later period than Wang Shih-cheng. The writer who may be taken as the leader of this "actual" school at the end of the sixteenth century is Hsü Wei (1520-93), who was not only an important political figure, but is also known as the author of several popular plays—*Yü-yang Lung, Ts'ui-hsiang Meng, Tz'u Mu-lan,* etc. Now we have already seen that at the beginning of the seventeenth century the only discoverable complete manuscript of the *Chin P'ing Mei* was procured from the Hsü family. This is a fact worth remembering. We have seen, too, that at the beginning of its career the book was regarded as the work of a "well known scholar of the Chia-ching period." Such a description is quite applicable to Hsü Wei. Another important figure in the same group was Feng Meng-lung (See p. xx), who besides editing and arranging popular stories, compiled and edited an anthology of plays, including several by himself. He also rewrote the old novel *P'ing Yao Chuan* ("Subdual of the Imps"). These men founded—if one may give it a Japanese name—a sort of Ukiyo ("Fleeting World") school of literature, which as its instrument did not disdain the living speech, and for its subject matter went to popular legend or everyday life. On the other hand, the school of the Wang Shih-cheng condemned their performances as trivial and undignified, and would neither read nor write anything that had not a direct bearing on the Classics.

Of possible candidates for the authorship of the *Chin P'ing Mei* I personally regard Hsü Wei as the strongest. It would certainly be worth while comparing the lyrics in his plays with the poems scattered about through the *Chin P'ing Mei* and seeing whether there are any correspondences. But this is a task which I must leave to specialists in later Chinese literature.

ARTHUR WALEY

Editor's Note:

Although the authorship of *Chin P'ing Mei* was long a matter of uncertainty—and it was still unclear at the time this introduction was originally written—C. T. Hsia, in his 1968 work *The Classic Chinese Novel,* showed to the satisfaction of most scholars that it was in fact written by Hsiao-hsiao-sheng.

NOTES TO THE INTRODUCTION

1. See Waley, *Burlington Magazine*, XXX, 1.

2. For Yen Sung as the stock villain of Chinese historical legend see the *Shên Hsiao Hsia*, which is No. 13 in the collection *Chin Ku Ch'i Kuan*.

3. 1506–60.

4. 1526–90 (We know from Wang Shih-cheng's tomb inscription that the "1593" of the Ming History is a mistake).

5. *Shang-chêng*, literally "Goblet Rules," ch. XIX, f. 6. verso, of his complete Works as published in 1829.

6. The existing *Yeh Huo Pien* has a preface dated 1606. But it contains a good deal of matter added later. The passage in question *(Yeh Huo Pien*, XXV, 35 recto) seems to have been taken from another work of Shên Te-fu, the Theatrical Miscellany *(Ku Ch'ü Tsa Yen)*, to which I have not had access. I translate the passage from the text given in the *Hsiao Shuo K'ao Chêng* of Chiang Jui-tsao (English title, Historical Study of Chinese novels, Commercial Press, Shanghai, 1919), as being obviously freer from error than the text of the *Yeh Huo Pien*.

7. In the province of Hupeh.

8. Probably a younger brother of Hsü Wên-ch'ang, i.e., Hsü Wei, 1520–93.

9. According to the Ming Shih (288, f. 3 verso) he passed his Local Examinations in 1603 and his Metropolitan Examinations in 1586. As the Local Examinations came first, one or the other of these dates must be a misprint. Metropolitan Examinations were held, so far as I can make out, in 1607, 1610, 1613. Those of 1610 must be the ones here referred to.

10. Also known as Feng Meng-lung, Lung-yu Tzu, and Mo-han-chai ("Ink-crazy Studio"). See Waley, *T'oung Pao, 1932*.

11. The difference has not, however, been noticed by European readers. None of the more obvious and striking characteristics of Soochow

dialect occur. Whether there is indeed any trace at all of Soochow influence in these chapters native philologians must decide.

12. Berthold Laufer, *Skizze der Manjurischen Literatur* (Keleti Szemle, "Revue Orientale pour les Etudes Ouralo-altaiques," Vol. IX, 1908, p. 32) has shown that the attribution of the translation to K'ang Hsi's brother is a mere piece of gossip. Wylie in his *Notes on Chinese Literature* (p. 202-3) repeats the attribution as though it were an ascertained fact, and other European writers have followed him.

13. See Chêng Chên-to, *Chung Kuo Wen Hsüeh Yen Chiu,* Chronological Tables.

14. See *Huang Ch'ao Chêng Tien Lei Ts'uan,* Ch. 390, f. 10 recto, and G. T. Staunton *Ta Tsing Leu Lee* (1810), p. 549. The *Hsiao Shuo K'ao Chêng Shih-i* mentions measures against improper fiction taken in 1652, 1709, 1714, 1736, etc. Concerning these I know nothing further.

15. Such as the *Wei Ai Shu Mu,* compiled by Imperial Order in 1779. There is what appears to be a copy of this in the British Museum, printed in 1782. Two more lists, the *Hsiao Hui Shu Mu* and the *Ch'ou Hui Shu Mu* were compiled in 1781. Finally in 1789 a general list of forbidden books *(Chin Shu Ts'ung Mu)* was compiled. It contains the names of about 150 works condemned on grounds of impropriety; among them the *Chin P'ing Mei.* The blocks of the *Wei Ai Shu Mu* were destroyed in a building set fire to by European troops at Canton in 1860.

NOTE ON LI YÜ AND LU NAN

Some editions of the *Chin P'ing Mei* have on the cover of the first fascicule the statement that the author of the book is Li Yü, dramatist, novelist, story-writer, and editor (in 1679) of the *Mustard Seed Garden Drawing Book*. He lived from about 1620 to 1690. Li Yü is considered by the Chinese to be a very disreputable person. One of his plays deals with sapphism, another with sodomy, and a third (the *Na Ho T'ien*) contains a lampoon on the personal appearance of the head of the K'ung family, 65th descendant of Confucius. He is just the sort of person who might (if he was still alive in 1695, which is uncertain) have had a hand in the reprinting of the *Chin P'ing Mei*. For translations from the work of Li Yü see Imbault-Huart, *Journal Asiatique,* VIIIe Sér., Vol. XV (1890), pp. 483-92. and Sir John Davis, *Contes Chinois,* pp. 51-106. The *Mustard Seed Garden* has been translated by R. Petrucci under the title *Encylopédie de la Peinture Chinoise*.

The preface to the Manchu translation (f. 3) suggests that the author of the *Chin P'ing Mei* may be a certain "scholar of Ming times" called Lu Nan ("Reed" and "Cedar"). The first character is occasionally, though rarely, found as a surname. If on the other hand the two characters form a "pen-name" (Lu-nan) it is one of very unusual formation.

CHIN P'ING MEI

VOLUME I

What is man, and what is power?
All things pass away.
The flutes are sprung, the harps unstrung,
The songs of old are long unsung.
They had their day.

What are glory and loveliness?
All things pass away.
The shattered lute falls to the floor,
The star of love is bright no more.
They had their day.

Now the jade terraces are still.
The autumn mists are drifting chill.
Cold and casual the moonlight falls
Into the long-deserted halls.
Those that loved and revelled must
Long ago have fallen to dust.

CHAPTER ONE: *In the Gladness of his Heart Hsi Men forms the Company of Ten. Wu Sung meets his Brother's Wife with cool Reserve*

Oʊʀ TALE is of what befell under the Sung dynasty, in the era of the Emperor Hui Tsung: in that epoch which bears the name of Chong Ho, "the Harmonious Reign." In that time there lived in Shantung, in the district of Tsing ho hsien, which belongs to the prefecture of Tung ping Fu, a young rake by the name of Hsi Men. This comely and jovial fellow, whose years were thirty, was amply blessed with strings of a thousand cash. His late father had formerly carried on a prosperous trade in drugs and medicaments in the provinces of Sze-ch'uen and Kwang-tung, which abound in herbs, and more recently he had possessed a large apothecary's shop in the market-town of Tsing ho hsien. There were five rooms in the front of his house, which was seven rooms deep; his household contained a multitude of servants; his stables were well filled with horses and mules. Hsi Men could therefore count himself, if not among the very wealthy and distinguished members of society, at least among the more affluent inhabitants of the district.

Pampered and spoiled from his early childhood, Hsi Men had early become accustomed to a dissolute mode of life, and he abhorred all book-learning. After the death of his parents, he devoted much of his time to "riding the waves of pleasure, caressed by the moon and the winds, spending his nights among blossoms and willows." Boxing and fencing, cards and dice, chess and the solving of riddles were his only accomplishments. A band of nine wild, smooth-tongued, useless fellows kept him company in his debaucheries. Of the nine Hsi Men was most intimate with Ying Po Kui. This Ying, a bankrupt silk merchant, now eked out a living by supplying the women's apartments of the local mandarins with fresh commodities. He was commonly known among the townsfolk as "Beggar Ying," and was something of an authority on chess, football, and dicing.

Another of Hsi Men's comrades was a certain Hsia Hsi Ta, the grandson of a former governor of the city. After the early death of his parents he had plunged into a life of disorder, destroying every prospect of an official career. An accomplished lutanist, he enjoyed a favored position in the circle of Hsi Men's intimates.

The other seven were Chu Shih Nien, Sun Tien Hua, Yuen Li Shou, Chang Shih Kia, Pu Chi Tao, Pai Lai Kwang, and Wu Tien En. The last named had once been District Surveyor for a term, and on being relieved of this post he busied himself as middleman and surety in the financial affairs of the local officials. In this capacity he had come into contact with the wealthy Hsi Men, who often appeared as money lender in such transactions.

These nine were able to profit greatly by Hsi Men's generous nature and his fortune, encouraging him on every occasion to pass his nights in tippling, gambling, and whoring.

> *Where the cups go gaily round*
> *A brother's vows are lightly taken.*
> *When the storms are raging loud*
> *Brotherhood will prove unshaken.*

In business affairs, Hsi Men displayed considerable acumen and ability. Not only were the officials of the district in his debt, but his influence extended to the sphere of a certain group of corrupt court officials, who are known to history as "the Four Exalted State Criminals." They were, of course, the omnipotent Chancellor Tsai Ching, the Marshal Yang Kien, and the two Lord High Eunuchs Kao Sui and Tung Kwan. It was thus no wonder that Hsi Men was regarded with the greatest respect throughout the district, for he had a finger in all the community's affairs, and a decision often turned on his word or recommendation.

In his first marriage Hsi Men had begotten one daughter, who

4

was betrothed, but as yet unmarried. His first wife had died, and he had recently wedded Moon Maiden, the twenty-five-year-old daughter of the Left Governor Wu of Tsing ho hsien. Moon Maiden, or rather Moon Lady, as she was called after her marriage, now held the rank of First Wife. Hers was a kindly and intelligent nature, and as far as outward appearance went she cleverly adapted herself to her husband's character, though this was fundamentally different from her own.

Other members of the household were two secondary wives, Li Kiao, and the thin, delicate Cho Tiu, former favorites of the flower-garden; and among the maidservants there were three or four pretty little creatures to whom Hsi Men occasionally granted his favors. But as though these were not enough his inordinate desires often drove him abroad "to rage with the winds and play with the moon-beams," and seduce the wives and daughters of other men.

> *With his neighbors east and west*
> *Gayly he tippled, richly fared!*
> *Gaudy peony, flower of the peach,*
> *Never a one was spared!*

"On the third day of the next month I celebrate with my nine friends our customary annual meeting. Make the necessary arrangements in good time, so that we may pass the day here feasting as befits the occasion. And engage a few singing girls," he said one day.

"I wish you wouldn't ask me to meet such a rabble!" replied Moon Lady, sulkily. "I ask you, are they human beings? This infernal crew of demons, released from the underworld to snap up the spirits of the departed here on earth—do you really mean to entertain them in our respectable house? You ought to have some regard for your Third Wife, who has not been at all well lately!"

"Dear Moon Lady, readily as I agree with you as a rule, in this case I cannot! Your unfavorable judgment of my friends may, as far as I'm concerned, hold good for the other seven, but please except Ying and Hsia. They are two capital fellows, absolutely de-

5

pendable. Moreover, this time I am planning something special for our meeting. Just coming together like this and then breaking up again isn't really worth while. No; this time we shall swear a solemn oath of brotherhood, whereby each will always find a firm support in the others."

"That sounds very pretty. My only fear is that the others will actually seek and obtain your support, but if the circumstances were ever reversed they would be of as little use to you as so many lifeless puppets."

"All the better for me, if I am always in a position to help the others," Hsi Men replied with a smile. "However, let that pass; I shall discuss further details with my friend Ying."

No sooner had he uttered the name than: "Uncle Ying and Uncle Hsia!" were announced by the little chamber boy, Tai A, a smart young fellow with bright eyes and finely-marked eyebrows. Hsi Men hastened to welcome the two visitors in the reception hall. Ying was wearing a somewhat disreputable quilted overcoat of sky-blue silk, but his black crêpe bonnet seemed to be fresh from the press, and his shoes and hose were immaculate.

"Where have you two been lately?"

"Oh, yesterday we paid a visit to Aunt Li, and we were admiring your Second Wife's little niece, whom we had not seen for a long time. I say, how the little girl has come on! She's going to be a regular beauty one day! Her mother urged us over and over again to look out for a handsome young husband when the time comes to deflower her. She is afraid that her daughter too might become your prey!"

"Is that so! Well, I must go and see for myself one of these days! And where else have you been?"

"Well, the day before we offered our condolences to the widow of our late lamented friend Pu Chi Tao, on the occasion of the funeral rites. She wishes us to thank you on her behalf for your funeral gifts. She is ashamed to invite you to her miserable poverty-stricken house to take part in the sacrifices to the dead."

"Yes, who would have thought that the poor fellow would come

6

to so sudden an end! Only a little while ago he presented me with a genuine gold-painted Sze-ch'uen fan, and I was just going to make him a gift in return. But now that he is dead—my gift must be paper spirit money!"

"All we can do now is to fill the gap he has left, so that we shall still be Ten," Hsia replied with a sigh. "Especially since we celebrate our annual reunion in a few days' time. For this occasion, I suppose we may count on your well-known hospitality, brother Hsi Men?"

"I have just been discussing it with my wife. This time, I have thought of something special. Tell me yourselves, has this coming together and breaking up again, this drinking and carousing, any real value? I propose that this time we hold our reunion in a temple, and that there, making a solemn invocation to the gods, we swear a formal oath of brotherhood, undertaking to give each other mutual aid as long as we live. I, of course, will buy the three victims for the sacrifice. The rest of you can contribute something toward the expenses, each according to his means. What do you think of my proposal?"

"Undoubtedly, a personal prayer to Buddha is of greater value than incense burned by one's widow. We must do what we can to co-operate!" said Ying, briskly. "But, please, do not for one moment forget that, in comparison with you, we others are only miserable rat-tails whose pitiful ulcers give damned little juice."

"You crazy dog, who would expect anything of you?" retorted Hsi Men, with a laugh.

"Your idea is excellent," Hsia admitted, with a bow. "But whom shall we choose to replace Pu Chi Tao? Our brotherhood must not be incomplete."

Hsi Men gave a meditative sniff, and suggested: "How about young Hua, the nephew of Lord High Eunuch Hua? Our family estates directly adjoin each other. When he goes walking in his garden, a thin wall is all that separates us. What is more, he has an open hand. I have often met him; I have only to send him a message, and he will come."

"Do you mean Hua Tze Hsu who visits little Wu Yi so regularly?" Ying asked excitedly.

"That is the man."

"Well then, tell him to come immediately. We shall be able to get many a fine feast out of him."

"You old beggar! Must you always be thinking of food? You'll die of a stoppage one of these days!" Hsi Men scolded him as the others burst into laughter.

He then called his boy, little Tai, and sent him with a message to his neighbor's estate.

"Where is this celebration on the third going to take place?" Ying inquired. "Here, or at a temple?"

"We have our choice between a Buddhist or a Taoist temple," Hsia replied. "Yung Fu Se, the Temple of Endless Prosperity, or Yu Huang Miao, the Jade Emperor's Temple; both are worth considering."

"Our league hasn't, properly speaking, anything to do with Buddhism," Hsi Men decided. "Besides, I am not acquainted with the head bonze of Yung Fu Se. On the other hand, the High Priest Wu in Yu Huang Miao is well known to me. I propose the roomy and more out-of-the-way Taoist temple."

"Wait a moment—the truth is that the bonze is not so much an acquaintance of yours, but a very close acquaintance of friend Hsia's wife," said Ying, teasingly. "For that reason I propose the Yung Fu Se."

"Must you always interrupt us with your rubbish, you dolt, when others are trying to talk sense?" retorted Hsia, with a smile.

Their conversation was interrupted by the entrance of little Tai.

"The honorable Hua was not at home," he told his master. "I delivered my message to his wife. She did not seem particularly pleased, but she sends you her greetings, and says that her husband cannot very well refuse your honored proposal, and that she will not fail to tell him to appear punctually on the third of next month. Then she gave me two tea cakes to eat on the way."

"A nice sensible woman," Hsi Men murmured complacently.

After drinking another cup of tea, the two visitors rose. "We shall notify the other six," they promised as they left, "and we shall collect the contributions; and you, Brother Hsi Men, will doubtless make all further arrangements with the priest Wu?"

"I will!"

"And be sure to have a few singing-girls there!"

"It shall be done!"

And amid laughter and jesting, the visitors took their leave.

On the morning of the first day of the following month, while Hsi Men was loitering in the apartment of his First Wife, a youthful messenger arrived from the neighboring house, bringing a gift of a beautifully polished, gold-lacquered box.

"My master," he said, "sends you many greetings, and regrets that he had just gone out the other day when you sent word to him, so that he could not receive your message personally. He will come punctually on the third, and sends you for the present an insignificant contribution. He would be obliged if, later, you would give him an account of his share of the expenses, so that he can make up the difference."

Hsi Men accepted the box. On the red strip of paper wrapped about it he read the words: "Enclosed one ounce of silver as contribution toward expenses."

"That's enough," he said. "Your master need make no further contribution. Just ask him not to make any other plans for the day after tomorrow, and to meet me here in good time."

"And convey my salutations to his wife," added Moon Lady. "I hope to see her here in a few days; I am looking forward to a good long talk with her."

She motioned to the maidservant, Jade Flute, to give the boy two hot pancakes. The messenger kowtowed and trotted off. Hardly was he gone when a second messenger arrived. This one came from Ying, and he, too, carried a gift box in his hand.

"On behalf of my master, I bring the total contributions."

Hsi Men glanced at the contents of the box—eight small parcels —and handed them over to his wife. Then he dismissed the mes-

9

senger and went in to his Third Wife. No sooner had he seated himself at her side than he was called back by his First Wife. The eight paper parcels lay unfolded before her.

"Just look! What magnificent contributions!" she cried, with a mocking laugh. "Your Ying at least has soared to the height of contributing one piece of silver and two cash. But in each of the other parcels there were only three to five measly coppers. Such rubbish, such dirty scraps—they might have been scraped off a cheap discarded bronze statue—have certainly never been seen in this house before! It would be a blot on our good name if we were to keep the stuff. We must send it back to them!"

"Let it pass!" said Hsi Men, soothingly. "It isn't worth troubling over. For all I care, you can throw the trash away."

On the following day he weighed out four ounces of good silver, and sent his servant, little Lai Hsing, to buy a pig, a wether, chickens, ducks, six jugs of Gold Blossom wine, and whatever else was needed for such a feast, as well as sticks of incense and paper money. It required three of them, little Lai Hsing, Lai Pao, and little Tai A, to carry everything to the temple and give it in charge of the priest Wu.

"Our master and his friends will be here tomorrow to take an oath of brotherhood," they told the priest. "They wish to spend the whole day here in feasting. Honorable sir, will you be so kind as to draft a suitable form of oath and make all arrangements for the feast?"

Punctually next morning the nine invited guests appeared before Hsi Men in holiday attire. They formed a circle and exchanged ceremonious greetings, quickly took a light breakfast, and set out together for the Jade Emperor's Temple.

On reaching the temple, they noted the spacious halls, the soaring roofs, the thick and lofty stone walls. Over the entrance portal an inscription of eight golden characters gleamed against a red background. Three winding paths led up to the temple. The interior was of translucent marble, wherein the eye lost itself. The Great Hall, whose rafters curved sharply upwards, was resplendent in gold and kingfisher-blue. In the center, enthroned in august majesty, sat the "Old Ancestor of Threefold Purity," while in the hall at the back of this, mounted on a black buffalo, was Lao Tse.

Passing through a door in the wall of the lesser hall, the visitors reached the domain of the priest Wu. On either side of the path were jasper-green lawns, bediamonded with flowers, and shaded by tall pines of a dark bluish-green, contrasting with the light halcyon green of bamboo. Raising his eyes, Hsi Men read on the two doors posts this inscription:

> *In these our spirit grottoes*
> *Time and space are forgot;*
> *Within our magic islands*
> *Pleasure and pain are not.*

The priest's dwelling contained three front rooms, wherein he was wont to attend to his clerical duties. In honor of the visitors the rooms were shining with cleanliness. In the central chamber hung a portrait of the "Jade Emperor of the Celestial Palace of Gold," while from the walls of the adjoining rooms the images of the "Genii of the Purple Palace" and of the four "Celestial Marshals," Ma, Chao, Wen, and Huang looked down in greeting. Standing before his oratory the priest received the guests with a bow and invited them to be seated and to drink tea.

After tea they made the rounds of the premises. At the sight of this or that saintly figure, the dissolute fellows could not refrain from facetious remarks. Now it was the tiger in the picture of the Celestial Marshal Chao, before which Pai Lai Kwang was standing.

"Friends, look at the tiger beside old Chao!" he cried. "He must surely be a vegetarian, otherwise such company would be rather uncomfortable!"

"Blockhead, he is one of the attendants of the Celestial Marshal!" said Ying, correcting him.

"Indeed! Well I, for one, could manage to get along without so dangerous a retainer!" bleated Hsia, his tongue protruding from his mouth in mock terror.

"What are you talking about?" asked Hsi Men, approaching the group before the picture of the tiger.

"Why, Hsia seems to be worried about this dangerous companion!" Ying answered dryly. "If you were half so timid, your eight voracious followers would have frightened you to death long ago!" At this there was general laughter.

"Now that the gentlemen are speaking of tigers," interrupted the priest, "it so happens that at present our neighborhood is afflicted with just such a monster. He has already attacked a great number of people, and among them ten huntsmen who have lost their lives in attempting to slay him."

"What!" exclaimed Hsi Men.

"Oh, indeed, have not the gentlemen heard of it? I, myself, had word of it only recently from one of my men whom I had sent to Hung hai chun, in the prefecture of Tsang chu Fu, to collect alms from our patron, the rich Lord Chai. On his way back through the forest on King Yang mountain, he caught sight of the brute, with its glaring eyes and white-striped forehead. Travelers and merchants no longer dare venture to cross the King Yang mountain alone, but travel in companies. Our District Magistrate has recently offered a reward of fifty ounces of silver to the lucky man who slays the beast. As for the poor foresters—what floggings they have suffered because they have not succeeded in capturing the monster!"

At the mention of the reward Pai Lai Kwang excitedly jumped into the air. "Hurrah! No later than tomorrow I shall go hunting! I won't let a handsome sum of money like that slip through my fingers!"

"And your life—I suppose that's of no value to you?" asked Hsi Men.

"What is life? Here today, gone tomorrow. After all, money is the main thing!"

"Splendid! I really must tell you an anecdote!" Ying's laughing voice was heard in the chorus. "A skinflint is struggling in the jaws of a tiger. His son, coming to the rescue, has already drawn his

12

knife and is about to stab the tiger. 'Stop!' shouts the miser; 'would you ruin a valuable tiger skin?'"

When the roars of laughter had subsided, the priest suggested that they should begin the ceremony, since the sacrificial foods had been made ready. He then produced a written document. "I have the oath here, duly drawn up. In what order do the gentlemen wish their names to appear?"

"Hsi Men's name must be first, of course," they cried unanimously.

"In order of seniority, Ying comes before me," protested Hsi Men.

"Oh, nowadays one goes by money, not by age!" Ying objected. "Besides, none of us enjoys more respect and esteem than yourself. The first place is yours by right."

"You rend my intestines," replied Hsi Men. But after some further resistance he accepted the glorious title of "Great Brother." The second place was accorded to Ying; the third to Hsia, while the fourth place was reserved, out of regard for his wealth, for the newly accepted Hua Tze Hsu. The others followed. In the order agreed upon the priest entered their ten names in his text. Then he lighted the incense, while the Ten solemnly stood before the image of the Jade Emperor, and in a loud voice he read as follows:

"On this the nth day of such and such a month and such and such a year in the era of the Harmonious Reign are here assembled on consecrated ground ten true believers from the district of Tsing ho hsien, which is part of the prefecture of Tung ping Fu in the province of Shantung, in the mighty Sung dominion; namely, Hsi Men Tsing, Ying Po Kui, Hsia Hsi Ta, Hua Tze Hsu, and so forth. . . . Having with freshly washed hands burned incense, after the illustrious example of the League of the Peach Garden, with fervor equal to that of the bosom friends Kwan Y Wu and Pao Shu Ya, mindful of the words of the holy Kung Tse: 'All men between the Four Seas should be brothers!' in all humility they announce their decision to form a brotherhood as fast and indissoluble as flesh and bone. With this purpose in mind, they approach this shrine with measured step, depose their tribute of sacrificial flesh and sacrificial paper money, bow themselves in due reverence, and offer up this prayer:

"'O worshipful Lord and Jade Emperor of the Celestial Gold Palace, and O ye Spirits of the Earth and district of Tsing ho hsien, and ye other Good Spirits of all five regions of the heavens, to whom homage is done this day, let the aroma of the incense we burn with uplifted hearts rise to your abodes, and do you graciously give ear to our vow:

"'Born, though we were on different days, we are prepared on the same day to die. May our alliance be forever untroubled. Happiness and joy we shall share in common, and in suffering, loyally help each other. The bond uniting us shall be constantly renewed. Who among us is rich and respected shall espouse the cause of the poor and wretched among us. With every day, with every month, be this covenant renewed! High as heaven, broad as earth, be our friendship. May long life, boundless felicity, and the favor of the gods be granted to us all!'"

At the end of the reading, the brotherhood bowed in unison, and then, one by one, according to rank, they bowed eight times before the image of the Jade Emperor. And with the burning of the paper money the ceremony came to a close.

In the meantime two tables had been laid with great bowls and platters, and the company sat down to the savory feast. The priest Wu took his place at a separate table. In the midst of their joyful carousal Hsi Men was called home by the prudent Moon Lady, on the pretext that the Third Wife had fallen into a deep swoon. Hsi Men excused himself, and left the banquet before its conclusion, accompanied by his neighbor Hua, since they took the same road home.

"There go both the rich fellows, leaving us poor beggars to our fate!" Ying called out after them. Their departure, however, in no way affected the holiday spirit of the brotherhood. "Stuffing a whole Tai Shan into their mouths, with no thanks in their hearts for the kindly provider, Mother Earth," they continued their revels until midnight, eating and drinking to the limit of their capacity.

The sun crept upwards over the boughs of the mulberry tree—
they drank.
Silently the mountains engulfed the beams of the sunlight—
and they drank.
At last the sickle of the new moon, peeping from behind the
treetops,
Saw them reeling homeward, leaning on the arms of strangers.

A few days later Hsi Men received a visit from his friend Ying.
"How is my third sister-in-law?" asked Ying.

"She is no better. I have just sent for the doctor again—but, tell
me, did you go on carousing much longer the other evening?"

"It was about the second drum beat when we broke up. Good
old Wu pressed us so urgently to remain that it was rather late
before we got away. We all had a splendid session. You may be
thankful that you decamped in good time. However, to come to
the point of my visit—I've brought you some astounding news."

"Out with it!"

"Just think, the tiger on King Yang mountain, the one that Priest
Wu was telling us about the other day, was killed yesterday by a
man who slew it with his bare hands."

"Nonsense! Tell that to someone else!"

"What? You don't believe me? Listen, I'll give you the exact
details!" And excitedly waving his hands, hopping restlessly from
one foot to the other, Ying proceeded to tell his tale:

"The man's name is Wu Sung, and he hails from the adjoining
district of Yang ku hsien; he's the younger of two brothers, and
for that reason, and also because of some unpleasantness, he left
his home, and for some time he was employed on the estate of the
wealthy Tchai in Hong hai kun. Upon recovering from some
illness, he set out in search of his elder brother. His way led him
over the King Yang mountain, where he suddenly came face to
face with the tiger. He belabored the beast with his fists and kicked
it to such effect that the tiger was left dead on the spot!" All this
Ying related in elaborate detail, with such lively gesticulations that

one might have thought that he himself had been present, and had slain the tiger with his own hands.

"And at this very hour he is about to make his triumphal entry with his quarry into the yamen of the District Intendant!" he concluded, quite breathless.

"Oh, we mustn't miss that. We will just have a quick breakfast first."

"There is no time for that; we shall be too late. No, we had better look for a good place on the balcony of some wineshop in the High Street, where we shall see him passing."

Hsi Men agreed, and calling to the servants that he would not be taking his breakfast, he hurriedly threw on a street robe, and seizing Ying by the hand, he dashed off with him.

On the way they met Hsia. "I'll wager you, too, are going to see the tiger!"

"You have guessed correctly. Come along with us!"

"Of course. The crowd is so thick in the main street that one can hardly get through it."

Before long the three had found good seats on the first floor balcony of a large wineshop in the main street. They had not been waiting long when they heard the approaching roll of drums and the braying of gongs. In the street below, the people began to crane their necks. A squad of huntsmen strode by in double file, bearing long spears with red tassels fluttering from the points, and behind them, cautiously borne by four men, and looking much like a sack covered with yellow silk, appeared the body of the tiger. Closing the procession, riding on a fine white palfrey, came the valiant warrior, the tiger slayer himself!

Ha, what a mighty hero! His body was at least seven feet in height. He had a broad face with a square jaw; his eyes were like glittering stars, and their steady, penetrating gaze seemed to rest on the distant horizon. His hand was gripping a heavy iron club. Tigers and leopards in their mountain fastnesses must indeed catch their breath if this giant, rising on the balls of his feet, should swing this iron bludgeon above his head. The bears in the caves and gorges would surely give up the ghost when this fist struck its hurtling blows! On his head the young hero wore a turban embroidered with the sign of the swastika, and adorned with two silver flowers. His body was protected by a coarse, patched hunter's doublet, spattered with blood; over this he wore an open, square-cut surcoat of red satin.

"One would need the strength of a thousand-pound water buffalo to deal with him!" Hsi Men whispered to his comrades, gnawing his fingernails in his excitement. Hastily sipping their wine, the three, with bated breath, expressed their admiration. So this was the hero of the day, the famous Wu Sung from Yang ku hsien!

The procession at last arrived before the yamen of the District Intendant. Wu Sung dismounted and strode into the hall, where the Intendant awaited him in the midst of the assembled officials. At the sight of this mighty hero, and the great dead beast, which was laid on the ground before the vermilion dais, the mandarin said to himself:

"What other man could have performed such a feat?"

Then, with an affable greeting, he turned to Wu Sung, and asked him to relate, from beginning to end, the exact sequence of the adventure. On either side of him the officials gazed and shuddered with horror as they listened.

The mandarin then presented the hero with a threefold draught of honor, and ordered that the proclaimed reward of fifty ounces of silver should be handed to him.

Wu Sung, bowing low, replied modestly: "It was not owing to my feeble strength, but rather to the blessed influences emanating from your Lordship, and to certain fortunate circumstances, that I was able to overcome the brute. I really do not deserve so rich a reward, and it grieves me that so many brave huntsmen have been punished so severely because of this tiger. Will your Lordship deign to hear my humble proposal? Let the reward be distributed among these good huntsmen, that the magnanimity of your Lordship may be radiantly displayed!"

"Let it be as the valiant hero wishes," the mandarin graciously decided.

Wu Sung then promptly distributed the silver. Moved by such humanity, such a sense of duty, and such comradeship, the mandarin resolved to employ Wu Sung in the public service.

"Your native district, Yang ku hsien, and my district of Tsing ho hsien adjoin each other," he said. "I am minded to appoint you my Captain of the Guard. It would be your special duty to wipe out the robber bands to the east and the west of the Tsing river. What do you say to that?"

Wu Sung thanked him on bended knees. "I shall do my utmost to prove myself worthy of your favor."

The mandarin motioned to his secretary, and had a commission made out, and Wu Sung was formally appointed Captain of the Guard.

The most respected inhabitants of the entire district came forward to felicitate Wu Sung, and for several days feast followed feast in his honor. In both districts of the prefecture of Tung ping Fu his name was on all men's lips.

> *The mighty champion, the hero bold,*
> *Deep in the groves of dark King Yang*
> *Struck, and the tiger reeled and fell!*
> *Then far and wide his praises rang!*

One day Wu Sung heard a voice calling him in the street.

"Hey, brother, don't you recognize me?"

He turned about, and there before him was Wu Ta, his brother, for whom he had long been searching.

> *The skin of his temples wrinkled in joy,*
> *His mouth opened in a smile.*

A bad harvest and the subsequent scarcity of food had caused Wu Ta to turn his back on his native town and migrate with his daughter, little Ying, to the city of Tsing ho hsien, where he leased a modest dwelling in Purple Stone Street. His weak body, servile manner, ugly features, and wrinkled skin, caused the neighbors to give him the nicknames of "Three-Inch Manikin" and "Bark Dwarf" and he was often a victim of their mockery and ridicule. He earned his living by marching up and down the streets all day with a hamper on his shoulders, offering hot tarts for sale. Business was not very good, and after a half-year's stay in Tsing ho hsien his meager savings dwindled to nothing. He had to give up his home and move into cheaper lodgings in the house of a certain Master Chang. There he lived in a little shop fronting the main street. While he continued to hawk his tarts as before, he was able, in his friendly, helpful way, to enlist the sympathies of the housekeeper, who interceded to have him exempted from paying rent.

Master Chang was a very wealthy sexagenarian. He possessed tens of thousands of strings of a thousand cash: but he had not a single son or daughter to call his own. His household consisted only of his wife, an austere, conventional old woman. There was not a drop of fresh young blood in the house to cheer his heart. Often, striking himself sadly on the breast, he would sigh:

"Poor childless old man that I am, what good do I get from all my money!"

And one day his wife had answered him:

"Very well, I shall commission a go-between to buy you two pretty young slaves. As far as I'm concerned they may entertain you from morning till night with their dancing and lute playing."

The old gentleman received this suggestion with joy, and a few days later a go-between brought two pretty young girls to the house. Unfortunately, the sixteen-year-old Pai Yu Lien died soon after her arrival. The other, the fifteen-year-old Pan Chin Lien, was the sixth daughter of a poor little tailor, Pan, who lived in the suburbs, to the south of the city. The name of Chin Lien, Gold Lotus, was given to her because of her precocious charms and her pretty, slender feet. After the death of her father the girl, barely nine years of age, had been sold by her mother into the distinguished household of one Master Wang, and had been instructed in singing and lute playing, and also in the arts of reading and writing. Hers was an exceptionally alert and versatile nature. When barely thirteen she knew already how to embellish her eyebrows and her eyes, and how to redden her lips and cheeks with perfect art. She could play on the bamboo flute and the guitar; she was proficient in all fine handwork and needlework, and had mastered the difficulties of the written language. Her carefully waved hair she wore attractively arranged in luxuriant masses. She drew her garments closely about her young body. And so she grew up to be a coquettish little beauty.

When Gold Lotus was fifteen, old Master Wang died. Her mother at once redeemed her from slavery for twenty ounces of silver and sold her to the house of Chang. There Gold Lotus perfected herself in manifold arts, and learned, in particular, to play the seven-stringed *pi pa*. She had now seen eighteen springs, and had blossomed into a perfect beauty. "A face of peach-blossom loveliness; two brows as finely curved as the sickle of the new moon." For a long while Master Chang had been itching to possess her, but his dread of his austere wife had always restrained him from plucking this precious blossom. Then one day, while his wife was visiting a neighbor, he finally succeeded. He had, indeed, to atone five times over for the short-lived rapture of this secret indulgence. He was immediately affected with: first, backache; second, running of the eyes; third, ringing in the ears; fourth, a cold in the head; and fifth, catarrh of the bladder.

Naturally the cause of his sufferings could not long be concealed from his wife, whereupon a violent scene took place, with words of abuse and blows for poor Gold Lotus. This grieved Master Chang deeply, and he decided to give her in marriage outside his household. He himself was willing to provide her dowry. On hearing this, his servants suggested their amiable lodger, the widower, Wu Ta, as a suitable husband for Gold Lotus. Master Chang reflected that this arrangement would enable him to visit Gold Lotus in secret from time to time, so he gladly accepted the proposal. The fortunate Wu Ta was not asked to pay a single cash piece;

he received his new wife absolutely free of charge. Even after the marriage, Master Chang was greatly concerned for the welfare of the young couple, and was always ready to aid the husband if Wu Ta happened to be short of money.

Whenever Wu Ta was away for the whole day, unsuspectingly hawking his tarts in the street, his benefactor, as soon as he saw that he was unobserved, would slip into his tenant's house in order to carry on his clandestine affair with Gold Lotus. Once the husband actually surprised his patron on such an occasion, but he dared not complain, for he told himself that he was merely clay in the old man's hands. The affair continued until one day Master Chang was carried off by a grievous catarrh of the bladder. His wife, who had long known of the affair, showed her displeasure immediately by turning Gold Lotus and her husband out of the house. And so Wu Ta had to seek new lodgings. He was fortunately able to rent a couple of small rooms in the house of a certain Wang, on the west side of Purple Stone Street. Once more he tramped the streets with his basket on his shoulders, selling his tarts, and earning a bare living.

Gold Lotus had nothing but contempt for her poor wretch of a husband. Angry words often passed between them, and in her rage she even cursed the memory of old Chang.

"Why, of all the men in the wide world, did he choose for me just this miserable creature, who meekly swallows every insult, who becomes so drunk from the smallest mouthful of wine that not even a cobbler's awl could tickle him awake! What crime did I, unhappy creature, commit in a former existence, that I should be punished by such a marriage?"

Sometimes, when alone, she would mournfully give voice to her woe in the song of "The Strayed Lamb on the Precipice":

"O error, O ill-starred entanglement!
Presumption it cannot be, and yet—
Dare the scurvy crow ally himself
With the glittering phœnix?

21

Am I not gold embedded in the filth of the gutter?
Though he liken himself to the finest copper,
Can copper compare itself with gold?
He is a lump of common quartz, whom chance
Allows to embrace my jasper body, smooth as a plump lamb.
I, growing on a dungheap, am a noble herb, exhaling
*   miraculous fragrance."*

Most honorable reader, it is clear that a lovely woman who wants a handsome lover may always procure one, if she be gifted with a little wit. For it is an old story that Beauty and Talent are seldom happily coupled. The demand for gold is often greater than the supply; in short, this Wu Ta might be an honest fellow, but he was none the less positively repulsive to his wife. In the mornings she could hardly wait until he had left the house with his tarts, so impatient was she to be alone for the rest of the day. She liked best to while away the time behind the balcony window, which overlooked the street, when she would perhaps lay melons on the floor from behind the curtain, since this allowed her to display her two enchanting "golden-lily" feet. She delighted to attract the attention of the elegant young idlers in the street. Soon there were daily promenades before her window, and the notes of strumming lutes, caressing words, and amorous allusions were wafted up to her. Someone, perhaps, would sing:

"Poor tender fillet of lamb,
Snapped up by the jaws of a cur!"

These and other such words flowed smoothly from youthful lips. Naturally the matter attracted attention, and in the end her husband was bound to hear of it. Wu Ta now decided that under the circumstances it would be unwise to continue to live in Purple Stone Street. One day, therefore, he suggested another change of residence.

"You loafer, you crazy simpleton!" his wife scolded. "Perhaps you would like us to live still more cheaply among strangers, and expose ourselves to still more ridicule from the neighbors? If you're resolved on moving, you might at least exert yourself to provide the necessary money, so that we could at last have a decent little house of our own!"

"And where am I to get the money for a high rent?"

"Pah! you helpless idiot! You filthy clod! Such a one dares call himself a man! If there is no money, you may pawn my jewels for all I care! We can always redeem them later."

Wu Ta promptly scraped together ten taels on credit and rented a four-roomed house in West Street—two rooms on the ground floor, two on the floor above, and a little garden. It was a quiet and attractive dwelling. When the moving was finally over and everything in order, Wu Ta once more walked the streets with his tarts, painfully earning his livelihood.

One day, in the course of his wanderings, he came upon his brother, Wu Sung. Overjoyed, Wu Ta invited him to his house. He led Wu Sung into the upper rooms, and, full of pride, introduced him to his wife.

"Here is the famous tiger slayer of King Yang mountain, the Captain of the Guard—your brother-in-law, Wu Sung!"

With folded hands, Gold Lotus looked up admiringly at her brother-in-law.

"Ten-thousandfold happiness!" she murmured, and they kowtowed slightly in mutual salutation. With shy reserve, Wu Sung noted her perfect beauty. The elder brother would take no excuses, but insisted that his guest must stay to dinner, and in order to supplement the modest provisions in the pantry, Wu Ta himself went out to make some purchases. Thus, for a little while his wife and his brother were left alone.

With secret rapture, Gold Lotus gazed at the pattern of physical manhood who was seated before her. The notion of strength so tremendous that it could strike down a tiger thrilled her.

"How is it possible," she marveled, "that these two should spring from one and the same mother! The one deformed as a stunted tree, only three-tenths man and seven-tenths an ugly demon! The other a hero bursting with vigor! Oh, he simply must come and live with us," she decided.

"Where are you living, brother-in-law?" she asked, her face wreathed in smiles, "and who attends to your housekeeping?"

"My position does not permit me to live too far from the yamen. I have taken a room in a tavern near by. And as to housekeeping, two of my men see to that."

"Dear brother, would you not rather live with us? Dirty soldiers to cook for you and wait on you, *brr*, how unappetizing! Here, your sister-in-law would prepare your food, and take the utmost care of your personal belongings."

"I am deeply obliged to you," Wu Sung replied, evasively, hesitating to accept her offer.

"Doubtless you have a companion?" she cautiously inquired. "You could live with her here without misgiving and undisturbed."

"I am not married," he answered.

"How many verdant springs does my brother-in-law count?"

"Eight-and-twenty years have I squandered in vain."

"Then you are five years older than I. Where were you living before you came here?"

"I spent last year in the prefecture of Tsang chu Fu. I never suspected that in the meantime my brother had settled here."

"Brother-in-law, I can't very well explain matters with a word. The truth is that since my marriage with your brother—he may have his good qualities in other respects—I have been forced to endure a great deal of mockery from the neighbors. Now if so valiant, so powerful a man as yourself were to live with us, who would dare to breathe a word against us?"

"Hm . . . my brother is a good-tempered man. . . . I, on the other hand, am very easily provoked."

"Come now!" she laughed—

> *"Only courage and strength*
> *Can give us peace!*

24

That's an old adage. I am a quick-tempered woman myself, and cannot endure to put up with affronts."

"On the other hand, my brother's gentle ways have so far been able to protect you from serious trouble."

Thus they sat talking, in the upper chambers of Wu Ta's house. One of them at least was secretly thrilled with desire. At last, Wu Ta reappeared on the scene.

"Dear wife, will you not go down and see to the food?"

"Listen to this simpleton!" she replied, crossly. "Is it mannerly to leave a visitor upstairs alone? Send for old Mother Wang next door, and let her attend to the cooking."

Wu Ta obediently trotted off and brought back Mother Wang with him; and finally they sat down to a table laden with fish, roast meat, vegetables, wine, and pastries.

"Pray be so gracious, brother-in-law, as to partake of our meager fare and our watery wine!" said Gold Lotus, offering the first cup to their guest.

"Accept my thanks, sister-in-law, and spare yourself, I beg you, all needless words of apology."

While the head of the house poured the wine, Gold Lotus placed the best portions of the food before their guest, and urged him, with her most winning smile, to help himself.

Wu Sung was a simple creature, who accepted all these attentions as marks of hospitality. He did not suspect that the woman before him had grown up in a servile condition, and that her amiability hid base intentions. Still, it did not escape him that from time to time her gaze caressed his body from head to foot, and more than once he could not refrain from bowing his head in embarrassment. And so, when the meal was over, he hastened to take his leave, and firmly declined her pressing invitation to remain.

"Some other time, sister-in-law!"

"But you are definitely coming to live with us, aren't you—? You know what I told you before—how much we have to suffer from the mockery of our neighbors! Your presence would mean so much to us!" she whispered urgently, at the very door.

"Very well, sister-in-law, since you wish it so much I will send my things over this evening."

"Your slave awaits you!"

CHAPTER TWO: *The Beauty spins a delicate Web behind the Door Curtain. Mother Wang in her Tea Room gossips to good Purpose*

Lotus face—
Bright as snow, the cool radiance of slender limbs—
A half-unfolded plum blossom,
She leans upon the door post.
Gazing from under the curtain
When first her eyes meet his,
Her cheeks flush red with shame—
Yet still she stands there!
But he is driven
To wander back and forth before her door.
To know her, to speak to her
What a bewildering thought!
To walk a little beside her!
Or only to linger near her!
To seat himself at her side!
Oh, rapture—even to embrace her!

THE FOLLOWING AFTERNOON Wu Sung moved into his brother's house. When the soldiers unloaded his luggage and his bedding, Gold Lotus experienced a secret satisfaction, as though someone had brought a costly treasure into the house. She insisted on rising next morning punctually at six in order that her brother-in-law might be ready for the early roll call at the yamen. She herself brought him hot water for washing. Before he left the house he had to promise that he would return for breakfast after roll call, and that he would not stop anywhere on the way.

At breakfast it irked him to see Gold Lotus serving him tea with her own hands.

"It troubles me, sister-in-law, to see you take so much trouble for me. Tomorrow I would rather detail a soldier to wait on me."

"But, brother-in-law, what an idea! Why should I not wait upon you? After all, you are one of the family! Of course, I have little Ying to help me. But I don't like her; she is too clumsy. And as for your soldiers, I couldn't bear the sight of them. They would only make a mess of my pots and my hearth."

"Then I must accept your gracious services."

Shortly after his arrival, Wu Sung gave his elder brother a few silver pieces to buy cakes and other dainties to send as gifts to the neighbors. The neighbors hastened to subscribe for a feast of friendship, and then it was Wu Ta's turn to show his appreciation by arranging for a feast. Thus, Wu Sung was able to improve his brother's relations with his neighbors.

Always courteous, Wu Sung did not forget to surprise his sister-in-law with the present of a length of gayly-colored satin for a new dress, which greatly delighted her.

With servile devotion, Gold Lotus, whether he returned from the yamen late or early, did her utmost to assure his comfort, and she lavished upon him the best that the kitchen could provide. He, in his simple and thick-skinned innocence, did not seem to be aware of any hidden purpose behind her attentions, and if ever she ventured a suggestive remark that made her intentions a little more obvious, he simply did not reply.

Wu Sung had been living for a month in his brother's house; in the meantime the winter had come, and for several days a biting November storm had been raging from the north. The whole sky was covered with dense, reddish clouds, and suddenly a mighty and beneficent fall of snow set in.

Ten thousand miles around
The russet clouds.

28

Out of the air
Beneficently floats a light curtain.
From the eaves the flakes
Whirl in a lovely dance.
Soon the snow lies heavy
On terraces and roofs.
The down-flowing silver
Merges into the silver of the heights:
Like sifting salt, like floating flour,
It fills all space.

The snow continued to fall until dusk. Far and wide the land-scape lay in silver splendor, as though heaven and earth, like monstrous rollers, had hulled mountains of rice. On the following day, when Gold Lotus had packed off her husband as usual to tramp the streets, she requested her neighbor, the widow Wang, to obtain some wine and meat. She had already kindled a charcoal brazier in her brother-in-law's room.

"Today I must succeed!" she told herself. "This time he shall not remain indifferent!"

For a long while she watched for his approach from behind the curtain, shivering with cold. At length, long past noon, she saw him coming through the snow. He stamped up to the door in an eddy of minute snow crystals. Gold Lotus pulled the curtain aside.

"It's cold enough today, isn't it, brother-in-law?"

"Thank you, sister-in-law, for taking so much trouble over me."

He entered the house, and removed his wide-brimmed felt hat. Gold Lotus offered to take it from him.

"Don't trouble yourself, sister-in-law!" he protested. He shook the snow from the brim and hung the hat on the wall. He took off his belt, and put on his parrot-green quilted cotton coat, which bore many patches. Then he went to his room, Gold Lotus following at his heels.

"I have waited for you in vain all the morning. Why didn't you come to lunch?"

"A friend invited me," he replied. "He really wanted to go on drinking, but I managed to get away."

"So that was it. Well, make yourself comfortable by the fire, brother-in-law!"

"Ah, that does a man good!" Wu Sung pulled off his greased boots, changed his socks, and slipped his feet into a warm pair of slippers. He pushed a bench close to the charcoal brazier and sat down.

Meanwhile little Ying, at her mistress's bidding, barred the doors, both front and back. Gold Lotus then proceeded to set a number of bowls of hot food on the table in Wu Sung's room.

"Where has my brother got to?" said Wu Sung, interrupting her preparations.

"He is out peddling his tarts. But we can begin without him."

"I think we ought to wait for him. There will still be plenty of time to eat."

"Oh, we needn't stand on ceremony for him," she replied.

Little Ying now appeared, carrying a pitcher of punch, which she set on the table. Gold Lotus also pushed a bench close to the brazier and sat down. Twice, in rapid succession, she handed Wu Sung a full goblet.

"Please drink it, brother-in-law," she encouraged him.

For the sake of courtesy, Wu Sung accepted the punch, and then poured some for Gold Lotus. She drank, and handed him a third goblet. Her dress had suddenly become displaced, so that the swell of her smooth bosom appeared; her loosely knotted hair came undone and fell upon her shoulders. Her lips were twisted into a roguish smile.

"Brother-in-law, it is said that you keep a singing-girl in a house not far from the yamen. Is that so?"

"Don't listen to such gossip! I am not that sort of man."

"Who knows? Perhaps you speak one way and think another?"

"Well, please ask my brother."

"Your brother? What does he know? He dreams his way through

life, as though he were half drunk! Would he have to peddle pastries if he had any wits?—Drink, brother-in-law!"

And she forced three more goblets upon him, and then a fourth. She herself had drunk three, and the insatiable lust of youth was blazing within her like a fire. Her speech became more and more undisguised. Despite all that he had drunk, Wu Sung was still nine-tenths sober. He had no thought of basely profiting by the occasion; he bowed his head, and was silent. Gold Lotus rose and went into the kitchen to pour out some more punch. She was absent for some time, and Wu Sung whiled away the minutes by raking together the glowing embers in the brazier. At last she returned. In one hand she held the steaming pitcher of punch; the other she placed upon his shoulder. He could feel a slight pressure from her fingers.

"You're so lightly dressed, brother-in-law. Don't you feel the cold?"

His thoughts were elsewhere, and he paid no attention to her. Suddenly she took the poker from his hand:

"Brother-in-law, you don't seem to understand how to handle this thing. Let me do it: I'll make you as hot as the stove itself!"

Inwardly Wu Sung had long been boiling with rage, but he held himself in check.

Gold Lotus did not seem to realize his restrained anger. She threw the poker aside, and hastily took a gulp from a fresh-filled goblet.

"Drink up, brother-in-law, if you have a heart!" she cried, holding out the half-emptied goblet.

Then Wu Sung seized the goblet and angrily poured the contents on the floor. And while he extended his other hand as though to repulse her, he shouted, as his eyes blazed with fury:

"Enough of these indecencies, sister-in-law! I am an honest man who has always stood upright on his two legs between heaven and earth, and kept his tongue inside his mouth. I am none of your dissolute swine who disregard all decency and human principles! Stop this nonsense! If you let yourself be bent like grass by every puff of wind, my eyes may recognize you as my sister-in-law, but my fists may forget it!"

Blushing all over her body, Gold Lotus endured his rebuke in silence. Then she called the maid, and bade her clear the table.

At last she stammered: "I was only jesting. How could I know that you would take me seriously? How coarse you are!"

She turned her back upon him and disappeared into the kitchen.

> *O joy, thinks the falling flower*
> *To be swept away by the flood!*
> *But the water flows unheeding*
> *And the blossom lies in the mud.*

Gold Lotus had realized that she would never succeed in captivating her prudish brother-in-law. On the contrary, she had met with resolute resistance. As for Wu Sung, he remained sullenly in his room, considering how he could escape from his situation.

It was the fourth hour of the afternoon when Wu Ta returned home with his pack over his shoulder, in a heavy fall of snow.

"Have you had trouble with anyone?" he asked in surprise, as he noticed that his wife's eyes were red with weeping.

"It is all the fault of your sneaking ways that I should have to suffer insults from vagabonds," she replied.

"Why, who has dared to insult you?"

"Who, indeed? Who should it be but this fellow Wu Sung? Kindhearted as I am, when he came home in this terrible snowstorm, I prepared something hot for him to eat and drink. As soon as he saw that you were not there, he began to make bold remarks. Little Ying can tell you that I am not accusing him unjustly."

"What! No, I cannot believe that of my brother. He has always been honor itself. But please oblige me by not shouting any more, or the whole neighborhood will hear you and laugh at us."

He left her and went to his brother. "I say, shan't we have something to eat?"

The younger brother did not answer, but sat brooding. After a while he rose and silently made for the front door.

"Hey, where are you going?" Wu Ta called after him. But Wu Sung went his way, stiff and silent. Wu-Ta re-entered the house and turned to his wife.

"I called after him," he explained to Gold Lotus, "but he didn't answer me; he simply stared in front of him and went off in the direction of the yamen. I don't understand what this means."

"You sloppy pancake—you miserable reptile!" she raged. "It's simple enough: the fellow is ashamed to meet your eyes, and that's why he has taken himself off! You see, he will send for his things; he won't want to stay here any longer. And he shan't, either! And don't you dare to attempt to persuade him to stay!"

"But people will make a mock of us if he leaves us so suddenly."

"You stupid, ugly little devil! And if he is allowed to insult me, will people mock at us any the less? Go on, go to him if you like; live with him, and write me a bill of divorcement! That will suit me well enough! I'm not anxious for your company!"

He did not dare to utter another word, but let her rage on. Just as they had at last begun to talk on indifferent matters Wu Sung returned, followed by a soldier who carried a yoke over his shoulder. Without a word, Wu Sung made straight for his room, waited while the soldier packed his belongings, and went, as he had come, without a word.

"But, brother, why are you leaving us?" Wu Ta called after him.

"Spare me the need of an explanation. Otherwise you might think I was competing with you unfairly," was Wu Sung's cryptic answer. "Let me go my way in peace. That will be best."

The elder brother asked no further questions, but allowed him to depart. Meanwhile, Gold Lotus was muttering to herself: "That's right! One's own relatives are always the worst debtors; that is an old story. This fellow here, instead of doing something to support his elder brother and his sister-in-law, as one might have expected, after he had become Captain of the Guard, actually dares to slander us! What a quince he has proved to be! A fine appearance, and nothing behind it! Thank heaven and earth that he is gone! At least we shall be spared the sight of the hateful creature!"

Wu Ta did not know how to reply to her words, but privately he rejected her judgment.

Wu Sung moved back to his former lodgings near the yamen. The elder brother had thoughts of going to see him there, but since his wife strictly forbade any further intercourse, he did not venture to carry out his intention.

About a fortnight later Wu Sung was called before the District Intendant. The mandarin wished to dispatch to the Eastern Capital the considerable treasure in gold and silver which he had accumulated in his two years of office in the district, and to entrust it to the care of a kinsman, Mandarin Chu, Commandant of the Palace. When, in the following year, the Intendant's term of office was completed, this treasure would serve to open the doors of the high dignitaries of the Court, and persuade them that he was not unworthy of an audience. If this valuable convoy was to reach its destination safely, an absolutely trustworthy, sturdy, and sensible man must be found. The Intendant, therefore, summoned Wu Sung, the Captain of the Guard.

"You are just the man I want," he told Wu Sung. "Now do not pain me by refusing this commission. You can rest assured that on your return you will be amply rewarded."

Wu Sung humbly thanked him and announced that he was ready for the task. The mandarin honored him with three goblets of wine, and dismissed him graciously with a present of ten ounces of silver.

That same day, Wu Sung went to his brother's house. An attendant carried a jug of wine and a basket of provisions. Wu Sung squatted down before the threshold. He would not enter the house before his elder brother had returned from his peddling.

Gold Lotus still retained a trace of affection for her brother-in-law. When she saw him return with a jug of wine, and various other good things, she thought to herself: "He must surely have

34

some liking for me. What other reason could he have for returning? Well, I'll find out soon enough."

Gold Lotus hurried to her room upstairs, and presently, freshly powdered, with carefully waved hair, and wearing a gayly-colored gown, she confronted her brother-in-law.

"Dear brother-in-law, it must have been through a misunderstanding that you have shunned our threshold so long. It has worried me greatly. I am all the more pleasantly surprised by your present visit. But why have you gone to so much expense? There was no need for that!"

"I have come simply to say a few words to my brother," he answered dryly.

When Wu Ta arrived they went upstairs and sat down at the table. Wu Sung let his brother and sister-in-law sit at one end of the table; he himself sat on a bench facing them. The soldier could be heard talking noisily in the kitchen. Then he came upstairs to wait at table. During the meal, Gold Lotus could not refrain from casting expectant glances at her brother-in-law. But he seemed to be completely absorbed in eating and drinking. At last he turned to his brother and solemnly addressed him:

"On behalf of the District Intendant I have to set out tomorrow on an official journey to the Eastern Capital. I can hardly return before the end of two months. Dear brother, you are rather soft and tender-hearted by nature. I am afraid that during my absence people may tease you, and perhaps try to injure you. Do not under any circumstances allow yourself to be drawn into arguments, but wait until I return and I will then set matters right. Further, if I were in your place, I should take out only six trays of tarts instead of the usual ten. Don't leave too early, and don't stay away from home too long. Don't take to drinking with your friends. Let down the curtain as soon as you get home, and lock your door early. That will save you a great deal of annoyance. Now, let's drink to it!"

The elder brother emptied the offered goblet.

35

"You are right; I shall do just as you say," he promised. Wu Sung handed a second goblet to his sister-in-law.

"Sister-in-law, you have such delicacy of feeling that I need not say much. You see what a kindly, innocent duffer my brother is, and how completely he relies on you.

> Simple and solid is worth more
> Than tinsel and empty show—

as the proverb says. Therefore, sister-in-law, make a comfortable home for your husband, so that he finds no cause for complaint,

> A fence must be strong and sturdy,
> Then no stray dog can enter."

As he spoke these words to Gold Lotus, a wave of purple, starting from her temples, flooded her whole face. Pointing a finger at her husband, she suddenly burst out in a rage:

"You stupid clod! What have you been saying about me that I should have to endure such insults? Because I don't wear a man's turban, do you think that I am worth less than one of you men? I am a wife as honest and dutiful as the ring of the gong when it is beaten! You can stand on my fist; a horse can walk over my breast, over my body! I am not a soft, lazy toad that has blundered into a bloody mess of pus and mucus and can't get out of the sticky mess! Not so much as an ant has crawled over our doorstep since I married you. So what is the meaning of this talk of a dog and a fence? Brother-in-law, desist from riddles and insinuations for which there is no foundation! A tile does not drop into emptiness, but falls somewhere on firm ground."

Wu Sung seemed to be amused by her outburst of temper.

"So you feel that you yourself are responsible for the peace of this house? That's all right, then. But you must put your heart into the business. However, I shall keep your words well in mind. On that understanding, sister-in-law, let us drink!"

But Gold Lotus angrily thrust the offered goblet aside, so that it overturned, and she ran quickly downstairs. As she ran she called back:

"Although you talk like an old fogy, you don't even know that the wife of an elder brother must be respected like a mother! When I married, I had never heard of the existence of a younger brother. Who knows how much truth there really is in your alleged relationship? In any event, it doesn't please me to see you play the master in this house, and make such unjust and disgusting insinuations!"

And sobbing loudly, she ran down the stairs.

> *Whether one bitterly blames her,*
> *Or admonishes her with kindly words,*
> *Like the waves in a storm*
> *She froths with impotent rage.*
> *How could this happen to her?*
> *She must blush red with shame!*
> *For the insolent brother-in-law*
> *She wishes but one thing: death.*

After this dramatic exit, the two brothers were in no mood to sit over their cups, and they soon took leave of each other.

"Brother, just give up your business for the time being, and as far as possible, don't leave the house!" said the younger man at the last moment. "What you need to keep going I will send you by a messenger. See to your doors and your gate! Do you hear?"

The following morning Wu Sung went to the yamen to receive final orders for his journey. He started on his trip to the Eastern Capital well armed, with his cargo of gold and silver laden on a camel.

For the next three or four days Wu Ta had to endure the scolding of his wife. He controlled his temper, patiently swallowed his anger, and let her rage on. For the rest, he followed his brother's advice and left the house with only half his usual batch of pies. Early in the afternoon he returned, and no sooner had he put down his tray than he shut carefully the front door, drew the curtains,

37

and sat down in the living room. This naturally evoked a fresh outburst of rage from Gold Lotus.

"You fool, you have now lost all, even all sense of time! To shut up the house while the sun is still high in the heavens! The neighbors will have something more to laugh about! They'll say we see ghosts in broad daylight! This comes, of course, of listening to your rake of a brother. He can't lay anything but addled eggs, but he cackles all the more loudly and impudently for that!"

"Let the people laugh!" Wu Ta retorted. "My brother is quite right. In this way we save ourselves from something worse."

"Bah, you lump of dirt!" she cried, and she spat contemptuously into his face. "Such a thing to call itself a man! You've no will of your own; you let yourself be led by others!"

"That's enough," he replied, defensively. "For me, my brother's words are virgin gold and solid rock."

So the new daily routine was continued. Gradually, after a few more violent outbursts, Gold Lotus's anger began to abate. She became reconciled to the new order. Indeed, she even adopted the plan of barring the door and drawing the curtains herself on her husband's return. Wu Ta noticed this change with no little satisfaction, though indeed on thinking it over he began to feel faintly suspicious. Has it not truly been said:

> However minute his precautions—
> Door bolted, and early home—
> Between him and her love
> Towers a wall of precipitous rock.
> One spark of youthful desire
> And the threads of marriage are snarled.
> Though he set her about with bars
> One day he finds the cage empty.

Life hastened onward, fleet as a spirited colt when it leaps over graves; swift as a weaver's shuttle the days and months flashed by. And with the end of the twelfth month, Yang, the Prince of Light, resumed his dominion, and now the season of plum blossom had arrived.

One seductively radiant spring morning, Gold Lotus decked herself in her newest and most dazzling finery. She waited only until her husband had gone to take her accustomed place under the awning before the door. It is an old story that the encounters willed by Fate are mostly brought about by trivial chances. In short, the young woman was in the act of adjusting the prop that held up the bamboo awning above the door when a sudden gust of wind caused the pole in her hand to swing aside, so that it grazed the head of a passer-by.

Startled, and yet amused, Gold Lotus looked more closely at the stranger. He had the air of a man about town, and was perhaps thirty-five years of age. His handsome figure was clothed in a tunic of thin green silk; on his head he wore a fine tasseled hat, decorated with golden arrows whose pendants tinkled faintly as he moved. Around his waist he wore a golden girdle with a border of jade; on his feet were cotton socks of dazzling cleanliness, and light, thin-soled shoes. In his hand he carried a gold-spattered Szc-ch'uen fan. Altogether he was a very Chang Shong, a second Pan An; in short, such a smart cavalier as every woman's heart must desire. Such was the man who stood under the awning as Gold Lotus inquisitively measured him with her glance.

When he felt the pole graze his head, he stopped short, and was about to make an angry protest. But when he looked up he found to his surprise that he was confronting a seductive beauty. Her thick black tresses were piled upon her head: the kiss-curls, like raven's feathers, contrasted sharply with the snowy whiteness of her temples; her blue-black eyebrows were curved like the sickle of the new moon. The almond-shaped eyes met his with a cool, clear gaze; the cherry mouth exhaled a fragrant breath; her little nose was like rose-colored jasper; her full, rounded cheeks were delicately pink; her figure was slender and pliant as the stem of a flower, which could almost be spanned with the hands. Her fingers were like tender onion-shoots, carved out of jade; her small waist was supple as an osier. And then that tender body, white as rice powder, those full firm breasts, those tiny feet, peeping forth like twinkling stars, those smooth thighs! And there was something else—something tightly closed, something firm and youthful, something dark and cushioned . . . I know not what. Ah, who could ever tire of gazing at such charms!

Dark splendor of tresses rolled in a heavy knot;
Waves of fragrance well forth from its recesses.
It is transfixed with delicate arrows;
On one side is a flower stem with twofold bud.
A comb is rakishly set in the knot at the back.
Words cannot describe the sweep of the eyebrows:
Slender willow leaves curving above two peach blossoms.
The tinkle of earrings is faintly audible.
Under the small wide-armed jacket
Of clinging blue-green muslin
Shows the gentle swell of the jasper bosom.
Over the tunic, slashed in the mode of Hunan,
A short skirt of taffeta glistens.
From the open sleeve peeps a gayly-flowered lawn kerchief,
A sachet of perfume swings at her waist,
Above her breast is a button, and one at her throat.
Roving downwards, the eye beholds
Two tiny, nimble, gold-lily feet:
Blessed the dust over which they float
In their white satin slippers, artfully quilted,
And light as clouds!
She moves, and the red silken hose are revealed,
Caught at the knee with a border of flowers and birds.
Now and again, as she walks or sits,
A breeze entices from her under garments
A breath of a strangely piquant fragrance,
A breath of musk and the scent of orchids.
Only to look at her!—Where is the man

Who would not long to swoon in her embrace?
And to be derided by her
Would truly be mortal anguish.

This unexpected sight caused the stranger's anger to take flight to the far land of Java. The scowl on his face changed to a gracious smile. The young woman, however, very conscious of her awkwardness, raised her clasped hands in greeting, and said, with a deep bow:

"A gust of wind made me lose my hold, so that the pole accidentally hit his lordship! His lordship must forgive me!"

Straightening his hat, the person thus addressed bowed so deeply that his head almost touched the ground: "It was nothing at all. The lady may be quite easy."

Mother Wang, the proprietress of the tea room next door, who had observed the whole performance, now intervened, stepping forward, and amiably grinning.

"The noble lord got a real swipe as he was passing by!"

"Entirely my fault!" the stranger insisted with a courteous smile. "I hope the lady has forgiven me?"

"Please, please!" Gold Lotus exclaimed. "The gentleman has no reason to ask pardon!"

"Oh, please, I beg you!" He spoke with the greatest submissiveness, trying to give his voice a ringing and melodious tone. But his eyes, thievishly desirous, accustomed for years to lust after flowers and grasses that quiver in the wind of desire, clung to the beauty's body. At last, but not without looking back some seven or eight times, he turned to go, resuming his indolent, swaying gait, and waving his fan.

Mild is the air, and heaven smiles;
He comes forth for a stroll.
About to pass under the awning
He sees her there, so lovely and abashed.
Hardly come, he turns away from her,
Sending back to her many a burning glance.

41

Ah, springtide love, barely awakened,
Has robbed him of sense and strength.

The stranger's elegant and worldly appearance, and his cultivated manner of speech had made a deep impression on Gold Lotus. Had he not caught fire from her, would he have turned his head seven or eight times as he left her? If only she knew his name and address! She could not help looking after him until he disappeared from her sight. Then, and only then, she drew in the awning, closed the door, and went inside.

Worthy reader, who do you think this stranger was? He was none other than the chief of that band of dissolute fellows whose pastime it was to rage with the winds and sport with the moonbeams; their leader in plucking the blue flowers of the night, and rifling their magic fragrance; our wholesale apothecary, the most highly-esteemed Master Hsi Men.

Still saddened by the recent death of his ailing Third Wife, whom he had just conveyed to her last rest, he had left the house this day in search of distraction. He felt a longing to see his friend Ying Po Kui, whose company would surely cheer him a little. And now, on his way to call on his friend, he had this unexpected adventure under the awning of a strange house. He gave up the thought of visiting Ying, and turned homewards. Once indoors, he abandoned himself to his thoughts. What an adorable little bird! How could he ensnare her? Mother Wang, the teahouse woman next door—she could do the trick! A few ounces of silver were nothing to him. Without even allowing himself time for his midday meal, he hurried back to the tea house of Mother Wang, and seated himself comfortably on a stool beneath the penthouse.

"Aha, the noble gentleman had just the right buttery tone when he was here just now!" said the worthy dame, teasingly, with a cunning smile.

"Worthy adoptive mother, come here; there is something I

simply must ask you. That little bird next door—whose wife is she?"

"Why, she's the younger sister of the Prince of Hell, the daughter of the Marshal of the Five Roads. Why do you ask me about her?"

"No nonsense! Please talk seriously."

"What, you don't know her? Her old man keeps the cookshop by the yamen."

"Ah, you must mean Yu San, who sells the date cakes?"

"No. If it were he, they would make quite a passable pair. Guess again, noble gentleman!"

"Do you mean the man who sells broth, Li San?"

"No, no. Even he wouldn't be a bad match for her. Guess again!"

"Well then, it might be little Liu Hsiao, with the crippled shoulder."

"Wrong again. Even he wouldn't be such a bad partner. Go on!"

"Worthy adoptive mother, I cannot guess."

"Aha! Then I'll tell you. Her husband is the pieman, Wu Ta."

"What! The Three-Inch Manikin, the Bark Dwarf?"

"No other!"

Hsi Men shook with laughter. But then he exclaimed, bitterly: "All the same, it is a pity this delicious mouthful of roast lamb should fall into the jaws of such a filthy dog!"

"Well, that's how it is always," sighed the old woman. "The dullest fellows ride the best horses and sleep with the loveliest women. The old man in the moon is partial to such unequal matches."

"Adoptive mother, how much do I owe you?"

"Nothing to speak of. Stay a little longer. We can settle the reckoning later."

"By the way, where is your son, Chao, employed at present?"

"If only I knew! The last I heard of him he had joined a traveling merchant from An Hui, and I haven't set eyes on him since then. I haven't the faintest idea to to whether he is alive or dead."

"A clever, wide-awake young fellow. You should have placed him in my care."

"Were my noble Lord to take an interest in him, his fortune would be made."

"We'll wait until he returns; then we'll talk of it again."

He rose and took his leave.

Less than four hours later he was back again at Mother Wang's tea shop. Taking a seat beneath the penthouse, he gazed fixedly at the door of the adjoining house.

"Would you like some plum broth?" the hostess inquired.

"Excellent idea. But plenty of vinegar in it, please."

A few minutes later, Mother Wang set before him a dish filled to the brim and a bowl. For a time he gave his attention to the broth.

"Adoptive mother, you know how to make this kind of plum broth to perfection. Have you much of it on hand?"

"What do you mean, on hand? This old woman has arranged marriages all her life."

"Who was talking about marriage? I was praising your plum broth."

"Excuse me, I distinctly heard you say how well I understood the art of matchmaking."

"Very well," he agreed, with a smile. "I have no doubt you could bring mountains together. Would you be inclined to play go-between for me some time? If you do the job well, there will be a big reward for you."

"It pleases the gentleman to jest with me! What if your First Wife should come to hear of it? She would surely half pull my ears off!"

"Don't worry about that. My First Wife is a kind, sensible creature. The fact is that among the various women I have at home there is not one who really appeals to me. Perhaps you know of someone who might suit me? If so, you can make your proposal in perfect confidence. Even a divorced woman would do. . . ."

"Only a little while ago I had someone who would suit the gentleman on hand, but I'm not sure. . . ."

"Speak plainly! I am greatly interested."

44

"Well, then, as far as her outward charms are concerned, she is more than perfect. The only thing is, she is rather advanced in years."

"Well, sometimes a ripe beauty is not to be despised. How old is she? I am not so particular about a few years more or less."

"She was born in the sixtieth year of the sixtieth cycle under the Sign of the Boar, so she'll be ninety-three years at the New Year."

"What an old windbag you are!" Hsi Men exclaimed with a laugh. "You must always have your stupid joke!"

"Well, we must wet our agreement!" said the old woman, encouragingly.

"That suits me. And make the drink sweet and strong!"

It was late in the evening when Hsi Men left his observation post and returned home.

"Adoptive mother, I will settle the account tomorrow. Enter it in your books for the present. Is that agreed?"

"That's all right, that's all right. Honor me again soon!"

At home, Hsi Men found that he had no appetite, nor could he sleep, so full was his mind of the unknown beauty. Moon Lady attributed his moodiness to his grief for the loss of his Third Wife, and took no special notice of it.

Next morning, no sooner had Mother Wang opened her shop than she saw Master Hsi Men pacing up and down the street not far from the house.

"He's in a mighty hurry!" she thought. "How the fellow hankers for the syrup I've smeared on his nose! Well, he's fleeced the whole district, and now he's fallen into my hands! He shall pay a pretty price for his pleasure!"

It should be remarked that Old Wang was quite untroubled by moral scruples. For years she had been an active procuress and matchmaker, and an expert nurse and midwife; and lastly, she was a resourceful receiver of stolen goods.

She now disappeared inside the shop, and busied herself about the tea kettle. It was not long before Hsi Men stepped in under the penthouse and took up his usual post of observation. Mother

Wang pretended that she had not seen him; she seemed to have no eyes for anything but the fire, which she was vigorously fanning.

"I say, adoptive mother, two bowls of tea!" her early customer called at last from the porch.

"Oh, it's you, noble gentleman!" she said, in pretended astonishment. "I haven't had the honor of your presence for the last few days. Please make yourself comfortable."

"Keep me company!" he invited her, as she set before him on the table two bowls of strong, dark-green tea.

"Ha, ha! I'm to keep you company!" she laughed in his face. "I hope you don't mean to seduce me?"

He could not help smiling; then he continued: "Tell me, has the fellow next door anything really good to sell?"

"Why, crisp biscuits, cabbage rolls, meat collops, puff pastries, mussel soup with dumplings, and warm spiced cheese."

"I suppose you are quite crazy! Come, let's talk sense for once! If your neighbor really makes decent pies I should like to buy forty or fifty of them."

"You had better wait until he comes out. It would seem less remarkable if you were to buy from him in the street rather than call at the house."

"There, of course, you are right." He emptied his bowl and went out into the street. He turned to the east, then faced about and walked toward the west; but again he turned, and again he passed the house. Seven or eight times he marched up and down, at last he re-entered the tea room.

"Ah, my noble gentlemen! What happiness! It is days since I've had the honor of a visit!" the old worm greeted him ironically.

He drew a shining silver coin from his pocket and handed it to her.

"Here, adoptive mother, in partial settlement of my score."

She pocketed the money, thinking: "All right, let the fellow go on believing he'll get her! This is enough to pay my rent tomorrow." Aloud, she said:

"It seems to me that there is something on your mind."

46

"Now how did you guess that?"

"It wasn't so difficult. Don't you know the old saying:

> *Comes a stranger to this place,*
> *Question not unduly:*
> *You must learn to read his face*
> *Would you know him truly.*

Ah, my dear gentleman, what strange and intricate histories such people as I have divined!"

"Listen: if you can really find out what is troubling me at this moment, I will give you a prize of five ounces of silver."

"Oh, it won't take me long to guess that! I will whisper it in your ear right away: if you have been running your legs off today and yesterday, it's because of a certain person next door whom you can't get out of our mind. Well, am I right?"

"My congratulations! you've guessed it. I must admit that since I saw her yesterday standing before her door, I have no longer any control over my three souls and my six senses. Day and night I can find no peace or rest. I have lost all desire for food and drink, and if I try to do anything, I feel as though I were paralyzed. Can't you give me some good advice?"

"Well, I'll speak quite plainly. If I were to depend on my miserable tea room for a living, I might as well hire a ghost as night watchman. It is now three years since a few poor bubbles of steam have evaporated from my tea kettle. I remember it distinctly; it was on a cold and snowy day at the beginning of June. Since then my shop has been without a patron. Under these circumstances, I naturally had to turn to some other means of support. I have been a widow since my sixty-third year. How were my boy and I to live? Well, I earned my living by negotiating marriages and acting as midwife and nurse; I sold old clothes on commission, and I did a bit of procuring; also, I know a bit about cauterizing wounds and diagnosing sickness with the sounding-needle."

"Good heavens, but you're a versatile woman! Well, if you'll

47

help me to an interview with my little bird, I'll pay you a fee of ten ounces of silver. That's as much as you'll need for your coffin."

"Ha!" said Mother Wang; "you were taken in at once! Why, I was only joking!"

CHAPTER THREE: *Mother Wang pockets her Reward for Matchmaking. Her Cunning procures forbidden Joys for our Libertine*

"THEN, WORTHY adoptive mother, ten good ounces of silver are yours if you can bring this about," Hsi Men repeated, urgently.

"Listen to me, my noble gentleman. In love affairs it's not so simple as that. What does 'love' mean today? Stolen love. And for that, six things are necessary: good appearance, money, blooming youth, ample time for loafing about, the gentle rigidity of a needle wrapped in cotton wool, and finally a something as strong as the thing of an ass."

"Frankly speaking, I can offer all six of these requirements. First, as regards my looks. I don't indeed wish to compare myself to a Pan An, but otherwise I can very well say—not so bad! Secondly, I have plenty of money to burn. As for youth, I may still count myself one of the younger generation. As for loafing, I've time and to spare. If it were not so, would you find me so diligent a visitor? And as to gentleness, well, I'll let a woman strike me four hundred times before I so much as clench my fist. And finally, as for the sixth point, since my earliest youth I have been at home in all the houses of joy, and have reared up quite a nice little monster."

"Then so far everything is in order. But there is still one difficulty, on which such affairs are most commonly wrecked."

"And that is?"

"Don't be angry if I speak quite frankly, but a love affair like this often goes wrong because one begrudges the last one per cent of the expenses. I know you are a thrifty gentleman who doesn't thoughtlessly waste his money. That's where the difficulty lies."

"You need not worry about that. I shall do exactly as you wish."

"Good! If that's how it is, I know of a nice little plan for bringing you and the little bird together."

"Really! Then out with it!"

"First of all you must go quietly home. Three or six months from now we'll discuss the matter further."

"Stop! This is absolute torture! Think of the reward that awaits you!"

"Not so hasty, noble gentleman! It is true that the little bird is of humble descent—old Pan, her father, is nothing more than a little tailor outside the South Gate; but she is intelligent and cultured; she can sing and pluck the guitar, throw dice, and play chess; she knows by heart all the songs of the hundred poets; and she is thoroughly skilled in all the arts of the housewife. She learned to sing and play the guitar in the house of old Chang. You've heard of the wealthy Master Chang: it was he who gave her, free and gratis, to the Three-Inch Manikin as wife. As she is much alone in the house, and never goes out, I frequently keep her company. She often asks my advice, and she calls me, quite familiarly, her 'adoptive mother.'

"If you want to get your way, then take my advice: first buy two bolts of coarse silk, one blue and one white, also a bolt of fine white silk and ten ounces of the best cotton wool. Have it all sent here to me. Then I'll go over to her and ask to see the calendar, pretending that I want to find a suitable day to send for the tailor. If she does not offer to do the work herself, well then, we must give up our plan. On the other hand, if she tells me that I needn't send for the tailor, and that she will gladly do the work for me herself, then we have won one-tenth of the game. If, at my suggestion, she comes here to do the work, two-tenths of the game is won. I shall then put wine and food before her and urge her to help herself. If she declines and leaves without touching the food, then we must give up our plan. If, on the other hand, she accepts without a word, then the game is three-tenths won.

"You mustn't come here the first time. You mustn't show yourself until the third visit, some time in the afternoon. Dress yourself in your best, and before you enter announce your arrival by clearing your throat. Say that it's a long time since you've seen me, and you would like to drink a bowl of tea. Then I'll invite you to come in. If she gets up as you enter, and if I can't persuade her to stay, then we must give up our plan. If, however, she doesn't stir, then the game is four-tenths won.

"I shall then introduce you as the giver of the material, and emphasize your innumerable virtues. You, for your part, must praise her skill and dexterity. If she is overawed, and cannot answer you, then we must give up our plan. But if she should begin to talk with you, half the game is ours. I shall then immediately remark how extraordinarily fortunate this meeting is, since I am indebted to both of you for the work she is doing—to you for the material, to her for the labor. I could flatter myself a little on my ability to bring distant mountains together, and then I could suggest that you might make this an occasion for standing some wine in honor of the lady. You will naturally take my hint, and give me the money to fetch the wine. If now, in spite of all persuasion, she insists on leaving, then we must give up our plan. If, however, she remains seated, then the game is six-tenths won.

"I shall take the money, and as I go I shall ask her to stay and keep the noble gentleman company. If she objects, and gets up, and insists on going, then we must give up our plan. If, however, she does not get up, then things are going in your favor, and the game is seven-tenths won. When I return, I shall lay the table nicely, and say to her: 'Come now, put aside your work and drink a cup of wine with us. The noble gentleman won't want to have spent his money in vain.' If she refuses to drink at the same table with you, and gets up to go, then our plan has failed. If, however, she objects only in words, and keeps her seat, then our prospects are good, and the game is eight-tenths won. As soon as I see that the wine is making her merry, and that the talk is tending in the right direction, I shall pretend that the wine is all gone, and then I shall go out again to buy some more, and you must give me more money for the purpose. As I go out, I shall simply lock the two of you in. If she is frightened and makes a scene, then you must give up your plan. But if she calmly allows me to lock the door, then the game is nine-tenths won.

"There is yet one-tenth more to win, but before that is won, there are, of course, considerable difficulties to be overcome. When you find yourself alone with her, you must press her with sweet and winning words, and don't be afraid to use the speech of hands and feet. Everything will depend on you. Brush a couple of chopsticks from the table with your sleeve, as though by accident, and when you stoop as though to pick them up give her leg a familiar pat. If she is outraged, and makes a scene, then I shall come in and help you out of the scrape. Of course, if that happens, we shall have to consider the game as good as lost. But if she puts up with all this without a word, then all the ten-tenths of the game are won. But will you show yourself grateful afterwards?"

"You have thought it all out magnificently, adoptive mother!" exclaimed Hsi Men, with enthusiasm. "You almost deserve a seat of honor in the 'Hall of Those who float on Clouds!'"

"There, there. I shall be content with the ten ounces of silver you promised me."

"Don't worry about that! Tell me, when is this plan to be carried out?"

"This very moment, while the Three-Inch Manikin is out, I shall go over to her and borrow the calendar and discuss the matter with her. Now, you have the silk and cotton sent here as soon as possible, and I shall have news for you this very night!"

"Rely on me! I shall keep my word," Hsi Men promised as he took his leave.

On his way home he bought three bolts of silk, and ten ounces of the best pure white cotton wool. He ordered his servant, little Tai, to wrap them up in a shawl and deliver them at once to Mother Wang. With unconcealed delight she received the gift, and immediately entered the neighboring house by way of the back door.

"The lady has not honored my wretched hovel for the last few days," she said, as she greeted Gold Lotus.

"I haven't been altogether well of late, so I haven't felt like going out."

"Have you perhaps a calendar in the house? This old woman would like to pick out an auspicious day for tailoring."

"What do you want to have made, adoptive mother?"

"Well, this old woman is plagued with ten woes and nine laments! The time has come to think of dying. And my son is not at home."

"Where is he, then?"

"He joined a traveling merchant and left for foreign parts. He has not written to me since, and from day to day I grow more anxious about him."

"How old is he?"

"Seventeen."

"Why don't you find him a wife? Then you would have someone in the house to give you a helping hand."

"That's true. Yet as long as I have to do without help I can't manage to go looking for a bride. But I shall talk to him about it directly he returns. Oh, I suffer so from breathlessness and coughing! I feel as if I'd been beaten all over. At night the pain is so bad that I can't close an eye. It is high time to think of my shroud. And now it happens that a kind and wealthy patron of mine, to whom I have been of some service from time to time, going to his house as sick-nurse, or finding him a maid or a concubine—this wealthy gentleman, in his thoughtfulness and sympathy, has presented me with the very stuff for a shroud. It has been lying on my shelves for over a year now. But I could never find the time to make it up. Still, in view of my condition I can't go on putting it off. Besides, it so happens that this is a leap year, with an extra long month, so that I can spare a few days for sewing. But first my tailor fleeces me outrageously, and then he leaves me altogether, with the excuse that he is swamped with work. These endless vexations! They are simply beyond words!"

"I don't know whether I could suit your taste; otherwise, adoptive mother, if you do not despise my help, I could find some time for you in the next few days."

"Oh, if only you would work for me with your precious fingers," the old woman said, "then I could die content! I have often heard people speak highly of your skill, but I did not venture to trouble you with my affairs."

"Why speak of trouble? You have my promise, and it is settled. Now take my calendar along with you and have someone select a lucky day."

"But, my dear little lady, please do not underrate yourself. Is it really necessary to get a stranger to read the calendar, when you yourself are so well versed in all the rhymed and unrhymed poetry of our hundred poets?"

"I have long forgotten all I ever knew," said Gold Lotus, jestingly.

"Excuses, excuses!" Mother Wang persisted, forcing the calendar upon her.

"Tomorrow and the day after are inauspicious," Gold Lotus declared, after she had studied the calendar for a while. "But the day after the day after tomorrow is a lucky day."

Mother Wang impatiently took the calendar from her hand and returned it to its place on the wall.

"Well, but why do we need an especially propitious day for it? The very fact that you are lending me a helping hand is enough so to speak, to kindle a lucky star for me!"

"As far as that goes, when a shroud is in question, an overcast day would really be more suitable for the work," Gold Lotus decided.

"As long as you are helping, any day will do for me, whether good or bad," Mother Wang eagerly agreed. "Then I may expect you tomorrow in my dreary abode?"

"Why, wouldn't you rather come here to me?"

"I should very much like to watch you working, but on the other hand, I have no one to look after the house in my absence."

"That is true. Then, tomorrow after breakfast."

That very evening Mother Wang told Hsi Men that he was to make his appearance on the third afternoon.

Gold Lotus kept her word. The following morning, as soon as her husband had gone out, she went to her neighbor's house. Mother Wang welcomed her with an especially strong bowl of tea, flavored with an infusion of walnuts and pine kernels. Gold Lotus measured and cut the material and began to sew. Old Mother Wang watched her intently, and loudly expressed her admiration. She was now past seventy, but she had never known such skill and dexterity. Towards noon the work was interrupted for a light meal, and then Gold Lotus was busy until the evening.

The Three-Inch Manikin crossed the threshold, with his pannier on his back, at the very moment when Gold Lotus re-entered the house. He noticed that her cheeks were slightly flushed.

"Where have you been?" he asked her.

"At Mother Wang's," she answered. "She asked me to help her to make her shroud. She kept me for dinner at noon."

"You should not have stayed for dinner. We are always accepting favors from her. It isn't that the mouthful of food is worth talking about, but still it's better that you should come home for your meals, so as not to be a burden to her. At all events, if you go there again tomorrow, give her a little money so that you can square the account.

> *The neighbors to whom we bid good day*
> *Are better than kinsfolk far away.*

That's an old maxim. We must keep on good terms with the woman. And if she refuses to accept anything in return, then you had better do the work at home."

Gold Lotus listened to him and was silent.

Next day she resumed her work in her neighbor's house. As noon approached she took from her sleeve three hundred copper cash and handed them to old Mother Wang.

"Here, adoptive mother, buy something to eat and drink with this."

"Why, what does this mean!" cried the old woman in surprise. "I have asked a favor of you—and now you want to put yourself to expense as well! Or perhaps my food isn't to your taste?"

"My imbecile of a husband wishes it. If you persist in spurning this little gift, I am to finish the work at home."

"Your honorable husband is a stickler for form, I must say. Well, if you wish, I will accept your gift," agreed the old woman quickly, for she saw that her scheme was in danger. She added a few coins from her own pocket, and bought some extra good wine and a few special delicacies for their dinner. Towards evening she bade farewell to her guest, with extravagant expressions of gratitude.

On the following afternoon the two women were seated at their sewing in Mother Wang's shop when they heard someone loudly clearing his throat outside, and immediately afterwards a voice called out:

"Hey, Mother Wang! It's a long time since I've seen you!"

The old woman screwed up her eyes.

"Who is that outside?"

"It's I," came the answer.

It was, of course, Hsi Men. He had hardly been able to wait for the third day, and now he punctually appeared before the tea shop in all his finery, with five ounces of silver in his purse, his gold-besprinkled Sze-ch'uen fan in his hand. Mother Wang bustled out to greet him.

"Ah, it is you. Do please come in; you are just in time to see."

And tugging at his sleeve, she ushered Hsi Men into the shop.

"Allow me, my dear little lady, to present to you the noble donor of the material, Master Hsi Men."

He, in the meantime, could not remove his eyes from this fresh, delicate face, over which was piled a cloud of luxuriant blue-black hair. She was wearing over her chemise of white lawn a slashed petticoat of peach-colored silk and blue satin trousers. As he entered she continued her sewing, and merely lowered her head a little. Hsi Men bent his back in a low bow and spoke his words of greeting in a musical tone. She laid her work aside and replied with a soft "Ten-thousandfold happiness!"

"Just think, my noble Lord," old Mother Wang interposed, "until now I have not been able to get to work on the material with which you honored me more than a year ago. And I have to thank the helpful fingers of this lady for the fact that the work is being done at last. And how her fingers can sew; how accurately stitch follows stitch! One can scarcely believe it! Just come closer, noble gentleman, and see for yourself!"

"Marvelous! Simply divine!" he exclaimed.

"Now don't be so sarcastic!" said Gold Lotus with a smile, sinking her head still lower.

"Might I ask to what family the lady is related?" he inquired, pretending ignorance, turning towards Mother Wang.

"See if you can guess!"

"I have no idea."

"Then I'll tell you. But first, take a seat," and she gave him a chair facing Gold Lotus.

"Do you remember, the other day, as you were passing a certain house, you got a good crack on the head?"

"Oh, you mean when the awning prop struck me? Yes, and I wish I knew whose house that was!"

Gold Lotus bowed her head still lower, roguishly murmuring: "I hope that you are no longer offended at my carelessness."

"What? Please tell me, what do you mean?"

"Why, this is the lady, and she is the wife of my neighbor, Wu Ta," said Mother Wang, completing her introduction.

"Alas! That I have been so remiss in paying you my respects!" murmured Hsi Men.

Now Mother Wang turned to the young woman.

"Do you know this gentleman?"

"No."

"He is the honorable Hsi Men, one of the wealthiest gentlemen in this district. He enjoys the honor of personal acquaintance with His Excellency, the District Mandarin, and his fortune is numbered in ten thousand times ten thousand strings of a thousand cash. The Great Dipper in heaven would not be big enough to hold all his money. The large apothecary shop near the yamen belongs to him, and in his granaries there is such a surplus of rice that it is rotting there in heaps. Everything yellow in his house is gold; everything white, silver; everything round, pearls; everything that gleams, gems; and there, too, are rhinoceros horns and elephant tusks; and his First Wife is a born Wu, daughter of Wu, the Left Commandant of the city. She is a clever, capable woman, as I know, for it was I who arranged the marriage. But, tell me, Master Hsi Men, why is it so long since you last came to see me?"

"My daughter's betrothal has kept me busy for the last few days."

He spoke of his domestic affairs, and the conversation was restricted to himself and Mother Wang, the old woman doing her utmost to emphasize the wealth and brilliance of her patron. Meanwhile Gold Lotus continued to sew in silence, with bowed head, but she listened as she sewed.

> *How women do change, alack!*
> *Now it is this, now t'other.*
> *The husband turns his back,*
> *And off they go to another!*

With satisfaction the experienced Hsi Men realized that the beauty was one-tenth won, and it grieved him that he could not take possession of her at once. However, it seemed wiser to bide his time, and allow the old woman to carry out her plan, step by step. Now the important stage was reached where Mother Wang could suggest to her patron, after some circumstantial preparation, that he should send for a good bottle of wine in honor of the lady. Hsi Men pretended to be surprised.

"Well, you have taken me unawares, but fortunately I happen to have some money with me. Please take this." He dived into his pocket, and brought out an ounce of silver.

Gold Lotus signed to the old woman that she must not take it, but her objection was only a matter of form, since, after all, she did not rise from her seat. The old woman, therefore, paid no attention to her, but took the piece of silver and turned to go.

"Might I ask you, dear lady, to keep the gentleman company in the meantime? I shall be back directly."

"I really ought not to, adoptive mother," Gold Lotus shyly objected, but she did not move.

And so they were left alone together. Both were silent. His eyes were steadfastly fixed on her, and she, bent over her sewing, could not refrain from taking an occasional glance at him. It was not long before Mother Wang returned. At a cook shop she had bought a fat goose, a duck crisply browned, roast meat, and freshly baked fish, and also various choice fruits, and wine of the best quality. And soon the table was set with succulent dishes. The old woman beamed encouragingly at Gold Lotus.

"Come now, put aside your work, and drink a cup with us!"

"Oh, no, that would hardly be proper for me. Do you keep the gentleman company!"

"My dear little lady, what nonsense! It is expressly in your honor that he has just washed his hands!"

And without waiting for an answer, the old woman placed a few savory dishes before Gold Lotus. At the beginning of the meal there was still some affectation on the part of the beauty, and some courteous formality on the part of her gallant, but after the third course, when Mother Wang left the room for a moment to fetch more wine, his manner became less constrained.

"How many blooming springs has the lady seen?" he asked.

"I am twenty-five."

"Then you are of the same age as my 'Lowly Intimate.' Her birth took place in the year of the Dragon, on the twenty-fifth of the eighth month."

"Too great an honor! To name me in the same breath as your First Wife is to place heaven and earth on a footing of equality."

"Oh, Madame Gold Lotus has had the most refined education," interposed old Mother Wang. "Not only can she ply her needle and thread to perfection; more than that, she knows our hundred poets and all our philosophers by heart, to say nothing of the art of writing, chess playing, throwing the dice and laying the cards, interpreting signs, and similar arts, in which she's a past mistress."

"Where else could one find so many virtues united?" exclaimed Hsi Men in admiration.

"H'm, this old woman doesn't wish to venture an opinion, but tell me, among all the women of your household is there one to compare with Lady Gold Lotus?"

"You are absolutely right. You see, I cannot explain myself in a word, but I've had the most infernal luck. I never succeeded in bringing the right woman home."

"How about your deceased First, of the house of Chen?"

"Oh, we won't speak of her. It's true she was of humble birth, but how clever and circumspect! I could rely upon her in every way. What a calamity, that death should have taken her from me three years ago! If she were still alive, things would not be at sixes and sevens in my house. Five, seven mouths to be filled, but no one takes the trouble to see to the housekeeping. The proper mistress is lacking. My 'Lowly Intimate' is constantly ailing and leaves the household to look after itself. That is really why I go out so much, since at home I have nothing but vexation."

"Don't take it ill, noble gentleman, if I speak rather frankly; but neither your former nor your present First Wife could compare with Madame Gold Lotus in outward and inward merits."

"True, nor in charm and vitality."

"Still, you have a little friend in East Street, haven't you? Why not let me act as go-between for her?"

"Oh, the little Chang, who sings so drearily. Since I discovered that she has taken to going round the corner I am no longer interested in her."

"And little Li Kiao from the house of joy? You have known her for some time, haven't you?"

"She is now my Second Wife. Unfortunately, she knows nothing about housekeeping. Otherwise I would have made her my First."

"Well, you've always got on excellently with little Cho Tin?"

"Oh, don't speak of her! She was my Third. A little while ago she fell ill and died."

"Oh, dear! Now suppose I knew someone exactly to your taste, would there be any objection if I were to come to your house with my proposal?"

"Since my parents are no longer among the living, I am my own master. Who could interfere with me?"

"I was only jesting. How should I find the right person at a moment's notice?"

"Why shouldn't you? Alas, that I should be so unfortunate in marriage!"

"Why, the wine is all gone!" said the old woman, suddenly interrupting the conversation. "It always gives out just when one feels most inclined to drink! Don't scold me for being so careless. How if I were to fetch another jug of wine?"

Hsi Men thrust his hand into his purse, and drew out the other four silver coins.

"Here, adoptive mother, take them all, so that we can have enough in case we run short again."

The old woman thanked him and set off on her errand, but not before she had cast a searching glance at the beauty. The three large goblets of wine whose contents had passed between her lips had not failed to take their effect upon Gold Lotus. Desire was now kindled within her. She had by no means missed the significance of the conversation, although she had listened in silence, motionless, with her eyes on the ground.

CHAPTER FOUR: *On the Magic Mountain she tastes of stolen Joys. In righteous Indignation Little Brother Yuen raises a Tempest in the Tea Room*

WITH AN INGRATIATING smirk, Mother Wang turned to the young woman. "I am just going to East Street, near the District Yamen; I know where I can get a first-rate wine. It will be some time before I return. Be so kind as to keep the gentleman company until then. There is still a little wine left in the jug there. Fill your cups from that when they are empty."

"Please don't go on my account. I don't need any more wine."

"Oh, you two are no longer strangers. Why shouldn't you drink another cup together? Don't be so faint-hearted!"

"Don't go!" Gold Lotus protested once more, but she did not stir from her seat.

Mother Wang opened the door, and fastened it again from the outside, tying the latch string to the door post. She then sat down outside it and began quickly to spin yarn.

The lovers were now shut up together. Gold Lotus had pushed her seat back from the table, and from time to time she glanced surreptitiously at her companion. Hsi Men was gazing at her fixedly with brimming eyes.

At last he spoke. "What did you say was your honorable family name?"

"Wu."

"Oh, yes, Wu," he repeated, absently. "Not a very common name in this district—Wu. Might the pastry dealer, Wu Ta, the so-called Three-Inch Manikin, be any relation of yours?"

She flushed red for shame. "My husband," she breathed, drooping her head.

For a moment he was stricken dumb, and looked wildly around as though he had lost his senses. Then, in a pathetic tone of voice, he cried: "What an outrage!"

"Why, what injury have you suffered?" she asked in amusement, eyeing him obliquely.

"An outrage to you, not to me!"

And now he began to pay court to her in long, flowery phrases, with many an "Honored Lady" and "Gracious One." Meanwhile, as she fingered her coat, and nibbled at the seam of her sleeve, she provided an accompaniment to his speech, without stopping her nibbling, in the shape of a spirited retort, or a mischievous sidelong glance. And now, on the pretext that the heat was oppressive, he suddenly drew off his thin, green silk surcoat.

"Would you oblige me by putting this on my adoptive mother's bed?" he begged her.

She turned away from him with a shrug.

"Why don't you do it yourself? Your hands are not paralyzed," she replied, merrily nibbling her sleeve.

"Well, if you won't, you won't."

With outstretched arm he reached over the table and threw the garment on to the stove on which the old woman slept. His sleeve caught on one of the chopsticks, and swept it to the floor, and—oh, how providentially!—the chopstick rolled under her dress! As he was about to fill her cup again, and to offer her more food, it was only natural that he should miss one of his chopsticks.

"Is this perhaps your chopstick?" she asked with a smile, pressing her little foot on it.

"Oh, there it is!" he said, in pretended surprise, and he stooped; but instead of picking up the chopstick he gently pressed his hand on her gayly embroidered slipper. She burst out laughing.

"What are you thinking of? I shall scream!"

He fell on his knees before her.

63

"Most gracious lady, take pity on a wretched man!" he sighed, while his hand crept upwards along her thigh.

Struggling and throwing up her hands, with outspread fingers, she cried: "Why, you naughty, dissolute fellow! I'll give you such a box on the ears!"

"Ah, gracious lady, it would be bliss even to die at your hands!"

And without giving her time to reply, he took her in his arms and laid her down on Mother Wang's bed. There he loosened her girdle, and disrobed her. And now, sharing a pillow together, they also shared their delight.

Consider, worthy reader, that he who first possessed Gold Lotus was a feeble graybeard, the old moneybag, Chang. Now, this feeble graybeard, always with a drop on his nose, and his diet of bean-flour gruel—what sort of pleasure could he afford her? Then came the Three-Inch Manikin. The extent of his powers may be left to the imagination. If now she encounters Hsi Men, one long familiar with the play of the moon and the winds, a strong and upstanding lover, must she not at last experience satisfaction?

> *Breast to breast—two mandarin ducks in love,*
> *Tumbling merrily about in the water.*
> *Head to head—a tender phœnix pair,*
> *Busy and gay, building their nest of twigs.*
> *She—fastening her red lips upon his cheek,*
> *He—firmly clasping her upturned head.*
> *Now the two golden clasps have fallen from her tresses,*
> *And the black cloud of her hair lies outspread over the*
> *   pillow.*
> *His vows, deep as the sea and exalted as mountains,*
> *And the thousand variations of his caress,*
> *Banish the last lingering trace of reserve,*
> *As a cloud is driven headlong by the wind.*
> *Overcome by his tender violence*
> *She utters a cry of bliss, like the song of the goldfinch.*
> *The sweet saliva gathers in her mouth*

And she thrusts out her tongue in voluptuous pleasure.
Through all the veins and arteries of her willow-lithe
*   body*
Heavily pulses the brimming, resistless tide of delight.
But now the panting breath of her cherry lips is more
*   languid,*
The dusk of twilight settles upon her eyes,
Her skin is agleam with a hundred fragrant pearls,
Her smooth bosom rises and falls like hurrying waves.
Now—all the sweetness of stolen love consumed—
Two lovers have completed their mating.

The cloud had poured forth its contents. The two lovers were just making themselves presentable again when old Mother Wang suddenly flung open the door and entered. She clapped hands as though in amazement, crying: "Hi, hi, here's a pretty business!" And turning to Gold Lotus, where she stood in confusion:

"I asked you here to sew, not to go whoring! The best thing I can do is to go straight to your husband and tell him the truth, for he'll reproach me all the more if he discovers it behind my back!"

And she turned as if to go, but Gold Lotus, red with shame, held her fast by the coat.

"Adoptive mother, have pity!" she pleaded softly.

"On one condition only: from this day you must meet Master Hsi Men in secret whenever he wishes; whether I call you early in the morning or late at night, you must come. In that case I will be silent. Otherwise I shall tell your husband everything."

Gold Lotus could not speak for shame.

"Well, what about it? Answer quickly, please!" the old woman insisted.

"I promise," came the hardly audible reply.

Now the old woman turned to Hsi Men:

"Noble gentleman, you have had ten-tenths of your desire—now remember your promise! Otherwise. . . ."

"Have no fear, adoptive mother, I keep my word!"

"There is still another point," the old woman continued. "I have your promises, it is true, but they are not worth much without visible proof. I propose that you exchange mutual pledges as evidence of your sincerity."

Hsi Men immediately removed a golden hair clasp and made it fast to the curls on the nape of Gold Lotus's neck. She, however, took it from her hair and hid it in her sleeve, for she feared that her husband might notice it and grow suspicious. For her own part, she did not want to provide any memento of the incident, but before she could prevent it Mother Wang had drawn a flowered handkerchief of fine Hangchow silk from her sleeve and thrust it into Hsi Men's hand. They drank a few more cups of wine, and then Gold Lotus rose and slipped home through the back door.

"Tell me, have I done well?" Mother Wang asked Hsi Men.

"Excellently! I am deeply indebted."

"And is she well versed in the art of love?"

"Oh, she is a very daughter of delight. . . . There is no describing it!"

"Then don't forget the reward you promised!"

"I shall send it to you as soon as I get home."

The old woman laughingly quoted the lines:

> *"The eye already sees the conquering banners wave;*
> *Now from afar the ear hears the triumphant blast!*

Still, I hope I shan't have to climb out of my coffin to collect the mourners' fees from you!"

Well, on the very next morning she was able to pocket her ten shining pieces of silver. Hsi Men brought them in person. It is an old story that money makes people accommodating. Mother Wang's black eyes sparkled with joy when they met the glitter of the snowy metal. Not contenting herself with the most effusive expressions of gratitude, she offered of her own accord to fetch her beautiful neighbor then and there. It was early in the day, and the

Three-Inch Manikin was sure to be still at home; however, she would risk a visit, and make arrangements with the young woman on the pretext that she wished to borrow a gourd ladle. And off she went next door.

Gold Lotus was just putting her husband's breakfast on the table when little Ying came in to say that Mother Wang had knocked at the back door and was asking for the loan of a gourd ladle. Gold Lotus hurried out at once, gave the old woman the required ladle, and invited her to come in. Mother Wang thanked her, saying that she could not stay, as there was no one in her house, but she gave the young woman a sly pinch, to make her understand that Hsi Men had arrived. She hurried her husband through his breakfast, and no sooner had he trotted off with his load of tarts than she raced upstairs to her bedroom and hurriedly threw on her best clothes, adorning herself in all her finery. Before leaving she gave orders to little Ying:

"I am going to Mother Wang's for a while. Take care of the house while I am out and let me know the minute my husband returns. Do you understand my orders? If you don't do just as I tell you I'll smash you to pieces, you miserable, common little thing!"

Hsi Men thought he beheld an apparition from heaven when Gold Lotus entered the room. Soon they were fondly sitting together, shoulder to shoulder and thigh to thigh.

"Did the honorable husband say anything yesterday?" Mother Wang asked casually as she brought them tea and wine.

"He asked if we had finished making your shroud. I said yes, and then I added that I still had to make the slippers and the stockings for your last journey."

Hsi Men took this opportunity to examine his beloved in detail. She seemed to him even more ravishing than before. How delightful, as she drank, was the red flush upon the white of her cheek! And the two ringlets of hair, that boldly curled over her temples, as though painted there with a brush! To him, she seemed to possess the unearthly beauty of the Moon Fairy.

In ecstasy he clasped her to his breast; the hem of her robe was lifted, revealing her neat little feet which were thrust into tiny black satin slippers. He lifted her robe still higher, and already his senses began to tingle. As lovers, they drank from the same side of the cup.

"How old are you really?" she asked.

"Thirty-five. My birthday is on the twenty-eighth of the seventh month."

"How many wives have you?"

"Besides my First Wife, I have three or four secondary wives. But not one of them really pleases me."

"And how many children have you?"

"Only a young daughter who is going to be married soon."

From his sleeve he took a flat silver box, gilded within, and containing a subtly perfumed tea and olive paste. He offered her some of the paste on the tip of his tongue. Sighing and moaning aloud with delight, they clasped each other closely. Old Mother Wang was discreet enough to leave them undisturbed at their amorous play. She busied herself with pouring their wine and bringing them food. Higher and higher rose the tide of their passion; and soon they were alone.

From this time onwards Gold Lotus met Hsi Men every day in Mother Wang's tea room. They clove together as firmly and inseparably as glue and lacquer. It is an old story that news of good works seldom goes beyond the threshold of the house, but reports of evil deeds are quickly circulated for a thousand miles around. In less than half a month the affair in Mother Wang's house was discussed in the streets and squares of the whole neighborhood. The one person who knew nothing about it was the husband, Wu Ta.

> With all his efforts directed to gaining his livelihood,
> How should he suspect betrayal and deceit in his home?

There lived in the district a fifteen-year-old lad with the family name of Hiao. Since he had come from the prefecture of Yuen

Chow he was commonly known as "Little Brother Yuen." He was a thoroughly wide-awake and wily little fellow. Except for his aged father, he was quite alone in the world, and he managed to make his living by selling fresh fruit in the many taverns in the neighborhood of the yamen. The wealthy Hsi Men was a patron of his, who would sometimes give him a few cash as pocket money, over and above the price of his fruit.

One day, as the lad in question was walking the streets with his basket of pears under his arm, he suddenly decided to seek out his patron, Hsi Men. On the way he got into talk with a garrulous fellow, who told him:

"Why, if you're looking for Hsi Men, I can tell you where to find him!"

"Where? Please tell me, old Uncle," said Little Brother Yuen.

"Well, he's carrying on as usual with Lady Gold Lotus. He meets her every day in Mother Wang's tea room in Purple Stone Street. You go there, my lad, and you'll find him there for certain!"

Little Brother Yuen thanked him for his information, picked up his basket of pears, and set off for Mother Wang's tea room. Mother Wang was sitting on a bench by the door, busily winding yarn. He set down his basket.

"My most respectful greeting, adoptive mother!" he said, looking her in the face.

"What do you want here?"

"I am looking for a certain fine gentleman, so as to earn a few coppers for my old father."

"What fine gentleman are you talking about?"

"Come, adoptive mother, are you joking? I mean Master Hsi Men, of course." Little Brother Yuen was already at the door. But Mother Wang seized him and held him fast.

"Where are you going, you little monkey?" she cried angrily. "There's no admittance here for such as you!"

"But I only want to fetch him out, to say a word to him."

"Stop, you little tramp! There's no Master Hsi Men here," Mother Wang stormed at him, now in a fury.

"Adoptive mother, don't gobble up everything yourself! Let me pick up a few miserable crumbs! After all, what harm have I done?"

"You dare to ask that, you intruder, you little criminal!"

Little Brother Yuen lost his temper.

"You're as clumsy as a horse's hoof, and as close as a wooden bowl for chopping greens that won't let a drop of water through! If you really want me to say all I know—only I'm afraid it might upset old Brother Pastry-Dealer!"

"He's crazy!" decided the frightened old woman, bursting into a rage: "You little monkey, have you come here just to make a row?"

"Well, if I'm a little monkey you are a stubborn old cow!"

Furious, the old woman grabbed him and gave him a couple of stinging blows on the ear.

"Ow, you're hurting me!" cried the little fellow.

"You whore's monkey-brat, you, if you make any noise, I'll give you a few more boxes on the ear!"

"You wicked, poisonous old reptile, what harm have I done you?"

In answer, the old woman dealt him blow upon blow, and finally forced him out into the street. She hurled his basket after him, so that the pears were scattered to all four quarters of the heavens and over the face of the earth. What could the poor little monkey do, but pick up the scattered pears as he made his escape, venting his rage in howls and words of abuse?

"Venomous old snake!" he hissed, shaking a fist at the tea room. "Don't be afraid, I'll pay you back for this! Never fear! I'll send a guest to your shop one of these days, and that will be the end of you!"

Then he picked up his basket, and trotted off.

He had disturbed the straw concealing the fox's earth,
And had alarmed a pair of ducks who were slumbering in
the sand.

CHAPTER FIVE: *Little Brother Yuen
devises a Plan to detect the amorous Pair. Wu
Ta swallows a poisonous Potion and comes to a
sorry End*

> *Regard with philosophic eye*
> *This whole romantic hue and cry,*
> *And what they call the smile of Fate*
> *Is seen to be ill luck too late.*
> *Are mind and heart of one accord?*
> *Then that is love, to use the word,*
> *Yet pleasure soon gives way to pain*
> *When hatred leads to self-disdain.*
> *These flowers are gaudy?—pass them by.*
> *These wilding grasses?—let them lie.*
> *Give me the real, the solid—these*
> *Are qualities that bring us ease.*
> *A simple housewife meets my wishes,*
> *Children, a few, and frugal dishes.*
> *Why this is better soon is told:*
> *You spare your nerves and save your gold.*

WHEN LITTLE BROTHER YUEN had been
thrashed by the old woman, he ran off with his basket of pears
under his arm to find the Three-Inch Manikin. Two streets further
on he ran into him.

"It's a long time since I've seen you," he greeted Wu Ta. "But
you've put on a lot of fat."

"I didn't know I had grown any stouter than I was."

"Listen: I wanted to buy some spelt a little while ago, but I couldn't find any anywhere. And then I was told I could get it from you."

"How so? I haven't got a poultry run."

"You don't say so! But perhaps you yourself are a waddling, overfed drake, so fat that his legs won't carry him, and who lets himself be stuffed into the cooking pot without a struggle?"

"Are you trying to tease me, you little bandit? My wife has no secret affairs with strange men; so why do you call me an overfed drake?"

"And I tell you straight: your wife *does* have secret affairs with strange men!"

Wu Ta seized the little fellow. "Tell me his name!" he cried.

"Ha, ha, I can't help laughing! Instead of shaking me you ought to bite the fellow next door!"

"Good little brother, tell me who he is! I'll give you ten tarts as a reward!"

"This isn't to be settled with tarts. No, this is going to cost you a proper banquet! After the third cup I'll tell you."

"What a sly rascal! Well then, come along!" and Wu Ta disappeared with the boy into a little wineshop near by.

When he had stuffed himself with food and drink, the little monkey at last agreed to speak.

"Just feel those bumps on my head."

"Hallo, where did you get those?"

"From that old bitch Mother Wang . . ." and Little Brother Yuen related the incident from the very beginning.

"I had to rile you a bit with my hints or I'd never have got you to ask me questions," he added.

"Is all this really true?" Wu Ta demanded.

"As true as you're a drake! The two of them just wait until you leave the house, and then they meet at Mother Wang's, and enjoy themselves. I'm not trying to fool you."

Wu Ta reflected.

"Little brother," he said, "I can't deny that just lately my wife

72

has been visiting old Mother Wang every day, but she says it is to help the old woman to prepare her funeral garments. I have noticed that my wife's face is always flushed when she comes home. Then there's something else that worries me. She's always so mean to little Ying, my daughter by my first marriage; she beats her, scolds her from morning till night, and sometimes gives her nothing to eat. Lately, too, she's often distracted and has a surly expression when she looks at me. So I was already beginning to feel just a little suspicious, and what you tell me confirms my suspicion. What do you say—shall I carry my load home now and surprise that lustful couple in the act?"

"You haven't much sense for your age. Do you imagine that the old bitch will allow herself to be intimidated by anyone? A fine chance you'd have with her! As soon as you showed yourself, she'd give an agreed signal and secretly let your wife out at the back door. Then you'd have to deal with Hsi Men alone, and he'd soon make you feel the weight of his fist. Besides, he has money, and influence; he'd twist the affair round and bring a charge against you. And then you'd have a lawsuit on your hands. No one would back you up, and you'd be risking your very life."

"You are quite right there—but then how am I to revenge myself?"

"Well, I haven't revenged myself on the old woman yet. Listen to me; I'll tell you how we ought to set about it. You go home today as usual; don't make a scene, and don't speak a word. To-morrow morning bake less pastry than usual. I shall be waiting for you at the first corner. You remain close at hand. As soon as I see Hsi Men go into the old woman's tea room, I shall make a sign to you. Then you come with me, and lie in wait close to the house. First I'll begin to tease the old bitch, and of course she'll try to beat me again. As soon as you see me sling my basket of pears into the middle of the street, you must rush up and force your way into the room, and shout: 'This is an outrage!' I shall hold fast to the old woman in the meantime. What do you say?"

"Excellent! I am in your debt, little brother. Here, take these two strings of cash. It is settled, then? Tomorrow morning we meet at the corner of Purple Stone Street."

Little Brother Yuen departed with his strings of cash, and several tarts as well.

Wu Ta settled the score, made a few purchases, and went home.

Conscious of guilt, Gold Lotus had discontinued her incessant bickering and abuse; she had lately assumed a covertly observant attitude.

"You've been putting a pint or two away, haven't you?" she casually remarked when he came home that evening.

"Three, to be exact. With a friend of mine, a broker," he answered calmly.

Otherwise the evening passed as usual. Next morning, Wu Ta started off on his daily rounds with his load of tarts. But this time he took only three trayfuls. His wife, whose thoughts were with her lover, never noticed that he had baked fewer than usual. She could hardly wait until her husband was out of the house before hurrying across to the tea room.

Just as they had arranged, Wu Ta found Little Brother Yuen waiting for him at the corner of the first turning out of Purple Stone Street.

"Well?"

"A little too early. You have time to make a short round, but don't wander off too far. The fellow is sure to arrive directly."

Wu Ta sailed away like a cloud. He quickly disposed of a couple of tarts, and returned.

"Now we're for it!" Little Brother Yuen informed him. "When my basket flies out into the street, that will be your time!"

And he made directly for the tea room. Impudently planting himself before old Mother Wang, he cried out: "Old Swine of a bitch, what on earth induced you to beat me yesterday, eh?"

The old woman, who could not suddenly alter her nature, shouted back: "You monkey, I don't want anything to do with you! Why have you come here abusing me again?" In a fury, she tried to fall upon him, but the little monkey, quickly hurling his basket

74

into the middle of the street, shouted loudly: "Come on, then!" seized her by the girdle, and butted her in the body with his head, so that she staggered and would certainly have fallen if the wall at her back had not supported her. While the little fellow rammed her against the wall with all his might, the Three-Inch Manikin, his coat girdled up high, came dashing up with long strides. The old woman was unable to bar the way, being held fast by the little monkey, and she had to content herself with shouting aloud: "Wu Ta is coming!"

Warned by her cry, the lovers within drew apart in alarm. It was too late for Gold Lotus to escape; she rushed to the door and tried to barricade it with the weight of her body. In the excitement of the moment, Hsi Men had crept under the bed.

"A fine business, this!" cried Wu Ta, as he vainly attempted to force the door inwards.

Gold Lotus, breathless from exertion, appealed to her cowardly lover.

"At ordinary times you can crow with the best," she scolded him under her breath, "and you boast of your mighty fist. But when it comes to the point you are good for nothing, and you tremble at the sight of a pasteboard tiger!"

If she had hoped by these words to compel Hsi Men to fall upon her husband, and enable her to escape, she had achieved her end. Hsi Men, whose honor was affronted, crawled out from under the bed.

"It was only that I lost my head for the moment," he excused himself. "I'll soon show you what I can do!"

And with a sudden jerk he tore the door open.

"Get out of here!" he roared at the Three-Inch Manikin. Wu Ta tried to close in on him, but he was met by so violent a kick in the pit of his stomach that the puny little fellow fell over backwards. Hsi Men seized this opportunity to make a hasty escape. When Little Brother Yuen saw that matters were going badly, he thrust the old woman aside and likewise took to his heels. Out of respect for Hsi Men the neighbors had not ventured to intervene.

Old Mother Wang now attempted to raise Wu Ta from the ground. But when she discovered that blood was trickling from his mouth, and that his face was white as wax, she ordered Gold Lotus to fetch a bowl of water; then she sprinkled the unconscious man until he came to himself. With their united efforts they lifted him on to their shoulders and carried him out of the back door to his own house. They took him upstairs to his bedroom, and laid him down on the bed.

Since nothing in particular resulted from this incident, the very next morning found the lovers once again at their usual rendezvous. They hoped that Wu Ta would die of his own accord before long. For five days the poor fellow lay sick in bed, unable even to sit up. In vain he asked for hot broth and cold water; in vain he called for his wife. She deliberately ignored all his requests. He was actually compelled to watch her adorn and beautify herself before she went out, and to see her return each time with flushed cheeks. Not even little Ying, his own daughter, was allowed to go near him. Gold Lotus warned her severely: "Don't you dare to speak to him or take him anything! Or you'll get something to remember, you wretched creature!"

The little girl did not dare to take the sick man a spoonful of soup or a drop of water, although he several times fainted from exhaustion.

One day he called Gold Lotus to his bedside, and said: "I know you are carrying on a love affair. I myself caught you at it the other day, and it was you who incited your lover to kick me in the stomach, and it is because of you that I am now hovering between life and death. Very well, amuse yourself as you will; I can't deal with you, and after all, it's all one to me if I die. But think of my brother! You know the sort of man he is. Sooner or later he will return and then . . . Now, I offer you this choice. Have some little compassion for me at last; help me, so that I can recover my health, and I won't breathe a word of this affair to him when he returns. But if you go on being so hard-hearted, then he shall know everything!"

Gold Lotus did not reply, but hurriedly went next door to consult old Mother Wang. Hsi Men, who was waiting for her, felt as though a bucket of icy water had been emptied over him.

"Damn it all!" he exclaimed, turning to Gold Lotus, "I never thought of this tiger slayer from King Yang mountain! On the other hand, I have loved you too long, and I cherish you too dearly —I can't possibly give you up. Mother Wang, is there no way out? Confound it all!"

"Look at him!" Mother Wang dryly remarked. "A man like that wants to take the helm, and he trembles in every limb! While I, a simple boatman, who punts along as I'm told, I'm not afraid!"

"Very well, I'm a useless fellow and I don't know what course to steer. But haven't you any bright idea?"

"I do know of a plan. But it all depends upon whether you want to be mates for good or only for a time."

"What do you mean by that?"

"Let us suppose that you separate for the present, allow Wu Ta to grow well again, and persuade him not to drop a word of the story to his brother; wait patiently until his brother has to go abroad on another commission, and then resume your relations. That's what I call mating for a time. If, on the other hand, you want to be mated permanently, to meet each other daily, and to risk all the consequences without misgiving, then I know of an excellent plan. Though, really, I don't quite like to speak of it."

"Truly, dear adoptive mother, you are as thoughtful for us as a brood hen for her chicks. Of course we want to be mated permanently."

"Well, in that case, all I need is a mere trifle, a little something that the gods permit to exist. It happens, however, that I cannot obtain it elsewhere than in your shop, my noble gentleman. So listen. The Manikin is now lying seriously ill. Take advantage of his hour of need. You have, of course, some arsenic in your shop? Leave a small quantity with Lady Gold Lotus. A pinch of it mixed in a medicine for stomach troubles, and it's all up with the little dwarf. The body will be decently burned, so that not a trace will

be left. Then you need not fear his brother's return. And after that
—there is a good old saying:

> *"First marriage—to please one's parents,*
> *Second marriage—to please oneself.*

Do you think this troublesome brother of his will interfere with
your wedding arrangements? He will not dare to protest, even in
silence. Wait one little half-year, until the widow's regulation period of mourning is over, and nothing further will stand in the
way of your marriage. And you will then be mated for good and
will belong to each other until death. What do you say?"

"Excellent in every detail, dear adoptive mother! I, too, know a
fine old adage:

> *"If you would breathe in joy with every breath*
> *You must not shrink before another's death.*

Enough! That's settled."

"Then it is agreed. We tear the weed out by the roots, so that
it can never grow again. And now, noble gentleman, make haste,
bring the stuff here and I'll soon show the young woman how to
use it. And afterwards, will there be a fat reward for old Mother
Wang?"

"There will be no haggling about that."

A little while later, Hsi Men handed a little package of arsenic
to the old woman. She turned to Gold Lotus.

"Now attend to what I say: Your husband has reproached you
again today, saying that you ought to help him to recover his
health. Behave as though you had taken his words to heart, and
assume an appearance of touching affection. If he asks you for
a medicine for the pain in his stomach, you are to mix a dose of
arsenic in his drink. Wait until a feverish ague sets in, then give
him still more of the drink. When the poison begins to work
properly, his bowels will burst and he will scream aloud with pain.
You must take care that no one hears him. Push him under the
blankets, and hold the edges down firmly. The next effect of the

poison will be that he will begin to bleed from all the seven openings of his body. He will also, in his convulsions, bite into his lips. So you must have ready a kettle of hot water and a washcloth. As soon as it's all over, be careful to wash off all traces of blood with the wet steaming cloth. When once we have sent him out of the house in his coffin and have safely reduced him to ashes, there will be nothing more to worry about."

"Very pretty! But my hand is weak. What if it should falter?"

"Then you have only to knock on the wall, and I'll come over and help you."

"Go to work very carefully," Hsi Men admonished the two women. "Tomorrow, at the hour of the fifth drum beat, I will come again." And with that he took his leave.

Gold Lotus, too, returned home at once. In her sleeve she concealed the package of arsenic, which the old woman had rubbed to a fine powder between her fingers.

Gold Lotus went upstairs and into the sick-room. The sick man's breathing was thin as a thread and his eyes had a look that spoke of resignation in the face of death. She sat down on the edge of the bed and forced herself to sob aloud.

"What are you crying for?" he asked in surprise. She pretended to wipe the tears from her eyes.

"In a thoughtless moment I went astray and allowed myself to be inveigled by this Hsi Men. Who would have suspected that the brute would give you a kick in the pit of the stomach? But I have discovered that there is a remedy for your pain. I have wanted to give it you before this, but I don't know . . . perhaps you distrust me, and will refuse to take it?"

"I trust you," he said, "and the whole affair shall be blotted out of our memories with a stroke of the brush if you will only help me. My brother shall never learn a word of it. So be quick and bring me this medicine!"

Gold Lotus took a few coppers, went at once to Old Mother Wang, and made the old woman give her the questionable remedy. She then returned with it to the sick-room.

79

"Here is the remedy that the physician prescribed for stomach pains," she said, handing him the medicine. "You are to take some of it at midnight and then lie down to sleep. I am to cover you well with blankets so that you may fall into a sweat, and perhaps tomorrow you will be able to get up."

"Good! But then I shall have to ask you to sit up for a little while, so that you can give me the medicine at midnight."

"Don't worry about that. I am going to look after you."

When it began to grow dark, Gold Lotus lighted the lamp in the kitchen and set a pot of water to boil on the hearth. She put a washcloth into the pot. She listened tensely for the night watch to mark the hour of the night. At last the third drum beat announced that midnight was approaching. Then she rose, emptied the powdered arsenic into a cup, and carried it upstairs to her husband, together with a bowl of hot water.

"Where have you put the medicine?" she asked him.

"Under the mattress, near the bolster. Be quick and give it to me!"

She drew the powdered medicine from the place indicated, dropped it into the cup, and diluted it with hot water from the bowl. Then she took a silver clasp from her hair, and stirred the mixture thoroughly. She propped up the sick man's head with her left hand, and with her right she held the drink to his lips.

"But what a nauseous taste!" he exclaimed after the first mouthful.

"The taste doesn't matter; the main thing is that it should do its work," she said soothingly.

As he opened his mouth for a second sip, she forcibly poured the entire contents of the cup down his throat. She then let him fall back on the pillow, with a hasty movement she leaped away from his bed.

"Woman, that burns me terribly inside!" he groaned aloud. "Oh, oh! I can't bear it!"

Now she quickly stepped to the foot of the bed, and rolled two blankets in such a way that even his head was completely and securely muffled.

"I can't breathe!" his smothered voice could be heard faintly beneath the blankets.

"This will make you sweat as the doctor prescribed," she comforted him. Once more the voice began to speak, and she was suddenly terrified lest he should extricate himself from the blankets. With swift determination she leaped upon the bed and set herself astride on his chest, and with both hands she pressed the ends of the blankets as tightly as she could against his head, and never relaxed her hold. Two smothered outcries, a death rattle, and the sick man stirred no more. Gold Lotus lifted the blankets a little. His teeth were clenched in his lips, and blood was trickling from the seven openings of his body. Then she was overcome with horror. With one bound she was off the bed and at the wall, beating on it wildly. It was not long before a loud hawking in front of the door announced that the old woman had come. Gold Lotus rushed down the stairs and let her in.

"Finished?" whispered the old woman.

"Finished!" was the low reply. "But I feel I've no strength left."

"I'll help you."

They went into the kitchen. The old woman rolled her coat-sleeves up high, poured boiling water from the kettle into a pail, dropped a washcloth into it, and carried the pail upstairs. She went up to the bed and pulled back the blankets. With the wet and steaming cloth she wiped away the blood from about the mouth and lips of the dead man, then carefully cleansed the other orifices. Together they lifted the dead man, having put his clothes on the body, and cautiously carried him down the stairs. In the hallway they laid him on an old door, combed his hair, put a cap on his head, and pulled on his coat, shoes, and hose. They veiled his face with white crêpe and spread a clean coverlet over the corpse. Finally they went upstairs once more and set the sickroom in order. When the old woman had gone, Gold Lotus crouched down beside the corpse, and for the sake of appearance began the mourning that is enjoined upon afflicted widows.

There are, for widows, three modes of mourning; weeping,

and uttering sudden outcries, which is called lamenting; weeping without an outcry, which may be called wet mourning; and finally, neither shedding tears nor wailing aloud, and this is dry mourning. Gold Lotus contented herself with this third mode, while she remained beside the bier for the rest of the night.

At the hour of the fifth drum beat, while the day was still dawning, Hsi Men entered the house of old Mother Wang. When he had heard all the details of the affair, he gave the old woman money to purchase a coffin, and to cover the expenses of the funeral. Then he bade her call his beloved.

"Now that he is dead," Gold Lotus asked him, "can I rely on you to save me from falling into the snares of the law?"

"But don't worry yourself unnecessarily!"

"And what if you should be untrue to me?"

"Then may I suffer as did Wu Ta!"

The old woman interrupted the conversation.

"There is only one thing to trouble about now, noble gentleman. Today, when we come to burying the corpse, we may perhaps have to deal with some scrupulous coroner who will want to sift the matter to the bottom. Our District Intendant, Master Hu Kiu, is a clever and discerning gentleman. It's to be hoped that in this case he won't refuse to supervise the inquest. . . ."

"Ha, ha, leave that to me. I shall deal with the good Hu Kiu in person. I am sure he will respect my wishes."

"Then make haste and notify him, for we must lose no time."

CHAPTER SIX: *Hu Kiu allows himself to be corrupted and deceives the Gods. Mother Wang, a busy Go-Between, gets a Wetting*

Some day, dear love, the parting comes!
Even gems, even pearls, split and fall asunder.
Forgotten are vows, though deep as the sea, exalted as the hills!
Is love to shield you like the eternal heavens?
Alas, from the mate of the phœnix to the hen pheasant
Is only a step!
All in vain does the good Siao Lang,
On her way to the House of Joy,
Turn her head for one joyless backward glance.
Though the new love outshine even the First Wife,
On her too waits division and an ocean of sorrows.

AT DAYBREAK, Mother Wang set out to purchase a coffin, incense, candles, a few pairs of silver-paper slippers, and other articles of pasteboard, such as are burned on the occasion of a funeral. Upon her return she lit a lamp, and placed it at the head of the corpse.

Presently the people of the neighborhood came in to view the corpse on its bier, and the young widow crouching beside it. For the sake of appearances she covered her lovely face with her hands, as though in grief.

"What illness did he die of?" the inquisitive neighbors wanted to know.

"Cramp of the stomach," the widow explained. "He grew worse from day to day, and last night, about the hour of the third drum beat, alas! he passed away. Alas, alas, what a bitter fate is mine!" and she broke into loud sobbing.

The onlookers naturally drew their own conclusions as to her part in the matter, but they asked no further questions, and spoke all sorts of consoling words: "The dead cannot be recalled to life. Life too must have its due. Don't mourn to excess, or you'll injure your health in this heat."

With feigned emotion, Gold Lotus then expressed her thanks, and the visitors withdrew.

Meanwhile Mother Wang had not been idle. She ordered the coffin, bought everything necessary for the funeral, and held it in readiness. She begged the District Intendant, Hu Kiu, to preside over the inquest, and finally she summoned from the Cloister of Gracious Recompense two bonzes who were to keep vigil that night and pray for the welfare of the dead man's soul.

Towards the eleventh hour of the forenoon the District Inspector Hu Kiu was walking leisurely to the house of mourning, having previously engaged two men to cremate the body. At the junction of Purple Stone Street and a crossroad he suddenly encountered Hsi Men.

"Whither, old friend?" Hsi Men cordially greeted him.

"Why, to the house of the deceased pastry pedlar, Wu Ta, whom we are burying today."

"Wait a moment, I have something to say to you." The other allowed his friend to lead him round a corner, and into a little wineshop. Hsi Men ushered him into an isolated booth on the upper story, and with exaggerated politeness waved him to the seat of honor. He then ordered a jug of warm spiced wine, and a few meatless dishes. Hu Kiu silently wondered at so much cordiality.

"He never condescended to drink with me before. And today, all of a sudden? There is something behind all this!" he thought to himself.

For a few minutes they ate and drank in silence. Then Hsi Men brought to view a glittering, snowy bar of silver. He placed it on the table before his companion, saying: "My good friend, do

84

not spurn, I beg of you, this humble token of my respect. I shall show myself still more appreciative in the near future!"

Hu Kiu made a gesture of protest with his hand. "What claim can this unworthy person lay to such generosity? I have never rendered the honorable gentleman an iota of service. How then can I accept a present of ten silver ounces? Perhaps, however, the honorable gentleman has some injunctions. . . ."

"That's all right. Put it away!"

"And what is the matter in question?"

"Nothing special. You ought to receive a bit of 'affliction money' for your mournful duties in the pastry dealer's house. By the way, will you do me the service of directing the proceedings at the cremation of Wu Ta's body, and, above all, see that it remains properly covered?"

"And is that your only request? I expected something prodigious. For that, why so sumptuous a donation?"

"If you do not accept this trifle, then I must consider your answer as a refusal."

Hu Kiu had the greatest respect for Hsi Men, being well aware of his influence with the authorities. He therefore pocketed the bribe, and the two presently parted company. Hsi Men asked the innkeeper to mark up the score and call for payment at the apothecary shop.

"Then, old friend," said Hsi Men at the tavern door, "I can count on your discretion! Later, I shall show myself still more appreciative of this favor."

He took his leave of the Inspector. The latter, with the shining silver ingot up his sleeve, reflected. "Of course, there is something at the bottom of all this. But what concern is it of mine? The money comes at a most opportune moment, and by the time the younger Wu returns, I shall have thought of some explanation."

Speculating thus, he arrived at the house of mourning. Outside the two corpse burners were already waiting for him, and indoors, on fire with impatience, was old Mother Wang.

85

"Of what disease did this man die?" Hu Kiu demanded of his assistants.

"From stomach cramps, so his wife says," they replied.

He lifted the curtain before the door, and entered.

"We have been waiting a long time for you," Mother Wang greeted him in the hallway. "Why do you come so late? The registrar of deaths arrived long ago."

"It's all right; I was delayed a little."

In a simple, colorless mourning robe, a white cloth bound about her head, and sobbing in simulated grief, the widow Gold Lotus entered.

"Do not grieve to excess, honored lady," the Inspector consoled her. "Your husband has now entered heaven."

Covering her eyes with her hands, and shamming tears, she responded: "Alas, how inexpressibly bitter is my fate! A few days ago he began to have some pain in the stomach, and now, already, he is dead! Alas, how bitter is my fate!"

As he examined her features, Hu Kiu thought to himself: "Formerly, I was always hearing that she could not bear the sight of her husband. And now . . . ? But what's that to me? Why did he ever marry her?"

Hsi Men's ten ounces of silver had taken effect. Casually the Inspector approached the body. The registrar of deaths read a sutra, and set up the little Banner of a Thousand Autumns. Hu Kiu raised the white crêpe pall, and inspected the dead man at closer range. He observed the swollen, bluish-green fingernails, the darkly discolored lips, the face, yellow as wax, with the eyes starting from their sockets. That here was indisputable evidence of an atrocious crime could not escape his notice, nor that of his two assistants.

"The discoloration of the face is supicious," they observed, "the lips show the marks of teeth, and there is blood in his mouth. . . ."

"Nonsense!" he silenced them. "That's the result of the heat. Come on, take up the body!"

And hurriedly, with seven hands and eight feet, they proceeded to lay out the body and put it in the coffin. Finally, the coffin was fastened down on both sides with the Nails of Long Life. Mother Wang presided over these doings, repeatedly urging the men to make haste, and she presented Hu Kiu with a string of copper cash.

"When is the coffin to be sent for?" he asked, after dismissing his assistants.

"The day after tomorrow, at the request of the widow. He is to be burned outside the city walls."

Hu Kiu took his leave.

That evening the mourners partook of a solemn feast, and the next day the bonzes of the Cloister of Gracious Recompense held a service for the welfare of the dead man's soul. At last, early in the morning of the next day, toward the hour of the fifth drum beat, a party of corpse burners arrived and carried the coffin outside the city walls. Several of the neighbors fell into line with the procession, which was headed by the litter of the widow, who was dressed in white mourning garments. Throughout the journey, with crocodile tears in her eyes, she played the role of the bereaved widow lamenting the loss of her beloved husband. Outside the walls the procession halted before the Palace of Terrestrial Transformation. A funeral pyre was set ablaze, and the coffin placed in the flames; in a little while it was completely and decently reduced to ashes. Whatever bones and other mortal remains had resisted the ravages of the fire were cast into the city moat near by. The ceremony was immediately followed by a dinner at Hsi Men's expense in the refectory of the Cloister of Gracious Recompense.

When Gold Lotus returned home, she went into a room in the upper story and set up a tablet to the memory of the dead, with the inscription "The Soul of My Deceased Husband, Wu Ta," and placed a burning water lamp at its foot. Around the frame of the tablet she fastened little gold and silver banners. She did not forget to lay before the tablet some spirit money of gilt and silvered pasteboard.

That very day she had an assignation with her lover. Mother Wang was sent away, so that now, for the first time, they could devote themselves undisturbed to indulgence in that pleasure which they enjoyed both vertically and horizontally. Their former delights in Mother Wang's tea room had always been marred by a certain furtiveness. But now, having the house at their disposal, they could at last give free vent to their desires, sleeping afterwards late into the morning.

At first, fearing the opinion of the neighbors, Hsi Men would visit the house by way of Mother Wang's tea room, but later, even when accompanied by his little serving lad, he dispensed with ceremony and went straight to the back door of Wu Ta's house. His relations with Gold Lotus became more and more intimate and impassioned; so that he sometimes did not go home for three, four, or even five nights in succession. This naturally caused intense indignation among the members of his household, who, both great and small, felt neglected and disdained.

The affair between Hsi Men and Gold Lotus had already continued for two months when, on the fifth day of the fifth month, the delightful Festival of the Dragon Boat was celebrated.

> *Willow leaves, streamers of emerald green,*
> *Swing to and fro.*
> *Like crimson dots of ink*
> *The fruit gleams from the crown of the pomegranate tree.*
> *The wind, softly soughing,*
> *Fans us with balmy coolness.*
> *There is merry tippling in every nest;*
> *Today is the Festival of the Dragon Boat.*

Hsi Men, on the occasion of the Festival, attended the Fair in the Temple of the Five Holy Mountains. On his way back he dropped into Mother Wang's tea room. His very first question concerned his beloved.

"Her mother is with her, just now, on a visit, and I'm afraid she won't be at liberty," the old woman told him. "But I'll go over and see."

She found mother and daughter together sitting over a cup of wine. Gold Lotus hospitably invited her to drink with them: "Come, we will drink to your future progeny!"

"Alas! I'm past all that—a poor, forsaken old creature! Perhaps it would be more fitting in respect of yourself, young woman!"

Gold Lotus replied jestingly:

"Young buds are for the most part empty;
Late blossoms are more fruitful."

The old woman cast a sidelong glance at Mother Pan; "Just see how bold your daughter makes with a respectable old woman like myself! But some day she will find the late blossom has its uses."

"She has always had an unruly tongue," said Mother Pan. "You mustn't think too badly of her!"

"Otherwise, she is a clever and capable, and indeed, I may say, an excellent little woman. Who knows, she may still make a good match!"

"Venerable Mother, if only we could depend upon you for that! Why, you can bring mountains together, they say!"

For a while they continued to talk of this and that. Mother Wang helped herself liberally, and her face was already flushed with the many cups of wine which she had swallowed in quick succession, when at last she remembered her errand. Unwilling to keep Hsi Men waiting any longer, she took her leave with a swift, significant look at Gold Lotus.

Gold Lotus pressed her mother to take her departure; then she hurriedly put everything in order for the reception of her lover, not forgetting to kindle a fragrant censer.

Once her husband was buried, Gold Lotus did not take her mourning very seriously. She soon relegated his soul tablet to a corner of the room, concealing it with a sheet of white paper. The prescribed offerings of food she of course consumed herself. Powdering and prinking and adorning herself for her lover was now her only concern. Not having seen him for a few days, she received him with some show of temper. "Faithless bandit, have you already coldly discarded your devoted slave? I suppose you have found some sweet young thing elsewhere, eh?"

"Business, my love, business! But I'm taking a holiday today, and I've brought you something nice from the Temple Market."

He beckoned to his boy, little Tai, who at his bidding opened a handbag and brought forth a number of gems and pieces of jewelry, pearls, kingfisher feathers in enamel, and the like, and also several lengths of cloth. Overjoyed, Gold Lotus accepted the gifts, and she begged Hsi Men to be seated, ordering little Ying to wait upon them. By frequent beatings, Gold Lotus had thoroughly intimidated the poor young creature, and she no longer felt it necessary to exercise restraint in her presence.

"But please don't put yourself out!" Hsi Men protested. "I have already given old Wang money with which to buy all that's needed, for I want to celebrate this day with you joyfully."

"Oh, it so happens that everything is ready now, for my mother came to see me today. We may have to wait a long time for Mother Wang, so let us begin at once." She tenderly nestled her head against his cheek, and pressed her thigh against his.

Meanwhile old Mother Wang, with her basket under her arm, was on her way to market. Now, the fifth month is known to be the month of showers. On her way, Mother Wang was caught in a thunderstorm. Black clouds suddenly overcast the face of the sun, which a moment before was shining brightly in the sky. The rain poured down as though from overturned tubs.

Gloomy clouds gather on the horizon,
The sable ranks encompass the heavens;
Like a monstrous besom the storm sweeps hither,
Swishing through the air, and a screen of cloud obscures the sun;
Drop after drop comes pattering down
Heavily striking the banana fronds.
Raging winds, with sudden-gathered force
Snatch at the ancient junipers,
And swift as lightning bare their roots.

Hoary mountain summits quiver.
The burning, sultry heat dispelled,
The fields drink the life-giving flood.
Down rush the streams, swollen with new waters,
Smiling stands the bamboo grove, freshly washed and green.

When the storm had abated, Mother Wang, who had found shelter under the wide eaves of a house, made for home at a run. With her clothes soaking wet, a red kerchief on her head, and her well-filled basket under her arm, she breathlessly entered the tea room.

"There they sit, dry and comfortable, enjoying themselves," she blustered. "Look at me—I'm dripping! You must repay me for this, noble gentleman!"

"Are you crazy?"

"No, I'm not crazy. This is going to cost you a bolt of sea-blue calico!"

"That's all right," Gold Lotus interposed: "here's a cup of wine to refresh you!"

The old woman gulped down three cups, one after the other, and went into the kitchen to dry her clothes at the hearth. She busied herself with preparing the meal, and soon a savory dish was ready, of finely chopped goose and chicken meat, with boiled rice and a variety of vegetables and fruits. The lovers sat thigh to thigh, eating out of the same dish and sipping from the same cup. Hsi Men caught sight of a guitar on the wall, a six-stringed *pi pa*.

"Play me a little tune," he begged. "I have heard how well you play the guitar."

"Oh, I used to practice it a little a long time ago, but I never got very far with my playing. You'll laugh at me."

Hsi Men took the guitar from the wall and pushed it towards her. Entranced, he watched her as she laid it on her knee. To him her fingers seemed carved of ivory, pliant as bamboo shoots, as they rested outspread or glided easily over the silvery strings. She began to pluck the strings gently as she sang, in a quiet voice:

"Bareheaded, in sweet disorder,
Her blue-black hair caught loosely
With a slanting arrow of bright gold,
She cries: 'Come, my little Mei Hsiang,
Bring me a robe from the clothespress!'
And then, like a second Hsi Shih, lovely and innocent,
She steps forth from her chamber, saying:
'Roll up the mat before the door,
Burn sticks of fine incense for the night'."

Hsi Men could not contain his delight in her playing and her song. He put his hand behind her neck and kissed her on the mouth.

"Who would have thought that you were so great an artist!" he exclaimed. "I know my way about all the flower gardens of the city, but there is no one there to compare with you!"

"You exaggerate," she answered. "Today you are heart and soul with your little slave—it is to be hoped that you won't forget her later!"

"Never!" he protested, stroking her cheek. "Never!"

Their mood soon grew more passionate. Infatuated as he was, he drew one of her gayly embroidered satin slippers from her foot, filled it with wine, and drained it. Then he barred the door; they undressed, and on the bed they abandoned themselves to the frolicsome delights of love. In their unbridled passion they were like two romping phœnixes, or two little fishes tumbling in the water. She proved herself a mistress of the joys of the couch, excelling in her wantonness and ingenuity any professional servant of love. Once more he proved a master of the amorous arts. Both were in their prime; she, in respect of her charms, he in respect of physical competence. While the amorous pair thus delighted themselves until a late hour of the evening, Mother Wang and little Ying sat patiently in the kitchen. At last Hsi Men decided to take his leave. On bidding her farewell, he presented Gold Lotus with

some ounces of broken silver. In vain she begged him twice and
thrice to stay. He put on his mask and departed.

> *Leaning against the door post*
> *She stood until it was night.*
> *A drifting petal, a wreath of smoke,*
> *He vanished from her sight.*

CHAPTER SEVEN: *She questions the Fates in her Affliction. A Bonze who comes to burn the Soul Tablet overhears Words of Lust*

Long since, the red light of dawn
Crept through the curtains.
At last, her arms half bared,
She rises wearily from her bed,
A closed blossom
Braving the sun.
Truly, when the night wind rages about one's chamber
It is difficult to rest,
And so tempestuous thoughts,
Of him, her only love, robbed her of sleep.

A MONTH PASSED, and Gold Lotus had never a glimpse of Hsi Men. In the meantime he led home a wealthy, thirty-year-old widow, Mong Yu Loh, to take the place of little Cho Tiu, his deceased Third Wife. He then raised his maidservant, Sun Hsueh O, to the rank of Fourth Wife.

Day after day the forsaken Gold Lotus leaned against the door post, gazing into space. Many times she sent her neighbor, Mother Wang, to Hsi Men, but the gatekeeper knew well enough on whose errand the old woman came, and deliberately ignored her. And little Ying, who was usually sent there whenever the old woman returned without result, could never bring herself to venture inside the spacious grounds, but merely prowled about outside. It went ill with her when she returned from her fruitless errand. Gold Lotus would scold her and spit in her face, and, as a punishment, she would force her to kneel for half the day and go without food.

One day, early in August, when the heat was at its greatest, Gold Lotus ordered little Ying to prepare a hot bath. Meanwhile she waited, sitting on a bench, clad only in a short, thin shift of muslin. Perhaps today he would come at last? For emergencies she had prepared a small basketful of crisp meat turnovers, made with her own hands. "Ungrateful bandit!" she murmured from time to time. Incapable of doing anything reasonable, in sheer boredom she stripped off one of her red satin slippers and tried to tell her fortune with it. She wanted to know whether he still thought of her:

> *Indeed, indeed, they were closely knit,*
> *But can one utter such things aloud?*
> *Better in secret to question Fate.*
> *Will the future perhaps bring him back?*

And here the poem about the Lamb on the Precipice may fittingly be quoted:

> *Her shoes, red cloudlets,*
> *Within which lie concealed two little feet,*
> *Two little feet in stockings of flowered silk,*
> *As delicate as lotus-blossom petals*
> *Lightly swaying above the waters.*
> *Tell me, O shoes, if he still thinks of me*
> *As I think always of him?*
> *How often, leaning on the door post*
> *I stand, and gaze, alas, and gaze!*
> *How cheerless, alas, how cheerless the nights*
> *Behind curtained windows, all alone!*
> *Vainly, from the pillows of my couch*
> *I cry, with wild longing, his name.*
> *Does opium keep him away, or the flowery lanes,*
> *That I must suffer lonely grief?*
> *Alas, my brows are fading, fading,*
> *But for whose sake now should I paint them?*

In what green pasture has he now
Tethered his little horse?
Truly, his is the rankest ingratitude.
But I deserve no blame—not I!

For a while Gold Lotus diverted herself by interrogating Fate; then she grew tired, and throwing herself across the bed she fell asleep. Two hours later she woke in an evil humor. Little Ying announced that her bath was ready. It now occurred to Gold Lotus to ask the little maid to bring in the basket of meat turnovers, and to number them with her slender fingers.

"I baked thirty of these. Now I find only twenty-nine. Where is the thirtieth?" she demanded menacingly.

"I don't know. Perhaps my mistress counted wrongly?"

"Not a bit of it! I counted them twice and thrice. They were especially intended for the gentleman. How could you have the impudence to take one for yourself? You lazy, greedy little slave! You'll get colic one day as result of your gluttony. It's all the same if one gives you a big helping or a small, you just wolf the lot! But you just wait; I'll teach you to obey me!" And spinning little Ying about, she promptly stripped off her clothes and gave her thirty lashes of her riding whip on her naked back.

"Now will you confess?" she shrieked at her victim, who squealed like a little pig before slaughter. "Or else be prepared for a hundred more lashes!"

"Yes, yes!" howled the maltreated child; "only stop whipping me! I did take one, but only because I was feeling quite stupid with hunger."

"I knew it! and you dared to accuse me of counting incorrectly! You dissolute hussy, you wretched, thieving creature! When your cuckold of a father was still alive you ought to have learned some sense, instead of making false accusations! Now he is no longer here, yet you dare to play your impudent tricks in my house! I ought to cut you to ribbons, you disorderly, good-for-nothing wench!"

She gave the girl another lash of the whip, then, pulling up her shift, she made the girl stand beside her, and fan a cooling breeze over her body. After little Ying had fanned her for a while, Gold Lotus broke out once more: "Turn your face this way! I just want to mark you with my nails!"

The little one obediently bent her face toward her mistress. With her sharp fingernails Gold Lotus scratched two bloody stripes over little Ying's cheeks.

She then let the poor little creature go. She herself stood before the mirror, calmly powdered her face, arranged her hair, and went to take her accustomed place beneath the awning over the door.

At this very moment she spied Master Hsi Men's boy, little Tai, riding by with a traveling bag under his arm.

"Hi, where are you going?" she called.

Now the lad was by no means stupid, and since his master had constantly taken him with him on his previous visits to Lady Gold Lotus, and since Lady Gold Lotus had often "moistened his palm" with small presents, he felt entirely at ease with her. He dismounted and came nearer.

"To the house of the Military Commandant," he replied in answer to her question. "I am taking him some presents."

"What is your master doing at home?" she asked, as she led him into the house. "Why is it one can't even catch a glimpse of his shadow? I suppose he has found a dainty morsel elsewhere?"

"Not that I know. Urgent business has made it impossible for him to find time to visit you."

"Oh! Business! That's no reason for neglecting me for a whole month—for not letting me have even a word from him! What sort of business?"

Instead of answering, the youngster grinned.

"Well, what sort of business?" she asked, more urgently.

"Let that be enough, when I say 'business.' What's the good of blowing on a fur if you only discover the mangy spots?"

"Dear little oily-mouth, I'll be angry with you to my dying day if you don't tell me!"

"Very well, I'll tell you, but promise that you won't give me away to my master."

"I promise."

"Well then, he has recently married Lady Mong Yu Loh——"

While the young fellow related the why and the wherefore of the business, from head to tail, the pearly tears began to roll down the beauty's fragrant cheeks.

The boy stopped, in some consternation. "You aren't large-hearted enough in your way of looking at such things; that's why I didn't want to tell you."

She leaned back against the door, sighed deeply, and said: "Little Tai, you don't know how we loved each other! Why has he so suddenly forsaken me?"

"Don't take it so tragically!" said little Tai, trying to comfort her. "His other wives at home think nothing of it."

"Listen!" she begged softly, and she began to sing:

"The faithless man, the splendid lover,
A month went by, and he came no more.
Beneath the sheets so finely embroidered
With pairs of mating ducks,
I sorrowed for thirty lonesome nights.
So loving was he on that last day,
That I, poor fool, am tortured with disappointment.
Well may you reprove me: I was too ardent.
What is lightly won is as lightly abandoned.
O sundered love
And vanished joy!"

When the song was ended she began to sob violently.

"Don't cry!" the lad tried to soothe her. "My master's birthday is coming soon and then he will surely show himself. Write him a few lines, and I'll take your message."

"Why yes! And I'll reward you with a pair of handsome shoes, made with my own hands. Then I shall expect him here on his birthday! But woe to you, my little oily-mouth, if he doesn't come then!"

She ordered little Ying to give him tea and a plate of meat pies. Then she went to her room for a strip of flowered letter paper, took the writing brush between her fingers, twirled and pointed the tip of soft sheep's wool, and in a moment she had written down a poem which she entitled: "Blossom Message."

> *From one, from one*
> *Who knows him well,*
> *This flowered scroll*
> *To him is sent.*
> *Does he recall*
> *How first he saw her?*
> *How, under the awning*
> *She stood afraid?*
> *Now he is false:*
> *She waits in anguish*
> *For him to bring*
> *That silken kerchief,*
> *That fragrant pledge*
> *To one who knows him. . . .*

She folded the strip into a square, sealed it, and handed it to little Tai.

"Guard this letter as a brood hen would guard her egg! I expect your master here on his birthday, whatever happens, do you understand?"

When the youngster had refreshed himself and was about to go, she slipped a few coppers into his hand.

"Tell your master I have been very angry with him, and if he doesn't come I shall get into my litter and go to him."

Little Tai promised to carry out her instructions, swung himself upon his pony and trotted off.

During the whole of the next day she sat and waited, but no

answer came to her letter: it was as though she had dropped a stone into the bottomless ocean. The seventh month was now nearing its end, bringing with it the birthday of her beloved. And the closer it drew, the more slowly did time seem to pass. A day prolonged itself into three autumns, and a sleepless night into half a summer. No news, not a word.

In her disappointment she often gnashed her silvery teeth, while the tears rose to her starry eyes.

On the eve of the birthday she sent for Mother Wang. She first entertained the voracious old woman, and then gave her a clasp of silver tipped with gold, which she took from her own hair. For she knew that the old woman's aid was not to be had without payment.

"Do me a favor and bring him here!" she pleaded.

"He certainly won't come today," the old woman answered. "Today he'll be feasting from morning till night. But I'll go early tomorrow morning."

"You won't forget?"

"How could I forget? When it concerns Master Hsi Men!"

Sated with food, her face flushed with wine, the old woman withdrew. Lady Gold Lotus, however, could not sleep that night, though she lay between soft and delicately perfumed blankets embroidered with pairs of amorous mandarin ducks. She spent the night idly trimming the wick of her silver lamp, sighing deeply. As the poem says:

> *There were lutes enough*
> *To while away*
> *The long night with music,*
> *But watching alone in an empty chamber*
> *It is so hard to play.*

She took her *pi pa* in her hand and softly sang a little tune, which she called "Tangled Silk Floss":

> *"To think that another*
> *Is adorning herself for him!*

Oh, rage makes me drunken,
Drives me insane.
Sorrowfully I lean
On the chest before the bed—
Why did he abandon me?
No reason occurs to me.
Faithless one! Thus to break his vows!
If mankind will not, may heaven avenge me!"

The first thing she did the next morning, when she rose after a troubled and sleepless night, was to send little Ying to the neighboring house to see if Mother Wang had kept her word. Little Ying returned with the comforting news that Mother Wang was gone, that she had set out early that morning for Hsi Men's residence.

And this was the truth. The old woman had made an early start, and for a long while she lurked about the gates of Hsi Men's estate. At last she caught sight of the attendant Fu, just as he was about to open up the apothecary shop. She went up to him, greeted him, and asked if his master was at home.

"You should have come sooner," Fu told her. "He was at home yesterday. It was his birthday, and a great many guests were here in his honor. At night he went out with his friends to enjoy himself. He must still be in some house of joy. . . . You will have to look for him there."

Mother Wang at once set out for the nearest street in which there were houses of joy—a turning not far from the yamen. And sure enough, there he was, riding along the street, escorted by a couple of boys. The ravages of the night before were plainly visible on his face. He rolled in his saddle, staring fixedly with his wine-bleared eyes.

"Ho, noble gentleman, you ought to drink a little more moderately!" the old woman cried. At the same time she caught hold of his nag by the bridle and brought it to a full stop.

"Oh, it's you, adoptive mother," he mumbled. "I suppose little sister Gold Lotus has sent you out in search of me? Ha, ha!"

She whispered a few words to him.

"That's all right," he interrupted. "My boy has already told me. I know she is angry with me. But now I'll go straight to her."

And continuing their conversation on the way, they set forth in the direction of Purple Stone Street. Now, when they were about to reach their destination, the old woman hurried ahead.

"You may congratulate yourself and thank me, young woman," she cried as she burst into the room. "Not an hour has passed, and I have already brought him to you!"

Lady Gold Lotus had not fully recovered from the shock of delight when Hsi Men himself entered, not yet sober, flirting a fan.

"What a rare honor!" she greeted him reproachfully. "I suppose you have discarded your poor slave altogether, since one can't catch a glimpse of your shadow? But of course, if you cleave to the New One as fast as glue and lacquer, then is there naturally no time left for this poor devoted slave."

"I do wish you wouldn't heed people's idle chatter! The 'New One'! Bah! I had a great many preparations to make for the marriage of my daughter, and that was the reason why I could not come."

"Don't try to fool me!" she frowned. "Swear by your sleek stallion's hide that you are still true to me and not in love with any 'New One'!"

"I swear it—and if I am false, may I be afflicted with ulcers the size of plates, and plagued five years with the jaundice, and bitten behind by a louse as big as a bricklayer's hod!"

"You rascal, a lot of difference that would make to you!" she cried, and she tore his fine new fringed cap from his head and dashed it to the ground.

Old Mother Wang was shocked; she picked it up and placed it reverently on the table. "But, my dear little woman," she interposed in an attempt to placate Gold Lotus, "it is not him that you should blame, but me, for not having asked him here before! That's how matters stand!"

Gold Lotus angrily ignored Mother Wang, and abruptly snatched

a broad, golden clasp from Hsi Men's pigtail. She examined the
ornament intently. It was moist with hair oil. On one side of it
she found these lines engraved in a cursive script:

> *Neighing on flowery hillsides*
> *Gold-harnessed ponies frisk.*
> *When apricot trees are in bloom,*
> *The chink of cups echoes through the*
> *jade chamber.*

The clasp was a gift from the newly wedded Jade Fountain, as
the two characters of her name Yu Loh clearly indicated. Gold
Lotus, however, fancied that it was the gift of some singing-girl.
She thrust it into her sleeve, and broke out angrily: "You incorrigible rake! Where is the brooch I gave you?"

"Alas, I lost it lately," he exclaimed, "when I was drunk and fell
from my horse. My cap rolled into the mud, my pigtail came loose,
and the brooch must have fallen out."

Scornfully, she snapped her fingers in his face: "You couldn't
fool a three year-old child with that!"

The old woman interceded once more. "Little woman, that's
enough of your scolding. Our little master suffers from long-
sightedness. He can see a bee relieving herself at a distance of forty
li from the city, but he stumbles over the elephant in front of his
door. You must keep this peculiarity in mind."

"Am I not already harassed enough, that you too should run
me down!" sighed Hsi Men.

At this point Gold Lotus caught sight of the gold-sprinkled
Sze-ch'uen fan of carved red ivory in Hsi Men's hand. She instantly
wrested it from him, and held it up searchingly to the light. On
the two flat sides she discovered the numerous imprints of teeth,
and versed as she was in all the intricacies of love, she naturally
suspected that it came from some beauty. Without a word she
broke it in two.

"But that's only a souvenir of my dear departed friend, Pu Chi
Tao," Hsi Men explained reproachfully, who had vainly attempted

to recover the fan. "I've always taken the greatest care of it. I used it for the first time a few days ago, and now you've broken it!"

For a while she continued to vent her anger on him. Now little Ying entered with the tea bowls. At the bidding of her mistress she set down the tray, and kowtowed before Hsi Men. Old Mother Wang decided that the moment had come for her to withdraw to the kitchen.

"You have been dinning abuse into his ears long enough. Now be sure not to neglect the main thing!" she croaked before disappearing.

While Ying was setting the table, Gold Lotus brought from the clothespress the birthday gifts which she had prepared for her lover and set them on the board before him: a pair of black satin slippers; a pair of scent sachets to be worn on strings; a pair of knee guards of dark red satin worked with pines, bamboos, and acanthus leaves— the three frost-defying associates of winter; a length of thin, green satin lining, as smooth as Shansi oil: a plaited girdle of bast and purple silk yarn; a pink sash; and a broad hairpin with a head wrought in the shape of twin lotus blossoms. On the hairpin were inscribed the verses:

Twin lotus blossoms
I pin in my beloved's hair.
May he never part with it,
And wear it for evermore.

Deeply touched, Hsi Men clasped her in his arms and kissed her. During the whole of that day and the following night he did not leave her side, and with wild abandon the lovers celebrated their reconciliation.

It is an old story that happiness is balanced by misfortune. On the following morning, at the breakfast hour, though the amorous pair had not yet arisen, a mounted messenger checked his steed before the house of the deceased Wu Ta. He came from Wu Sung. In the meantime Wu Sung had discharged his commission in the Eastern

Capital. He had delivered to the Palace Commandant, Chu, the letter from the District Intendant, together with the camel load of presents. A few days later, with a letter of reply, Wu Sung set out on his journey home. The summer was over, and autumn drew near as he traveled homewards. Continuous bad weather delayed him on the way, so that the double journey took a full three months. During the whole of this time, whether waking or sleeping, he was haunted by a strange unrest, an unwonted anxiety concerning his brother. Wu Sung resolved to send one of his men ahead to announce his coming to the District Intendant, and immediately thereafter to deliver a letter to Wu Ta. And now this messenger had arrived. He found the house of the elder Wu closed, and was about to knock on the door when neighbor Wang, who happened to be standing outside her house, asked him what he wanted.

"I have a letter from the Captain of the Guard, Wu Sung, to be delivered to his brother."

"He's not at home. The whole household is at the cemetery. Give me the letter; I can deliver it to him when he returns, just as surely as you would yourself."

The messenger handed her the letter, saluted her, and rode off.

Old Mother Wang hurried with the letter to the lovers in the neighboring house.

"Up, up, good people!" she cried as she burst excitedly into the room. "A messenger has just come from Wu Sung. He himself will be here directly. The messenger brought a letter for Wu Ta. I took the letter myself and sent him on his way. Now, we cannot waste any time. This situation calls for a quick decision."

Had Hsi Men been told anything else, he probably would not even have heard it. But at this news he felt as though his head had been split asunder, as though he had suddenly been dipped into a tub of melting snow. In a moment both he and Gold Lotus had leaped from their bed and thrown on their clothes. In the living room they deciphered the letter. Wu Sung wrote that he would be back in the middle third of autumn at the latest. The lovers were panic-stricken. Trembling in every limb, they appealed wildly to the old woman for advice.

"The matter is quite simple," Mother Wang reassured them. "As I have already said, there is an old adage which runs:

> *"First marriage—to please one's parents,*
> *Second marriage—to please oneself.*

"Furthermore, the law forbids a brother and a sister-in-law to live alone under the same roof. The hundred days of mourning since Wu Ta's death will soon be over. Now all our little lady needs to do is call in a couple of bonzes to perform the customary ceremony of burning the soul tablet, and then, in due time, before Wu Sung's return, have my lord Hsi Men lead her home, in a litter, as his bride. Then the fellow will be faced with an accomplished fact, and for the rest, I shall know how to manage him. You, however, will be united for the rest of your lives. Well, now, what do you say? Haven't I planned it splendidly?"

"Splendid indeed. And thus shall it be done!" Hsi Men eagerly agreed, and thus reassured he sat down to a hearty breakfast with Gold Lotus.

The sixth of the eighth month arrived, the last of the hundred days of mourning after Wu Ta's death. Hsi Men, supplied with several ounces of broken silver, went to the house of Lady Gold Lotus. Presently six bonzes appeared from the Cloister of Gracious Recompense. They were to hold a day-long service for the soul of the deceased, and in the evening they would burn the tablet according to the ritual. The High Priest, with a load of prayer books, arrived early in the morning, at the hour of the fifth watch of the night. He set up a platform for prayer and hung up an image of Buddha. He then busied himself in the kitchen, helping Mother Wang with the preparation of the sacrificial foods. Meanwhile, however, Hsi Men was enjoying himself in bed with Lady Gold Lotus.

At length the company of bonzes was assembled in full force, and soon there resounded throughout the house the whirring of spirit cudgels, the rolling of drums, the ringing of bells, and the mumbling sing-song of invocation. In the meantime, Gold Lotus, far removed from all thoughts of piety and moderation, was lying in bed with her lover. Though it was now midday she had not thought of rising. The ceremony, however, required her presence on the prayer platform as chief mourner, to kindle sticks of incense, sign the prayer formulæ, depose evidence of having kept her vows, and do reverence to the image of Buddha. Accordingly, she rose, washed herself, and curled her hair; then, clad in plain but attractive mourning apparel, she advanced to the prayer platform and gracefully bowed before the image of Buddha. As soon as the saintly friars beheld her their devotion to Buddha and their inner composure vanished. Before such charms they were helpless; they lost all control of themselves, and became soft as cheese; and then one and all were seized with a heat as of stallions, and a lustfulness as of apes.

The chief of the band, distracted and wanton,
Forgets how he ought to invoke the divinity.
He stumbles in his speech, can hardly collect himself;
Instead of sutras he begins to stammer nonsensical rubbish.
And the others also are completely beside themselves!
One, brandishing the censer, with fumbling hand,
Overturns the flower vase so that it falls to the ground.
A second, instead of a taper, holds an ashtray in his hand.
A third, appointed to recite the formulæ of oaths,
Instead of the Sung realm, tells of the realm of Tang.
And he who was to extol the blessed peace of the dead
Babbles forth praises of the widow alone.
The abbot, like one possessed, seizes his neighbor's hand
And beats time with it as with a drumstick.
Here a novice, losing all self-control,
Beats upon a brother's tonsure as on a drum.
All virtue gained in severe monastic discipline
In this moment dwindles to naught.

Yet were one a thousand times more iron-willed
Here he would none the less have fallen.

After Lady Gold Lotus had burned the sticks of incense, affixed her signature to the formulæ, and acquitted herself of her reverences before the image of Buddha, she withdrew to her chamber, and swiftly returned to Hsi Men's couch to resume the interrupted delights of love. In defiance of all the pious prescriptions of abstinence, she partook freely of wine and meat highly seasoned with garlic. Hsi Men instructed old Mother Wang to see that the baldheads did not disturb Gold Lotus again.

But the thoughts of the baldheads were still with the pretty young widow. During the midday pause they went back to the cloister for a frugal meal. When the recess was over, it happened that one of them returned to the house of mourning before the others. By chance the room wherein the priests had discharged their liturgical duties was divided from the bedroom of the young widow only by a flimsy wooden partition. The bonze stepped over to wash his hands in a bucket of water that stood beneath the bedroom window when he suddenly became aware of a suspicious whispering and panting, of sighs and moans, of grunts and stifled outcries—in short, of all the unmistakable sounds that betray the act of love. Pretending still to be washing his hands, he stood on the spot and listened. And now there came to his ears, quite clearly, broken phrases, uttered in a woman's voice.

"Darling!—Take care, you're hurting me!—Oh, they'll be back directly, and they'll hear us.—Let me go! Go away, quick!——"

And then in masculine tones:

"Don't be afraid! Now the stove door is open, I must just burn another quickly. . . ."

If they could have dreamed that their words had been overheard with eager sympathy by a baldhead in hiding!

When the whole company was again assembled, and the ritual tom-tom was heard anew, the eavesdropper whispered to the brother nearest him, who passed on the gossip that in the next room the Lady Gold Lotus was enjoying herself with a man. What strength took possession of their limbs, how excitedly the knaves began to toss their hands and kick their feet! At length the ceremony neared its end. Towards evening the soul tablet and the funeral gifts of pasteboard were solemnly carried out to be burnt before the door. Lady Gold Lotus had long before this curled her hair in the usual fashion and dressed herself in a pretty, gayly-colored robe. She stood behind the curtained window, leaning on Hsi Men's shoulder, and watched the bonzes outside as they burned to ashes the soul tablet and the image of Buddha. Old Mother Wang made herself useful by sprinkling the sacrificial wine and kindling the fires. The bald-headed rogues leered with lustful eyes at the curtained window opposite. They could see the shadows of the beauty and her gallant, closely pressed against each other, and brooding on the tender bedroom scene that they had thus glimpsed in broad daylight, they fell into a heat and drummed on their drums and beat on their gongs like men possessed. Suddenly a gust of wind wafted the headdress of the High Priest to the ground, so that his round shining tonsure, rimmed about with black, was revealed. No one stooped to pick it up, so absorbed were they in their drumming and mumbling. In truth, a laughable spectacle!

"Master," said old Mother Wang, turning to one of the bonzes, "everything has long been burnt to ashes. Why are you still ringing your bells and beating your drums?"

"There is still something to be burned behind the stove door," was the reply.

Hsi Men understood the allusion. He hastily bade the old woman give the bonzes their fee and dismiss them. The High Priest was anxious to express his gratitude personally to the beautiful donor. But Gold Lotus declined.

"Well then, in that case, we'll leave her in peace!" growled the monks, and grinning, they went their way.

> *Ay, ay, there are times when walls have ears.*
> *And no window is safe from prying eyes.*

CHAPTER EIGHT: *The Two secretly enter into Wedlock. Laboring under a Misapprehension, Wu Sung slays the the Agent Li*

THE NEXT DAY Gold Lotus invited old Mother Wang to a farewell dinner, and committed little Ying to the old woman's care and protection.

"If only I knew how we could contrive that Wu Sung should never learn of our marriage!" said Hsi Men anxiously.

"Just you leave that to me, noble gentleman!" the old woman reassured him. "If he presumes to force his way in here, or tries to go snooping around, I shall have something to say to him!"

Hsi Men took courage again, and with good grace he presented the old woman with three ounces of silver. That evening he had all the young woman's possessions packed in chests and coffers and removed to his own house. A certain amount of old rubbish, such as broken tables and benches, worn-out clothing, and so forth, was left for the old woman. On the next day—it was the eighth of the eighth month—he had his beloved, festively arrayed, brought home in a litter. Mother Wang, the boy, little Tai, and four lantern bearers formed her escort. Of course, all the inhabitants of Purple Stone Street were well acquainted with the true facts of the case. But with all of them in awe of Hsi Men's money and influence, who would dare to meddle in his affairs? Public opinion, however, expressed itself pertinently in a lampoon which appeared on this occasion.

> *Fie, Master Hsi Men, what sort of doings are these!*
> *Such a marriage is truly ridiculous.*
> *First you commit adultery and then go wooing!*
> *Never again will your name be clean.*

In a red litter, decked out like a bride,
Your whore is brought to your home.
No relative of hers brings her to you,
Only an old procuress.

In an isolated corner of the park, to which access was obtained through a concealed postern, Hsi Men had the three lower rooms of a two-story pavilion made habitable for his beloved. The surroundings were beautified with flower beds and potted plants. It was a pleasant and absolutely secluded little spot, where scarcely a soul passed all day. Hsi Men devoted especial care to the furnishing of the bedchamber, on which he expended no less than sixty ounces of silver. He purchased a large bed of black lacquer, with gold figures, and curtains of red silk worked with a design of gold circles, a costly dressing table, inlaid with floral designs of gems and ivory, and several softly-padded arm chairs covered with a gay damask.

Moon Lady, his First Wife, had hitherto had two maids, Spring Plum and Jade Flute, for her personal service. Hsi Men gave orders for Spring Plum to move into the pavilion of Gold Lotus, where the girl was to do her bidding and address her respectfully as "Mistress." He also bought for six ounces of silver a kitchenmaid, whose name was Autumn Aster; and for Moon Lady, for five ounces, he bought a maid called Little Jewel, to replace Spring Plum. Gold Lotus received the rank of a Fifth Wife, since Hsi Men had previously increased the number of his wives by a third and a fourth.

On the day after she had entered Hsi Men's household, Gold Lotus, with her hair carefully curled, and wearing her finest apparel, presented herself in Moon Lady's apartment in order to introduce herself to all the female members of the household, great and small, who were assembled there. Moon Lady, from her place in the seat of honor, looked curiously at the new wife, and her impression was: "Love of life from head to foot, sensuality from foot to head." This emanation of vitality and sensuality that seemed to surround her person evoked the impression of a shimmering pearl rolling in a crystal bowl. She had the look of a branch of red apricots bathed in moonlight.

When Moon Lady had silently observed the new wife for a time she told herself:

"Whenever little Tai came home raving of Wu Ta's wife, I was always skeptical. Now that I see her for the first time face to face, I can easily understand why she makes the men go crazy."

Gold Lotus threw herself at the feet of Moon Lady, performed a fourfold kowtow, and presented the customary slippers of welcome. Next, according to their rank, she greeted the other wives in sisterly fashion: Sunflower, Jade Fountain, and Snowblossom. Then Gold Lotus modestly stepped to one side. Moon Lady ordered a chair to be brought for her, and informed the maids and servants that they were to honor Gold Lotus as their "Fifth Mistress."

From her chair, Gold Lotus, without turning her head, surreptitiously observed the other four wives. First of all there was Moon Lady, whom she judged to be about twenty-seven; her face was smooth and white as a silver bowl; her eyes were round and fresh as apricots. Her movements were lithe and gentle; her bearing dignified, and her speech concise and measured. Then there was Sunflower, the former singing-girl from the house of joy; she was a rather plump, comfortable beauty; doubtless a high-class courtesan, yet far inferior to Gold Lotus in the technique of love. Jade Fountain, the Third Wife, was thirty. She was like a pear blossom; her waist was supple as an osier, her figure ample and seductive. On her face, round as a melon, there were tiny freckles here and there that by no means detracted from her natural beauty. Under her petticoat her two little feet were as small as Gold Lotus's own. And finally Snowblossom, who had grown up in the house as a maidservant. Very slender, and rather undersized, she was as proficient in the art of cooking as in dancing and juggling with plates. With one rapid glance, Gold Lotus did her best to impress their characteristics on her mind.

From the third day, Gold Lotus developed the habit of rising early and punctually paying a morning visit to Moon Lady, when she obligingly relieved the First Wife of all sewing and manual work. It was never necessary for Moon Lady to press her to do anything. Alert and willing, Gold Lotus always set to work of her own accord. In her relations with the servants, she never spoke of Moon Lady otherwise than as the "Great Mistress." With her little attentions and her affectionate manners, she quickly won the sympathy of Moon Lady. Before long the First Wife was affectionately calling her "Sister Six," for Gold Lotus had actually been the youngest of six sisters. This was not altogether pleasing to the other three wives. Behind Moon Lady's back they often gave vent to their jealousy.

"She makes nothing of us, who were here first, yet she's as intimate as possible with this newcomer, who has been in the household only a few days!"

Since Gold Lotus had been a member of his household, Hsi Men had suddenly become domesticated. He never went beyond the limits of his large and beautiful garden, or the spacious park. Hsi Men and Gold Lotus clove together like size and lacquer, and each night they renewed the ecstasies of sensual delight.

In the first third of the eighth month, Wu Sung arrived in the district of Tsing ho hsien, and reported at once to the District Intendant, to whom he handed the written reply from the Palace Commandant Chu. In recognition of his faithful services, Wu Sung was hospitably received by the Intendant, who rewarded him with ten ounces of silver. Wu Sung then hastened to his quarters, attired himself from head to foot in his finest apparel, and set out in search of his brother. The news of Wu Sung's return created consternation among the neighbors in Purple Stone Street, and apprehension caused the cold sweat to drip from their brows.

"Alas, now there'll be a family catastrophe! The star of ill omen is visible again, and there is no way of avoiding it!" the neighbors exclaimed.

On arriving at his brother's house, Wu Sung lifted the mat over the door and stepped in. He called out: "Brother!" No answer. "Sister-in-law!" No answer. He thought: "Have I been stricken deaf, that I can hear no answer."

Presently he spied little Ying, who was sitting on the veranda and sewing. He called to her. At his unexpected appearance she was so frightened that the words stuck in her throat, and when he asked where his brother and sister-in-law were, instead of replying she began to cry. Just then Mother Wang caught sight of him. She resolutely subdued her fears and came hurrying across.

"Where the devil is my brother, and why isn't my sister-in-law at home?" he roared at the old woman.

"First take a seat, and then I will tell you everything in detail," she replied. "Now then, your brother was carried off by a malignant disease, in the fourth month, soon after your departure."

Wu Sung wanted to know exactly, even to the day, when and how his brother had died, and with what remedies he had been treated.

"On the twentieth of the fourth month," lied old Wang, "he was seized for the first time with severe cramps in the stomach. Eight or nine days he lay sick. He took every possible remedy, but all attempts to cure him and all exorcisms failed. And he passed away, but his memory is not forgotten."

"How did he come to be afflicted with these stomach cramps? He never suffered from them before. I do not understand."

"Captain, now you are asking me too much. The decrees of Heaven are beyond man's reckoning. One must accept the fact that fortune and misfortune alternate like day and night. This very evening you may with cheerful heart, draw off your boots and stockings, and yet you are not sure that early the next morning you will draw them on again. Who can be proof against the vicissitudes of fate?

"When your brother was taken ill there wasn't a copper cash in the whole house. His wife was as helpless as a crab without legs. Where was she to get the money for a burial place? Thanks to the magnanimous intervention of a wealthy gentleman in the neighborhood who had been on friendly terms with her husband, she was enabled at all events to buy a coffin. Three days the coffin stood in the house for decency's sake. What else was there for her to do after that, but to have it carried outside the city walls and reduced to ashes?"

"And where is my sister-in-law now?"

"She is only a frail young woman, who found herself suddenly deprived of all support, and so, having conscientiously observed the prescribed hundred days of mourning, she took her mother's advice; she is married again, to a gentleman from the capital. She took all her belongings with her, except the young maid, whom she left in my care. I was only waiting until you came back so that I could turn the young person over to you. And that settles the matter as far as I'm concerned."

Wu Sung heaved a long, deep sigh. He left the old woman without a word, and returned to his quarters. He put on the worst clothes he could find, and sent one of his men out to buy coarse hempen material for a mourning coat, with cotton socks, a mourning hat, and various sacrificial articles to offer up to the spirit of his departed brother, such as fruit, sweets, incense-tapers, paper images, spirit money, and the like. All these things he ordered to be brought to his brother's house. There he set up a soul tablet anew, placed before it the various offerings, together with a bowl of good sacrificial wine, hoisted a gayly-colored paper death flag, and lighted the incense. In the evening, at about the tenth hour, he solemnly bowed his head before the soul tablet. Holding an incense taper in his hand, he invoked the spirit of the dead man.

"Brother, your soul cannot be far from here. In your lifetime you were weak and yielding. I still do not see clearly how you came to die. If anyone has wronged you, then reveal it to me, your younger brother, in a dream, that I may avenge you and wash away the affront!"

Wu Sung sprinkled some wine in honor of the departed, and set fire to the paper figures. Then he broke out into loud lamentations. As he made his way to his brother's house many people had expressed their condolence by wailing. Now, in the whole neighborhood, there was no one who did not loudly join in the chorus of lamentation. When he had finished bewailing the dead, he, with his men, and little Ying, partook of the sacrificial foods and wine. For the night he ordered two sleeping mats to be laid out, one for his guardsmen in the courtyard under the open sky, and one inside for little Ying. He himself chose for his couch a place opposite the table on which stood the soul tablet of the dead man. Until the hour of midnight Wu Sung was unable to sleep. Restless and sighing, he tossed from side to side. The guardsmen, however, had long been fast asleep, and were snoring. Wu Sung raised himself on one arm and looked about him. The flame in the glass death lamp on the table before him was flickering, half extinguished. He sat up on the mat and spoke aloud to himself.

"In his lifetime he was so weak and compliant; I suspect that there was something queer about his death. . . ."

In the midst of his meditation, there suddenly came an icy draught from under the table on which the soul tablet was standing.

> *Neither body nor shadow,*
> *Neither mist nor smoke,*
> *A phantom swirl,*
> *A ghostly breath,*
> *Icily it creeps hither,*
> *And shudderingly penetrates flesh and bone.*
> *Oppressive is the gloom,*
> *Dimly burns the lamp.*
> *The flapping death flag*
> *Throws flickering shadows on the wall;*
> *Now flapping across the table*
> *It scatters a heap of paper shavings.*
> *Concealed in darkness,*
> *In obscure night,*
> *The dead man's spirit*
> *Keeps solitary vigil.*

Wu Sung's hair bristled as the icy breath suddenly blew over his face. Now it seemed to him that he could vaguely see a human form creeping from under the table on which the soul tablet stood, and he seemed to hear a voice that said: "Brother, they have wronged me!"

He moved closer, to see more clearly, and question the apparition, but the face disappeared. The icy breath, too, was gone. Reeling, Wu Sung fell back on the mat. Then he tried to collect his thoughts.

"Strange! It seemed to be a dream, and yet I was not dreaming. His spirit was about to reveal something to me when my mortal breath dispelled it. There is something wrong here."

He listened. The night watchman's drum rolled three times—it was midnight. He turned his head, and looked toward the place where the guardsmen lay. They were sleeping soundly. At that moment he would have been glad to talk to someone, for he felt troubled in his soul. Now he had to keep his lonely vigil till morning. At last, at the hour of the fifth drum beat, he heard the first cock crow. In the east the dawn spread slowly. The guardsmen arose, and set about cooking their morning broth. Wu Sung washed himself and rinsed his mouth, and then withdrew with his men, leaving the house in charge of little Ying. On the way, he questioned the people of the neighborhood whom he encountered. He wanted to discover the cause of his brother's death, and to learn whom his sister-in-law had married. The neighbors were acquainted with every detail of the affair, but, fearing to incur the displeasure of the rich and powerful Hsi Men, they withheld their information.

"Inquire at Mother Wang's. Ask the pear seller, Little Brother Yuen, or the District Inspector, Hu Kiu; they'll tell you everything," was all they would say.

Wu Sung set out at once in search of Little Brother Yuen. It was not long before the little monkey, a wicker basket under his arm, came running towards him. Little Brother Yuen had just been buying rice.

"Good day, Little Brother Yuen," Wu Sung greeted him cordially.

"Captain, you come a step too late," the lad told him. Little Yuen knew at once what Wu Sung wanted. "Unfortunately I cannot do as I should like. I have to look after a sixty-year-old father, who is all alone in the world. So you can hardly count upon me for your lawsuit."

"My dear Little Brother, come along with me!" Wu Sung led him into a tavern near by, and ordered two sumptuous dinners. Then Wu Sung began:

"I see that, in spite of your youth, you know what a good, dutiful son owes to his old father. To be sure, what I can give you is not much, but here"—and he thrust five ounces of broken silver into the lad's hand—"here is a little gift for your dear father. When the matter is settled you should receive ten ounces more, and then you will have a small capital, and can start a business. But now tell me! Did my brother quarrel with anybody? Who is the man who conspired against his life? Whom did my sister-in-law marry? Out with it, and keep nothing back!"

Little Brother Yuen put the shining pieces of silver into his pocket, thinking: "Father can live on that for five months, so there's no danger if I say what I know in court."

"Very well, I'll speak," he said, "but I hope you won't work yourself into a fury over it!"

And he related in great detail what had been going on in the tea room, and described his fight with old Mother Wang, and how the Three-Inch Manikin had been violently kicked in the pit of the stomach by Hsi Men, and how, a few days later, he had died suddenly.

"And whom did my sister-in-law marry?"

"Hsi Men took her away in the marriage litter."

"You're not deceiving me?"

"I am willing to swear to it before the authorities."

"Good! Be at the courthouse early tomorrow morning. I'll need you as witness. And now, where does this Hu Kiu live?"

"You're too late for him. Three days ago, on the news of your return, he went off on a journey—no one knows where."

They finished their meal, and Wu Sung let the lad go.

The next morning, Wu Sung got Master Chen to draw up a

formal indictment. With this in his hand Wu Sung went to the courthouse, where Little Brother Yuen was waiting for him.

Wu Sung strode into the hall where the District Mandarin was publicly administering justice, knelt down in the gangway, and cried in a loud voice, "Injustice!"

At this the Mandarin requested him to present his indictment. Wu Sung handed it over, and briefly accused the missing Hu Kiu of accepting bribes and suppressing the truth, and old Mother Wang, of procuring and inciting to murder, and finally, Hsi Men, of adultery and of the murder of Wu Ta. He referred to the testimony of Little Brother Yuen, whom he had brought with him.

The Mandarin was greatly embarrassed, since both he and his officials were closely associated with Hsi Men, and he immediately withdrew to take private counsel with his subordinates. Without exception they advised him to prevent legal proceedings. Accordingly when he returned to the courtroom he announced:

"Wu Sung, as officially appointed Captain of the Guard you ought to be better acquainted with the statutes. No action against an adulterer may be taken when either of the married couple is missing. Nor can a charge of murder be upheld without an official examination of the body. Your case is based solely on the verbal testimony of this young fellow. That is not sufficient evidence. I should be suspected of prejudice, and be thought irresponsible, if I were to open a trial for murder on such evidence. You have been rather too hasty. Think the matter over once more calmly."

Wu Sung was not satisfied with this. He demanded that Hsi Men, Lady Gold Lotus, and Mother Wang should be arrested and brought into court. If his accusation should then be proved groundless, he was willing to pay any penalty that might be imposed.

"As to that I can decide only after mature consideration," the Mandarin informed him. "If possible I will comply with your demand. For the present, stand up."

With that, Wu Sung was dismissed. He returned to his quarters taking with him Little Brother Yuen, whom for the moment he would not allow to go home. He wanted, at all events, to have his witness at hand.

As soon as the news of Wu Sung's proceedings were reported to him, Hsi Men became alarmed. It was evident that he must act at once. Accordingly he dispatched his two trusty retainers, Lai Pao and Lai Wang, with large sums of money. That very same evening he succeeded in buying the favor of the Mandarin and all his officials.

Next morning Wu Sung unsuspectingly returned to the yamen. He was astounded when the Mandarin returned his written indictment.

"You must not pay too much attention to such libels!" the Mandarin admonished him in a fatherly tone. "You surely would not wish to make an enemy of Master Hsi Men? The matter is far too obscure for me to intervene in my official capacity. There is an old proverb that runs:

> *"My eyes indeed beheld it,*
> *But even eyes may err.*

Still less can one put any faith in belated rumors! No, no! Let us have no undue haste!"

And the jail keeper, who was present, added:

"Captain of the Guard, in your own official capacity, you ought to be familiar with the statutes, and to know that a charge of murder cannot be proceeded with until it has been accurately ascertained what marks of injury or disease the body exhibits, and what lethal instruments or other evidences of the deed are forthcoming. In this case there is no body to be inspected. With such lack of evidence how can you expect to set the law in motion?"

Wu Sung answered defiantly: "Then according to Your Excellency's interpretation, the injustice suffered by my brother is not to be redressed? But I maintain that my accusation is justified."

He took up his indictment and left the court. He dismissed his witness. He absolutely refused to resign himself to the situation.

Lifting his eyes to the heavens, and gnashing his teeth, he sighed and wrathfully murmured to himself:

"That harlot! What sort of fellow should I be to swallow this disgrace!"

And making a sudden resolve, he set out for the apothecary shop. He would seize that villain, Hsi Men, and chastise him with his own hands. In the counting house of the apothecary shop he saw the manager, Fu. He burst into the shop and roared: "Is your master on the premises?"

"No. What's the trouble, Captain?" answered Fu.

"Come outside with me. I have something to say to you."

Fu, who knew well enough with whom he had to deal, did not dare to refuse his request. He came out of the shop, and followed Wu Sung into a side street. There Wu Sung suddenly faced about. He grabbed Fu by the collar, and in menacing tones, his eyes rolling horribly, he demanded: "Do you wish to die, or do you prefer to live?"

"Captain, I am entirely at your service," stammered the terror-stricken Fu, quaking in his boots. "Why are you so furious? Has my insignificance ever offended you?"

"Answer me, if you value your life! Where at this moment is that fellow Hsi Men? And when exactly did he add my sister-in-law to his household? Speak, or——!"

"Captain, please do not be so angry! I am only Hsi Men's employee, serving him for a monthly salary of two ounces. I am concerned only with the shop; what do I know of what goes on behind his curtains? I know only that he has just gone out with an acquaintance to drink a pint of wine in the big wineshop in Lion Street. That's the absolute truth. Why should I lie to you?"

Wu Sung loosened his grip, and set him free. While Fu still stood there, terrified and unable to move a step, Wu Sung was already hurrying with long strides toward the Lion Street.

On the upper floor of the wineshop in Lion Street below the bridge, Hsi Men sat drinking with Li, the secretary of the yamen. This Li was notorious as eavesdropper and go-between in connection with lawsuits which were pending in the local courts or in those of the prefecture, being well paid for information which he sold now to the one party, now to the other. He also arranged for the bribing of officials, and in this way obtained money from both sides. He was therefore familiarly known as "Agent Li."

On the day when the Mandarin dismissed Wu Sung's indictment as invalid, Agent Li rushed off to Hsi Men with the joyful news. Hsi Men rewarded him with five ounces of silver and invited him to the wineshop. In the best of spirits they sat drinking their wine, until Hsi Men happened to look out of the window and up the street, when he suddenly caught sight of Wu Sung, rushing over the bridge and up to the wineshop like an avenging spirit.

Terror-stricken, Hsi Men attempted to flee. But the way down to the street was already barred, so he hastily took refuge in the back rooms of the upper floor. He excused himself to his guest, saying that he had to leave the room for a moment.

In the meantime Wu Sung had entered the wineshop.

"Is Hsi Men here?" he asked the host.

"He's sitting upstairs with a friend."

Girding up his coat, Wu Sung dashed up the stairs. There he saw a man sitting in the company of two painted singing-girls. Hsi Men was nowhere to be seen. But Wu Sung recognized the man as Agent Li, and immediately understood what had happened. Without a doubt, this man had brought Hsi Men the news that his indictment had been dismissed. He was overcome with sudden rage. Going close up to Li, he roared:

"Hi, fellow, where have you hidden Hsi Men? Out with it, or you'll feel the weight of my fist!"

Poor Li was stricken dumb with fright. He stood there trembling like an aspen leaf and could not utter a sound. His silence still further enraged Wu Sung. With one kick he overturned the table in front of Li. Plates, dishes, and cups rolled to the ground with a loud crash of breaking crockery. The two painted beauties fainted. Li, now aware of his terrible situation, tried to escape. But Wu Sung seized him at once.

"Stop, fellow! Where are you going? You won't speak, eh? Good! Then my fist must make you talk!"

With that Wu Sung struck him a smashing blow in the face. Li groaned aloud in pain.

"Hsi Men has only just left the room. What have I to do with your affairs? Let me alone, will you!"

But the infuriated man was no longer to be restrained. With a jerk he flung open the window, and the next moment Li found himself held out over the street in the grip of a powerful hand, while a merciless voice roared: "You wanted to go out, did you? Very well, you shall!"

With a dull thud, Li's body landed in the street below. But Wu Sung rushed off to the back premises in search of Hsi Men.

From his hiding place, Hsi Men heard the uproar. His courage failing him, reckless of his life, he leapt over the eaves and down into the courtyard of the adjoining house. When Wu Sung could not discover his intended victim he believed that Li had purposely deceived him. Leaping wildly down the stairs and into the street, he saw Li lying stiff and motionless, already half dead. Only his eyes still moved. In uncontrollable fury, Wu Sung kicked him twice. With a last groan, Li gave up the ghost.

"But that's the secretary, Li," the bystanders said to Wu Sung. "What has he done to you? Why have you killed him?"

"I had intended that for Hsi Men. This fellow was with him, and so he fell into my hands."

And now the wardens of the local ten-family and hundred-family associations came upon the scene. Since homicide had been committed, it was their duty to intervene. But they did not dare to lay hands on the dreaded Captain of the Guard. They simply surrounded him, so that he could not escape from them. Then, with Wang Luan and the two painted beauties, they escorted him to the yamen. Of course, the whole of Lion Street was in an uproar, and throughout the city the incident was the talk of the day. As usual in such cases, exaggerated rumors were started, and it was soon reported that the slain man was none other than Hsi Men.

CHAPTER NINE: *The Champion of Justice is banished to Meng Chou. Wives and Concubines divert themselves in the Water Pavilion*

In the eighth month, in midmost autumn,
Cool is the breeze and caressing.
Now on lakes and ponds
The water lilies bloom.
Sisters, big and little,
Chatter as they bake their cakes.
Happy couples wander
In park and woodland.
They pluck flowers and branches
To grace beautiful vases,
And at home in the evening
Make merry over wine.
Three cups, and already
The walls of sadness are overthrown.
Alas, no sooner are we sober
Than sadness walls us in again.

WHEN HSI MEN leaped from the window, he landed in the courtyard of the adjoining house, which belonged to old Fu, a physician. As Hsi Men crept cautiously along the wall, he was suddenly seen by a maid who had come out into the courtyard to attend to a call of nature, and who, having reached a remote corner, was in the act of placing her magnificent posterior in position. At her loud screams of "Burglar! Burglar!" old Fu came running up.

"Oh, it's you, noble gentleman!" he exclaimed, smiling, as he recognized Hsi Men. "Well, you may be thankful that Wu Sung didn't catch you. He slew your friend, and they've taken him to the District Court. The affair will undoubtedly cost him his head. You need have no fear; you can now go home in peace. As far as you're concerned, the matter is settled."

Greatly relieved, Hsi Men thanked Fu for the welcome news. Then, with rolling gait and head erect, Hsi Men strolled homewards. As soon as he reached the house he told Lady Gold Lotus the whole story. The two could not restrain their joy. They clapped hands with delight, for now they believed that they were entirely out of danger. Following Gold Lotus's advice, he sent his trusty servant Lai Wang to the District Mandarin with a sumptuous gift of fifty ounces of pure silver and a complete wine service of silver gilt. And to all other officials who were in any way concerned, Hsi Men sent a splendid gift of money. There was not one among them who spurned Hsi Men's generosity.

The next day Wu Sung was led before the District Intendant. But now the Mandarin's manner had changed, and he harshly upbraided Wu Sung:

"Fellow, yesterday you made false accusations against respectable and peaceable citizens. I treated you with constant consideration. In return you yourself now violate the law and slay a man in broad daylight!"

"I really had a score to settle with Hsi Men," was Wu Sung's only defense. "This other man, unfortunately, happened to thwart me. He had hidden Hsi Men, whom I was pursuing, and would not tell me where he was. In my rage I forgot myself and killed him. I am ready to atone for my crime. I only hope that Your Excellency will have Hsi Men also arrested, so that the injustice done to my brother may be fully requited."

"Nonsense! You must realize to whom you are speaking! The murder of the Secretary Li is an altogether different matter, and has nothing whatever to do with Hsi Men. But I see that you won't confess without a thrashing."

At a sign from him three or four court beadles leapt in a flash upon poor Wu Sung, threw him face downwards on the ground, and began to belabor him with a couple of bamboo cudgels. When they had given him twenty strokes Wu Sung reproachfully reminded the Intendant of the many good services which he, as Captain of the Guard, had rendered him. In vain; Wu Sung was made to suffer fifty strokes more, and to undergo the torture of the finger press. Then a heavy wooden collar was put about his neck, and he was led back to prison.

All the officers of the prison, and even two officials of the yamen—namely, the Sub-Intendant and his assistant—were in sympathy with Wu Sung, for they regarded him as an old friend and an honest and upright man. But gladly as they would have helped him, they had one and all been bribed by Hsi Men, so at first their lips were as if glued together.

But a few days later they resolved, on behalf of their imprisoned friend, who was incessantly clamoring for justice, to draw up a fictitious record of a confession, so worded that the prisoner's situation would be alleviated while the dreaded Hsi Men would still be uncompromised. First, however, an inquest was held upon the body of Li. The jail keeper and several witnesses of the homicide from the Street of the Lion were present. It was then discovered that the forehead, the left side of the chest, the pit of the stomach, and the abdomen of the deceased exhibited purple extravasations. As the case was represented in the fabricated confession, Wu Sung had quarreled with the deceased Li over a debt which the latter owed him, and in his anger he fatally injured the deceased by kicks and blows of the fist. This confession, with an accompanying report of the incident, was sent to the Prefect of Tung ping fu for further consideration. Wu Sung, together with the witnesses, the taverner Wang Luan, and the two singing-girls who had been in Li's company, was forwarded to the capital of the prefecture, Tung ping fu.

The Prefect Chen hailed from the province of Honan, and was

celebrated far and wide for his upright administration. Without delay he proceeded to the examination of Wu Sung's case. He ordered the accused and the witnesses to appear before him. He carefully read both the report signed by the Intendant of Tsing ho hsien and his four subordinates, and the fictitious confession accompanying it. The report stressed the fact that Wu Sung had vainly demanded payment from Li of an old debt of three thousand cash and had killed him in a drunken rage. No reference whatsoever was made to Hsi Men.

"How did you come to kill this man?" asked the Prefect, at the opening of the trial.

"Venerable Master, to kneel before your tribunal is as soothing and refreshing for me as the sight of the sun in heaven to one who has been long deprived of it. May I speak freely and openly?"

"Speak out!"

Thereupon Wu Sung truthfully described the course of events, not without mentioning the name of Hsi Men.

"Since I could obtain no justice at the District Court, I decided that I myself would avenge my brother," he concluded. "My wrath was intended for Hsi Men. By an unfortunate error I slew Li. I would gladly suffer death for my brother's sake."

"That is enough; now it is all clear to me," said the Prefect, and he at once had twenty strokes of the light bamboo administered to the District Secretary Kien Lao, as one of the five signatories of the false report.

"A fine official, that Mandarin of yours!" Chen remarked sarcastically. "To make justice simply an article of commerce!"

The Prefect next examined the witnesses. Taking up his brush, with his own hand he completely altered the alleged confession. Turning to his subordinates on either hand, he told them: "Wu Sung wished to avenge his brother. He is an honest and highminded fellow, and must not be regarded as on the same level as common murderers."

At his command, the heavy collar was removed from Wu Sung's

shoulders and exchanged for a lighter one, such as is customarily assigned for trifling offenses. The witnesses were dismissed to their homes. The whole affair was referred back to the District Mandarin for renewed investigation. The Mandarin was directed in particular to interrogate, in public session, Hsi Men, Gold Lotus, Mother Wang, Little Brother Yuen, and Hu Kiu; to ferret out all the facts in the case without respect of persons, and to draw up a new and final report.

Wu Sung was known throughout Tung ping fu as an honorable man, and not a single warder or turnkey in the prison dreamt of demanding a copper of him. On the contrary, they took pains to ease his confinement with gifts of wine and roast meat.

Meanwhile a spy of Hsi Men's reported to his employer the latest developments in the case. Hsi Men was terrified and trembled in every limb. He realized that any attempt to corrupt the Prefect was out of the question. The matter must be tackled from a new angle.

He immediately dispatched his trusty Lai Wang, with instructions to ride day and night until he reached the Eastern Capital, where he would present a petition to Marshal Yang, who was a good friend of Hsi Men's. Marshal Yang in turn must intercede in Hsi Men's favor with Tsai, the Chancellor, and the tutor of the Imperial Prince. Chancellor Tsai was the patron of the Intendant Li of Tsing ho hsien, whose reputation and career were now seriously imperiled. Chancellor Tsai at once addressed a private letter to Prefect Chen, begging the Prefect to refrain from all further inquiries touching Hsi Men. Now, Chen was indebted to Chancellor Tsai for his promotion to the Prefecture. This obligation and the fact that Marshal Yang had the freedom of the Court and access to the ear of the Son of Heaven, resulted in the partial surrender of Chen. He pronounced sentence against Wu Sung, decreeing that the former Captain of the Guard was to atone for his crime, not indeed with death, but with forty lashes on the back, with branding, and, finally, with banishment to a military station on the frontier, two thousand *li* distant. The investigation in respect of all other parties involved was suspended.

And so the next day found Wu Sung once more kneeling before the purple-draped tribunal. The Prefect ordered the forty lashes to be administered as the sentence required, and then had the wooden collar replaced by an iron collar riveted about the condemned man's neck. In addition to this, two rows of characters were branded upon his face.

Escorted by two guards, he was first of all brought back to Tsing ho hsien, where he was granted sufficient time to settle his domestic affairs and dispose of his possessions. He generously gave the proceeds to the two guards; they were to regard the sum as traveling expenses; and he also appointed a reliable man from among his deceased brother's neighbors to act as guardian to little Ying. He promised to give evidence of his gratitude if the Court, by granting a reprieve, should make it possible for him to return. The general sympathy felt for Wu Sung throughout the neighborhood was so great that several wealthy families supplied him with money, wine, and provisions. At last the day came for his departure, and with his guards he began the long march on the highroad to Mong Chou, beside the Great Wall.

Hsi Men felt as though he had been relieved of some terrible internal obstruction when he learned that his formidable enemy had been banished to the frontier. It seemed to him that a heavy stone had been removed from the pit of his stomach. Such an occasion had to be celebrated as it deserved, and he had the Water-lily Pavilion, in the park, to the rear of the house, attractively furnished, and the paths carefully swept. Screens and gayly colored curtains helped to beautify the pavilion. A troupe of musicians, dancers, and singing-girls was engaged for the entertainment. At this banquet in the Water-lily Pavilion Hsi Men's five wives, surrounded by the entire staff of domestics, were present.

> *From precious bronze basins*
> *Swirls the aromatic smoke.*

In deep bowls and vases
Chrysanthemums greet the eye.
Rare carvings are displayed
From Kwangsi, land of ivory;
And shimmering strings of pearls,
Gathered on Kwang Tung's shores.
In crystal bowls are heaped
Dates and pears.
Goblets of blue-green jade
Are brimming with rarest vintages.
A heady fragrance rises
From pitchers of red gold.
Chopsticks are plunged into food
Worth ten thousand cash:
Boiled dragon liver
And stewed phœnix giblets,
Black bears' paws
And tawny camels' feet,
And the finest of dragon-phœnix tea paste
To stimulate the palate anew—
Truly a feast unparalleled,
Worthy of the wealthiest of the wealthy.

During the banquet, the page, little Tai A, ushered into the pavilion two gay and pretty children, a boy and a girl. Each child carried a box.

"The neighboring house of Hua has sent some flowers for the ladies," announced the page.

The children kowtowed before Hsi Men and Moon Lady, then modestly stepped back and said: "Our mistress sends Hsi Men's lady some cakes and some flowers for her hair."

They opened the boxes and set them down before Moon Lady. One contained golden-yellow cakes with fruit filling, sprinkled over with pepper and salt, such as are eaten at Court. The other was filled with freshly picked tuberoses. Moon Lady was obviously delighted

"Your mistress has again put herself out for our sake," she said, and she had some sweets brought for the children. She also gave the little girl a handkerchief, and the boy a hundred coppers. She asked the children their names, and then cordially sent them home.

"Recommend me to your mistress and give her many thanks!" Moon Lady bade them.

"Mistress Hua is really too kind," Moon Lady said to Hsi Men. "She has repeatedly shown us such little courtesies. I regret to say that I have not yet made any return."

"My friend Hua married her barely two years ago," Hsi Men told his First. "He has always praised her good character. His praise is certainly justified. Otherwise, she would never tolerate two such pretty young servants in the household."

"I have only once met her personally," Moon Lady continued. "That was at the funeral of the old High Eunuch Hua. She is, if I remember correctly, somewhat under the average height. Her face is rather round, but her eyebrows tell of breeding. I should judge her to be twenty-five at the most."

"You know, she was first a concubine of the Imperial Secretary-in-Chief Liang from Ta ming fu. She brought her present husband a pretty fortune when he married her."

"We must certainly return her courtesies at the very next opportunity."

Worthy reader, the said Lady Hua was a Li by birth. On the day she was born her parents happened to receive a present of a pair of vases decorated with fishes. They decided to call her by the name of Sister Ping, or Sister Vase. She was taken as concubine by the Secretary-in-Chief Liang, who was the son-in-law of Chancellor Tsai, of the Eastern Capital. Liang's First Wife was extremely jealous by nature: she had had many a beautiful maid or concubine strangled and buried in some remote corner of the park. For safety, Liang kept little Sister Vase beside him, in a wing of his library, with a reliable maid to guard her. On a night of the first month of the third year of the Harmonious Reign, while Lord Liang and his First Wife were passing the time in the Pavilion of the King-fisher Blue Cloud, he was suddenly murdered and every member of his family was slain. Sister Vase and her maid alone, in the terrible confusion, succeeded in escaping. She fled to her own family in the Eastern Capital, taking with her a hundred large Western pearls, and a pair of deep-blue turquoises, two ounces each in weight. These jewels she had snatched up and concealed on the night of the tragedy. Later, through the kindness of the Lord High Eunuch Hua, she was installed as First Wife in the house of his hitherto unmarried nephew, Tze Hsu. When old Hua was promoted to the post of Commissioner for the Defense of the South, he took the young couple with him and kept them beside him. And later, when he resigned his office on account of ill health, and retired to his native district, to Tsing ho hsien, he brought them back with him. After his death his entire property, which was considerable, passed into the hands of his nephew.

The nephew, Hua Tze Hsu, was one of the nine companions who had joined with Hsi Men in the Jade Emperor's Temple to swear eternal brotherhood. It was now his daily habit to foregather with Ying Po Kui, or Hsia Hsi Ta, or some other member of this Brotherhood of Ten, and arrange common orgies in taverns and houses of joy. And the other Brothers, who, with the exception of Hsi Men, were all poverty-stricken starvelings, naturally encouraged the wealthy Hua to continue his dissipations and to squander his money. And so it happened that he often stayed away from home for three or even five nights running.

> *How pleasant in the spring to stroll*
> *Along the purple street,*
> *Drink deep at the Red Tower*
> *To the music of lutes and flutes.*
> *For what is the use of grieving?*
> *Enjoy this brief today!*
> *So long as we dare to hope*
> *He is a fool who does not make merry!*

The banquet in the Water-lily Pavilion continued until the evening. At a late hour Hsi Men entered the chamber of his favorite. He was slightly drunk, and the wine awakened in him a desire for the delights of love.

Gold Lotus arranged the bed, and lighted incense in the bronze basin. Then they helped each other to undress, and slipped under the silken hangings. But Hsi Men was not in the mood for the usual game of clouds and rain. He was aware of Gold Lotus's proficiency in playing the flute, and he had only to hint at his desire. . . .

Suddenly he called for tea, and at once the maid, Spring Plum, appeared. Embarrassed, Gold Lotus hastily drew the bed curtains. Hsi Men smiled.

"Why are you embarraseed before her? Lady Ping, next door, is not in the least disconcerted when her husband enjoys himself with one of her handmaids. By the way, the older one is of the same age as our Spring Plum. The one who brought you the flowers today is the younger. Pretty young things, both of them. What a sly chap, this Hua! Who would have thought him capable of making up to such extremely young girls!"

Gold Lotus gave her husband a casual, scrutinizing glance.

"What a rascal you are! But I'm not going to quarrel with you. Of course, every word you have just spoken was uttered with Spring Plum in mind. Very well, take her! Why all this beating about the bush? This talk of the mountain when you are thinking of the mill behind it? You need not point to other women as examples. I am not one to object; no, not by any means! Tomorrow, if you wish, I'll make way for your little one for a time."

Hsi Men was charmed. "Child, how clever you are at providing for my comfort! I have really every reason to love you!"

And so they continued to enjoy each other in complete harmony. When the flute play slowly died away, they at last fell asleep, head pressed closely to head, thigh to thigh. Not without reason is it said:

Would'st thou fetter thy love with thine arts,
Then, little woman, play the flute!

Gold Lotus kept her word. She spent the next day with Moon
Lady so that Hsi Men might be undisturbed in his possession of
Spring Plum.

Red peach blossoms:
The Spring wind blustered by,
Picked one out for himself,
And crumpled it sadly.
Young green willows:
The Spring wind came that way,
Picked one out for himself,
And bent it cruelly.

From that hour, Spring Plum enjoyed the special favor of her
master. She was no longer compelled to drudge away at menial
tasks, to lift heavy cooking pots in the kitchen, or to sweep the
dusty hearth. Her only duties were to make the beds and to serve
tea. Whatever clothes and jewelry she desired, Gold Lotus gave
her out of her own belongings. She also taught the maid the art
of strapping her feet. Spring Plum, apart from her attractive appearance, was a clever, capable little thing; she was witty in repartee,
always cheerful, and fond of a jest: very different from lethargic,
unpractical Autumn Aster, who was also in the service of Gold
Lotus, and had to take many a beating at her hands.

Sparrows with crumpled plumage,
Swallows with blood-flecked throats,
Swoop through the air and alight,
Bent upon noise and strife.
All birds: and their countless numbers
Are one in their power of flight.
But alien in kind, and strangers by choice
Each species hates the rest.

CHAPTER TEN: *Gold Lotus incites Hsi Men to chastise Snowblossom. Hsi Men deflowers Cinnamon Bud*

GOLD LOTUS, now that she was the favorite, became more and more domineering and capricious. Distrustful by nature, she could no longer find peace by day or by night. Her suspicions were readily aroused, and she was continually spying and peeping from behind walls and hedges. One day, being put out of temper by some trifling matter, Gold Lotus scolded her maid Spring Plum. Little Spring Plum was rather hot-tempered, and by no means inclined to accept a scolding patiently. She ran out of the pavilion and into the kitchen. There she could give uninterrupted expression to her rage at having been corrected. In a fury, she drummed with her little fists on the tables and benches. Her behavior elicited from Snowblossom, who, as usual, was supervising the work of the kitchen, the would-be playful remark: "You funny little thing, can't you arrange to have your hysterical fits somewhere else?"

Spring Plum, who was already sufficiently provoked, now lost her temper completely.

"I'll have no one make such insolent remarks to me!" she hissed.

Mistress Snowblossom wisely ignored her.

Spring Plum ran to her mistress, who was resting in the front apartment. She railed bitterly against Snowblossom, wildly exaggerating the incident by embellishments of her own.

"Just think, Mistress, she said that you yourself handed me over to the master so that you might retain his favor!"

Her story naturally caused Gold Lotus no little displeasure.

Gold Lotus was feeling tired and languid. That morning she had risen earlier than usual. Moon Lady was attending a funeral, and Gold Lotus had accompanied her part of the way. She lay down again to sleep. Then she rose and went back to her pavilion. On the way thither she met Jade Fountain.

"Why so listless and silent?" Jade Fountain asked her, unsuspectingly. "Are you tired?"

"I feel a little tired, yes. Where have you been?"

"In the kitchen."

"Did that woman in the kitchen tell you anything?"

"No, I don't think so."

Gold Lotus tried to conceal her annoyance, and was silent. They sat down together, and for a while they passed the time with needlework. Then they decided to play a game of chess. No sooner had they begun to play than Hsi Men entered the room. He gazed with satisfaction at the two lightly, but always carefully dressed women. How attractive was the silver net over their hair! How charming the kiss curls on the temples, the earrings of blue sapphire, the red-embroidered ducks on their slippers! How pleasantly the red and silver of their collars stood out from the white of their thin, silken garments!

"As exquisite as two expensive flower girls, not to be had under a hundred ounces of silver!" he could not help exclaiming, in a jesting tone:

"Please, please! Flower girls, did you say? There may be some elsewhere in your household, but not here!" Gold Lotus retorted sharply.

Jade Fountain rose, tactfully seeking to withdraw. But he caught her and drew her back into the room.

"Where are you going? No sooner do I come than she runs away! What have you two been doing while I was out?"

"At all events, nothing wrong. We've been playing chess," Gold Lotus replied. She helped him put the chessmen away. "You're back very early from the funeral."

"Yes, I wanted to escape the ceremonial feed in the temple, and then this oppressive heat! So I got out of it before the end."

"And Moon Lady?" asked Jade Fountain.

"She is coming later in the litter." He sat down. "I see you were in the middle of a game. What stakes were you playing for?"

"Oh, we were simply playing for the sake of the game."

"Good, I'll play a game with each of you, now. The loser must pay an ounce of silver for a feast."

"But we haven't any money on us," objected Gold Lotus.

"That doesn't matter. You can give me a hair clasp as a pledge."

He played first with Gold Lotus. She lost, and he was just about to set the pieces again for a game with Jade Fountain, when Gold Lotus suddenly rose, jostled the board so that the pieces fell over in confusion, and ran out of the room and into the park. Hsi Men followed at her heels. At last he found her hiding under a bough laden with fragrant blossoms. She was leaning on a rock at the edge of the water-lily tank.

"So you've hidden yourself here, my soft-spoken little darling!" he cried, breathless from running.

She looked at him with a roguish twinkle in her eyes.

"Villain, to pursue me so, merely because I've lost! You wouldn't dare do that to her!" Opening her little fist, she playfully cast a handful of blossoms over him. Hsi Men slipped under the boughs, took her amorously in his arms, and gently laid her on the rocky brink. Once again she had succeeded in kindling his desire for her body. In the midst of their lustful tongue play they were surprised by Jade Fountain.

"Get up and go to Moon Lady, she has just come home!" she called to Gold Lotus.

Gold Lotus disengaged herself from Hsi Men, and hurried away with Jade Fountain in order to greet Moon Lady as was incumbent on her.

"You have been able to amuse yourselves?" asked Moon Lady, calm and self-contained as ever.

"Yes, Sister Five lost an ounce of silver playing chess with our revered master, so tomorrow there will be something good to eat. Won't you risk a game, too?"

137

Gold Lotus soon took her leave, in order to rejoin Hsi Men in the pavilion. She thoughtfully had a hot bath prepared for him, and when evening came they diverted themselves like two merry little fishes in the water.

Although Moon Lady held first rank among Hsi Men's five wives, her delicate health usually prevented her from fulfilling the obligations imposed by her rank. When visits were to be paid, Li Kiao, the Second Wife, usually took her place. It was Li Kiao, Lady Sunflower, who managed the household budget. Snowblossom, the Fourth Wife, supervised the kitchen and the staff of servants. This explanation will enable the reader to understand what follows.

Hsi Men once more spent the night with his favorite, Gold Lotus. In a generous mood, he promised to go immediately after breakfast to the Temple Market to buy Gold Lotus some pearls. When he told Spring Plum to fetch breakfast from the kitchen—ordering lotus-seed tarts and silver carp soup—the little girl suddenly refused. She absolutely would not go to the kitchen.

Gold Lotus explained to Hsi Men: "There is someone in the kitchen who says I induced the little one to let you have your way with her, which proves that my love for you is mere hypocrisy. This person is trying to strike at me by reviling others. You had better not send the little one to the kitchen. Send Autumn Aster instead!"

"Who is this person?"

"The question is superfluous. All the cooking pots in the kitchen are witnesses."

Hsi Men sent Autumn Aster to the kitchen. A long time passed; time enough to have cooked and eaten two breakfasts. Autumn Aster did not return. Hsi Men, his patience exhausted, was losing his temper when Gold Lotus decided to send Spring Plum after all.

"Go and see where that creature is loitering. She must be waiting to watch the grass grow."

Unwillingly Spring Plum obeyed. She found Autumn Aster standing in the kitchen, waiting.

"You naughty girl!" Spring Plum scolded her. "Our mistress will have your feet chopped off! What is keeping you here? Master Hsi Men has lost his temper. He is in a hurry to go to the Temple Market. I am to fetch you back at once——"

She was about to say more, when Snowblossom angrily interrupted her.

"Silly wench! A kettle is made of iron, isn't it? Do you think the soup in it will get hot of itself? The tarts, too, are not yet nearly done. One mustn't eat undercooked food; it gives one worms in the stomach!"

"Impudence!" cried Spring Plum, flaring up. "Do you think I came here for pleasure? Master Hsi Men will be furious when I tell him!"

She seized Autumn Aster by the ear, and dragged her out of the kitchen. "I have much more reason to complain of you, you insolent creature!" Snowblossom angrily shouted after her.

"Whether you complain or don't complain, it's all the same to me!" Spring Plum called back. "But you won't succeed in sowing dissension in this house!"

And she rushed off in a fury. Yellow with rage, she dragged Autumn Aster before her mistress.

"What is the matter?" Gold Lotus inquired.

"Ask her! When I came into the kitchen, she was standing about looking on. The other was taking as long to prepare a little breakfast as it takes to make doughnuts. When I told her that the master was in a hurry for his breakfast, that wretch burst out and called me a slave wench, and made other ugly personal remarks, even insulting our master! She seems to think the kitchen is intended for scolding and back-biting instead of for cooking!"

"What did I tell you?" cried Gold Lotus, turning to Hsi Men. "We ought not to have sent Spring Plum to the kitchen. That woman tries to quarrel with everybody. She insinuates that Spring Plum and I have appropriated you for ourselves, and won't let you out of our bedchamber. To endure such insults from that woman!"

Her words produced the desired effect. Hsi Men angrily rushed into the kitchen, and kicked Snowblossom repeatedly. "You common, malicious bag of bones!" he cried. "What do you mean by abusing the girl I sent to fetch my breakfast and calling her slave wench? Look at your reflection in your own puddle!"

No sooner was his back turned than the poor woman unbosomed herself to Lai Pao's wife, who was working in the kitchen with her.

"You were here! You saw her come snorting in like an evil spirit! But did I say the least thing to her? She simply runs off with the other maid, tells tales to our master, turns white into black, and encourages him to abuse me for no reason at all! But you just wait, I'll keep a lookout for her! Just let that impudent slave wench come here again! It'll be the worse for her, that's all!"

In her anger she did not stop to consider that her words might be overheard by Hsi Men, who was listening outside the door. Suddenly, convulsed with rage, he stood before her, and soundly boxed her ears.

"You vicious, accursed slave!" he shouted. "You say you didn't insult her? With my own ears I heard how you abused her!"

And he beat and buffeted her again, until she shrieked with pain. Then he stormed out of the kitchen.

Moon Lady, who was having her hair dressed, heard the disturbance in the kitchen, and sent her maid, Little Jewel, to learn the cause of the trouble. Little Jewel came back with the story.

"He never ordered pastries for breakfast before!" said Moon Lady. "But that doesn't matter; they must be made as quickly as possible, and in any case Snowblossom mustn't scold the little girl without reason."

She sent Little Jewel to the kitchen again, to urge Snowblossom to hurry. After this interlude Hsi Men at last got his breakfast, after which he left the house for the Temple Market.

Snowblossom could not get over the treatment she had suffered, and as soon as Hsi Men left the house she went to Moon Lady to vindicate herself. She did not suspect that Gold Lotus was creeping after her, or that she hid herself under the window, where she could overhear everything that Snowblossom said to Moon Lady and to Sunflower, who was also in the room.

"You have no idea what this man-crazy woman, who has monopolized Hsi Men, says and does behind our backs," Gold Lotus heard her declare. "One doesn't blame a woman for carrying on all night with her husband once in a while. But this woman simply can't exist without a man. People like that are capable of anything. Didn't she get rid of her first husband by poisoning him? Who knows what mischief she may hatch against us yet? After all, she can't bear the sight of us, this creature who rolls her black eyes like a cackling hen, at every man she sees!"

"All this began harmlessly," Moon Lady quietly replied. "You only had to send the child back with the breakfast, and everything would have been all right. Why, then, this unreasonable abuse?"

"May I be stricken bald and blind if I ever abused her! Don't you listen to her if she comes here after me! Very likely she'll tell you that I tried to stab her in the back with the kitchen knife! Since she has had Hsi Men in her power she has grown so arrogant and presumptuous. . . ."

"The Fifth Wife is outside," Little Jewel warned her; and a moment later Gold Lotus walked in. Looking steadily at her enemy, she began:

"Suppose I really had poisoned my first husband, then you shouldn't have allowed Master Hsi Men to receive me into his household. You would then have reason to complain that I prevent him from enjoying himself with you. As far as Spring Plum is concerned, she is not my property. If it doesn't suit you that she should wait on me, she can wait on Moon Lady again as far as I'm concerned. I shouldn't then feel that I was involved if you chose to quarrel with her. As a matter of fact, it is quite permissible nowadays for a widow to marry again. But I can go, if you wish; I can simply ask him to give me a letter of divorcement when he comes home."

"I don't really understand what you two have against each other,"

Moon Lady intervened. "But in any case, if you were all a little more sparing of words, everything would go smoothly."

"There you have it!" cried Snowblossom, angrily defending herself. "With a mouth like hers, that spills over like a raging torrent! How can one deal with her? And if her tongue were to be cut out before Hsi Men's very face she could still make him believe the contrary by rolling her eyes! If she had her way, we other women, with the exception of yourself, perhaps, would all be driven out of the house."

Moon Lady listened calmly to the accusations and insults which the two wrangling women hurled at each other. When it seemed that Snowblossom was about to spring at Gold Lotus's throat, Moon Lady ordered Little Jewel to take Snowblossom out of the room. Gold Lotus returned to her pavilion. She threw off her clothes, and washed the rouge and powder from her cheeks. With disheveled hair, a wild look in her eyes, and her flowerlike face stained with tears, she cast herself on the bed. She lay there until evening. At last Hsi Men returned. In perplexity, he asked her what had happened. Sobbing loudly, she told him, and demanded a letter of divorcement.

"When I came here it was not a financial speculation but an impulse of my heart," she protested. "And now I must suffer insult upon insult. A husband poisoner, that's what she called me to my face. It would be better if I had no one to wait on me, for how can I expect a maid to remain in my service when she has to put up with continual abuse on my account . . . ?"

Hsi Men did not wait for her to finish. His three souls each took a mighty leap, his five senses bounded high as heaven. Like a whirlwind he swept down upon Snowblossom. He seized her by the hair of her head, and his short bamboo cudgel whistled through the air as he dealt her blow after blow, until Moon Lady caught and held his arm.

"You ought, all of you, to exercise a little self-control!" she gently reproached poor Snowblossom. "You shouldn't needlessly provoke your master!"

"You accursed, treacherous bag of bones!" Hsi Men roared at Snowblossom. "I myself heard you insult her in the kitchen! If you molest her again I refuse to be responsible for the consequences!"

He went back to the pavilion to give Gold Lotus the present which he had promised to bring her from the Temple Market. It was a set of pearls weighing four ounces. Gold Lotus was content. He had taken her part and had avenged her. She now stood higher than ever in his favor. She had only to ask for whatever she might crave, and she received it tenfold. Had she not reason to rejoice?

A few days later it was the turn of Hsi Men's neighbor, Hua Tze Hsu, to entertain his friends. They all arrived in full strength. The board was laden as sumptuously as ever. Entertainment in the form of dances, singing, and luteplay was provided by two delightful singing-girls whose talent and charm would have done honor to the Imperial Peach Grove.

> *They are swathed in snowy silk,*
> *Their lustrous hair is gathered into clouds.*
> *Their mouths are cherry, apricot their cheeks,*
> *Slender their hips as osiers.*
> *It is a rare delight to behold them:*
> *Orchids in the midst of common flowers.*
> *As a blackbird sings in the boughs,*
> *So softly flow the notes from their lips.*
> *Like the phœnix flitting among flowers,*
> *So nimble and graceful is their dance.*
> *Their songs, sung to old melodies,*
> *Resound like music of the heavenly spheres.*
> *Their dancing roots the moon to her place,*
> *High or low, in haste, or at rest,*
> *And checks the onrush of the clouds.*
> *All things attentively give ear*
> *To such harmonies as these.*
> *Sickness is banished, pain assuaged.*

in ordered beauty, as the wild ducks fly,
Note follows note in melody.
The red-toothed plectrum plucks the string,
Lily-stem fingers twang the lute.
Delightfully, and in perfect accord, the new refrains
Set to old melodies, echo among the pillars.

After the second song the girls laid their instruments aside. Swaying like blossoming branches in the wind, they approached the table and performed a kowtow. Hsi Men was so enraptured that he called his boy Tai and told him to present three silver coins to each of the singing-girls.

"Who are those two girls, really?" Hsi Men asked his host. "They certainly understand their art." Before Hua Tze Hsu could reply, Beggar Ying cackled, noisily as ever:

"The noble gentleman must surely be suffering from a total loss of memory. Why, the one with the twelve-stringed lute is Silver Bird, our friend Hua's darling from the house of joy, and the one with the six-stringed *pi pa* is Lady Cinnamon Bud, whose praises I have often sung. The noble gentleman has her aunt, Sunflower, as Second Wife, in his own house, and does not even know his dear little niece!"

"Oh, so that's who the little thing is!" said Hsi Men with a smirk. "I haven't seen her for three years. Well, well, how she has filled out!"

"How are your mother and sister?" he asked little Cinnamon Bud, later in the evening, when she came coquettishly tripping across to where he sat in order to fill his cup. "Why have you never come to visit your aunt?"

"Mother has not been well this last year," she answered. "Until today I have not been free to leave the house. Sometimes I have to help my sister to entertain. For the last six months she has had a friend, a stranger from the Chiang Su district. When he receives guests in his house I have to go there, and I even have to stay away from home for two or three days at a time. So I have had no time to visit you, glad as I should be to see my aunt. But why have you avoided our house so long? You never send my aunt to see us!"

Hsi Men sensed an invitation in her words. After a moment he said: "Suppose two of my friends and I were to take you home tonight?"

"You must be jesting. Your noble foot would never deign to cross our humble doorstep."

"I'm not jesting," he replied, and to prove that he was serious, Hsi Men drew from his wide sleeve a fine handkerchief and a box of perfumed tea paste, and made her a present of both.

"When do we leave?" she asked. "I think we might send my companion ahead, so that mother will be prepared to receive you."

"We'll go as soon as the others have gone."

It was not long before the guests rose from the table, and lantern in hand, took their leave. Hsi Men, Beggar Ying, and Hsia Hsi Ta waited until they had gone. Then they mounted their horses, and escorted Cinnamon Bud in her litter to the quarter of the flower gardens.

> *Cellars, pits, mantraps are lurking,*
> *Enchanted grottoes secretly await their prey.*
> *Piles of brick enclose them*
> *Gloomy as prison walls;*
> *As livestock in the slaughteryard,*
> *So here human flesh may be had at will.*
> *They who are strangers to the bliss of freedom,*
> *Here dumbly support the misery of existence.*
> *Without, sign upon sign, in huge characters,*
> *Lures the visitor in.*
> *Within, the old procuress*
> *Pockets her flower money.*
> *Such wares, worthy masters,*
> *Are not readily supplied on credit.*

At last they reached the house of Mother Li. The litter disappeared into the entry. Cinnamon Bud's elder sister came out to greet the visitors and graciously invited them into the guest room. Soon Mother Li came shuffling in, leaning on a cane, her back bent and stiff with rheumatism.

"Good heavens!" she cried: "What gust of wind has blown hither the noble husband of my sister?"

"Do not be angry with me, Mother Li, but all this time the pressure of business has made it impossible for me to pay you a visit."

She turned to his companions. "These two gentlemen haven't been seen here for quite a long while either."

"No time," replied Beggar Ying. "But today we happened to meet your little one at Brother Hua's, and so we brought her home, and at the same time embraced the opportunity of a brief visit. But now out with the stuff, quickly! We're dying for a few good bowls of wine."

They sat down. Mother Li cleared the table, served food and drink, and lighted the festal tapers. Cinnamon Bud came in, dressed more charmingly than before. The two sisters entertained the guests with dancing and music; they played on the dragon flute, and beat the rhinoceros drum. Their slender limbs swayed in rhythmic unison. Here music was blended with youthful grace, and of them it could not be said that "the springtime of life was uselessly dissipated." They resembled silver vases whereupon the golden sunbeams played. Hsi Men begged that they might hear a song from Cinnamon Bud. He spoke to the elder sister. "My friends have heard so much of your little sister's singing. Would you be so kind as to ask her to give us a song?"

"Yes, yes," cried Beggar Ying, in agreement. "I'll keep perfectly quiet, too. And I'll borrow a little of my friend Hsi Men's brilliance, to polish my ears, so that not a note shall escape me!"

Mother Li and the two girls, of course, realized that Hsi Men was merely beating about the bush, and that he was actually burning with impatience to deflower Cinnamon Bud. Strict reserve seemed necessary, so that a better price might be secured. Cinnamon

146

Bud smiled, but did not stir from her seat. Her sister begged her friends to excuse her.

"She has been very carefully educated; and a girl so modest cannot sing at a moment's notice."

Hsi Men understood. He laid a silver bar, five ounces in weight, on the table. "Just a trifle for rouge and powder," he said. "Later, she shall have a few pretty gold-embroidered silk dresses."

Cinnamon Bud rose. She thanked him for the present, and told a servant to put it away in a safe place. At last she condescended to sing. Young though she was, she showed no haste, no excitement. She accompanied her song with graceful gestures, while, peeping from her sleeve, a silk handkerchief with red and silver fringe fluttered gayly as a blossom dancing on the waves. What she sang was a strophe from the song, "The Cloud-Rider."

> Calm and splendid he descends,
> Forcing his way through the murky vapors
> That dismally fill the flower garden.
> His presence transforms
> The choking fumes into fragrant breezes.
> The knitting of his brows
> Makes men tremble with fright.
> What value a staff of finest jade,
> In dirt, in mud, in slime—?
> Yet one sings, and her song
> Makes all her listeners shiver,
> Giving them a taste of the sacred bliss,
> That once King Hsiang experienced in a dream,
> In a dream, King Hsiang.

When the song was ended Hsi Men was in such a state of rapture that he hardly knew what to do. He passed that night in the room of the elder sister, but he had determined that he would be the first with the still intact virgin. The next day he sent his boy, little Tai, to a silk merchant's, to order four costly dresses for Cinnamon Bud, at the price of five hundred ounces of silver. Sunflower, Hsi

Men's Second Wife, was overjoyed when she heard that her niece was to have the honor of being deflowered by Hsi Men. For this festive occasion she gave Mother Li, her sister, a silver bar fifty ounces in weight, as a contribution toward the expenses of food, music, decorations, and clothing. For three days the deflowering of Cinnamon Bud was toasted and celebrated. Hsi Men's friends came to congratulate him, and to present their contribution, which amounted, all told, to the magnificent sum of five copper cash. They again seized the welcome opportunity of gorging and guzzling to their hearts' content at Hsi Men's expense.

> *Song, music, dancing, women—*
> *Merrily it goes the livelong day.*
> *Hurrah! for one's own dear carcass*
> *Let another's gold be lavished!*
> *Why should one rise from the table*
> *When wealth is one's host?*
> *Temperance is a medicine*
> *That suits best the table of Poverty.*

CHAPTER ELEVEN: *Gold Lotus abandons herself to a Slave. Astrologer Liu aids her with his Magic and does a good Stroke of Business for himself*

Trembling in root and branch,
A lonely sapling stands.
The dew that bathes it at dawn
Is soon dispelled by the wind.
Upon her unshared couch
Wakes a forsaken woman.
She has no lover to caress
Her delicate young body.

For a fortnight Hsi Men remained with Cinnamon Bud in the house of joy. Not once during that time did he show his face at home. Moon Lady had repeatedly sent his boy and his horse to bring him away. Mother Li, however, had always contrived to detain him by the simple expedient of hiding his clothes.

His five wives felt shamefully forsaken and cast aside. All but Gold Lotus could patiently bear this misfortune. Gold Lotus, however, whose blooming springs were still far from the tale of thirty, and whose ardent longing for love blazed fathom-high, could not endure the absence of her mate. Each day she carefully curled her hair, and powdered and rouged her face, and polished as a well-cut gem she stood at the door of the pavilion and longingly watched for his coming. When the yellow twilight came without him, she returned, disappointed, to her chamber. But the loneliness that brooded over the pillows and bed hangings exasperated her, and robbed her of her sleep. She formed a habit of rising in the middle of the night, and wandering restlessly through the park. Sometimes she would glide over the moss and the flowers, and gaze into the lotus pond that shimmered in the moonlight.

When Jade Fountain entered Hsi Men's household she brought with her a handsome and intelligent young servant, by name Kin Tung. He was then about sixteen years of age. Hsi Men employed him as gardener's boy, and allowed him to live in a lodge beside the garden gate. Whenever Gold Lotus and Jade Fountain spent the day in one of the arbors, plying their needles or playing chess, they would often call upon him for trifling services, and he was always obliging and pleasant. He kept a constant lookout for the master of the house, so that he might announce Hsi Men's return in good time. Gold Lotus liked the smart young fellow, and often invited him into her pavilion, and gave him food and wine. She ended by wanting him always beside her, from morning to night.

The seventh month came, and Hsi Men's birthday was at hand. Moon Lady made another attempt to tear him away from "the region of smoke and flowers," and again she sent the boy with his horse. Gold Lotus secretly gave little Tai a written message for Hsi Men. She told him to hand it to his master in private, and to beg Hsi Men in the name of his beloved to return home at once.

Little Tai surprised Hsi Men in Mother Li's house, as he was drinking merrily with his arm around a painted singing-girl. He was surrounded by his inevitable retinue of boon companions.

"What are you doing here? Has anything happened at home?" Hsi Men asked the boy.

"Nothing in particular."

"Have you brought Lady Cinnamon Bud anything to wear?"

"Here."

Little Tai opened his bag which he carried in his hand, and took out a rose-colored silk blouse and a blue slashed petticoat. Cinnamon Bud was delighted with the garments. She took the messenger downstairs, to reward him with a snack and a cup of wine. When he returned, he bent close to Hsi Men's ear and whispered: "I have a message from your Fifth Wife. She begs you not to delay, but to come home at once."

Before Hsi Men could take the letter that the lad was holding out to him, Cinnamon Bud had snatched it.

"No doubt a love letter from some beauty!" she told herself, while she curiously examined the writing. "Read it aloud!" she bade Chu Shih Nien, when she found that she could not decipher the rows of black characters, which were drawn with the brush on a strip of gayly colored silk.

Chu Shih Nien unrolled the silk and read. It was an ode called "Flowers Broken by the Storm":

> *Whether in the pale twilight,*
> *Or in the sunlit day,*
> *My thoughts are of him.*
> *I feel such anguish*
> *As one hardly feels*
> *At the sight of the beloved lying dead.*
> *I grieve for him,*
> *And am like to die of sorrow.*
> *Lonely is the pillow,*
> *Dimly flickers the lamp.*
> *The moon looks in*
> *Through the half-open window.*
> *Alas! How can a heart*
> *Even of iron*
> *Be insensible to its beams?*
> *Alas, how can I, wretched one,*
> *Survive the frosty night?*
> *Your loving concubine, the Sixth Daughter*
> *Pan greets you.*

Cinnamon Bud hardly waited to hear the end. She rose from the table and withdrew to her room. She threw herself upon her bed, and with her face pressed into the pillow she soon fell asleep. Hsi Men seized the strip of silk, the cause of her annoyance, and tore it to shreds. Then he angrily kicked the boy twice, for all to see, and sent him home. Twice he sent for Cinnamon Bud, but she did not come. He lost patience, and ran upstairs to speak to her himself. He went up to the bed, lifted her in his arms, and spoke soothingly to her.

"Little Sister Cinnamon Bud, don't distress yourself! This letter really doesn't matter. My Fifth sent it. She wants me to run home and discuss a few matters with her; that's all."

"Don't believe him! He's trying to deceive you!" bleated Chu Shih Nien, who had followed Hsi Men. "The writer is his latest sweetheart—an extremely dangerous rival for you. Don't let him go!"

Hsi Men laughingly gave him a buffet. "You accursed joker, you drive one to despair with your crazy interruptions!"

Cinnamon Bud answered ironically: "You are making a mistake, Master Hsi Men. Since you are so well provided for at home, you do not need to take the virginity of strange girls. You should remain decently at home. You have been with us long enough. It is high time now for you to run away home!"

Hsi Men clasped her tenderly to his bosom, and remained.

In the meantime poor little Tai had gone home. Distracted and weeping, he went to Moon Lady to report what had happened. Jade Fountain and Gold Lotus were in the room.

"Have you brought your master?" they asked eagerly.

"All I got was kicks and curses," he answered. "He says he'll smash everything in the house, if you send for him again."

"That is really too bad of him," said Moon Lady, turning to the other wives. "He doesn't want to come; very well. But why does he beat the poor little fellow?"

"He may kick him as often as he likes, for all I care. But why is he angry with us?" Jade Fountain asked indignantly.

"He needn't imagine that a common wench like that can really love him," said Gold Lotus, disdainfully. "Girls of that sort have eyes only for his money. How does the proverb run?—

> *Not even a whole ship's cargo of gold*
> *Can fill the maw of a house of joy."*

She did not suspect that her words were overheard by Sunflower, who was listening outside the window. Sunflower was by no means pleased to hear Gold Lotus express such contempt of Cinnamon Bud, her niece. From that moment Gold Lotus had a new enemy.

> *Words work a twofold wonder:*
> *Gentle words melt even ice;*
> *Speak one angry word among them,*
> *Hot turns chilly in a trice.*

Sadly, Gold Lotus went back to her pavilion. The time passed with intolerable slowness. An hour seemed to her a month. At last she made up her mind. Hsi Men would not come home that night, she was certain. As soon as it was dark she sent her two maids to bed. Then Gold Lotus went into the park, as though she were going to take one of her nightly strolls. But this time she had a definite goal: the cottage of the young gardener, Kin Tung. Quietly she invited him to come to her pavilion. She let him in, carefully bolted the door, and set wine before him. She pressed him to drink until he grew tipsy. Then she loosened her girdle, disrobed, and abandoned herself to him.

> *Eternal rules she disregards,*
> *Rules that nature herself proclaims:*
> *The high must ever shun the low,*
> *Noble from base be strictly severed.*
> *Emboldened by her desires,*
> *She fears not her master's wrath;*
> *Hot with unbridled desire*
> *She obeys only her own voice.*
> *In the park of the hundred flowers*

She allows her base impulse to rule her,
Making a brothel of the house
Where chastity should prevail.
But what is honor, what reputation?
Love is her pastime.
The ignoble seed of an ass
Is allowed to defile her jasper body.

Every night from now onwards Gold Lotus admitted the gardener's boy to her pavilion. Early in the morning, before it grew light, she sent him away. She gave him, as tokens of her favor, a golden headband, three silver hair clasps, and a silken perfume sachet. She naturally believed in the discretion of her young lover. She never suspected that the lad often went off to drink and dice with his fellows, and then he would boast of his good fortune. In short, one day the wind of rumor blew into the ears of her two enemies, Snowblossom and Sunflower; it seemed that in her present marriage Gold Lotus was no more faithful than in her first. They went at once to Moon Lady and told her what was rumored about the hated Fifth. Moon Lady would not believe the story.

"It's simply that you two can't bear the woman," Moon Lady decided as she dismissed them.

One night Gold Lotus forgot to lock the kitchen door. Autumn Aster came to the kitchen late that night, and when she opened the door she discovered Gold Lotus in the arms of the gardener's boy. She told Little Jewel of this next morning, and she, in turn, informed Snowblossom, who rushed off to Sunflower with the news. Sunflower and Snowblossom then went once more to Moon Lady.

"We have her own maid as witness this time," they told her, "and if you will not tell Master Hsi Men, then we shall inform him. He might just as well live with a scorpion as with this woman."

Moon Lady begged them not to spoil his birthday with this gossip. On the twenty-seventh of the seventh month, two days before the celebration, Hsi Men returned home. Sunflower and Snowblossom went at once to tell him of Gold Lotus's infidelity.

Bitter gall mounted to the heart of Hsi Men. The thousand domestic and commercial matters that awaited his attention were instantly forgotten. He bellowed for the guilty Kin Tung. Lady Gold Lotus, warned of the gathering storm, had just time to summon the youth to her pavilion. She warned him to admit nothing, and she hurriedly took back her gifts to him, the headband and the hair clasps, but in her excitement she forgot the silken perfume sachet.

Now the sinner was kneeling before his master in the front hall, and the examination began.

"Do you confess, you miserable scoundrel?"

Kin Tung was silent.

"Tear the clasps from his hair and show them to me!" Hsi Men cried to the four servants, who, armed with cudgels, had stationed themselves on his right and his left; but they could discover no clasps.

"Where have you hidden the gold ring and the silver clasps?"

"I have never had anything of the kind."

"Perhaps your memory is failing!—Off with his clothes!"

Powerful hands laid hold upon him and stripped off his jerkin and trunk hose. There, dangling from the waistband of his drawers, was a gayly-colored silken perfume sachet. Hsi Men at once recognized the sachet that Gold Lotus had often worn.

"Ha! and where did you get this, fellow?"

Disconcerted, Kin Tung stood silent and trembling. Then he lied: "I found it one day, as I was sweeping the garden."

Hsi Men gnashed his teeth with rage. "Bind him and give it him properly!" he cried to the servants. Thirty times the heavy bamboo cudgel crashed down on Kin Tung's back, until his skin was burst, and his body dyed with blood. Then Hsi Men ordered Lai Pao to tear two tufts of hair from above the youth's temples. After this he was driven from the house.

Gold Lotus felt as though she were being dipped into a tub of icy water when she heard the shrieks of pain from the tortured lad. Then Hsi Men crossed her threshold. In her terror she trembled in every limb; the blood stopped flowing in her veins; she could no longer breathe. Nevertheless, she roused herself to a supreme effort and calmly helped him off with his outer clothes as usual. A sudden blow landed on her face. Hsi Men called Spring Plum, and ordered her to close the outer gates, and to let no one into the pavilion.

With a horsewhip in his hand, Hsi Men took his seat on a stool in the courtyard. Curtly he ordered Gold Lotus to take off her clothes and kneel down. She obeyed silently, with bowed head.

"Now, infamous woman, out with the truth!" he commanded. "The scoundrel has already confessed everything. No evasions! How often have you played the whore with him here in my absence?"

"Oh, heavens, do not allow me, an innocent woman, to be murdered!" she wailed. "Truly I have done nothing wrong while you were away. During the day I sat over my needlework with Jade Fountain; in the evening I bolted the door and went to bed early. I have never made use of the side door. If you do not believe what I say, ask Spring Plum!"

And raising her voice, she called the maid.

"But I am told you gave him a golden headband and three silver hair clasps! Your lies are useless!" he shouted angrily.

"They do me deadly injustice!" she protested vehemently. "The whole story has been invented by that villainous wretch, who cannot endure me because you have granted me a little of your favor. May her tongue be cut out at the roots! May she die a miserable death! The headband and the clasps you gave me are here! Convince yourself! If there is a single article missing, then trust me no longer! If that little scoundrel has told you anything else, he lies in his throat!"

"That's all very well about the clasps and the headband. But this"—he drew the silken perfume sachet from his sleeve—"do you recognize *this?* How did this happen to be on *his* person, under his clothes? Do you still persist in your denials——?"

His words added fuel to his anger, and now he brought the horsewhip down on her smooth, fragrant skin.

"Dear Master," she pleaded, writhing in pain, "spare the life of your slave! She will speak! I lost this sachet in the park one day. My girdle came loose just as I was passing the Kashmir Thistle Arbor with Jade Fountain. The sachet fell to the ground, but I did not notice that it was lost until later, and then I could not find it. Could I dream that that little rogue would pick it up? Never, never, I swear by all that's holy, did he receive it from my hands!"

Hsi Men was at a loss. Her words confirmed the gardener boy's story. As Hsi Men looked at her, in her rosy nakedness, like a lovely blossom lying on the ground, beautiful even in her pain, alluring even in her tears, compassion took possession of nine-tenths of his heart, and in a moment his wrath fled to distant Javaland.

Spring Plum was told to come in and to sit on his lap.

"It now depends upon you whether I spare your mistress. Tell me, has this story of her affair with the gardener's boy any truth in it?"

The smart little maid, who was anything but a fool, answered briskly:

"What you are thinking is out of the question. I was with my mistress all day long. We were as inseparable as lip and cheek. The whole story of the gardener's boy is invented from beginning to end, and is simply a malicious plot. You shouldn't let people stuff your head with such ugly gossip!"

Her words took effect. Hsi Men threw the horsewhip away and told Gold Lotus to put on her clothes. He bade Autumn Aster lay the table and serve food and wine. Gold Lotus knelt before Hsi Men and offered him the first cup.

"I forgive you!" he said. "But in future, when I am away from home, make use of your solitude to cleanse and purify your heart.

Close the gates and doors in good time! Refrain even in your thoughts from any irregularities! If further complaints come to my ears, I shall not spare you."

"Your slave hears your command," she answered, and she performed four kowtows. And with that the incident was closed.

But her resentment over the treatment she had suffered gnawed deep into Gold Lotus's heart. On Hsi Men's birthday, two days later, when troops of guests came to the house, Gold Lotus did not appear. And when Cinnamon Bud and her aunt came to the pavilion in order to pay their respects to the Fifth Wife, Gold Lotus ordered Spring Plum to bolt all the doors, so that Gold Lotus was enclosed as though in an iron barrel. The visitors, red with embarrassment, were forced to go away.

When Hsi Men came to her that evening he found her in a dejected state; her cloudy hair was disheveled, her flowerlike face was pale and drawn. Humbly she went about her duties; she loosened his girdle, helped him to undress, and bathed his feet in lukewarm water. But late at night, in an interval between the accustomed delights of the bed, the intolerable feeling of shame that oppressed her compelled her to speak to him.

"My Ko ko, who is there in all your household that loves you so truly and sincerely as I do? All the others are women whose love is as perishable as the dew, women who without a second thought would sit down to a new wedding feast in the event of your death. I am the only one who understands you completely. If only you would try to understand me! Don't you see that all these accusations were inspired by hate and envy, aroused by the fact that you have shown a slight preference for my company? I shouldn't be surprised if new schemes were being laid for stabbing me in the back. And now you have heartlessly shamed and humbled the only one who really loves you! Didn't the proverb occur to you:

"The domestic fowl if roughly handled
Flutters here and there in bewilderment.
The lot of a wild fowl is easier:
She can fly, for the heavens lie open.

158

"Don't you realize that in maltreating me you have maltreated your best and truest hen? When recently, in the house of joy, you kicked little Tai, I did not utter a word of blame. Moon Lady and Jade Fountain can testify to that. My only concern was, and is, that you may ruin yourself with these strange powder-faces. Do understand me! That kind of creature loves only your money, not your person. Don't be influenced by that sort of woman. Depend on me, your truly devoted slave!"

Thus she cleverly bedded him in a warm nest of tender words.

But in spite of Gold Lotus's warnings, his impulses drove him again, a few days later, to Mother Li's premises. Cinnamon Bud, who was entertaining some visitors, withdrew to her room when Hsi Men was announced. She washed the rouge and powder from her face, took off her brooches and rings, threw herself on her bed, and buried her head in the pillows.

Hsi Men had to wait for some time before old Mother Li appeared.

"We haven't had the honor for a long time, noble Brother-in-Law!" she greeted him.

"Yes, the disturbance occasioned by my insignificant birthday kept me at home."

"I hope that the visit of my little one did not inconvenience you!"

"On the contrary. Where is she, by the way?"

"Alas, she's changed so since she came back from your house. She must be upset over something or other. She lies in bed all day, and nothing will induce her to get up. So far she hasn't once left her room."

"That's strange. Then I'll just go up and look at her."

He asked to be shown to Cinnamon Bud's bedchamber at the back of the house. There he saw her lying on the bed with loose, disheveled hair, her face pressed into the pillows. She did not move when he entered.

"What ails you?" he asked. "Why have you been in such low

spirits ever since you came to see me a few days ago? Has anyone given you cause for distress?"

For a long while she did not speak. When he kept repeating his question, she burst out: "What do you want with us when you have your Fifth? But even though I have grown up in a public house of joy, I too have my advantages, and I need only stand on my toes a little to overtop such an honest wife as she is. Recently I went to your house, not by formal invitation but as a kinswoman, to offer my congratulations. Your First received me most graciously, gave me clothes and trinkets, and asked me to visit her again soon. Shall it be said that we in our flower gardens have no notion of manners and good breeding? I went with my aunt to pay my respects to your Fifth also. What did the Fifth do? She shut herself up in her pavilion and told her maid to inform us that she was not to be seen. Is that the way to behave? Is that good breeding?"

"Don't take it so to heart!" said Hsi Men soothingly. "She was not quite in her right senses that day. But if she ever snubs you again she'll get a sound thrashing."

Cinnamon Bud laid her hand across his lips. "Ruffian, you wouldn't go so far as to beat her?"

"If you only knew!" he laughed. "How do you suppose I could otherwise keep peace and order among my wives? Twenty, thirty lashes of the whip! And if that's not effectual, then off with their hair!"

"Oh, you're just trying to impress me. How soon does your severity change to tenderness when you are with her? I am not there to see. You would have to show me a lock of hair cut from her head by way of evidence, before I would believe in your celebrated severity."

"Then rest assured, you shall believe in it!"

At dawn the following day he took leave of Cinnamon Bud. She reminded him: "Don't come here again without you know what! Otherwise you will suffer a shameful loss of face!"

He arrived home still half seas over, and still completely under the spell of her last words. Without lingering in the front rooms of the house, he went straight to Gold Lotus's bedchamber. She noticed that he was not quite sober, and was even more attentive than usual. He sat down on the edge of the bed and ordered her to pull off his shoes. She had hardly performed this humble service when he suddenly commanded: "Take off your clothes! Kneel down!"

A wild terror seized her and she broke into a cold sweat. She knelt, but would not take off her clothes.

"Master, at least enlighten your slave with a word of explanation!" she pleaded. "I would rather die than endure this daily torment! Why can I never please you, though I try in a thousand ways? This slow torture with a blunt knife is more than I can bear!"

"Off with your clothes, or you'll get something!" he threatened. Then he shouted to Spring Plum: "Bring the whip!"

But Spring Plum would not obey him. He repeated his command. At last she slowly opened the door, and tremblingly approached him. But when she saw her mistress kneeling on the floor beside the bed, and noticed the overturned lamp under the table, she stood still, unable to stir from the spot.

"Sister Spring Plum, help me! He wanted to beat me again!" her mistress cried in a despairing voice.

"Don't trouble yourself about her, little oily-mouth!" cried Hsi Men. "Rather hand me the whip that I may chastise her!"

The little maid could no longer contain her indignation.

"Aren't you ashamed of yourself, Master? What harm has she done you? With no excuse, just because of other people's gossip, you fall upon her like a hurricane raging across the plain at obstacles that don't exist. Who is to understand you or respect you? I, at all events, won't help you."

And she rushed out of the room.

Hsi Men laughed a dry, embarrassed laugh. Then he turned to Gold Lotus, who was still kneeling.

"Come here! I won't beat you. I want only a trifle from you. Will you give it to me?"

"Dear Master, my whole body belongs to you. Whatever you want, that you shall have. Only I don't know what you have in mind."

"I want a lock of your beautiful hair."

"Why?"

"For a hair-net."

"Really? Very well, you may have a lock. But promise me that you'll make no improper use of it."

"I promise."

She loosened her hair, and Hsi Men cut off a thick and beautiful lock. He wrapped it carefully in paper and thrust it into his pocket. Gold Lotus laid her head on his breast.

"You know I want to do everything you wish," she said, tearfully. "Only I beg of you, don't be so unreliable and variable! I won't say a word if you are nice to other women. Only don't treat me so brutally!"

The following day Hsi Men went to Cinnamon Bud and triumphantly handed her the black, lustrous, luxuriant tress of Gold Lotus's hair.

"Well, have I kept my word? It took a considerable effort before I persuaded her. Without trickery, too, I couldn't have succeeded. Ha, ha! I had to make her believe I needed the strand for a hairnet!"

"There's something more than that in it, to judge by the fuss you make of it! If you are so afraid of her, you need not have bothered. Well, give it to me! You may have the rubbish back when you go."

She signed to her elder sister to keep company with Hsi Men for a moment. She herself disappeared into her room with her booty. She pulled off her slipper and arranged the tress of hair as padding in the sole. To trample her rival's hair underfoot would give her constant satisfaction.

Day after day passed and Hsi Men did not return. Since the last incident, which cost her a beautiful lock of hair, the forsaken Gold

Lotus was oppressed with melancholy. She would not set foot outside her pavilion. All food was distasteful to her. Moon Lady, who was worried about her, decided to call in Mother Liu, who was regularly consulted by Hsi Men's household in such cases. Mother Liu prescribed two black pills daily and a strong unseasoned broth in the evening. She then suggested that her husband should be called in to cast Gold Lotus's horoscope.

"Does he know how to foretell the future?" asked Gold Lotus with interest.

"Why, of course. He may have to go about the streets with his blind man's drum, but there are three things he knows his way about. Firstly, he can read horoscopes and conjure spirits. Secondly, he can cauterize boils with red-hot needles. And thirdly, he knows all about spells."

"Spells? What kind of spells?"

"Suppose parents and children can't get on together, suppose a brother and sister are always quarreling, or a wife and concubine living at daggers drawn, then my old man supplies a written spell which has to be burned to ashes, mixed in some liquid, and swallowed. In less than three days everything is all in order. His magic not only enables him to cure illnesses and drunkenness—he can make trade flourish, he can make the fields produce a hundredfold, he can make a business of any kind prosper. Since he has a special knowledge of the stars, he is commonly known as Liu the astrologer."

Gold Lotus listened with strained attention. She had tea and cakes brought for the old woman, and gave her some pieces of silver when she was ready to go.

"Here are three pieces of silver for your fee," said Gold Lotus. "The other five are to cover the cost of the paper amulet and whatever else you need. So I'll expect you tomorrow at breakfast time. Don't forget to bring your husband with you."

Mother Liu came early next morning, bringing her blind husband. The old rogue told Gold Lotus to give him the four twofold astronomical signs of the hour, the day, the month, and the year of her birth. He kneaded invisible figures with his fingers, and then droned out the findings of the horoscope with abstruse astrological formulae. Gold Lotus gathered only that the constellation of her marriage star was inharmonious, and that she was to guard against the tongues of small-minded people.

"Master," she said, "I should be deeply obliged to you if you would now set your magic working. There are only two things I want. To be safe from the gossip of mean-spirited people, and to have my husband love and respect me; that is all I ask."

The blind rascal answered her: "Cut a slip of wood from the trunk of a willow tree, carve it into the figures of a man and woman, write on it the four twofold signs of the birth hours of yourself and your husband, wind both figures about with seven times seven red silk threads, wrap them in a strip of red crêpe, and place the whole upon your husband's eyes at night. Put a few sprigs of wormwood over his heart, pierce his hands with a needle, and smear glue between his feet. And lastly, hide a spell written in cinnabar red in his pillow, burn another, and mix the ashes in his tea. Within three days the desired effect will be produced."

"Might I ask the meaning of these spells?"

"I will tell you. Placing the figures wrapped in red silk over the eyes of your husband will have the effect of making you appear in his eyes as lovely and desirable as a Hsi Shih. The sprigs of wormwood will kindle new love for you in his heart. The prick of the needle will prevent him from ever raising his hand to strike you, even though you have done wrong. And the glue will keep him from setting foot again in places of unbridled lust."

Gold Lotus was satisfied. She gave the old magician his fee, and a pair of beautiful hair clasps. On the morrow Old Mother Liu brought the spells and the various accessories which were to be applied according to the blind man's prescriptions. When Hsi Men returned Gold Lotus had everything ready. She gave him tea with the ashes of the charm in it; she hid a cinnabar-red spell in his pillow. She forgot nothing. The results seemed in accordance with the predictions of the blind magician. Two days later Gold

Lotus and Hsi Men were on the best of terms and enjoying themselves like little fishes in the water. But, worthy reader, it is not without reason that a married man is warned against letting his wife have secret dealings with bonzes and nuns, with Tao priests and soothsayers, with nurses and matchmakers. A good old proverb runs:

> *Let not your guests behold your wife,*
> *And secretly lock the postern gate.*
> *Restrict her to courtyard and garden;*
> *So intrigue and misfortune will pass you by.*

CHAPTER TWELVE: *Mistress Hua casts unseen Threads over the Wall. The Handmaid Pear Blossom spies through a Chink in the Window*

ONE DAY Hsi Men received an invitation to the house of his neighbor, Hua Tze Hsu. When he went there, at noon, he was so wrapped in his thoughts that as he crossed the outer court he almost collided with Mistress Hua, who was standing on the raised platform inside the second entry. He had seen her only once before, when visiting his friend's country estate. Today, for the first time, he looked at her closely. On account of the heat she was dressed lightly. Her thin blouse left the throat uncovered, and closed over her bosom as loosely as the two halves of a split lotus root held together by fragile fibers. Beneath the hem of her white skirt, like the tips of two little tongues, peeped out two neat little red satin slippers, embroidered with a phœnix pattern. Her hair was bound in a silver net, and at the lobes of her ears glittered earrings of rubies set in gold. Her full figure was of medium stature, and her face was oval and full as a melon. Her brows were delicately penciled, and here eyes made Hsi Men's senses soar to the heights of heaven.

She answered his low bow with a soft *Wan fu*: "Happiness ten thousandfold!" and at once withdrew. A maid ushered him into the reception room and pressed him to take a seat. A moment later Mistress Hua's charming face appeared again from behind the door.

"Please wait a moment," she begged him. "My husband has just gone out on a business errand and will soon be here."

The maid brought him tea. Then he again heard Mistress Hua's voice behind the door.

"May I ask a favor of you, noble gentleman? If my husband wants you to drink wine with him today in a certain place, will you, for the sake of my honor, see that he does not stay away too long? For the moment I am all alone in the house with my two maids."

Hsi Men had just time to promise her, "Sister-in-law, I will not fail—" when Master Hua's return was announced. His wife at once disappeared from the door. Master Hua had sent for Hsi Men only in order to propose an immediate visit to Mother Wu's house of joy. For Hua's beloved, Silver Bud, was that day celebrating her birthday, the twenty-fourth of the sixth month. With the beautiful Lady Hua's request in mind, Hsi Men, at an early hour of the evening, brought his extremely intoxicated friend home, having done his best to reduce him to that condition. When the drunken man had been got safely indoors and Hsi Men was about to take his leave, Mistress Hua came into the reception room to thank him for escorting her husband. "Of course my lunatic of a husband has drunk too much again!" she said. "How kind of you to see him home!"

Hsi Men bowed. "Please, please. Any command of yours is at once buried in my heart like a bronze inscription, engraved upon my very bones. Besides, we were going the same way. My only regret is that I was unable to prevent him from remaining as long as he did. It took all my powers of persuasion to induce him to leave. And on the way, as we came by the Hall of the Pleasure-Star, Mother Chong's place, I had great difficulty in preventing him from entering. For when he saw little Darling Perfume standing in the doorway—she's really a pretty little thing—he felt strongly inclined to go in. If I had allowed him, he would have remained there all night. But how can a man neglect such a lovely young wife as you! It is really inexcusable of the stupid fellow!"

"You are right. I am really quite ill with worry on account of his feather-headed ways. May I hope that for my sake you will to some extent keep an eye on him in the future? I should thank you from the bottom of my heart!"

Now, Hsi Men was this sort of person: if he was tapped on the head, there was instantly an echo from the soles of his feet. Thanks to his years of experience in the play of the moon and wind, he at once understood that by her words the beautiful Mistress Hua had opened a convenient passage into the haven of love. With a meaning smile he replied: "Set yourself at ease, Lady Sister-in-Law! I shall watch over him most rigorously!"

She thanked him and withdrew. Hsi Men slowly sipped his tea, flavored with foam of apricot kernels, and contentedly went home.

From now onwards he proceeded systematically. Whenever he and his friend Hua went to a house of joy, his boon companions, Beggar Ying and Hsia Hsi Ta, were instructed to detain the other at his cups, and, if possible, keep him away from home all night. Hsi Men would leave quietly, and going home, would stand outside the door of his house. As soon as he saw his beautiful neighbor and her two maids at the door opposite, waiting for Hua, Hsi Men would stroll up and down in front of her house, turning now to the east, now to the west, and clearing his throat to attract attention, occasionally darting a glance into the shadows of the gateway. She, on the other hand, would retreat shyly indoors whenever he passed, but as soon as he had gone by she would cautiously emerge again, and peer after him with wistful eyes. Each waited anxiously for the other to make the next advance.

One evening when he was standing outside the door the maid Apricot Blossom came over to him.

"Is there anything your mistress wishes of me?" he asked eagerly.

"Yes, she would like to speak to you," she whispered. "The master isn't at home."

He quickly followed the maid, and was shown into the reception room.

"You were so kind the other day—" his neighbor greeted him. "Have you by any chance come across my husband today or yesterday? He has been away for two days now."

"Why, yes, we were at Mother Chong's yesterday," he said. "I left rather early on business. I haven't seen him today—and I really couldn't say where he is just now. I am only thankful that I myself did not remain, for then I should deserve the severest criticism for keeping my promise so indifferently."

"Oh, his lack of consideration is driving me to despair! Must he always continue to rove among flowers and willows, and never come home?" she cried.

"In other respects he is the best and most amiable of men . . ." Hsi Men sighed hypocritically. Fearing to be surprised by her husband, he soon took his leave.

Next day, Master Hua came home. His wife greeted him with bitter reproaches. Then she added:

"Our honorable neighbor, Hsi Men, has been unselfish enough to look after you a little; otherwise you would ruin yourself completely. We ought to show our gratitude by some little attention. Such things preserve a friendship."

Friend Hua obediently packed four boxes with little presents, and sent them, with a jug of his best wine, to the house next door.

When Hsi Men explained to Moon Lady the reason for these presents, Moon Lady answered sarcastically:

"Well, to think of that! You are trying to guide him into a decent way of life! You had better give a little thought to your own way of life! It is just as if a clay Buddha were to teach an earthenware Buddha how to behave. Don't you yourself spend the whole day racketing about? However, for the sake of politeness we must return this courtesy. See whose signature is on the letter. If it is his wife's signature then I must reply with an invitation to her. If it is the signature of Master Hua, then you must answer it."

"It is his signature," replied Hsi Men. "I will ask him to come here tomorrow."

After Master Hua had been sumptuously feasted for a whole day, it was once more his wife who suggested that a few paltry gifts were not a sufficient return for the generous hospitality which he had enjoyed. The approaching Chrysanthemum Festival, on the ninth day of the ninth month, afforded a convenient opportunity. And so neighbor Hua invited Hsi Men and four of their friends to come to the chrysanthemum show in his house. Two dancers were engaged to entertain the party, and as usual they did themselves well.

> *This is the season when the nimble hare*
> *Speeds over the fields in zig-zag bounds,*
> *When tree and sward glow spattered with red.*
> *Rare fragrance rises from yellow flowers.*
> *What care we for the raven's mournful flight?*
> *One must rightly understand the season's favors.*
> *Let us rejoice with wine and comely wenches,*
> *While our beloved ones watch behind the curtain!*

It was about the hour when one takes lantern in hand when Hsi Men rose from the table to leave the room for a moment. Outside the door he almost collided with Mistress Hua, who had chosen a dark corner near the spirit wall for her observation post. She quickly withdrew to the side door on the west of the house. Immediately afterwards her maid, Apricot Blossom, emerged from the darkness and approached Hsi Men.

"My mistress begs you," she whispered, "to be temperate in your drinking and to leave early. Later she will send you another message."

In his joy Hsi Men almost forgot to do what he had left the house for. When he returned to the table he pretended to be drunk, and as far as possible refused more wine.

Meanwhile Mistress Hua, impatiently walking up and down behind the curtain, had to wait for some little time. The first watch of the night was already past, and she saw Master Hsi Men still sitting at the table, nodding his head as though half-asleep. Beggar Ying and Hsia Hsi Ta seemed nailed to their seats. They did not even stir when Chu Shih Nien and Sun Tien Hua went home. Mistress Hua was beside herself with impatience. At last Hsi Men rose to go.

"Little Brother, why can't you sit still?" his friend Hua asked reproachfully. "You're not very courteous to your host today."

"I'm tipsy and can hardly stand on my feet," said Hsi Men, thickly. Supported by two servants, he made his way to the door, simulating the rolling gait of a drunkard.

"I don't know what's wrong with him today," grumbled Beggar Ying. "Doesn't want to drink and gets drunk on a couple of drops. But that shouldn't prevent us from having a few more rounds. We are getting along excellently without him."

"Impudent rascals!" Mistress Hua, behind the curtain, murmured angrily; and she sent for her husband.

"Please oblige me by taking yourself and those two fellows off to your house of joy," she said. "There you can go on soaking for all I care. But here I should like to be spared this deafening racket and uproar. Do you expect me to waste my whole night burning the lamp, and keeping the fire alight? I have no notion of doing such a thing!"

"I should like to go out, but then you'd reproach me afterwards."

"For all I care you need not come home till morning," she replied.

Master Hua did not wait to be told twice, and his two companions were no less delighted, so shortly before midnight they left with the two dancers. The servants Tien Fu and Tien Hsi followed.

Hsi Men went out in the darkness and sat under an arbor close to the wall between his grounds and those of Master Hua. There he waited impatiently for the message from Mistress Hua. Suddenly he heard the sound of a dog barking. A door creaked. Then silence. After a moment he heard the mewing of a cat on the top of the wall. He looked up and saw the maid Pear Blossom. She leaned over and beckoned to him. Quickly he pushed a table against the wall, placed a bench on top of the table, and climbed over. On the other side there was a ladder leaning against the wall. He was ushered into a candle-lit room. In a light house dress, bare-headed and with loosened hair, his beautiful neighbor appeared, pressed him to take a seat, and presented him with a cup of welcome.

"I was almost dying with impatience!" she continued, after a few polite and flowery phrases of greeting. "Neither of the impudent fellows whom my husband had invited made the least motion to leave. At last I gave him to understand that he could go on with his diversions if he chose, but in a house of joy. So I got rid of the troublesome crew."

"But what if Brother Hua should suddenly come home?" inquired the prudent Hsi Men.

"Oh, I've granted him leave until the morning. Besides, both the servants have gone with him. I am all alone with my two maids, except for Mother Bee, my old nurse, who keeps the door, and is thoroughly discreet and absolutely dependable."

His fears allayed, Hsi Men, without another thought, gave himself up to the pleasure of the moment. Shoulder pressed to shoulder, thigh to thigh, he drank out of the same bowl with her, out of the same goblet. Pear Blossom poured while Apricot Blossom served. After the meal the two lovers went to a bedroom fragrant with perfume, and there, under bright silken curtains, they abandoned themselves to the joys of the couch.

Lady Hua had carefully shut the parchment-covered double window in order to elude any possible curious glances from outside. But she had not reckoned with the artfulness of her maid, Pear Blossom. This inquisitive, seventeen-year-old creature could not refrain from sneaking up under the windowsill, and, with a hairpin, boring a peephole through the twofold pane of parchment. And now she perceived, in the light of the lamp and the tapers, a something that outlined itself on the bed hangings like the shadow of a great, queerly-shaped, struggling fish. Then that queer being came to rest; it split into two halves, and these words fell on her ear:

"How many flourishing springs do you number at present?"

"Twenty-three. And what is the age of your First?"

"Twenty-six."

"Three years older than I am, then. I should be delighted to pay my respects to her and present her with some trifling gift. But perhaps she has no wish to make my acquaintance?"

"Have no fear. She has a most kindly character."

"Suppose she has remarked your nocturnal excursion, how will you answer her?"

"Oh, all my wives live some distance from the house; they could not possibly have noticed anything. Only the Fifth dwells in a garden pavilion close by. But she will take care not to meddle in my affairs."

"How old is the Fifth?"

"Just as old as the First."

"In case the Fifth does not disdain my insufficient self, I should like to enter into a bond of sisterhood with her. Tomorrow morning I shall present her and the First with two pairs of slippers which I fashioned with my own hands."

She took two golden clasps from her hair and gave them to Hsi Men. "But don't let my husband see them!"

They remained together until the first crowing of the cock, when a pale glow in the east indicated the approach of dawn. Thereupon Hsi Men returned home as he had come. For future assignations they had agreed upon a secret signal. A cough and the throwing of a wall tile over the wall would give him to understand that the coast was clear.

Hsi Men went to the pavilion of Gold Lotus, who was still in bed.

"Where have you been all night?" she asked him.

"At Mother Wu's place with Brother Hua. I went along with him only to oblige him."

She believed him, yet the shadow of a doubt lurked in her heart.

One afternoon, as she sat sewing in an arbor with Jade Fountain, a tile suddenly fell to the ground just in front of the arbor. Startled, Jade Fountain drew in her feet and lowered her head; Gold Lotus, accidentally glancing in the direction of the adjacent park wall, had a vague glimpse of a sunlit face that rose and immediately disap-

173

peared. She nudged her companion and pointed to the spot in question.

"Sister Three," she asked quietly, "doesn't the estate of neighbor Hua lie on the other side of that wall? And it was surely Mother Bee who peeped over the wall and immediately disappeared when she saw us sitting here. I distinctly recognized her. Do you imagine that she wanted merely to look at our flowers?"

All that evening she kept a secret watch over Hsi Men. Having paid her a short visit in her pavilion, when she asked him if he would have something to eat or drink, he absently declined, and presently excusing himself he went off into the park. Burning with curiosity, she followed him at a distance. He turned his footsteps in the direction of the wall. All at once she saw the same face which she had seen in the afternoon peer over the wall, and immediately afterwards Hsi Men placed a ladder against the coping and cautiously clambered over. She returned to her pavilion, full of thought. For a long while she paced restlessly up and down her room. When at last she lay down it was only to lie wakeful throughout that night.

In the early hours of the morning Hsi Men appeared in her room and sat close beside her on the edge of her bed. Peeping at him from between her half-closed eyelids, she could plainly read embarrassment and the consciousness of guilt on his face. She sat up and seized him by the ear, looking him sternly in the eyes.

"You faithless wretch!" she scolded him. "Confess where you have been all night! But please, no evasions! I know all about your little game. Yesterday afternoon, as I sat sewing with Jade Fountain in the arbor, we accidentally noticed the signal which they gave you from the other side. I did not understand, when you recently told me that your friend Hua had dragged you out in the middle of the night to a house of joy, that you meant, of course, the cuckold's own house! Come now, how often have you played the fool with the wanton next door? If you make a frank and honorable confession I shall hold my peace. But if you try to deceive me with a single word, I'll disgrace you utterly as the ungrateful scoundrel that you are! Then you shan't find as much as a clod of earth to give you a modest grave!"

Hsi Men saw that he was caught. He preferred to make himself as small as a dwarf. He fell on his knees before her and humbly pleaded: "Darling little oily-mouth, no scandal, I beg of you! I will confess everything!" And when he had confessed, he concluded:

"Besides, she will soon pay you a friendly visit, and the First also, and will felicitate you both and present you with slippers which she has made with her own hands. And with you she would like to enter into a bond of sisterhood."

"Bah, as though I thought anything of that!" she retorted. "Such attentions are merely meant to facilitate her access to your house. I am too experienced to let anyone throw dust in my eyes, and I've no desire to observe her witchcraft at close quarters. Tell me frankly, how often have you been with her?"

Hsi Men could not contain himself for laughing.

"You funny little woman, you would plague a man to death with your questions! Don't disturb yourself, I beg of you. Tomorrow she will come and dutifully kowtow before you and present you with a pair of friendship slippers. Yesterday she obtained the foot measure of Moon Lady, and for the time being she sends you these trifling gifts by me."

He removed his hat, and took from his hair the two brooches given him by Mistress Hua. They were precious ornaments of chased gold, in the form of the auspicious symbol Shu, encrusted with blue turquoises, which signify long life. In his day, the old High Eunuch, her husband's uncle, had worn them at Court.

"Well, how do you like them?"

Gold Lotus was pacified.

"Very well, I shall say no more. On the contrary, I'll help you to discover how the wind blows whenever you feel any desire for her. What do you say now?"

"What a sensible little woman you are!" he said, in commendation. Overjoyed by this sudden change of attitude, he clasped her tenderly in his arms. "And do you know, that woman yonder does

175

not love me in a calculating way. It is really love at first sight. And as for you, tomorrow you shall have a ravishing new dress as a reward."

"Listen: I haven't too much faith in your honeyed tongue and your sugary words. I would rather you promised me three things, if you want me to tolerate this affair of yours."

"I will promise anything you like!"

"Well then, firstly you must keep away from the houses of joy. Secondly, you must obey me and do whatever I tell you. Thirdly, whenever you have been with her you must tell me just exactly how things went. And you are not to keep anything back! Do you promise?"

"With pleasure!"

From this time onwards, whenever he had been with Lady Hua he made a practice of faithfully informing Gold Lotus of all that had taken place. Not only what he had eaten and what he had drunk, but also whether Lady Hua's body was fair in complexion, and whether it felt as soft to the touch as flowered damask; whether she was as accomplished in wine drinking and card playing as in the play of the moon and the wind; she wanted to know everything.

Once he brought over a valuable silken frieze which the old High Eunuch Hua had carried off from the Imperial harem. It was a long, scalloped strip of silk, bordered with gold, upon which a painter had depicted with the utmost perfection twelve different erotic scenes. The twenty-four naked male and female figures, the twelve couples engaged in satisfying their vernal impulse, were painted with unearthly beauty.

Gold Lotus carefully examined it by the light of the lamp. Then she folded it up and gave it to Spring Plum for safe keeping, as though it were now her own property.

"But I must have it back within two days," Hsi Men protested humbly. "It is a precious souvenir of our neighbor's, and I brought it only to show it to you."

"I shall not give it up!" she answered defiantly. "I shall study those paintings every day."

176

"Now listen, if you defy me I shall open your little fist by main force," he threatened.

"Just you try! I will not give it up—you can tear me into little bits first!"

"What's to be done, then?" he said good-humoredly. "Very well, keep it and look at it to your heart's content. As far as that goes, there are other curious things over there that I'll show you some time."

"Splendid! And now, as your reward, I will open my little fist of my own accord."

And with undiminished vigor they surrendered themselves to the fugitive delights of the couch.

Worthy reader, from time immemorial there have been certain magic formulæ of mysterious efficacy. At any rate, since Gold Lotus had had recourse to the spells of Liu the Stargazer, Hsi Men was as though transformed in respect of his relations with her. Rancor and neglect gave way to favor and love; instead of sorrow and shame she experienced only satisfaction and triumph. He no longer dared to chastise her. And though she had perpetrated the wildest deviltries, he would have drunk the water in which she washed her feet, so completely was he bewitched.

CHAPTER THIRTEEN: *Chagrin carries off Brother Hua. At the Lantern Show five Beauties divert themselves on a Balcony*

ONE AFTERNOON Hsi Men came to Moon Lady in a state of complete consternation. "Just think, they've arrested Friend Hua!" he announced excitedly. "The four of us, quite unsuspecting, were tippling at Mother Chong's—you know, where Fragrant Waters lives—when suddenly a couple of beadles from the yamen appeared and marched him off without a word of explanation. Naturally, the rest of us were not a little startled. I ran off to Cinnamon Bud at once and lay low in her room half the day. In the meantime I managed to obtain some information. It seems that Hua's three brothers have lodged a complaint against him with the Prefect of the Eastern Capital, in respect of an inheritance, and in the course of the proceedings they have managed to get a warrant of arrest issued against him. Well, that's not so bad, after all, and so, reassured to some extent, I have ventured out of my hiding place."

"So it has come to that! This is the result of the company you keep, and the way you go racketing about!" Moon Lady rebuked him. "This time you have come off scot free again, but I see a day coming when you will be mixed up in a brawl and have your muttonhead beaten to a jelly. It's time you made up your mind to turn over a new leaf! But unfortunately I know your vacillating character. At home you listen to me, but you are no sooner outside than you prick up your donkey's ears and believe what any flower-girl whispers to you. My advice is just wind in your ears, but you respect the words of strangers as though they were sacred inscriptions in bronze."

"Ha, ha, did you say beat me?" Hsi Men laughed confidently. "The man to do that would need at least seven foreheads and eight spleens!"

"It is easy to talk big at home!"

Their conversation was interrupted by the entrance of the boy Tai. By her servant Golden Willow, Mistress Hua had sent word to ask that Master Hsi Men would come to her at once. Hsi Men stood irresolute for a moment. Then he turned towards the door.

"Next time, perhaps, you will have no one to give you a word of good advice," Moon Lady warned him.

"Inasmuch as we are such close neighbors we cannot very well decline her request. Let me deal with this," he insisted, and he left the room.

Mistress Hua came to meet him, negligently dressed, with a face bewildered and as white as wax. She fell at his feet and wailed:

"Alas, noble gentleman, I am completely at my wits' end. For Buddha's sake, not for that of his unworthy servant, stand by me as a friend and neighbor! My husband would never listen to me. Instead of thinking of his household he was always in the town. And now the disaster has come. I was about to consult the servants as to what I could do to rescue him. But what can I do, I, a woman, whose feet are hampered like those of an ungainly crab? Ah, I could die of rage when I think of him! And if they beat him to a jelly in the Eastern Capital it will only serve him right! But I am thinking of the good name of old Kung Kung. For his sake I implore you to have pity on me, and prevent this matter from coming to a public trial and a scandal!"

"Sister-in-law, do please get up! It's not so bad as all that," said Hsi Men reassuringly. "But to begin with, I don't know all the details of the affair."

"You must understand that my husband is the second of four brothers, blood nephews of old Kung Kung. Old Kung Kung, before he died, had entrusted his whole fortune in bullion to me exclusively, because he did not think my husband dependable enough. The other three nephews avoided the old man, because he was accustomed to thrash them with his stick for the slightest offense. When the old man died last year, the three nephews received their share of household goods and furniture, but the treasure remained in my possession, undivided. I repeatedly urged my husband to indemnify his brothers in money for their share of the treasure, but he never troubled his head about the matter. Now they have taken him by surprise."

"So you see, it is merely an ordinary squabble over an inheritance," said Hsi Men. "That's a matter of no great consequence. You really need not be so anxious, Lady Sister-in-Law. Of course, I am entirely at your service, and I shall consider Brother Hua's affairs as though they were my own."

"You have certainly relieved my mind. In my opinion the first thing to be done is to obtain the support of the authorities. Of course, I shall gladly place the necessary means at your disposal."

"No excessive expenditure will be necessary. The decision rests with the Prefect of Kai fong fu, Marshal Yang. He is one of the clients of Chancellor Tsai. Master Tsai, however, is hand in glove with my relative Marshal Yang. They are both important people at Court and have direct access to the Son of Heaven. It is to these two that we must address our petitions, in order that they may influence the Prefect Yang in your husband's favor. Of course, we shall not gain our ends without offering a few presents to the Chancellor. On the other hand, presents for the Marshal would be superfluous. He is my relative, after all."

Mistress Hua disappeared for a moment into her bedchamber, opened two chests, and bade her maids carry to Hsi Men, in the guest chamber, sixty bars of silver, of the total weight of three thousand ounces.

"I place this at your disposal," she said.

"Why so much? Half would suffice."

"Whatever surplus there may be, I beg you to consider as your own property. Besides this, I have hidden behind my bed several caskets and chests containing court robes, ceremonial bonnets, jade girdles, rings, and other valuable ornaments which I should be glad to consign to your care, for the sake of security. May I?"

"What if Brother Hua should miss these things when he comes back?"

"Oh, he knows nothing at all about them. Old Kung Kung entrusted them to me personally, and I have never whispered a word about them to my husband."

"Then I shall go across at once and send my people to fetch them."

At home he took counsel with his First. Moon Lady advised that servants should fetch the silver in ordinary food hampers, while the chests and boxes could be lifted over the wall at night, in order to avoid attracting undesirable attention in the neighborhood.

Hsi Men followed her advice, and ordered four servants to bring the silver bullion in plain hampers. At night the chests and boxes followed. On one side of the wall Mistress Hua and her two maids pushed and heaved, while on the other Hsi Men, Moon Lady, Gold Lotus, and Spring Plum tugged and hauled. No male servant was present. Everything was carried unobserved into Moon Lady's chamber.

On the following day Hsi Men's son-in-law, Chen, departed with a petition for his uncle, Marshal Yang. A servant, Lai Pao, was dispatched in all haste to the city of Kai fong fu. The letter which he carried had the immediate effect of bringing about a complete understanding between the Marshal and Chancellor Tsai, as well as the latter's protégé, the Prefect of the Capital.

And then came the day of the public action against Friend Hua in the prefecture. Upwards of a thousand persons knelt on the ground when the Prefect entered the great Hall of Justice. During his detention, Hua had learned from Hsi Men, who had written to him, what was being done. His examination was brief and lenient. When the Prefect inquired as to the residue of his uncle's property, he explained that there were still two residential estates in the city and a country seat. The furniture and household goods had already been apportioned, while all the ready money had been consumed by the expenses of a worthy funeral. The Prefect declared himself satisfied with this statement, and proclaimed:

"In the case of officials who are employed in the more intimate service of the Court, it is difficult to ascertain the extent of their possessions. Very often such officials lose their property as easily as they acquired it. Inasmuch as that portion of the personality which was in cash is no longer existent, I decree that the District Mandarin of Tsing ho hsien shall put up the three estates to public auction, and that the proceeds shall be divided among the plaintiffs."

The three plaintiffs, who had hoped for more, were by no means satisfied with this decision. They threw themselves on their faces before the scarlet dais, and pleaded that the defendant should be held in custody until he delivered up the cash inheritance of whose existence they were positive. But the Prefect snorted angrily: "Why did you not press your claim immediately after your uncle's decease? The matter is superannuated. What is the meaning of this belated complaint?"

And Friend Hua was set free without having received a single stripe.

> *Wealth stands by wealth,*
> *Influence does more than effort.*
> *To him who hath shall be given*
> *While poverty clamors in vain.*

When Mistress Hua learned of the outcome of the trial, she sent for Hsi Men in order to take counsel with him. She proposed that he should acquire the adjoining estate before it fell into strange hands. Hsi Men then discussed her proposal with Moon Lady. Moon Lady had her misgivings. She felt that such a proceeding would attract attention, and would certainly arouse the suspicions of Friend Hua. So Hsi Men postponed his decision for the time being.

Soon after this Friend Hua returned home, and the public auction took place of the estates that had formerly belonged to old Kung Kung. The second estate, situated on "Peace Place" in the main thoroughfare, passed into the possession of the Imperial house for seven hundred ounces of silver. The country seat outside the southern city gate was acquired by the River Prefect Chow for seven hundred and fifty ounces of silver. For the estate adjoining Hsi Men's property, valued at five hundred and forty ounces, no purchaser could be found, for no one dared to forestall Hsi Men. Friend Hua repeatedly offered it to his neighbor, but Hsi Men always pleaded a lack of means as his excuse.

As the District Mandarin was urging a speedy settlement of the business, Mistress Hua resolved to send old Mother Bee to Hsi Men. He might, she informed him, take the purchase money out of the silver treasure which she had recently entrusted to him. To this Hsi Men agreed, and without further delay he bought the adjoining estate. The total proceeds were equally divided into three equal parts and paid over to the three plaintiffs. For poor Hua, however, there was nothing left.

Tortured with anxiety, he asked his wife whether she had received from Hsi Men an account of his employment of the sixty bars of silver which she had placed at his disposal. Perhaps there was still something left which would enable them to buy a home somewhere else in the city and at least keep body and soul together. This suggestion met with a cool reception at her hands. For five days he was compelled to endure her scolding.

"You stupid devil! All this time you could find nothing better to do than knock about from one house of joy to another, and pass your nights among flowers and willows! At home you let everything go to the dogs. Who is to blame for our ruin, but yourself! What could I do to save you, I, an honorable woman who has never set foot in the streets alone? You should be thankful that in our necessity and disgrace the honorable Hsi Men stood by us like a friend and a neighbor! Regardless of the cold season of the year, with its terrible sandstorms, he sent his people to the capital and arranged everything for you. And today, when your trial is happily a thing of the past, when you are on your legs again, and can call yourself a free man, and breathe the open air, you behave like a man who has just been sick unto death and now complains of a trivial boil, and you plague me with petty questions of money! Didn't you yourself write me a note from the jail, saying that I was to employ the money for your deliverance? I should have done so even if you had not written."

"It is true, I did write such a note. But nevertheless I cannot help hoping that there is still something left of that money."

"Pah! there's no use wrangling with a blockhead like you. Had you exerted yourself in time you would not have fallen into the trap the others set for you. Now you complain of excessive expenses. You behave as though you couldn't imagine where the three thousand had gone. Do you imagine that such noble princes as the Lord High Secretary Tsai and Marshal Yang are to be sated with a mouthful or two? And do you imagine that the Prefect let you go unpunished for nothing plus nothing? Instead of sulking here you would do better to give a feast of thanksgiving to your high-minded benefactor, who, without being related to you, or under any obligation to you, took on himself all this trouble and vexation, only for your sake, and so sweep yourself clean with the broom of gratitude!"

There was no withstanding such a torrent of words, and Friend Hua chose the better part of silence.

The following day Hsi Men, not unmoved by Hua's low spirits, sent him a few trifling gifts. Friend Hua responded with an invitation to a thanksgiving dinner. He proposed to take this opportunity of demanding an accounting of the balance of his money, and apart from what Hsi Men might remit to him, he meant to ask him, as his friend, to add one or two hundred ounces towards the expense of a new home. But he foolishly allowed his wife to know of his intention. The first thing she did was to advise Hsi Men, through the medium of old Mother Bee, by no means to accept the invitation, but to send over a cooked account, explaining that the money in question had all been expended in bribes. Thus poor Hua waited in vain for the arrival of his friend. He repeated his invitation twice and thrice, but Hsi Men remained invisible. He had simply retired to the pleasure-house district. When Hua was informed that Hsi

Men was away from home, he fainted from sheer vexation and dis-appointment.

Worthy reader, when once a wife is inwardly estranged from her husband not even the most energetic of men can exercise any influence over her or detect her secret intentions. He might as well try to bite through nails. It is an old saying that women should be entrusted only with the care of household affairs. What endless evils have not resulted when women have been permitted to meddle in matters outside the home!

But was not our good Hua himself to blame for this state of affairs? How can a man who constantly neglects his home expect his wife to be a paragon of virtue?

Hua eventually succeeded in scraping together, from his friends and acquaintances, a sum of two hundred and fifty ounces of silver, and he was thus enabled to buy a house in Lion Street. Unfortunately he did not long enjoy its possession. The constant worry of the last few weeks, and a severe cold on his chest, brought him to bed shortly after the removal. For reasons of economy he denied himself a doctor, dragging himself about from day to day, until finally he breathed his last. He had attained the age of only twenty-four years!

The prescribed mourning period of five weeks was not yet over when the widow resolved to visit her former neighbors. Her thoughts had been dwelling less on the soul tablet of the deceased than on Hsi Men. The birthday of Gold Lotus, which fell on the ninth day of the first month, afforded her a welcome pretext.

When she stepped down from her litter it could be seen that the austere mourning white of her outer garments and her widow's veil of grass linen was mitigated by a gold-embroidered petticoat of blue silk and a splendid diadem of pearls. She performed her four kowtows before Moon Lady, who thereupon introduced her to Hsi Men's wives in the order of their rank. Tien Fu, her only remaining manservant—for Tien Hsi, at the commencement of his master's illness, had secretly made off with several ounces of silver—and old Mother Bee, were all her retinue. Old Mother Bee brought a bag full of birthday presents for Gold Lotus. Mistress Hua was soon on the friendliest of terms with the four women, especially with Gold Lotus, whom she addressed as "Sister" from the very first.

Since it was quickly seen that she had an amazingly strong head for liquor, a joyous drinking-bout was soon in progress, and in the evening the four hostesses would by no means allow their guest to go home. They pressed her to spend the night with Gold Lotus in the garden pavilion. Hsi Men had not appeared until a late hour of the evening. He and his friends had had a "wet session" all day in the Imperial Jade Temple.

In celebration of her birthday Gold Lotus was wearing in her hair the golden Shu brooches which Hsi Men had given her. When Moon Lady chanced to comment on these ornaments, Mistress Hua offered to present her and the three other women with brooches of the same design, and the very next day, at breakfast time, old Mother Bee, whom her mistress had sent home the evening before, appeared with a parcel from which Mistress Hua took four pairs of golden brooches, of the same fine craftsmanship as that which Gold Lotus was wearing, and presented each of the four women with a pair. This prompt generosity did not a little towards winning for Mistress Hua the whole-hearted sympathies of Hsi Men's household. They asked for the date of her birthday; and when it was discovered that it fell on the fifteenth of the first month, the day of the Lantern Festival, it was unanimously resolved that a return visit should be paid to her on that occasion. They were eager to take this opportunity of observing the festivities at close quarters, for Mistress Hua's house in Lion Street was just opposite the Lantern Market.

When at last, toward evening, Mistress Hua stepped into her litter in order to return home, she could not suppress a secret feeling of satisfaction. She was confident that by this visit she had insinuated herself into the good graces of Hsi Men's wives, and that she need have no fear of opposition from that quarter should Hsi Men wish to install her in his household as his wife—for this was the goal that floated before her eyes. As far as Hsi Men was concerned, there was one circumstance that went far to confirm her hopes: she had noticed that preparations for building were being made between Gold Lotus's pavilion and the adjoining estate. The wall between the two estates had already been broken through, and she had heard from Gold Lotus that the geomancer had viewed the site and had recently announced that the new buildings might be commenced as early as the second month. The park was now to be extended to include the new property; in the foreground there was to be an artificial hill, crowned with a belvedere; and behind this a new one-storied dwelling would be erected.

"All for me," Gold Lotus had added with a complacent smile.

"For me," thought Mistress Hua, and held her peace.

Punctually on the day preceding the fifteenth, Hsi Men, in the name of his First Wife, sent Mistress Hua a jug of rare wine, several dishes of ready-cooked food, a plate of long-life noodles, a bowl of long-life peaches, and a quilted, gold-embroidered silk robe. In response there came five invitation cards addressed to Hsi Men's wives, and one secretly addressed to him, warning him to postpone his visit until late in the evening. With the exception of Sun Hsueh O, Snowblossom, who was to take care of the house, all the wives accepted the invitation. On the afternoon of the fifteenth, they proceeded to Lion Street, each seated in a litter and followed by a numerous retinue.

Mistress Hua's new house measured four rooms across and three deep. At the back it overlooked a park which was part of an estate belonging to kinsfolk of the Imperial house. In front, where it looked out upon the Lantern Market, it rose to the height of two stories, with a spacious balcony room.

It was in this room that Mistress Hua had ordered the festal table to be laid. All about the table were set screens tastefully painted with mountain landscapes; while from the ceiling and before the windows many-colored lanterns were cheerfully swinging. After taking a snack at four little tables downstairs, the company ascended to the upper room and took their places at the festal table. Two singing-girls entertained them with songs and dances. But the general attention was naturally directed to the festive activities outside, and soon the five beauties were struggling together at the balcony window, peeping through the bead strings of the curtain at the street below.

The Lantern Market, with its dozens of crowded stalls, opened from the street in front of the house, and like two turbulent mountain torrents the throngs of holiday-makers came streaming from east and west along Lion Street. What a varied spectacle it was! What a gay profusion of shapes and patterns was displayed by these splendid lanterns, some for sale, hanging in rows in the stalls, some on tall staves and poles, serving to decorate the square, some carried by the people, in the hand or at the end of a stick, like miraculous blossoms or great luminous pearls—all hovering and gliding through the black crowds in a magical, ceaseless ebb and flow. Every species of flower was represented; from the gleaming water lily to the pale ice flower, to say nothing of human and animal forms! What quaint and strange conceits were there! Here young licentiates, handsome Confucian novices, and respectable housewives, with all the decorous bearing and deportment of the days of the good old Emperor Shen Hung; there corpulent monks with pious full-moon tonsures but lustful expressions. Here was the hideous old Chung Kwei, the stern judge of the underworld, flanked by a couple of smart courtesans; and there the rich hypocrite Liu Hao, sitting on a golden three-legged toad as he devoured his own jewels. Here were heavily laden camels, silver lions, apes, and white elephants, entering the city gate with rare treasures on their backs; there many-legged crabs, sharks with mighty jaws and long gill slits, darting through the blue waves, and gulping down green seaweeds and silver butterflies; here iridescent chameleons and salamanders playing in the sand, and other such gay follies; there Lao tse's four disciples holding out the mysterious volume containing the formulæ of mercurial remedies and the elixir of life; while dangerous neighbors from the frontiers figured as peaceful envoys bringing tribute, or pacific villagers were shown as warriors eager for battle; and other such crazy devices.

All classes of society were represented among the frequenters of the market, from the bored young aristocrat who impatiently stamped his foot when further progress through the crowd was impossible, or the gayly-dressed patrician wives and daughters who walked sedately hand in hand, and fled from the turmoil to the upper stories of the adjacent tea rooms, beautifying and enlivening the whole picture with the colorful splendor of their garments. Of course, the usual fortune teller was not lacking, offering to predict for the passers-by, from the form of the clouds or the conjectures of the stars, what luck the new year would bring; nor the down-at-heel student, who, raised above the crowd, recited poems and stories; nor the wandering monk, incessantly beating his cymbals with the heels of his hands, and seeking to edify the people with Tripitaka texts; nor the itinerant baker with stacks of New Year pancakes; nor the dealer who offered for sale dry branches covered with artificial peach blossoms; nor any of the other queer characters who are accustomed to throng a New Year's market.

For a while the five beauties surrendered themselves to the impressions of the lively picture offered by the motley crowd at their feet, listening to the roar and hum of innumerable voices, accompanied by the rumble and clatter of heavy cartwheels. Then Moon Lady, Sunflower, and Mistress Ping withdrew to the inner part of the room, and took their places at the table. Gold Lotus, however, together with Jade Fountain and the two singing-girls, lingered at the window, for they could not take their eyes from the scene. Gold Lotus felt in a wanton frame of mind. Turning up the long sleeves of her white silk coat so that her delicate onion-shoot fingers were visible, adorned with six golden rings in the form of stirrups, she leaned far out over the balcony railing and amused herself by spitting out on the heads of the promenading crowd below the husks of the melon seeds which she was constantly nibbling. Meanwhile her tongue was not still for a moment, but accompanied the observations of her eyes with childish, gay remarks and clear, ringing laughter. No wonder, then, that those below soon began to take notice of the beauties at the window! They stood stock-still, and blocked the thoroughfare, lifting curious glances to the balcony, and giving voice to expressions of admiration and wondering conjectures.

189

"They surely belong to some princely harem," ventured one of a group of dashing young men.

"They are probably princely concubines from the estate over there, which belongs to the Imperial house," a second voice was heard to suggest.

"Or little daughters of joy whom some generous patron has invited here for the Lantern Festival," declared a third.

"Nonsense! I'll tell you who they are!" a fourth speaker interposed. "Unless they are concubines of the Prince of Hell himself, they belong to the harem of wealthy Hsi Men; you know, the one who owns the apothecary's shop near the yamen, and who has all our officials, from the highest to the lowest, in his debt. The one with the green-bordered golden jabot I don't know, but the other, the pretty one with the red-bordered golden collar, is undoubtedly the former wife of the pastry cook Wu Ta, the Three-Inch Manikin, whom Hsi Men dispatched into the next world with a kick in the belly. I expect you remember the whole ugly business, that had its beginnings in Mother Wang's tea room? Later on the brother-in-law, Wu Sung, tried to settle accounts with Master Hsi Men, but through some misunderstanding he killed Commissioner Li, and was punished by being exiled to the frontier. Nothing has been heard of him for the last two years——"

Gold Lotus was overcome by a feeling of uneasiness. She could not hear what followed, for Moon Lady called to her and Jade Fountain to come from the window, and they sat down to the banquet. Later in the afternoon Moon Lady and Sunflower took their departure. Gold Lotus and Jade Fountain remained, as they wanted to wait for the lighting of the lanterns.

Hsi Men had chosen this day for a spree with Beggar Ying and Hsia Hsi Ta. He too made the Lantern Market his goal. But since he did not wish to be seen from Mistress Ping's house, he would not venture into the market itself, but contented himself with viewing the lanterns of silken gauze in the stalls close at hand. On the way back at a street corner, the three unexpectedly met Sun Tien Hua and Chu Shih Nien, who reproached them bitterly for not having invited them as well. A wearisome discussion followed as to the program for the rest of the day. It ended with their going in a body to Mother Li's place. Hsi Men, who would have been glad to keep the evening free, because of his secret appointment with Mistress Ping, reluctantly accompanied them.

CHAPTER FOURTEEN: *Censor Yu upsets a pretty Scheme. Mistress Ping settles Accounts with Doctor Bamboo Hill*

HSI MEN was obliged to spend some hours with his friends in Mother Li's house. But neither the arts and charms of Cinnamon Bud and her sister, nor the other diversions with which his companions whiled away the time—such as tippling, dicing and ball-play—had any attraction for him today. There he sat, feeling thoroughly bored, waiting for a message from Lion Street. At last, when it was already dark, his boy Tai appeared. Bending close to his master's ear, Tai informed Hsi Men in a low voice that Moon Lady and Sunflower had gone home, and that Mistress Ping bade him delay no longer. Hsi Men covertly instructed the boy to lead his horse to the back door and there wait for him. For a little longer he remained sitting beside Cinnamon Bud, but he refrained from drinking. Then he withdrew, under the pretext that he must go outside for a moment. He went through the back door into the courtyard, sprang on his horse, which was standing ready, and flew off like the wind. He left word for his friend, Beggar Ying, that urgent business had summoned him home.

When he reached Mistress Ping's house the fact that the gate was closed told him that the guests had gone. Reassured, he knocked. He was admitted by old Mother Bee. Wearing a simple house dress, with her hair wound in a knot on the top of her head, and carrying a taper in her hand, Mistress Ping advanced smiling to the head of the stairs to meet him.

"You very nearly walked into your Third and your Fifth," she whispered, "They left only this minute. And where do you come from?"

Hsi Men told her about his jaunt through the streets, and how his friends had dragged him to Mother Li's place; and finally, how he had resorted to a subterfuge in order to elude them.

She thanked him for his gifts, and ushered him into a festively illuminated guest chamber, where the bronze braziers, freshly filled with glowing charcoal, and the bright tapestries on the walls, radiated warmth and comfort, while the blue-gray wafts of ambergris vapor, rising in curious undulations, like the curves of a cryptic script, filled the room with aromatic fragrance.

Mistress Ping fell to her knees, performed a kowtow, and solemnly began:

"Since the death of my unworthy husband I am all alone. Wherever I look, nowhere do I see kith or kin to cherish me. You, noble lord, are today my only support. If I do not appear altogether ill-favored and inferior in your sight, grant me the privilege of preparing your couch and arranging your blankets! Let me be a sister to your wives! Then I should die with sweetness in my heart!"

There was a pleading expression in her eyes, which were glistening with tears. Hsi Men took with one hand the cup which she offered him, while with the other he gently raised her to her feet.

"Your loving words shall remain engraved on my heart like a bronze inscription," he said. "As soon as your period of mourning is over I will take counsel. In the meantime, don't worry! Now let us celebrate your happy birthday!"

And they sat down to the sumptuous repast that old Mother Bee had prepared. The two maids, Pear Blossom and Apricot Blossom, served the dishes and poured the wine. Tai now appeared, and politely kowtowing, offered his congratulations. Mistress Ping saw to it that the boy was generously feasted in the kitchen. When she asked him what he would say at home about the absence of his master, he replied: "I shall simply say that the Master is spending the night at Mother Li's place, and will be home tomorrow morning." This ready reply pleased her so that she presented the lad with two silver pieces for "melon-seed money," and promised to make him a pair of slippers as well.

The two amused themselves for a while with dice and dominoes, then retired to the bedchamber. Pear Blossom had to prepare the couch, and set fruit and wine within reach. Since her husband's death, Lady Ping had permitted Hsi Men to make use of both maids, so the lovers observed no restraint in their presence. They undressed, and under the purple hangings, snuggling shoulder to shoulder on the bed, they continued for a time to drink and to play dominoes.

"How is the building getting on?" Mistress Ping suddenly inquired.

"It won't begin until next month. The whole adjacent property is to be converted into a park. All the present buildings will be pulled down. Only a three-roomed pleasure pavilion will be built there. In front I'm having a hill made, which will have a round belvedere on the summit."

She pointed to the wall behind the bed.

"There I have hidden in tea chests forty pounds of aloes, two hundred pounds of white ash-tree wax, and eighty pounds of pepper, as well as two jars of quicksilver. I should like you to send for these things and turn them into cash. The proceeds I should like to place at your disposal as my contribution towards the cost of the building. It is my most heartfelt desire to come to you as soon as possible! I cannot do without you!"

Tenderly, with his handkerchief, he dried the tears that had risen to her eyes, and answered:

"Have patience until your period of mourning is over. In the meantime the new pavilion will be finished. I don't know where I should find accommodation for you before then."

"Could I not live with the Fifth for the time being? I am on excellent terms with her, and with the Third as well. They are both so attractive, and they are as like as two sisters. The First, on the other hand, I cannot endure. There is something in her glance that repels one at once."

"Oh, no, she in particular is kindness itself!" cried Hsi Men, laughing. "Would she otherwise tolerate so many wives about her? But

194

to change the subject, I have designed the new pavilion as your future home. It will be accessible only by two secret side doors, so that you will be completely undisturbed. What do you say to that?"

"Oh, my Ko ko . . . !" she sighed blissfully, as she sank into his arms. This time their wanton phœnix play lasted until the fourth drum beat. Their desire was insatiable, and dawn was already break, ing when they finally surrendered themselves to sleep.

The morning was far advanced when they awoke, but they did not feel like leaving their bed. They took their breakfast there, and eagerly returned to their loves. But ere long they were distracted by the voice of the boy Tai outside the window. Five spice merchants from the Southern Province had come to town, he informed his master. They had brought a consignment of goods with them, and they wanted a hundred ounces of silver for it, payable in six months. Moon Lady had sent him to find his master, as the merchants wanted Hsi Men to sign the contract personally.

"You didn't by any chance let out that I am here?" Hsi Men demanded.

"No. I said that the master was staying at Mother Li's place."

"Uncle Fu, the dispenser, can see to the business just as well. Why am I bothered with it?"

"The merchants refuse to be satisfied with Uncle Fu's signature."

"Business always comes first," Mistress Ping interposed. "Moon Lady will begin to wonder if you don't go."

"These cursed provincial hucksters have probably lost their mar, ket, or they'd hardly bring their goods to one's very door," he muttered irritably. "When one is in a hurry they usually keep one waiting for delivery. Anyhow, there are other apothecary's shops in the district as well as mine. When I need them they'll come soon enough."

"In business one should never spare one's legs," Mistress Ping advised him. "If I were you I should go. Many delightful days are still before us, innumerable as the leaves of a willow tree."

Reluctantly he followed her advice, rose leisurely, made a careful toilet, ate another breakfast in peace and quiet, put on his mask, mounted his horse, and cantered home.

In the apothecary shop he accepted the goods, examined them, had them weighed, made a payment on account, signed the agreement, and sent the five merchants on their way. When this was done, he visited Gold Lotus.

"Where were you hiding yourself yesterday?" she greeted him. "But no humbug, please, or I shall raise such a clamor that you will fall to dust!"

"Where could I have been?" he asked. "In the afternoon I went with my friends to see the Lantern Festival, and then we went to Mother Li's, where I stayed overnight."

"Yes, your spirit, perhaps, but not your body! No, you faithless vagabond, you cannot deceive me! Do you think I didn't notice yesterday how a certain somebody was up to her tricks in order to get rid of us and lure you in? You have been making love to her all night! Your boy, the smart little rascal, has told me everything. It's true that he told Moon Lady that you'd gone to Mother Li's with your cronies. But when I cross-examined him afterwards he laughed and confessed that you were with Mistress Ping in Lion Street. I should just like to know how the sly rogue has discovered that we two have no secrets from each other, so that he need hide nothing from me."

Seeing that he had been detected, Hsi Men renounced further evasion, and conscientiously related all that had happened; how Mistress Ping had complained to him of her forlorn state, had told him how uneasy she felt at night when she lay alone in her chamber and heard the lewd fox goblins clamoring in the adjacent park and throwing stones over the wall, and had implored him to take her into his household as a concubine and lodge her with Gold Lotus until the new pavilion was ready. All this he reported faithfully and in full detail.

Gold Lotus reflected for a while. "Let her come," she said finally. "In any case I am rather tired of my seclusion. I hardly ever see the shadow of a human being. Her companionship will do me good.

After all, a harbor has room for many ships, a street for many wagons. But, of course, Moon Lady will wish to have a voice in the matter."

"The only scruple I have," he concluded, "is the fact that her term of mourning has not yet expired."

Soon after this conversation Hsi Men found a broker who was willing to purchase from him Mistress Ping's store of aloes, pepper, ash-tree wax, and quicksilver. Of the three hundred ounces of silver that were realized, Mistress Ping retained for herself one hundred and eighty; the remainder she placed at Hsi Men's disposal, as her contribution to the cost of building the pavilion. A calendar expert was then consulted, and the eighth day of the second month was decided on as the date for beginning operations. The task of supervising the work and procuring materials Hsi Men left to his steward, Lai Chao, and his private secretary, Pen Se. This Pen Se was an intelligent, vivacious, and versatile fellow, who had originally been in the employ of a Court eunuch, but had been dismissed from his post for a dereliction of duty. He was engaged for a time in a distinguished household, had there been smitten with a young concubine, and had abducted and married her. He had then set up for himself as a buyer of old clothes. Finally he had made the acquaintance of Hsi Men, who had come to have a high regard not only for Pen Se's business ability, but also for his talents as an entertainer; for he was a highly skilled performer on the cithern and the flute. Hsi Men had recourse to Pen Se's judgment on all possible occasions; he employed him as negotiator in respect of loans, entrusted him with the stock-taking and valuation of his pharmaceutical wares, and lastly, found him indispensable as a sort of private secretary.

These two, Lai Chao and Pen Se, were given five hundred ounces of silver for the purchase of building stone, bricks, timber, and other materials, and on the eighth of the second month the work of building began. First the wall dividing the two adjacent estates was leveled, and the whole group of houses which Brother Hua had formerly inhabited was torn down. The observation hill was then raised, and finally work was started on the new pavilion.

It was a month later. Mistress Ping had once more sent word for Hsi Men to come to her, for the hundred days' term of mourning was about to expire, and she wished to consult him concerning the ceremonial of burning the soul tablet, and also in respect of her removal, and the sale of the house in which she was living, and several other matters. At last she repeated, urgently, and with tears in her eyes, her former request that he would send for her before the completion of the new building, and allow her to live with Gold Lotus for the time being.

"If it were granted me to live with you only for a day, I would gladly die!" she said. "Spare me the continued torture of seeing the days creep by like years!" she implored him. "There is still a full month before my period of mourning is over, and I cannot endure it here any longer!"

Complying with her request, he again discussed the situation with Gold Lotus.

"As far as I'm concerned, she can have two rooms here," Gold Lotus declared indifferently. "But Moon Lady will want to have her say in the matter. After all, in your domestic affairs, I am only a humble tributary stream, unsuitable for navigation."

So Hsi Men sought out Moon Lady and told her Mistress Ping's request. Moon Lady advised him quite decidedly against granting it. In the first place, the period of mourning was not yet over; in the second place, it seemed to her that it would excite suspicion if he took to himself the widow of one who had been his intimate friend, especially as he had already acquired her former home, and had secretly received from her, for safekeeping, various effects of value; such circumstances might easily be misconstrued. She feared above all the eldest Hua, a malicious, intriguing fellow, who would take any opportunity of creating a scandal.

Hsi Men reflected in silence. Then he once more took counsel with Gold Lotus. "What shall I tell her now?" he asked in perplexity.

"That's very simple. Tell her you have spoken to me, but with the best of goodwill one can't find accommodation for her in my pavilion, as the different rooms are packed full of household goods and pharmaceutical wares. You would not know where to find room for her things, but you will see to it that the work of building is hurried on, and as soon as the painter has finished his varnishing and lacquering she can move in. As far as that goes, you would get nothing of her while the two of us were living at such close quarters. Your diet would be neither meat nor vegetable!"

"Excellent. I'll put that to her," he exclaimed with relief, and he at once made his way to Lion Street. Poor Mistress Ping was forced, willy-nilly, to console herself with looking forward to the fifth month. By that time, she was told, the building would be finished, and she could then definitely move in.

Two months elapsed. The building operations had made excellent progress, and the new estate was nearing completion; the mound had been raised, and only the belvedere had still to be begun.

The day came when house doors are decorated with wormwood and magic formulæ, namely, the fifth of the fifth month, which was the day of the Dragon Boat Festival. Mistress Ping invited Hsi Men to her house, to partake of the customary drumsticks wrapped in rushes, and also to advise her on various matters concerning the imminent expiration of her mourning period. It was decided that the ceremony of burning the soul tablet should take place on the fifteenth of the month. When that had been performed he would appoint a convenient day for her removal to his establishment.

"Will your three brothers-in-law be present on the fifteenth?" he inquired. He was still apprehensive of the three brothers whom he had helped Lady Ping to overreach.

"I have invited them for form's sake," she replied.

On the fifteenth, while Mistress Ping's house was filled with the uproar created by the twelve bonzes from the "Cloister of Merciful Recompense" who officiated at the ceremony of burning the soul tablet, Hsi Men passed the time at Beggar Ying's. There it was just as noisy, for Beggar Ying was celebrating his birthday.

and the ten sworn Brothers had one and all assembled. In the place of the deceased Hua, Hsi Men's confidant, Pen Se, had been taken into the brotherhood, in order to make the company of ten once more complete. Two youthful actors, a younger brother of Silver Cup, and an elder brother of Fragrant Waters, on this occasion defrayed the cost of the entertainment.

It was late in the afternoon when Tai bent down to his master's ear and whispered that Mistress Ping begged him to come to her. Hsi Men merely gave the boy a glance of understanding. But this incident had been noted by Beggar Ying. When the boy withdrew, Beggar Ying followed him outside, and said:

"You good-for-nothing carrion! Confess! What was it you whispered to your master just now? Out with it, or I'll twist your ear off. Have I so many birthdays in the year that I should allow my guests to be spirited away in broad daylight? Who sent you? Was it your mistress or the little one at Number Eighteen?"

"No one sent me," Tai lied. "I just thought it was time to call for my master——"

"Really? Well, if I ever discover that you have deceived me, you may be sure that I'll be even with you!"

He treated the boy to wine and cakes, and then returned to his companions.

Presently Hsi Men came downstairs and took the boy aside. "Were any of the Huas there?"

"Only the eldest and his wife, but they have gone already. Mistress Ping gave her sister-in-law two dresses and ten pieces of silver. The woman was delighted and thanked her with a kowtow."

"Did they have anything to say about the remarriage?"

"Not a word. They asked if they might pay their respects to her in her new home on the third day after the reception, that's all."

"Good, I feel reassured. And how about the mass for the soul of the departed?"

"The soul tablet was burnt under favorable auspices, and the bonzes have already gone."

"Very well, I'll make my excuses. Have the horse in readiness!"

Tai went out into the courtyard to get the horse, when Beggar Ying suddenly intercepted him. He had overheard the whole conversation.

"That's a pretty story to have to listen to, and you, you accursed piece of offal, never told me a word of it!" he shouted at the disconcerted youngster.

"Don't make such a row about it, you crazy fool!" said Hsi Men, trying to silence him.

Of course, his departure was now out of the question. Beggar Ying dragged him back to the festal board, and announced to the assembled company the great news that Hsi Men was about to lead home a sixth wife. "And not a word of it to his friends!" he cried. "A nice sort of fellow! He ought at least to have taken us into his confidence, so that we should have known what to say if the elder Hua had made any trouble. Doesn't he know that for him we would go through fire and water?"

"As a punishment, we'll denounce him to Cinnamon Bud and Silver Cup," one of them suggested. "Then he can be prepared for a friendly reception at their hands!"

"Very well," cried Hsi Men, laughing. "You must know, then, that Mistress Ping is to be my wife! The matter is settled."

"Ho, and that means another big feast, when we come to congratulate you!" exclaimed Hsia Hsi Ta, with enthusiasm. "And this time you won't get off with less than four dancing-girls!"

"It goes without saying that I shall expect you to celebrate the event," said Hsi Men, confirming their hopes.

"Why wait so long?" suggested Chu Shih Nien. "We must drink to the joyful event here and now!"

And the whole troop came thronging about Hsi Men, and went down on their knees before him. Beggar Ying, as the master of ceremonies, tendered Hsi Men a cup which Hsia Hsi Ta had filled to the brim, while Chu Shih Nien waited on him with a heaped-up plate in his hand. Simultaneously the two singing-boys intoned a festal chant. Three times Hsi Men had to empty the cup, and then they all took their places at the table again. It was late in the evening before Hsi Men at last succeeded in stealing away from the circle of his befuddled companions. Mistress Ping, in holiday attire, ushered him into a dazzlingly lighted guest chamber. Nowhere was there a trace of mourning to be seen.

"Did the Huas have anything to say?" was his first question. She confirmed what Tai had told him—that they had refrained from making any criticism whatever, and had announced their visit of felicitation for the third day after her installation.

"Very good, let them come!" he growled. "But woe betide them if they say a word too much!"

"Let them dare to pick a quarrel!" she said.

Together they drank from the great silver goblet which the maid Apricot Blossom constantly replenished with a heady Southern wine.

Mistress Ping was in a merrier mood than usual, for she believed that she was now near the goal of her desires. "Do your friends know how matters stand with us?" she asked.

"Beggar Ying guessed half and the rest they squeezed out of me. They want to congratulate us, and they are rejoicing already at the thought of the inevitable feast."

The strong Southern wine began to take effect. They held each other in a close embrace, each inhaling the other's breath. Their faces, pressed together, glowed like twin apricots in an enchanted garden.

"My ko ko, take me home to yourself soon! Don't leave me to spend my nights here alone and lamenting!" she whispered.

And she exacted a promise that the fourth day of the next month should be the day of her entry into his household.

A few days before this date she once more bade him come to her in Lion Street. He was to admire the new mirror, which had just come from the silversmith, and which she had chosen as her wedding present to him. They were once again in the best of spirits; they partook freely of the flowing bowl, and in the gathering twilight they withdrew to the silent intercourse of the couch.

Toward the hour of the first watch of the night, when they were absorbed in their delectable occupation, they were startled by a violent knocking at the door. It was the boy Tai. He was greatly excited; he wanted to come in and speak to his master. Annoyed by the interruption, Hsi Men had him brought into the adjacent room.

"Master, the First Wife begs you most urgently to hurry home at once; the matter is of the greatest importance," the boy's voice sounded from behind the curtain. "Your daughter and your son-in-law have arrived unexpectedly with a lot of luggage."

"Tonight of all nights!" Hsi Men grumbled angrily as he hastily pulled on his clothes.

"What brings you here?" It was in a tone of surprise that he greeted his daughter and his son-in-law, who were waiting for him in the reception room at the back of the house, amidst piles of luggage. His son-in-law, Chen Tsing Ki, kowtowed awkwardly and briefly informed him:

"Uncle Yang, the Marshal, has fallen into disgrace. Censor Yu has denounced him before the Throne. He is at this moment under arrest in the Southern City jail. All his kindred and his dependents are involved in his misfortune, and are sentenced to be sent into exile on the frontier with wooden collars about their necks. Yesterday Uncle Yang's steward arrived from the capital and brought us news of the disaster. My father advised your daughter and myself to take refuge with you for the time being. He has already set out for the Capital, in order to obtain further particulars from Aunt Yang."

"Did your father entrust you with a letter for me?"

"Yes, here it is." He drew a letter from his sleeve.

Hsi Men opened it and read:

"The Patriarch Chen Hung bows his head and presents his most respectful greetings to his highborn cousin Hsi Men.

"On account of the defeat at the frontier passes in the District of Yung Chow, for which the War Minister was to blame, inasmuch as he failed to send up reserve troops, it has pleased the

Illustrious One, on the basis of a denunciation by the Censor Yu, to regard our kinsman Marshal Yang as in part responsible for the reverse, and to order him to be imprisoned in the Southern City jail. His family and all his dependents are to be banished to a penal colony on the frontier. I consider it advisable for the time being to consign to your care my unworthy son and your beloved daughter. I myself am departing for the capital to obtain more detailed information. In the eventuality of any action on the part of the local yamen, I am sending you through my son five hundred ounces of silver which you must employ as you see fit. I shall be grateful to you for your good services until the last tooth falls out of my head.

"Written under the lamp in precipitate haste on the twentieth of the midsummer month.

CHEN HUNG."

As Hsi Men read this missive, a terrible fear took possession of his limbs. Nevertheless, he told himself that he must act at once. First of all he ordered three rooms of the eastern wing in front of the main hall to be made habitable for the young couple. All the valuables in their luggage Moon Lady must take into her safekeeping. He appropriated for himself the five hundred ounces sent by old Chen. That same evening he sent to the office of the adjacent yamen, and at the cost of five ounces of silver he was able to obtain an exact copy of the report of the affair, which had in the meantime arrived from the Capital.

The actual facts were these: A group of censors, with Censor Yu at their head, had seized the opportunity offered by the check on the frontier to lay before the Throne a general complaint against the factious Chancellor Tsai Ching and his followers, Marshal Yang among them. The Son of Heaven had indeed been moved to pity, and had retained Chancellor Tsai in his office, but the Imperial rescript had decreed, through the State tribunal, the imprisonment and conviction of Marshal Yang. Moreover, a large number of families who belonged to Yang's faction were to be banished to the frontier within a month, with the wooden kang about their necks.

Among the names of these unfortunates Hsi Men read, to his terror, the name of Chen Hung. He felt as though a thunderbolt had fallen beside him. Marshal Yang, his noble patron at court, overthrown! His daughter's father-in-law exiled! There was a roaring in his ears, and his breath could find no outlet through his nose.

Terror oozes from his pores,
From the seven doors of his heart.
Past six ribs, to the lungs,
His liver flutters up and down.

It was some time before he could collect himself. Then he set to work. Sleep, of course, was not to be thought of. He summoned his two trusty servants, Lai Pao and Lai Wang, and gave them secret instructions. By daybreak they both departed for Kai fong fu, with a donkey-load of gold, silver, and jewels. Next morning the two builder's foremen were directed to stop all work on the buildings in the park and dismiss all the workmen. Further, the doorkeeper was given strict orders to keep the entrance door locked until further notice. No one was to go in or out of the house without the most urgent cause.

Meanwhile Hsi Men paced restlessly up and down in his room. The more he pondered the more his uneasiness increased, like a centipede in the moist heat. His affair with Mistress Ping had receded from his mind far into the ninth celestial sphere.

Moon Lady, who saw with concern that his knitted brows did not relax, nor his gloomy features lighten, endeavored to console him: "This is after all the affair of the Chen family. What concern is it of yours? Let each find for himself the means of compounding with his creditors and enemies."

"You don't realize what this means!" he replied bitterly. "It concerns my own daughter and my son-in-law, who have taken refuge with me! Our worthy neighbors look sufficiently askance at me without this trouble! It is the old story. Chase the tender lamb and the wild colt is frightened. If once this paltry rabble should grow nasty and go to extremes, I would not vouch for my safety nor for

yours. One may sit quietly at home behind locked doors, and disaster will suddenly break in."

When two days had elapsed without a word from Hsi Men,
Mistress Ping sent Mother Bee to make inquiries. But the old
woman found the house closed. For a long while she waited at the
entrance, but she could not catch so much as a glimpse of the front
teeth of a single inmate, so she trotted off, completely mystified. On
the twenty-fourth, the day upon which the wedding gifts were to
be exchanged according to agreement, old Mother Bee was once
more dispatched. She was to deliver the silver mirror, Mistress
Ping's present to Hsi Men. Once more she found the gate closed.
She took up her post under the curved eaves of a house directly
opposite the gate, and waited. This time she was rewarded. It was
not long before the boy Tai stepped out into the street, holding by
the bridle a horse which he was leading to water. He recognized
her directly and came toward her with a friendly greeting. "What
brings you here, Mother Bee?"

"My mistress sends me. I have to deliver this mirror. Besides, she
wants to speak to the honorable Hsi Men. Why is everything so
quiet?"

"Oh, Master Hsi Men has been very busy these last few days.
If you like, I will take the mirror inside with me. But first I must
water the horse. Will you wait here outside for an answer?"

"Certainly, dear little brother. I'll wait here. And do you tell him
that my mistress is very angry with him."

Little Tai tied the horse to the trough and vanished into the
house. It was a long while before he appeared again. "Master Hsi
Men bids you convey his thanks to Mistress Ping for the mirror,"
he informed the old woman. "Let her be patient for a few days
longer and then he will come in person."

But the few days which Mistress Ping was to wait were stretched
out into weeks. The fifth month expired, and it was already the
middle of the first third of the sixth month, and still no news of
Hsi Men! By day she looked for his return and at night she lay
tormented by her dreams. He did not come.

Listlessly she strokes her brows;
The thought of adorning herself distresses her.
Gloom weighs upon her jasper bosom.
She sighs and bears her misery alone.

Once she dreamed quite distinctly that he had knocked on the door. She opened it, and overwhelmed with joy she led him into her room. They had chatted together to their hearts' content, jesting and telling each other how they had suffered. Then, inextricably embraced, they knew the bliss of a night of love. Next morning, when she woke at cockcrow, and was about to rise, she discovered that the place at her side was empty. She uttered a piercing scream and fell into a swoon. Startled by her cry, old Mother Bee came hurrying in. "Have you locked the door safely? He must have gone out this moment," the poor woman said, when she had recovered consciousness.

"You must be wandering in your mind," said the old woman, shaking her head. "Not a shadow of him has been here."

Her dreams were often haunted by lewd fox goblins in the form of men, who wastefully lured the subtle virtue from the marrow of her bones. Her fresh color was visibly fading, and as she was taking less and less nourishment, and hardly ever rose from her bed, she grew paler and thinner from day to day. Old Mother Bee could no longer bear to see her thus.

"I have asked the doctor to call and examine you. May he come in?" she announced one day.

Mistress Ping, her face framed in a cloud of disheveled hair and pressed against the pillow, lay motionless, in a state of apathy. Old Mother Bee admitted the doctor and quickly straightened the bed-clothes. Doctor Kiang, nicknamed "Bamboo Hill," a short, artful, sprightly little man about thirty years of age, approached her bed, felt her pulse, and noted her breathing. During this examination none of the delectable charms of her person escaped him.

"In the estimation of this humble adept," he said, formulating his diagnosis, "your illness results from the fact that the veins of the liver and of the uterus have burst and flooded the intestines. As a consequence you are completely under the sway of the six desires and the seven passions. In your body the Yang principle is at variance with the Yin principle. One moment you are too cold, the next moment too hot. You suffer from an intermittent fever and an oppressive melancholy. In the daytime you feel weary and relaxed, and long only to sleep. At night, your soul is so restless that it will not remain in its tenement, and in your dreams you hold intercourse with spirits. A speedy cure alone can save you from perishing of consumption. Your life, alas, hangs by a finespun thread of silk!"

"I should be obliged to you if you would prescribe a remedy for me," she replied despondently.

"Trust to my skill. The medicine I shall prescribe for you will make you well again."

He pocketed his fee of five silver bits and took his leave. Old Mother Bee accompanied him to his dispensary in order to obtain the prescribed medicine. That evening Mistress Ping took the remedy, and immediately afterwards she felt a decided improvement. She was able to sleep again, her appetite gradually revived, and in a few days she had completely recovered from her illness. She decided to invite Doctor Bamboo Hill to a feast of thanks. And Doctor Bamboo Hill, in whose heart her glance had from the very first kindled presumptuous hopes and desires, was only too glad to accept the invitation.

It goes without saying that her elegant appearance, the luxuriously furnished table, and the heavy fragrance of musk and orchids which filled the house, positively bewildered him. In the course of the meal, he was pleasantly surprised when the maid Apricot Blossom presented him with three ounces of silver on a plate with a gilt pattern. At the same time Mistress Ping lifted a jade goblet full of wine, and said:

"With your kindly assistance I have successfully overcome my recent illness. As a token of my gratitude, I take the liberty of offering you this simple cup of watery wine. Once more, thanks, many thanks!"

"I did no more than my professional duty dictated," he stammered, and with a sidelong look at the shining pieces of silver: "How have I deserved . . . ?"

"Take them, do!" she urged him with a smile. "It is only a trifling token of my gratitude."

After some further affectation he allowed himself to be persuaded; overjoyed, he slipped the three ounces of silver into his pocket. Three cups had been sufficient to inspire him, who all this time had been taking surreptitious glances at her well-groomed loveliness, with the courage to speak.

"May I ask you how many springs you have flourished?" he cautiously inquired.

"I have uselessly dissipated twenty-four years," she replied.

"You are young, beautiful, cultured, wealthy, able to satisfy every craving of your heart. How, in spite of all these, could you give way to melancholy?"

She answered with a faint smile: "Frankly speaking, ever since my fool of a husband departed from this world, I have been quite alone. The solemn silence that constantly surrounds me—can you wonder that I should grow dejected and fall ill?"

"How long is it since your husband's death, may I ask?"

"He died in the eleventh month of last year—of an inflammation of the lungs. Yes, it is already eight months since then," she sighed.

"Did you never have occasion to call in a physician before?"

"Yes, I once consulted Doctor Hu from the Main Street."

"Oh, Hu, whom they call 'Devil's-mouth,' who lives in the house of the eunuch Liu? Why, he's nothing but a quack, a common charlatan! He never attended our medical academy. What can he know of the pulse? You should not have consulted him."

"He was recommended to me by the neighbors. However, I have never sent for him since my husband's death."

"Have you a son or a daughter?"

"Neither."

"A pity, a pity!" he sighed sympathetically. "In the bloom of life, to be quite alone! Of course that would make you lose heart! Have you never thought of joining your path to that of another husband?"

"Yes, indeed, and my remarriage is already arranged. In a very short time I hope to cross the threshold of my new home."

"And may I ask, who——?"

"Master Hsi Men, the owner of the apothecary shop near the local yamen."

"Ah! Ah! That man! But, gracious lady, how could you think of such a thing! As his family doctor I am well acquainted with his affairs. He is the man to whom everybody stands indebted, the man who buys and sells people's opinions, who has the last say in the politics of the district. Apart from his numerous maids and servants he always has five or six wives in his household. And if one of them ceases to please him he beats her with a stick, or simply sells her to some outsider through the agency of a go-between. The man is the ringleader of an infamous band of wife seducers and girl kidnapers! It is a good thing that I am in time to warn you: marriage to that man would simply be placing your head in the tiger's jaws. You would be bound to regret it bitterly in the end. Moreover, he has lately been implicated in some criminal business affecting the family of his daughter's father-in-law. Don't you know that his daughter and his son-in-law are hiding in his house? This is why the building operations in his grounds have been interrupted and the workmen discharged. The prefecture and the yamen have received from the Capital a decree of banishment against all his relations. Who knows but that he too will be involved presently, and all his possessions confiscated? What will become of his wives then? They are greatly to be pitied!"

Mistress Ping was struck dumb. She remembered with alarm the property which she had entrusted to Hsi Men's safekeeping. Now she realized why he had been invisible for so long. And she reflected that perhaps it would be more to her advantage to marry a pleasant, amiable, entertaining individual like this Doctor Bamboo

Hill. But of course, she did not know whether he would be prepared to marry her.

"I am infinitely grateful to you for your kindly advice," she said after a long pause. "And I would gladly consider your suggestions if you should be able to recommend any friend of yours as a husband."

"I shall be very pleased to keep my eyes open for you. Only I don't yet know what type you would prefer."

"His outward appearance would be immaterial if only he resembled you in other respects."

At this, Master Bamboo Hill could hardly contain himself for rapture. He jumped high into the air and plumped down on his knees before her.

"Oh, gracious Lady, I cannot conceal the fact that in my women's apartment there is no one with whom I, unfortunate being, can share my crust of bread. Nor have I any offspring. My life is as dismal as that of a lonely pike. Were you to take compassion on me I would joyfully contract a lifelong alliance with you."

She smiled and raised him to his feet.

"If we are to speak seriously of marriage, I must first know your age and how long you have been living as a lonely pike. Besides, you must send the customary middleman and provide for the customary wedding presents."

Once more he plumped down before her.

"I am twenty-nine years old and was born on the twenty-seventh of the first month in the hour of the hare. The simple woman whose only hair ornament was a thorn, and whom I called my wife, I lost last year. My lowly hut, alas, is cold and empty. If you deign to bestow on me your golden consent, what need have we of that man of ice, the middleman?"

"Ah, if it is the expense to which you object, I myself will conclude the formalities. I will send my old Mother Bee to act as intermediary, and you can omit the wedding presents. I shall select a suitable wedding day, and you will simply move into my house. Is that agreeable to you?"

He beat his forehead against the floor: "Then the happiness of all my three existences would be assured. You would not only be wife to me, but father and mother as well."

With that the marriage compact was concluded, and drunk with wine and bliss; Doctor Bamboo Hill sought his cold hut at a late hour that evening.

The very next day old Mother Bee discharged her commission, and on the eighteenth of the sixth month, a lucky day of the first degree, Doctor Bamboo Hill moved into Mistress Ping's house. On the third day after the nuptials she handed him three hundred ounces of silver, which enabled him to open a brand-new dispensary in the front rooms on the ground floor. And whereas hitherto he had wearily made his rounds on foot, henceforth he visited his patients proudly riding on a mule.

Sometimes the daring whisper of the spring breeze
May gently ripple the surface of a stagnant pool.

CHAPTER FIFTEEN: *Gold Ingots induce Chancellor Li to save the House of Hsi Men from ruin. Gold Lotus leads young Chen astray*

 I N THE MEANTIME, Hsi Men's two envoys pressed onwards to the Capital, Kai fong fu. The rising sun threw a purple glow across their path as they began their day's march. They did not reach their destination before the setting sun reddened the dust at their feet. At last they passed under the towering "Gate of Ten Thousand Generations," and, completely exhausted, they went to their lodgings. After they had slept off the fatigue of the journey they set out in the morning to acquaint themselves with whatever news was current in the streets and byways. They learned from the popular gossip that a sentence of exile had already been pronounced against the former War Minister Wang, who was responsible for the disaster on the frontier, whereas the preliminary examination of Marshal Yang was still in abeyance. Thus they knew that they had not come too late.

Their next goal was the palace of Chancellor Tsai. They had been there twice before and knew the way. Now they stood under the arch of the marble shrine on the Street of the Dragon's Strength, where they could peer across at the adjacent entrance to the Palace. They had not waited long before they saw a man in a green jerkin come out and hurry off in an easterly direction. Lai Pao recognized Marshal Yang's house steward, and was about to call out when he remembered that his master, Hsi Men, had prudently given him strict instructions to avoid all contact with the household or staff of the indicted Marshal. The steward was therefore permitted to go his way.

Finally the two advanced toward the portal and made for the doorkeeper's lodge.

"Is the Ancient Commander at home?" they asked the doorkeeper, after courteously murmuring their greetings.

"The Ancient Commander is still in attendance at the audience in the palace," he answered. "What is your desire?"

"May we speak to the Intendant Ti?"

"Uncle Ti is not at home either."

Lai Pao realized that there was not much to be got out of the taciturn old fellow without the inducement of chinking metal. He therefore dug into the pocket of his sleeves and handed him a piece of silver.

The laconic doorkeeper became astoundingly loquacious. "Is it the 'Ancient Commander' or the 'Great Commander' to whom you wish to speak?" he asked. "In the first case you must apply to the 'Great Intendant,' Uncle Ti, in the second case to the 'Little Intendant,' Uncle Kao An. Each has his clearly defined functions. As I said before, the Ancient Commander is attending the audience at Court, but his son, the Great Commander, the Secretary-in-Chief, Tsai Yu, is at home. If you wish to speak to him I will announce your arrival to his Intendant Uncle, Kao An."

"Tell him that we belong to the following of Marshal Yang," whispered Lai Pao confidentially.

Having instructed them to wait in the forecourt, the doorkeeper disappeared inside. After some time he returned, accompanied by the Little Intendant. Before the latter could open his mouth, Lai Pao had presented him with ten pieces of silver.

"We are in the service of Marshal Yang and we made an appointment with his house steward to make a joint call on the Ancient Commander in order to solicit further information. On the way here we somehow missed each other. Presumably the house steward has already been here?"

"Yes, he left just a moment ago. The Ancient Commander has

not yet returned from the audience. But if you wish to speak to the Great Commander I can show you in. Come this way!"

And he led them across the spacious reception hall, through a door set in a corner of the far side of the room, and thence into a smaller reception hall divided into three parts, with an entrance facing the south. All round this building ran a green-lacquered wooden balustrade, and from the blue-green background of the gable-end there stood out in high relief a red tablet inscribed with large golden characters, painted with the emperor's own brush. The inscription read: "The Psaltery Hall of the Great Secretary, endowed by the Emperor."

Tsai Yu, like his father, the Chancellor Tsai King, enjoyed the special favor of the Emperor Hui Tsung. Apart from his high position as Great Secretary of the "Hall of Prosperous Harmony" he occupied the post of Minister of Public Worship, and as "Guardian of the Palace of the Great Unity" he enjoyed the privilege of reprimanding the Emperor.

Kao An, who had gone ahead, now motioned the two to enter, and they presently stood in the presence of the Secretary, who sat enthroned on his chair of state on a raised platform. Keeping a respectful distance, they knelt down and performed their kowtows.

"Where do you come from?" he asked.

"We belong to the household of Chen Hung, near relatives to Marshal Yang, and have come to solicit further information concerning the Ancient Commander."

Lai Pao, the spokesman, drew a list of gifts from his sleeve and delivered it into the hands of the Secretary, who scanned it with a fleeting glance. When his eyes read: "Five hundred ounces of gold" he gave Lai Pao a sign to come closer.

"Listen!" he said under his breath. "In consideration of the rumors set on foot by the censors, the Ancient Commander has withdrawn from the affairs of State for a few days. Therefore if you wish to learn further details regarding the progress of the affair, you must apply to the Right Chancellor Li. As far as Marshal Yang is concerned, I can only tell you that there is talk in the Palace of the Holy One exercising clemency towards him, and of settling the matter by means of a trifling reduction of rank. On the other hand, the various members of his family and his followers who were indicted with him will be more severely punished. You will hear further particulars from the Right Chancellor."

Lai Pao, somewhat embarrassed, performed another kowtow. "I have no friends in the Palace of the Right Chancellor. May I, in my helplessness, hope for your magnanimous support?"

"Go to the wall on the north bank not far from the bridge over the Celestial River. You will see a great gate with a watch tower. There you must ask the way to the Palace of the Right Chancellor, Great Secretary of the 'Hall of the Tutelary Government,' and Associate Minister of Public Worship, Li Pang Yen. Anybody there will be able to tell you the way. I will also give you a letter of recommendation and provide you with one of my own servants as escort."

He wrote a few lines and told the Intendant Kao An to accompany them. He had also to take charge of the list of presents.

Chancellor Li, arrayed in his red robe of state, with a jade girdle round his waist, was in the act of alighting from the litter which had brought him home from the audience chamber when the three visitors were announced. At first only Kao An was admitted, but a moment later the others were invited to follow.

Kao An submitted his master's letter of recommendation, together with the list of presents, while Lai Pao and Lai Wang deposited the treasures which they had brought on the platform at the Chancellor's feet.

"Since you are recommended to me by the Great Secretary Tsai, these courtesies are really superfluous," observed the Chancellor, with a glance at the gold bullion. "Furthermore, the views of the Holy One with regard to the case of Marshal Yang have taken a lenient turn. Your master is now out of all danger. Only certain of his retinue will be somewhat severely dealt with and sent into exile, for on this the censors have insisted."

He beckoned to one of his officials and ordered him to produce from the archives the censors' bill of indictment and the list of those to be banished. He then allowed the two envoys to see the list for themselves. It was headed by the name of the deposed War Minister Wang: beneath this were the names of several of his followers, and then the names of a number of persons who belonged to the retinue of Marshal Yang, who had been pardoned. In this series of names, however, they discovered, to their horror, not only the name of Chen Hung, but also, directly below it, that of their master, Hsi Men Ch'ing!

". . . These hirelings, these bloodhounds and vultures"—thus read the indictment intended for presentation before the Throne—"these criminals have dared to clothe their foxlike forms with the borrowed majesty of the tiger. We, the Censors, propose that they be delivered over to the Supreme Court of Justice. They shall then either be sent to the distant wilderness of the frontier where they can make themselves useful by combating the devils of the swamp and the forest, or they shall undergo capital punishment in order that the laws of the land may be satisfied——"

Lai Pao and Lai Wang fell trembling to the ground.

"The actual truth is that our master is Hsi Men Ch'ing," they confessed. "Will the Ancient Commander deign to open his heart as high as the heavens and as wide as the earth and save our master's life?"

Kao An likewise fell to his knees and added his entreaties to theirs. Chancellor Li deliberated. He was offered the magnificent sum of five hundred ounces of gold as the price of a single name on the list of proscriptions. It seemed to him a profitable affair. It would cost him no more than a slight revision of the fatal list. A wave of the hand—a table and writing implements were set before him. With a few adroit strokes of the brush he joined together the two characters of Hsi and Men to make the character *Ku*, and changed the character Ch'ing into the similarly formed character *liang*. The characters now read: "the one guilty of suborning officials—" and the name of Hsi Men was in this ingenious manner effaced from the list. The Chancellor then wrote a brief note in answer to the Secretary; after which the three suppliants were given each five pieces of silver and were graciously dismissed. Rejoicing in the success of their mission, Lai Pao and Lai Wang returned to their lodgings, paid their reckoning, and on the very same day set forth on their homeward journey.

Arrived in Tsing ho hsien, they delivered a detailed report to their master. During their narration, Hsi Men felt as if he had been dipped in the proverbial tub of ice water, but when they had ended the proverbial stone dropped from his heart; and beaming with joy he ran to Moon Lady, to inform her of the fortunate outcome of the affair.

> *He saw the sun of his happiness*
> *Sink shrouded in the west.*
> *Now he beholds it rise again,*
> *Climbing upwards through the boughs.*

Two days later the building operations in the park were once more in full swing, while the massive gates of the main portal stood wide open, and there was a coming and going as in former days.

One day the little groom Tai, while riding through Lion Street noticed, to his surprise, in Mistress Ping's own house, a splendid dispensary, newly opened and fully stocked with drugs and medicaments. The handsome red-lacquered signboard outside the shop did not appeal to the public in vain, for the vermilion counter within proved to be altogether too small for the host of customers.

Hsi Men smiled incredulously when the boy brought him the news, and gave the matter no further thought. Tai had as yet no knowledge of Mistress Ping's second marriage, and spoke only of her having opened an apothecary shop and having engaged a manager.

It was in the first third of the seventh month, when a golden west wind had brought with it a life-giving rain and a refreshing coolness, that Hsi Men decided to enjoy a little jaunt on horseback. As he rode he fell in with Beggar Ying and Hsia Hsi Ta.

"Why is it we haven't seen you for so long?" they greeted him. "We passed your house several times but always found the gates tightly shut. We didn't want to disturb you, so we went our way. Has anything unusual happened? How do matters stand with your coming marriage? You know we are greatly looking forward to the promised feast."

"There you touch on a painful subject," Hsi Men replied. "For some time now I have been involved in an unpleasant business concerning my cousin, Chen Hung, and so, unfortunately, I have been obliged to postpone the date of the wedding."

"Why, we had no idea of that. We are inexpressibly sorry. So much the more reason then for a little celebration in honor of our meeting after so long a time. How about three cups at little Sister Silver's? They will help to wash away the traces of your distress."

And paying no heed to his protestations, they closed in upon him, and the three proceeded in company to Mother Wu's place. When late that evening Hsi Men was riding home, half-tipsy, Mother Bee ran across the road at the entrance to the Eastern Avenue. He reined in his horse. "Hey, where are you going in such a hurry, Mother Fong?"

"To the temple outside the gate," she answered. "I have to burn spirit money for my deceased master, as custom prescribes at such times."

"How is your mistress? Tell her that I am coming to see her tomorrow."

"Your question and your visit can no longer have any point. Another has already cleaned out the marriage pot."

"What! Do you mean to say that she has married someone else?"

"Now, listen! She waited for you, heaven knows how long, and she sent you, by this old person, the silver mirror that was to be her wedding present. You were no longer visible—you kept your gate closely barricaded and would not let this old person in. So my mistress just married another."

"Whom?"

"Doctor Bamboo Hill."

And the old woman related, from beginning to end, the whole course of the affair: how Mistress Ping had been pestered of nights by lewd fox goblins, and had fallen seriously ill, how she had been cured by Doctor Bamboo Hill, whom she had ended by marrying, and to whom she had given three hundred pieces of silver wherewith to open a dispensary.

Hsi Men's consternation was so great when he heard this that he nearly fell from his saddle.

"What a wretched business!" he thought to himself. "If it had been anyone else I might have put up with it. But to think of her taking that wizened little manikin, that blockhead, that impotent turtle! What a wretched business!"

Furiously he lashed his horse and galloped off.

At home, amidst general laughter, Moon Lady, Jade Fountain, Gold Lotus, and Hsi Men's daughter were enjoying a game of horses in the moonlit courtyard of the front hall. When they heard him coming they all, with the exception of Gold Lotus, disappeared into the rear apartments. Complaisant as ever, Gold Lotus helped him out of his boots while he leaned against a pillar.

"Silly wenches!" he berated her. "To go prancing about and wasting your time on such childish games!"

In an evil humor he kicked her out of his way, and omitting to say good night to Moon Lady, he staggered off to the library in the west wing, where he ordered his bed to be made up for the night. After making a few insulting remarks to the maids in attendance, he laid himself down to sleep.

In the meantime, completely intimidated, the four women stood together debating the incident. Moon Lady rebuked Gold Lotus.

"You saw that he was drunk. Why didn't you keep out of his way? No, when he was already close at hand, you had to irritate him by laughing, and then you pulled off his boots for him! No wonder he went up into the air like a grasshopper!"

"That he should abuse the three of us, one might, after all, overlook," Jade Fountain interposed. "But to call his own daughter a wench was tactless."

"Of course, as always, I am to blame for everything!" said Gold Lotus, sulkily. "Whom does he pick out for his kicks? Me! Do you still talk of favoritism?"

"Why didn't you persuade him to kick me too?" the exasperated Moon Lady retorted. "After all, if there is anyone who is favored above the rest, it is you. Your remark was extremely illogical. But one can't utter a word of reproach to you, your babbling tongue goes to work at once and twists everything about."

"Sister, I meant no harm," said Gold Lotus, seeking to appease her. "For some reason or other he was in a bad temper and happened to vent his spleen on me."

"Certainly, but why must you get in his way? You could have left him alone to vent his rage on a dog!"

Jade Fountain suggested the only means of putting an end to this senseless bickering. "Let us question his boy," she proposed. "He may know why our master is displeased. This morning when he left the house he was in the best of tempers. What can have happened to make him blow so dismal a tune upon his return?"

Her suggestion met with approval; Tai was summoned, and from him they learned the cause of Hsi Men's ill-temper.

"It was certainly highly unbecoming, to say the least, of this woman to marry again so soon after the death of her first husband!" was the self-righteous criticism of Jade Fountain.

"In our day and age," Moon Lady rejoined with drastic emphasis, "who asks if a thing is becoming or unbecoming? There are actually women so low that they will carouse and carry on with strange men during their very period of mourning. That I should call supremely unbecoming and shameless!"

Gold Lotus and Jade Fountain felt the unmistakable barbs of this speech, which was aimed at them. And as they both had good grounds for feeling that the reproach was deserved, they took their leave in some embarrassment and withdrew to their apartments.

Hsi Men resolved to give his son-in-law, young Chen, an opportunity of making himself useful. From now onwards he was to share with Pen Se the work of supervising the building operations, while his predecessor Lai Chao might take his ease in the less strenuous post of gatekeeper. Thus Chen was occupied all day on the building site at the rear of the park, and took his meals there or in the room which he and his wife inhabited in the front of the east wing. Without his father-in-law's express permission he never ventured to set foot in the central hall, the principal living room of Hsi Men's establishment, which explains how it was possible for him to be a member of Hsi Men's household for some time without coming face to face with any of his wives.

One day Hsi Men was away from home. He was accompanying the provincial judge, Ho, on a portion of his circuit. It was then that Moon Lady observed to Sunflower and Jade Fountain: "Hitherto I haven't taken the least notice of young Chen. The poor fellow has to work hard all day long in a strange house, rising early and going to bed late. How would it be if we were to give him a little refreshment while he is at work? Only, I am not sure whether I should be doing what is right. I might be accused of meddling in things that don't concern me. On the other hand, I don't like to see the young fellow altogether neglected."

"Sister, you are in charge of the household," said Jade Fountain, who approved of the suggestion. "If you don't take his part, who will?"

Accordingly, Moon Lady ordered a sumptuous repast from the kitchen, and at noon she invited young Chen into the central hall.

"I see you day in, day out, never taking a moment's rest, wearing yourself out at the building site," said Moon Lady, in a friendly tone. "So I am taking advantage of today's opportunity, when the master is away from home, to prepare a little refreshment for you, and invite you to drink a cup of watery wine."

"Many thanks for your kindness," murmured young Chen. "The few duties I have to discharge are really not worthy of mention."

Moon Lady had sent for Chen's young wife, who was to keep him company. However, some time elapsed before she appeared. From the adjoining room could be heard the characteristic sharp clicks produced by the placing of dominoes.

"Who's playing dominoes?" he inquired.

Moon Lady peeped into the next room.

"Hsi Men's daughter and the maid, Jade Flute."

"You see, that's the way she behaves!" he sighed. "You send for her, and she calmly goes on playing dominoes in the next room!"

At last the curtain was pushed aside, his young wife entered, and coolly took her place at the table facing him.

"Does your husband also understand the game of dominoes?" asked Moon Lady.

"He has just the barest notion," she answered flippantly. "He can just about tell a perfume from a stench."

Moon Lady had known the young fellow only as a courteous and dutiful son-in-law. She had no notion that he was as skilled in the composition of poems and essays as in the manipulation of dice and knucklebones, chessmen and dominoes.

"Well, then, we'll go into the next room and he can join in a game," Moon Lady good-naturedly proposed.

"It would hardly be seemly," he said, modestly declining. "I would rather that you two played!"

"Oh, please! After all, you are one of the family! What is there in that?" Moon Lady reassured him.

So they went into the adjoining room, where Jade Fountain was lounging on a crimson divan, absorbed in a domino solitaire. She rose as they entered, and was about to withdraw, but Moon Lady detained her.

"Young Chen is not a stranger. You can welcome him with propriety," she said. And turning to him: "This," she said, "is your sister-in-law Three."

Young Chen bowed hastily, and Jade Fountain murmured: "Tenthousandfold happiness!"

The three women now began a game of dominoes. At first Chen stood unassumingly to one side, simply looking on. But soon the spirit of the play seized him, and helping his young wife to make her moves, he showed by his ingenious combinations that he could do much more than "just about tell a perfume from a stench."

In the middle of the game the curtain parted. Gold Lotus entered, smiling, a silver net stretched over her curls, a fresh flower perched coquettishly over her left temple.

"Why, Brother Chen!" she cried merrily. "I was just wondering who could be here."

Chen turned towards her, captivated by the silvery music of her voice. Her glance sent the hot blood to his heart, dazzled his eyes, and banished his reason. It seemed to him that he suddenly stood before one who had been his beloved in a previous existence.

"This is Sister Five," said Moon Lady, introducing her.

Chen advanced a few paces towards her, and with hands crossed over his breast he bowed as deeply as his backbone would permit.

"Sister Five, come over and see this duckling who swims like an old experienced drake!" said Moon Lady, jestingly.

Gracefully cooling her face with her white silken fan, Gold Lotus stood beside Moon Lady and advised her as to her moves.

At this moment Hsi Men's arrival was announced. The game came to an abrupt end, and young Chen was hastily spirited away through a side door by the maid, Little Jewel.

Dismounting from his horse, Hsi Men went directly to the building site, to see how the work was getting on. Then he repaired to Gold Lotus's pavilion.

"You're back rather early," Gold Lotus observed.

"Yes, I accompanied him only as far as the outskirts of the town. You know—the Provincial Judge Ho, who has been promoted to be Border Prefect of the Hsin Ping march. He paid me the honor of a farewell visit, so for decency's sake I had to escort him part of the way. Not exactly a pleasure in this heat!"

"There is going to be quite a commotion in the house the day after tomorrow," he remarked at supper. "The work on the belvedere is now so far advanced that we can hold a feast in celebration of its completion. The house will be full of guests. Quite a number of people will want to bring their red strips of congratulation. There will be plenty to do in the kitchen."

By this time it was evening. Spring Plum had already brought the lamp. Exhausted by his ride in the heat, and overcome with drowsiness, the result of the many cups of wine which he had hurriedly poured down his throat, Hsi Men went early to bed. Soon his snores droned through the room like the distant roll of thunder.

It was the end of July, and the night air was oppressively sultry. Gold Lotus, at his side, could not sleep for the heat. Her attention was attracted by a metallic whirring which sounded from the mosquito trap, covered with a net of jade-green gauze. Naked as she was, she rose from the couch, and held up the lamp to the mosquito net. And there she saw a dragon fly entangled in the net. She freed the insect and singed it in the flame. As she did so there came into her mind that passage of the ode "The Walk through the Sedge" in which the poet speaks of the dragon fly in an ambiguous sense:

Swelling and smooth, its body
Narrows gently to a point.
When it hovers above the grasses,
It sounds like the shrilling of a flute.
In the saffron twilight
It may well befall
That it runs to its destruction
Through the red open door.
Alas, now the tender body
Batters the green gauze net,
And the trunk greedily plunges
Deep into the lip-red syrup.
Thus entangled in sweet toils,
It emits a hundred notes,
And the people asleep in the chamber
Wake, and forget their sleep, and listen.

While these words ran through her mind, her eye ranged over the naked form of Hsi Men on the couch. An irresistible craving overcame her. She stooped over him and caressed him.

"Crazy wench!" he growled. "Can't you give a man peace even in his sleep!"

But raising himself in bed, he feasted his eyes on the perfect lines of her curving body. Gold Lotus had her way.

Their sport might have lasted the length of time required to consume a meal, when he felt afar off the advent of the familiar and agreeable thirst. Straightway he called for the maid Spring Plum to bring him wine. She was to place the candle on a bench behind the bed curtain, so that the light should not dazzle their eyes. Then she was to take her place at his head, the wine jug in her hand.

"You good-for-nothing rascal!" Gold Lotus scolded him. "What new crotchet is this? What has the child to do here?"

"I learned this at Sister Ping's," he said laughing. "There the maid Pear Blossom had to stand beside me and give me wine. It heightens the pleasures of the cup."

"Well, I don't want to quarrel with you, but kindly spare me this talk of Sister Ping! We meant well by her and reaped nothing but unpleasantness from her. She could hardly wait to marry again, and by acting as she did she completely ruined your temper. And who has to suffer for that? I! Upon whom did you recently vent your spleen? On me! When you came home that night, drunk and beside yourself, whom did you kick? Me! And on top of that I have had to put up with all sorts of reproaches."

"Who has been reproaching you?"

"Your First."

And she told him of the altercation which she had had with Moon Lady at the time. The First had croaked at her like a dropsical frog.

"You women misunderstood me at the time," he reassured her. "I was not in the least angry with you. But you can understand how greatly it annoyed me that she had preferred a thing like that wizened manikin, that turtle, that damned Doctor Bamboo Hill, to myself! And that snarling cur, the elder Hua, never said a word against the marriage! And on top of everything, she gives that knave of a husband of hers money to open up a shop and compete with me! And the business is prospering! In short, you can understand how fed up I was that day."

"Why didn't you take her into your house from the beginning? You know I was in favor of it. But of course, you have ears only for your First, and she dissuaded you."

An angry wave of red mantled Hsi Men's cheek. Moon Lady become suddenly abhorrent to him.

"From tomorrow onwards I will never look at her again!" he said, resolutely.

How devastating an effect a few slanderous words may have on the relationship of those who by their very nature ought to cleave together! Whether it be the prince and his most faithful minister, or the father and his son, or the husband and his wife, or brother and brother, it is always the same old story: once give heed to the malicious insinuations of others, and the breach is there! How could such idle curtain gossip as this estrange Hsi Men from his good and faithful First, a woman above all suspicion?

At all events, from that very hour he was her bitter enemy. He never gave her a glance, never exchanged a word with her. And Moon Lady, for her part, took no further notice of him, nor did she inquire into his coming and going. If he chanced to enter her room, she would busy herself with whatever came to hand. She avoided looking at him, and allowed the maids to answer in her stead. In short, their relations were completely cold and meaningless.

Gold Lotus, on the contrary, felt that her position in Hsi Men's household was more firmly established than ever, and her animal spirits were greatly stimulated by the knowledge. And now she had cast her eyes upon young Chen. When she had met him a few days earlier at the domino party, she had taken more than a superficial liking to the lithe, handsome, intelligent young fellow. Then and there she had resolved to win him for herself. However, as long as Hsi Men was at hand she controlled herself. But once she was certain that he was out of the house she would invite young Chen to her pavilion, drink tea with him, chat with him, and play a game of chess with him.

Now came the day when the completion of the new buildings was to be celebrated. The morning brought to the house a vast number of friends and acquaintances, of boxes of fruit and red strips of congratulation. The workmen received their presents, and a luxurious banquet was prepared for the guests. In the afternoon, when the bustle and confusion was finally over, and the last guest had departed, Hsi Men, who had risen early, and was worn out by the exertions of the day, retired to one of the rooms at the back of the house and lay down for a nap. Now young Chen appeared in Gold Lotus' pavilion, and asked for a cup of tea. Gold Lotus was lying on the divan, thrumming on her six-stringed *pi pa*.

"Why, you were at the banquet; you had half the day for eating and drinking. How can you still have any appetite?" she asked in astonishment.

"To tell you the truth, I have been on my feet since early this morning. I had no time to think of eating and drinking."

"Is the Master at home?"

"He lay down to sleep at the back."

She called Spring Plum and ordered a meal with wine and dessert for her visitor. While he was enjoying his food, she continued to thrum on her *pi pa*.

"What are you playing? Won't you sing me a song?" he boldly asked.

"You are not asking much, my dear fellow," she drawled. "What if I were to report this to Master Hsi Men?"

He fell on his knees before her.

"Sister Five, have compassion on a poor young man!" he pleaded in comic consternation. "I will never again be so presumptuous!"

She raised him to his feet with a smile that was full of promise.

From that hour the intercourse between the two become more familiar from day to day. Frank and unconcerned, he went in and out of her pavilion, chatting with her easily and intimately, sometimes leaning on her shoulder or casually stroking her back. This was done in a nonchalant way, as though all was just as it should be. If only the good Moon Lady, who esteemed him for his youthful innocence, had suspected what a rampant libertine she had let loose in the house!

CHAPTER SIXTEEN: *Grass Snake and Road Rat administer a Thrashing to Doctor Bamboo Hill. Mistress Ping is inflamed with a renewed Passion for Hsi Men*

A FEW MONTHS LATER the new buildings stood complete to the last shingle and shone in the glory of their fresh paint. For the housewarming Hsi Men organized a magnificent feast that lasted several days. But we will not linger over the details of this banquet.

One day in the early part of the eighth month, about the tenth hour of the morning, Hsi Men set out for the country seat of the new Provincial Judge, Hsieh, which lay on the outskirts of the town, there to take part in the celebration of the Judge's birthday. Hardly had the hoofbeats of his horse ceased to echo in the gateway, when Moon Lady, accompanied by the four other wives, and by Hsi Men's daughter, set out in a body for a leisurely inspection of the new pleasure ground. And in truth, once they had passed through the lofty grille, wonders without end lay revealed to their eyes.

Here and there, above the somber blue-green of cypress and the kingfisher green of bamboos, little hills emerged, some sloping gently, and some precipitous, but leveled at the summit to make room for a belvedere. Every season of the year had contributed its charm to the park. There stood the "Hall of the Migrating Swallows," which in the springtime would afford a close view of a coppice of peach and of plum trees, that would vie with one another in the splendor of their blossom. Yonder slumbered in seclusion the "Glen of the Woodland Stream," where in the summer the water lilies and lotuses would unfold their beauty. Here rose the high

"Tower of Green-Covered Heights," whose surroundings, in autumn, would be ablaze with golden chrysanthemums. And here, in the "Hall of Hidden Spring" the rare winter calycanthus would stretch forth its blossoming boughs. Quiet waters trickled past islands resplendent with flowers. Over richly carved gateways hung branches laden with fruit. The narrow, drooping leaves of the willow danced lightly in the wind, flowing into curves like the delicate sweep of a maiden's eyebrows. Before the "Hall of the Migrating Swallows" gayly-colored lanterns would sway to and fro on the evening of the Lantern Festival. Behind the "Hall of Hidden Spring," the first apricot shoots would shyly venture to pierce their silver coverlet of snow. On the rocky shores of the lake veins of gold and silver ore glittered in masses of roughly-hewn quartz. From parapets and balustrades gems of many colors peeped forth like tender bamboo shoots. Red-breasted swallows came skimming through the curtained portals and under the roofs of the halls, while yellow cockatoos whirred shrieking through the green shade of the trees. Moon-shaped openings in the walls were not absent, nor a floating ark, nor a wattled arbor of fragrant Kashmir thistle roots, nor somber groves of pines and cheerful bamboo alleys, nor meandering streams and rectangular ponds, nor flights of steps flanked with shrubs and palms, nor basins full of rare fishes, nor fluttering, many-colored butterflies. In short, a park that could compare favorably with the "Peony Grove" of the old Tang Emperor, the view of which was said to bring a smile of amazement to the rigid features of a Bodhisattva absorbed in pious meditation.

With Moon Lady at their head, the six beauties wandered along the winding paths of the park, now perhaps breaking a way through the tall grass and reclining on the fragrant sward, now kneeling beside the flower beds the better to admire some rare floral wonder. By the edge of the quiet ponds they diverted themselves by feeding the goldfish, or startling the gayly-colored butterflies with their round fans. Now Moon Lady proposed the lofty "Pavilion of Cloudy Rest" for their goal, and engaged in a game of chess with Jade Fountain and Sunflower, while the other three women climbed to the top of the lookout in order to feast their eyes on the magnificent panorama. Their enraptured gaze swept over the clumps of clustering peonies and the hedges of roses, over the boughs of crabapple trees and the thickets of Kashmir thistles, over the frost-defying bamboos and the evergreen cypresses. Here, indeed, was the abode of perpetual Spring!

When at last they had gazed their fill at the scene before them the party assembled in the observation pavilion for a picnic repast. Moon Lady sat at the head of the table, with Sunflower facing her. The other four women took their places on either side, in strict accordance with their rank.

"Why, I've quite forgotten to invite young Chen," said Moon Lady, and she sent Little Jewel to ask him to join them. Presently he appeared, and took his place at a little table behind his wife.

He was sporting a crimson coat of flowered silk; on his head was a crêpe bonnet of celestial blue, on his feet a pair of smart black satin slippers. After they had refreshed themselves with several cups of wine, Moon Lady, Sunflower, and Hsi Men's daughter resumed their interrupted game of chess, while Jade Fountain and Snowblossom climbed the observation tower. Gold Lotus was left alone. She decided to inspect the lotus pond that lay at the foot of the hill, and there she beguiled the time by striking at butterflies with her fan. Quite unobserved, the libertine Chen had crept after her, and now he stood just behind her. Suddenly she heard his voice from close at hand:

"Why, Sister Five, you don't know much about chasing butterflies. Let me help you."

Startled, she turned and surveyed him with a sidelong but scrutinizing glance.

"Rascal, you scared me to death!" she gently rebuked him.

Smiling, he stepped up to her, and without more ado he clasped her in his arms and kissed her. Pressing her hands against his breast, she feigned a feeble resistance.

"Sister Five!" At this moment she heard Jade Fountain's voice calling her from the observation tower. "Come up here quickly! I have something to tell you."

Gold Lotus hastily disengaged herself from her importunate admirer and climbed up the hill. Young Chen, however, slipped back to his quarters. He was at once joyful and despondent. And while he pensively went his way, swayed by conflicting emotions, the mood of the moment inspired him with the following verses:

> *Fresh blossoms slanting in her hair,*
> *She stands before me evermore.*
> *Those crimson lips of hers*
> *Have no need of rouge or pencil.*
> *No sooner have I beheld her*
> *Than I long to behold her again.*
> *Her eyes seem to tell the love*
> *That her mouth refrains from speaking.*
> *It is true that her eyes said "Yes,"*
> *But I long for the spoken word.*
> *It is true that she seemed to repel me,*
> *But her struggles were like caresses.*
> *Whether she lingers beside me*
> *Or flees me on hurrying feet*
> *Always, always I ask myself:*
> *When will she grant me fulfillment?*

Hsi Men was a well-known personage not only in the upper classes of society, but also in the more questionable quarters of the good city of Tsing ho hsien. All the underworld knew him, and many of its members could boast of having received substantial "benefits" from his hand. Among these were two notorious bandits, who in their own circle were known as "Grass Snake" and "Road Rat." They were criminals of the type known during the Sung dynasty as "Sluggers," and nowadays as "Cudgelers." That evening, on his way back from the country seat of Provincial Judge Hsieh, Hsi Men, as he trotted through a narrow suburban lane, saw these two fellows sitting outside a pot house, playing dice. A sudden thought flashed through his mind. He reined in his horse and called to them. They at once came running up to him and greeted him with a slight genuflection.

"Where from, noble gentleman?"

"From the birthday feast of the honorable Provincial Judge Hsieh. By the way, I have a little job for you."

"Noble gentleman, in the past we have often had the honor and the favor. You know that for you we would go through fire and boiling water, we would die ten thousand deaths."

"Very well, come and see me tomorrow morning. We will speak further of it then."

"Why tomorrow? Speak at once, noble gentleman!"

Hsi Men stooped his head to the level of their ears and related in an undertone the story of Mistress Ping's remarriage.

"Brothers," he concluded, "I should be damnably pleased if you would give this accursed Doctor Bamboo Hill what he richly deserves."

He pulled out a purse from his underclothing and shook out the contents—five ounces of broken silver.

"Here is a trifle for the present. If you do the job promptly there will be more."

Grass Snake would not accept the money.

"We are still in your debt, noble gentleman. Indeed, if you had asked us to sail to the Eastern Sea and steal from the blue sea-dragon the topmost horn of the crest on his back, or to break a front tooth from the jaw of the tiger of the Hua Shan Mountain, that would be a different matter. But for a trifle like this! No, we can't take anything for that."

"Good, then, I won't trouble you," Hsi Men replied abruptly, and he ordered his boy Tai to put the money back in his purse. At the same time he gave his horse a flick of the whip, and made as though to ride off. But Road Rat caught hold of the reins.

"You don't know the gentleman's way," he told his comrade. "He takes it as a refusal if we reject his gifts." He knelt on the pavement, made a kowtow, and addressed Hsi Men: "Noble gentleman, you can go home quietly and wait for the job to be done. We'll do our very best within two days at most. You shall have something to laugh about!"

"And when it is done, perhaps we may hope that the noble gentleman will obtain for us, as a reward, a tidy post under His Excellency Hsieh," added Grass Snake.

"Done!" Hsi Men promised, and he trotted off.

Home again, he felt inclined for an evening stroll in the park. He found Gold Lotus clearing away the signs of the banquet in the observation pavilion. The other women had hastily withdrawn to their apartments at the news of his arrival.

He was in a jovial mood, and today Gold Lotus seemed to him more desirable than ever. After he had partaken of some slight refreshment he drew her to his side and kissed her tenderly. The maid, Spring Plum, was told to bring some strong sweet wine, and while Gold Lotus, with her coat girded up, made herself comfortable on his lap, they both drank from the same cup. Now and again she would adroitly spurt a few drops of wine from her own mouth between his lips. Then she slipped a young and still hairy lotus kernel into his mouth.

"Brr! But that's bitter, and its bristles stick in one's throat!" he said, making a wry face.

"Whatever your loving wife gives you, you must eat! It foretells good fortune!"

And she followed the lotus kernel with a fresh nut. He understood what she meant. Not one of his five wives had yet presented him with offspring!

He pressed his head to her bosom. She opened the fine cambric chemise, so that her round breasts, soft as butter, smooth and gleaming as flawless jade, were revealed. Greedily he allowed his lips to rove over their swelling curves. Then he drew himself up.

"Listen, I have some news for you," he said, well pleased with himself. "There's going to be some capital sport tomorrow. Doctor Bamboo Hill, you know, who has opened a new dispensary for Lady Ping, will be able to open up his face as a fig shop tomorrow!"

"How so?"

Hsi Men told her of his plot with the two rascals whom he had met in the suburb outside the city wall.

"What things you think of!" she said, with a laugh. "By the way, isn't that the doctor who attends us here from time to time? He is really a polite and modest little man. Whenever he greets anybody he makes an incredibly low bow. I am really sorry for him."

"Ha ha! He knows well enough why he bows so low before you women. It's so that he can get a closer look at your legs!"

"Oh, do you think so? I can hardly believe that. Such a learned man! He couldn't possibly be guilty of such thoughts."

"You know only his prepossessing exterior. Behind that he's a most accomplished rogue."

Two months had now passed since Lady Ping had received Doctor Bamboo Hill into her house as her husband. If at first he had hoped to win her love by his arts—by means of stimulating drugs and sympathetic nostrums—he was very soon completely disillusioned. For deep in her heart she was thoroughly infatuated with Hsi Men, and her faint liking for the little man passed as swiftly as a sudden whirlwind or a shower of rain. His physical nearness not only left her cold but was even repulsive to her. Indeed, the various love charms which he pressed her to employ she dashed to the ground, tramped underfoot, and consigned to the refuse heap.

"You ugly tree frog, you loathsome earthworm!" she would cry in her fury, whenever he sought to cajole her into employing some magical remedy. "You have not an ounce of vigor in your loins, so spare me this rubbish! For me you are a scrap of rotten meat; to see you is to lose one's appetite. You are a wax-tipped spear, a dead tortoise! Get out of my sight!"

She often drove him out of her bedchamber to pass the night in the shop. Day and night she brooded over the reason why Hsi Men had not received her into his household; and when by exception she was not thinking of him she would sit over her abacus and reckon up her possessions under her breath. One day there had again been a stormy scene between the husband and wife, and Doctor Bamboo

235

Hill, his belly full of wrath, had retreated to his shop. Hardly had he taken his place on the stool behind the counter when two strangers of a vicious and dissolute appearance entered and casually took their seats on the customers' bench.

"Have you 'dog-yellow' in your shop?" asked one.

"You must mean 'ox-yellow' or 'ox-bezoar.' I stock that," replied Doctor Bamboo Hill. "There is no such thing as 'dog-yellow.'"

"Well, then, I should like to buy a couple of ounces of 'Ice-ashes.'"

"You are pleased to jest. Or else you are confusing 'Ice-ashes' with 'Ice-chips' or camphor. I can supply you with good Persian camphor."

"Joking aside," said the second customer, turning to the first, "probably the shop has only just been opened, so that the stock isn't quite complete. We will just have a word with him. Look here, Friend Bamboo Hill, don't act any longer as though you were asleep or dreaming. You remember, of course, the thirty ounces of silver which you borrowed from this gentleman two years ago, when your wife died. Well, now he wants you to repay him with interest. We learned some time ago that you intended to marry again and to open a dispensary here. We therefore granted you a short respite. But now, out with the cash!"

Doctor Bamboo Hill stared at the speaker with startled eyes. "What! I am supposed to owe this gentleman money?"

"Don't get excited, my little friend! There isn't the smallest hole where you can lay the fly-blow of your indignation!"

"But I don't even know this gentleman's name! I've never seen him before! How could I possibly owe him money?"

"Stop and think! Just remember how formerly, as a poor itinerant doctor, you used to run up and down the streets with your belled staff, puffing your pills and ointments! Well, who paid the expenses of your wife's funeral? This gentleman here!"

"My name is Lu Hua," said the so-called gentleman, who was none other than Grass Snake, introducing himself. "At that time I placed at your disposal thirty ounces of silver. With interest your present indebtedness amounts to forty-eight ounces, and I want it repaid in full."

"Why should I pay it?" cried the indignant Doctor Bamboo Hill. "Where is the note of hand? Where are the sureties?"

"If you please, it was I myself, Chang Shong, who went surety for you," said Road Rat, "and here is the note of hand."

And out of his sleeve he pulled a sheet of paper, which he held up before the eyes of the bewildered doctor, whose face grew wax-yellow with rage.

"You dogs, you accursed bandits, you're just trying to hold me up!" he shouted.

For answer, Grass Snake, reaching over the counter, dealt the doctor a sudden blow in the face that knocked his nose askew. He then seized a fully laden showcase and pitched it out of doors, so that the medicine bottles and pill boxes rolled across the street.

Lifting his voice, the dismayed Doctor Bamboo Hill summoned his old servant Tien Fu to his aid. But no sooner did Tien Fu enter the shop than he received so violent a kick that he speedily withdrew. The doctor was then dragged out from behind his counter and held fast.

"Brother, you have waited so long already!" said Road Rat to Grass Snake. "Can't you grant the good doctor a further respite of two days? He might be able to procure the money by then. Hey, what do you think of that, my little friend? Perhaps he might abate a little of the interest if you paid up with good will."

"I'll prosecute the blackguard!" cried Doctor Bamboo Hill, in a passion.

Another smashing blow in the face.

"I'm afraid you've been drinking—and so early in the morning!" Road Rat jeered at his victim, who was staggering and had lost his cap.

His loud cries of help brought in a police patrol. The three men were fettered together and led off to the yamen.

Meanwhile, behind the curtain, Mistress Ping had witnessed the proceedings with a secret and malignant satisfaction. When the three men had been led away she ordered old Mother Bee to take in the signboard and close the shop. The boxes and bottles lying about the street had long ago been picked up and appropriated by passers-by.

It was not long before news of the incident had come to Hsi Men's ears, and that very hour he sent a confidential messenger to his good friend, the Provincial Judge Hsieh, before whose court the case would be heard next morning. He had taken good care that judgment would be pronounced in accordance with his wishes.

"So then, you are Kiang, called Bamboo Hill!" said Judge Hsieh, opening the hearing next morning. "Why do you refuse to pay your debt, and why, into the bargain, do you calumniate the man who lent you the money? Your conduct is abominable."

"I don't understand this at all. I never borrowed anything from him," was the doctor's defense. "When I tried to talk reason to him he began to beat me and damaged my shop fittings."

"Lu Hua, what have you to reply to this?"

"Two years ago he borrowed money from me. He needed it to pay for his wife's funeral. For two years he kept putting me off. In the meantime he opened a thriving dispensary. When yesterday I insisted on payment he began to rave and abuse me. However, here is the note and there stands the surety."

The judge unfolded the proffered slip and read: "The executor of this promissory note, Kiang, called Bamboo Hill, practicing physician in the district, in order to defray the expenses of his deceased wife's funeral, has borrowed and received from Lu Hua thirty ounces of white silver at the rate of three per cent monthly interest. Payment to be made within twelve months. Chang Shong is surety. In case of dispute, this note is to serve as evidence."

Angrily Master Hsieh pounded on the table.

"There's the proof!" he cried. "You're nothing but an obdurate, grudging debtor who dares throw doubt on the clear text of a legal document!"

A curt order, and three or four court beadles pounced on the poor doctor, and laid on thirty strokes of the heavy bamboo cudgel. They then closed in on him and dragged him to his house. They had been instructed to make forcible collection of the thirty pieces of silver. In case the money was not forthcoming, the defendant was to be consigned to the debtors' prison. Groaning and moaning, the victim implored his wife to pay the thirty ingots of silver for him. At this Mistress Ping spat in his face.

"Not a single cash did you bring into our marriage, and now you want me to pay your debts as well!" she snorted. "If I had only seen through you in time I would have taken good care not to marry you, you loathsome, insupportable turtle!"

The four beadles, hearing this speech, were on the point of dragging the doctor back to the yamen, when he threw himself on his face before Mistress Ping, and by the most moving appeal sought to rouse her compassion. She would win, he declared, a mountain-high blessing from heaven if only she performed this one act of charity for him, and preserved him from being beaten to death. She relented; and after tearing up the note, Grass Snake and Road Rat went off in triumph, with thirty bright new ingots of silver.

They went without delay to Hsi Men, whom they found in the lookout pavilion, and proudly informed him of their successful stroke of business. He commended them, entertained them lavishly, and magnanimously confirmed them in the possession of the thirty ounces of silver—which, after all, did not come out of his pocket— as their reward for the pains which they had taken. He graciously promised that should he ever have need of such services again in the future, he would surely remember them. His satisfaction soared to the very clouds next day, when he heard that Mistress Ping, without more ado, had driven his unhappy rival out of the house, as penniless as he had come, and had definitely closed the competing dispensary. Such, indeed, was the very truth. On the doctor's departure, Mistress Ping could not refrain from ordering old Fu to pour the customary pail of water under the house door, as a visible confirmation of the fact of their divorce. She sighed with relief as his hated figure disappeared, and she reproached herself bitterly for having ever contracted this overhasty marriage. From this moment all her thoughts and hopes were centered again on Hsi Men. Leaning against the doorpost, she watched and waited, longing for news of him.

Moon Lady's birthday had come round—the fifteenth of the eighth month—but since Hsi Men was still not on speaking terms with her, he had gone to spend the day with Cinnamon Bud, expressly in order to avoid the household festival. He had taken with him Beggar Ying and Hsia Hsi Ta. Cinnamon Bud's elder sister happened to be at home, so the five entertained themselves all day with drinking and dicing, or diverted themselves in the courtyard at the time-honored and popular bottle-game, which consists in deftly tossing arrows by hand through the neck of a bottle. Towards evening Tai arrived with Hsi Men's horse.

"Any news from home?" he asked the boy.

"Nothing out of the common. Most of the guests have already gone. Through Mother Bee, Mistress Ping from Lion Street sent Moon Lady her congratulations, together with various presents."

"You're very hot. Have you been drinking?"

"Yes. Mistress Ping told Mother Bee she wanted to see me, and I've just come from there. She gave me two large bowls of wine. That's why I'm rather hot. Mistress Ping told me all her troubles. She bitterly reproaches herself for ever having taken Doctor Bamboo Hill into her house. With all her heart she begs you to forgive her, and to come to see her, and she wants at any cost to move over to you. She begged me most urgently to bring her an immediate answer from you. It does seem to mean a lot to her, Master, for she's much thinner than she used to be."

"That confounded woman! What more does she want of me?" Hsi Men muttered sullenly. "But I don't care! Go to her and tell her outright that I've had enough of this visiting and this tiresome coming and going. I shall choose a convenient date for the marriage and then send the litter. Let that be an end of the matter!"

"Then may I take her your answer at once? I've brought Ping An with me, so that he can take my place in the meantime."

240

"Very good, go!"

Mistress Ping inwardly shouted for joy when before the day was over Tai brought her the glad tidings. "What a good messenger you are, dear little brother!" she praised him. "I shall always be grateful to you!"

And she hurried into the kitchen, quickly prepared a meal with her own hands, and treated him to the best wine. And then he had to promise to help her old servant Tien Fu when it came to removing her effects.

The very next day she hired five porters, and began the work of removal, which took no less than five days, so large was her stock of household goods. Without informing Moon Lady, Hsi Men ordered Mistress Ping's belongings to be brought into the new pleasure pavilion, and fixed upon the twentieth of the eighth month for the marriage day.

Accordingly, on the afternoon of the twentieth he dispatched the large marriage litter, with its red silken hangings, to Lion Street. Four of his own servants, together with eight men bearing great red lanterns, made a dignified retinue. Mistress Ping, for her part, sent old Mother Bee and her two maids to announce her coming. She waited until old Mother Bee returned, then entrusted the key of her house into Mother Bee's and Tien Fu's keeping, and blissfully took her place in the red litter.

Hsi Men, although he had not gone out that day, had nevertheless abstained from making any festive preparations, such as would have been proper on the installation of a "New One." This very first day, he resolved, he would teach her a lesson. In his everyday indoor clothes he sat in the lookout pavilion and calmly awaited her entry.

Mistress Ping was not a little astonished when her litter was set down under the main portal and nobody came out to receive her. According to the precepts of the marriage ritual, as long as no accredited woman of the house appeared to greet her, she dared not step over the threshold, and must therefore wait outside.

Finally, Jade Fountain, moved to compassion, ran to Moon Lady and implored her to conduct the "New One" over the threshold. "You are the mistress in the house; that you should welcome her is an obligation imposed upon you by your position. Hsi Men will surely be angry if you fail to do so. The poor woman has been waiting before the threshold for half a day, and nobody has gone out to welcome her. That's hardly the proper thing to do."

Filled with comprehensible resentment against the "New One," Moon Lady hesitated for a moment. But in the end her fear of Hsi Men prevailed over her resentment, and with a sigh she rose, and slowly set her lily feet in motion towards the door. So that after a seeming eternity of anxious expectation, Mistress Ping at last found herself lifted from the litter, and escorted on Moon Lady's arm to her new home in the park, where the two maids, Pear Blossom and Apricot Blossom, had already prepared the nuptial chamber. But all that evening and all night Lady Ping waited in vain. Hsi Men did not come, but passed the night with Gold Lotus.

Not until the next morning did Hsi Men appear outside the pavilion, and call her forth in order to lead her to the inner apartments, and formally introduce her as the "Sixth" to his other wives and handmaidens. But this second night also she spent lonely and forsaken in her chamber. For Hsi Men spent the night with Jade Fountain.

Now when the third night had passed, and Hsi Men still continued to keep aloof, she gave way to dull despair. It was about midnight when the two maids, asleep in the next room, were awakened by a pitiful moaning. Disquieted, they rose, and entered the adjacent chamber, and beheld, in the dim light of the low-burning oil lamp, their mistress, clad in all her wedding finery, dangling from a transverse beam of the bedstead, her throat in the noose of her silken girdle.

With loud shrieks the two women ran out into the park and fetched Gold Lotus and Spring Plum, who lived next door, to the rescue. Gold Lotus, cool and determined, seized a pair of scissors and with one vigorous snip cut the noose above the neck. Together they caught the falling body and laid the unconscious woman on the couch. And lo, a miracle! After a while a little white foam issued from her mouth. She was breathing! Fortunately for her, in her excitement she had failed to knot the noose with sufficient care, and it had not drawn tight enough to strangle her.

Spring Plum was now dispatched to inform Hsi Men. She found him, still dressed, in Jade Fountain's company, drinking and chatting merrily. Jade Fountain had just been reproaching him for avoiding his bride for three nights running. She would be seriously affronted, Jade Fountain warned him.

"You just let me manage this affair!" he replied. "I must school her first. She's a bit too inquisitive by nature; too fond of nibbling at the dishes and peeping into the cooking pots. Without a word to me she married that Doctor Bamboo Hill. For that she will have to make amends. She must learn that I am a different sort of man from that fellow, and that I don't have to run after her!"

"You may be right; but after all, she was the victim of a delusion, and I feel sorry for her."

At this moment loud and excited voices outside broke in on their conversation. Jade Fountain at once sent her maid, Fragrant Orchid, to discover what was wrong.

"The Sixth has hanged herself," Fragrant Orchid announced, in consternation. "The Fifth bids the Master come at once!"

"You see, I warned you! You wouldn't listen to me and now the misfortune has come," said Jade Fountain reproachfully to Hsi Men, and, lantern in hand, she dashed out of the room, to inform Moon Lady and Sunflower. While Hsi Men remained sitting where he was, completely at his ease, the three women hurried through the moonlit park to the new pavilion. They found the Sixth lying on the couch, pale and exhausted, but already to some extent recovered. Gold Lotus sat beside her, supporting her head and shoulders.

"Have you given her some hot ginger soup, Sister Five?" was the practical Moon Lady's first question.

"It was the first thing I did after I took her down," replied Gold Lotus.

"That's good. Now what she needs above all else is sleep."

And the three women, with many sympathetic sighs, but relieved at heart, returned to their own apartments.

"Don't allow yourselves to be taken in by her!" Hsi Men told his assembled wives next morning. "She planned the whole business, just to call attention to herself. I don't believe she had any serious intention of committing suicide. And I shan't let her off so easily. This very evening I shall go to her and make her sling herself up again before my own eyes, and if she flinches she'll get a taste of the horsewhip."

The wives preserved a troubled silence, but their apprehension for the wretched Sixth wrung a handful of perspiration from each of them. Sure enough, that very evening, with a horsewhip concealed in his sleeve, Hsi Men betook himself to the new pavilion. Gold Lotus and Jade Fountain crept after him, and expectantly took up their listening posts outside one of the side doors. Hsi Men had ordered all doors to be locked.

When he entered he found Mistress Ping sobbing on the bed, her face buried in the cushions. She did not stir, which vexed him at the outset. He first dismissed her two maids, and then calmly sat down on a stool.

"If you really want to hang yourself, why do you choose my house for the purpose?" he burst out angrily. "You could have done that in the house of your last husband—that idiot, that turtle! I didn't ask you to come here, I didn't lure you to my house. But never mind, I shan't hinder you! Here's a rope; now hang yourself! I should like to see you hang!"

He flung the rope which he had brought with him into her face.

Mistress Ping was overcome by a mortal terror. She suddenly recalled what Doctor Bamboo Hill had once told her of Hsi Men—that he was the head of a dangerous band of wife abductors and maiden ravishers. Perhaps the doctor had been right! Perhaps she had now really fallen in a trap, into a fiery pitfall? She uttered a wild shriek of terror.

"Off that bed! And off with your clothes! Down on your knees!" he cried wrathfully.

244

As she appeared to hesitate before obeying, though actually she was merely paralyzed with abject dread, he seized her and brutally dragged her from the couch. At the same time he pulled the whip from his sleeve and gave her three lashes. Then she resigned herself to her fate, and in fear and trembling threw off her clothes. He made her kneel completely naked on the bare floor, and in this position, he compelled her to listen patiently to the long lecture into which he launched. Why had she put no faith in him? Why could she not bide her time? Why had she married in such precipitate haste? Above all, how could she bring herself to prefer, before him, a wizened, deformed little manikin like Doctor Bamboo Hill? That had filled him with the profoundest indignation. And to crown the infamy of her conduct, she had set up a rival dispensary!

"I am sorry," she said, softly. "But remember, I beg of you, that you never let me see you; day and night I waited in vain. My sleep was haunted by lewd fox goblins who clamored in the neighboring park, and startled me out of confused dreams, in which I seemed about to embrace you. I was ill, my mind was deranged. Ask old Mother Bee, ask both the maids to tell you how ill I was. It was then the wretched fellow came to my house and took advantage of my suffering condition to talk me into doing as he wished. Oh, how bitterly I have had to atone for it! Won't you at last understand, and forgive me?"

He was not yet completely mollified.

"I've been told that you advised that confounded doctor to bring an action against me for the valuables which you committed to my safekeeping," he harshly accused her.

"That's not true!" she protested vehemently. "May my body wither away if I ever suggested such a thing!"

"Really?" His face lighted up. "Perhaps you wanted to come to me simply to regain possession of your belongings, eh? And once you have them again, you intend to slip away to another man? Let me tell you that if that's your plan, you have reckoned without your host! I shan't let you slip out of my hands so easily again! But now, to be quite frank with you: the whole incident of your husband's alleged indebtedness, his thrashing in the shop, his conviction—all that was my plan, my work! It's just as well that you should know!"

"Oh, I am so glad that I need not yet depart for the dismal plains of death!" she cried with a sigh.

"There is one more thing I want to hear from you: which of us is the stronger, the doctor or I?"

"How can you even ask? To compare you would be to compare heaven with a lump of dirt! The wretch can't be called a man at all! If you must seek for a comparison, rather ask to be compared with the late Hua Tze Hsu. But then why did I pine for you so, even when he was alive? You are the only balsam, the only medicine for my wounded heart!"

Hsi Men was appeased, and his old feeling for her returned. He threw the horsewhip from him, raised her gently to her feet, and helped her into her clothes.

"Everything is now all right again, child!" he said, and he clasped her tenderly in his arms.

CHAPTER SEVENTEEN: *The Fool exhibits his Bride to hilarious Feasters. In the House of Joy Jealousy drives him into a frenzy*

IN THE ODE "The Walk to the Hermit's Grotto" we read:

Down flowery paths,
And past the hedgerows
Two beauties creep along.
See! The piercing thorn
Has slit their coat seams.
Now, with heads bent to one side,
They listen and peer,
How sweetly sounds
From the budding branches
The twitter of birds!
A respectable pair of swallows,
Is scared from the family nest.
Let them flutter about the hedge,
While we take a sly peep at their brood.

While in the pavilion Mistress Ping's urgent pleading gradually transformed Hsi Men's harshness into compassion, his upbraiding into caresses, Jade Fountain and Gold Lotus stood outside the eastern door and listened. All the doors were bolted and barred, and Spring Plum alone was allowed to enter. She stood in the courtyard and awaited Hsi Men's commands. With anxious interest the two women peered through a narrow chink which they had made in the door. They could faintly perceive a portion of the candle-lit bedchamber, but unfortunately they could not understand a word of the conversation, for the distance was too great.

"The little girl is better off. She can hear every word," said Gold Lotus regretfully to Jade Fountain.

As a matter of fact, little Spring Plum had taken up an excellent listening post underneath the bedroom window. Treading lightly, she now approached the side door where the two women were standing.

"What's happening inside?" Gold Lotus inquired softly through the door.

"He has ordered her to take off her clothes and kneel down on the floor. When she hesitated, he grew angry and gave her a few cuts with his horsewhip."

"Did she take off her clothes?"

"Yes, and she went down on her knees all naked. He is taking her to task now."

"Sister Five, he may overhear us, if we go on talking here," Jade Fountain observed apprehensively. "We had better go to the western door."

And she pulled Gold Lotus along with her to the western door, which was further removed from the bedroom. There they stood whispering softly, cowering in the shadow of the wall to avoid being picked out by the mellow beams of the full August moon, which was just rising above the horizon. They could hardly wait until Spring Plum should come to the door to inform them of further developments. But Spring Plum did not come.

"I am only too familiar with such scenes as these," Gold Lotus whispered to her companion, with a touch of malignant joy in her voice. "What I have had to suffer from him! No matter how loving you are to him, you can never know what to expect from his caprices."

At this moment they heard the gate open, and immediately afterwards Spring Plum appeared on the moonlit path, passing close by them.

"Where are you going, little one?" they called to her out of the darkness.

Spring Plum smiled and continued to walk on.

"Will you come here, you impudent hussy? I simply must have a word with you!" said Gold Lotus imperiously.

The little maid stopped and approached the two lurking in the shadow.

"For a long while she cried and tried to appease him," she related. "And in the end he relented; he lifted her to her feet, helped her into her clothes, and embraced her. Now I have to go to the main kitchen to order some food and wine."

"All empty thunder and no rain, then!" said Gold Lotus, who was disappointed, to Jade Fountain. "Didn't I tell you he was absolutely incalculable?"

"Why must you go to the main kitchen precisely?" she demanded of Spring Plum, with displeasure. "The New One has her own kitchen, hasn't she? If you should get at cross purposes with the Fourth again, I assure you I shan't take your part this time."

"That won't be necessary," the little one retorted saucily. "I do what my master Hsi Men commands me to do."

And with a laugh, she skipped off.

"How briskly the wench can hop about when she has the errands of a stranger to run!" Gold Lotus called after her reprovingly. "When I, who am after all her rightful mistress, want anything of her, she behaves as though she were dead, so slothful and indolent is she. But for the New One she runs like a mouse in front of a cat."

"I have just the same trouble with my maid, Fragrant Orchid," Jade Fountain consoled her. "Whenever I tell her to do anything she can hardly be moved from the spot. But if it's for the Master, oh, then she can run!"

After a while Spring Plum, accompanied by Little Jewel, came out of the kitchen, the one carrying a jug of wine, the other the food, and Gold Lotus could not refrain from berating the girl once more: "Little wretch, did you understand me? I say you are not to wait on that old rat! You are to wait on me alone, do you hear?"

The little maid laughed mockingly and proceeded unconcernedly on her way. Gold Lotus, however, stole back to her pavilion and in an evil humor retired to her solitary couch.

> *Ah, how the disk of the full moon gleams!*
> *And yet what use are its familiar rays*
> *When for the couch of a strange woman*
> *My lover ruthlessly forsakes my side?*

At breakfast the next morning, Mistress Ping unlocked one of her chests and permitted Hsi Men a peep inside. It was filled to the brim with valuable robes and magnificent jewelry. On the top of the robes were the hundred large Indian pearls which she had salvaged when she fled from the house of her first husband, the Great Secretary Liang. She now took from the chest a magnificent dark blue sapphire in a golden bezel.

"Old Kung Kung himself wore this on his court cap," she said. "It weighs close on a half an ounce. Please take it to the goldsmith and have him make a pair of ear pendants out of it."

Then she brought out a gold hairnet, nine ounces in weight.

"Do your wives wear such hairnets as this?" she asked him.

"No, two or three of them have silver ones."

"I should not like to outshine them too conspicuously. Take the net to the goldsmith, too. Let him break it up and make something different out of it. He shall make a nine-linked necklet, each link to represent a phœnix holding a pearl in its beak. Let him use any surplus gold as encrustation on a jade figure of Kwan Yuen, inlaid in a golden Swastika symbol. I should like to wear the whole as a brooch. It is to be made exactly like Moon Lady's brooch."

"Very good." Hsi Men nodded and slipped both the valuable ornaments into the pockets of his sleeves.

When he stepped out into the park a little later, he saw Gold Lotus standing before the eastern door. Her hair was disheveled and she wore her meanest apparel.

250

"Where are you going?" she asked.

"I have to attend to something in the city."

"Why are you running away so fast? I particularly want to speak to you."

Hearing the note of entreaty in her words, he obliged her by turning back. She grasped him by the arm and led him into her pavilion. There she sat down and drew him close to her with both hands.

"I don't want to quarrel with you, but you're a droll fellow to run from me so, as if you were a little boy caught in the act of stealing jam. It seems to me you're trying to hide something from me."

"Let me go, please! I have urgent business on hand. We can continue the conversation when I have attended to it." He rose impatiently and sought to disengage himself; but her hand, sliding along his sleeve, came into contact with something hard and heavy.

"What is that? Let me see!" she begged.

"That? Why, just my purse!"

She did not believe him; she darted her hand into the pocket of his sleeve and triumphantly brought to light the gold hairnet.

"Well, look at that! And what are you going to do with it?"

"Oh, she asked me whether you too had such golden trinkets. When I told her that you hadn't, she thought it would be better not to outshine you too much. She told me I had better take it to the goldsmith to be made up into something else."

"How heavy is the thing? And what's going to be done with it?"

"It weighs nine ounces. She would like to have a nine-linked necklet instead, each link to represent a phœnix holding a pearl in its beak. And whatever gold is left over is to be used as encrustation on a jade figure of Kwan Yuen, to be inlaid in a gold Swastika symbol. She wants to wear just the same kind of brooch as Moon Lady."

Gold Lotus made a rapid calculation.

"About three and a half ounces of gold at the outside for the necklet, and for the brooch one and a half will be ample. There will be four ounces of gold left over. With that you must have just such a phœnix necklet made for me too! Please, I beg you!"

"I'm afraid your calculation is incorrect. The brooch is to be a thoroughly substantial piece of work."

"Let it be as substantial as you like—two or three ounces will certainly be left over, and that's enough for a phœnix necklet," she insisted.

"What a woman you are! You know how to squeeze a profit out of everything, even if it's no bigger than a pinpoint."

And with a laugh he freed himself from her embrace.

Mistress Ping's dramatic entry into Hsi Men's household was not regarded very favorably by the rest of his wives, who stood coolly aloof from her, and subjected her every action to a merciless criticism. When she ventured to ask Hsi Men to send one of his own servants to guard her house in Lion Street, even the usually equable Moon Lady was incensed, regarding the request as an unheard-of piece of arrogance and presumption.

When that morning, while Hsi Men was discharging his commission at the goldsmith's, she appeared, in conformity with polite usage, before the assembled wives, she had to endure many mocking and ironical remarks. Even the two maids, Little Jewel and Jade Flute, permitted themselves several impudent comments. She felt profoundly embarrassed, alternately flushing and turning pale; she breathed a sigh of relief when at last this trying visit was over, and she was once again alone in her pavilion. Soon after this Hsi Men came in.

"Moon Lady thinks that your servant, Lai Wang, whom you were going to send to Lion Street, cannot very well be spared, and his wife is unwell," she said, in a rather disheartened tone. "Perhaps it would be better if you sent someone else, and then only every other night, in order to relieve Tien Fu from time to time."

"Very well, I will send Ping An every second night," he agreed.

On the twenty-fifth the great banquet took place which Hsi Men had promised his friends, and to which they had so long looked forward. No less than four dancing-girls, among them Cinnamon

Bud and Silver Bud, as well as their brothers, Li Ming and Wu Hui, both gifted singing-boys, provided entertainment for the numerous male guests. In the afternoon they amused themselves in the park and the belvedere with songs and dances and various games, and in the evening seven tables were laid for the principal feast in the great banqueting hall.

During the meal, when the guests were already in the most festive of moods, Beggar Ying rose to his feet and requested amidst the boisterous applause of his fellows, that the 'New One' might show herself in the hall, in order to receive the homage of the guests. He and his friends would behave quite properly for once. For that matter, owing to the presence of her brother, the elder Hua, and of Moon Lady's brother also, it was incumbent upon her to show herself. Hsi Men endeavored to persuade Beggar Ying to withdraw his proposal; but in vain. The guests besieged him with their entreaties, until at last he sent his boy Tai to summon Mistress Ping. It was a long while, however, before Lady Ping could be prevailed upon to come, and then only after much urgent persuasion on the part of Gold Lotus and Jade Fountain.

Arrayed in festive red, her tresses heavy with pearls and golden clasps, she finally appeared in the doorway, supported by her two maids, like a spray of blossoms swaying in the breeze. The four dancers, playing upon their flutes and their lutes, composed her retinue. The path which her feet were to tread was laid with highly-colored rugs and soft carpets. A cloud of fragrance, odorous of musk and orchid, hovered about her, and as she moved a gentle rustling was heard, like that of the wind playing in the foliage of young bamboos. Her gait was divine as that of the fairy from the Palace of the Moon.

Her appearance silenced all conversation in the hall. The guests rose from their seats, responding to her slight nod of the head with low and repeated bows.

Meanwhile, hidden behind a screen, Gold Lotus, Jade Fountain, and Sunflower, surrounding Moon Lady like a bamboo hedge, observed with burning curiosity the scene in the banquet hall, while

253

they listened to the tender strains of the music that rose and fell like the cooing of a pair of courting phœnixes.

"This wedding music seems to me extremely tactless and in very bad taste," Gold Lotus whispered in Moon Lady's ear. "If these two are really going to regard their relationship as an intimate, life-long union, as the music would seem to signify, then what is to become of you, Sister?"

The stab went home. The good-natured Moon Lady felt a bitter taste in her mouth, as though she had bitten upon a cypress kernel. The fact is that she was greatly vexed to see how the 'New One' was being toasted and admired by Hsi Men's friends.

"You are right," she replied. "What good do I get from all my virtue, from my chaste life within these walls? We live but once. A man who has been so amazingly favored by fortune as Hsi Men cares not a straw for my womanly virtues. For such as we death is the best fate."

At this very moment little Tai brought them Hsi Men's commands; they must all retire to their apartments. Naturally, they were by no means pleased with this order, and they vented their resentment on the messenger, addressing him in the most uncomplimentary terms.

A little later Mistress Ping herself left the hall, the four grateful singing-girls, to each of whom she had given five pieces of silver and a gold-fringed handkerchief, clustering round her and flattering her. "Noble Lady" they babbled, "Esteemed Lady," while their hands admiringly stroked the folds of her magnificent robe, or inquisitively fingered the valuable ornaments with which her tresses were adorned.

Moon Lady was sitting listlessly in her chamber when Tai and Ping An entered. They brought her, on behalf of Hsi Men, in commemoration of the festival, various presents, such as dress materials, fruits, sweetmeats, and money.

Moon Lady, hardly condescending to glance at the servants, asked them indignantly: "What is this stuff doing here? Take it to the front of the house, please, to the Fifth!"

"The master meant it expressly for you," they replied gently.

Moon Lady brusquely waved them away and told Jade Flute to lay the boxes containing the presents on the bed.

Immediately thereafter she received a visit from her elder brother, who had left the table in order to stretch his legs in the corridors.

"Sister, I hear that for a long time you have not been on speaking terms with your husband," he said, in a tone of friendly admonition. "I want to advise you most earnestly to change your attitude towards him. After all, he has honored me with his invitation today, and he has just shown you a mark of attention. If you persist in defying him you will lose the affection he used to feel for you. Be a little more compliant; don't oppose him in future, and you will find that he will be quite friendly again."

"You don't understand the situation. The New One is a rich woman. I, on the contrary, am in his eyes merely the daughter of a poverty-stricken official. As such I am naturally neglected. What profit have I of all my wifely virtues? It is just that he is inwardly estranged from me. But don't distress yourself on that account; I have plenty of company without him."

Though she strove to speak bravely, she could not repress a few tears.

"I cannot share your point of view. After all, we have no reason to be ashamed of our family. Really, you must try to live on better terms with him! We should both be gainers."

Their conversation was interrupted by the entrance of a servant, who informed him that he was missed at the table.

From that day onwards Mistress Ping was Hsi Men's avowed favorite. He took hardly any notice of his other wives. Gold Lotus suffered most from this state of affairs. All her efforts were now directed toward sowing dissension between Moon Lady and the Sixth. In Moon Lady's company she inveighed against Mistress Ping, while to the latter she would speak of Moon Lady as an insufferable person; and Mistress Ping who was easily influenced, now became extremely friendly with Gold Lotus.

Hsi Men's prosperity was considerably increased by his union with the rich Mistress Ping. But even without this, his was a brilliant establishment. His fields were blessed with fertility, and fortune smiled upon all his commercial undertakings. He had therefore no need to stint his household expenditure. On his country estate, as in his town house, everything was perfect and in meticulous order. His granaries were filled to bursting, he had mules and horses in herds, and he had a whole battalion of servants. Besides Tien Fu, whom he had taken over from Mistress Ping (his name being changed to King Tung), his domestic staff was increased by two new servants. The maids, Spring Plum, Jade Flute, Pear Blossom, and Fragrant Orchid enjoyed his special favor, and were handsomely rewarded with clothing and finery. He also engaged, at a monthly salary, the young and talented musician Li Ming, Cinnamon Bud's brother. He had to apply himself diligently to giving the four maids daily music lessons; so that Spring Plum learned the pear-shaped six-stringed *pi pa,* Jade Flute the twelve-stringed psaltery, Pear Blossom the viol, and Fragrant Orchid the five-stringed guitar.

Hsi Men's superfluous capital required investment. He therefore decided to open a pawnshop next door to his apothecary shop, and for this purpose he set aside two thousand ounces of silver as loan capital. He entrusted his steward, Fu, and his secretary, Pen Se, with the management of this new enterprise; while his son-in-law, Chen, exercised a general supervision and took charge of the key of the strong room. While the upper story of Gold Lotus's pavilion served as a warehouse for the pharmaceutical products, a room in the upper story of the new pavilion was fitted up for storing the pledged articles, and provided with the necessary wardrobes and chests of drawers.

The new venture met with immediate success, and very soon clothing and ornaments, antiquities and curios began to accumulate in the store room. Young Chen discharged his duties with zeal and devotion; he was on his feet early in the morning, and allowed himself no rest until late at night. Conscientiously he kept an account of the incoming and outgoing moneys, and the issuing and accepting of pawn tickets. Hsi Men had every reason to be satisfied with him.

"My dear son-in-law," he said one day, as they were dining together in the front hall, "I am very well satisfied with your progress. I am glad to think that in business matters I can depend upon you completely. Your father, too, in Kai fong fu, will be happy to hear this. If one has no son of one's own, one must look to a son-in-law for support; that is an old saying. And should male offspring continue to be denied to me, then one day all my property will pass to you and your wife."

"My dear father-in-law," young Chen replied modestly, "I have already much to thank you for. When misfortune struck my family you provided my wife and myself with a place of refuge in your house. I shall hardly be able to repay you for all your goodness. Moreover, I am still young and inexperienced: I hope that it will be long before you have to realize your intention."

This answer pleased Hsi Men exceedingly, and from that time forward he promoted Chen to a position of greater trust, allowed him to undertake important personal correspondence, and at feasts and banquets he brought him into contact with influential people. Hsi Men never dreamed that this crafty fellow was to become a needle in the wadding, a positive thorn in the flesh.

It was in the first third of the eleventh month that Hsi Men, after a long absence, once more paid a visit to Mother Li's establishment. Together with Beggar Ying and Hsia Hsi Ta he had taken tea at Chang Shih Kia's, and towards evening, as he was riding homewards with his friends through a heavy snowstorm, he allowed them, when they reached the neighborhood of Eastern Street, to persuade him to make a passing call on Cinnamon Bud.

"In this desolate weather one is doubly inclined to refresh oneself with the sight of a precious winter calycanthus blossom," said Beggar Ying, and Hsia added: "Ying is perfectly right. You have been neglecting her for months. Why do you make the beauty a monthly allowance of twenty pieces of silver?"

But when they had made themselves comfortable in Mother Li's warm guest room, a disappointment lay in store for them. The winter calycanthus blossom, the sight of which was to bring them joy, did not make its appearance. They were forced to console themselves with the society of Cinnamon Bud's elder sister and old Mother Li.

"Where's the little one?" Hsi Men asked impatiently.

"Ah, noble gentleman, for weeks past she has longed for your coming every day. Well, since you never put in an appearance, she could not imagine that you would come today, so she went off in the litter to see her fifth aunt, in order to felicitate her on her birthday."

This, of course, was a lie. As a matter of fact Cinnamon Bud had not set foot outside the house; at this very moment she was comfortably seated in a private room at the back of the house amusing herself with her new friend, a young silk merchant from Hangchow. He had recently arrived from Hangchow with his father and a shipment of silk, and having two days earlier sold the greater part of the shipment for a thousand ounces of silver, he had then given his father the slip. Providing himself with ten pieces of silver and a handsome dress of rich satin, he had hurried off to Cinnamon Bud. This was the second night he had spent with her. When Hsi Men had arrived so unexpectedly, old Mother Li had speedily called the couple out of the front guest room, and had taken them to a small secret chamber at the back of the house.

"Well, bring us something to drink for the time being! We can wait until the little one returns," Hsi Men replied peevishly when he heard the unwelcome news.

For a time the men amused themselves with drinking and throwing the knuckle bones whilst Cinnamon Bud's elder sister did her best to distract them by singing a few songs.

Then Hsi Men rose and went out into the back yard to relieve himself. There, as luck would have it, he heard merry laughter proceeding from a little room situated in the east wing of the house. Overcome with curiosity, he crept under the window of the room in question, and furtively peeped inside. There he beheld Cinnamon Bud, drinking and dallying with a young man. The square cap on the latter's head betrayed the fact that he hailed from the Southern provinces.

At the sight a blazing fire seemed to rise from Hsi Men's body to his head. Like a man possessed he stormed into the guest room, seized the table, and overthrew it, so that plates, dishes, and cups rolled across the floor and were shattered into shards. Then, with a shout, he called in the two servants who had accompanied him, and ordered them then and there to smash everything in the house, sparing neither the windows, the doors, nor the walls.

"Where's that fellow, that Southern scoundrel?" he roared into the courtyard. "Out with him! And bring a rope! Bind him and the powder-face together! And shut them up in the gate-chamber so everybody can see them!"

Young Ting was by no means a hero; indeed, he was so terrified by the threatening cries that he hastily crawled under the bed. Cinnamon Bud threw him a glance full of contempt.

"Pah! What's all the commotion about?" she asked nonchalantly. "We often have to go through scenes like this. After all, Mother's there. Come out of that and let him roar!"

But old Mother Li sought in vain to appease the infuriated man, and to lie herself out of the situation. He raged like a ravening wolf, and there was no quieting him. Only with difficulty could his friends restrain him from attacking the old woman herself. At last his fury abated, and with a solemn oath that he would never again set foot across the threshold of the house, he mounted his horse and rode off into the wintry night.

CHAPTER EIGHTEEN: *Moon Lady pours Tea made with fresh Snow. Beggar Ying conveys an Invitation from the Flower Garden*

WHEN HSI MEN arrived home late that night the weather had already cleared. The constellation of the Great Bear shone brightly from the northern quarter of the firmament. Hsi Men crossed the inner courtyard, stamping over the soft and glittering layer of fine white crystals, and made his way towards the gate that led into the women's apartments. He noted with astonishment that the gate stood half-open, which was something unusual at this late hour. Hurriedly he concealed himself in the shadow of a buttress close to the gate and waited to see what would happen.

And then he saw Little Jewel come out. She carried a low altar, which she set down not far from the gate, in the covered gallery which, open on one side, ran the length of the wall. Hsi Men did not yet know that ever since the beginning of their quarrel, Moon Lady was accustomed to fast thrice monthly and to perform seven kowtows before the constellation of the Great Bear, at the same time burning incense, hoping to bring about a change in her husband's attitude.

When Little Jewel had set the usual requisites for burning incense on the little table, Hsi Men saw Moon Lady, in ceremonial dress, approaching with measured step. She carefully swept the ground about the table with a broom; then she knelt down on a cushion, lit a fire in the incense bowl, and kindled a stick of incense. Turning towards the northern heavens she bowed seven times, and he distinctly heard her murmur a prayer:

"I, the humble handmaiden of the line of Wu, see with sorrow

260

how my spouse, Hsi Men, casts away his heart in the houses of wine-bibbing and flowers. Of all his six wives, not one, alas, has been able to present him with male offspring. When he is dead there will be no son to sweep his grave clean or to offer consoling sacrifices to his departed spirit. Day and night is my heart troubled. Who will now be the prop of his old age? In the sight of the nocturnal firmament, I implore thee, O propitious constellation: lend me thy splendor and succor me, let his heart turn once more towards this humble handmaiden, in order that he may be blessed with offspring to continue his line. This is the sincere prayer of this humble handmaiden."

Even before Hsi Men had heard her to the end he was overcome with a feeling of profound shame. What injustice he had done this woman, who was praying for him in the cold winter night, revealing such a loyal and devoted character!

He could no longer contain himself in his hiding place against the wall; but with long, quick strides he stepped up to her, and deeply moved, he threw his arms about her. She was not a little startled when he appeared before her so suddenly and silently in the snow-covered courtyard. Indeed, for a moment she sought to escape from him and make off through the gate. But he held her fast in his powerful arms.

"Sister, I've been a fool. Until this moment I didn't know what a good soul you were," he said, with emotion. "How unjustly I have behaved to you! I regret my fault with all my heart and soul!"

At first she maintained a cool reserve.

"I suppose you have mistaken the door in the snow," she said, in a casual tone. "After all, I'm the bad woman who has long been unworthy of your love, and the sight of whom is hateful to you. What have you to say to me now?"

He did not answer, but took her by the hand and led her silently to her room. By the light of the lamp he scrutinized her closely. For the first time he remarked how tastefully she was dressed, how perfectly her yellow jupon matched her red coat, how becoming was her sable toque, how delightful was her brooch—a jade image of Kwan Yuen, in a golden setting! Was she not truly lovable? The very low bow which he now made before her was more than a mere courteous formality.

"My eyes have been stricken with blindness hitherto," he said, in a voice which spoke of genuine devotion. "My ear was deaf and heedless of your well-meaning words. How grievously have I sinned against you! How could I pay attention to common pebbles and neglect this glorious jade! A thousand, ten thousand times I beg your forgiveness!"

"I am not accustomed to meddling in your affairs, so I don't know how I came to give you well-meaning advice," she replied obstinately. "I am content to live quietly in my rooms, and I shall be glad if you will trouble yourself no further about me. I have no conveniences to offer you here, and I would beg you to leave the room as soon as possible. You don't wish me to call the maid to show you the door?"

"I have been terribly upset today, and I came here through all the snow on purpose to open my heart to you. Come, do be kind!" he pleaded.

"What does it matter to me if you were upset? I don't wish you to open your heart to me. Please confide in anyone else!"

Since she lowered her eyes and avoided looking at him, he crouched before her like a dwarf in order to enter her field of vision. Finally he knelt at her feet, croaking the words: "Dear Sister, precious Sister!" again and again, in the lamentable, broken voice of a hen that has just had its throat cut.

Still she refused to look at him. "Your puppyish whining and cringing is unbearable. I shall call the maid," she said, and she summoned Little Jewel.

Hsi Men scrambled to his feet in embarrassment, and anxiously considered how he could get rid of the girl. "Be quick and bring in the incense table that you left standing outside. It will be covered with snow," he said.

"It was brought in long ago," was the pert answer.

Moon Lady could contain herself no longer: "You impudent

knave, aren't you ashamed of such pretences even before the maid?"
she scolded him, repressing her laughter.

In the meantime the maid had tactfully withdrawn. Hsi Men immediately fell on his knees again, and once more began to whimper.

At last Moon Lady relented. "Well, I suppose in a hundred
years or so I could try to put up with you again," she said, jestingly,
and she allowed him to sit beside her. Jade Flute was ordered to
serve tea, and with that they concluded peace. Hsi Men gave her
a circumstantial account of his exasperating experience at Mother
Li's, and he confessed how he had raged and had sworn a solemn
oath never again to set foot over the threshold of a pleasure house.

"You yourself ought to know what to do and what not to do.
At all events you have learned now that your good ringing gold
won't prevent such a person from having another man. You can't
muzzle the feelings, even though you bind the body with a hundred
cords, and seal them too!"

"You are right," he agreed thoughtfully. Then he dismissed the
maid, undressed himself, and lay down on the bed. Moon Lady
understood the beseeching expression in his eyes.

"It can't be very comfortable lying like that," she said with a
roguish smile. "But if you really must take your ease on my bed,
pray do so! But don't imagine for a moment——!"

Instead of answering her he rose, embraced her passionately, and
drew her down on to the bed.

Early the next morning, Jade Fountain appeared in front of
Gold Lotus's pavilion.

"Is Sister Five already up?" she asked the maid, Spring Plum.

"She's just curling her hair. Please come in!"

Jade Fountain entered, and found Gold Lotus sitting at her
dressing table, busily arranging her fragrant clouds of hair.

"Sister, I have important news! Have you already heard?" Jade
Fountain exclaimed, quite breathless.

"What great news could I have heard here, far from any drop
of human saliva? Well, what has happened?"

"Just think, when he came home late last night he went to

263

Moon Lady and made it up with her! He slept with her all night long! What do you say to that? My little Fragrant Orchid learned it from his boy early this morning in the kitchen. Yesterday evening he was in Mother Li's place with a couple of friends, intending, as a matter of fact, to take his pleasure with Cinnamon Bud. Then and there he caught the hussy with another man, and in his fury he smashed all the furniture to pieces. Through the snowstorm, in the middle of the night, he came riding home, foaming with rage. And by chance Moon Lady was in the courtyard just then, burning incense. He listened to her unseen, and then there was a sudden reconciliation. There was no end of talk, he fell on his knees before her and whimpered like a dog. She went for him at first, but afterwards she magnanimously forgave him. Isn't that touching?"

"The hypocrite!" said Gold Lotus, contemptuously. "If she had been in earnest she could have said her prayers quietly in her room by herself. Why this public exhibition in the courtyard? All calculation, of course! She told herself that she might very possibly be surprised by him at her devotions, and that would make a great impression on him. Well, we see once again that hypocrisy's the best policy. By sitting quietly and comfortably in one's room and taking care not to give one's husband any good advice or to tell him any candid truths—that's the way to win affection!"

"I shouldn't call her a hypocrite, exactly," said Jade Fountain, seeking to defend Moon Lady now that she was attacked. "She certainly has a good heart, and she always wants everything to be in perfect harmony. It is just that she's a rather awkward speaker; she can't rightly express what she feels. But do make haste and get ready! We'll go to the Sixth together. It goes without saying, we shall have to arrange a little banquet in honor of Moon Lady, to celebrate this happy occasion. I thought each of us could contribute one and a half ounces towards the expense. The Sixth, of course, must give double the amount. After the banquet we'll all go out to see the snow in the park, and then for the rest of the day we'll do nothing but drink and play and make merry. Oh, it's going to be splendid!"

"Agreed. But let's hope that Hsi Men has no other plans for today!"

"He will hardly go out in the snow. When I passed the First's bedroom no one was stirring within. They had only just opened the door so that Little Jewel could take in water for washing."

Gold Lotus quickly finished dressing, and set out with Jade Fountain for the new pavilion. The Sixth was still asleep in bed when they arrived.

"Sister Three and Sister Five are here," announced Pear Blossom to her mistress, and almost as she spoke the two entered the room.

"Up, Sister, up! Still in bed at this hour, sprawling like a slothful dragon!"

Gold Lotus, always ready for a jest, slipped a hand under the bedclothes, and feeling a silver perfume ball, she quickly drew it out, crying, with a laugh: "Look, the Sixth has given birth to a ball!" Then she pulled the bedclothes right off, so that the Sixth lay revealed in all her rosy nudity, and at last made ready to get up.

"Sister Five, stop your crazy jokes! We've got to talk sensibly to the Sixth," said Jade Fountain, scolding Gold Lotus. While Lady Ping was dressing she related in all its particulars the great event that had taken place in the household.

"And today there's to be a joyful celebration!" she concluded. "You, of course, must make a double contribution toward the cost of the feast, since after all you are to blame for the whole story. Had it not been for you, he wouldn't have neglected Cinnamon Bud until she became unfaithful to him."

The Sixth acquiesced, and ordered Pear Blossom to fetch a bar of silver from the treasure chest. Gold Lotus ascertained its precise weight on the scales, which was more than the required three ounces.

"Sister Five, I'll run to the back of the house and collect contributions from Sunflower and Snowblossom," Jade Fountain proposed. "Do you keep Sister Six company in the meantime."

And so for an hour Gold Lotus watched Lady Ping making her ceremonial toilet. Then Jade Fountain reappeared.

"A difficult job it was to get round those two! I expected as much," she reported. "That woman, Snowblossom, began to grumble straight away. She was only a luckless creature anyhow, and no man ever came to her chamber! She wanted to be left out of the party, if you please! It took all my arts of persuasion to induce her at last to sacrifice this silver hairpin. See what it weighs, will you, Sister Five?"

Gold Lotus laid the pin on the scales.

"It's not an ounce," she said disdainfully.

"And Sunflower?"

"Gave me a downright refusal at first. True, she had charge of the household budget, but everything was so accurately calculated that there was nothing for extra expenses. At last, when I was running off in a temper, she called me back and brought out this piece of silver."

Gold Lotus weighed it. "That's not the full weight either. What a scurvy pair! There's no help for it, we must just make up the difference out of our own pockets."

They added jointly to the contributions, so that the sum of three ounces was made up. Then Tai, after he had been exhaustively cross-examined as to the incident at Mother Li's on the previous day, was sent into town with Lai Hsing, to purchase the best Golden Blossom wine, some fowls, and various other delicacies.

In the reception room at the back of the house, which was comfortably furnished with carpets, screens, and curtains, and pleasantly warmed with braziers, the banquet was held at the hour of noon. Hsi Men had enriched the board with a jar of Jasmine Perfume wine from his own private cellar. He sat with Moon Lady at the head of the table, while his five other wives and his daughter took their seats on either side. Young Chen once more had a place assigned to him at a little table not far from his wife. After this long interval the whole family found itself once more united and in harmony. Moon Lady was toasted as she deserved. Flattering speeches and jests were exchanged across the table, the guests vied with one another in merriment, and bygone discords were forgotten in the jollity of the occasion. The four handmaidens, Spring Plum, Pear Blossom, Jade Flute and Fragrant Orchid, provided the music, and gave proof of the progress which they had made under their master, Li Ming. That they should have sung the Pomegranate Blossom Song was due, of course, to the instigation of the wanton Gold Lotus. For the pomegranate is universally familiar as a symbol of great fecundity. Hsi Men, who understood the allusion perfectly, could not refrain from calling playfully to Gold Lotus:

"From you, of course, one can pluck only sterile blossoms!"

While they cheerfully dined and chatted indoors, outside the windows there was a whirling as of great flocks of cotton, as of dancing pear-blossom petals. What a beautiful spectacle was this snowfall!

At first the flakes float one by one
Like stray pussy willows.
Then they teem like down
When a goose-feather bed is shaken.
Now they come sweeping and creeping
Like crabs over the ground.
Soon white layers accumulate
Of powdery crystals.
The wanderer's coat is wet.
And he brushes them off his face
Like one who waves his hands
To ward off a swarm of bees.
See, from bush to bush
The undulating masses
Might well be the fabled dragon
About to soar off into the clouds.
Whoo! a sudden gust of wind
That makes the wanderer hunch his shoulders
And shudder
Flaps against his forehead

Like a feather the white crane
Has lost in flight.
Now it is clearing yonder,
And under the break is a gleam
As of rice husks after the thrashing.
The smooth earth lies
A sea of silver.

For some time the whole company diverted themselves by watch‧
ing the frolicsome play of the snowflakes outside the window. Moon
Lady now rose, and accompanied by Little Jewel, who was told to
bring a teakettle, she stepped out into the snow-covered courtyard.
With her own hand she swept a portion of the path clear of its
white coverlet; then she filled the kettle with fresh snow, and with
her own hand she poured tea for the group assembled round the
table. On this occasion she employed a special blend of the noble
Phœnix and the mild Lark's Tongue teas.

In the jasper crock
Light puffs of crystalline vapor;
From the golden bowls
A mild, rare fragrance mounts.

While they were enjoying the beverage which Moon Lady had
prepared for them, Cinnamon Bud's brother, the young musician,
Li, was announced.

"Most opportune!" cried Hsi Men to his boy. "Bring him in!"

Li Ming entered, kowtowed before the company, and remained
modestly standing at the door.

"Whence do you come?" asked Hsi Men.

"From Eunuch Li, who lives in the north of the city not far from
the Wine and Vinegar Gate. There are some children there to
whom I give lessons in music. On the way back it occurred to me
that several pieces of music which I had the honor of rehearsing in
your esteemed house did not as yet sound quite harmonious. So I
did not wish to miss the opportunity. . . ."

"Excellent. You can play something for us. But first refresh yourself."

And Hsi Men led him to a little table apart from the banquet table and cordially offered him a bowl of tea.

After Li Ming had refreshed himself, he took the twelve-stringed psaltery in his hand, approached the table, and sang the song: "Spring Meeting in Winter."

When he had ended Hsi Men amiably beckoned to him to approach his chair, and ordered Jade Flute to fill a silver goblet three times over with wine, which Li Ming drank on his knees. He also ordered four plates of various meats from the banquet table to be served to him on a tray. Li Ming retired to his place, ate with relish, wiped his mouth clean, and once more took up his position against the wall, not far from where Hsi Men was sitting. Hsi Men now told him, under his breath, what had happened at Mother Li's the night before.

"Oh, this is the first I have heard of it; I haven't been there for a long time. I am convinced," said Li Ming, glibly, "that it was entirely the old woman's fault. You ought not to be angry with Sister Cinnamon Bud on that account! I shall speak to her, and everything will be all right again."

Hsi Men did not contradict him. When at the first hour of the evening they rose from the table, and Hsi Men bade the young musician farewell, he whispered to him:

"But don't tell her that you were here today!"

An injunction that Li Ming naturally took care to understand in the contrary sense.

It was on the following morning, while Hsi Men was still at breakfast with Moon Lady, that Beggar Ying and Hsia Hsi Ta were announced. Hsi Men at once laid aside the slice of cake which he was nibbling, and rose to welcome his early callers.

"Let them wait!" said Moon Lady peevishly. "All this haste for the sake of such devil's envoys! What can they be wanting of you, anyhow? Of course, they'll ask you to go out with them. That would be crazy enough in this snowy weather! Moreover, today is the eve of Jade Fountain's birthday."

"Send the cakes and tea into the front room; I'll finish my breakfast with them," Hsi Men insisted. He had a presentiment that the two were bringing him some sort of message from old Mother Li's establishment, towards which, in spite of everything, he still felt powerfully attracted. As a matter of fact, this was so: the two friends had come on behalf of Cinnamon Bud. Early that morning she had sent them a roast goose and a jug of wine, and had earnestly begged them to propitiate Hsi Men by fair means or foul.

"We reproached her most seriously," the two friends began. "We reminded her what innumerable benefits you had bestowed upon her house. It was inexcusable to have an affair behind your back with a Southern scoundrel like that, and for no better reason than that you hadn't shown yourself for a few days. Our words made a deep impression. With tears in her eyes, and on her knees, she implored us to intercede with you on her behalf, and you ought not to refuse her request to drink a cup of watery wine at her house."

"That's all very well," said Hsi Men. "But I am not going there again."

"We understand your resentment perfectly. But you are actually doing Cinnamon Bud an injustice. She was truly not to blame. This young Ting was really the friend of her elder sister. But just on that unlucky evening he wanted to arrange a little celebration in honor of a young countryman (the son of the shipowner in whose vessel he had come with his father and a consignment of silk two days before from Hangchow). He had paid a good ten ounces in advance, and Mother Li naturally didn't want to offend her generous guest when we called so unexpectedly, so she felt that she was bound in courtesy to let Cinnamon Bud keep him company. And so, in her very natural confusion, she spirited the two away into the back room, and then tried to conceal their presence from us. It was simply an unlucky coincidence; nothing more. There was never the least familiarity between the two. They were just sitting innocently together, we assure you! Now the misunderstanding is cleared up, and you needn't be angry any longer with the little one."

"There is no question of being angry. But I have sworn a solemn oath never to go there again. Give her my best wishes, and tell her I thank her for the invitation, but she need not trouble herself, as there are some trifling affairs that detain me at home."

The two friends fell simultaneously on their knees.

"But, dear friend, you need not forswear yourself in the least, if you just pay her a short visit as a matter of courtesy. Who is asking more than that of you?"

Thus they entreated and plagued him until he yielded. All his good intentions were forgotten again, and when he had finished his breakfast, to the great grief of the good Moon Lady, he left the house with his two friends.

The house of Li had taken all pains to give him a worthy welcome. Kneeling, and simulating the most heartfelt contrition, Mother Li greeted him at the threshold of the house. Besides Cinnamon Bud and her elder sister, two pretty singing-girls awaited them. Cinnamon Bud was arrayed in her finest apparel, and she devoted herself exclusively to Hsi Men, pouring him one cup of wine after another, and overwhelming him with a hundred endearments.

"Well you might let us have a cup too, once in a while," Beggar Ying scolded, pretending to be offended. "We talked our mouths sore to fetch him here. Is this your gratitude? If he hadn't come you would have cried your little eyes blind, and tomorrow no one at all would have cared for you. You are behaving as meanly as one who has begged a pious sutra from a bonze, and then falls on the poor man and belabors him. Now, come here and give me a luke-warm kiss for my reward!"

And he had already clasped her about the neck and snatched his well-earned tribute; but the violent movements of the struggling pair upset a full cup of wine, the contents of which poured over Hsi Men's coat. This little accident broke the last bonds of constraint which had at first weighed upon the company. Soon the room resounded with laughter, jests and quips were bandied to and fro, and Hsi Men's rancor was banished to distant Javaland. None the less, Moon Lady's admonitions exercised such an influence over him that he summoned up the will power to return home early in the evening. At home a great banquet was being held as a prelude to the celebration of Jade Fountain's birthday. In perfect harmony, and playing all sorts of cheerful round games, they sat up together until a late hour. That night Jade Fountain was the chosen one to whom fell the honor of sharing her couch with Hsi Men.

CHAPTER NINETEEN: *Lotus Petal carries on an amorous Intrigue with Hsi Men. Gold Lotus spies upon them in the "Grotto of Hidden Spring"*

HSI MEN'S SERVANT, Lai Wang, had a charming little wife, whose name was Lotus Petal. The daughter of the coffin dealer Sung, she had been married originally to a cook who had often been engaged to help in Hsi Men's kitchen. Lai Wang had usually to fetch him whenever he was wanted, which was frequently the case, and so he made the acquaintance of the cook's charming wife. It often happened that he found her alone in the house, and so, beginning with gossip and dalliance, there soon developed a secret intrigue between the two. After the cook had been knifed in a brawl by one of his fellows, Lai Wang had taken his mistress to live with him, and had presented her to Moon Lady, ostensibly as his newly-married wife, and the good Moon Lady had granted him the permission he craved—namely, that Lotus Petal, whose practiced hands could be profitably employed in needlework, might henceforth live in the house. Further, she had bestowed a considerable marriage portion upon the couple.

Lotus Petal was a pretty, sprightly little creature of just four and twenty years, and with her faultless proportions—being neither too tall nor too short, neither too plump nor too thin—her fresh, blooming complexion, and her dainty little feet, she was just the sort of creature to drive men crazy and disturb the peaceful atmosphere of a respectable household.

She very soon succeeded in winning the affection of Hsi Men's wives and their handmaidens, and although at first she was innocent

273

of personal adornment, within a month she had studied her mistresses so attentively that she knew just how to do her hair and dress herself in the best of taste. In short, she had only to cross Hsi Men's line of vision, to kindle within him an ardent desire to possess her.

In order to effect his purpose he had dispatched Lai Wang to Hangchow at the beginning of the eleventh month—that is, a few days before the date of which we are writing. There he was to have tailored, as a birthday present for Hsi Men's noble patron, the Chancellor Tsai Ching, a complete wardrobe for every season of the year, from the serpent-embroidered robe of state to the ordinary everyday coat, at a total cost of five hundred ounces of silver. Hsi Men calculated that Lai Wang would be away for at least six months. Within this time he would surely accomplish what he wished!

Today, on Jade Fountain's birthday, Hsi Men was nowhere to be seen. He contented himself with standing behind the curtain of the reception room at the back of the house, where all his wives, with a number of congratulatory guests, were assembled round the banquet table, and looking on. Among the maids in attendance he discovered his Lotus Petal. "What singular taste, this slashed crimson skirt under a cinnabar-red coat!" he reflected. "These two shades of red don't match each other at all." At the same time it occurred to him that here was an opportunity of making the young woman's acquaintance.

He beckoned to Jade Flute.

"Is the young woman in red the wife of Lai Wang?"

"Yes."

"How can anyone dress with such lack of taste? I wish you would speak to your mistress tomorrow; she simply must provide her with a differently colored skirt."

"She borrowed the red skirt from me," said Jade Flute in a slightly injured tone.

One afternoon a day or two later it so happened that Moon Lady was away from home on a visit to a neighbor. Hsi Men had just returned from a drinking bout, and was about to step through the inner door that led to the women's apartments when he collided by chance with Lotus Petal. Flushed with wine as he was, he seized her without further ceremony, and pressed his lips upon her mouth.

"Listen, if you're nice and do what I want, you can have as many clothes as you like," he said thickly.

Laughing, she disengaged herself, and fled without a word in reply. Hsi Men, however, made his way to Moon Lady's sitting room, where he came upon Jade Flute.

"Take her this piece of blue satin," he told her under his breath, "and tell her to make herself a skirt out of it. That crimson stuff she was wearing recently over a cinnabar-red coat didn't suit her at all."

Jade Flute was shrewd enough to grasp his meaning. When Lotus Petal unfolded the length of beautiful blue satin, gayly embroidered with flowers of every season of the year, she asked the bearer: "But what am I to say, if the First wants to know where I got my new skirt?"

"You needn't worry about that," Jade Flute reassured her. "Our master will himself find an explanation. And he says you can have a great deal more if you are nice to him. It's fortunate that Moon Lady is away today."

"Am I to wait for him in my room? And when?"

"He would rather not go to you in your room. It might be noticed by the servants. However, you might slip into the park without attracting attention, and wait for him in the 'Grotto of Hidden Spring.' There you can be quite unobserved."

"But the Fifth lives close by!"

"Oh, she and the Third are at present in the new pavilion with the Sixth, playing chess."

As a matter of fact, Gold Lotus and Jade Fountain were at that moment in Lady Ping's pavilion, and all three were playing chess. Presently the maid, Little Phœnix, appeared and announced Hsi Men's return. Thereupon the three broke up their game of chess, Gold Lotus and Jade Fountain retiring to their several quarters. The impatient Gold Lotus, however, could not long endure waiting in her pavilion, and resolved to go in search of Hsi Men. When she came to the gate that led to the women's apartments she saw Little Jewel standing before it.

"Is your master in?" she asked. Little Jewel shook her head and pointed with her finger in the direction of the park. Gold Lotus understood and turned back. No sooner had she approached the gate of the new park than of a sudden Jade Flute came rushing up, and placed herself before the grille as though to prevent her entrance. Gold Lotus at once took offense. Angrily she thrust the maid aside and opened the grille.

"You mustn't go just now. The master does not wish to be disturbed," Jade Flute ventured to warn her.

"Silence, you scrap of dog's meat!" Gold Lotus cried in a fury. "Do you imagine that I'm afraid of him?"

And she at once hurried into the park. But her search was fruitless. Nowhere could she discover him whom she was seeking, and whom she suspected of having made a tryst with Jade Flute.

She now directed her footsteps past the "Grotto of Hidden Spring," when there came to her ears the tones of human voices from within, the voices of a man and of a woman. In a moment she was at the entrance to the grotto, and she was just in time to see Hsi Men and Lotus Petal break apart from a close embrace on the divan, hastily endeavoring to repair the extreme disorder of their dress. With a deep blush of shame on her face, Lotus Petal attempted to slip by and make her escape into the open.

"What are you doing here, you rancid carrion?" Gold Lotus reviled the girl.

"I was just looking for Snow Bud," she stammered in alarm, and she dashed off like a streak of vapor.

"Shameless scoundrel that you are! So you are her Snow Bud!" cried Gold Lotus, storming at the culprit, who was still nervously fingering his belt. "In broad daylight you dare to carry on with a miserable slave wench! If she hadn't made off so quickly I would have boxed her ears for her! Now confess, how long has this been going on? And no humbug, if you please! or I tell Moon Lady the whole story, and she will see that that sow, that hussy, gets her due!"

"Pst! Not so loud, or the others may hear us!" He smiled with embarrassment, seeking to appease her. "And to tell the honest truth, this was the first and only time. It just happened——"

"Oh, I don't believe that! But I shall soon find out for myself, and woe to you, you scoundrel, if you have been imposing on me!"

"Oh, let well alone!" he said, laughing, and he drew her out of the grotto into the park. Having cross-examined the maids, when she ascertained that he had really told her the truth, and that his intrigue with Lotus Petal had begun that very day, innocently enough at first, with the gift of the piece of blue satin, she was quickly reconciled, and preserved a discreet silence in respect of the whole affair. Even Jade Fountain, her greatest confidant, never had an inkling of the matter. On the other hand, Gold Lotus adopted the tactics of patronizing Hsi Men's latest favorite, and of calling upon her for all kinds of personal service. And so, thanks to her generous tolerance, Hsi Men was able to continue his secret meetings with Lotus Petal.

As time went on it naturally struck observers that Lotus Petal had suddenly begun to dress with far greater elegance than of old: that she carried whole ounces of shining silver about with her, and was a regular customer of the peddlers who loitered outside the gateway, offering hairpins and enamel feathers for sale. Again, the warmth with which Hsi Men had interceded with Moon Lady on her behalf could not escape attention, nor the manner in which he praised her skill in preparing tea, nor the fact that he insisted that she should be exempted from menial work in the kitchen, in order to share with Jade Flute the light duties of a maid in attendance on Moon Lady. Worthy reader, experience has long taught us that the gentry should never demean themselves with the common herd. For if the distinction between high and low be obliterated, then all domestic discipline vanishes with it, and presumptuous encroachments are the final result.

On the morning of the eighth day of the twelfth month, Hsi Men, together with Beggar Ying, was to attend the obsequies of a common acquaintance. The horses were already saddled, but Beggar

Ying, who was to call for Hsi Men, kept him waiting. Li Ming happened to be present, and in order to while away the time Hsi Men, ensconcing himself beside his son-in-law in front of the warm stove in the reception hall, asked the young musician to conduct his household orchestra, which consisted of the four maids, Spring Plum, Pear Blossom, Jade Flute, and Fragrant Orchid. At last, in the midst of their performance, Beggar Ying appeared. The four girls modestly wished to withdraw at once, but Hsi Men ordered them to remain.

"You needn't run away from Friend Ying! Go and bow to him prettily!"

The four beauties obediently curtsied to the visitor, and performed a respectful kowtow. Enraptured by this charming reception, Beggar Ying, greeting them in return, stuttered forth his *Wan fu* an unconscionable number of times.

"The fortunate fellow! Who can be compared with him?" he sighed in admiration. "To have about him four such lovely little sisters, like hyacinths in glasses, standing in a row on the window-sill, each one prettier than the next! What a pity that I come with empty hands! I was in such a hurry! But the next time I shall take the liberty of presenting you with a trifle for rouge and powder."

The four hyacinths had their own opinion as to that, and withdrew giggling. Hsi Men, together with Beggar Ying and young Chen, hastily partook of a little breakfast, which, apart from the never-failing boiled rice, comprised ten different meatless courses and three cups of heady Golden Blossom wine. He then departed with Beggar Ying. Before leaving the house, however—generous man that he was—he did not forget to order a substantial meal, consisting of the abundant remains of the breakfast dishes, to be served to young Li in the western wing.

For a while the four hyacinths played at various games in the same room in which their music master was enjoying his breakfast; then they retired to the eastern wing, in order to afford Hsi Men's daughter, Lady Chen, the pleasure of their company. Spring Plum alone stayed with Li Ming, as she wanted to practice a little longer on the lute under his direction. Stimulated by the rich repast and the excellent wine, Li Ming, seeing that he was alone with his charming pupil, thought to avail himself of this favorable opportunity. Approaching her closely, he boldly felt for the little hand that lay concealed in the folds of her capacious sleeve. But he was making a mistake. Spring Plum angrily drew back.

"How dare you dream of touching me, you abominable tortoise!" she spat at him. "Whom do you think you are dealing with? I dare say you *would* like to eat and drink your fill here, and then go poking your dirty dibble into other people's flower beds! But wait till Master Hsi Men returns! I'll tell him, and then you'll learn something! You'll be driven out of the house, you abominable tortoise!"

And after hurling a few dozen more verbal tortoises at his head, she tucked up her dress, flounced out of the room, and ran as fast as she could run, still scolding as she went, to the back hall, where Gold Lotus, Jade Fountain, Lady Ping and Lotus Petal were playing chess.

"What's the trouble, little dumpling?" asked Gold Lotus, glancing up at her.

Flushed and out of breath, Spring Plum told her story. "At first he grinned impudently, and then he was in a fright when I began to rage at him and ran away. It was lucky for him I did, or I would have boxed his ears. My fingers were itching to slap his face green and blue for him! A wretched tortoise like that!"

"Don't excite yourself so, little one!" said Gold Lotus equably. "It's bad for your complexion. Wait quietly until Master Hsi Men returns. He'll show the saucy knave the door. I saw through the fellow long ago; he infests other people's houses in order to seduce the daughters. But now the jug's full."

"But the second mistress, his aunt—she's sure to lay the blame on me," Spring Plum declared, rather despondently.

That same evening the gatekeeper Lai Hsing received strict orders that he was henceforth to refuse admittance to the young musician, Li Ming.

The furtive, hasty meetings with Lotus Petal, at which the initiated Jade Flute had usually to play the part of sentinel, and whose delights were greatly diminished by the constant dread of detection, could not satisfy Hsi Men. One evening toward the end of the twelfth month he spoke to Gold Lotus:

"Dear little oily-mouth, I should like to sleep with Lotus Petal tonight. Couldn't it be arranged here in your pavilion?"

"What! You are really oozing with perversity at every pore! But I won't quarrel with you. If you are positively lusting to amuse yourself with that lecherous wench, you may, for all I care. But where am I to make up a bed for you? I don't know where to find room for it. Besides, Spring Plum would hardly agree. Ask her and see!"

"Very well, I see it doesn't suit you women. I shall have to make the best of the 'Grotto of Hidden Spring.' But it's devilish cold there. Please see that the grotto is heated and have some bedclothes sent up!"

Gold Lotus could not suppress her laughter. "Look at the amorous King Hsiang, going to bed with his fairy on a cold winter's night among the bare, dripping rocks!"

But she did his bidding, and that very hour she sent her maid, Autumn Aster, to the grotto with the bedclothes. She had also to take a brazier filled with charcoal and to kindle a bright, cheery fire. In the meantime, Lotus Petal was given due notice by Jade Flute, and after she had finished waiting on Moon Lady she lingered for a while before the inner gate. When not even the front teeth of a solitary human being were to be seen she flitted into the park like a wreath of vapor. Hsi Men, candle in hand, was already awaiting her at the grotto.

This time King Hsiang's vigil
For the fairy is not long.
The magic mountain bestows its blessing,
And sheds the longed-for rain.

As she entered the grotto Lotus Petal encountered an icy draught, that made her shrink and shiver. The heat of the charcoal brazier could not do much to dispel the accumulated cold of three winter months. A thick layer of dust covered floor, table, and chairs. However, the aromatic clouds of smoke ascending from two incense tapers, together with the mellow light of the lamp and the red glow of the charcoal in the brazier, did do something to mitigate the dreary atmosphere of the inhospitable chamber. The two lovers made themselves as comfortable as they could in the improvised bed on the divan, the only possible resting place in the whole grotto. Hsi Men's wadded overcoat of sable had to serve as a counterpane.

While the lovers, locked in a close and passionate embrace, quickly forgot the cold, someone was standing and freezing outside the oriel window. Urged by an insuperable curiosity, Gold Lotus had silently crept hither, making her way over the hoar-frosted moss and through thickets armed with piercing thorns, in order to play the eavesdropper on the amorous couple. Now she heard merry laughter from within, and then she distinguished Lotus Petal's voice: "To think that I have to seek you in this icy cellar, in a dismal retreat like this! Are you so poverty-stricken that you can't find a better place? Why, the very saliva in one's mouth turns into icicles!"

And a moment later: "We can't sleep in this cold. Let's talk. Just look at my pretty little feet! In the whole house I can't find a pair of shoes to fit me. Wouldn't you like to have a pair made to measure for me some time?"

"If that is all you want!" he replied. "Tomorrow you can have a whole assortment in every color. I shouldn't have thought your feet were even smaller than those of my Fifth."

"Pah! However could you compare me with her! I tried her shoes on recently. My own found room to spare in them. Hers are only more handsomely worked."

"This is getting interesting," the eavesdropper outside said to herself. "I must see whether she has anything more to say about me!"

"How many autumns has your Fifth really frittered away?" she heard Lotus Petal ask presently. "And was she still a virgin or already married when you took her?"

"She had already met someone else."

"So she's been used to double harness a long time, has she? Of course, she's one of the rootless sort, who have to 'make their bed on the dew and feed on the air,' as the saying goes," said Lotus Petal disparagingly.

"Insolence!" the listener at the window muttered to herself. "Unheard-of impudence to speak of me as 'making my bed on the dew and feeding on the air!' To say nothing of 'frittering away my autumns!' If I were to tell the other women how this slut reviles us behind our backs there would be a pretty to-do! But for his sake I'll control myself. I'll soon find an opportunity of telling her what I think of her!"

And she ran off in a rage. But at the garden gate she came to a stop, took a silver brooch from her hair, and jammed it into the lock, in such a manner that the gate could no longer be opened from inside.

Next morning, when Lotus Petal wanted to slip out of the park unnoticed, she discovered, to her alarm, that the gate was bolted. In vain she shook it; it would not open. There was no help for it; she had to call Hsi Men to her assistance; and as he too was unable to force the gate, he had to shout over the fence to summon the maid Pear Blossom, who happened to be within call. Pear Blossom at last succeeded in opening the gate, after she had extracted the silver brooch which had been jammed into the lock. Hsi Men recognized it at once for the property of his Fifth, and now it was quite clear to the lovers that they had been overheard during the night by Gold Lotus.

Oppressed by the demons of a bad conscience, Lotus Petal scurried off to her room, which was in front of the house. In the courtyard upon which her room opened she nearly ran into the servant Ping An. He eyed her with an impudent grin. She pulled herself up. "What's there to laugh at?" she demanded severely.

"No need to lose your temper if one laughs a little!"

"You must have some reason for laughing so early in the morning."

"Dear sister-in-law, I understand why you are so touchy. You haven't been able to eat these three days past, you're so full of love, and now you see flowers dancing before your eyes. Your room was empty last night, wasn't it?"

A sudden red flushed her cheeks. "Why should it have been empty, you silly tattler? You must be seeing ghosts, you accursed son of a gallowsbird!" she stormed at him.

"All the same, with my own eyes I saw you locked out just now!"

"That may be. I've been with the Fifth early this morning!"

"Oh, yes! And the Fifth left you floundering, so that you couldn't stir from the spot any more than a crab on dry land! She also told us how prettily you can do the splits, and she says she'll send you out to the gate to buy a fan, so that you can fan your mouth dry, as it's . . ."

Convulsed with rage, Lotus Petal rushed across the yard and fell upon him.

"You filthy outcast, you! You wait, I'll tell someone of you, and you'll pay for your insolence!"

"I know whom you'll tell! Someone up and down whose branch you can clamber so well!" jeered Ping An.

Beside herself with fury, she raised her clenched fists to strike him in the face, when in the nick of time Tai issued from the near-by pawn shop. He at once sprang between them and separated the squabbling antagonists.

"But, sister-in-law, you surely weren't going to strike him!" he said, trying to quiet the infuriated Lotus Petal.

"Haven't I had sufficient provocation? That venomous reptile has insulted me so that I feel sore with rage!"

In the meantime Ping An had made off.

"Don't take it so to heart, sister-in-law!" said Tai, gently admonishing her. "You had better go to your room and tidy yourself up. Your hair is just anyhow!"

She felt in the purse at her girdle and gave him a few small pieces of broken silver. "Dear little brother, be so kind as to fetch me a tureen of thick, strong broth!"

"Gladly."

After she had refreshed herself, washed, and dressed her hair, she went out to give Moon Lady her customary morning greeting, after which she sought Gold Lotus.

Gold Lotus was sitting before the mirror, arranging her hair. She did not deign to favor her caller with so much as a glance. Eager to be of service, Lotus Petal dusted the mirror, poured fresh water into the washbasin, and in other ways endeavored to make herself useful.

"May I take off your bed slippers and undo your foot bandages?" Lotus Petal asked, in a timid voice.

"No! I have my own servants for that!" was the curt reply. "Autumn Aster! Where are you hiding, you silly thing?"

"She's sweeping the snow from the door outside. But Spring Plum is close by. Shall I call her?"

"Don't trouble yourself about her, but go! Go! Go to Master Hsi Men and wait on him! He will be delighted. What have you to do with such as we? After all, we are just wretched creatures who have to 'make our beds on the dew and feed on air,' who 'have long been broken in to double harness,' aren't we? Your case, my most esteemed sister-in-law, is entirely different. You, of course, were brought home by Hsi Men in the marriage litter as an honorable bride. You are his lawfully wedded wife. You have not 'frittered away your autumns' as we have, of course!"

Completely crushed, Lotus Petal sank to her knees. She saw that she was convicted of guilt. There could be no disguising the facts here.

"My fate lies in your hands, mistress. Be merciful!" she humbly pleaded. "It was because I thought at first that it was with your consent that I yielded to his solicitations. I know that in the rear apartments your word is law, and you are sovereign over all of us. Whatever I am I owe to your favor. Never again, I swear it, shall I venture to make game of you. Should I ever slander you by a single word, may I die a miserable death, then may my body break out in boils and ulcers set as close as hairs!"

"That will do," Gold Lotus interposed, moved to clemency once more. "You see, however, that not the smallest grain of sand escapes my notice. As far as I'm concerned, you may continue your intercourse with him. But once for all, I forbid you to say irresponsible things about me when you are with him. If you ever again take it into your head to trample on me with your straw-soled shoes, I promise you, I'll give you a kick in the belly that will make you caper. Be reasonable, Sister, and have done with your former malice!"

"I swear I will! But I'm afraid you rather misunderstood my words last night."

"I understood them well enough, you silly creature! And let me tell you another thing: there are men for whom not even ten wives are enough. Hsi Men is one of them. Do you think for a moment he finds you, me, the First, the Third, and the Sixth enough? Besides us, outside his own household he has his various powder-masks. But from me he conceals nothing; he tells me of every adventure. At the time when his First was full of grievances against him, he spent a lot of his time away from home. But when he came home he always told me everything candidly. So don't imagine that you can keep anything from me!"

Lotus Petal stood silent for a while, and then, completely subdued, she slipped out of the room.

Confident in the favor which Hsi Men bestowed upon her, Lotus Petal took greater liberties from day to day. She was especially fond of loitering in the gateway and buying the trashy wares of the passing peddlers. Thus it was natural that she should often come into contact with the steward, Fu, young Chen, and the secretary, Pen Se, who were employed in the two shops outside the gate; and she soon began to address the three men with a familiarity which was hardly befitting her servile condition. She disrespectfully called the steward Fu "Old Fellow," young Chen she addressed as "Son-in-law," and the secretary, Pen Se, as "Old Number Four," playing upon the character Se in his name, which signified "four."

Often enough, when the three were attending to customers, or reckoning up their accounts, they had to put up with Lotus Petal's sudden incursions. She would ask them to run into the street then and there, in order to keep a lookout for this or that peddler, because she was in urgent need of this or that. Her appetite for powder and rouge, scissors, ribbons and handkerchiefs, enameled feathers and fresh flowers for her hair, melon seeds, and other delicacies, which she would generously share with the other servants, was really enormous. And Hsi Men saw to it that she always had money. Under her short skirt she wore close-fitting hose of bright red satin, and in the pockets of her sleeves not one, but three flasks of perfume were concealed, and two boxes of tea paste. All her efforts were concentrated on keeping on the best of terms with Gold Lotus, whom she rightly regarded as the most influential of all of Hsi Men's six wives.

Her duties about Moon Lady were limited to paying her the conventional respects early in the morning. Apart from this she danced attendance exclusively on the Fifth; and the Fifth, for her part, required her not only to wait on her, but also to keep her company. She played chess with her, plied her with wine, and even invited her to table when Hsi Men was staying in her pavilion. All this for the love of Hsi Men.

> *The willow catkins love to fly with the wind,*
> *And the peach blossom travels with the racing*
> *stream.*

CHAPTER TWENTY: *While in his Cups Lai Wang talks himself into Perdition. Lotus Petal swallows Shame and hangs herself twice*

THE EVENING of the Lantern Festival saw Hsi Men and all his wives once more united at the festal board. Many gayly-colored lamps decorated the reception hall at the back of the house, in which the banquet was held. In one corner of the spacious room, at some distance from the banquet table, young Chen sat at his own little table. Spring Plum, Pear Blossom, Jade Flute and Fragrant Orchid provided the chamber music as usual, and four other maids had to wait on the company. At the entrance to the salon, Lotus Petal had made herself comfortable outside the door of the hall behind a screen in the gallery that led to the wings. There she sat at ease in her chair, whiling away the time indefatigably nibbling melon seeds, the husks of which she spat out on the floor all around her, with a total lack of discretion. Her whole duty was to warn the male servants, who had to bring food and wine from the kitchen, whenever anything was required at the table. Once there was a call for punch, whereupon she shouted so loudly that her voice could be heard in the hall: "Hey, Tai and Hua Tung, hurry up with the punch! Where are you hiding, you bandits? Do you call that attending to your duties?"

Of course, when poor Hua Tung entered with the bowl of punch, he was sharply reprimanded by Hsi Men, using the very words which he had just heard Lotus Petal employ. As the servant left the room he spoke reproachfully to Lotus Petal.

"You thoroughly deserved to be blamed," she retorted. "Why aren't you on the spot when anything is wanted in the hall?"

"Oho! and these husks all over the floor—I suppose the master would have nothing to say to that?"

"Better pay my husband the money you have owed him since the sixth month!" she cried angrily. "And if you don't sweep these husks away at once, I'll complain of you!"

What could the browbeaten menial do but fetch a broom and obey? This was the manner in which she was accustomed to deal with her equals.

Soon after this Hsi Men noticed that no punch had been served to young Chen at his little table.

"Go and take him something to drink!" he said to Gold Lotus.

And Gold Lotus was only too willing to comply with his request. Putting on her most winning smile, she approached young Chen's table. "Friend, at the express command of your lord, the devoted slave brings you this goblet of punch. Accept it you must, whether you will or not!" she said roguishly, and with a meaning glance she proffered him the brimming goblet.

"Stay a moment, Sister-in-law Five! I should like to enjoy this draught at leisure!" he replied, gazing into her eyes.

Gold Lotus cautiously edged herself into the interval between the candles on his table, so that she was only dimly visible from the main table. While with her left hand she offered him the goblet, with her right hand she gently stroked the back of the hand which he extended to take it. He responded with a gentle pressure on her foot.

"Be careful, little one! What if Hsi Men should see us?" she admonished him, but she smiled, and did not move. Unseen by those at the round table, the two indulged for a while in the silent sport of amorous gestures and tender glances. They never suspected that on the other side of the room two eyes were watching their every movement with eager attention.

"The hypocrites!" thought Lotus Petal, as she spied through the peephole in the screen from the adjacent doorway. "Before us maids she's so wonderfully demure, and here she is dallying with this young fellow on the sly! Well, let her just try to take me to task again!"

On a fine afternoon in March Hsi Men's wives took advantage of his absence to saunter in the park and exercise their limbs, which were languid with the spring, on the swing. Two by two they took their places on the brightly lacquered seat—first Moon Lady and Jade Fountain, then Mistress Ping and Gold Lotus. Sunflower was not in the mood for such diversions, and Snowblossom remained in the kitchen as usual.

"Now we'll swing three at a time!" Jade Fountain proposed. "Sister Five, you stand up on the seat!"

"But no one is to laugh!" Moon Lady added.

Lotus Petal and Spring Plum had to push the swing, and the three swung merrily up and down, their delicate hands holding fast to the ropes.

> *Rosy cheek on rosy cheek,*
> *One soft shoulder against another,*
> *Delicate hands cling to the cords,*
> *The tiny pairs of feet swing up and down*
>   *together.*

Gold Lotus took a special delight in this diversion, and laughed hilariously from her airy height. Even as Moon Lady warned her again she slipped on the smooth surface of the board, lost her footing, and was within an ace of falling off the swing, together with the Third. Luckily she was able to grasp the ropes in time to save herself.

"Did I not warn you just now? When you swing standing up you should never be frivolous, or your legs will go limp, and you will fall," said Moon Lady, admonishing the others. "I remember a thing that happened in my childhood. It was about this time of the year, a little before the Tsing Ming festival, and we children were amusing ourselves on our swing in the garden—we were four girls, counting the little Chow from next door. Little Chow stood up on the swing, and through her own carelessness she suddenly slipped, and she fell astride the narrow edge of the seat with such violence that she tore something in a certain part of her anatomy. How shall I put it?—later on, when she married, her young husband sent her back to her parents directly after the bridal night, because she had already lost her virginity, he declared! What a calamity for the poor thing! Since then I've had a wholesome respect for swings."

"Sister Three upset our balance!" Gold Lotus explained. "Now let me swing with Sister Six alone!"

The two were gently swinging to and fro when young Chen came up. "So you're hard at work swinging!" he observed.

"You come just at the right moment, Son-in-law," said Moon Lady. "You can make yourself useful and give both your sisters-n-law a good swing. The maids aren't quite strong enough."

Now young Chen was as sharp of hearing as a wily old bonze who can hear the bell sounding even before it is struck.

"With pleasure!" he answered; with a few hasty strides he took his place behind the swing.

"Hold fast, Sister-in-law Five!" he cried to Gold Lotus, audaciously seizing her fluttering skirt. Then he pushed her so energetically that the swing flew high into the air.

"Push me like that, too!" begged the Sixth, who this time was standing up on the seat.

"Not so hasty, Sister-in-law! You must wait your proper turn! I can't oblige two at once—one with my hands and one with my feet!" he cried.

He now lifted the skirt of the Sixth a little so that her red undergarment was exposed, laid his hands about her plump hips, and gave her a violent push.

"Not so rough!" she laughed from above his head. "Or I'll fall! I can hardly keep my feet!"

"Why, you haven't been drinking, have you?"

Thus for a while suggestive remarks and covert allusions were bandied to and fro; then the two got down from the swing to make way for Lotus Petal and Jade Flute. Standing sure-footed on the board, by the well-timed pressure of her supple thighs, and without the help of young Chen, Lotus Petal contrived to give such an impetus to the swing that she flew up and down as though moved by the hands of spirits.

"See how splendidly she swings herself!" Moon Lady exclaimed to the others.

That same afternoon, while Hsi Men's beauties were diverting themselves with the swing in the park, the servant Lai Wang returned from his journey to Hangchow with several sumpter loads of chests and coffers, packed with the clothes which were intended as a birthday gift for the Chancellor Tsai. On his way to the back of the house he met Snowblossom.

"Ah, you're back again!" she greeted him. "No doubt you suffered severely on your journey from the inclemency of the weather and the wintry fogs and sandstorms. All the same, you're looking very well! You've grown positively corpulent since I saw you last!"

"Is the master home just now?"

"No, today he's gone for an excursion with his friends. His wives are amusing themselves on the swing in the park."

She invited him into her room for a cup of tea. "Have you had anything to eat yet?"

"No, not yet. I just wanted to pay my respects to the First, and then wash and tidy myself up a little. Is my wife in the kitchen? How is it that she's nowhere to be seen?"

Snowblossom curled her lips in a frosty smile. "In the kitchen, forsooth! Your wife has grown to be a fine lady in your absence. The only duties she still condescends to perform are those of a companion."

Their conversation was interrupted by the appearance of Moon Lady, who had been informed of Lai Wang's arrival. She bade him good-day, inquired as to the progress of his journey, and presented him with two flasks of wine.

"Now go to your room," she graciously told him; "refresh yourself, have a wash, and rest until Master Hsi Men sends for you."

Accompanied by his wife, Lotus Petal, who had at last made her appearance, Lai Wang retired to his chamber. Lotus Petal indolently helped him to unpack and change his clothes, and prepared a meal for him.

"How fat you've grown, you black rascal!" were her only words of endearment.

Towards evening Hsi Men returned home and received from Lai Wang a formal account of his journey.

"By a stroke of luck I was able to make the return journey in the mandarin's junk," concluded Lai Wang. "So I was able to save the cost of porters and sumpter mules, and escape the tolls. The garments you commissioned me to obtain are carefully laid out in the western wing."

Hsi Men expressed his satisfaction, gave the man a few ounces of silver as payment for his services, and dismissed him.

On the following day Lai Wang sought a private interview with Snowblossom, when he gave her various pretty things which he had brought back with him. Two cambric handkerchiefs, two pairs of flowered half-hose, four boxes of the best Hangchow powder, and twenty boxes of rouge. Snowblossom showed her gratitude by unreservedly acquainting him with what had taken place in the house during his absence.

"During the whole of the last four months your wife has been carrying on like this with Hsi Men. Jade Flute has done duty as go-between, and the Fifth has given them her pavilion as their love nest, having first caught them together in 'The Grotto of Hidden Spring.' Later they slept together in the pavilion of the Fifth, spending whole days and nights there; once they were there from morning till night, another time from night till morning. She has received clothes, jewels, and money from him in abundance. And hardly a day goes by without her spending money."

Lai Wang changed color. "I was wondering about all the clothes and jewels in her chest. When I asked here where they came from, she simply said she had received them all as gifts from the First," he exclaimed savagely.

Lai Wang was fond of a good glass of wine. By the evening he had already had a considerable quantity of wine in order to assuage the grief that was gnawing at his entrails. Half intoxicated as he was, he felt impelled to open his wife's chest and rummage about among the contents. And now he came across a magnificent piece of blue flowered satin.

"Where did you get this rag?" he asked his wife, watching her narrowly.

Lotus Petal laughed uneasily. "Stupid question! From the First, of course. How else do you suppose? She wanted me to make myself a skirt out of it. But I haven't had time to do it."

"And this other rubbish, here? I advise you to tell the truth!" he said, with a threat in his voice.

"You crazy idiot, did you imagine that I picked the stuff off a refuse heap? Every bird has its nest, every creature its den. Am I not a person with relations of six degrees of kinship? The ornaments were lent me by an aunt, if you must know!"

Smash! His fist struck her full in the face.

"What, you cursed drab, are you still trying to lie yourself out of it? I have my witnesses, who have seen you abandon yourself to a certain swine, who has none of the five fundamental human qualities. That wretched slut, Jade Flute, played the go-between; it was she who brought you this blue satin trash and took you to the grotto in the garden. Later, you carried on with him in the pavilion of the accursed Fifth for whole days and nights together. Now you know!"

Lotus Petal began to howl aloud.

"Wicked man that you are, to strike me! What harm have I done to you? What evil tongues have turned you against your wife? I come of a respectable family, and if I have taken even one false step I wish I may cease to bear my honorable name! The First gave me that piece of blue satin. It was in the eleventh month, on the birthday of the Third; I was wearing a crimson skirt of Jade Flute's under my cinnabar-red coat. The First didn't like the combination of colors, so she gave me the material for a new skirt. Heavens, to misjudge me so! It's enough to drive one mad!"

"Very well, then I've been all worked up about nothing," growled Lai Wang, seemingly appeased. "Now be quick and make my bed. I want to sleep."

So once more Lotus Petal had weathered the storm. She could hardly wait until night came. Then she hurried off to find Jade Flute.

"Who's been blabbing?"

Jade Flute knew no more than Lotus Petal. But very soon after this a twofold coincidence was to betray the tell-tale. A few days after Lai Wang's return, Moon Lady sent her maid, Little Jewel, for Snowblossom. At first Little Jewel could not find her anywhere, when she suddenly saw her coming out of Lai Wang's room. The maid naturally thought she had gone there to discuss something with Lai Wang's wife, but when she entered the kitchen immediately afterwards there was Lotus Petal, chopping meat! On another occasion, when Hsi Men, who was then in the inner courtyard, which was surrounded by the individual apartments of the women, shouted for Lai Wang, he saw his servant tumbling out of Snowblossom's room, visibly embarrassed. It was, therefore, evident that Snowblossom and Lai Wang were on confidential terms, and that only Snowblossom could have been the informant.

One evening Lai Wang got thoroughly drunk again. This naturally loosened his tongue, and in the servants' room, before some of the other servants, he began to inveigh loudly against Hsi Men.

"It all began with that blue satin stuff he sent my wife by that wench while I was away. That's how he got round my wife. At first they met in the garden grotto, and after that in the pavilion of that damnable Fifth! But let him as much as tread on my little finger, and I'll see to it that my knife goes in white and comes out behind him red. And that damned trollop, the Fifth, can expect the same treatment! You'll see, I'm a man of my word! Didn't the woman murder her first husband, Wu Ta, by poisoning him?

Who helped her out of her fix then, and used his money to see that her brother-in-law, Wu Sung, was first sent to jail and then to the frontier? That scoundrel, Hsi Men. Ay, how I hate him, the rascal, the woman hunter! He and the Fifth must both die!"

Thus spoke Lai Wang, with heavy tongue, heedless of the fact that among those listening was the doorkeeper, Lai Hsing. An inveterate hatred had long existed between the two, and the first thing Lai Hsing did, early next morning, was to approach Gold Lotus.

"What's the trouble? Where's your master?" she asked him.

"The master has gone out; he had an appointment with Uncle Ying," he replied briefly, and then, hesitating, and with a doubting glance at Jade Fountain, who chanced to be present, he continued, speaking softly:

"I have important information to give you. But can I count on your silence? I don't want it to be known that the information comes from me. Besides, you are not alone. . . ."

"Don't be afraid. Say what you like! Sister Three is no stranger to me."

Lai Hsing now related in detail what Lai Wang had declared in his cups the previous evening. How he had denounced Hsi Men as a swine, and her, the Fifth, as a poisoner, and how he hinted in threatening terms at a knife that would go in white and come out red. And so he had come to warn her.

The two women listened, horror-stricken. Gold Lotus turned pale and clenched her silvery-white teeth so tightly that one could hear them grinding.

"He deserves to die, this mutinous slave!" she exclaimed. "Have I ever done him any harm? What have I to do with this affair between his wife and his master? The dangerous fellow must be turned out of the house without delay. Our lives are not safe any longer!"

And turning to Lai Hsing: "As soon as your master comes home," she said, "when he sends for you, you must tell him exactly what happened. Do you understand?"

"You can rely on me!" he answered obediently, and withdrew.

"Has Hsi Men really had any dealings with that servant woman?" asked the unsuspecting Jade Fountain. Gold Lotus could not do otherwise than enlighten her.

"That lump of carrion!" Jade Fountain cried, indignantly. "So that's why she was so obsequious and importunate, and made such a fuss—just so that she could rob us more safely behind our backs! Ought we to tell him about the matter at all? It would be more considerate to the First to say nothing about it. But if the slave should ever carry out his threat, we shouldn't be able to explain why we were silent."

"Leave it all to me!" Gold Lotus replied decisively, once more completely self-possessed. "In a case like this forebearance is out of the question!"

When Hsi Men appeared in Gold Lotus's pavilion that evening, he found her sitting distractedly on the edge of the bed with her cloudy hair disheveled, her fragrant cheeks wet with tears, and her eyelids red and swollen.

"Why, what is the matter?" he asked in astonishment.

She told him. "If you allow this knave to go on saying such things about us your face will lose all refulgence, and if we don't take steps at once to stop his murderous hand, we are both as good as dead!"

"From whom could the scoundrel have heard the story? Is he on intimate terms with anyone at the back of the house?"

"You must ask Little Jewel."

Hsi Men went at once to the front of the house, and bade Lai Hsing repeat the whole story to him in the privacy of his study. He found that Gold Lotus's statement was fully confirmed. Then he interviewed Little Jewel, from whom he learned that no one but Snowblossom could have been the informant. The first thing he did was to see that Snowblossom received a thrashing, and that her freedom of movement should be restricted by the removal of her upper garments. Henceforth she was to busy herself only in the kitchen and mix only with the female servants. All intercourse and conversation with the male servants was strictly forbidden.

He took the first opportunity to talk the matter over with Lotus Petal. She viewed the whole affair in a much less tragic light.

"Why, that's just the bombastic sort of thing he says in his cups. He's not nearly as bloodthirsty as you'd think from what he says. I'll vouch for him. After all, he depends on your goodwill, and he's not such a fool as to saw away the branch that he's clinging to. Don't pay any attention to such talk! By the way, who told you the whole story?"

"My Fifth. And Lai Hsing confirmed what she said."

"Oh, that fellow! Then I am not at all surprised. You know he can't get over the fact that you recently entrusted my husband with the buying of provisions for the larder, which was formerly his job. There's always a little to be made on such purchases; so he feels that my husband has done him an injury, and hates him. No, you need not take his talk so seriously. But perhaps it would be best if you could somehow get him out of the house without hurting his feelings. Entrust him with a few ounces of silver, so that he can carry on a little business on his own account in some distant town. If I know the man, that is what he'd wish, and then we should both be free to meet early and late without being disturbed."

"I really believe you're right," Hsi Men agreed; he was easily influenced. "For that matter, I might send him to the Eastern Capital with the birthday presents for Chancellor Tsai. To be sure, he has just come back from Hangchow, and for that reason I really intended to send Lai Pao. But you are quite right. And when he returns from the Eastern Capital I shall give him a thousand ounces and send him back to Hangchow. There he can open a silk business on my account. What do you think?"

"Yes, yes!" she cried, delighted, and she threw her arms about his neck. "That's a fine idea!" For a while his tender kisses sealed her mouth. Then she pleaded: "How about the silver hairnet you promised me? How much longer must I wait for it?"

"Tomorrow, child. The first thing tomorrow I'll go to the silver-smith; I'll run to eight ounces. But what if the First wants to know where you got it?"

"Oh, I've thought of an excuse long ago. I shall simply say that my aunt lent it to me."

On the following day Hsi Men sent for his servant, Lai Wang.

"I have decided to send you to Kai fong fu. You are to convey my birthday gifts to Chancellor Tsai. You will start on the twenty-eighth of this month. Have your baggage ready in time. And when you return, I shall send you to Hangchow. There you are to open up a silk mercer's business on my account."

Highly honored by this twofold mission, Lai Wang performed a kowtow of thanks, and straightway began to make preparations for the journey.

His antagonist Lai Hsing, however, speedily sought out Gold Lotus, and informed her of the new turn of events. Gold Lotus resolved to take counsel with Hsi Men at once, and dashed off to the belvedere in the park, where she had been told that he would be found. But there she discovered, instead of Hsi Men, young Chen, his son-in-law. He was busy pasting strips of paper on gift-boxes and sealing them.

"Where is the master, and what are you sealing there?" she asked.

"He was here a moment ago. He wanted to see Moon Lady. These are the presents for the Chancellor."

Gold Lotus ran down the steps of the belvedere and hurried off to the exit from the park. On the way she met Hsi Men, and carried him off to her pavilion.

"Are you really sending this Lai Wang to the Eastern Capital?" she asked.

"Yes."

"And so you have allowed that servant girl to cajole you! Once again you take no notice of my words. And later on you mean to let him open a silk mercer's shop in Hangchow! You intend to entrust a thousand good ounces to your bitterest enemy? Have you no eyes in your head? Do you think the fellow will employ the money for your benefit? Not a cash of it will you ever see! On the other hand, if you allow him to remain in this house, your life is in danger, and these eyes of mine cannot always keep watch over you! My Ko ko, understand me rightly! I am not actuated by jealousy. You may have the wench for all I care. But I tremble for your money, for your life. The fellow must be put out of the way! A weed must be exterminated root and branch, or it always grows again!"

Once more her words brought about a complete change of mood. It seemed to him as though he had awakened from a dream.

"I have reconsidered the matter overnight," he said to Lai Wang the next day. "You have just returned from one journey, and I really cannot expect you to undertake the fatigue of another journey immediately. I shall send Lai Pao. Take a few days' rest; then I will give you some money, so that you can hire a manager and open a small business along the street."

What could Lai Wang do? A servant must bow to the will of his master. He agreed to Hsi Men's proposal, and in his chamber he strove to stifle his vexation by copious draughts of wine. After he had drunk himself into a state of intoxication he once more began to inveigh against Hsi Men and to utter wild threats.

"Will you stop gnashing your teeth, you snarling cur!" cried Lotus Petal, angrily rebuking him. "You are talking the most irresponsible nonsense. Walls have cracks and partitions have ears! You had better lap up your pea soup!"

And she saw to it that he went to bed early. While he was sleeping off his drink, she ran to Jade Flute, and through her asked Hsi Men to meet her outside. In a remote corner of the courtyard behind the kitchen she had a private interview with him. Jade Flute kept watch as usual.

"A fine sort of fellow you are!" she began reproachfully. "No sooner have we agreed upon the course to be followed than you turn the horse about again! Now you suddenly decide to send Lai Pao, and my husband is to stay at home. You are no better than a ball that one bounces up and down; as limp as a wick that one screws up or down! The next thing you'll do will be to erect a temple to the God of Lies. What reliance can one have on your word?"

"Now, now! It is not as bad as all that," he laughingly reassured her. "I have merely reconsidered the matter in view of the fact that he would be a total stranger in the Chancellor's palace, while Lai Pao knows his way about there. But he can carry on a nice little business here just as well as anywhere else."

"What were you thinking of?"

"Of a wineshop. That would be most in accordance with his inclinations."

"As far as that goes, I think it would!" said Lotus Petal in a satisfied tone; and she went back to her quarters, to give the welcome news to her husband.

A few days later Hsi Men summoned Lai Wang to his study. On the table before him lay six sealed packages of silver.

"I did not wish to expose you so soon to the hardships of another journey, when you had only just returned from Hangchow. Moreover, you are a stranger in the Chancellor's palace, so I have sent Lai Pao in your place. But now take these six packages. They contain three hundred ounces of silver. Engage a manager and open a wineshop a little way up the street. I think it will be to your advantage. The business will make quite a comfortable monthly profit."

Overjoyed, Lai Wang thanked him with several kowtows, took the six packages, and hurried back to his wife.

"He means us no harm, after all. With these three hundred ounces I can build us a snug little nest," he announced, beaming with pleasure.

"You see, you black bandit! But no more grumbling after this! Do you hear? And pull yourself together a little in future and don't drink so much!"

He promised to obey her, gave her the six packages for safe-keeping, and proceeded at once to look for a suitable manager. But when he returned home that evening his drunken condition proved that he had not taken his promise too seriously. Nor had he been able to find a manager. Worn out by his excesses, and by running about the town, he soon retired to rest. And almost as soon as he began to nod his wife slipped quietly out of the room. Jade Flute had asked her to meet her in her room at the back of the house. She never dreamed that Jade Flute was luring her away at Hsi Men's request.

It was about the ninth hour of the evening when Lai Wang woke from his sleep. The effects of intoxication had not yet passed off, and his mind was still befogged. In this hazy condition he thought he heard Snowblossom's voice calling from outside: "Up, brother Lai Wang. Up! Your wife is betraying you again with that shameless fellow in the park! How can you lie there and sleep?"

Lai Wang opened his eyes to their widest extent, and gazed about him. His wife had disappeared.

"So, she dares to play her tricks before my very eyes!" he snarled wrathfully. Leaping from his bed, he dashed out, making for the park. Suddenly, as he was about to turn the corner of the western wing, a stool hurled out of the darkness caught him between the legs and made him stumble. At the same time he heard a clatter on the stone flags beside him as though a knife had been dropped. Next moment five servants pounced upon him, and loud shouts of "Thief!" echoed through the silent courtyard.

"But I am Lai Wang, the servant Lai Wang!" he cried, struggling vainly to tear himself from their grip. "I was only looking for my wife. What do you mean by falling on me like this?"

He received no answer, but was dragged into the front hall. It was brightly illuminated. Enthroned on a raised platform sat Hsi Men, dark and menacing.

"Bring him here!" he brusquely ordered.

Lai Wang knelt down before him, and conscious of his innocence, he immediately began to make a speech in his own defense, which was so defiant that it sounded more like a denunciation. "I woke as I was sleeping off my drink, and finding that my wife had disappeared from the room I went out to look for her. What harm is there in that? Why am I treated like a common thief?"

Thereupon his bitter foe, Lai Hsing, advanced towards the platform, and with a malignant smile he laid before Hsi Men a long daggerlike knife.

"We took that from him," he said.

"Aha, he was actually intending to commit a murder!" roared the judge. "No beast can be so treacherous as a man! In the benevolence of my heart I had actually placed three hundred ounces of silver at his disposal, so that he might comfortably establish himself in some steady little business, and live a life of ease, and in return for my kindness he prowls about in the dead of night seeking to murder me! Why else should he have had this knife upon his person? Ho there, men!" he cried turning to the five servants: "take him to his room and make him fetch the three hundred ounces he received from me!"

In the meantime the report of this nocturnal episode had come to the ears of Lotus Petal, who sat, quite unsuspecting, chatting with Jade Flute. When in her alarm she rushed back to her room she found it full of people. Her husband had just been brought in, and they were searching for Hsi Men's three hundred ounces. Lotus Petal was beside herself.

"This is the result of your accursed drinking!" she cried, weeping. "How often have I warned you! Now in your drunkenness you actually dare to attack people knife in hand!"

She extracted the six as yet unopened packages of money from the chest, and the men, with Lai Wang in their midst, withdrew.

Hsi Men had the six packages laid before him. He opened them in the light of the lamp, one after the other, and behold, the contents of only one package were seen to be silver; all the rest contained bars of common lead.

"This into the bargain! Worthless lead substituted for my good silver!" Hsi Men cried in feigned indignation. "Where have you hidden the five other packages?"

Lai Wang now lost what little composure he had left.

"But, master!" he stammered, in his agitation, "how could I have substituted anything for your bars of silver? Really, I don't know how. . . ."

"Enough! You have not only tried to murder me, you have tried to rob me as well. And if the evidence before me is not enough, I have a witness as well. Lai Hsing, step forward!"

Lai Hsing knelt before the platform and related how one evening in the servants' hall he had overheard the drunken Lai Wang utter loud threats against Hsi Men's life, making sinister allusions to a knife that was to go in white and come out at the back red.

"That will do," said Hsi Men curtly. "Bind him and lock him up in the gatehouse for the night. Tomorrow I shall draw up a bill of indictment and have him brought before the yamen."

The wretched Lai Wang, having listened to his enemy's deposition with mouth agape, and unable to utter a word in self-defense, was being led out of the hall when Lotus Petal rushed in, in a state of the greatest excitement, her hair disheveled and her clothing disordered.

"This is all your doing, master!" she vehemently protested, as she threw herself at Hsi Men's feet. "Why is he treated like a common thief? I myself took the six packages into safekeeping. The original sealing strips have never been touched. How could the packages have been changed? You are doing him an injustice, master! Let him be given a thrashing, for all I care, but why do you want to drag him before the Court?"

"Calm yourself," Hsi Men replied as mildly as possible. "This affair doesn't concern you in any way! It is not only since yesterday that I have had this bold and dangerous villain under observation. The knife that was found on him tonight has finally convicted him. You knew nothing of all this."

He beckoned to the servant, Lai An, and quietly bade him take Lotus Petal to her room, treating her with all possible consideration. But the woman could hardly be moved from the spot.

"Hatred darkens your judgment, master!" she began again. "You honor the image of Buddha, and offend the poor bonzes. It is true

303

that he may have talked nonsense when he was drunk, but never in the world would he be capable of such crimes as you accuse him of!"

Hsi Men was becoming impatient, and in vigorous tones he ordered Lai An to pick her up and take her to her room. Thus ended this nocturnal episode.

The next morning he drew up a formal bill of indictment, to which Lai Hsing had to attach his signed deposition. In vain Moon Lady attempted to intercede, and to persuade Hsi Men to settle the matter by inflicting a punishment at home, instead of insisting on a public trial. Once more, Gold Lotus proved to be the stronger. Hsi Men remained inexorable.

"Come, what can a woman like you understand of the elements of higher reason?" he snorted, his eyes rolling in his head. "I am to spare my murderer? That would be a fine thing!"

That very morning he had Lai Wang arraigned before the Provincial Judge. Moon Lady, blushing with shame at the rebuke which she had received, withdrew to the rear apartments.

"Everything here is in confusion," she said to the other wives, with unmistakable reference to the absent Gold Lotus. "The house is bedeviled by a nine-tailed vixen. Some conscienceless person has talked him into all this. It is unheard of, this treating a good and faithful servant like a criminal, without any valid reason! His evidence is as faulty as a pasteboard coffin. He is really incapable of reason; he is simply bewitched by some magic potion!"

"Calm yourself, child!" she said to Lotus Petal, who, dissolved in tears, was kneeling at her feet. "A few judicious questions before the tribunal, and the innocence of your husband will be evident at once."

"In his present state of mind he is not accessible to reason," said Jade Fountain, also endeavoring to console the girl. "As soon as he calms down a little we shall intercede with him on behalf of your husband."

But they reckoned without Gold Lotus, who, from behind the scenes, directed the course of events, and was firmly and ruthlessly resolved to pursue to the very end the path upon which she had entered.

Not in vain had Hsi Men seen to it that a nice little list of presents was slipped into the hands of his good friend Hsieh, together with the bill of indictment. Thus the public trial of Lai Wang proceeded quite otherwise than the good Moon Lady had imagined.

What did it avail the unfortunate man that he should seek to explain to the judge how his wife had betrayed him with Hsi Men, and how the latter had engineered the whole nocturnal assault with the intention of putting him out of the way? What did it avail him that he filled the court with his lamentable cry of "Injustice! Injustice!"

"Is this your gratitude, wretched slave?" Master Hsieh wrathfully upbraided him. "Is this your gratitude to your kind master, who not only showed you the favor of permitting you to live under the same roof with this woman as your wife, but even placed at your disposal a magnificent sum of money wherewith you might furnish yourself a comfortable little nest?"

But neither the torture of the finger press nor the agony of twenty strokes of the heavy bamboo could wring from Lai Wang the required confession, so Master Hsieh adjourned the court, and sent the prisoner back to jail, in order that imprisonment might make him more tractable.

Hsi Men was well content with the outcome of the trial so far. He gave his servants strict orders that they were not to take any food or bedding to the jail for their imprisoned fellow-servant. No one, moreover, was to give Lotus Petal the slightest information as to how the prisoner was faring.

"They won't be too hard on him; a few days in jail, and then he will be set free," he added, to reassure the servants.

Ever since her husband's committal, Lotus Petal had neglected her appearance. Her hair was no longer curled; no water touched her pale and unrouged cheeks; she refused food and drink, and sat behind locked doors on the edge of her bed and wept. Her condition filled Hsi Men with genuine solicitude. Repeatedly he sent Jade Flute to console her.

"You need not alarm yourself," Jade Flute assured her. "Your husband has been guilty of a piece of folly while drunk. They will treat him leniently and release him after a few days in prison." But Lotus Petal remained incredulous and inconsolable. Her faith in Hsi Men's promises had once before this been grievously shaken. Not until Lai An, whom she had sent to the jail with food, assured her that her husband was well treated, and that his release was only a question of a few days, did she pluck up courage and dry her tears.

One day Hsi Men passed by her chamber. She was standing in front of the door, under the eaves. Since there was no one in the kitchen she asked him to enter.

"How do matters stand with my husband?" she asked urgently.

"My child, for the sake of yourself and your good name I have sent the judge a petition of pardon," he lied. "I have seen to it that he will be spared further torture, and will soon be released. And once he is out again, I will still help him to start some little business. All for your sake!"

She fell upon his neck.

"I thank you for being so considerate of my good name. If only they let him out! What happens to him after that I leave to you. And I shall tell him that if he will get drunk again, then all is over between him and me. Then you can send him somewhere else and find him another wife for all I care. After all, I am not his property for all eternity!"

"Excellent, my heart! And I happen to know of a suitable little home for you, opposite the Kiao house. It shall be our love-nest. To-morrow, however, I shall write to the Provincial Judge and ask for your husband's release. And now don't be sad any longer, my darling! It spoils your good looks!"

He parted the loosely-hanging garment beneath which, at this warm season of the year, she wore only a chemise and no pantaloons, and made use of this favorable opportunity to play the amorous drake for a while. Before his departure he gave her two ounces of silver and solemnly swore to live and die with her.

At this fresh proof of Hsi Men's favor and goodwill, Lotus Petal believed that she could no longer doubt the sincerity of his words, and in her joy she straightway fell into the error of talking to the maids and menservants about Lai Wang's impending release, as though the matter were as good as settled. The maids naturally spread the news further, and so it came to the ears of Jade Fountain, who in turn made haste to inform the Fifth.

"Just think, he is going to help him to obtain speedy release, and he is going to furnish a three-roomed apartment opposite the Kiao house, and buy her a maidservant, and present her with a silver hairnet costing eight ounces of silver, and, in short, treat her exactly like one of us!" was what the Third had to tell.

"Oh, really?" said Gold Lotus, coldly. "Well, leave her in possession of her faith! I, at any rate, will no longer be called Pan's daughter if ever I permit him to make her his Seventh."

"What can you do to stop him? He is deaf to all argument, and Moon Lady puts up with anything," rejoined the other, doubtfully.

"There is nothing heroic about your character. Mine is a warrior's nature. Do you think I will obligingly let that wench get the better of me? I would rather die!"

"I admit that I am faint-hearted. I shouldn't have the courage to anger him by any sort of opposition."

That evening, while Hsi Men was sitting at his desk in the "Malachite Cabinet" in the park, writing the draft of the petition which he intended to present to the Provincial Judge on behalf of Lai Wang, Gold Lotus entered unexpectedly. Quickly glancing at the document over his shoulder, she asked: "What are you writing there?"

Taken by surprise, Hsi Men was forced willy-nilly to confess that he was engaged in drawing up a petition of pardon for Lai Wang. She sat down beside him.

"You really don't deserve the name of man! You let your ship drift rudderless, the sport of every wind. Once again you have allowed that slave girl to cajole you. Haven't you seen how she cleaves to her husband, regardless of the fact that you stuff her daily with sugar and honey? Haven't you considered what an obstacle he will be after his release, when you want to take your pleasure with his wife? You'll get neither meat nor vegetables; you'll be the butt of your family, the laughing-stock of your servants! No, if you want to possess her without fear of disturbance you must first of all re· move the husband!"

Her words induced him to draft then and there a new petition to the Provincial Judge, requesting him to make the prisoner tractable by thrashing him, and to pass judgment upon him within three days. Now, of all the Court officials, down to the very turnkeys in the jail, there was not one who had not benefited by Hsi Men's generosity. Who then would have dared to disregard his wishes? Luckily Secretary Yin was a humane and upright soul. He steadily refused to formulate the decree providing for the application of torture, which Hsi Men had demanded of the judge. In the end he and the judge talked the matter over, and Master Hsieh, who felt that his hands were tied by this opposition, adopted an expedient which had regard for the secretary's scruples as well as for Hsi Men's request. He ordered the prisoner to be given another forty strokes, and then to be transported to his birthplace, Sze-chow.

And so the day came when Lai Wang, was brought out of the dungeon where he had languished for half a month, and a wooden kang was placed round his neck. Under a convoy of two guards, he set out on his march to distant Sze-chow. The wretched Lai Wang was desperately low-hearted. His limbs, from the recent beating he had received, felt like jelly; his clothes were in tatters, and he had not a penny in his purse. And now he was faced with an exhausting journey.

"Brothers, take compassion on my misery!" he implored his guards. "Bring me first to the house of my former master, where my wife is living. I will ask her to provide me with clothing and money, so that we may not lack for food on the way."

"Are you out of your senses?" the guards replied. "Do you imagine that your former master—who instituted these proceedings against you—will permit your wife to open a coffer for your sake or to take a step out of the house? Have you no other relations anywhere?"

"Brothers, let me at least stand and wait a while in the gateway of Hsi Men's house. Perhaps one or another of the visitors entering the gate will take my part and intercede with him on my behalf," Lai Wang pleaded.

The guards complied with his request, and brought him to Hsi Men's house. Inasmuch as Beggar Ying dwelt close by, Lai Wang endeavored to gain admittance to his presence. But Beggar Ying refused to see him, and denied that he was at home. Neighbors Chu and Yuen then came along. They were moved to pity by his supplications, and put in a good word for him with Hsi Men. But Hsi Men closed his ears and sent out five of his men with cudgels to drive Lai Wang from the threshold.

The guards finally led their prisoner to the house of his father-in-law, the coffin-dealer Sung. The latter had mercy on him, and gave him an ounce of silver, a string of copper cash, and a bushel of rice. And then began the long journey on the hot and dusty highway to Sze-chow.

In the meantime, Lotus Petal, waiting impatiently in her chamber, knew nothing of all this. For Hsi Men had warned his servants to expect twenty blows of the cudgel if any one of them should venture to drop a single word as to Lai Wang's fate in her presence. From day to day she hoped to see him free and for the time being she continued to send a daily basket of food to the prison. And the servants, to whom she sometimes gave a message, took the basket also, for the sake of appearances, in order to consume the contents behind her back. When they returned the empty basket, and were questioned, they would lie to her, saying that he had enjoyed the food, and hoped to be liberated in two or three days' time.

This deceitful performance had long been continued, when one day there came to her ears a vague rumor blown by the wind, that her husband had already been released from prison, and had that day stood in the gateway, vainly seeking to obtain some clothing from her. He had then been led away to an unknown destination. In her dismay she questioned one servant after another, but not one dared to tell her the truth. Last of all she came upon Tai A. He was about to accompany Hsi Men on horseback, when she saw him passing her chamber on his way through the courtyard.

"Little brother, I implore you to tell me how things stand with my husband!" she urgently pleaded. "When will he be released?"

"I will tell you, sister," Tai said in a low voice. "He is already out. He was sentenced to another forty blows, because he would not confess, and now he is being taken back to his native Sze-chow. You will never see him again. But, I beg of you, do not betray me. We have been strictly forbidden to let you know about this."

When Lotus Petal heard these tidings all her other cares and worries evaporated. She barred herself in her chamber and wept bitterly.

"Alas, my poor husband!" she sobbed; "what have you done to deserve such injustice at the hands of your master, whose mood is as unstable as a pasteboard coffin! This is your reward for your faithful service! Now you have not even a single coat to wear on your long journey! And your wife has been most shamefully deceived! She has been kept imprisoned as though at the bottom of a well, so that she might be unaware of what was going on about her!"

She wept herself into a state of utter despair. Then, seizing a towel, she fastened it to the lintel of her bedroom door, and forming a running noose, she hanged herself.

Fortunately I Chang Tsing, the wife of the servant Lai Chao, whose apartment was separated from Lotus Petal's by a thin partition, had long since become aware of her loud sobbing and wailing. When, after a last smothered shriek, all sounds from the adjoining room suddenly ceased, she had a foreboding of evil; she dashed out of her room, and when her knocking brought no answer, she called Ping An to her assistance. The latter forced a window without further ado, and clambered over the sill. There he saw the wretched Lotus Petal hanging from the lintel. He took her down at once, loosened the knot, and opened the door. I Chang Tsing, however, had hurried to the kitchen, and was quickly at hand with that sterling household remedy, a warm infusion of ginger. In the meantime the report of this unhappy incident had spread to all the rear apartments, and presently Moon Lady, Sunflower, Jade Fountain, Lady Pen Se, Jade Flute, and Little Jewel were gathered in a compact circle, watching with eager interest and sympathy as I Chang Tsing fed the beneficent infusion, sip by sip, to poor Lotus Petal, who was lying apparently lifeless on the ground. Presently a feeble sigh came from her lips. She was still alive.

"But, child, you were otherwise so brave! How could you ever take this desperate course? Tell us why?" Moon Lady gently urged her.

Only a faint moaning was audible, which slowly grew stronger, until it finally developed into a convulsive sobbing. Unable to elicit a word from her, Moon Lady surrendered her to the care of Mistress Pen Se and Jade Flute, and withdrew with the other wives and the maids.

Lotus Petal steadily refused to be helped to her bed, and was still lying on the ground in the middle of the room when at last Hsi Men entered.

"Carry her to her bed!" he ordered.

"She won't let us," Jade Flute explained.

"Dear obstinate child, you will catch your death of cold on the damp ground: do be reasonable!"

She shook her head, and then, in a feeble voice, she made her bitter complaint:

"Spare me your 'dear child!' It isn't honestly meant. First you torture me to death and then you assure me of your sympathy. That's how your 'dear child' strikes me. Everything about you is a lie. Did you not assure me daily that he would soon be released? Yes, they've released him, only to drag him far away. You even begrudged my bidding him farewell. Why didn't you send us both away together? What place have I now in this house?"

"But, my dear child, his fate cannot affect you in the least," he said, reassuringly, with an embarrassed laugh. "He was a murderous villain who deserved his punishment. Why trouble yourself about him? You shall want for nothing."

He departed, and presently sent the servant Lai An with a jug of wine and a box of sweetmeats, which arrived just as Lotus Petal was being helped into bed.

"Take that rubbish away; I won't have it!" she cried passionately. "I shall dash his wine to the ground before I drink a single drop of it!"

"But, sister-in-law, you can't spurn his gifts! It is I who would be blamed," protested Lai An. He set the jug and box on the table and beat a hasty retreat. It was with the greatest difficulty that I Chang Tsing could prevent Lotus Petal from making good her threat, and in a violent struggle with the frenzied woman I Chang Tsing received a bite on the finger.

Hsi Men had ordered Jade Flute to share Lotus Petal's room at night. He promised himself that Jade Flute, her confidant of bygone hours of love and happiness, would have an especially soothing influence on her distressing state of mind.

"Be reasonable, sister!" Jade Flute was to say to her. "You are in the bloom of youth, at the height of your beauty; you are a blossom just fully unclosed. You have the good fortune to be beloved by your master. Why continue to lament a common slave? You have bewailed him long enough."

But Lotus Petal remained inconsolable, and refused all nourishment. Thereupon Hsi Men sent Gold Lotus, who found the girl no less inflexible than before. With vexation, she told Hsi Men of the failure of her mission.

"She is too devoted to her former husband. She is so obstinate in her constancy that she is totally inaccessible to reason!"

"Constancy, did you say?" Hsi Men asked with a laugh. "Would she have deceived the cook, her first husband, with Lai Wang if she had been of so constant a nature? But all this trouble is the result of one of the servants having let out the secret in defiance of my prohibition."

And he ordered all the male servants to assemble in the hall.

"Which of you is guilty of having blabbed to Lai Wang's wife?" he demanded imperiously. "If the culprit confesses of his own accord, he shall go unpunished. Otherwise he will receive thirty strokes and be dismissed from service."

At this Hua Tung knelt down before him.

"Master, I saw her speak to your boy Tai when you were about to go out riding, and Tai had some conversation with her."

"So? Where is that boy? Bring him here!"

But Tai was not to be found. The prudent fellow had fled from the scene of the impending storm, and hurried off to Gold Lotus's quarters. There he fell on his knees and implored her to protect him.

"What do you mean by bursting in here so abruptly?" said Gold Lotus, who was engaged in performing her ablutions, reproving him. "It is enough to startle one!" In the end, however, she graciously permitted him to remain. It flattered her vanity that anyone should seek her protection.

For a time Hsi Men raged and thundered in the hall, but when Tai was nowhere to be found he himself set out in search of the culprit. And now, horsewhip in hand, he came storming into the pavilion like a whirlwind.

"Is the boy here?" he cried in a passion.

Gold Lotus paid no attention to him. He searched through one room after another, and finally discovered his victim cowering behind the bedroom door. Already his arm was raised to strike when Gold Lotus seized his hand, snatched the whip from his fingers, and threw it on the bed.

"You ought to be ashamed to strike an innocent lad!" she remarked coldly, eyeing him with a withering glance. "Is it the fault of this poor fellow that the wench is so attached to her husband?" And troubling herself no further with the infuriated Hsi Men, who stared at her with eyes starting from his head, she calmly

313

continued, addressing herself to Tai: "Be off, and in future attend to your own business, and don't meddle in the affairs of others! However, if you should be in danger of a beating, remember I am here to protect you!"

Hsi Men slunk out of her apartment, a defeated man.

But when Gold Lotus perceived that her lord would not renounce his love for Lotus Petal, she resolved to put an end to the disagreeable situation by vigorous action. Accordingly, one day she sought out Snowblossom, and convinced her that Lotus Petal laid the entire blame for her husband's misfortune at Snowblossom's door. She it was who had carried on a flirtation with Lai Wang and had upheld him in his hostile attitude towards Hsi Men. Her tattling had been the main cause of Lai Wang's expulsion, and it was on that account that Hsi Men had punished her with a beating and confinement to her room.

Leaving Snowblossom with a heart full of suppressed rancor, she went to Lotus Petal, and now, conversely, she began to speak ill of Snowblossom, who, according to Gold Lotus, was maligning her throughout the rear apartments, saying of her, for example, that she was none too scrupulous about a point of conjugal fidelity, and had herself helped to drive her poor husband from the house, so that she might carry on her love affair with Hsi Men undisturbed; that her mourning was only simulated, her pretended tears mere drops of water, which she deliberately sprinkled on her face. In this way did Gold Lotus sow dissension between the two women, hoping before long to see an explosion of the ill will accumulated on either side.

It was the evening of the eighteenth of the fourth month, Sunflower's birthday. Hsi Men was away from home. His wives and the guests sat round the table in the back hall. Lotus Petal had gone to bed early. She was sent for repeatedly, but failed to appear, until Snowblossom went to discover the reason for her absence.

"You're a fine one, to make us beg for your presence in this way!" she exclaimed, when she found Lotus Petal lying in bed.

Her face hidden in the pillows, Lotus Petal pretended to be asleep.

"Oh, your thoughts are again with your husband, are they?" Snowblossom continued, maliciously. "You would have done better if you had concerned yourself about him before! After all, it is your own fault if he has been driven out of the house, very likely to die a premature death."

In a flash Lotus Petal was on her feet. For these were the very words she had recently heard from the Fifth!

"So! If I am to blame for his being driven out, why were you thrashed and confined to your room?" she burst out passionately. "You, and you alone, with your tattling, are to blame!"

"Miserable slave of a whore!" the other hissed.

"Good, I am a slave of a whore, but you are the whore of a slave! Did you not have secret relations with my husband? It is always more honorable to be the whore of a master than that of his slave!"

Snowblossom responded with a box on the ear, and the altercation developed into a heated battle. In the nick of time I Chang Tsing rushed in, threw herself between the combatants, and dragged Snowblossom out of the room with her. But for a time angry invective and counterinvective were exchanged at long range, until finally the appearance of Moon Lady put a stop to the squabble.

"Have you no manners at all?" she upbraided them. "Could you not at least show more consideration for our guests? What will Master Hsi Men say when I tell him!"

Snowblossom made off at once.

"Put your hair in order quickly and accompany me back to the hall!" Moon Lady bade Lotus Petal, who stood before her with disheveled locks.

Lotus Petal obeyed without a word. But after Moon Lady had brought her to the entrance of the hall she turned back and locked herself in her room. There she threw herself on her bed and let her tears flow unchecked. For a long time she lay thus and wept. The deeper the shadow of twilight in her room, the more heavily did the burden of a nameless sorrow weigh upon her. At last, while in the festively illumined hall the others were sitting over their

315

wine, and merrily conversing, she rose mechanically, knotted two foot bandages together, made a noose, fastened it to the lintel, and hanged herself. When they broke into her room some time later she was already quite dead.

"The little fool! There was no helping her. She was simply born to misfortune," Hsi Men concluded, shrugging his shoulders, when late that night he stood before the corpse.

And so Gold Lotus had triumphed once more.

CHAPTER TWENTY-ONE: *In the Malachite veranda Mistress Ping reveals a tender Secret. In the Vine Arbor Gold Lotus and Hsi Men celebrate*

LAI PAO HAD RETURNED from a successful journey to the Eastern Capital, bringing Hsi Men a flattering invitation from the Chancellor Tsai. The Ancient Commander, on receiving Hsi Men's gifts, had expressed the desire to greet the giver in person, in the capital, on his birthday: that is, on the fifteenth day of the sixth month.

Naturally, Hsi Men felt very greatly honored. In his joy at the invitation he immediately took from his treasury a further three hundred ounces, and ordered the best silversmith in the city to make for this price a valuable centerpiece in silver repoussé, consisting of four male figures, over a foot in height, representing the four seasons, and holding a Shu symbol over their heads; and also a ewer in gold repoussé in the form of the Shu symbol. Further, he selected two jade peach dishes, and also four ceremonial robes of the best Hangchow brocade, embroidered in five colors with a serpent design. Two of these robes, and indeed by far the finest of them, came out of one of Mistress Ping's chests. All these things he dispatched in advance in the care of Lai Pao, a few days before his own departure for Kai fong fu. Lai Pao had to leave with the baggage on the twenty-eighth day of the fifth month.

It was the first day of the sixth month. A broiling heat lay in the air. A blazing disc of fire, the midday sun hung suspended in cloudless space. It was a heat to smelt metals, to calcine stones.

From the South
The god of flames
Pelted the fiery dragon,
Setting ablaze
The halls of heaven.
In a glowing oven
The countries languished.
Between the five mountains
Not a wisp of cloud.
Will not the fiery wheel
Roll onward?
When at last will the evening
Send forth the golden breeze,
Like a cooling broom
To sweep away the heat?

Owing to the heat, it was some days since Hsi Men had set foot outside the house. On this particular morning he sat uncombed and comfortably clad, with collar wide open, on the airy height of the belvedere, in the malachite veranda, watching the gardener lads, watering can in hand, sprinkling the flower beds.

He had just called their attention to a bed of roses which were limply hanging their heads and dying of thirst, when Gold Lotus and Mistress Ping climbed slowly up to the belvedere. Over the plain white of their thin cambric shifts they wore a jupon of gold lamé, fitting closely to the body. Gold Lotus was without a hood, and in its place she had wrapped about her head, to protect it from the scorching sun, one of those "blue cloud veils" that are woven in Hangchow. Merrily chattering and walking hand in hand, the two beauties approached as gracefully as two blossoming boughs swaying in the breeze.

"You don't look exactly prepared to receive callers!" they cried to him, jestingly.

"To tell the truth, I haven't yet combed my hair. I was so taken up with the flowers. Just send someone up here with a comb and a washbowl! I'll make my toilet here at once."

Gold Lotus told the servant Lai An to put down his watering can and hurry. Then she went over to the bed of roses, which had just been watered, and was about to pluck a rose for herself.

"Don't do that!" said Hsi Men, "I wanted myself to present you each with a rose."

He had already plucked a few half-opened roses, and had them ready in a porcelain vase. But the greedy Gold Lotus, who did not care to receive the same favors as his other wives, anticipated his gift, and with her own hands took the finest buds from the vase in order to fix them in her hair. So he gave one to Mistress Ping only.

In a little while Spring Plum and Autumn Aster appeared with brush and comb, looking glass and water. Hsi Men took three more roses from the vase.

"Here, these are for my First, Second, and Third," he told Spring Plum. "And I should like my Third to come here. She might bring the four-stringed moon lute with her."

"I tell you what, I'll go myself and bring Sister Three," Gold Lotus suddenly proposed, and she went off with Spring Plum. But her departure was only a maneuver. At the garden gate she suddenly left Spring Plum.

"I have changed my mind. I'm going back now," she said. "Don't forget to send Sister Three with the lute!"

And she returned by another path to the belvedere.

In the meantime Hsi Men had sent Autumn Aster away. She was to fetch the jasmine soap which she had forgotten. So he was left alone in the malachite veranda with Mistress Ping. In the expectant silence of this sultry hour the nearness of her lightly-clad body had a doubly stimulating and perturbing effect upon his sensitive nerves. As she took a few casual steps in the direction of the slanting rays of sunlight he clearly perceived, gleaming through the diaphanous texture of her red cambric pantaloons, the swelling curves of her thighs, the jadelike pallor, the snowy shimmer of her flesh. It was enough to kindle at a moment's notice an irresistible desire to possess her. Comb and wash-hand basin were forgotten. He drew her towards him without a word, lifted her on to the divan, turned up the hem of her robe, and stripped off her innermost garments. . . .

While the two were abandoning themselves to the ephemeral delights of their passionate union, Gold Lotus had quietly approached the pavilion, and she presently stood unperceived behind the screen at the entrance to the malachite veranda, listening with bated breath. Now she could hear his tremulous voice, his passionate words of endearment.

And after a time the woman's voice reproved him:

"Not so violent! I'll confess it: for the last month I've felt that I am pregnant. So treat me just a little tenderly!"

"Is it possible? My dear!" he cried, enraptured. "But why didn't you tell me at once? Then I would not have been so rough!"

His panting breath, his moaning exclamations had just died away, and the echo of her last parrotlike screech was silenced, when the woman listening without heard footsteps approaching her from behind. It was Jade Fountain.

"Well, Sister Five, is there anything special to be seen there?" she cried unsuspectingly while still at some distance from the belvedere.

With a gesture of the hand, Gold Lotus silenced her, and they entered the pavilion together. Startled by their unexpected appearance, Hsi Men was so embarrassed that he did not know what to do with his hands and feet.

"But you have not washed yourself or done your hair, and I have been gone quite a long while!" exclaimed Gold Lotus, examining the pair with a cool and critical glance.

"Yes, I was just waiting until the child brought the jasmine soap," he stammered, and he busily began to wash himself and arrange his hair.

"Well, what have you been doing? And have you brought the lute?" he asked Jade Fountain, when he had completed his toilet.

"Spring Plum will bring the lute. I was threading beads for a piece of embroidery that Moon Lady wants to wear tomorrow, on the occasion of a birthday visit."

Almost immediately Spring Plum appeared with the lute, announcing that she had delivered the three roses as requested. Now she had to lay a tea table and bring a few refreshments, such as plums cooled in melting ice, and slices of melon. Then the company gathered round the table. Gold Lotus pushed her chair away, and sank down upon a round porcelain footstool.

"You'll catch cold on that chilly thing," said Jade Fountain.

"What if I do? What does it matter? I after all, have no need to be thinking about the little living creature in my womb," said Gold Lotus, significantly.

Hsi Men pricked up his ears and glanced surreptitiously at Mistress Ping.

"And now for a little music!" Hsi Men proposed that Jade Fountain and Gold Lotus should sing together the song of "The Red Prince of Flame sets the great Void afire." Jade Fountain was to play the moon lute in accompaniment, and Gold Lotus the *pi pa*. But Gold Lotus was unwilling to play.

"No, I don't want to!" she said, obstinately. "We two are to do all the work, and you two will have all the pleasure! No!—Unless Sister Six will play an instrument too."

"But she can't play!"

"Then let her at least give us the tempo with the castanets!"

"Very well. But you are really exciting yourself over a midge bite."

So Spring Plum had to run and fetch a pair of red ivory castanets. Then delicate jadelike fingers were outspread over the tensely-strung strings of shark gut, and the trio sang the poem of "Wild Ducks above the Dunes." The maid Apricot Blossom stood beside them, wafting a cooling breeze toward them with a fan.

When the song was ended Hsi Men gave each of the three beauties a goblet of wine, and they once more sat down to the table.

In the meantime the heavens had become overcast with clouds, rising darkly from the southeast. In the northwest was the dull rumbling of thunder. And now a brief but violent thunder shower came pattering down. Soon, however, the sun broke through again, conjuring up a rainbow in the heavens, beneath which the last drops flashed downwards like a glittering curtain of many-colored gems. At the same time a gentle breeze arose, which brought the coolness for which they were longing.

Now the maid, Little Jewel, appeared, to ask Jade Fountain if she would go to Moon Lady; she positively must thread the beads in time.

The whole company decided to escort her, and while they were walking towards the gate of the park they sang together a long and lovely chant in praise of summer rain. Hsi Men joined in to the extent of clapping his hands to give the tempo.

At the park gate he detained Gold Lotus, who had intended to accompany the other wives.

"Take care! The flagstones are slippery with the rain. Hold on to me, so that you don't slip, as you did recently when you were swinging," he said affectionately.

"But Sister Three and Sister Six are quite able to walk alone!"

"We'll enjoy this beautiful weather beside the lake, and amuse ourselves a little with the bottle game," he added. The other two wives were already out of hearing. Gold Lotus took the lute from Spring Plum, and strolled towards the lake with him, strumming on the lute as she walked. Wandering along the rocky bank of the lake, they passed a pomegranate tree whose blossoms, thanks to the beneficent influence of the thunder shower, had just unclosed in all their glory. Gold Lotus broke off a blossom, and fixed it in her hair above one temple.

"Oh," she cried, suddenly, feigning to be overcome by a slight faintness, "I feel so weak, and flowers are dancing before my eyes, just as though I had been fasting for three days!"

Hsi Men anxiously embraced her, and proceeded to lift her on to his shoulders.

"My dear child, you mustn't die and leave me! You have hardly had a glimpse of the world yet!" he said, in a jesting tone.

"Oh, it's not quite as bad as that. But I should like to put the lute down and recover my breath a little."

She laid the lute on the ground beside a flowerbed. Then she began, quite suddenly:

"I don't hold it against you in the least, that you should have enjoyed yourself today with Sister Six. No, no, I don't in the least wish to interfere with your pleasures! But I do hope you won't think less of me now."

"But what are you thinking of? And in any case, how am I supposed to have amused myself with Sister Six?"

"My lad, you can't fool me! Am I a senseless clod? You ought to know me by now! Do you imagine I really went running off to Sister Three this morning, in order to give her your rose? Ha, ha! Why, I was listening! And I heard everything she said to you in the malachite veranda!"

"What a woman you are!" he cried, laughing, as he laid her gently on the flowers and pressed his lips to hers. "Call me your dear Ta ta! At once! Or I won't let you get up!"

"My dear Ta ta!—All the same, you love another!" And laughing, she allowed him to pull her to her feet. With the lute under her left arm, and singing the last verse of the hymn to the summer rain, she strolled beside him along the narrow path that wound among the emerald fishponds, past the Kashmir Thistle Arbor, to the Vine Arbor. And there they decided to remain.

> *Above the stone balustrade*
> *Four airy walls of trellis*
> *Are woven about*
> *With close-set leafage.*
> *Once it was all aglow*
> *As with the purple fleece*
> *Of a bank of thyme, exhaling*
> *The spicy breath of autumn;*
> *But now the pale green pearls*
> *Are gathered in cloudlike masses.*

Like the many-colored crystal ornaments
That hang on a charger's breast,
Like the liquid, gleaming glaze
On a roof of colored tiles.
A gold-besprinkled arbor,
A mysterious spring
Wherein the sweet sap
Exhales a magic perfume.
A present from the lands
Of the mysterious West.

In the arbor there stood at present only four porcelain stools and a three-necked flask, containing the darts with which the bottle game is played. But now came Spring Plum with a jug of wine, and behind her Autumn Aster, carefully carrying with both hands a large food basket, on the lid of which a dish of fruit salad was all but splashing over.

"You have already almost run your lungs out of your body this morning, little faggot!" said Gold Lotus to Spring Plum. "Why do you come running out again?"

"To think that one has to hunt you up here!" complained the little maid. "You keep one running all over the place!"

She remained in order to wait on them, while Autumn Aster withdrew. Hsi Men opened the big basket. It contained a meal of eight separate courses in eight little dishes, each dish being neatly bestowed in its own compartment; and also a small silver flask of wine, two small golden goblets in the form of lilies, and two pairs of ivory chopsticks.

Hsi Men arranged all these things as well as he could on two of the stools, placed side by side, while he and Gold Lotus sat on the other two. They ate and drank with appetite, and from time to time they amused themselves by casting darts at the three-necked flask.

Having quickly drunk a good deal of wine, Gold Lotus began to feel slightly intoxicated; her cheeks assumed the delicate red of the peach blossom, and her sidelong glance had the moist gleam of the autumnal waves. When Hsi Men sent Spring Plum to fetch more wine, she told the little maid to bring her a few mats and cushions, for she was feeling tired, and wished to lie down for a time. After a while Autumn Aster appeared once more, heavily laden with mats and cushions. Gold Lotus made her arrange a comfortable resting place on the ground; then she was allowed to go.

"Shut the gate of the park after you!" Gold Lotus commanded. "And you needn't come back unless I send for you."

Now the two made themselves comfortable. First Hsi Men took off his coat and hung it over the balustrade, and when he returned from a brief excursion to the shrubbery beside the peony bed he found Gold Lotus lying absolutely naked on the mats. Her red satin shoes were her only clothing. She was cooling herself with her fan.

The sight of Gold Lotus heated Hsi Men's blood to boiling point. Hastily he threw off the rest of his clothes, and sat down on one of the porcelain stools. At first he amused himself, as he sat there, by poking at her with his toes. Then he removed even his satin slippers, and having done so he suddenly conceived the peculiar notion of lashing her feet, by means of her foot bandages, to the two posts of the back entrance to the arbor, one foot being bound to each post, at some distance from the ground. Like a backward-rearing dragon with uplifted forelegs, there she lay and had to suffer his amorous onset.

In the midst of his efforts he was startled by the appearance of Spring Plum. In consideration of the strange position in which she discovered the pair, she silently set down the wine jug at the front entrance to the arbor, and in obedience to the backward gesture of Hsi Men's waving hand, she discreetly withdrew to the neighboring "Pavilion of the Resting Cloud," where she sat down and amused herself by playing a solo game of chess.

But Hsi Men, stimulated by her nearness to fresh desires for novel delights, hastily tore himself away from Gold Lotus, and all naked as he was, he ran with great strides along the stony path and past the rocky shore of the lake to the "Pavilion of the Resting Cloud." When Spring Plum saw him coming she hastily slipped out of the pavilion and fled along a narrow path which led past the "Grotto of Hidden Spring," and plunged into a dense shrubbery, where she thought she would be safe from observation.

However, he soon discovered her hiding place, and now, parting the branches, he stood before her, hot and panting after his run.

"I have you at last!" he cried, laughing. Then he lifted her in his arms like a bundle, and carried her back to the Vine Arbor. Then she had to sit in his lap and drink a goblet of wine with him. The little maid glanced with amazement in her eyes at Gold Lotus, who was lying on the mats in the same position as before, her feet bound fast to the doorposts of the back entrance to the arbor.

"This is a pretty crazy thing to do in broad daylight!" she ventured to remark. "Suppose anyone were to come this way?"

"Oh, nonsense! We purposely got Autumn Aster to bolt the gate. I hope you didn't leave it open? And now look here, little oily-mouth, I'll show you a new sort of bottle game. It's called 'Shooting with Golden Bullets at the Silver Swan.'"

He took from the dish of iced fruit salad three hard yellow egg plums and proceeded, taking careful aim, to throw them at the prostrate woman. Three times he threw, and three times he struck the target.

"Oh, you're shooting me dead!" shrieked the drunken woman, writhing with laughter, while he poured himself three large beakers of "Five Fragrant Joys" wine, which he awarded to himself as a prize for his accurate shooting.

"Give her something to drink too, and cool her with your fan!" he ordered the maid, speaking thickly. "I want to sleep now."

He dropped heavily on to the mats, and in a moment he was asleep. Spring Plum, however, disgusted by the scene, took this opportunity of creeping past the sleepers with silent tread, and vanishing like a wisp of vapor.

But an hour later Hsi Men was awake again, and as he woke his lustful desires revived.

When he had once more satisfied them he released Gold Lotus from his embrace. She lay limply on the mats, completely exhausted, and hardly able to breathe; the tip of her tongue seemed cold as ice. At last he released her feet, and helped her to assume a comfortable, half-sitting posture. Gradually life returned to her.

He helped her to dress; then, while Spring Plum and Autumn Aster removed the dishes, he escorted her to her pavilion.

"Today I have conquered her," he told himself.

CHAPTER TWENTY-TWO: *The favor of Chance deals young Chen a Trump Card. Gold Lotus incites Hsi Men to a noontide Skirmish in the Orchid Tub*

NEXT MORNING, when Gold Lotus wanted to change her bed shoes for the red satin slippers which she had worn the day before, one of the slippers was missing. She looked for it right and left, but could not find it. The two maids had to make a thorough search through all her rooms; it was not to be found.

"Perhaps you lost it yesterday evening in the park?" Autumn Aster timidly suggested.

"You stupid creature, do you suppose I came home with bare feet?"

Then, after some reflection: "A ghost must have spirited it away," she said. "Spring Plum, go into the park with her and help her to look for it. If she doesn't find it I'll make her kneel in the court-yard with a stone on her head as punishment."

After some time the two maids returned. They had not found the slipper. They had made a special search in the neighborhood of the Vine Arbor, but in vain.

"Then go into the courtyard and take your punishment!" said Gold Lotus severely, to Autumn Aster.

"Oh, mistress, let me look once more in the park!" Autumn Aster pleaded. "If I don't find it you can have me beaten as much as you like."

"You are talking nonsense," Spring Plum interposed. "The park is thoroughly swept every morning. Every pin is picked up; to say nothing of a red slipper!"

"Kindly leave it to the mistress to decide whether or not I shall look again! Who asked you to poke your nose in?" said Autumn Aster, aggressively.

"Very well, have another look!" Gold Lotus commanded.

This time they searched even more thoroughly than before, but once more, in vain. Spring Plum angrily gave the younger maid a couple of slaps, and was about to return.

"Oh, but it has just occurred to me that we haven't yet looked in the Snow Grotto," Autumn Aster protested, excitedly, clinging to Spring Plum's sleeve.

"You mean the 'Grotto of Hidden Spring,' which our master has heated sometimes, so that he can sleep there? Our mistress wouldn't in any case have gone there. But we can just have a look, for all I care."

Accordingly they went to the grotto, where they peeped behind the bed and under the table, examined every corner, and left nothing unopened. At last only a small book box was left. Autumn Aster began to rummage about in it; Spring Plum, on the other hand, was for disregarding it.

"How should one of our mistress's slippers find its way into a dusty book box? It's full to the very top with visiting cards! Come along, we are wasting our time here!"

She had already turned to go out, when she heard the other rejoicing: "Here it is!"

Spring Plum reluctantly turned back and looked incredulously into the box. And there, truly enough, quietly lying beside some incense sticks, a red satin slipper peeped out of its paper wrappings.

"That is actually the mistress's shoe," she said, "but how did it find its way in here? This is very peculiar!"

And she ran quickly to the pavilion with her find.

"We have found it!" Spring Plum reported. "In the 'Grotto of Hidden Spring'! It was in a book box, under a heap of visiting cards; it had been put away with some incense sticks!"

Gold Lotus took the slipper in her hand and compared it with the one which had remained in her possession. It was the same red stuff, the same pattern of embroidered flowers, the same white silk lining, the same green heel, the same blue metallic eyelets. Yet, one moment . . . on closer examination there was one trifling difference: in one slipper the strap was a bluish green, in the other it was kingfisher blue.

Gold Lotus tried on the slipper which had been found, and she then discovered that it did not fit her; it was too small. She realized at once that this shoe must have belonged to the late Lotus Petal, for of all the women of the household only Lotus Petal could boast of smaller feet than Gold Lotus's own.

"It is not my slipper," she said, turning to Spring Plum. "Take that miserable creature into the courtyard and make her kneel, and lay a good big heavy stone on her head!"

Poor Autumn Aster wailed and pleaded in vain; she had to allow herself to be led out into the courtyard, where she was made to kneel on the hot flagstones, and there she had to expose her head to the burning rays of the sun, burdened with the weight of a rough, heavy stone.

Gold Lotus, however, slipped on another pair of shoes, and since she found it too hot in the downstairs rooms she went upstairs, and told Spring Plum to bring her toilet table and her washbowl after her. She would make her toilet in the airy balcony room.

That same morning young Chen had just left the shop, in order to walk awhile in the shady park, when by the entrance gate he encountered little Iron Bolt, the son of the servant Lai Chao, who was playing in the sand. The butterfly net in young Chen's hand naturally attracted the boy's attention.

"Master Son-in-law, give me the net!" he pleaded.

Young Chen had to refuse his request. He had already promised the net to someone else, but he would give him another one later.

"No, I want that one!" the child pleaded again. "I'll give you something pretty for it!"

"What will that be? Let me see it!"

The little monkey forthwith felt inside his coat and brought out a red satin slipper, embroidered with a floral design.

"Where did you get that?" asked the other, in astonishment.

The little monkey giggled slyly.

"Master Son-in-law, I know something—shall I tell you? Yesterday evening I was playing at the end of the park, near the shore of the lake. When I came near the Vine Arbor I saw how the master had bound the Fifth by the feet against the back entrance to the arbor and was having his fun with her. Later on, when they had gone, I slipped into the arbor. I wanted to ask Spring Plum to give me some fruit if there was any left, but she had gone already, and then I found the slipper in the arbor."

Young Chen held the pretty thing in his hand for a while, examining it closely; here was the delicate curve of the crescent moon, and there the tender flush of the water lily. Now he measured it against the length of his palm.

"That's it—barely three inches," he said to himself. "It can only be hers."

"Give it to me!" he said aloud to the little monkey. "Tomorrow you shall have a beautiful butterfly net."

"But you'll really keep your promise?"

"You can rely on my word!"

Triumphantly he dropped the slipper into his sleeve pocket and went his way.

"Heaven has dropped this shoe into my lap," he reflected. "I've had a few skirmishes with her already, but always, when I was near my goal, she has slipped out of my hands like a wave. But this time I have her in a corner. She shan't slip through the bed curtains and escape me."

One has but to know when the proper moment has come
And the thread of itself will pass through the needle's eye.

He went straight to Gold Lotus's pavilion. As he passed through the courtyard he saw Autumn Aster in the scorching sun, her head burdened with a heavy stone, kneeling on the hard flags.

"Why, little one, sent to the penal colony?" he cried, jestingly, and he compassionately freed her from her burden.

Gold Lotus, in the balcony room, hearing a strange voice in the courtyard, said to Spring Plum:

"But who was that? And look, he has even had the impudence to take the stone off the wench's head!"

Spring Plum hastily ran downstairs.

"The Son-in-law is here," she shouted up from the courtyard. "I've put the stone back on her head."

"Oho! Bring Master Chen upstairs!" Gold Lotus commanded.

He entered. The two front windows were wide open, and the blinds were drawn up.

Gold Lotus was sitting before the mirror, doing her hair. Some of the heavy tresses, gleaming like black oil, were still hanging down her back; they were so long that they touched the floor. He took his seat beside her on a little stool, and he now had leisure to observe her closely.

Presently her task was ended. The silver net fitted snugly over the orderly masses of cloudy fragrance, amidst which, here and there, a pearl glistened, or a bright enamel flower. Against her cheeks lay the bold, fourfold curve of her side curls.

She rose, and once more washed her hands. Then Spring Plum had to clear away the toilet table and bring tea. All this time her guest sat smiling, and never spoke a word.

"Why do you smile, friend?"

"Because you have lost something that you value and cannot find it."

"And if I have lost something, what is that to you, you rascal? And as far as that goes, how do you come to know . . .?"

"But, Sister-in-law! I come here with the best of intentions, with the soft liver, the patient knees of a faithful sumpter mule, and you attack me so crossly! That being so, I had better leave you."

He rose, and was actually making for the door. Gold Lotus held him back.

"Rascal, I quite understand: now that your dear Lotus Petal isn't here, you remember my existence. But speak out: what have I lost?"

Smiling, he drew the red satin slipper from his sleeve pocket.

"Now, whose property can that be?" he asked.

"Then you've stolen it, you scamp! And the poor girl is innocent, and has had to suffer for nothing!"

"Stolen it? No! It came into my hands in quite a different way."

"Of course you stole it! Who else but you would dare to slink into my room like a thieving rat?"

"Please, please! It is quite two days since I have been here."

"Just you wait, you insolent fellow! I shall tell Master Hsi Men."

"You may, for all I care. I suppose you think you can frighten me by saying that?"

"And what if I tell him that you made love to his beloved Lotus Petal, seven or eight times or more? But now give me the slipper, and confess candidly how you came by it, if you didn't steal it. I've got you completely in my power!"

"Dear Sister-in-law, you are such a sensible woman! We are quite alone here: don't be so cold. Let us have a nice little talk. If you absolutely must have the slipper, very well! But no thunder without lightning: you must give me something for it!"

"And what is that?"

"Give me at least the handkerchief that is peeping out of your sleeve!"

"That? No, I can hardly do that. He knows it too well, he would recognize it at once. Be patient; wait until tomorrow; you shall have another handkerchief."

"Sister-in-law, I have set my heart on this one. I wouldn't exchange it for a hundred others," he said, in a pleading tone.

She could not help laughing. "You intolerable rogue! You wear one out with your insistence! Here you are!"

And she gave him what he desired: the fine white cambric kerchief with the openwork hem, on which her name, Pan Chin Lien, was embroidered in letters of silver, and whose actual purpose was to dry her fragrant skin on hot nights.

"But hide it carefully! Above all, don't let your wife see it; she has a malicious tongue."

He bowed low and murmured his thanks. Then he gave her the

red satin slipper, and told her how the boy Iron Bolt had originally found it in the Vine Arbor, and how he, Chen, had fortunately obtained it from the boy. A slight flush crept over her cheeks.

"The little rascal! Steals my property and plays the eavesdropper! That would earn him a fine thrashing, if I were to tell Master Hsi Men!"

"No, no! Please don't tell him! If you do I shall be involved."

"Is one to show indulgence to a scorpion?"

They were still debating the point when a servant, sent by Hsi Men, appeared with the message that young Chen was needed in the front hall, as his father-in-law wished him to write some letters of congratulation. Gold Lotus hastily pushed him downstairs.

After he had gone she made Spring Plum bring her a light cane, with which to chastise Autumn Aster, for this matter of the lost slipper was highly disagreeable to her.

"But I found the slipper, so why should I be beaten?" the little maid objected in vain.

"This is the real slipper—take a good look at it!" said Gold Lotus, angrily, holding the slipper which young Chen had brought her close to the maid's face. "It was this you ought to have been looking for, you stupid creature!"

Autumn Aster stared at the slipper for a long while, as though she had lost her wits. "But that's strange," she stammered, quite bewildered. "Now you have three of the same pattern!"

"What are you talking about? Do you want to persuade me that somebody else's slipper is my own? Am I by any chance the three-legged toad in the moon?"

And she made Spring Plum give her fellow servant ten strokes with the cane. During this painful procedure the little maid clung weeping to her angry mistress's knees, and cried, pointing to Spring Plum:

"If she hadn't left the gate of the park open no one could have gone in and taken your slipper. She alone is to blame!"

"Did you ever hear such a thing!" cried the incriminated maid, in self-defense. "To try to throw suspicion on me too! It was you who had to bring the mats and cushions away from the Vine Arbor yesterday, so you ought to have kept your eyes open for the missing slipper. If it had been a brooch or a ring there would be something in what you say, but one can't very well overlook a red slipper! Your mistress is much too merciful. You've richly deserved twenty to thirty strokes!"

And poor Autumn Aster had to stifle her chagrin and once more suffer injustice. Moreover, Gold Lotus made her search the Grotto for the mate to Lotus Petal's slipper. In this she finally succeeded.

And that little monkey Iron Bolt had to atone no less dearly for his escapade. When that same afternoon Hsi Men learned from Gold Lotus what he had done he boxed the little boy's ears and kicked him until he squealed like a stuck pig, and lay more dead than alive on the steps of the terrace where the master had found him playing. When at last he recovered consciousness and told his parents why he had been thus maltreated, his mother, I Chang Tsing, could not refrain from rushing off to the kitchen, where she broadcast her indignation to west and east, with loud objurgations and fierce gesticulations.

"This accursed woman!" she began as she raved against Gold Lotus. "She'll come to a bad end one of these days! What harm had my boy done to her? The little fellow is barely twelve yet; he's a fledgling still, and one ought to make allowances for him! How could anyone leave him half dead and all bleeding just because of a silly childish scrape? The Fifth and her tortoise are not without their faults! If one were to reckon up the list of their sins—why, one would never have done!"

When a few nights later Hsi Men was sleeping in Gold Lotus's pavilion he noticed that she was wearing a pair of new green satin slippers with red heels.

"But, my darling, what are those ugly things you are wearing?" he asked, disapprovingly.

"They are only bedroom slippers. Since the little slave had soiled one of my red slippers with his dirty fingers I don't care to wear the red pair."

"Then I'll give you a new pair. You know I always think you look so charming in red slippers."

"Really? Oh, that reminds me of something I wanted to say to you."

She made Spring Plum bring her the pair of slippers which had been found in the "Grotto of Hidden Spring."

"Do you recognize these shoes?"

"I don't think so."

"Don't behave like a proud cockerel who doesn't recognize his hens after the event! These once belonged to your Lotus Petal! A pity they should ever be worn by the dirty feet of a wench like that! They were in a book chest, hidden under a heap of visiting cards, wrapped up with a lot of incense tapers."

And pointing to Autumn Aster, she continued:

"And this stupid creature wanted to persuade me they were mine! I gave her ten strokes with the cane for her insolence. Here!" she said, turning to Autumn Aster, "I give them to you; you can wear them yourself."

"But, mistress, they are much too small for me!" Autumn Aster shyly ventured to object. "They would barely go on my big toe!"

"What, you dare to contradict me? You ought to be flattered at wearing the shoes of one of your master's former mistresses! But perhaps your master would not have put them away so carefully if they had not been a valued memento?"

Autumn Aster was obediently departing with her present when Gold Lotus called her back.

"Bring me a knife!" she ordered. "I'd rather cut them to pieces. Their place is the rubbish heap."

And turning to Hsi Men: "See, how nicely one can slash them to ribbons! Does it hurt your feelings?"

"Oh, I'm not that sort!" replied Hsi Men, laughing, with assumed indifference.

"Oh, it doesn't hurt your feelings? Can you take your oath on that? Then why did you preserve them so carefully? Only so that you might think of the person who wore them, whenever you saw them; yes, again and again! Or is a woman you have loved so soon regarded with indifference, so quickly obliterated from your memory? In that case, you monster, have I perhaps to expect the same treatment from you?"

"Come, that's enough!" he said, smiling, and seeking to appease her. "After all, she was always very pleasant and respectful to you."

And he stifled her further objections with an affectionate kiss.

Next morning Gold Lotus was sitting on the steps of the terrace before the Malachite Veranda, diligently preparing to begin work on the new slippers. Her work basket stood open beside her. She had spread a sheet of paper over her knees, on which she was drawing, with deft strokes of the brush, the outline of her design for the new slippers.

"What are you drawing?" asked the Sixth, who had come to keep her company.

"My new red slippers. Outside, red satin; inside, a flowered white silk, quilted. On the toes a parrot will be embroidered biting at a peach."

"I have some red satin that would do, I'll fetch it and help you with the sewing," offered the Sixth.

She brought the satin, with needles and silk, and set to work beside Gold Lotus.

"You know, Sister Three might help us too. She wanted to make herself a new pair some time or other. I'll bring her," Gold Lotus suggested, and presently she returned hand in hand with Jade Fountain.

The Third took from her work basket a half-completed pair of black satin slippers.

"Whom are you hoping to excite with those?" asked the ever-suspicious Gold Lotus, in a casual tone.

"I excite anybody! No, I'm already an old woman beside you fresh young pearl blossoms! The clouds which I ought to evoke must be packed away in hard, wire-stitched sheepskins, through which not a drop will trickle!" said this ripe woman of thirty, in a resigned though jesting tone.

337

Now the three women began to ply scissors and needle in earnest. One helped the others with good advice, and incidentally they discussed the latest household events. Amongst other things, the incident of the red slippers was mentioned, and Gold Lotus listened attentively as the Third related how I Chang Tsing, the mother of Iron Bolt, had railed against her in the kitchen and the servants' quarters.

"She outpoured a whole ocean of abuse over you and Hsi Men and the Son-in-law. It was nothing but 'that female,' 'that tortoise,' 'that young ram.' And it seems that you were by no means blameless. At first we couldn't make very much of her scolding, but then Hsi Men's daughter sent for the boy, and we learned what it was all about. It's a good thing that Moon Lady wasn't there just then, or she would have had plenty to say about you!"

"Did she ever say anything against me?"

"Didn't she just! She complained of a nine-tailed vixen who had bewitched the whole household. It was on your conscience that the faithful Lai Wang was driven from home, and that his wife hanged herself. And now you'd been moving heaven and earth on account of a mere trifle, on account of a lost slipper, and you had a poor boy who'd been pilfering a little beaten until he was half dead. You ought to have looked after your shoes yourself. But apparently you were dead drunk in the Vine Arbor. Otherwise it was impossible to understand how you could have gone off with only one shoe. You had upset the whole household on account of a mere trifle."

"Oh, and if a servant intends to stab his master, is that a mere trifle? Sister Three, you were there when Lai Hsing warned us of the danger that threatened Hsi Men. Can we be expected to have the wife of a murderer waiting on us all day? And suppose I had not spoken? I should simply have been an accessory to the intended crime. No, those who are guilty invite punishment; those who borrow must satisfy their creditors; if people hurt me I hurt them. Who knows, if I had not acted in time I should long ago have been drowned in the river." Gold Lotus had spoken with heat, and her cheeks were flushed.

338

"Sister Five," said Jade Fountain consolingly, "we three understand one another and have no secrets from one another. But please oblige me by keeping to yourself what I have told you!"

Gold Lotus, however, took little heed of her admonition. That very evening Hsi Men was told the whole story, and the consequence was that the following day the servant Lai Chao, with his wife I Chang Tsing and the boy Iron Bolt, had to leave the house. One thing at least Moon Lady was able to do for them: they were allowed to live, for the future, in Mistress Ping's house in Lion Street, where they could replace the servant Ping An as caretakers of the property. Ping An was employed instead as a gatekeeper in Hsi Men's establishment. Once more Gold Lotus had triumphed over a troublesome adversary.

The fragile crimson threads with which she held Hsi Men bound to her person proved to be tough and strong as iron wires, and he, on the other hand, was indefatigable in the invention of ever fresh modifications of the sport of love.

One afternoon he was sitting in the belvedere of the open "Hall of the Assembled Horizon," waving a banana-leaf fan, and surrendering himself to the mood of the silent park, which lay beneath him, filled with sweet odors, brooding in the heat of the noontide sun; a mood whose charm is evoked by the poet, when he says:

Above the green shade
The dazzling glow of noon.
Towers and stone terraces
Rise silent from still waters.
The zephyr stirs the curtain,
With a faint crystalline tinkle.
The heavy fragrance of roses
Is wafted through the halls.

The maid Spring Plum had just set before him a dish of iced-fruit salad.

"What is your mistress doing?" he asked.

"She has told Autumn Aster to prepare a bath for her. In the meantime she is lying down for a little while."

"Oh, then I'll surprise her."

He swallowed the rest of his fruit salad, rose, and laying his hands on the maid's shoulder, turned her towards the postern gate which led to Gold Lotus's pavilion, and walked on beside her.

Silently he entered the bedroom. He found Gold Lotus asleep on her fine new bed, which was decorated with scrollwork in gilt metal. Since she had seen a bed of this kind in the bedroom of the Sixth she had given him no peace until he obtained another of the same kind for her. Sixty good ounces he had paid for this showy piece of furniture. It was surrounded by a skillfully carved wooden rail, and on either side of it stood a new screen, whose embroidery showed the same scrollwork motive, in addition to the usual sprays of flowers and peacock feathers. The crimson hangings were fastened to the tester of the bed with massive silver nails. Hsi Men had not grudged payment.

Gold Lotus, clad only in a thin, rose-pink lawn brassière, was lying on a cool mat, under a thin red silk coverlet, her head resting on a cushion embroidered with a pattern of mandarin ducks. She was fast asleep. The sight of her instantly aroused his desire. He gently pushed the maid Spring Plum to the door, hastily stripped off his clothes, and lifted the coverlet. And before she had time to open her starlike eyes in alarm, he already had what he desired of her.

"You rascal, how did you get in? Really, you startle one to death! I was having such a pleasant sleep."

"Well, it's only me! You behave just as though I were some youthful stranger!"

"Go along with you! What impudent intruder with seven stars and eight gall bladders could find his way into my bedroom, to which only you have access!"

Since Gold Lotus, when listening recently beneath the Malachite Veranda, had heard Hsi Men expressing his admiration for the smooth hips and buttocks of the Sixth, she had secretly obtained an oil subtly perfumed with jasmine, and with this, during the last few days, she had liberally anointed her body. Now, as she lay before him in her rosy nudity, it seemed to him that her skin was softer and smoother than usual, and that it exhaled a peculiarly delicious perfume. And further, the new deep crimson bed slippers which she was wearing attracted his attention.

"I was told you were going to take a bath," he said presently.

"That is so. And you can bathe with me."

She told the maids to bring in the large bathtub and fill it with orchid-scented water. Then they both got into it, and began to splash about like two jolly little fish. After they had amused themselves thus for a while he pressed her back against the sloping side of the tub and repeated his former feat.

At last he was satisfied. They dried each other, each pulled on a short, light smock, and they stretched their pleasantly-relaxed limbs upon the bed. Before they gave way to sleep they refreshed themselves with a little fresh fruit and sweet pastry. Gold Lotus also wanted a mouthful of white wine. But as Autumn Aster was offering the brimming silver goblet to her mistress, Hsi Men remarked that it was icy cold. Gold Lotus angrily seized the goblet and flung the contents full into the unfortunate maid's face.

"You clumsy creature, how dare you offer your master such freezing stuff! You are positively good for nothing!" she cried to the startled girl. "Spring Plum, take her into the courtyard and make her kneel and do penance!"

"But the master has been asking every day for iced wine!" said the maid, in self-defense, between her terrified sobs. "How could I know that he had changed his mind today?"

"Accursed wench, must you always answer back?" Gold Lotus cried, striking her on the mouth. "Spring Plum, give her ten good slaps, right and left!"

"Mistress, I don't want to soil my hands on her dirty hide!" Spring Plum objected. "But I'll put a good big stone on her head outside in the courtyard."

And so poor Autumn Aster had once more to kneel on the hard

flags of the courtyard in the blazing afternoon sun, with the grievous burden of a heavy stone on her head. It was fortunate for her that Sunflower had just been obliged to engage a fresh maid. On the advice of the Sixth, Gold Lotus decided to buy the fifteen-year-old Summer Blossom from the Second for seven ounces, and to take her into her service in the place of Autumn Aster, who was sent to the big kitchen as kitchenmaid; so that she was rid of her moody mistress.

CHAPTER TWENTY-THREE: *Chancellor Tsai distributes Offices and Dignities. Hsi Men becomes the Father of a Son, and a Mandarin*

I N THE MEANTIME, after a hot and fatiguing journey, Lai Pao, with his companion Wu Tien En, who was Hsi Men's friend and brother-in-law, had safely reached the Eastern Capital with his heavily-laden mules and the boxes of birthday gifts. The travelers alighted at a hostelry outside the "Gate of the Ten Thousand Generations," and on the following morning they went with their mules to the palace of the Chancellor Tsai. The new porter, who did not know them, would not at first admit them. When, in reply to his questions as to who they were and where they came from, Lai Pao explained that they were envoys from Master Hsi Men of the city of Tsing ho hsien in the province of Shantung, and that they were bringing birthday gifts for the Ancient Commander, the porter replied testily: "Don't you fellows know where you are, that you have the impudence to demand admission here? The Ancient Commander has only one over him and millions under him. Hardly any can enter here but the Three Councillors of State and the eight Ministers; hardly any but princes and rulers. What has the Ancient Commander to do with your master, who lives far away in the wilderness by the eastern gates of the Empire? Be off with you!"

It so happened that a few of the palace servants were standing by, who had made Lai Pao's acquaintance on the occasion of his former visit. One of them now came forward, and said, in a conciliatory tone: "Don't take offense! He is the new porter, who has only been a few days in service, so that he doesn't know you. If you wish to speak to the Ancient Commander, I will ask Uncle Ti to come out."

Lai Pao promptly drew from his sleeve a parcel of silver, containing an ounce, which he handed to the obliging speaker.

"I don't want anything," said the latter, declining it. "But add another ounce to it and give it to the doorkeeper and his assistant, so that they will know you in future."

Lai Pao immediately followed his advice, whereupon the porter's face was transformed by a friendly grin.

"So you come from Tsing ho hsien? Well, well! Now just you wait a bit. I'll send in your name at once to Intendant Ti. The Ancient Commander has just returned from the 'Palace of Ethereal Purity,' and is resting a little in the library."

And he disappeared indoors. After a long interval he returned in the company of the Intendant Ti. Uncle Ti was wearing cool bast sandals over his light stockings, and a coat of thin blue silk, such as the Taoist priests are accustomed to wear. He had met Lai Pao on the occasion of his former visit.

"You have been here before, with presents for the Ancient Commander, have you not?"

Lai Pao made a kowtow and offered him, with one hand, his visiting card, and with the other a packet of thirty ounces of silver, wrapped in Nanking silk.

"My master sends you his greetings," he said, "and begs that in lieu of a more worthy gift you will not disdain this insignificant trifle as a sign of his friendly feelings."

"I really ought not to accept your gift, but I should not wish to offend you. . . ."

The heavy package disappeared in his sleeve as he glanced over the list of presents which Lai Pao now handed him. "Come with me!" he said.

He led them to a second gate, on the western side of which were three waiting rooms for visitors. Here he made them sit down and refresh themselves with tea. After some time they were summoned to the presence of the Ancient Commander in the outer reception hall. They knelt before the dais on which the Chancellor sat, while the Intendant laid the visiting card and the list of presents before him. In the meantime some of the servants had unpacked the presents and brought them into the hall, where they spread them out on the dais. Now the tankards of gold repoussé in the form of the character Shu glittered yellow, the jade goblets shone with a pale luster, the four genii of the silver service, representing the four seasons, gleamed with a white radiance, and the satin robes, with their pattern of embroidered snakes, dazzled the eye. Here the noble wine of Tang yang sparkled in golden pitchers; there, in silver bowls, were piles of delicious fruits. Must not the heart of the recipient be enlarged by such a spectacle?

"I cannot possibly accept these presents!" said the Chancellor. "Take them away!"

The two envoys quickly made a few kowtows.

"Our master sends these inconspicuous trifles merely as a feeble token of his devotion. The Ancient Commander can distribute them as he pleases."

"That is another matter. Then I will accept your gifts for my people."

He signed to those about him, and the heaped-up treasures were carried out.

"Your master has repeatedly paid me attentions. I do not really know how I should express my gratitude. Has he any official rank?"

"Our master is a simple citizen, without any rank."

"Indeed. It so happens that by the Emperor's grace I have a few blank patents of appointment in hand. I could appoint your master supplementary District Judge, in order to fill the vacancy caused by the removal of a certain judge. What do you think?"

Lai Pao beat his forehead upon the floor.

"For the favor of such promotion my master would thank the Ancient Commander until old age had powdered his hair white and broken his body into fragments."

The Chancellor sent for a writing table, and a few blank patents. One of these he completed in the name of Hsi Men. "To be supplementary District Judge in Shantung with the title of a Gold Staff Warden," the preamble read.

"And you two have taken strenuous pains to bring me these birthday gifts," the Chancellor continued. "Who is the companion, Lai Pao, whom I see kneeling behind you?"

"My master's brother-in-law, Wu Tien En."

"Indeed, his brother-in-law. Well, I will requite his zeal for duty. I appoint him postmaster of Tsing ho hsien."

And he filled in a second form with the name of Wu Tien En.

The delighted Wu Tien En, in token of his gratitude, struck his head upon the floor so violently that it sounded as though garlic were being pounded in a mortar.

The Chancellor now filled in a third patent, and before the worthy Lai Pao realized what was happening he was appointed Gate Commandant in the palace of Prince Yuen in Tsing ho hsien.

"Here, take your appointments," said the Chancellor benevolently. "Go with them tomorrow to the Ministry of the Interior and the War Ministry, have your names entered there in the official registers, and obtain your patents and official seals. And you, Ti, see that they are given some wine and something to eat in the west wing. Pay them, too, ten ounces of silver from my treasury, so that they shall need for nothing on the journey."

With this they were graciously dismissed. Intendant Ti led them to one of the reception rooms in the west wing of the inner gate, and had a sumptuous meal set before them. He waited until the visitors had eaten their fill; then he moved a little nearer to Lai Pao, and began in a confidential tone: "I had a small personal petition to lay before your master. But perhaps he will not look into the matter?"

"But, Master Ti, how could you even for a moment doubt the goodwill of my master! After all, we owe our gracious reception by the Ancient Commander entirely to your kind introduction. Whatever it may be, tell me your wish without misgiving; my master will not fail to attend to your desires."

"Well, then, to speak quite frankly, I want a young consort. My homely wife is now nearly forty, and often indisposed. Unhappily,

346

our marriage is childless. On the other hand, my service under the Ancient Commander gives me little time to attend to such personal affairs myself. In short, if your master would have the kindness to look about for a fresh young creature, say about fifteen or sixteen years of age, and not without certain personal merits, the price would not matter as far as I am concerned. . . ."

"Oh, my master will not fail to do so. . . ."

In the meantime the letter of reply to Hsi Men, confirming the receipt of his gift, had been duly prepared in the secretariat. Intendant Ti handed it to Lai Pao, together with the ten ounces from the Chancellor's treasury, and to this he added five ounces on his own account for each of the two envoys. At first they would not hear of accepting his gifts.

"We have only just profited by the benevolence of the Ancient Commander. How could we. . . ."

"That has nothing to do with the question. I am sure you will not wish to hurt my feelings." And he insisted that they should accept his five ounces. A secretary, whom he told off to accompany them, would see that on the following day the necessary formalities, such as the registration and preparation of the patents and official seals, were effected without delay in the two Ministries. They repaid him with a banquet and three ounces, and on the following day they were ready to begin their homeward journey.

On one of those midsummer days when one slinks along in the heat like a dog, Hsi Men, his wives, and the household musicians, were assembled in the airy "Hall of the Assembled Horizon" to partake of a joyful banquet. All the wives were there, with the exception of the Sixth.

"Where is your mistress hiding herself?" Moon Lady asked of the maid Apricot Blossom.

"She has a bad pain inside today, so she didn't feel like going out."

"Oh, she can't be as bad as all that. Go quickly and bring her here; she ought to listen to the music."

"What is the matter with her?" Hsi Men inquired.

347

"She complains of pains in the body, and she has taken something for them. She will come directly." And speaking quietly to Jade Fountain, she said: "She's already well into the eighth month. Her time will soon have come."

"It's much too early for her confinement," said Gold Lotus, decidedly.

"Very well, then she can just come and listen to the music," echoed Hsi Men.

And presently the Sixth appeared.

"No doubt you have been sitting in a draught and have caught a little cold," said Moon Lady, solicitously. "A sip of hot wine will do you good."

At Hsi Men's request the four musicians—Spring Plum, Jade Flute, Fragrant Orchid, and Pear Blossom—began to sing the song, "When summer's heat is threatening." But Mistress Ping was able to listen only to the first verse. With a faint moan she rose while the maids were singing and crept back to her pavilion.

"She's in labor," reported the maid, Little Jewel, whom Moon Lady had sent after her.

"I said as much!" cried Moon Lady. "But as usual, the Fifth knew better. And we haven't even sent for the midwife!"

Hsi Men ordered Ping An to run like the wind and fetch Mother Tsai. The feast was abandoned, and all hurried off to the pavilion of the Sixth.

"How do you feel, sister?" asked Moon Lady, compassionately.

"As though my bowels were turning over, as though a great toad were struggling inside my body."

"Raise yourself up a little, so that the fruit can find its way out more readily, and isn't suffocated."

"Has anyone been sent for the midwife?" asked Moon Lady, turning to those about her.

"Ping An has gone," said little Tai.

"How ill-advised, to send that dawdling old man! The matter is urgent! Quick, run after him and bring the woman here with all possible speed!"

So Tai had to mount a mule, and follow the other at a gallop.

"This excitement!" Gold Lotus whispered contemptuously to the Third, whom she drew out of the house, to a shady spot under the projecting eaves. "All that crowd in the one room is enough to stifle you. This fuss about an unborn child! As though they expected to see a young elephant!"

At last, and just at the critical moment, Mother Tsai, the midwife, appeared.

"Which of these ladies is the mistress of the house?" she asked, of the assembled women. Someone pointed to Moon Lady. The old woman went up to her and made her bow.

"No ceremony now, please!" Moon Lady objected. "It was high time you came!"

Mother Tsai went up to the bed and felt Mistress Ping's body.

"It's *so* far," she declared. "Are the swaddling bands ready?"

"They are all ready in my room," replied Moon Lady. "Little Jewel, run and fetch them!"

"Shall we go in again and look on? The old woman is there," said Jade Fountain, turning to Gold Lotus.

"You go, if you want to. I'll stay here," replied Gold Lotus, coldly. "After all, what is there to see when a woman is confined?"

So Jade Fountain continued to keep her company, and they began to exchange doubts and conjectures as to whether Hsi Men was really the child's father. Now Little Jewel hurried past them with a bundle of swaddling bands and pillows, tied up with silken tape.

"The First had really got those ready for her own use," Jade Fountain whispered to her companion. "Now the Sixth has got ahead of her."

Presently the wailing of a child was heard from the bedchamber, and then Mother Tsai appeared in the doorway, announcing, with a portentous expression: "A little boy has arrived. Just inform the master of the house; he ought to pay handsomely for the glad tidings!"

Hsi Men, to whom Moon Lady brought the joyful news, quickly washed his hands and fell upon his knees, expressing his thanks to

Heaven, Earth, and his ancestors by an extravagant offering of incense, while he prayed that they would bless and protect mother and child, bath and swaddling bands. There was only one person who did not join in the general rejoicings. Gold Lotus, on hearing that a man-child was born, had withdrawn resentfully to her pavilion. She bolted the door, flung herself upon her bed, and wept bitterly. This happened on the twenty-third day of the sixth month of the fourth year of the "Harmonious Government" (1115).

In the meantime, Mother Tsai, having bitten through the navel string, had carefully swaddled the child, and washed the mother, for whom she prepared a strong, stimulating broth. Then, her work being done, she was able to refresh herself, making a good meal, at Moon Lady's invitation, in the First Wife's own room, and to pocket a fee of no less than five ounces. Hsi Men also invited her to attend the feast in celebration of the washing of the newborn child, which would be held two days later, and on her departure he gave her a fine length of satin.

Now he himself went at last to the mother's bedside, in order to inquire into the welfare of his wife and child. His delight in the beautifully formed little creature, who was distinguished by an exceptionally fair complexion, was boundless. He spent the whole night in the pavilion of the Sixth, and was never weary of gazing at the child.

Early the next morning servants were dispatched in all directions, in order to publish the joyful news to kinsfolk and neighbors. For this reason they had to distribute no less than twenty ceremonial boxes of noodles. The first visitors to present their congratulations, covering two full paces at every stride, were Beggar Ying and Hsia Hsi Ta. Hsi Men shared a dish of "long life noodles" with them in the belvedere; then he sent them away. That day there were all sorts of things to be seen to. Above all, a suitable wet-nurse had to be engaged. She was soon found. The wife of Neighbor Pi brought to the house the young wife of a servant of hers. She had lost her child a month earlier, and now her husband, who had been enrolled for military service, had to leave her and proceed to the front. Moon

Lady took a fancy to this strongly-built, neatly dressed young woman of thirty, so she bought her from her neighbor for the price at which she was offered—namely, six ounces—and established her in Mistress Ping's pavilion, where she was to feed the child night and morning. She was given the name of Ju I—"As you like it."

In the very midst of this day's confusion Hsi Men's two envoys returned from the Eastern Capital. Now there was another joyful surprise. Hsi Men was appointed District Judge with the title of Gold Staff Warden! From the corners of his eyes a beaming smile spread over his whole countenance as Lai Pao spread before him on the table his fine official seal, in duplicate, and the various ministerial notifications of his appointment. He hastily gathered up all these treasures, and ran off to the rear apartments, in order to feast his eyes upon them in the presence of his wives.

"It has pleased the Ancient Commander to exalt my house and to appoint me supplementary District Judge," he solemnly announced. "I now bear the title of Gold Staff Warden, and am a mandarin of the fifth class! And you," he added, gallantly, turning to Moon Lady, "can henceforth adorn your hair with the gold flower of a mandarin's wife! Two joyful events in less than a fortnight! Good fortune as exalted as the clouds is vouchsafed to our house! But the stout little fellow whom the Sixth has given us shall tomorrow, at the ceremony of his washing, receive the name of Kwan Ko—'Little Brother Mandarin!'"

Bad iron will sometimes gleam with a false luster
While sterling gold, being hidden, cannot glitter!

CHAPTER TWENTY-FOUR: *Gold Lotus makes young Chen howl for Mercy, while Intendant Ti repeats in Writing his request for a young Virgin*

A MONTH HAD PASSED. It had brought much unrest and confusion to the household of Hsi Men. First of all, there was Master Chow, who, with his seven apprentices, had set up a regular little tailor's shop in the eastern wing of the house, in order to complete Hsi Men's official wardrobe in time by several days of feverish activity. Then new visiting cards had to be written. Innumerable visits of congratulation had to be received. Then came the day selected by the astrologers—an auspicious date of the first order—when Hsi Men, with great pomp, entered upon his official career. And this was followed by three banquets of unprecedented sumptuousness; one for kinsfolk and neighbors, an official banquet for Hsi Men's colleagues, and finally, on the day of which we are writing, an unceremonious friendly feast for the nine Brethren.

While in the front of the house Hsi Men's comrades were carousing and jesting with the four flower-girls who had been invited to entertain them—Cinnamon Bud, Little Silver, Darling Fragrance, and Jade Clasp—Gold Lotus was sitting glumly before her mirror, adorning herself in vain. She felt, with increasing anxiety, that since the birth of the child her hold upon Hsi Men was diminishing. His visits were growing rarer and rarer, while he spent night after night in the pavilion of the Sixth.

Now she had finished arranging her hair. Yawning with boredom, she rose and strolled out into the park. The loud whimpering of a child fell upon her ear, causing her to direct her steps to the pavilion of the Sixth.

"Is anything the matter with the little one?" she asked the nurse.

"He is longing for his mother. She is still in the big house."

"There, there!" said Gold Lotus, laughing, as she stooped over the child's cradle. "Such a little fellow, only just born, and he knows his mama already! Wait a moment, I'll take you to her!"

"Mistress, you had better not take him out! He's afraid of you, and he'll soil you," the nurse warned her.

"Be quiet, you lazy lump!" said Gold Lotus, peremptorily. "I'll carry him on the pillows. What can happen then?"

And lifting the child from the cradle, she carried him to the house, now snuggling him against her bosom, now carelessly tossing him in the air.

"See what I'm bringing you!" she cried, laughingly, to Moon Lady, who was resting on the veranda outside her sitting room. "The little man is looking for his mama."

And once more she merrily tossed her burden high above her head.

"But Sister Five, how can you handle the child so carelessly! You will give him a positive tiger of a fright!" said Moon Lady reprovingly. "His mother is indoors. Sister Six, come out! Your baby wants you!" she cried.

Startled, Mistress Ping came rushing on to the veranda. "You should have left the child in my room with the nurse," she said reproachfully. "It was most unnecessary to bring him here. And I see there are wet patches on your dress. It serves you right."

"He was crying for you so," said Gold Lotus, in some embarrassment, seeking to excuse herelf.

Mistress Ping took the child from her, placed him in safety against her motherly bosom, and carried him back to the pavilion.

"How could you let the child out of your sight and allow the Fifth to carry him off!" she scolded the nurse.

"She took him from me against my will."

She was able gradually to quiet the child and lull him to sleep.

But in the middle of the night he seemed to be suddenly terrified by a bad dream; he began once more to whimper pitifully; he shivered as though with ague, and broke out into perspiration. In vain did the nurse offer him the breast to soothe him. He turned his little head away and cried still more pitifully.

"What is the matter with the child?" asked Hsi Men, anxiously, when he entered Mistress Ping's bedchamber late that night, the last of his guests having taken his leave. She did not quite like to accuse Gold Lotus, and merely shrugged her shoulders. Naturally, the innocent nurse had to endure an undeserved reprimand. Then Hsi Men hurried off to consult with Moon Lady. She, again, though perfectly well aware of the cause of the child's sudden indisposition, was careful to spare Gold Lotus, saying nothing of the prank which she had played.

"I will send for old Liu tomorrow," she proposed.

"Keep that silly woman with her crazy cauterizing needle out of the house!" he protested. "We had far better send for a sensible children's doctor."

"Oh, for a creature like that, barely a month old, you can't have a children's doctor!"

And next morning, when Hsi Men had gone to his office at his usual early hour, she insisted on sending for the well-tried Mother Liu. The medicine which the old woman gave the child was, as a matter of fact, effectual. He fell into a deep sleep, and when he woke he readily accepted the nurse's breast. A stone fell from Mistress Ping's heart. But a little later, when Moon Lady entered the room to inquire after the child, the two women exchanged a meaning glance.

"Didn't I say so?" Moon Lady observed. "She's a nine-tailed vixen, who has bewitched the whole household!"

That day as Hsi Men was taking his midday meal with Moon Lady, Beggar Ying was announced. Hsi Men kept him waiting for some time in the belvedere.

"What does he want of you again today?" asked Moon Lady. "He was here only yesterday."

"He's come on a matter of business," explained Hsi Men. "A silk merchant of his acquaintance from Huchow, who happens to be passing through the town, wants to unload his wares on me. He is asking five hundred ounces—fifty more than I have offered him. He is pressing for a settlement, and Beggar Ying has come on his behalf in order to complete the transaction. And I shall complete it; I have decided to open a silk mercer's shop in our house in Lion Street. The position has one great advantage—just behind the house is Prince Yuen's estate, where our Lai Pao puts in his little bit of service as gatekeeper. Thanks to his position, so conveniently near the house, he will be able to send us many aristocratic customers, and at the same time he will be able to look after the business a little, so that he can still go on working for me."

"But you will have to look out for a suitable manager."

"I have done so. An acquaintance of Ying's, a certain Han Tao Kwo, will be my manager. He knows his way about the silk trade, and Ying recommends him as being thoroughly capable and trustworthy. Since he hasn't enough capital to set up for himself he is glad to accept the position of manager under me."

In the meantime Beggar Ying, who had promised himself a good deal of incidental profit from the conclusion of this agreement, waited in the belvedere, burning with impatience, and swallowing bowl after bowl of tea. Young Chen was keeping him company. At last Hsi Men appeared, and with him Lai Pao, dragging a number of heavy purses, which contained four hundred and fifty ounces of silver. At the sight of the purses Friend Ying's eyes grew round with delight.

"Now, get on with it!" Hsi Men urged him. "Take the money to the dealer! And then we can hire carts at once and have the stuff taken to the shop. Today is an auspicious date for such business."

Beggar Ying, accompanied by Lai Pao, hurried off to the inn outside the city gate, where the dealer from Hu Chow was staying. Then, behind Lai Pao's back, Ying once more haggled desperately with the dealer, with the result that the purchase price was finally knocked down to four hundred and twenty ounces. Twenty of the remaining thirty ounces he pocketed as commission, while he generously shared the residue of ten ounces with Lai Pao. Then carts and coolies were hired, and the bales of silk were removed to Lion Street. A few days later the agreement was signed appointing Han Tao Kwo as manager. The new manager was a thick-set man of forty, with a full, round face and a flexible mouth which poured forth torrents of words. He and Lai Pao were given a considerable sum as working capital, with which to pay wages, dyers' charges, cost of fixtures, etc., and before long the newly-opened shop began to flourish under their twofold management, and the daily turnover was considerable. Hsi Men had no premonition that the new manager would be of valuable assistance to him in another sphere than the commercial.

Gold Lotus had not forgotten, and could not forget, how impudently young Chen had played against her the trump card of the lost scarlet slipper. One day in the eighth month she found an opportunity of revenging herself. She was visiting the Sixth with her mother when the maid Spring Plum was called out. Young Chen was downstairs; he wanted to fetch some things out of the pledge chamber in the Fifth's pavilion. Spring Plum had to accompany him and open the outer door of the upper story. The business of the pawnshop in front of the house had continued to increase, so that Hsi Men had been obliged to install a second repository in Gold Lotus's pavilion.

In obedience to one of her sudden caprices, Gold Lotus called after the maid: "When he has got his things out bring him here; I invite him to take some refreshment."

But young Chen was not at all anxious to accept her invitation. There was a press of clients at the pawnbroker's counter; he had no time to spare.

"Bring him here whatever the circumstances!" Gold Lotus commanded, when Spring Plum told her that young Chen had refused her invitation. And she sent the maid Apricot Blossom with her by way of reinforcement. At last the two maids dragged the refractory visitor into the house. He had to set down his pledges in a corner and take a seat, and then he had to drink a large and brimming bowl of tea.

"One little bowl, or two at most," he objected; "but this great basin—why, the people in the shop are waiting for me!"

"Let them wait!" said Gold Lotus, and she insisted that he must empty the great bowl. Then a few beakers of wine were set before him, and as a matter of politeness he was obliged to crack a few unshelled nuts with his teeth.

"Sister-in-law, have pity on me!" he pleaded. "If father-in-law catches me in business hours all flushed with wine. . . ."

"I thought you were not afraid of him?" she said, coldly. "Didn't you at some time or other say something to that effect?"

At last, during a lively conversation, at a moment when Gold Lotus's attention was diverted, he picked up his parcels and quickly slipped out of the room.

"He has left the key of the store room behind him," said Spring Plum, when he had gone.

"Give it here!" Gold Lotus commanded, and she quickly concealed it under her clothes.

"And don't you betray me! I want to keep him on the rack a bit first!"

Very soon young Chen returned, inquiring most anxiously for the lost key.

"What have we to do with your key?" said Gold Lotus, coldly. "Of course, you have dropped it over there."

"No, I distinctly remember that I brought it here. It must be here. Please help me to look for it! The clients are waiting. If it isn't found I shall have to have the door burst open."

Gold Lotus could hardly refrain from laughing at his consternation. Like an ox circling round the millstone, he sought round the room with his anxious gaze. Suddenly he saw a scrap of the key ribbon protruding from under the petticoat of the Fifth. He tried to seize it, but she was too quick for him, and in a moment the key was tucked away in her sleeve.

"I wonder what Master Hsi Men would think of you if he learned that your key is in my possession? Eh?" she asked, mockingly, gloating over his terror. He fell at her feet and implored her, in a voice as lamentable as that of a dying hen, to stop tormenting him.

"Not until you have sung me a nice song. You are so fond of singing at your work in the shop. Why should the shop assistants be the only people to enjoy your voice? We should like to have a chance of enjoying it too."

And although he was by no means in the mood for singing, he had, willy-nilly, to do his best with one of the songs from his repertoire. But even then her longing for revenge was not satisfied. He had to sing a second song; then she let him go.

"If I wanted to, I could keep you singing until far into the night. And I should only have to tell the person of whom you say you are not afraid that you boldly forced your way into my room after losing the key in a state of drunkenness. It would go badly with you. You know my maxim: 'Who torments me, him I torment.' Now we are quits. Go!"

As Hsi Men was not expected to return before the evening, that afternoon Moon Lady, together with the Second, Third, Fifth, and Sixth wives, went to look over the estate of Neighbor Kiao, which Hsi Men had recently purchased in another part of the city. As ill luck would have it, Moon Lady, in ascending to the upper floor of the house, slipped on the stairs and fell. She retained her grip of the stair rail, and escaped without external injury, but she was so overcome by the shock that she got into her litter immediately and was carried home. On the way she began to suffer violent internal pains; for she was pregnant. Mother Liu, who was hastily sent for, declared, with a rueful wag of the head, that the fall would undoubtedly have cost the life of her sixth months' child, and that now, for the sake of her own health, she must resign herself to an abortion. So Moon Lady swallowed a double dose of the black purgative pills and the infusion of wormwood which the old woman gave her, and that very night she gave birth to a dead and already fairly well-developed child. It was a male child! Poor Moon Lady! With this her proud hope was shattered. And Hsi Men must never learn how near she had been to her goal.

Since Hsi Men had become the father of a son, and a mandarin into the bargain, his whole mode of life had undergone a far-reaching transformation. Twice a day he betook himself to the yamen, where he consulted with his colleague Ho, or sat on the bench beside him. And his new position involved many other official duties, which took up much of his time, and were very tiring. In short, there could be no further question of his former carefree and dissolute way of life. On the contrary, the society of his former drinking companions and sworn confederates gradually became so obnoxious to him that his gatekeepers were given strict orders to deny them admittance if the comrades of his once joyful days should visit him uninvited. Only Beggar Ying and Hsia Hsi Ta had access to him at any time, as of old. But even the flower gardens of the five streets and the seven lanes had to dispense with the honor of his frequent presence. He had to put them out of mind, like so many other things that had once seemed to him important.

Yet in the press of business he had quite forgotten another matter which ought to have seemed important enough even under his now altered circumstances. One day a mounted messenger appeared from the Eastern Capital, bringing a letter from Intendant Ti of the Chancellor's palace. It ran as follows:

"The ancient Ti in the Eastern Capital bows his head and offers his greeting to the great Hsi Men, promoted to the 'Hall of the Silk-blossoming Talents.'

"Long since, crouching before your threshold, I have gazed up at you in admiration as to the summit of the august Tai Shan or the constellation of the Great Bear. Even before I was granted the precious enjoyment of your personal acquaintance you have repeatedly put me to shame with abundant proofs of your favor, thereby pledging me to eternal gratitude. The exalted intimation which you recently vouchsafed me was engraven upon my heart like a bronze inscription, and you may be convinced that I have at all

359

times done all that was in my power to support you, as though you had been a worthy and venerable commander of a hundred and ten years.

"As regards the little matter with which I troubled you recently, in reliance on your infinite kindness, I presume that in the meantime you have settled this for me. While I beg you to accept the accompanying ten ounces of gold as a sorry expression of my gratitude, I trust, in humble expectation, that you will forthwith favor me with an adequate reply. . . ."

When Hsi Men had read this letter to the end he clicked the tip of his tongue against his palate an infinite number of times, and exhaled a long sigh of regret. Then, turning to Moon Lady:

"How could I," he said, "have forgotten this affair! We must send for a go-between at once."

Moon Lady, who so far knew nothing of the matter, wanted to know of what affair he was speaking.

"When Lai Pao took my presents to the Chancellor, Intendant Ti gave him a message for me. He asked me, since he was childless, and his only wife was already nearly forty, and always ailing, to find him a young girl for a concubine. The price needn't be considered, and it didn't matter if she were rich or poor. The main thing was that she must be young—fifteen or sixteen or thereabouts—and good to look at. He would indemnify me for all expenses, and in return he would always do his utmost to promote my interests with the Chancellor. It is really a very important matter. How could I be so forgetful! But with all this official business! And then I've rather lost sight of Lai Pao, in this new job of his, so that he couldn't remind me of the matter. It's too annoying! And the messenger left word that he will call for my answer tomorrow afternoon, as he has to go on at once. What on earth am I to do? Master Ti must already be wondering about me. The girl must be found by tomorrow. How would it be if I were simply to send our Apricot Blossom?"

"Now, don't go rushing off as though you had a forest fire at your heels! After wasting three months without attending to the matter, you can't settle it from one day to the next. And you really can't send him a common maidservant. Master Ti will want something better than that; we can't consider anyone but a carefully-guarded girl of good family. You must give the matter a little further consideration, and wait patiently until the go-between has found some-one suitable."

"But the messenger wants his answer tomorrow."

"If only that were all! Treat him generously, and tell Master Ti to wait a little longer! Say in your reply that the girl is already found, but that her trousseau isn't ready yet. You'll send her to the capital very shortly."

"Excellent. It shall be done."

Young Chen had immediately to write a carefully-worded reply, and on the following day, when the messenger appeared, he was received by Hsi Men in person, sumptuously entertained, and sent on his way with a present of five ounces.

Moon Lady, however, dispatched old Fong and Mother Pi and a few other matchmakers in search of a suitable maiden.

Three days later, as Hsi Men was riding through the city, he saw old Fong in the distance, and sent his boy to fetch her.

"Well, Mother Fong, what about the young lady? Not found yet?" he cried.

"What a hunt I have had for her today! But there was nothing suitable. And then at last, by pure chance, I found the very thing for you. If I hadn't by chance invited her mother to drink a bowl of tea with me yesterday as she was passing I shouldn't have got her today. I assure you, a creature of the hundred per cent class! A pedigree filly, and barely fifteen! The way she droops her head, and the way she does her hair, it would delight the brush of any artist! That slender body! Those tiny feet! That smooth little face! The tiny little mouth! A divine creature! 'Darling' is her name, and she was born on the day of the Dragon Boat Festival. Don't imagine that I'm exaggerating! You'll fall in love with her yourself once you've seen her!"

"Now, no joking! This time the little girl is not for me. Do you know for whom she is destined? For the enormously wealthy Intendant Ti, in the palace of the Chancellor Tsai! He has chosen her for his concubine, and hopes for a son to continue his line. I received from him the honorable commission to discover the fitting maiden for him. You will not lose by it if my choice is in accordance with his desires. Whose daughter is she? And have you already procured the cards with the eight characters of her birth?"

"Whose daughter is she? Well, you needn't look far afield! She's the child of the manager of your silk shop, Master Han Tao Kwo, by his first marriage. And if you wish I will consult her father and fix a day on which you can see her for yourself."

"Do so: settle the matter with him, and get the cards with the eight characters."

Two days later old Fong came to him with the required eight cards. The maiden in question was indeed the daughter of his manager, Han Tao Kwo; fifteen years of age, and born on the fifth day of the fifth month.

"I have spoken to the old man," Mother Fong reported. "He thinks that since it is you who are taking his daughter from him it can only be for her happiness. But he doesn't know how he, in his poverty-stricken hovel, can get the necessary trousseau together."

"Tell him he needn't spend a copper. As for clothes, linen, jewelry, I'll see to all that myself, and I'll place twenty ounces at his disposal into the bargain. He might just see to it that she has suitable shoes and slippers. And further, you can inform him that I should like him to escort his daughter to the capital in person; that would be better than entrusting her to the care of a maid. For the rest, you can tell him that Master Ti's chief desire is to get a son by his daughter, so that she would be received like a chief wife, and she can look forward to a carefree, brilliant, and honorable career."

"And when should he be ready to receive your visit?"

"I shall call on him tomorrow. But he is not to put himself to any trouble. A bowl of tea will be quite enough. I shall leave as soon as I have seen the girl."

"But you wouldn't wish to hurt his feelings. He wouldn't like to be deprived of the opportunity of receiving you in a proper manner."

"Nonsense! Official business must have precedence!"

On the following afternoon, when Hsi Men, accompanied by two servants, and assured against recognition by the wearing of a mask, alighted before the modest home of the Hans in the muddy Ox-hide Lane, he was received only by the lady of the house, the "Sixth Wang," by name, and her young daughter; for the head of the house was employed all day in the silk shop. However, old Fong was present, to wait on them and pour the tea.

Hsi Men, though a man of decidedly luxurious tastes, was amazed to encounter, in the person of the Sixth Wang, a woman of quite exceptional beauty. He could hardly vouchsafe a glance for the daughter at her side; he had to stare and stare, with unmoving gaze, at her youthful stepmother. She was tall and slender, and the symmetry of her figure was perfect. The natural amiability of her features, the smooth freshness of her cheeks, made powder and rouge superfluous. Her eyebrows were curved like the graceful contours of distant hills, in her eyes lay the moist gleam of the autumn wave, and the least opening of her little mouth, fragrant as sandal, was enough to send bees crazy, and butterflies rampant, and make them unroll their probosci in lustful desire.

For a while Hsi Men stood silent, absorbed in mute admiration. Now he turned his gaze upon the daughter. She too was a flawless beauty, and yet, so it seemed to him, she was nothing to look at beside her still lovelier stepmother.

Now, at her stepmother's bidding, the girl bowed before Hsi Men like a blossom-laden bough swaying in the breeze, and having made a fourfold kowtow she discreetly withdrew to one side. Hsi Men had perforce to take a seat, and while his mouth pensively sipped the bowl of tea which was offered to him, his eyes, peering over the rim of the bowl, continued to devour the beauty before him. Now he beckoned Tai A, and made him take from a saddle bag two lengths of flowered silk, four golden rings, and twenty ounces of silver. All this old Fong had to lay upon a tea tray, and offer to the Sixth

Wang. The Sixth Wang placed the rings on her daughter's fingers, told her to thank the giver and take her leave of him, and pushed her out of the room.

"Send your daughter to my house the day after tomorrow," said Hsi Men, as the beginning of a brief and businesslike conversation. "She can then have her whole trousseau made in my house. You can use these few bits of silver to get her some suitable shoes and slippers."

"That we are able to hold up our heads, that our feet can walk on firm ground—this we owe solely to your favor," she hastened to reply. "And now you magnanimously take our child and overwhelm us, into the bargain, with rich presents! How can we ever thank you?"

For a time there was a mutual exchange of courtesies; then Hsi Men rose and left the house. And he took home with him a nice little scheme, complete in all particulars.

Two days later Mistress Han appeared with her charming stepdaughter, who until her departure was a guest in Hsi Men's household. Master Chow had to come once again with all his journeymen and make a complete bridal trousseau of the splendid silks—white, and red, and green, and gleaming with gold, heavy and fragrant—which Hsi Men himself had selected and purchased. Hsi Men also provided new chests in gold lacquer, a large toilet mirror, vases and jugs, copper wash bowls, a bathtub, bronze braziers, and all else that went to the furnishing of a cultured lady's chamber.

On the tenth day of the ninth month "Darling" set out on her journey to the Eastern Capital, in a traveling carriage with closely-drawn curtains, to which four mules were harnessed. Her escort consisted of her father, Lai Pao, as Hsi Men's confidential man of business, four outriders, and two guardsmen from the District Yamen, armed with bows and arrows.

CHAPTER TWENTY-FIVE: *Hsi Men gains possession of the Sixth Wang. In the snowy Night Gold Lotus plays the Pi pa*

ONE EVENING, a few days after Darling's departure, Hsi Men met old Fong in the Street of the Lion. He gave her a piece of silver.

"This is for your trouble in the matter of Han's little daughter. Have you seen his wife at all in the meantime?"

"I have visited her every day, so that she should not feel too lonely. For the first two or three days she was very unhappy and wept incessantly. Now at last she is calmer. She wanted to know whether I had already received my fee from you. I told her that I had not yet been to see you, and that you were altogether taken up with your official duties, but that you had promised me a good reward as soon as Father Han had returned from the capital."

"That goes without saying. But one thing more"—and he looked round to make sure that no one was near; then he bent down to the old woman's ear and continued, under his breath: "When you go to see her again just tell her I send her my greetings, and that if I had time I would like to pay her a longer visit some day—and stay half the day, do you hear? And go and see her at once! To-morrow I'll come again for my answer."

The old woman responded with a crafty smile. "A fine fellow you are! First you discover a decent young maiden, sewn up, one might say, in an impenetrable hide; you unearth the treasure of a carefully-guarded virgin, and now you begin to stalk her mother! Well, it's too late to do anything today. But possess yourself in patience until tomorrow; I'll draw a thick leathern mask of impudence over my face, and speak. In the meantime I am sure you will be curious to learn something more about her. Well, she is a younger sister of our Master-butcher Wang in the back street, the youngest of six sisters, which is why she is called the Sixth Wang. She is twenty-three years of age, and she was born under the constellation of the Viper. You have already realized how attractive she is, but if only you could see her today! Well, tomorrow I shall have something to tell you."

That very evening the old woman slipped round to Ox-hide Lane to call on the Sixth Wang. After the conversation had turned for a time upon the savory dish of noodles which had been cooked the previous evening, and had now been warmed up again, and the handsome young woman had shed a few tears, scalding as vinegar, over her loneliness, Mother Fong began to speak in a matter-of-fact way of the purpose of her visit.

"Yes, yes," she sighed, sympathetically; "it's an old story:

"A son in the house, and the neighbors are full of interest,
If it is a daughter, not a tear is shed.

"But wait until your daughter has found her feet in the capital, and has brought a little son into the world; then it will go well with you parents, and the day will come when you will bless this old person. Of course, I can understand that just at present you feel lonely. Don't you sometimes feel rather nervous in the evenings, being all alone in the house?"

"Are you asking that? I suppose you are making fun of me."

"Well, for the present I'm here. But there may be times when I can't come. How would it be if I were to send someone to keep you company—someone whom I can recommend? Would you like me to do that?"

"What someone do you mean?"

"Why, who else but our good Master Hsi Men? Now listen! He came to see me a little while ago, and while we were talking I could see how he pitied you in your cheerless solitude. He would very much like to keep you company for a half a day some time or other. What do you say to that? No one would know anything about it.

366

If you once let him in at your door, you needn't worry any more about clothes and food and servants. You would have everything. And if you really got on together he could give you a nice house, much nicer than this out-of-the-way hole in the grubby Ox-hide Lane."

"But he already has several wives in his house, as beautiful as goddesses! How could he want an unattractive creature like myself?"

"How can you think so poorly of yourself? With a passionate man love is like the sun, which follows its course to the west and rises again in the east! It was plainly the will of Providence that he should have seen you the other day! Since then he can't get you out of his mind. Would he have given me what he did if he hadn't been in earnest? I am here at his express wish, so you may as well know it!"

The young woman drew a long breath, and sighed heavily. "Well, if he really thinks me worthy of attention I will expect him here tomorrow."

Hsi Men was beside himself with delight when on the following day old Fong informed him of the favorable result of her visit. He then and there weighed her out six ounces of silver.

"Here, this is for a few necessary little purchases."

The old woman took her basket, and quickly procured various things to eat and drink, in order that the modest cuisine of the Sixth Wang might be worthy of the half-day's visit of a pampered voluptuary.

Early in the afternoon Hsi Men rode forth, masked and accompanied by two servants. He kept Tai A to wait on him; the other had to take his horse, for the time being, to the house in Lion Street. The Sixth Wang, in her best clothes, freshly washed, and with her nails carefully clipped and polished, received him in a veranda room at the back of the house. The whole house was shining with cleanliness, and there was not a speck of dust on the chairs and tables.

The conversation began with the customary formalities: "I owe my lord more thanks than I can ever express for all the kindness that he has shown my daughter."

"I have hitherto neglected to wait upon you and your husband. I trust I have not offended you."

"But how can there be any question of offense, when we have received nothing but benefits from you!"

She made four kowtows, and then old Fong gave them tea. The outer door of the house was closed, and there Tai A stood on guard. Directly they had drunk their tea the young woman invited her guest into her bedroom. She had made it look as comfortable and hospitable as possible. Over the kang, to one side of the door, which had a parchment window, she had hung, by way of bed curtains, four artistically-shaped pieces of silk of various colors. On one of the walls, instead of a standing screen, she had fixed a strip of cloth, closely embroidered with flowers and bees and cockatoos. Here and there about the floor smoldered braziers containing embers of fragrant cedarwood. The rest of the scanty furnishings of the room consisted of a toilet table, with mirror, a few vases, a wash bowl of cheap tinware, and a single arm chair. In this chair Hsi Men seated himself.

The Sixth Wang offered him a brimming bowl of tea with a beaten-up mixture of walnuts and bamboo shoots; then she herself sat down on the edge of the bed. They spoke briefly or at greater length of various domestic matters. Hsi Men did not like to see her busying herself with the tea tray, "You really must have a young maid," he said.

"Well, I cannot deny," she promptly agreed, "that since my daughter has left me I find it very trying to have to do everything with my own hands."

"That can easily be avoided. I will commission Mother Fong to engage a young maid for you tomorrow. Let me see to paying her wages."

"But how I take still further advantage of your goodness! Already I am deeply indebted to you."

He was secretly delighted to note how easily and correctly she spoke. And at this moment old Fong brought in the ready-laid table.

"Hey, Mother Fong, a young maid is wanted in this house," he said. "See if you can find one tomorrow!"

"Oh, you ought to thank him nicely for that, little lady!" said Mother Fong, turning to the Sixth Wang. "And I know where I can find one. My sister-in-law Chow in the southern city would be glad to find a situation for her thirteen-year-old daughter, but she wants four bars of silver. If the noble gentleman is agreeable. . . ."

"That's settled," said Hsi Men, and the young woman thanked him with a hasty *Wan fu.*

Now they proceeded to dine. The Sixth Wang was about to hand her noble guest the first goblet of wine with a new-fashioned ceremonial curtsy, but this he would not allow.

"Enough of ceremonies!" he said, gallantly raising her, on which she smilingly breathed another *Wan fu.* After old Fong had cleared the table she discreetly withdrew to the kitchen, where with the assistance of Tai A she did justice to the abundant remains of the meal.

Meanwhile, in the bedroom, after a few goblets of wine, the conversation was becoming more intimate. First they drank together from the same side of the goblet. Then the young woman moved her low stool nearer and nearer to his chair. He laid his arm about her neck and kissed her with a passionate tongue-kiss, while she let her hand fall as though by accident on his lap. In mutual desire the hot waters of their passion bubbled over. Now she unsheathed herself, and he too stripped off his clothes. With a sense of blissful relief he was conscious of her soft flesh, her smooth skin. The Sixth Wang was acquainted with variations of the game of love which offered even the greatly experienced Hsi Men unfamiliar delights.

It was with high satisfaction that he parted from his new darling as the night was falling.

On the following day, in accordance with his promise, he gave old Fong the requisite four ounces for the thirteen-year-old daughter of her sister-in-law Chow. That very day she had to enter upon her new duties in the house of the Sixth Wang, taking the name of "Bright Silkling." The delights of the previous day had made such a deep impression on Hsi Men that two days later he again found his way to Ox-hide Lane. And thereafter visit followed upon visit.

So far his wives had no suspicion as to his latest diversion, for he always reached the house punctually by the first drum beat. This time he did not even take Gold Lotus into his confidence. But it occurred to Mistress Ping that her old Fong was never to be seen nowadays. She had even sent for her in vain, once, twice, and thrice. The old woman had always made the excuse that she was busy out of doors all day. Or she was simply not to be found. At last, one day, the servant Hua Tung managed to catch her in the street and drag her off to her mistress's pavilion.

"Well, well, where are you spending all your time?" asked Mistress Ping, in some surprise. "One doesn't see so much as your shadow nowadays. I have already sent for you several times in vain. There is a heap of clothes to be ironed, and linen to be washed; I want you to give my maid a little help."

"If only you realized how overworked I always am!" said the old woman, by way of excuse, in a consequential tone. "After all, I've got my own affairs to attend to. One can't be scribe and soldier, salt merchant, and stone mason all at the same time!"

"You old fraud! Well, the First will have something to say to you!"

But before old Fong ventured to present herself to Moon Lady she ran off to the kitchen, in order to learn how the wind was blowing. There she found Jade Flute, one of Moon Lady's maids.

"Well, are you here at last, Mother Fong? The Sixth is fit to bite the flesh off your bones, she is so angry; she couldn't even get a sight of the edge of your shadow!"

"You think so, do you? Well, she was quite pleasant, as a matter of fact; I've just come from her."

"Well, you'll get it all the worse from the First. She has asked over and over again what you were doing about the grapes which you were supposed to be getting for her."

"Then she'll ask in vain. The wine merchant had already left for his home in the South. You can give her back her money; here it is."

"No, no, you give it her yourself!"

But the crafty old woman preferred to keep the money in her pocket when she presently confronted Moon Lady. She knew that lady's simple good nature, and she had not calculated wrongly. Moon Lady listened patiently to her specious explanation, in respect of the wine merchant, who was supposed to have left the town already, and would return in the third month of the following year, when he would bring two different kinds of prime vintage grapes; then she said:

"Very well, keep the money in the meantime and get me a basket of each kind of grapes next year!"

And she gave the old woman tea and cake, and unsuspiciously dismissed her.

"Well, did she give you a proper scolding?" asked Mistress Ping, when old Fong came to see her again after her visit to Moon Lady.

"On the contrary, I explained everything so cleverly that she was amiability itself, and even treated me to tea and cakes," said the old woman proudly.

"Then you've your impudent tongue to thank for that. She ought really to have pinned you down in your lies like a fat June cockchafer. But now you'll stay here and busy yourself with the washing!"

"Tomorrow, mistress, tomorrow. This afternoon I simply must pay an urgent call at the house of a friend of mine."

And off she went, covering two paces with every stride. What she wanted to do was to get to the Sixth Wang's house as quickly as possible, for she fully expected that Hsi Men would be there. And she was right; for when she slipped past the side door of the front reception room Tai A was standing there, and he called to her, under his breath: "Be quick! He has sent Ki Tung out for wine already."

And at this moment Hsi Men was indeed sitting beside the Sixth Wang.

"The wine one is served in this house has no flavor," he was saying: "So today I have had some brought from my own cellar. You will like that better. It was given to me by a Court eunuch. 'Clear Bamboo-leaf Dewdrops,' it is called, and there's really something in it; an admirable wine; it strengthens one like medicine."

She saw at once that this was an opportunity to profit by, and she replied, apologetically:

"Well, what sort of wine can one get in this seedy neighborhood! I have to send all the way to the main thoroughfare, where the big shops are . . . "

"Wait until your husband is back," he interrupted, rightly guessing at what was passing through her mind; "then I'll stump up a few ounces and buy you a nice little house in Lion Street. It's a better residential quarter, and your husband won't have far to go to the shop, and that again will be all to the good of my business."

"Oh, yes, that would be splendid!" she agreed vivaciously. "And then we shouldn't have such reason to dread the gossip of the common people as here. My husband is the least of our troubles; he won't disturb us."

One day at the beginning of the tenth month Lai Pao and Han Tao Kwo returned from the Eastern Capital. Intendant Ti had been absolutely delighted with the maiden whom Hsi Men had chosen for him, and had entertained the envoys for two whole days with magnificent hospitality. In addition to an enthusiastic letter of thanks, and a magnificent black horse from the Tunguz steppe, he had given them fifty ounces of consideration money for Hsi Men, and to them personally he had given twenty ounces as traveling expenses.

Hsi Men read the letter of thanks with great satisfaction. It told him that Master Ti regarded him henceforth as a brother and ally, and would do all that lay in his power to promote his interests. Now, when Han Tao, with a respectful kowtow, was about to hand the fifty ounces of silver to his employer, Hsi Men magnanimously refused it. "Keep the money as a well-deserved reward for the good education which you have bestowed upon your daughter!" he said; and as Han modestly protested against the acceptance of so magnificent a present, he added: "I shall be seriously angry with you if you don't accept it. However, don't spend it. I have a plan to propose by which you could invest it to advantage. I'll discuss it with you later."

At home, the Sixth Wang welcomed her husband with heartfelt delight. While he was brushing off the dust of the highway and unpacking his box, she made him describe all the incidents of the journey, and above all she wanted to know how her daughter was received in her new home.

"Oh, splendidly," Han replied. "She has three rooms of her own and two maids to wait on her; as for clothes, linen, and jewelry, she lacks for nothing. On the day after her arrival she was introduced to the First Wife. Master Ti is happy to possess her. He kept me and Lai Pao for two days as his guests, and he treated us and our servants with so much wine and so many choice dishes that we simply couldn't swallow another mouthful. Finally he gave me fifty ounces of consideration money for Master Hsi Men, and just think—Master Hsi Men was so nobly generous as to give me the money! He absolutely insisted that I should keep it, though I protested twice and thrice. Here it is."

His wife, highly gratified, took charge of this considerable sum.

"Just one thing," she said. "We ought to give good old Fong an ounce of silver. She has taken such touching care of me during your absence, and has consoled me in my loneliness."

At this moment Bright Silkling entered the room, bringing tea.

"But who is this?" he asked in surprise.

"Our new maid. She is called Bright Silkling. Come here, child, and make a pretty kowtow to your master!"

Bright Silkling made her kowtow as custom required, and disappeared into the kitchen. Of course, the Sixth Wang had to explain to her husband how she, in her humble home, could suddenly permit herself the luxury of a servant; and as she knew him to be broadminded and free from prejudice, she told him frankly and unreservedly of her profitable intercourse with Hsi Men; how he

373

had first helped her to engage a servant, and had then promised her a fine new house in the Street of the Lion.

"Ah, now I understand why I was to accept the fifty ounces, but not spend it!" said Han, with twinkling eyes. "Of course, the money is intended for the new house."

"And you may be sure it won't stop at fifty," she continued. "There'll be many an ounce to add to these. Well, if we get a fine house for it, and perhaps a few clothes and jewels for me, I'll gladly let him tumble my body a little!"

"If he comes again tomorrow while I am in the shop be as nice and affectionate to him as ever, and behave as though I knew nothing about it. We must take proper advantage of this splendid opportunity to pick up a little money without working for it!"

"Of course it suits a useless scamp like you to eat a ready-cooked meal! If only you knew what your poor wife has to go through before the meal is ready!"

The husband and wife gazed at each other for a moment, and then burst into peals of laughter.

As a matter of fact, before a fortnight had elapsed Hsi Men had bought a nice little home for the Hans, in Lion Street, to the east of the Marble Bridge. For this he paid one hundred and twenty ounces. It was two rooms wide and four deep. At the front there were two reception rooms; then came two devotional chambers, one designed for the exhibition of a statue of the Buddha, and the other for the reception of the ancestral tablets. Behind these were two living rooms, and finally the kitchen and a stove room.

When the neighbors learned that the newcomers were the manager of the rich and powerful Hsi Men and his wife they hastened to congratulate them on their installment in their new house, bringing them tea and boxes of cakes and pastry by way of welcome. Han they cordially addressed as "Big Brother," and his wife as "Sister-in-law Han." The common people of the neighborhood called them "Uncle" and "Aunt."

When Hsi Men paid one of his friendly afternoon calls on Mistress Han—which he did at least once a week—the husband was

374

considerate enough to spend the night at the shop, for he did not wish to disturb his employer at his diversions. On the contrary, he encouraged his wife to be thoroughly affectionate and forthcoming to her visitor. Hsi Men was able to run in and out of the Hans' house just as he liked, morning or evening. Like the fire in a charcoal brazier, so his affection for the Sixth Wang burned with a steady heat. And the neighbors, who naturally realized what was happening under the Hans' roof, kept a watch on their tongues and were silent. Who would have dared to fall foul of the much-moneyed and influential Master Hsi Men?

Autumn had passed; out of doors it was beginning to freeze. Gold Lotus, sitting in her pavilion, suffered more and more, as day followed day, from the chilling solitude that now brooded over the kingfisher-pattern pillows, and between the lotus-embroidered hangings of her couch.

Once more there fell one of those monotonous evenings when she stood leaning against the spirit wall before the entrance to her pavilion, waiting and waiting and watching in vain. Now it had grown quite dark. She withdrew, sighing, to her bedchamber, lit by a silver lamp, stretched herself upon the couch, laid her *pi pa* across her knees, and began, in a low voice, to improvise a mournful strain:

> *"With sorrow in my heart*
> *I lean against the shrine.*
> *Why now should I disrobe?*
> *A lonely couch is mine!"*

She stopped and listened. Outside, from the ridge of the roof, she could hear the melodious humming of the æolian harp. And was not that the hard rap of the iron door ring against the outer door? Spring Plum had to run quickly and see whether Hsi Men was outside. But the little maid returned shaking her head.

"Your ear was deceived, mistress. The wind was blowing icicles against the door."

Gold Lotus fingered the strings again, and resumed her song:

375

> *"Without, the storm*
> *Is raging again;*
> *There drums on the window*
> *An icy rain."*

It was dark in the room; the lamp was threatening to go out. She laid her lute aside and rose wearily, in order to lift the charred wick and light fresh sticks of incense. Then, with a sorrowful heart, she continued to sing:

> *"With careless hand*
> *I trim the wick*
> *And hold a brand*
> *To the incense stick.*
> *Oh, if the night*
> *Would pass away!*
> *And yet I shrink*
> *From the empty day.*
> *How long shall I wait?*
> *How long this pain?*
> *Is all my youth*
> *To be spent in rain?*
> *The fires of grief*
> *In my heart are hot,*
> *But what recks he*
> *Of my desolate lot?"*

That evening Hsi Men was the guest of his colleague, Judge Ho, who wished to show his gratitude for a horse which Hsi Men had given him. It was late when he started upon his homeward way, and the night was foul with driving rain and snow. A layer of white sparkled on his cap and furs, and he stamped his feet as he entered the pavilion of the Sixth; for the very first thing he did, on returning home, was to look in on the mother and her child. This had now become a fixed habit. The Sixth helped him out of his dripping cloak, and sent the maid Pear Blossom for tea and a hot snack.

"Is the little one already asleep?" was his first question, while he slipped into a comfortable dressing gown and changed his wet boots for warm slippers.

"He has just gone to sleep. He had such fun this afternoon. You are home very early?"

"The worthy Ho made a tremendous effort with his dinner, in return for the horse I gave him recently; he had even sent for two smart young actors to entertain us. But in this horrible weather I preferred to leave a little earlier than usual."

"Would you like a little hot millet brandy? You must be frozen."

"Thanks, I feel more like drinking some decent wine. That home-brewed stuff I was given this evening, that Chrysanthemum wine, tasted as horrible as it smelt."

In the meantime Pear Blossom had laid the table and brought a few hot dishes. Beside the table a freshly-filled charcoal brazier emitted a grateful warmth. And so they sat down and set to, enjoying together comfort of a winter evening at home.

Gold Lotus had no idea that Hsi Men had returned home. In her disconsolate mood she was quite unable to sleep; and a vague hope that he might even yet come to her helped to keep her awake. So, with loosened hair, she sat buried in the cushions, the bed curtains half drawn and the lamp dimly shining, whiling away the time by strumming on her *pi pa* and singing:

> *"Must I not hate thee*
> *O heartless friend,*
> *Who dost so cruelly*
> *Thy love offend?"*

Once more she was overcome with a nervous disquietude. She called Spring Plum.

"Go quickly and see whether your master has come yet," she said.

It was some time before the maid returned.

"He has been home a long time!" she announced. "He's sitting comfortably with the Sixth and drinking wine with her!"

Gold Lotus felt as though her heart were pierced with a number of daggers simultaneously.

"Faithless bandit!" she repeated, over and over again, half under her breath, between her angrily clenched teeth, while her little fists beat fiercely upon the pillows and tears of rage started from her eyes. Then she again seized her lute, and sang with increasing power, so that her voice resounded through the silent park, and was heard in the adjacent pavilion of the Sixth:

> *"Grief with hard talons*
> *Grips at my soul.*
> *In my desolate bosom*
> *It burns like a coal.*
> *Sweet peaches are here,*
> *Sour berries there;*
> *Only the blind*
> *Could confuse such fare.*
> *How long shall I wait,*
> *How long this pain?*
> *Is all my youth*
> *To be spent in vain?*
> *The fires of grief*
> *In my heart are hot,*
> *But what recks he*
> *Of my desolate lot?"*

Hsi Men listened to the last lines of this song.

"Who is singing to the lute so late at night?" he asked in astonishment.

"It will be the Fifth; no doubt she finds herself unable to sleep," replied Mistress Ping. "We ought to ask her to keep us company for a time."

And she sent the maid Apricot Blossom across to the other pavilion, while Pear Blossom quickly laid a third table.

Presently Apricot Blossom came back alone. "She will not come," was her message.

378

"Go once more and tell her that Master Hsi Men and I beg her to come," said Mistress Ping.

"She has bolted the door, and she says she has already blown out the lamp and has laid herself down to sleep," was the new message.

"That's just talk. Come, we'll go ourselves and fetch her," said Hsi Men to Mistress Ping, and together they went through the dark park to the neighboring pavilion. After repeated knocking the door was opened an inch or two, and Spring Plum could be seen through the narrow chink. Hsi Men, with a vigorous push, flung the door open and drew Mistress Ping in with him. They found Gold Lotus still dressed, but with loosened hair, lying on her couch behind the half-drawn curtains, the *pi pa* by her side.

"You queer little woman, must one ask you three times before you'll come?" said Hsi Men.

Gold Lotus raised herself to a sitting position, and so she remained for a long while, motionless, absorbed in silent reflection. At last she opened her lips: "Why do you wish to drag me, unhappy that I am, from my cold, self-chosen solitude? Be so good as to leave me alone. I really did not wish to disturb you to no purpose."

"You are talking like a toothless old grandmother of eighty! It's ridiculous!" growled Hsi Men. "The Sixth wanted to play a game of chess with you. Don't you feel like it?"

"Do oblige me by coming!" begged Mistress Ping. "And we'll drink another good beaker of wine together."

"Do go, Sister, and leave me alone!" replied Gold Lotus. "I really haven't been feeling well these last few days; I am living only on thin gruel, and I only want to rest all day."

"But why didn't you tell us long ago? Then I could have sent for a doctor," Hsi Men interposed, anxiously.

"If you don't believe me—Spring Plum, bring the mirror!"

She took the mirror in her hand, and regarded herself attentively for a while by the light of the lamp.

"Well, don't you see how thin I have grown in the face?"

Hsi Men took the mirror in his hand, looked at himself, and observed, in a jesting tone: "That's queer, the mirror doesn't make me look thin!"

"With the happy, carefree life you live you have no reason to grow thin, but rather fat!" she scolded him, already half reconciled by his jesting tone.

He pressed himself against her, laid his arm round her neck, and kissed her tenderly. Then, feeling her body, he observed, with comic earnestness: "Really, child, you have actually grown thin!"

"Oh, how cold your hands are!" she said, shaking herself. "But no wonder; you are just a lump of ice, and you don't realize how I am suffering."

After a long argument they succeeded in persuading her to get up and accompany them. And when they had played a game of chess together and drunk themselves into a good humor with a few beakers of wine, Hsi Men decided, on Mistress Ping's advice, to share his bed that night, after so long an interval, with his Fifth.

CHAPTER TWENTY-SIX: *A covetous Servant attempts his Master's Life. Hsi Men reveals himself as a venal Judge*

THAT NIGHT Gold Lotus lavished a hundred endearments on him, covered him with a thousand caresses. She seemed positively to regret, so great was her affection, that she could not creep into his body and be enveloped by it. Her tears flowed so abundantly that a leviathan might have bathed in them. Her words overflowed with tenderness and devotion. By all this she hoped to win back his heart. But in vain; when the new day dawned his thoughts long fluttered back to the Sixth Wang, and Gold Lotus was already forgotten.

Indeed, on her birthday, which fell on the ninth of the first month, he did not even deem it necessary to call on her, if only for a moment. On the contrary, he spent the whole day with Beggar Ying, Hsia Hsi Ta, the elder brother of Moon Lady, and the elder brother of Mistress Ping, in the Temple of the Jade Emperor, where with great pomp and elaborate ceremonial the solemn proclamation of a temple name for his little son was celebrated, a name which was to protect him from sickness and the influence of evil spirits. At Hsi Men's request not only the High Priest Wu, but all the sixteen brothers of the temple were invited to the performance of this ceremony; and the sumptuous banquet which formed its inevitable accompaniment was so protracted that Hsi Men preferred to spend the night in the temple.

That evening, therefore, Gold Lotus sat with the five other wives and six congratulants in Moon Lady's apartments, waiting in vain for Hsi Men's return, and finding the long hours of waiting tedious beyond expression.

When the talkers had dealt exhaustively with the recent events in the household, a general wish was expressed that the two nuns, Ta and Wang, from the neighboring Kwan Yin convent—who were never absent from any family celebration in Hsi Men's house—should recite, speaking in alternation, a legend of the saints. Their monotonous delivery, interrupted from time to time by the rattle of the prayer drums, exerted a gently somnolent influence on the hearers, so that one by one—and first of all Gold Lotus—the listeners vanished from the room in the course of the narration, and sought their couches.

Only Moon Lady, whose simple heart was especially receptive of the doctrine of Buddha, held out to the last, and did not go to sleep until Sister Wang, with whom she was sharing her bedroom that night, had told the legend to the end. In the meantime the fourth watch of the night had passed and the cock had already crowed. But it was to be some time before the good Moon Lady fell asleep.

"Why are you so solemn all the time?" asked the nun, suddenly. "One never sees you making merry."

"Can one be cheerful if one has had so sad an experience as mine?" And Moon Lady related how in the eighth month, while looking over the house of Kiao, she had slipped upon the stairs, and so had suffered a miscarriage.

"Was the fruit already developed, then?"

"It was an almost fully developed seven months' child, and a man-child too!"

"That is sad indeed, dear lady. Who knows what a fine man he might have become! But this child of the Sixth, who has been so short a time in the household—what good can come of that?"

"It will be as Heaven disposes," said Moon Lady resignedly.

"Oh, but one can do something to help. The Abbess Pi knows a recipe. She tried it last year in the case of a Ministerial Secretary's wife, Mistress Chen. This Mistress Chen was about your age, and she was childless; she had had only a number of miscarriages. But last year she tried the magic draught of the Abbess Pi, and she recently gave birth to a fine, healthy little son. There is only one drawback to the recipe."

"And that is?"

"One needs the afterbirth of a first-born child. This afterbirth has to be washed in wine, then dried, and burned to ashes. These ashes are then mixed with the other ingredients of the draught, and on the seven-times-seventh day of the sixty-day cycle it must be washed down with yellow wine, on a fasting stomach, unnoticed by men and spirits. Exactly a month later you will feel that you are pregnant."

"To what convent does the Abbess Pi belong?" Moon Lady wanted to know.

"Originally to the 'Cloister of Earthly Seclusion.' Recently she has become the Abbess of the 'Cloister of the Flowery Doctrine' in the Southern suburb. She is seventy years old, and she can expound all the sutras, and has all the legends of the saints at her finger ends. She could recite legends to you for a month on end. She is always visiting the very best houses for that purpose, and sometimes the people keep her for half a month as their guest."

"You simply must ask her to pay me a visit."

"Willingly. And I'll prepare the drink for you. Only I don't quite know where I am to get the one thing that is so difficult to obtain."

"I'll give you money for it."

"Good. Then I'll let you know as soon as I have prepared the draught. It won't take half a month."

"But this must be a secret between us!"

"Rely on me for that!"

On the following afternoon, as Sister Wang was taking her leave, Moon Lady pressed an ounce of silver into her hand. "Later on, when you have prepared everything, you shall have more."

Honored reader, those who live in great houses should beware of allowing such nuns to enter the inner chambers and become intimate with the women of the household. Their spiritual devotions and their pious narrations of legends are often but a pretext for "spending heat and stealing cold" behind the back of the master of the house. What mischief cannot they cause!

As always at the season of the New Year, so this year also there were great doings in Hsi Men's household during the days preceding the Feast of Lanterns. Almost immediately after Gold Lotus's birthday preparations had to be made for the great reception on Mistress Ping's birthday, which fell on the fifteenth of the first month, the day of the Feast. In the meantime, all the wives were invited for the thirteenth day to the house of their wealthy neighbor Kiao.

A few days before this date Gold Lotus declared, briefly and positively, that she would not accept this invitation, for she had nothing to wear, and refused to make herself ridiculous. There was no help for it: Hsi Men had to send for Master Chow and his journeymen, and ask him in all haste to make new dresses for his six wives—altogether thirty garments. And when a few days later he told the maid Spring Plum that she and Pear Blossom and Jade Flute and Fragrant Orchid must be ready to act as wine tasters on the fifteenth, and must be really nicely dressed, the cunning little thing followed her mistress's example, declaring that she would not on any account show herself at the banquet table, for she had nothing to wear, and did not want people to laugh at her. So Master Chow had to appear once more with all his journeymen, and quickly prepare sixteen new dresses for the four favorite maids.

So the day of the Feast of Lanterns, which was also Mistress Ping's birthday, was celebrated with great pomp. In addition to four singing-girls, Hsi Men had engaged, in honor of his guests, the theatrical troupe, numbering twenty players, of the Imperial Prince Yuen, his neighbor in Lion Street, and he had had a stage built in the western wing, which gave on to the front reception hall. A performance was given of that famous drama, "The Story of the Western Pavilion." The day concluded with a magnificent firework display, under the supervision of Pen Se and young Chen. The fireworks were let off outside the gate, and they attracted a closely-packed throng of spectators, who surrounded the house.

Hsi Men himself avoided all the domestic confusion. He preferred to stroll through the Lantern Market with Beggar Ying and Hsia Hsi Ta, afterwards diverting himself with the Sixth Wang in his house in Lion Street.

Apart from the usual festivities, this first month of the year was marked by two important events. One of these was of a domestic nature. When on the thirteenth day of the month his wives visited the home of his rich neighbor Kiao, they took with them his little son, together with his nurse, Ju I. Master and Mistress Kiao had only one child, a daughter, three months old. While they were at table the nurse, Ju I, took the little boy to the nursery, where she laid him, in his cushions, on a bed, close beside the little daughter of the house. When after dinner the whole company entered the room to see the children, they discovered, to their joyful surprise, that the two children had freed themselves from their cushions and were now blissfully treading each other with their tiny hands and feet.

The assembled womenfolk of the two families were of course agreed that this was a sign from Heaven, and declared that the two children were betrothed.

Moon Lady immediately sent a servant home to bring a quantity of red silk, with which the walls of the reception hall of the Kiao's house were draped, as an outward token of the joyful event. And the very next morning the Kiao family sent handsome betrothal presents to the house of Hsi Men.

Now Hsi Men was confronted with an accomplished fact. For decency's sake he had to give presents in return for those received, and announce his consent to the betrothal. But as a matter of fact he did not approve of the overhasty choice of his wives. It was true —he explained to Moon Lady—that Neighbor Kiao was rich and respected, but he was only a plain citizen, without official rank, so that he was not the social equal of Hsi Men. And his disapproval must somehow have come to the ears of the Kiao family, for two days later, when the Kiaos were the guests of Hsi Men's household, the septuagenarian grandmother, Kiao Wu, in the course of conversation, let fall a casual remark to the effect that one of her nieces was an Imperial concubine of the second rank, and the mistress of the Eastern Palace; which was apparently meant as a hint that Hsi Men's family was not really the social equal of her own.

The second important event related to Hsi Men's official position.

And here the narrator must go back a little. At this time there was living in the city of Kwang ling, which was in the district of Yangchow, in the province of Kiang nan, a wealthy private scholar, whose name was Miao Tsien Hsiu. He was forty years old, and he had only one daughter, who was young and unmarried. Since his chief wife was constantly ailing and bedridden, he left the care of the household to his favorite concubine, a certain Tiao Ki, who had originally been a singing-girl, and whom he had purchased for the great price of three hundred ounces.

One day an aged monk from the "Cloister of Gracious Recompense" in the Eastern Capital knocked at his door. He had been sent out to collect money for a new monastery gong. The wealthy Master Miao was no miser; he gave the wandering monk fifty ounces. When the monk thanked him, but declined the gift, saying that half the sum would be ample, he replied, smiling: "No, keep it! Half the money is for Buddha; the other half is to feed his servant on his travels."

The monk, who was eager to show his gratitude for such kindness, did so by giving him a piece of good advice as he took his leave: "Master, your left eye lies too deep in the orbit. It threatens you with death out of doors. If I may advise you, do not leave your house until this year is at an end. You have been so kind to me: pray allow the poor monk, in his gratitude, to make use of his art of looking into the future. Once more, pray be warned: do not undertake any journeys!"

And with this he went his way. About half a month later Master Miao, while taking a stroll in the park behind his dwelling house, happened upon his servant, Miao Tsing, engaged in intimate dalliance with his concubine, Tiao Ki. Enraged by such impudence, he gave him a good beating and told him to leave the house. But the servant pleaded so urgently for mercy that he allowed his heart to be softened, and ended by retaining the man in his service. Yet since this time the servant had cherished a secret hatred for his employer.

Master Miao had a cousin, Huang by name, who like himself was a native of the district of Yangchow, and like himself, had a thorough knowledge of the Confucian scriptures. He had achieved the degree of Doctor of the second rank, and in the Eastern Capital he filled the post of a metropolitan Under-Prefect. From this cousin Master Miao received one day a letter which contained a cordial invitation to visit the capital. This journey was to serve a twofold purpose: it was to be a pleasure trip, but it would also enable him to consult his cousin in respect of his entry into the official career. Master Miao was delighted by this proposal, and he told his wives: "Kai fong fu is the Imperial residence; there are all manner of things to see and do there. It has always been my dearest wish to pay it a visit. This invitation of my cousin's is most seasonable."

But his First Wife advised him against the journey.

"Have you already forgotten the monk's warning?" she said. "You ought not on any account to undertake a journey. It is a long way to the Eastern Capital; who knows what might happen to you during the journey? So far there has never been any talk of your entering the service of the State. And you would leave behind you a sick wife and a young daughter, with no one to protect them, and a large household, without anyone reliable to manage it! No, please don't make this journey!"

Master Miao became really angry; he refused to listen to her objections.

"Why did they hang a bow and arrow on the door when I was born? I am a man; am I to be afraid of a pleasant journey? It's no use looking at the world through the window all one's life. No, I have confidence in my heart and plenty of money in my purse. Why should I not achieve honor and success? This is a splendid notion of Cousin Huang's; there are no two words about it."

And that very day he gave orders for his baggage to be packed. A small junk was chartered, a few chests full of gold and silver were taken on board, and on the auspicious day, in the last third of autumn, the journey to the Eastern Capital was begun. Master Miao was accompanied by the servant Miao Tsing and a young lad, An Tung.

After some days' passage through the canal they reached the province of Shantung.

An old proverb says: "Who has few servants has few vexations."

One night, as the junk dropped anchor in a quiet backwater of the River Tsing, not far from the city of Tsing ho hsien, Master Miao laid himself down and fell into a peaceful sleep: but his servant was still awake, hatching a sinister scheme against his employer. He could not get over the fact that Master Miao had caught him in the park and had physically chastised him. "Here is my opportunity for revenge," he thought. "No doubt the two junk-men will co-operate if I promise to divide the booty with them. It would be best to let him disappear in the water. Then the next thing will be to help his sick wife at home to die as quickly as possible. Once she is dead the lovely Tiao Ki and all his property will be mine."

He spoke to the two boatmen immediately.

"My master's leather trunks contain a thousand ounces of silver, and in the camphor-wood boxes there are bales of silk and clothes worth two thousand ounces," he told them. "If you will help me each of you shall receive his third."

Chen San and Wong Pa—as the two boatmen were called—grinned at each other; then they replied: "We ourselves thought of doing what you suggest a long way back."

And with that the deal was concluded. It was midnight; Master Miao and the lad An Tung lay fast asleep in the central cabin. Then the servant Miao Tsing, at the stern of the vessel, raised the cry of "Robbers! Robbers! Robbers!" shouting at the top of his voice. The two sleepers, waking with a start, leaped from their beds and rushed on deck. Thereupon Chen San sprang at Master Miao, stabbed him in the throat, and threw him head first into the water. At the same time the lad received a heavy blow on the head from Wong Pa's cudgel, and as he staggered on a few steps he was pushed violently backwards, so that he too fell overboard into the water.

Without troubling any further about their two victims, the three scoundrels gave their immediate attention to the contents of the trunks and chests. "If we two were found in possession of such bales of silk and such fine garments we should be suspected immediately. With you it is rather different. You are a member of his household; no one would think it extraordinary that you should have them. So you take the silks and the clothes and leave us the cash." Thus spoke the pirates.

Miao Tsing agreed to this proposal, and after the division had been made on these lines the junk proceeded on its voyage, and at his request it continued upstream. At the customs barrier of Lin tsing he went ashore with his baggage, and while the two boatmen, with the junk, started on the return journey, he took his chests overland to the district capital, Tsing ho hsien. This was the nearest large trading center at which he could turn his goods into ready money.

Alighting at a good hostelry outside the city wall, he began gradually to take his booty to market.

But not in vain has it been said:

> *Whatever human minds intend*
> *'Tis Heaven that decides the end.*

It is true that Master Miao had to pay with his life for his foolishness in laughing at a well-meant warning; but his boy, although he was at first stunned by the blow of the cudgel, was able to keep his head above water by swimming, and had the good fortune to be rescued by a passing fishing boat. The old fisherwoman to whom the boat belonged began by giving the exhausted lad some warm clothes, and something to eat and drink; then only did she allow him to tell his story.

"What will you do now?" she asked compassionately, when he had finished. "Do you want to go back to Yangchow? If you don't, then you could, if it would be agreeable to you, stay with me and give me a hand with the fishing."

"That is what I would rather do," An Tung agreed, joyfully. "For what should I do in Yangchow without my poor master?"

"Good, then for the present you'll stay with me. And I'll wash my old eyes and see if I can't find out where your master's murderers have gone."

One day about the New Year the old fisherwoman went with her protégé to the fishmarket of Tsing ho hsien, in order to sell a hamper of fish. There, amidst the crowd of purchasers, An Tung suddenly perceived the two boatmen, Chen San and Wong Pa. Although it was broad daylight, they were already market-merry, and each of them was wearing one of the fine suits of his former employer.

Tung secretly nudged the old fisherwoman: "Those are the men," he said quietly.

"Good, we'll follow them."

They never lost sight of them, but saw how they bought some fish, and then went aboard their junk, which was tied up against the hither bank of the river; then they cooked their fish, and settled down on the deck to enjoy their feast, in the course of which they often addressed themeves to a huge pitcher of wine.

"We'll draw up an indictment as quickly as possible. They shan't escape us! The day after tomorrow is the Feast of Lanterns, so they'll hardly be thinking of leaving yet," said the old woman, and she quickly dragged the boy back with her to her boat.

An Tung hastily drew up an indictment, and took it that very hour to the yamen of the River Prefect Show. The River Prefect paid no attention to the indictment, since it bore no distinguished signature, and passed it on to the District Judge, Hsia. He, in view of the serious matter of the charge, which was one of robbery with murder, could not do otherwise than comply with young An Tung's request. On the following day he dispatched his bailiffs, who with An Tung's help discovered the junk in question, and arrested the two pirates.

The unexpected appearance of this witness to the murder, whom they had believed to be dead, so dismayed them, when they were examined before Judge Hsia, that they confessed their guilt at once, and it was not necessary to apply torture. Moreover, they named the servant Miao Tsing as the real instigator of the crime. They were accordingly committed to jail; An Tung, as a witness, was kept in custody, and bailiffs were dispatched to seize the person of the servant Miao Tsing.

Now the proceedings were adjourned for a couple of days, on account of the Feast of Lanterns, as during the holiday the courts and offices were closed. During the interval a messenger employed at the yamen, an acquaintance of Miao Tsing's, managed to warn him secretly of the warrant for his arrest. In deadly fear, Miao Tsing gave up his room at the hostelry and took refuge in the house of his friend the broker Yo San, who lived in Lion Street.

It so happened that this house adjoined the house of Hsi Men's manager, Han Tao Kwo; moreover, Yo San's wife was the intimate friend of her neighbor, the Sixth Wang. They used often to visit each other. The broker Yo San was immediately struck by the worried expression of his guest. Now, when he had questioned him and learned how matters stood with him, he declared that the case was not so serious; Miao Tsing could make his mind easy.

"You must know that Neighbor Han Tao Kwo is the business manager of the powerful and wealthy Master Hsi Men. Moreover, Master Hsi Men is the colleague of the District Judge Hsia. It so happens that he is on very intimate terms with the family, and is most accommodating and obliging in respect of any request which Master Han or his wife may make. You have only to expend a little money and this unfortunate affair will be canceled. I, or rather my wife, will not fail to go next door and speak a word in your favor."

Delighted by these words, Miao Tsing fell on his knees. "Oh, if you would take my part I would richly reward your kindness. As a matter of fact, I have not very much money with me. For the present, I hope the fifty ounces of silver and the two new robes of flowered damask which I brought with me in my haste will be sufficient."

He quickly wrote out a list of presents, which Yo San gave to his wife, together with the articles entered upon it.

Mistress Yo San was told briefly how the matter stood; then she hurried off next door to speak to the Sixth Wang. The Sixth Wang was delighted to receive the most welcome gifts, and promised that she would do her utmost.

But two days went by, and Hsi Men, absorbed in the preparations for the festival, had no time to visit the house in Lion Street. At last, on the evening of the seventeenth day, the Sixth Wang saw Tai A riding past the house. She quickly beckoned him in.

"Where were you coming from?"

"From Tung ping fu. I had to accompany my master; he wanted to take the Prefect some presents, and his New Year's congratulations."

"Tell him, then, that I beg him most urgently to come here for a consultation."

And the Sixth Wang showed the lad the list of presents, and explained what was doing.

"Worthy Mistress Aunt," said Tai A, thoughtfully, "it seems to me that the matter isn't as simple as you suppose. The two pirates have both confessed already, and the few ounces would hardly suffice to set the legs of a petty official scribe in motion. I, at all events, should have to ask for twenty ounces at least if you wanted me to speak to my master."

"You accursed little oily-mouth, you'd be doing well if you got a free meal out of it!" said the Sixth Wang, laughing. "And I can very well dispense with your help if you are afraid!"

"It isn't that, Mistress Aunt, but such an affair needs mature consideration." Well, the Sixth Wang understood his hint, and she immediately set before him some savory dishes and a few beakers of good wine. At last, having agreed to convey her wishes to Hsi Men, he proceeded on his way.

And late that evening Hsi Men managed to find his way to the house in Lion Street.

The Sixth Wang had warned her husband beforehand that Hsi Men would probably be calling, and Han Tao Kwo was obliging as usual; he did not come home at all, but spent the night at the shop. She accordingly had her visitor to herself.

Before she began to speak of the business in hand she made a few discursive remarks by way of leading up to it.

"So your little son is betrothed, I hear? I am sure that greatly delighted your household."

"It doesn't delight me so much. It was the women who arranged it. It was an overhasty business altogether, this betrothal."

"I understand; now that you have accepted a high official post, the Kiaos, although in other respects they may be most estimable people, can no longer offer a suitable alliance to your household."

"Well, we'll say no more. What's the use of wasting words over it now?"

She invited him from the chilly veranda room to her bed-chamber, where a brazier was emitting a grateful warmth. As soon as she saw that he was gradually feeling a little warmer she proceeded to speak frankly, expounding her neighbor's request.

Hsi Men listened quietly; then he wanted to know on what terms Miao Tsing expected to purchase his immunity. The Sixth Wang showed him the list of presents, and produced the fifty ounces and the two silken robes from a chest.

Hsi Men burst out laughing.

"Is that all? A common robber who has instigated a murder wants to buy himself off with such trifles? You must understand what a desperate case he is in. The two pirates, his accomplices, are arrested, and have already confessed everything. They will lose their heads. There is a witness who was present on the occasion of the crime. No, the fellow can't get off for a ridiculous price like that. You ought not to have accepted such a trifling amount in the first place. After all, he has goods worth two thousand put away somewhere. Where has he hidden his treasure?"

At this the Sixth Wang ran into the kitchen and sent Bright Silkling next door, returning Miao Tsing's presents. The maid was to tell her neighbor that the case was hopeless; she did not wish to have anything more to do with it.

Miao Tsing felt as though he had been tumbled into a tub of ice. Once more he besought Yo San's wife to go next door and intercede for him. He was ready to give up the whole two thousand ounces which his goods were worth if only he could get off with his life. After a brief discussion Yo San's wife decided to make another appeal to her neighbor.

"He offers Master Hsi Men the half of all his goods, of the value of a thousand ounces," she told the Sixth Wang in her kitchen. "But if Master Hsi Men prefers to receive cash, then he asks for a delay of three days. In that time he can dispose of the goods, and then he will bring Master Hsi Men the thousand ounces in person."

The Sixth Wang returned to the bedroom, where she told Hsi Men of Miao Tsing's new offer, and handed him the new list of presents.

"That is a different matter," said Hsi Men, with a satisfied air. "I can manage to postpone the execution of the warrant for his apprehension for a few days longer. For the rest, I agree that he had better bring his present to my house, in cash."

Miao Tsing could hardly contain himself for delight when Yo San's wife returned with this consoling message.

That very night his friend the broker had to go rushing off in all directions, in order to bring to the house as many purchasers as possible. And within three days he had actually managed to dispose of all the goods. The amount realized was one thousand seven hundred ounces.

Once more Miao Tsing sent a present to the Sixth Wang next door, but this time it consisted of a hundred ounces and four gowns of the finest quality; and then, on the evening of the nineteenth, he made his way to Hsi Men's house. He was followed by a few porters, carrying a carcass of pork and four wine pitchers filled with silver ingots. Hsi Men's servants were already informed of the purpose of his visit, so he was admitted without more ado, and led through the gloomy park to the belvedere, where Hsi Men awaited him. On the way he did not fail to distribute, right and left, a few tokens of goodwill, so that the servants Tai A, Ping An, Shu Tung, and Kiu Tung received ten ounces apiece.

Hsi Men had given express orders that no lamps or lanterns were to be lit. The interview took place in absolute darkness, except that the moon, which was just rising, provided a faint illumination. Miao Tsing flung himself on the ground before Hsi Men, and began: "You have graciously deigned to extricate me from my distress. Until my bones fall asunder, until my body crumbles to dust, I shall think of you with gratitude."

"That's all very well. I haven't yet quite completed the investigation of your affair," replied Hsi Men. "In any case, the depositions of the two boatmen under arrest incriminate you seriously, and you will do well to disappear as quickly as possible; in fact, this very night. At your request I have decided to allow you to escape. And in order not to hurt your feelings, I will accept your present, and share it with my colleague, Master Hsia, who has also, of course, a say in your affair."

He sent for a bowl of tea, which Miao Tsing had to drink standing, timidly leaning against the park wall under the pines. Then he was dismissed. He hurried back to Lion Street, quickly packed his things, took his leave of his friendly hosts, hired a couple of pack mules, and slipped out of the city gate as the day was dawning, in order to make his way back to Yangchow.

> *Speedy as a watchdog*
> *Loose upon the plain,*
> *Nimble as a little fish*
> *Escaping through the seine.*

Riding home from the yamen next day, as Judge Hsia was about to part company with Hsi Men in the High Street, the latter lifted his whip, as a sign that he wished to consult the Judge about something in his own house. The Judge therefore accompanied him to his house, where Hsi Men led him to the belvedere in the park. After they had made themselves comfortable, had disposed of a sumptuous dinner, and had several times emptied the golden wine beaker, Hsi Men began to speak in all frankness of the case of Miao Tsing.

"The fellow recently forwarded me a couple of petitions through the wife of his host, and sent various presents to my house. I did not wish to decide the matter independently, which is why I asked you here today to discuss the case."

He handed his guest Miao Tsing's list of presents.

"I shall be guided entirely by your valued judgment," said his colleague, after he had glanced at the list.

"What I propose is that we restrict the proceedings to the trial of the two pirates. Above all we must find out where they have hidden the stolen property. We will leave Miao Tsing out of it altogether, and we can release the witness, An Tung. If the corpse of the vanished Miao Tsien Hsiu should actually be found later on we could still revert to his evidence. The presents, of course, are properly yours."

"By no means, my dear colleague!" said the other, with ceremonious politeness. "You have taken all the trouble of this affair upon yourself. How should I accept them? In other respects I am in entire agreement with your proposal."

For a long time they debated the matter; then they agreed to divide the presents, and after they had well wetted their bargain Judge Hsia took his leave, and Tai A had to follow him, carrying five hundred ounces carefully packed in innocent-looking food boxes.

An old proverb says: As fire is to the roast, so is gold to the magistrate.

On the following day—all the minor officials of the court having in the meantime received from Yo San considerable payments on behalf of Miao Tsing—the two pirates were brought up for trial, and when, in the course of their depositions, they began to refer to Miao Tsing as the actual instigator of the murder, they were angrily interrupted by Hsi Men: "You accursed bandits!" he shouted at them, "for years you have been carrying on your piratical trade, as your regular activity, on the creeks and rivers, under the disguise of peaceable boatmen. Now, in your vexation at having been convicted, you want to involve an innocent third person in your guilt. Ho, An Tung, witness, come forward and speak out: who was it that struck your master, and who flung him into the water?"

"It was close on midnight," said An Tung, "when we, my master and I, were awakened from sleep by Miao Tsing's loud cries for help. As we rushed on deck from the cabin Chen San stabbed my master in the throat with a knife, and then threw him overboard. Wong Pa gave me a blow on the head with a cudgel, and pushed me so that I too fell into the water. What became of Miao Tsing I don't know."

"Good; the evidence of this witness is conclusive. Does it contain a single word incriminating Miao Tsing? No. So spare yourself the trouble of making your crazy accusations! Confess rather where you have hidden the stolen property."

He had the finger press applied to the two men, and ordered that they should be given thirty blows with the bamboo cudgel. Under the influence of this question by torture they confessed, shrieking: "We got a thousand ounces; half we have used, and the rest we have hidden here and there."

They were led away, and the proceedings terminated. The two judges drew up a protocol, which they sent, together with the two accused, to the prefect Hu of Tung, a close friend of Hsi Men's. On the strength of the protocol he passed sentence of death upon Chen San and Wong Pa, and for the rest he took no further steps in the matter.

An Tung, as witness, was released. However he was by no means satisfied with the decision of the court, since he had strong suspicions of Miao Tsing, but he journeyed to the Eastern Capital and sought out the cousin of his murdered master, the Sub-Prefect Huang. He told the latter how the two pirates had clearly and positively described Miao Tsing as the instigator of the murder, and how by bribing the judges Miao Tsing had contrived to have the charge against him withdrawn. Justice demanded that the crime of the treacherous servant, who according to the evidence of the pirates had made off with all his master's goods, should receive its merited punishment.

That very evening Master Huang set down the evidence of the lad An Tung in writing, and with an accompanying letter of explanation he addressed it to Master Tsong, who was Censor for the province of Shantung. He then gave the lad money for his journey and sent him with the two documents to the Censor Tsong in Shantung.

Master Tsong, who was making a tour of inspection through Shantung, had stopped in the prefectorial city of Tung chang fu. He was a Doctor of the first degree, and was known and feared for his strict integrity. An Tung wisely decided that he would not entrust his plaint to the Censor's subordinates. Such creatures seldom bestirred themselves until their palms were well greased. He preferred to lodge his accusation with the Censor in person, during the public session of the court. He therefore summoned up his courage, and one morning he punctually appeared before the courthouse in the prefecture where the Censor was about to officiate. Now the gong was booming inside the courthouse, as a sign that the Censor had taken his place at the judge's bench and had opened the session. The two halves of the entrance door of the courthouse were flung open, and three servants of the yamen emerged in single file, bearing banners with different inscriptions.

On the first banner was written in large characters: "Suits of members and kinsmen and relations by marriage of the Imperial house and the immediate high Nobility." On the second banner were the words: "Suits of the Civil and Military Mandarins." The third and last banner bore the inscription: "Suits of the Hundred Families." An Tung, with a number of other persons, attached himself to this banner and followed it to that part of the hall in which standing room was set aside for clients from the ranks of the people.

He waited patiently until all the other people had been dealt with; then he boldly stepped forward and threw himself upon the ground before the vermilion dais on which the Censor sat enthroned.

"What does this mean?" asked the harsh voices of the yamen beadles on either side of the judges' bench. In reply, An Tung drew forth the letter of the Sub-Prefect Huang and held it out, with up-lifted hands, toward the judge's bench.

"Take it from him and bring it here!" An Tung heard the Censor say. Several beadles obediently rushed at the kneeling man, snatched the document from his hands, and laid it on the judge's bench in front of the Censor. The Censor opened it and read:

> "Huang in the Capital
> To his former Comrade
> The Pillar of the State
> Tsong.

"Now it is already a year since the illustrious season of our companionship expired. How greatly I miss the nearness of the good fellow-traveler! When last autumn I received the jewel of your letter my soul for a moment went a-wandering and was once more united with your own. How great was my joyful satisfaction to learn that you had been elected Censor for the province of Shantung! It is your office publicly to reprove unfaithful servants of the State who use their power to violate justice and to ensure their personal advantage. For this reason I ought not to fail to call your attention to the still-unpunished crime of a certain Miao Tsing, committed against his master, the honorable Doctor Miao Tsien Hsiu of Yangchow. I trust that when you come to Tung ping fu you will look into this case, in order that justice may be duly satisfied. The bearer of this letter, a certain An Tung, will place in your hands a detailed indictment.

> Written in mid-Spring
> hoping for the day when we shall meet again,
> HUANG."

399

"Is there a written indictment?" asked the Censor.

"Have you a written indictment on you?" echoed the yamen beadles from the right and the left of the judge's bench, surrounding the kneeling man. An Tung felt in his bosom and brought out the indictment. The Censor read it. Then he seized his writing brush, and wrote on it a message for the Prefect of Tung ping fu, directing the latter to make inquiries in respect of the corpse of Miao Tsien Hsiu, who had been murdered in his district, and to report on the result of his inquiries. The lad An Tung was ordered to proceed to Tung ping fu, and there hold himself at the disposal of the authorities to the end of identifying the corpse. An Tung made a kowtow and took his departure by the side exit.

Master Tsong put the indictment and his directions in an envelope, sealed it with the long seal of office, and instructed the Assistant District Superintendent Ti from the district of Yang ku hsien to deliver the letter to the Prefect of Tung ping fu.

This Ti, a native of Honan, was a man of a somewhat crabbed and independent nature, who sometimes committed the greatest stupidities in the course of his investigations. But he was incorruptible.

Master Ti's itinerary took him past the district capital of Tsing ho hsien. Now, as he was riding along the bank of the River Tsing to the west of the city wall, he encountered a curious natural phenomenon. Close before his horse's head there suddenly rose a sharply-pointed cone of dust, which persistently whirled along the highway in front of him, and refused to make way for him. Impressed by this spectacle, Master Ti reined in his horse and ordered some of his retinue to ride after the conical whirlwind. After a while the men returned and reported that the whirlwind had moved on in the direction of the new river port, had come to a standstill at a certain spot, close to the undergrowth on the river bank, and had then dissolved. Master Ti now rode to the spot indicated, and made some of the people at work in the neighboring fields dig up the soil with their spades and mattocks. And lo, at the depth of a few feet the corpse of a man was laid bare. And the throat of the corpse revealed a wound, as though made with a knife.

Now an official coroner was fetched from the city, who had to make a written report of the discovery. Then Master Ti ascertained that the nearest human dwelling to the site of the discovery was a Buddhist convent, the "Cloister of Maternal Charity." He summoned all the inmates of the convent and subjected them to a strict examination. What they deposed was this: One evening in the tenth month of the previous year, while they were setting the Lanterns of the Dead floating downstream, a dead body was washed up on the river shore, just where they were assembled. Actuated by neighborly love, they had pulled it out of the water and had dug a dry grave for it. Apart from this they had no information concerning the corpse.

This offered the worthy Master Ti an excellent opportunity for distinguishing himself as a master of bold deduction.

"Of course, you are at the bottom of this sinister story!" he cried, accusing the flabbergasted monks. "You scraped a grave for the man here, having previously robbed and murdered him. And now you want to get out of it by pretending that the river washed him ashore!"

And without allowing them to speak a word in refutation of this charge, he made his myrmidons give them each a hundred blows of the rod, while the Abbot had also to suffer the torture of the finger press. He then threw them all into prison, and proud of his achievement, reported to the Censor Tsong.

But Master Tsong, after considering the matter at length, was unable to agree with Master Ti's conception of the case. "If the monks had really killed the man, why didn't they simply throw him into the river, instead of deliberately burying him close to their convent?" he asked himself. "By so doing they undoubtedly proved that their conscience was clear." And he promptly released them from custody.

Soon after this An Tung arrived in Tung ping fu, and reported at the Prefecture, as the Censor had bidden him. He was taken to the public morgue, and there, in the body cast up by the Tsing river and recently exhumed, he recognized his former master.

"It is my poor master!" he cried, in distress. "I recognize him by the wound in the throat." His evidence was reported to Master Tsong, who had the two pirates brought up for trial once more. They adhered to their former statement, that they had been incited to commit the murder by Miao Tsing. The Censor thereupon issued a warrant for the arrest of Miao Tsing, and at the same time he drew up an impeachment of the two judges who had protected the principal criminal in return for money, and had therefore degraded justice to the level of a purchasable commodity.

Since the Sixth Wang had become unexpectedly the possessor— thanks to Miao Tsing—of a hundred ounces of silver and four fine new dresses, she had found herself unable to rest by day or to sleep by night. She was continually dinning into her husband's ears the most varied proposals as to how all this money be employed to best advantage. Then rings and brooches were purchased; sixteen ounces were expended on a hair-net alone; the tailor had to come and run up this or that article of clothing for her; and finally, discovering that she needed another servant, she engaged a new maid, Spring Perfume by name.

One day, when Hsi Men was visiting the Sixth Wang, he had gone into the courtyard for a natural purpose, when he perceived that on the adjacent site there was a moon terrace from which one could obtain an unimpeded view of his manager's courtyard. The idea disturbed him, and he asked the Sixth Wang to which house this moon terrace belonged. "To the house of our neighbor Yo San," she replied.

"Well then, send them word that they are to pull down their moon terrace as quickly as possible. It is detrimental to the undisturbed occupation of your house. If they won't do it of their own free will I shall put the building police on to them."

The Sixth Wang thereupon consulted her husband.

"The Yo Sans are good neighbors and friends of ours. We could hardly persuade them to knock down their moon terrace because Master Hsi Men wants them to," she considered.

"I know a way out," said her husband. "We'll simply plant a few trees there, to screen the outlook. And besides that we'll build a moon terrace ourselves. We can use the upper platform for fermenting wine, and underneath we can build a decent privy and a stable, in which Master Hsi Men can stable his horse when he comes to visit you."

"Oh, but what do we want with a moon terrace? We should do better to put up a respectable brick building with a couple of living rooms."

"Very well, and we'll have one room on top of the other, so that the view of the people next door will be completely blocked."

And so a further thirty ounces were sacrificed for the building in the courtyard.

On Hsi Men's own property the building operations seemed never likely to come to an end. For months the workmen had been busy at his country seat outside the city gates, where the hereditary burial ground of his family was situated. They had heaped up a new hill, and built on the top of it a belvedere with living rooms. Since the birth of his son and his appointment as District Judge he had never found time to go there and sacrifice to his ancestors.

Now, however, after the new entrance gate, flanked by peach trees and willows, was completed, and the spirit avenue leading to the Hall of the Ancestors, which ran between steep banks, planted with pines and cypresses, he resolved to make a ceremonial offering to his ancestors on the sixth day of the third month—the day of the Tsing ming festival.

A few days beforehand he sent a considerable number of his friends and relatives written invitations to take part in the ceremony. On this occasion the day was to be observed with especial pomp. Large supplies of food and wine were sent out betimes, while a troupe of actors, and the four singing-girls, Cinnamon Bud, Little Silver, Jade Clasp, and Sweetheart, were engaged to entertain the guests.

It was a long procession of some thirty palanquins which passed out of the Southern Gate on the morning of the Tsing ming festival. Among the guests invited were Hsi Men's wealthy neighbor Kiao, Moon Lady's two brothers, a brother of Mistress Ping's, Beggar Ying, Hsia Hsi Ta, Pen Se, Han Tao Kwo, young Chen, and a dozen wives of friends and kinsmen. Beside Hsi Men, his daughter, and his six wives, the four favorite maids, Spring Plum, Jade Flute, Pear Blossom, and Fragrant Orchid took part in the excursion. Even Hsi Men's little son, who was still in his first year, had come with his nurse Ju I. Moon Lady had been strongly opposed to bringing him, because old Liu, to whom she was still wont to apply for medical advice, had urgently dissuaded her against it, but Hsi Men had only laughed at her, and had replied that he wasn't going to obey the orders of an old quack like that.

But when the company had assembled about the sacrificial terrace, which was built of white jade, and when, during the ceremonial sacrifice, the music suddenly struck up with the booming of gongs and trumpets, the child was so frightened that he timidly hid his little head against his nurse's breast, and hardly dared to breathe. Moon Lady, who noticed this, quietly warned Mistress Ping, his mother.

"Let the nurse take him further back, where it's quiet; the sound of the music is frightening him. It was an irresponsible thing to do to bring the child at all. But once more, no one would listen to me."

At Mistress Ping's request the musicians stopped playing until the nurse, covering the child's ears, had carried him out of hearing.

After the sacrificial rites were accomplished, and a written prayer had been read and burned, so that the flames might convey it to the spirits of the departed ancestors, Hsi Men invited the male guests to dine in the reception hall, while Moon Lady escorted the female guests along a flowery path, which ran between solemn cypress groves and cheerful bamboo thickets, to the belvedere on the new hill.

There, as the guests were dining, a troupe of actors displayed their

404

art, while the male guests were entertained with song and dance by the four singing-girls, who at frequent intervals poured wine for them. The four maids undertook the duty of pouring wine in the belvedere. After the meal the guests wandered at will about the spacious park. Gold Lotus, in company with Jade Fountain, Hsi Men's daughter, Cinnamon Bud, and Little Silver, amused herself on the swings.

Behind the belvedere were three rooms which Hsi Men had furnished sumptuously with couches and divans, toilet tables and alabaster mirrors. A splashing fountain provided pure drinking water, and on the walls, which were white as snow, hung inscribed rolls and pictures, nor were lutes and a chessboard forgotten. These comfortable rooms were intended for the female guests, who could rest and make their toilet here undisturbed.

To one of these rooms the nurse Ju I had brought her little charge, where she laid him, packed in his cushions, on a gold-besprinkled couch. The maid Pear Blossom, who had accompanied her, sat on the edge of the couch and played with the child. Suddenly Gold Lotus entered, waving in her hand the blossoming branch of a peach tree.

"Why are you not upstairs in the pavilion, serving the guests?" she asked Pear Blossom.

"My mistress asked me to look after the little one. There are still three maids to serve the guests."

In the meantime the nurse, who had been put on her guard by previous experiences, had taken the child into her arms directly Gold Lotus appeared. Gold Lotus bent over the child and said, jestingly: "Little coward! you were so terrified by the songs and trumpets just now that you couldn't utter a sound!"

She took him out of his blankets and cushions, pressed him to her bosom, and kissed him. While she was thus caressing the child young Chen, pushing the curtain aside, quietly entered the room. He went up to Gold Lotus, and began, like her, to caress and tease the child, and it was a curious fact that his nearness gave it confidence, so that it began to crow with delight. Then he took it from

405

Gold Lotus and kissed it lovingly. Gold Lotus noted with envy how the child seemed to trust young Chen. "When I kiss him he's angry and ruffles my hair," she remarked.

"Didn't you once tell me I didn't know how to kiss?" he asked, with a challenging smile.

She had an apt rejoinder on the tip of her tongue, but in view of the presence of the nurse and the maid she confined herself to striking him lightly with the handle of her fan. He seemed to find the touch of the fan most delightful, for he wriggled like a carp about to swallow a crumb.

"Oh, but that hurts!" he cried, laughing. "I've got such thin clothes on. You ought really to treat me more tenderly, Mistress Sister-in-law!"

"You scamp, you deserve no mercy! If you cheek me again I'll treat you much more harshly!"

Meanwhile the nurse had once more taken the child, and with the maid she withdrew into the next room, in order not to disturb the two at their amorous dalliance.

Now they went out into the open air, for they saw Jade Fountain, Hsi Men's daughter, and Cinnamon Bud approaching, and did not wish to be surprised indoors together. Gold Lotus allowed young Chen to precede her, and quietly pressed upon his head the branch of peach blossom, which she had bent into a wreath.

"What have they been doing to your hair?" asked his wife, laughing.

He felt his head, and in mute bewilderment removed the wreath.

Towards evening all returned to the city in an orderly procession: first the women's palanquins, escorted by four servants, then Hsi Men, followed by four guards, with the male guests, all on horseback; the cook bringing up the rear, with a number of porters carrying the food baskets.

At home a surprise awaited Hsi Men. He had barely dismounted when he was told that during the day Judge Hsia had asked for him in person, and had subsequently sent two messengers to inquire for him. He wished most urgently to speak to Hsi Men, who could not imagine what urgent occasion could have brought Master Hsia to the house.

"Did he leave any message?" he asked his body servant Shu Tung who was helping him to disrobe.

"Only that the matter was one of the greatest importance, and that he positively must speak to you today."

While Hsi Men was revolving all sorts of doubts and conjectures in his mind, Li Ping entered and announced: "Master Hsia has just come."

Hsi Men hastily ran to greet him in the front reception hall. "I am infinitely sorry that I missed you on your previous visit. I spent some time outside the city, in order to sacrifice to my ancestors and sweep the dust off their graves. Pray excuse my lack of foresight."

"If you please, I must speak to you in absolute confidence. Shall we be quite undisturbed here?"

Hsi Men preferred to take his guests into the outlying belvedere, and gave orders that during the consultation none of the servants were to enter the pavilion.

"This morning," Master Hsia began, "I received, quite unexpectedly, a visit from our District Superintendent Li. He informed me that the Censor for the province of Shantung intends to denounce us both to the Throne. His indictment is already on its way to the Eastern Capital. I immediately procured a copy of the indictment, and have brought it with me. Here it is."

"Petition to the Throne
    from the Censor for the Province of Shantung,
                   Tsong.

"In older days, when Master Kung Tse set down his Spring and Autumn Annals, the Ruler was wont from time to time to make a journey of inspection through his empire, in order to propagate in all directions light relating to the wise intentions of a good government, and help the population to achieve higher culture. Nowadays it is our office, as Censor, to continue this good old custom, and in particular to ensure that justice is done, and to stigmatize unsuitable officials and propose them to the Throne for punishment.

"Having been commissioned a twelvemonth since thoroughly to investigate the province of Shantung in this connection, I am obliged, at the close of my year's period of office, to bring a further accusation against two judicial officials. The one is Hsia, District Judge of Tsing ho hsien in the Prefecture of Tung ping fu . . . long known to be susceptible of bribery . . . the scandal of the bureaucracy . . . merciless as a raging hurricane to poor malefactors . . . obsequious expression and pliant, slavish knees when he is paid by wealthy scoundrels. . . . The other is Hsi Men, Assistant Judge of the same district . . . from the very first hail-fellow-well-met with the people of the markets and back streets . . . obtained his office by underhand devices . . . so ignorant that he cannot tell corn from turnips . . . of disreputable private life . . . allows wives and concubines to cross the street without protective curtain and behave themselves unseemly . . . drinks with daughters of joy before the eyes of passers-by on the balcony of his house on the Lantern Market . . . has illicit relations with the wife of his business manager Han . . . under cover of darkness received bribe moneys from the criminal Miao Tsing. . . .

"These men are both unworthy to hold office, and I ask for an injunction to the competent ministries, to examine the grounds of this accusation and to take the requisite measures, in order that the principles of a pure administration may be safeguarded and that the fair fame of the Imperial Government may not be prejudiced. . . ."

Hsi Men gazed at his companion in consternation.

"What now?" asked Master Hsia.

"There is nothing left for it," replied Hsi Men, after a few moments of tense deliberation, "but to send with all possible speed to the Ancient Commander in the Eastern Capital and purchase his support."

Master Hsia was entirely of the same opinion, and he left immediately, in order to make the necessary arrangements at home.

The very next morning, at an early hour, Hsi Men's confidential agent Lai Pao and Master Hsia's servant Hsia Shou made a hurried departure for Kai fong fu. Lai Pao carried with him three hundred ounces in bullion, as well as various articles of gold and silver jewelry, and precious stones, and a letter for the Intendant Ti. Hsia Shou had two hundred ounces of gold and two fine silver pitchers packed away in his trunk. For Hsi Men, the commotions of the night were aggravated by his anxiety concerning his child. The nervous excitement resulting from the protracted excursion persisted all night. The child would neither sleep nor accept his nurse's breast. He lay back among his cushions, tossing restlessly to and fro as though distressed by some alarming object. His anxious mother asked Moon Lady to advise her.

"Didn't I advise you not to take him?" said Moon Lady. "The child is not yet a year old. But this obstinate man is unteachable."

She sent for her old Liu, while Hsi Men called in a children's doctor. There was a constant opening and shutting of doors all that restless night. Fortunately old Liu considered that the child's condition was not such as to cause anxiety.

"Some sort of fright has entered his body," she thought. "Perhaps the 'Marshal of the Five Highways' met him on the road. I'll give him something that will soon quiet him."

And indeed the vermilion pills which she made the child swallow, dissolved in a broth prepared with rushes and lotus leaves, had such an effect that he soon quieted down and fell asleep. In her gratitude Mistress Ping gave the old woman an ounce of silver. Old Liu returned later accompanied by her husband, the blind astrologer, and in the belvedere she made him secretly recite his incantations for the child's benefit, and perform a dance to exorcise devils.

By dint of forced marches, traveling day and night, the two envoys, Lai Pao and Hsia Shou, reached Kai fong fu in the short time of six days, and delivered their presents to the Intendant Ti. Not idly had Master Ti promised to support Hsi Men as though he had been an Ancient Commander of a hundred and ten. After he had read Hsi Men's letter he assured the messengers that there was no occasion for **uneasiness.**

"The Censor's indictment has not yet been received here. When it arrives I will speak to the Chancellor and make sure that it is simply pigeon-holed by the competent Ministry—that is, the War Ministry—and left unanswered and completely ignored. Master Tsong's period of office has practically elapsed. Just tell your employers that they can be quite easy in their minds."

He hospitably entertained the two messengers, and gave them each five ounces of silver as traveling expenses, whereupon they set off with all speed for home.

Hsi Men, who awaited their return beside himself with impatience, felt himself freed from a grievous burden by the good news which they brought him.

"But how comes it that the Censor's dispatches had not yet reached the capital at the time of your arrival there?" he asked in astonishment.

"We got there first by covering the distance to Kai fong fu in only five days. No doubt the dispatches have arrived by now. For on the way back we met on the highway a troop of mail riders with bells on the horses' necks and yellow mailbags strapped to the saddles. Presumably they were the Censor's couriers."

"Well, that's all over as far as I'm concerned," said Hsi Men with a laugh. "They'll arrive too late."

He dismissed Hsia Shou with greetings to his master, Judge Hsia, and rewarded his servant Lai Pao with five ounces, two bottles of wine, a great roast, and a day's holiday to sleep off his fatigue.

CHAPTER TWENTY-SEVEN: *Father Fan provides Hsi Men with some miraculous Pills. The Nun Pi mixes a magic Draught for Moon Lady*

O N THE FOLLOWING DAY Judge Hsia, his colleague, hastened to pay Hsi Men a visit of thanks.

"Without your enlightened intellect and your powerful support I really should not have known how to get over the difficulty," he said, full of honest gratitude.

Hsi Men smiled, feeling pleasantly flattered.

"The Censor can allege what he likes. Our Ancient Commander in the Capital has also a lucid understanding."

And over their cups, merry and carefree, they celebrated until late in the night their fortunate salvation from a great peril.

Since nothing resulted from his indictment of the two dishonest judges, it was of course clear to Censor Tsong that the Chancellor Tsai King had allowed himself to be corrupted. Full of righteous wrath, he profited by the audience in which he was received by the Son of Heaven on the conclusion of his year's period of office in order to lay upon the steps of the Throne a new indictment, in which he most violently assailed the Chancellor in respect of unsocial commercial statutes which he had recently promulgated. The new regulations concerning the salt monopoly and the public granaries, he argued, would advantage only a few wealthy persons, and were calculated to melt all the fat of the rural population; so that if the peace of the Empire was not to be seriously imperiled the statutes in question must be repealed.

But his well-meant representations were without effect. The Chancellor at that time had unrestricted access to the ear of the Son of Heaven, and was able to parry the attack of his adversary. He was also able to contrive that Master Tsong should be transferred, as Prefect, to the province of Shensi. But the new Censor for the province of Shensi, a certain Sung Pan, was the brother-in-law of the Chancellor's son, the Chief Secretary Tsai Yu. This Censor, on the secret instructions of the Chancellor, applied himself to spying upon the private life of the hated Tsong, even going so far as to employ the latter's servants as spies; and he intrigued so long against him that Master Tsong, weary of all these vexations, and in order to escape legal proceedings in which he was bound to be the loser, left his office and his family in the lurch and retired to a remote mountain solitude. But that happened later.

About this time Hsi Men received the simultaneous visits of two dignitaries, which, though a great honor, involved him in great expense. The aforesaid Censor Sung, on his way to the province of Shensi, happened to meet, in Tsing ho hsien, the adopted son of the Chancellor Tsai Shen, who was about to take up his post as treasurer of the salt works in the two provinces of Huai. On the urgent recommendation of the Intendant Ti, Censor Sung had intended, on passing through the city, to wait upon the respected, wealthy, and therefore most noble Master Hsi Men. But Tsai Shen, who had already enjoyed Hsi Men's hospitality some months before this, was eager in any case to renew his former acquaintance, and so the two mandarins resolved to pay him a common visit.

Hsi Men had timely information of their intention, and had made adequate preparations for a brilliant reception. Naturally the two mandarins' palanquins, accompanied by a great retinue, attracted considerable attention in the city, and Hsi Men was once more the focus of the day's gossip. What an important person he must be— was the general opinion—if two distinguished stranger mandarins interrupted their official journeys especially to wait upon him!

This time Hsi Men surpassed himself in hospitality. Not only did he entertain the entire retinue of his two guests; he also sent a wealth of provisions aboard their traveling junks, including fifty bottles of wine each, five hundred cakes and pastries, and enormous roasts, a hundred pounds in weight. And when Master Sung, a lively Kiang hsi man, who could not sit still through a single act of a play, insisted on leaving as evening approached, Hsi Men gave him a whole menu, together with all the gold and silver plates and dishes, packed in twenty food baskets, as a present to speed him on his way. There were two great earthenware crocks of wine, two whole sheep, two silver mugs with handles, two silver wine beakers, two silver dishes, a pair of ivory chopsticks, two pairs of gold-leaf flowers, and two red silk tablecloths. And the Salt Treasurer, Tsai Shen, received the same attention. This day cost Hsi Men nearly a thousand ounces.

Master Tsai Shen did not take his leave until the following day. Hsi Men arranged for him to spend the night in the Malachite Veranda, and there he contrived a special surprise for him. When late that evening he entered the festively illuminated rooms of the Malachite Veranda, two charming young maidens greeted him, smiling and curtsying. They were Golden Ring and Sweetheart, whom Hsi Men had secretly sent thither in honor of his guest. Their stimulating society and his abundant draughts of wine inspired Master Tsai Shen's poetical powers. He wished to prove that not in vain had he emerged from the Palace examination of the previous year as the first among the blossoming talents, as Chuang yuen. He accordingly took his brush, added character to character in dexterous, serpentine curves, and to begin with immortalized himself by an eight-line stanza on the wall of the chamber. And then Sweetheart, whom he had chosen for his bedfellow that night, cajoled him until he seized the brush again and dashed off a four-line stanza on her gold-painted fan.

It goes without saying that Hsi Men succeeded in deriving some advantage from so significant a visit. Master Tsai Shen, as Salt Treasurer of two great salt-producing provinces, had control of the supplies of salt to the wholesale merchants. Now Hsi Men, with his neighbor Kiao, had long been engaged in the wholesale purchase and resale of salt as a profitable branch of commerce. So when he was far gone in his cups he introduced his confidential servant Lai Pao to his guest, and announced that Lai Pao would shortly be visiting Yangchow, where the Salt Treasurer discharged his functions, as his accredited agent. Upon this Master Tsai Shen smilingly promised to give him a full month's start of the other wholesale purchasers. Hsi Men would then be in a position to get rid of his consignments at a time when the market was still tight, so that he would be able to obtain a higher price. Under these circumstances it was well worth his while to indulge in a somewhat lavish hospitality.

On the following day Hsi Men insisted upon escorting Master Tsai Shen through the city gate, and as far as the temple of Buddha at Yung fung se, where he had prepared for his guest a sumptuous farewell breakfast. Then the last ceremonious courtesies were exchanged, the last profound obeisances; Master Tsai Shen stepped into his palanquin, in which he was carried to his traveling junk, and Hsi Men returned alone to the deserted table in the temple. After the fatigues of the last two days the monastic silence that surrounded him here was especially soothing, and he decided to prolong his stay. The appearance of the abbot roused him from his contemplative mood.

"What is your age?" he asked, noting that the monk's eyebrows were white as snow.

"The insignificant bonze has numbered four and seventy years," replied the Abbot.

"And how many friars have you here?"

"Thirty."

"H'm! There's plenty of room for you; your monastery is a fine, spacious building as far as size goes, but it still has a somewhat unfinished look."

"Your eyes have not deceived you. Our cloister is a foundation of the River Prefect Chow, but unfortunately the money gave out while it was being built, so that it has remained in a half-finished condition."

"Indeed, so Master Chow is your patron? Of course, his country seat is not far away. Well, you apply to Master Chow and ask him for further help. I am prepared, for my part, to contribute something to the cost of building." He handed the abbot an ounce of silver.

"Here is a slight compensation for the trouble I have caused you today."

The Abbot thanked him obsequiously.

"Pardon me for making no preparations for receiving you worthily. Your visit was so unexpected."

"That is all right. But now I just want to go out for a moment."

The Abbot bade a young novice open the doors leading to the rearward portion of the monastery. Having done his business there, Hsi Men looked about him. He saw, at some distance from the cells of the monks, a large, quintuple hall, dedicated to purposes of devotion, to whose silence the friars withdrew when they wished to abandon themselves to *dhyana,* to sacred meditation. Inside he saw kneeling quite a number of "cloud-wandering monks," bowed over their sutras, holding in their hands the hollow wooden fish, the symbol of sleeplessness, with which the day and night watches are struck. Without definite purpose, but actuated by mere curiosity, Hsi Men sauntered into the hall and looked about him.

One of the kneeling monks attracted his particular attention: a lean, emaciated figure, whose fleshless limbs protruded like sticks from the folds of his patched, reddish-brown cassock. There was a fanatical glitter in his eyes, which were as round as those of a leopard. His bare tonsure was surrounded by a ring of hair that had the appearance of being waxed, while under his chin grew a tangled, untended beard. He seemed to be a true *Arhat,* one of the elect disciples of the Buddha, as he crouched upon his bench, so withdrawn from the world in his ecstasy that he did not even notice that the mucus was dropping from his nostrils like two slender rods of jade.

"To judge from his singular appearance and behavior," thought Hsi Men, "he seems to be an especially advanced adept. I'll wake him up and question him." And with a loud voice he cried to the monk: "Hi, Master, what is your name, and where do you come from?"

But he had to repeat his question twice before the monk awoke from his ecstasy, slowly sat up on his bench, stretched himself, blinked his eyes, and at last sprang to his feet with a jerk. Turning to Hsi Men, he nodded his head a few times and at last replied, in a hoarse, croaking voice:

"I am Father Fan and I come from far in the Western countries. In the forest solitudes of India, on a towering summit, stands the 'Cloister of the Cold Hall,' to which I belong. I have wandered hither with the clouds. I am experienced in the art of dispensing medicine and healing the sick. What does the noble lord desire?"

"Indeed, so you have an understanding of medicine? Have you by chance a serviceable tonic or restorative for men?"

"I have, I have."

"Good, then I should like you to pay me a visit at once. Will you come with me?"

"Come with you, come with you."

"Then we'll go."

The monk fished out from under the bench a ragged iron-shod staff and a double bag filled with medicine bottles. He thrust the staff between the two bags, swung it, with its dangling load, over his shoulder, and followed Hsi Men to the monastery gate. There Hsi Men beckoned to his boy, Tai A.

"Get a couple of mules for yourself and the Master and ride on ahead with him," he ordered. "I shall overtake you on the way."

"By no means, master," the monk interposed. "I need no horse or mule, yet I shall arrive on foot quicker than you will on horse-back."

"He must really be an adept in the higher arts to make such a bold assertion," thought Hsi Men, and he agreed that the monk should go on foot; but for safety he sent Tai A with him, as he was afraid that the monk might give him the slip.

This day—it was the seventeenth of the fourth month—was the birthday not only of Sunflower, Hsi Men's second wife, but also of his secret mistress, the Sixth Wang. As the Sixth Wang felt a longing to spend the evening in Hsi Men's company, she sent her younger brother, Wang Tsing, to inform Tai A of her desire. But Tai A was still absent, so Wang Tsing decided to wait for him at the main entrance. He may have been standing there for an hour when Moon Lady and Sunflower appeared. They were escorting Mother Li, who had been paying her daughter a birthday visit, back to her palanquin. When Moon Lady saw the strange fifteen-year-old boy standing in the gateway she asked him where he came from and what he wanted. Wang Tsing made an embarrassed kowtow; then he replied: "I come from the house of Han and I am waiting for Brother An."

Since several of Hsi Men's servants bore the name of An, Moon Lady wished to know which Brother An he was referring to. The servant Ping An, who was standing there, and who was afraid that the boy might blurt out the truth and betray the secret of his master's relations with the Sixth Wang, pushed him quickly aside and replied for him: "He has been sent from the house of Han, and he wants to ask Tai A if Master Han Tao Kwo is coming home today."

Moon Lady, satisfied with this reply, returned to the inner apartments.

At last the expected youth arrived, accompanied by the monk Fan. He was quite out of breath, and dripping with perspiration from head to foot. The monk, on the contrary, did not betray the slightest trace of fatigue or effort. Ping An immediately gave Tai A the message of the Sixth Wang.

"The business might very well have turned out badly," he added: "Moon Lady happened to come up, and if I hadn't at once intervened and spoken for the boy, giving a harmless answer, I think the cloven hoof would have been apparent. If she should ask you anything, take good care that your reply agrees with what I told her."

Tai A was hardly attending. All that he cared about was to cool himself with his fan.

"It's enough to spoil one's whole day," he muttered angrily to himself. "Why should I have had to run home with this accursed baldhead? The fellow never let me rest a moment, all the way from the monastery to this house. The master expressly placed a mule at his disposal, and the crazy monk insisted on walking in this heat! My soles are worn through as if they'd been held to a grindstone, and my legs will barely carry me. I'm completely winded by this senseless racing."

"Why has the master sent the baldhead here?" Ping An wanted to know.

"How should I know? Some sort of quackery!"

While they were still talking, Hsi Men arrived with the rest of his retinue.

"What, are you there already, Master?" he cried in astonishment, as his eyes fell on the monk. "You can't have got here by natural means!"

He dismounted from his horse and led the monk into the front reception hall. While he was changing his clothes his visitor had time to take stock of his surroundings, which spoke of wealth and splendor. How lofty were the dimensions of this stately hall, how spacious were the great courtyards! At the entrance, like the hairs of a beard, hung the glittering strings of the green bead curtain, which displayed a design of frogs seated upon a tortoise. The floors were covered with lionskins and long-piled carpets. In the middle of the hall was the mighty circle of the many-legged, wide-spreading table of ebony, that shone as though oiled. In the center of the table, enclosed in circular frames, were plates of precious ornamental stone from Tal li fu in the province of Yunnan, resting, like the Buddhistic universe, on a Sumeru mountain summit as foundation. Round the table stood armchairs decorated with lizards' heads, of massive, thickly-veined cedarwood. On the walls, outstretched between reddish-brown bamboo rollers, were picture scrolls bordered with silken damask which showed an agatelike pattern.

"Will the Master be pleased to drink wine?" asked Hsi Men, as he returned to the hall after changing his clothes.

"Meat and wine, both are equally welcome to the simple mendicant monk," replied his famishing guest, with resignation.

Hsi Men sent a suitable order to the kitchen. Now it happened, as this was Sunflower's birthday, that the kitchen was overflowing with special culinary triumphs and delicacies, so that dish upon dish, bowl upon bowl, plate upon plate was brought in, and the simple monk disdained nothing, while his appetite seemed to have no limits. With playful ease he disposed of the appetizing entrées, with indefatigable endurance he worked through the solid roast meats of the middle courses, and he did not lay his chopsticks aside until he had polished off the entire menu of a sumptuous banquet. In the meantime he dealt valiantly with the liquor set before him, drinking it off at a single draught, emptying the small goblet or the great beaker with equal facility, whether the contents were rice spirit or wine. So he ate and drank, until his eyes protruded from their orbits. At last he had had enough.

"The simple mendicant monk is full to bursting," he said; whereupon Hsi Men had the table cleared, in order at last to talk business.

"What about the restorative you promised me?" he asked.

"I have it with me. It is an ancient prescription of Master Lao tse, who prepared it in accordance with a recipe of the fairy Hsi Wang Mu, the Queen-Mother of the West. Since you have treated me with such generous friendliness you shall have some pills."

He felt in his leathern medicine bags and brought out a hollow gourd, from whose belly he rolled on to the table a hundred and ten pills.

"Each time one pill! Never in any case more! And swallow it down with some corn spirit," he said. Then he took from another gourd a box containing perhaps something over a fifth of an ounce of a red salve.

"With this you must anoint yourself. Each time you must rub on just two-thousandths of an ounce! The supply will just suffice for a hundred and ten treatments."

"And what is the effect of your remedy?"

"Its use will convey you with the speed of the wind to the 'Grotto, of Eternal Spring'; it will give your loins twofold, nay, tenfold vigor, will make your hair and beard grow, anchor your teeth more firmly, and increase the keenness of your sight. Your desire will be measureless. In one night you will be able to deal with ten women. No courtesan's sensuality will be equal to yours. And if you are in danger of collapsing during the contest, a drink of cold water will suffice to revive your powers, and fill the orchid chamber with the breath of spring for the rest of the night."

Hsi Men listened eagerly. Now he wanted to know the recipe too, so that he himself could prepare the pills and the salve. For his wisdom already foresaw the time when his provision of the remedy would be exhausted. He was willing to pay any price for the recipe. And in confirmation of his promise he then and there pushed thirty bright ingots across the table. But the monk would not betray the secret of the prescription, and refused the thirty ingots with a laugh.

"I have renounced the world and taken the vows of poverty. With the clouds I drift hither and thither; what should I do with earthly treasure? I am leaving you the pills and the salve out of friendship, because you have shown me such great favor. I do not want your money!"

And he made ready to depart.

"Then at least take a length of cloth for a new cassock!" said Hsi Men, persuasively, and he bade his servants bring in a bale of cloth. This useful gift Father Fan accepted with gratitude; then, striking his clenched fists together in a gesture of farewell, he swung the staff with its dangling load of medicine bags over his shoulder and took his leave. At the threshold he turned once more and said: "Never take more than one pill at a time! Remember that, remember that!"

Among the visitors who had come to congratulate Sunflower on her birthday was the nun, Sister Wang, and this time, in pursuance of her promise to Moon Lady, she had brought with her the Abbess Pi from the "Cloister of the Flowery Doctrine." This worthy lady was accompanied by two pretty little novices of fifteen, whose names were Miao Fong and Miao Kue, meaning "Glorious Phœnix" and "Glorious Pleasure." She was dressed in a long tea-colored horsehair robe, and over the bluish-gray bloom of her shaven head she wore a clean white monastic cowl. She was tall and corpulent. Between her piglike eyes, which were bedded in fat, yawned a wide mouth, the very look of which told the observer that it was accustomed to chewing words and mangling sentences. Moon Lady treated her with especial courtesy; and respectfully addressed her as "Commandress," while she politely accosted Moon Lady as "Bodhisattva of the House," or "Noble Lady." While all were partaking of tea and special vegetable dishes, and listening devoutly to her conversation, Moon Lady saw the servant Shu Tung passing the window, carrying various dishes and goblets which he had taken from the table in the front reception hall and was now carrying to the back of the house.

"Has the wine-drinking and meat-eating monk gone already?" Moon Lady asked him as he passed the window.

"He has just taken his leave. The Master is now escorting him to the gate."

Sister-in-law Wu wanted to know what monk was this.

"My husband brought him back with him from the Yung fu se monastery, where he gave the Salt Treasurer Tsai a farewell breakfast this morning," said Moon Lady. "This remarkable monk has relieved us of quite a little wine and meat, as though there were no such things as monastic precepts, but he wouldn't take the money which my husband wanted to pay him for some medicine or other."

"Yes, it's difficult to refuse good food and drink," the Abbess interposed, with a laugh. "We nuns, of course, display a little self-control in that respect, but these friars don't all take the regulations so seriously. But they are very bad monks. In the Tripitaka it is written: What one wastes in luxurious living in this life one must make good in a subsequent existence."

"Good gracious!" said Sister-in-law Wu, in dismay, "then we who are spending the whole day here in feasting and luxurious living will have to atone for it abundantly in our subsequent existence!"

"Well, well, good people like the Bodhisattva of the house are naturally an exception," the Abbess rejoined, in a flattering tone. "They have earned their luxurious mode of life by good behavior in a former existence. As one sows in the spring, so one reaps in the autumn. It is just the same with the happiness and unhappiness of our various existences."

While the Abbess was dispensing her trite wisdom to the devoutly listening women, Hsi Men had escorted the wandering monk Fan to the gate and had bidden him farewell. Now, as he was returning to his apartments, Tai A came up to him and told him, under his breath, that Lady Han had sent her younger brother to say that he simply must visit her that evening on the occasion of her birthday feast.

This invitation suited Hsi Men admirably. Now he would have an excellent opportunity of testing his restorative. He immediately sent a jug of the best wine to Lion Street, and a little later he himself made his way thither.

"If they ask for me at home," he told Tai A, who in the meantime had to go back with his horse, "just say that I had to go through the accounts in Lion Street."

The Sixth Wang welcomed him joyfully and thanked him for the wine.

"I had quite forgotten it was your birthday," he said in apology. "It's a good thing you sent me a message! Here. . . ." And he gallantly handed her his birthday gift, a pair of golden brooches in the form of the character Shu. He also gave her half an ounce of broken silver.

"Weigh off a tenth of that and let my boy get a little Southern corn spirit," he said.

She was clearly surprised. "You positively want corn spirit? Perhaps you have drunk good wine until you are tired of it?" she said, jesting, and she sent Kiu Tung to get what he wanted.

As soon as Tai A had returned his master's horse to its stall he threw himself on his bed, for he was still worn out with the effort of keeping up with Father Fan, and there he rested for an hour. It was already nearly night by the time he had recovered himself. He rose hurriedly and went to the lamp room, for he needed lanterns to light his master on the homeward journey. Moon Lady, who saw him standing outside the lamp room, asked him:

"Whom is your master visiting? This afternoon, soon after the monk had gone, he went out without bidding me good-by."

"He is not visiting anybody. He wanted to go to the shop in Lion Street and look through the accounts."

"But he wouldn't need half the day for that!"

"Perhaps he has stopped somewhere for refreshment."

"Get away with you! He wouldn't do that unless he had someone with him. Now what is behind this? Who knows?"

She made Little Jewel give him the lantern he wanted from the lamp room, and impressed it upon him that he must remind his master that his second wife, Sunflower, was celebrating her birthday.

Tai A nodded obediently, and made his way to Lion Street with Hsi Men's horse and a little boy whose duty it was to carry the lanterns. Since his master was still with the Sixth Wang, behind locked doors, he went into the kitchen and enjoyed the supper which old Fong had prepared for him.

"Listen, Mother Fong!" he said, during a pause, teasingly: "you are really in the employment of our sixth lady, Mistress Ping. How would it be if I were to tell our Sixth that you are serving Mistress Han behind her back?"

"Don't you dare, you little monkey!" said old Fong, earnestly, giving him a slap. "I could never face her again if it came out! So you just hold your tongue! Do you understand?"

The rascal, delighted to have frightened her so, applied himself to his supper with renewed gusto. While he was eating Kiu Tung had stolen away unperceived, and had crept under the window of the bedroom in which his master was diverting himself with the Sixth Wang. He noted with interest how Hsi Men washed down a red pill with a draught of corn spirit, and then anointed himself with a reddish ointment, which he took from a silver box. The Sixth Wang too had watched his proceedings with interest, and she said, laughing: "Now I understand why you wanted corn spirit!" And he, most agreeably surprised by the astonishing result, told her what he owed to Father Fan and his restorative. Now the two lovers devoted themselves with enthusiasm to the accustomed sport, and it seemed to them that they had never yet experienced such bliss as on this occasion. The Sixth Wang was utterly ravished.

"My Ta ta, I could die of bliss!" she moaned, in ecstasies of pleasure. "Move the lamp a little nearer!"

"I tell you what," he said; "I'll send your old man this very day to the salt works at Yangchow with my servant Lai Pao, and later on to the silk factories at Huchow. Then we shall be quite alone."

"Yes, yes, dear Ta ta, send him somewhere! I don't know how to bear it with that tortoise in the house. But who will manage the Lion Street business in his absence?"

"Friend Pen Se will fill his place."

All this Kiu Tung was able to see and hear from the window, and now, to his great regret, Tai A clapped him on the shoulder and disturbed him in his exciting observations.

"Oh, what's the good of just listening and watching!" said Tai A, disdainfully. "We had much better take this opportunity and slip off to Butterfly Lane for a bit. I know a house there, Mother Lu's, where they've got two smart new wenches. Little Gold and Rival they're called, and they're eighteen at most. They'll make the time pass pleasantly."

And he dragged his comrade off to Butterfly Lane, where they played the gallant for a time with Little Gold and Rival, and did their best to show themselves intelligent pupils of their lord and master in amorous matters, until the little lantern bearer gave them the agreed signal which told them that Hsi Men was dressing himself and preparing to take his leave, and duty called them back to Lion Street.

In the meantime Hsi Men's wives were gathered about the two nuns, listening to their tales of convent life, or to the sacred hymns which the two young novices were asked to sing. Moon Lady was annoyed by Hsi Men's protracted absence, and she blamed his boy,

Tai A, who had certainly deceived her again. Her suspicion was confirmed when, impelled by curiosity, she went to Gold Lotus's bedroom and found that the drawer of the wardrobe behind the bed in which he usually kept his amorous panoply was empty.

"Who knows where he is now?" she asked dejectedly.

"Of course, in some flower garden," said Gold Lotus, casually. Which of the wives would have guessed at the Sixth Wang?

At last Hsi Men returned, but instead of going immediately to the living room in which his wives were assembled, he went straight back to the pavilion of the Sixth. It was not realized that he was there until Kiu Tung brought his hat and his outdoor robe to the maid Little Jewel, asking her to put them away.

"Where is your master now?" asked Moon Lady, in astonishment.

"He has gone to the pavilion of the Sixth," replied Kiu Tung.

"But is that a way to behave, not showing himself at all?" said Moon Lady, vexedly. "We are expecting him here." Mistress Ping rose immediately and hurried off to her pavilion.

"What do you want here now?" she asked reproachfully. "It's your Second's birthday today, and she expects you to come and congratulate her."

"Oh, there's time for that tomorrow!" he said, laughing indifferently. "I feel a little overcome with wine."

"Well, but a cup more or less is no great matter!" said the Sixth, and she dragged the protesting man off to the sitting room.

"What have you been doing all by yourself until this hour of the night?" asked Moon Lady.

"I've had a few drinks with friend Ying."

Moon Lady was appeased. "I thought at once that you wouldn't be drinking alone, as that stupid Tai A imagined."

And in order to avoid further awkward questions he very soon took his leave, having for the sake of appearances drunk a congratulatory beaker with Sunflower, and returned to the pavilion of the Sixth.

The Sixth was already lying down when he entered the room. The child was lying beside her, and was already fast asleep.

That did not matter to Hsi Men; he thought only of his pleasure. His restorative pills had a lasting effect. Whoever took one of them continued to feel the desire for a woman for a whole day. Despite the spirited contest which he had only just fought with the Sixth Wang he felt no trace of exhaustion.

He therefore immediately sent the maid Pear Blossom out of the room, and tried to get into bed with the Sixth. But she resisted him. "Go to one of the others today!" she begged him. "The little one is sleeping so sweetly: you'll disturb him."

He put his arms round her neck and kissed her.

"Your slave wants to sleep with *you*," he said beseechingly. "And if you don't do as I ask I shall die of unsatisfied desire!"

"Oh, do be reasonable! Go to the Fifth!"

"I don't know why, but today I'm just crazy for you!"

"You idiot, I can't help laughing. Where have you been drinking your sense away today? Well, I'll oblige you, but if I die for it you'll have me on your conscience!"

And yielding to his piteous plea, she finally did as he desired. But first the maid Pear Blossom had to take the child to the nurse in the next room. And so Hsi Men was able to convince himself for the second time that evening of the miraculous power of his pills.

In the meantime the other wives had gone to bed. The two nuns were spending the night in Moon Lady's bedroom. When the three were alone Sister Wang produced a medicine bottle.

"Here is the draught I promised you," she told Moon Lady mysteriously.

"To be drunk on the seven-times-seventh day of the sixty-day cycle, mixed with yellow wine!" added Sister Pi. "If you sleep with your husband the same night your womb will assuredly be blessed with a little boy. But you mustn't speak of it to anybody!"

Moon Lady hastily took the bottle from the nun.

"Many thanks!" she murmured. "And on my birthday, in the first month, I'll be sure to pay you if you'll call."

"It was not easy to get that certain ingredient," Sister Wang reminded her. "At last Sister Pi succeeded in getting round a midwife of her acquaintance, who supplied her with the afterbirth of a first-born man child. We washed it perfectly clean with wine, dried and roasted it, rubbed it through a sieve, and mixed it with the draught."

Moon Lady took the hint and hastened to give the nuns an ounce of silver apiece.

"If it has the desired result you shall have stuff for a new robe too," she promised. And once more the old proverb was confirmed:

> *You've a cargo of truth, and buyers to find,*
> *You'll hardly succeed in a ten days' grind.*
> *When you want to be rid of ten cargoes of lies*
> *You won't need a day, for everyone buys!*

CHIN P'ING MEI

VOLUME II

CHAPTER TWENTY-EIGHT: *Beggar*
Ying startles a pair of Lovers in the Grotto.
Gold Lotus tastes secret Bliss with young Chen

NEXT MORNING Moon Lady was just sitting down to breakfast with the wife of her elder brother and the two nuns, when Hsi Men unexpectedly pushed the curtain aside and entered the room. Sister-in-law Wu quickly took the two nuns by the hand and retired with them to Sunflower's apartments.

"Was that Sister Pi?" Hsi Men inquired of Moon Lady, in a tone of surprise. "What is that accursed carrion, that female baldhead doing here?"

"You ought to control your tongue a little better," Moon Lady reproved him. "What has she done to you that you should speak of her so disgustingly? And how do you come to know her at all?"

"Don't I just know her! That's the old woman who fouls heaven and earth and turns her convent into a brothel. She once arranged for the youngest daughter of the Ministerial Councillor Chen to meet a young lover in the 'Cloister of Earthly Seclusion,' and took money for it. The affair became known afterwards and came up before me in court. I made the young couple husband and wife, but I had the old procuress's robe pulled off and gave her twenty strokes with the rod. Moreover, she had to revert to her lay status, as being unworthy of holy orders. How is it she is wearing the nun's robe again today?"

"Oh, nonsense! She's a most orthodox person and lives a life of the greatest piety."

"Her piety consists in letting men through the convent gates at night!" he said, derisively.

"Oh, do stop exuding such wickedness! I don't want to hear anything about her. When are you sending your people to the salt works at Yangchow?" she asked, in order to divert the conversation from a painful subject.

"The day after tomorrow, on the twentieth of the month; that's a favorable day for traveling. I am sending Lai Pao and Han Tao Kwo, and Tsai Pen will accompany them as neighbor Kiao's agent. They'll take five hundred ounces from each of us. We can get a fine consignment of salt for that."

"And in Han's absence who is managing the silk business in Lion Street?"

"Pen Se."

Hsi Men was called out of the room. Han Tao Kwo and Lai Pao had come to receive the money for the salt and their traveling expenses. Hsi Men accompanied them to the belvedere, where the money was paid out and made up into parcels and bundles. While they were thus employed Beggar Ying presented himself.

"What are you stowing away there?" he asked inquisitively.

"The salt money," Hsi Men replied. "My messengers start for Yangchow on the twentieth."

"Oh, that will be a profitable business for you. One may congratulate you beforehand," said Beggar Ying. He discussed various business matters with Hsi Men; then he suddenly blurted out: "Have you by any chance heard the scandal about Cinnamon Bud?"

"I know of no scandal."

"Then listen. The third son of our respected ex-Minister Wang has married one of the beautiful nieces of the Head Eunuch Liu Huang in the Eastern Capital. Last New Year he and his young wife were living in the capital with his uncle by marriage, and on this occasion he was presented with a sum of a thousand ounces. After his return here he ran through it all in the company of our Brother Chu Shih Nien and Brother Sun Tien Hua, in the houses of joy, mostly with the help of Cinnamon Bud. And further, he deflowered little Tsi Hsiang from the house of Tsi in Second Lane. Being distressed by his way of life, his young wife attempted suicide by hanging. When this came to the ears of the irate Wang he got the Prefect of Tung ping fu to issue a warrant of arrest against Chu and Sun and little Tsi Hsiang and Cinnamon Bud. Chu and Sun were arrested yesterday; but both the girls were able to escape in time. Cinnamon Bud wanted to come to you yesterday and beg for your support. I wonder she hasn't been yet. She besought me to put in a word for her when I saw you."

He was in a great hurry; he rushed off again after he had unburdened himself of his news. At the main entrance he actually encountered Cinnamon Bud, who was just alighting from her palanquin. He greeted her and informed her in passing that he had already prepared Hsi Men for her visit.

Hsi Men had her shown into Moon Lady's sitting room. There she stood before him in her modest tea-colored dress, nervously dabbing her forehead with a white lace handkerchief, her flower-like face pale and bewildered, her cloudy hair carelessly dressed. She wore no jewelry.

"Oh, this misfortune!" she began. "Truly, one can quietly sit in one's room unsuspicious of evil, and disaster forces its way in. Only think, Master, yesterday Chu Shih Nien and Sun Tien Hua came to see us, bringing with them a young man who was a total stranger, Wang by name. My sister was not at home, and mother had gone out too, in order to congratulate my aunt here on her birthday. Oh, if only I had gone with her! I meant to come a little later, but Chu and Sun kept on hovering round me and bothering me not to go out, but to give their companion a little of my society. In the meantime they wanted to pay you a hasty visit. But they had hardly got out of the door before they were surrounded by a crowd of people and led away. At this young Master Wang fled out of the courtyard gate, and I followed him, and ran into the neighboring house, and took refuge with Mother Chu. Mother was naturally scared to death when she came home and learned from our servant what had happened during her absence. Early this morning some police from the yamen appeared and banged on the door; they exhibited a warrant of arrest and wanted to carry me off. I was to be taken to the Eastern Capital, to be examined there. Isn't that terrible? Oh, Master, take my part, or I'm lost! And you, dear mistress," she said, turning to Moon Lady, "do, I beg you, say a good word for me!"

Hsi Men smilingly raised her from her kneeling position; then he asked her: "Was there any name besides yours on the warrant for your arrest?"

"Yes, there was the name of little Tsi Hsiang, whom young Wang had deflowered. If he has spent money in her house, and got into debt, is that anything to do with our household? If he ever left so much as a copper coin with us may my eyes fall out of my head, and if Tsi Hsiang was deflowered in our house then may my body be smitten with as many great boils, each big as a plate, as it now has hair follicles!"

Moved by compassion, Moon Lady intervened on her behalf.

"Spare her the necessity of such terrible oaths!" she said to Hsi Men. "You see how urgently the poor thing needs your help."

"Have they already arrested Tsi Hsiang?" he asked.

"No, she is hiding herself in the house of Prince Yuen."

"So? Then I'll take you in here for a few days, and I'll intercede for you immediately with the District Superintendent Li."

And he made Shu Tung quickly write a letter and take it to Master Li. In this letter he said that he would stand surety for Cinnamon Bud, and he accordingly asked that she should not be arrested. Before long Shu Tung returned with a reply.

"Master Li writes," he declared, "that in any other matter he would gladly be of service to you. But in this case there is an express order from a higher authority in the capital, which he cannot very well circumvent. However, in view of your intervention he will postpone the execution of the warrant a few days longer. But he will be held responsible by the authorities in the capital."

"A pity!" said Hsi Men, with a sigh of regret. "A pity that I can't send Lai Pao. But he must start the day after tomorrow for the salt works of Yangchow. I have no one just now whom I can send to the capital."

"Let the other two go to Yangchow for the present and send Lai Pao to Kai fong fu," Moon Lady proposed. "After all, he can still

432

go to Yangchow after his return. You see how frightened the girl is."

Cinnamon Bud made a humble reverence before her and Hsi Men, by way of seconding Moon Lady's intercession.

Hsi Men reflected awhile; then he sent for Lai Pao.

"I have changed my mind," he said. "You will not go to Yangchow with the others on the twentieth. I want you to make an urgent journey to the Eastern Capital; and you will have to start tomorrow. You must seek out Intendant Ti and persuade him that whatever the circumstances, he must cancel the warrant of arrest that has been issued against Cinnamon Bud."

Cinnamon Bud quickly dropped a curtsy to Lai Pao, to which he responded with a bow. "You can count on me, little cousin," he assured her.

Hsi Men immediately made his scribe, Shu Tung, write a letter to the Intendant Ti, and to the letter he added a parcel of twenty ounces, which Lai Pao was to deliver at the same time. Cinnamon Bud generously gave him five ounces from her own pocket.

"A trifle for the journey," she said. "When you return my mother will be particularly grateful."

Hsi Men would not allow Lai Pao to accept this money from Cinnamon Bud. He made her take it back, which she did, thankfully enough, after a show of resistance. In its place he gave Lai Pao five ounces from his own pocket. The girl bowed to Lai Pao, saying: "Many thanks, cousin, for being so willing to take all this trouble for me. I hope you will start soon, so that you won't be too late."

"I am off early tomorrow, at the hour of the fifth drum beat," he promised, and he took his leave, in order to proceed to Lion Street, where he warned his colleague Han Tao Kwo that he would not be able to accompany him on the journey to Yangchow on the twentieth.

"When I have executed my commission in the Eastern Capital I shall follow you to Yangchow. Where shall I find you there?" he asked Han.

"Master Hsi Men has told us to take up our quarters in the hostelry of Wang Po Ju by the harbor. It is a large house, in which Master Hsi Men's father used often to stay. You must ask for us there."

"Sister-in-law, have you anything to give me or any message to send to your married daughter in the capital?" Lai Pao asked the Sixth Wang.

"You can take these two hair clasps and these two pairs of slippers for Darling," she said. "And please ask how things are with her, so that we need not be anxious about her."

He promised to do so, took the parcel containing the presents for Darling, and hurried home, there to make preparations for his journey.

In the meantime Cinnamon Bud, surrounded by Hsi Men's wives, was sitting in Moon Lady's room. She was overwhelmed with questions, and was not a little proud to be for once an object of general interest and sympathy. Her original hesitation had soon vanished, once she had realized that Hsi Men would protect her, and had been replaced by her usual cheerful insouciance. Indeed, she even felt in a mood to ask for a lute and sing a song. But this was too much for the sensible Moon Lady.

"Child, how can you be in a mood for singing in such a situation!" she said, shaking her head.

"Oh, well!" said Cinnamon Bud, lightly, "since I know Master Hsi Men is protecting me I have no further anxiety."

"One can see at once that she comes from a flower garden," said Jade Fountain, ironically. "How quickly such people can alter their expression! She came just now with a mournful expression and brows knitted with anxiety, and was so excited that she couldn't drink a bowl of tea, and now she's quite happy again, and as cheerful as if nothing had happened."

But this did not prevent Cinnamon Bud from passing her jade fingers nimbly over the strings and warbling a little song.

Now Kiu Tung appeared, and announced that the master had betaken himself to the pavilion of the Fifth. Gold Lotus, of course, would have liked to leap to her feet and run out of the room, but since three guests were present she had for decency's sake to remain seated. Moon Lady noticed her disguised restlessness, and smilingly bade her begone. Gold Lotus tried to look as indifferent as possible while she took her leave of the visitors, and then hurried off to her pavilion as fast as her feet would carry her. And that evening she was the third person upon whom Hsi Men tested the power of his miraculous pills.

It was two days later. That afternoon Hsi Men was sitting in the belvedere with his friends Beggar Ying and Hsia Hsi Ta, enjoying a festive banquet, the pretext for which was a fat pig which a friend had recently sent him, together with other presents, and which had that day been killed. Cinnamon Bud was there to cheer them with her singing and playing.

Meanwhile Hsi Men's wives were assembled on the eastern promenade, where they were drinking tea.

While they were sitting there and gossiping, they saw Barber Chow, bending low, creeping quietly and timidly along the wall at the other side of the courtyard. He was in attendance on Hsi Men's household that day, and already, at noon, he had dressed Hsi Men's hair and thoroughly massaged his body, manipulating it in accordance with the rules of breath gymnastics. Now he was creeping about the premises looking for some further task.

"He's come just in time," cried Mistress Ping. "Hi, barber, you might cut my little boy's hair!"

The little man hastily ran forward and made his kowtow before the assembled ladies.

"The master has already expressed the same wish."

"But we ought first to consult the calendar, to see whether this is a suitable day for hair cutting," Moon Lady objected. "Dear Sister Five, be so good as just to look in the calendar!"

Gold Lotus sent the maid Little Jewel for the calendar.

"Today is a favorable day for cutting the hair," she announced, after studying the calendar for some time.

Accordingly the maid Ju I was told to bring the little boy with her, a basin was filled with warm water, and while Little Jewel, with a towel over her arm, held the little boy, Barber Chow, having unpacked his box of implements, carefully began his responsible task under the sympathetic eyes of the women, who watched the operation with excited interest. The timid little boy began to whimper at the first snip of the scissors, and when the barber continued his work without heeding this protest the child, as was his habit when he was afraid, held his breath until his face was crimson, and did not utter another sound. Quite alarmed, and realizing that the child must be almost suffocated, his mother cried to the barber: "Stop, stop, the child is stifling!" whereupon the timid barber, equally alarmed, scrabbled his things together, and hastily made his escape. A fine proof of the calendar's "reliability"!

When the child no longer felt the strange hand and the cold scissors touching his little head, he at last ventured to breathe again, and all those about him drew breath at the same moment. While his mother fondled and patted him and spoke to him encouragingly, Moon Lady said to her: "Sister Six, you can surely cut the child's hair yourself. After all, he's no hero. Why did you need to send for the barber?"

Then, turning to Gold Lotus, she continued: "Sister Five, now that you have the calendar in your hand, could you just see on what day of the month the seven-times-seventh day of the sixty-day cycle falls?"

"On the twenty-third," replied Gold Lotus, after zealously searching the calendar. "Why do you want to know?"

"Oh, I just want to know!"

Foolish Moon Lady! She had just seen how unreliable the calendar was, and in the same moment, full of credulous trust in the delusive promise of Sister Pi, she consulted it anew!

In the meantime the feast in the belvedere, amidst merry jests and joyful outcries, had come to an end. Beggar Ying and Hsia Hsi Ta, who were greatly exhilarated, had happily settled down to a game of dice; Cinnamon Bud, whose lovely recitatives had been constantly interrupted by the wanton words and bad jokes of Beggar Ying, had stolen away into the park at a mute gesture from Hsi Men, and a little later Hsi Men himself contrived to leave the table unremarked, and to creep after her. She had gone to the rocky edge of the fishpond, where, gathering flowers, she awaited him, hidden by the bushes. The two topers, absorbed in their dice-throwing, at last began to wonder why Hsi Men did not return.

"Where has your master gone?" they asked Hua Tung, the servant who was waiting on them.

"He went to the back of the pavilion first, but he's gone out again."

"Extraordinary: he really ought to be back again," muttered Beggar Ying. "Well, I'll just have a look for him; in the meantime you remain here," he said, turning to his companion. And while the latter invited Hua Tung to play a game of chess with him, in order to pass the time, he sauntered off into the park, looking about him in all directions.

Hsi Men had not gone to the back of the belvedere at all, but had simply rushed off to the pavilion of the Sixth, swallowed a magic pill, and proceeded to look for Cinnamon Bud. He found her at last by the rocky bank of the fishpond, hidden in the bushes, and he dragged her off with him to the "Grotto of Hidden Spring." Having barred the door, he sat down on the small divan with her and tenderly lifted her on to his lap.

In the meantime Beggar Ying searched pavilion after pavilion and arbor after arbor in vain for his vanished friend. He crept through the Blue Grotto, searched the Kashmir Thistle Arbor, peeped into the Vine Arbor, and at last came to the "Grotto of Hidden Spring," concealed amidst the bamboos and cypresses. There he stood listening. He had distinctly heard someone laugh close at hand. Then he spied footprints in the sand; he followed them, and a few paces further on came to a bead curtain, trickling down through a niche in the rocks. When he parted the strings he found that he was standing before a door whose two halves were just ajar, so that he could look into the grotto through the chink. But as it was dark inside Beggar Ying preferred to press his ear to the door and listen. Now he could distinguish Cinnamon Bud's voice.

"Ta, ta, do something quickly!" he heard her say. "Anyone might come along and find us here."

Crash! At that very moment Beggar Ying flung the door open and with a loud cry leaped into the grotto before the pair, whose limbs were closely entangled. Hsi Men was just in the ecstasy of delight. Now he hastily attempted to free himself from his partner.

"Quick, bring some water! Here are two people glued together!" cried Beggar Ying, in jest.

"You impudent intruder! To startle us so!" scolded Cinnamon Bud, while she hastily pulled on her clothes.

"Crazy dog, out with you!" cried Hsi Men, reprovingly, half angry, half amused. "You really ought not to indulge in such jests!"

"But first please tell me, do tell me, little lady! What if I run off to Moon Lady and tell her that you've stolen her husband in return for her kind intercession? What then, eh?"

"That would be like you, wouldn't it? Be off with you, now!"

"Good, I'll go, but I demand at least a kiss as hush money."

And he quickly flung his arms round her neck and kissed her; then he turned to the door.

"Will you be so kind as to close the door behind you?" Hsi Men called after him. "What if one of the servants were to pass this way and see us!"

No sooner was he outside and the door closed than the two within resumed their interrupted sport. Then they dressed themselves and cautiously crept out of the grotto, following different paths, he to the pavilion of the Sixth and she to Moon Lady's apartments.

On the following day Hsi Men was invited to the country seat of his friend the former Head Eunuch, now the owner of the brickfield from which he usually obtained the materials for his building operations. This estate was a good thirty *li* from the southern wall of the city, so that Hsi Men did not go to the yamen first, but decided to spend the whole day in the country.

At home his wives took advantage of his absence to organize

a little banquet of their own, and enjoy the beauties of the park. First they dined in the belvedere; then they continued their drinking in the "Pavilion of Cloudy Repose," passing the time with chess and the bottle game and all sorts of other pastimes.

"Where is your husband, then?" Hsi Men's daughter asked Moon Lady.

"He had to go into the city again on business, in order to collect some debts that were overdue. He will soon be back."

After a while young Chen appeared, and was made to take his place at the table and join in the games and the conversation.

"I have collected the two hundred and fifty ounces that was lent to the merchant Hsue and given it to your maid Jade Flute in five bags," he informed Moon Lady, who was accustomed to keep Hsi Men's cash in her trunks.

After the beakers had been emptied a few times the company sorted itself into two groups. Moon Lady, Sunflower, and Cinnamon Bud settled down to a game of chess, while the other women, feeling the need of exercise, swarmed through the park like a flock of gayly-colored butterflies. Gold Lotus had attached herself to neither group, but, waving her white satin fan, wandered, in search of coolness, to the shady banana grove on the slope of the artificial hill.

She was just stooping to pluck a lovely red flower that was gleaming in the grass not far from a projecting wall, when she heard young Chen behind her, softly calling her. He had secretly followed her.

"Sister-in-law Five, may I venture to help you? The turf is slippery here; take care you don't slip! It would wring my heart!"

Gold Lotus turned her head and looked up at him with a sidelong glance, from eyes in which lay the moist gleam of the autumn wave, the result of copious draughts of wine.

"Rogue, you've been following me!" she said, smiling. "What if someone were to see us! Would it really pain you if I lost my footing?"

"I swear to you. . . ."

"Have you at all events the handkerchief on you that you wanted to get me in the city today?"

"Here it is," he said, drawing a fine lawn kerchief from his sleeve pocket. "And what do I get in payment?"

At the same time he bowed his face close to her shoulder, whereupon she waved her fan at him vigorously, in order to drive him back. It so chanced that at this moment Mistress Ping, with her child in her arms, and the maid Ju I beside her, were wandering along the path leading to the hedge of fig trees. She had recognized Gold Lotus in the distance, but could not see Chen, who was standing behind the Fifth, and she imagined that the vigorous waving of the fan was due to the presence of a butterfly.

"Have you got him, Sister Five?" she cried. "Do be so kind as to give him to my little one to play with!"

Young Chen, startled by her voice, crouching low in order to escape observation, and sliding three or four paces backwards, crept into a rocky cleft in the hillside.

"Unfortunately he got away. By the way, has Cousin Chen given you the promised handkerchief yet?"

"Not yet."

"I have mine already. He wouldn't give it to me in front of his wife, so he passed it to me secretly beforehand. Would you like to see it? Then come over here."

Mistress Ping came forward and sat down beside Gold Lotus, on the moss-grown edge of the lawn, below the dense banana thicket, in order to admire the new handkerchief.

"It is beautifully cool and shady here," said the Sixth. Then she called to the nurse, who was standing at some little distance: "Just run to Pear Blossom and tell her to bring a few pillows, and a mat for the little one, and also my dominoes. I should like to play a game of dominoes here with the Fifth. You can stay in the pavilion and look after the house."

Before long Pear Blossom brought the desired articles. With the mat and the pillows Mistress Ping prepared a soft couch on the grass for her little boy; then she began to play dominoes with Gold

440

Lotus. Since she felt thirsty Pear Blossom was sent off again to bring tea. The two women sat alone for a time, playing dominoes; then Jade Fountain signaled to them from the elevated "Pavilion of Cloudy Repose."

"Sister Six, you might come up here," she cried. "Moon Lady wants to speak to you."

Mistress Ping rose in obedience to the summons.

"Be so kind as to look after the child a little until I return," she asked of Gold Lotus, as she went.

No sooner did Gold Lotus find herself alone than she went quickly to the cleft into which Young Chen had crept.

"She has gone; you can come out," she cried softly.

"Sister-in-law, just come closer for a moment and look at the great mushrooms growing here!" he responded, as softly.

Gold Lotus entered the glimmering twilight of the crevice. Now she could feel his knees, and his hot breath. . . .

In the meantime Mistress Ping had reached the "Pavilion of Cloudy Repose." There she found Moon Lady playing at the bottle game with Jade Fountain and Cinnamon Bud.

"Come, Sister, you must have a game with us," Moon Lady challenged her.

"But there is no one down there to look after the child," she objected.

"Oh, Sister Five is close by. Nothing will happen to him."

"Sister Three, do you go down and look after the child for a little while!" Moon Lady suggested.

"Oh, then you had better bring him straight up here. And you," said Mistress Ping, turning to Little Jewel, "can go with her and bring the mat and the pillows after her."

When Jade Fountain and Little Jewel came to the resting place under the banana grove they found the child quite alone, trampling with his little hands and feet and whimpering pitifully. But close to the edge of the mat a great black cat was crouching. As the two women approached it disappeared like a wisp of smoke.

"But where is Sister Five? It is really irresponsible of her to leave the child alone like this!" said Jade Fountain, disapprovingly. "Now, of course, he has been frightened by that horrible black cat."

At this moment Gold Lotus quickly slipped out of the crevice, and joined the others with an unconcerned expression.

"I had to disappear for a moment. A harmless cat is really no reason for your eyebrows to turn white and your eyes red with excitement!"

Fortunately Jade Fountain did not investigate the crevice. She took the child into her arms, sought to quiet it by her caresses, and carried it quickly to the "Pavilion of Cloudy Repose," while Little Jewel followed her with the mat and the pillows. In order to deal with any comments, Gold Lotus accompanied them.

Meanwhile young Chen, as soon as he had made sure that no one was visible, crept cautiously out of his hiding place and made for the belvedere, following the path which ran beside the fig-tree hedge. He was only half satisfied with this afternoon's experience. He had been able to kiss and caress his beloved, but he had not achieved his ultimate purpose.

Now, as evening fell, and Hsi Men did not return, he again strolled out into the park, restlessly wandering along the paths and through the shrubberies, searching with burning entrails for his beloved. And his pains were to be rewarded; he found her at last, in a hidden nook of the valley behind the artificial hill. Lost in thought, her fragrant cheek resting on her left hand, she was sitting alone on a moss-covered rock in a dense thicket, listening to the murmur of the brook that was rippling past her. "A pity that I have no bowl in my hand, so that I could throw a splash of water over her from behind," he thought.

Gliding silently through the green shade, he crept close up to her from behind; then, suddenly seizing her two hands, he boldly pressed his lips to her mouth.

"Oh, beloved from a former life!" he groaned. "Why were we disturbed so quickly and inconsiderately by the Third this afternoon? I could have died with rage!"

She had turned round with a start. But her alarm was mingled with joy when she saw that her assailant was young Chen.

"Rogue, to frighten me so! Will you let me go at once? If anyone were to see me!"

But he had no intention of releasing her; on the contrary, his hands crept downwards and began to busy themselves with her girdle. She struggled, but her resistance was half surrender. Now he had successfully loosened the knot of her girdle.

"You impudent rascal!" she exclaimed, under her breath. "But you shan't have your way as easily as you imagine!"

"Oh, beloved of my former existence, listen to your slave!" he pleaded. "If you wanted to have my heart or liver stewed or roasted, for you I would gladly cut it out! But this time do for once listen to me!"

She, already inundated by the red tide of lustful desire, defended herself awhile, for the look of the thing, against his passionate embrace. Then, leaning against the red lacquer balustrade, they stood intimately embraced, tasting the long-desired union. But the inconvenient posture prevented him from attaining his end, so he begged her to lie down on the ground. For this time he was resolved to enjoy the favorable moment to the full. But she was afraid lest someone should unexpectedly pass that way; also, she did not want to disarrange her hair.

"Not today," she told him softly. "Another time you shall have your will." So she remained in her inconvenient posture against the red lacquer balustrade, and he continued to groan "Tjin tjin," while she sighed "Ta ta." But now they heard, behind the adjacent wall, the crunch of approaching steps on the gravel, and men's voices. Quickly, and all too soon, they released themselves from their embrace and started asunder. The voices were those of Tai A and Shu Tung, who were searching the park for Moon Lady, in order to announce Hsi Men's return.

Hsi Men was staggering perceptibly as he dismounted from his horse. He had come from a long and difficult session. He went, this time, to the apartments of Moon Lady; he affectionately put his arms about her as he entered, and behaved as though he wished to share her bed that night. But Moon Lady reflected that the famous seven-times-seventh night of the sixty-day cycle, which had been recommended by the learned nun, was the night of the following day; so she resisted him.

"I don't yet feel quite well again today, so do please oblige me by sleeping with someone else tonight," she begged him.

"I understand; my drunkenness offends you," he mumbled. "Well, for all I care I'll go."

"You really need not take offense. It is not on account of your condition; no, it's only. . . . You understand. But I shall expect you tomorrow."

He therefore did as she requested, and spent the night in the pavilion of his Fifth.

The following day was for Moon Lady a day of dedication. After rising early, and dressing herself, she made Little Jewel set up an incense table with the usual equipment; and behind it was suspended a picture roll on which the goddess Kwan Yin was portrayed, robed in white, with a child in her arms. After the contents of the bronze censers had been ignited she lit a stick of incense and bowed herself four times to the West, as that quarter of the heavens from which the doctrine of Buddha had come. Thereupon she unrolled a manuscript, and read, with twenty-four reverences, the twenty-four paragraphs of a Buddhistic sutra.

Now she took from a trunk the phial containing the magic potion which the nuns Pi and Wang had prepared, and placed it on the incense table. Four further bows followed: then she uttered a short prayer:

"Exalted Heaven! Hear the prayer of the humble daughter of the house of Wu, and enable her, by thine aid, and by the power of the draught provided by the nuns Pi and Wang, ere long to rejoice in a male offspring!"

At this point Little Jewel had to heat some yellow wine and pour it into a beaker. Moon Lady took the beaker in her hand, poured the magic potion into it, and stirred the two liquids together; then she knelt, with her face turned toward the West, and drank the contents. The draught left a slightly acrid after-taste in her mouth, which choked her at first and made her cough. Finally, she made four more reverences; then the ceremony was completed. All that day she did not leave her apartments. That evening, when Hsi Men came to visit her, he found her waiting for him, beautifully dressed, in her elaborately furnished bedroom, which was full of pleasant odors. Little Jewel had to bring in a light and specially chosen supper.

"Confess that you couldn't keep me here last night because of my drunken condition?" he asked her, smiling.

"No, I really was rather unwell," she said untruthfully, since the nuns had insisted that she must not confide the secret of the magic potion to anyone. "How can you be so suspicious? A long-wedded pair like ourselves have no secrets from each other!"

He applied himself with a good appetite to the fish and the roast duck, and after he had drunk himself, with the help of ten beakers of wine, into the desired mood, they once more betook themselves to the nuptial couch which they had not shared for so long, and there they tumbled as happily as the merry little fishes in the water.

CHAPTER TWENTY-NINE: *Hsi Men is twice received by the Chancellor. He goes to great Expense for a Friend*

S̲INCE HIS LAST two encounters with Gold Lotus, both of which were prematurely interrupted, young Chen was inspired by a single longing: namely, at a third meeting to effect the long-desired consummation of the work which he had begun. So, when a few afternoons later he knew that Hsi Men was the guest of his friends Beggar Ying and Chang Shih Kia in the City Park pavilion outside the city walls, he took this opportunity of stealing away from his work and sauntering about the park.

For a long while he stood at watch before the "Grotto of Hidden Spring," in the hope that the feet of his beloved would sooner or later stray into this neighborhood, so well provided with hiding places. But since his hope was disappointed, he suddenly made up his mind and went straight to her pavilion. Without meeting her maid, or anyone else, he passed through the entrance unhindered, and reached the threshold of her sitting room. He stood still for a moment and listened. She was singing. And these were the words that fell upon his ears:

> *"Almost as soon as he briefly possessed her*
> *He had forgot that he ever caressed her."*

He naturally took this as referring to himself. . . .

> *"How could I ever forget you, beloved?"*

Breaking into her song with these words, he suddenly rushed into the room and gathered her to his breast.

"Beloved, you mustn't be angry because I haven't shown myself just lately," he said. "But I couldn't get away from the business, and I had no opportunity of wandering about the park. Today, however, Hsi Men has gone to the City Park with his friends Ying and Chang, so I was able to come. I stood a long while before the Snow Grotto and waited for you in vain. I have almost died of longing for you."

"Quiet, quiet!" she admonished him. "The walls have ears. We must be careful."

She looked through the window into the park. There, at some distance, she saw Little Jewel, with a length of white cloth over her arm, sauntering easily toward the pavilion. But when she was close to the house she suddenly turned and hurried back.

"That's queer!" said Gold Lotus, thoughtfully. "She was coming here. Why did she suddenly turn round? Perhaps she had forgotten something. In that case she will certainly come again."

"Go, go quickly!" she urged her lover. "I don't want any unpleasantness."

And there was nothing for it but that young Chen must make his escape as quickly as possible. Gold Lotus was right: Little Jewel had been sent by Moon Lady with the stuff for a petticoat, which she intended as a present for one of her acquaintances. Gold Lotus was to embroider it, and Little Jewel had forgotten the pattern. This was why she suddenly turned back. And this time her forgetfulness was the salvation of the two lovers. When she appeared again some time later young Chen had long made his escape.

One afternoon in the first third of the fifth month the eagerly-expected Lai Pao returned from the Eastern Capital.

"Well, what about Cinnamon Bud's affair? Did you speak to Intendant Ti?" Hsi Men inquired.

"He received me, and after he had read your letter he sent me with a note of recommendation and a secretary to the Prefect of Police, Chu, who was investigating the affair. Master Chu, after glancing through the note of recommendation, declared that since intercession had been made from the Chancellor's palace he would suspend proceedings and would not undertake any further arrests.

The persons already in custody would be detained a few days longer, in order to afford some satisfaction to the plaintiff, the Chief Eunuch Lia Huang, and would then be discharged without punishment. Eunuchs are rather inclined by nature to seize upon a thing eagerly, and then to let it go, so to speak, between head and tail, and they are easily appeased."

"Then little Tsi Hsiang can congratulate herself on being saved from arrest," interposed Beggar Ying, who happened to be calling on Hsi Men.

"And our friends Sun and Chu, thanks to my vigorous intervention, have got off in their sleep!" added Hsi Men, laughing, after he had read Intendant Ti's reply to his letter.

"Master Ti has something else to tell you," said Lai Pao, completing his report. "As I was leaving he charged me to inform you that this time you positively must come to Kai fong fu on the occasion of the Chancellor's birthday, and bring him your congratulations in person. Besides, Master Ti himself wants to see you."

"I am not really prepared for the journey," said Hsi Men, "but since the invitation is so urgent I must make up my mind to it for once. You have a fatiguing journey behind you, Lai Pao. I give you two days' leave. Thus you can have a thorough rest and recover your strength. But after that you must get ready for the journey to Yangchow."

He was dismissed, and Hsi Men rose to his feet, in order to notify Cinnamon Bud, who was in Moon Lady's apartments. She had already heard the favorable news, and as he entered she hastened, beaming with delight, to make a kowtow of thanks before him and Moon Lady.

"You have rescued me from a position of great distress," she said. "How can I ever thank you?"

"It was a matter of course that we should stand by you once you had sought refuge in our house."

"After all, I had a right to appeal to you for help, since I was quite innocent in the matter. But how is it that this woman, this Tsi Hsiang, is profiting by your favor and your intervention? In her house money is raked in at such a rate that it's no wonder young Wang was ruined. It's entirely her fault that I was dragged into the business. She doesn't deserve to get off like this without punishment."

"Certainly the girl has had the most scandalous luck," Hsi Men laughingly agreed.

And after promising to return very shortly with her mother, in order to pay a ceremonious visit of thanks, the young woman took her leave, hurrying back to her flower garden.

The auspicious day so carefully selected in the calendar, on which Hsi Men had decided to begin his journey to the Eastern Capital, had dawned at last. He had chosen the four younger servants, Kiu Tung, Tai An, Shu Tung, and Hua Tung to accompany him. All his wives had helped him to pack, and the numerous boxes and bundles in which the birthday presents for the Chancellor were bestowed made no less than twenty loads.

On the evening before Hsi Men's departure a farewell banquet was held. The last night he spent with Moon Lady. Next morning the long caravan moved off. In front of the procession was a mounted herald, who had to hurry on ahead in order to warn the posting stations along the road of his master's approach, and to arrange betimes for shelter for the night. Then came the baggage train, consisting of the mules and porters who had to carry the thirty loads of baggage. In the middle of the train came Hsi Men, in a light traveling palanquin. The four mounted servants brought up the rear.

Before he entered his palanquin, Hsi Men paid a final visit to the pavilion of the Sixth, who had been unwell for some time, and was confined to her bed, and took an affectionate farewell of her and his child.

"Take the medicine which Doctor Yen has prescribed for you regularly," he bade her, "so that you will be quite well when I return."

"'Take care of yourself on the journey, and come back safely!" she replied, shedding a few tears in farewell.

The rest of his wives escorted him to the main gateway, and gazed after the departing palanquin until it had vanished from sight.

Without untoward incident, Hsi Men, after a ten days' journey, reached the "Gate of Ten Thousand Generations" and entered the Eastern Capital. On the way he had encountered numerous mandarins' palanquins, whose occupants, like himself, all had the same purpose—to bring their congratulations to the Chancellor Tsai King on his birthday.

It was evening when Hsi Men's palanquin passed the marble pailou in Dragon Energy Street, and before long it was set down in the inner courtyard of the Chancellor's palace, in front of the dwelling of Intendant Ti, in which Hsi Men took up his abode.

Master Ti welcomed him with a special feast, whose refinement even the Chancellor's table could not have excelled. After drinking a few beakers of wine Hsi Men began:

"I have brought a few inconspicuous presents for the Ancient Commander. Of course, I am not so unduly bold as to assume that he would ever vouchsafe them a glance. I can only hope that he will regard them as a faint expression of my genuine and filial reverence, and will not disdain them. And I have, moreover, a special request to make of you, dear cousin. It has long been my heartfelt desire to come into closer personal contact with the Ancient Commander, as a 'dry' son. I should not have lived in vain if only this desire were fulfilled. Might I, in this connection, hope for your approval and intercession?"

"Why not? We are, it is true, high officials and dignitaries, but we are also men, who are gratified by human respect and affection. Once again, as I perceive by your list of presents, you have made an exceptional effort. I am convinced that the Ancient Commander will not only be glad to receive you, as his adopted son, in his more intimate circle, but also that he will see to it that you are promoted to a higher rank."

This answer filled Hsi Men with proud anticipation, and it was in the highest spirits that he withdrew, after rising from table, to

450

the magnificent guest chamber which the master of the house had had prepared for him in the library building. Here no comfort, no luxury was forgotten; though he did feel that there was one thing lacking—that he, who was wont to embrace a woman every night, should have to sleep alone in his stately bed.

Hsi Men was awake betimes the next morning, and he could plainly hear the doorkeeper shuffling along the corridors and across the courtyards, unlocking door after door, gate after gate. For at night Master Ti was accustomed to locking the doors of all the rooms. At the ninth hour two servants appeared in Hsi Men's room, bringing warm scented water for washing, and towels. Hsi Men dressed himself and proceeded to the sitting room, where Master Ti, who was already awaiting him, invited him to the breakfast table.

The capacious, red-lacquered dumb waiter which a servant brought from the kitchen offered him, in small bowls, a choice of no less than thirty delicious dishes. There was also a mild phœnix tea to be sipped, and a light wine was poured from silver pitchers.

"My dear Master Cousin, do not let me disturb you at your breakfast," said Master Ti, rising. "Excuse me, I beg you, for a while, as I wish to offer my greetings to the Ancient Commander. When I come back I will present you to him, and will have your gifts laid before him."

After a little while he bustled in again.

"The Ancient Commander is just dressing in his library. Outside, in front of the reception hall, there is already a crowd of people come to congratulate him; all the officials of the Court, the civil and military mandarins, are there to a man. I have announced your presence to the Ancient Commander, and have contrived that he will receive you before all the rest of the visitors. We can go at once."

Hsi Men, who had already dressed himself in his best, heard this with satisfaction, and allowed his amiable host to assume the office of leader. Since the audience hall lay at some distance, they proceeded thither in their palanquins. Behind them came the Intendant's porters and servants, carrying the twenty loads of presents.

As they passed the various outer courtyards Hsi Men saw how the congratulants—mandarins of every rank—were standing shoulder to shoulder and back to back, pressing onwards toward the Court, and he was privately grateful to his host for contriving that he should have precedence of this crowd. Before the entrance gate of the Chancellor's own Palace Hsi Men alighted from his palanquin, made a deep bow, and allowed Master Ti to lead him in.

He noticed that the central wing of the triple gate was locked, and that the visitors all entered through the smaller side wings. The central entrance, he was told, in answer to his question, was reserved for the Son of Heaven alone.

Their way now led through various courtyards and double gates, before which armed guards were stationed, who saw to it that the many persons who came and went did so in the proper order of precedence. Each individual sentinel bowed to Master Ti by way of salute, and asked him who the stranger was, to which Master Ti replied that he was a personal relation who had come from Shantung to the birthday reception.

Their path now turned aside from the straight line which it had followed hitherto, in the direction of a stately building with brightly-colored barge boards and carved joists and glittering golden-yellow shingles. As they approached it, sounds like the music of the heavenly spheres fell upon Hsi Men's ears, proceeding from some hidden source.

"How does there come to be music in a place so remote from men?" he asked in astonishment.

"The Ancient Commander has a house orchestra of four and twenty young singers and dancers," his companion informed him. "Whether a devil dance is required, or a pious hymn to Kwan Yin, or the moon-fairy pantomime of the old Tang Emperor Hsuan Tsung, the girls can provide every sort of program. Three times a day the Ancient Commander makes them play table music: at breakfast, at dinner, and at supper. Apparently he is now at his breakfast."

452

And sure enough, a delicious waft of fragrance came to their nostrils, blending with the sonorous waves of the delightful music.

"We need hurry no longer; we have reached our goal," added Master Ti.

And after they had passed through an open semi-circular promenade, they found themselves standing before a lofty and magnificent hall. On wide lawns, to the right and left, amidst delicious flowers and evergreen shrubs, flocks of rare birds disported themselves, cranes stalked about on their long legs, and peacocks trailed their shimmering tails. It was a brilliant and colorful picture at which one was never tired of gazing. But Hsi Men had no time to linger and admire.

Being informed that the Chancellor had just gone into the hall, the two men entered, Intendant Ti going first, and Hsi Men following him, bearing himself with the greatest dignity. And now he stood before an armchair covered with a tiger skin, facing the entrance, in which was enthroned the Ancient Commander, clad in a great robe of state, monkey-red in color, and embroidered with a design of serpents. Behind him, protected by a screen, yet plainly visible, was a bevy of some thirty beautiful young women, sumptuously clad, nervously waving their fans or swinging their silken kerchiefs, and watching with tense interest the proceedings in the middle of the hall.

Intendant Ti, as he led Hsi Men forward, stepped to one side. Hsi Men prostrated himself and made four kowtows, whereupon the Chancellor rose, acknowledged his greeting with a slight bow, and sat down again. Now Master Ti went up to the chair, stooped over the Ancient Commander, and whispered something in his ear. Hsi Men knew that this whisper referred to his desire to become the Ancient Commander's adopted son. Now, after Ti had returned to his former place, he made four more kowtows, and the Ancient Commander remained seated: by which he knew that the Chancellor had adopted him, and now regarded himself as his father, who need not respond to his son's greeting. So Hsi Men, opened his mouth and made a little speech:

"Venerable Father, in commemoration of the happy consecration of this day your undutiful son has come hither and has brought with him a few insignificant trifles which he begs that he may lay at your feet, merely as a slight token of the fact that he has cherished respectful thoughts of you a thousand *li* away."

The Chancellor gave a sign to those about him to bring a chair for Hsi Men, and invited him to take a seat, which he did, with a bow. While he was offered tea, Ti hastily ran to the entrance, and gave a sign to the porters, who were waiting outside with the gifts. Now they appeared with their twenty loads, opened the woven bast cases, and laid out the treasures contained in them before the dais on which the Chancellor was seated. Here were piles of magnificent garments and bales of cloth, sparkling golden goblets, gleaming jade beakers, ten great pearls, splendid jade girdles, and the yellow glitter of two hundred ounces of gold ingots.

The Chancellor, with the list of presents in his hand, regarded with satisfaction the treasures heaped up before him, deigned to utter a brief word of thanks, and graciously commanded his Intendant to have the presents taken to the treasury. He also, as a mark of distinction, had wine set before the donor. But Hsi Men knew that it was not fitting that he should linger, since the Chancellor was expecting many more visitors. So he contented himself with sipping the wine as a matter of form; then he rose and begged leave to withdraw.

"This afternoon I expect you as my guest," said the Chancellor, in gracious invitation, and he even accompanied Hsi Men a few steps in the direction of the entrance. Once back in Master Ti's house, Hsi Men divested himself of his robe of office, dined, and lay down awhile, in order to be rested by the afternoon.

When he visited the Chancellor's palace for the second time, again in his official robes, he was accompanied by his four servants, and Tai A had to bring with him a box full of small packages of money, which he was to distribute among the Chancellor's attendants.

That the Chancellor had invited him to his table that day was a mark of special distinction, for properly this day was set apart

454

for the reception of congratulants, and the many visitors who were coming and going all day were dispatched one by one with a beaker of wine. The actual banquets were held on the next three days; on the first day the banquet for the members of the Imperial House and the Head Eunuchs; on the second day the banquet for the Ministers and the chief municipal authorities of the capital; on the third day the banquet for the rest of the higher and lower dignitaries. Since Hsi Men had come so far, and had offered such an exceptional wealth of gifts, the Chancellor granted him the honor of dining with him today, apart from the other guests.

He received his guest before the threshold, under the projecting eaves; which, again, was a special distinction, and he even wished Hsi Men to enter before him. But this his guest would by no means do, so there was a long contest of courtesies. At last the Chancellor took the lead, and Hsi Men reverently followed him, stepping like a dancer and humping his back. While they exchanged a few cordial words of greeting, such as are used between father and son, and took their places at two small separate tables, the four and twenty beauties of the house orchestra made their appearance and began to play the table music.

With his own hand the Chancellor offered his guest a brimming beaker, which the latter, in his modesty, was at first unwilling to accept, but finally, after vigorous resistance, he emptied it standing. Then he, in his turn, gave a sign to his servant Shu Tung, who stood beside him waiting for orders, whereupon the servant placed upon the table before him a golden goblet which Hsi Men had brought from his home, and which had the form of a peach blossom. Having filled this with wine, Hsi Men bore it to the table of the Chancellor, offering it to him on his knees, with the words: "May the Venerable Father be vouchsafed a thousand years!"

It could be seen from the Chancellor's expression that he was moved and rejoiced by such courtesy and decorum.

"Stand, my son!" he said, and he drained the offered goblet. The precious vessel itself was naturally intended as a gift.

The meal continued until the coming of twilight, but its many surprises and its costly delicacies will not be described in detail. Hsi Men did not fail to give each of the Chancellor's servants who waited upon him a small parcel of money. At last he considered that the moment had come for him to take his leave. With the polite assurance that he could never again dream of troubling the Venerable Father with his disrespectful visit, he made his farewell reverences and returned to the house of Intendant Ti, where he retired early to rest after the fatigues of the day.

After eight days in the capital, which were occupied with paying visits and entertaining guests, he was suddenly seized with an urgent longing to return home, to return with the swiftness of an arrow. He therefore bade his servants pack his things, took leave of his host, who moved heaven and earth to persuade him to remain, and took the road for Shantung.

Meanwhile his wives had spent the days of his absence quietly and sedately in their apartments, passing the time by diligently sewing and embroidering. The cheerful round games which they were accustomed to play, the merry garden parties, were for the time being banished from the order of the day. Gold Lotus was the only exception. Gay and careless as ever, without heeding the opinion of others, she strolled through the park every day, rouged and powdered and beautifully dressed, and haunting the neighborhood of the "Grotto of Hidden Spring," in the hope of encountering young Chen. And he, again, was always with her in her thoughts; and as often as time and circumstance permitted he too made his way into the park, so that there were many secret trysts, many secret kisses and embraces. But still, to his great chagrin, by reason of the many peeping eyes and listening ears of the great household, he was never able to drain the delight of these encounters to the long-desired end.

One day a hot and dusty Tai A entered the room in which Moon Lady and the other wives were sitting, flung himself on the floor, and announced Hsi Men's arrival.

"I had to ride on ahead; his palanquin is barely twenty *li* from the city wall, and will be here in a few hours."

His news was the cause of joyful confusion and bustle. Hasty toilets were made, orders relating to the banquet of welcome were sent to the kitchen, and then all the wives betook themselves to the front reception hall, where they waited to greet the homecomer.

A last he alighted from his palanquin and smilingly entered the circle of waiting women, greeting each in the order of her rank.

"Is the child still well? Have you taken Doctor Yen's medicine regularly, and are you better?" was his first question as he turned to Sister Six.

"The child has been quite well, and I feel a slight improvement since I have been taking the medicine," Mistress Ping replied.

Then he told them of his visit to the capital. That night he spent with Moon Lady, and it is needless to say that on this occasion the two spouses found the long withheld rain doubly refreshing.

The first visitors on the following day were Beggar Ying and Chang Shih Kia, the latter of whom had been endeavoring for some time to recover the favor of his wealthy confederate. In silent admiration they listened to all that Hsi Men had to tell them of the splendors of the capital, and of his magnificent reception by the Chancellor. As they were leaving Chang gave him to understand that he had a small request to make.

"Out with it, then!" said Hsi Men, encouragingly, as he noted the other's embarrassed expression and his hesitating speech.

"For a long while I have been anxious to exchange my present uncomfortable dwelling for a better one. But that would cost something, and money is scarce. Could I count on your friendly assistance? Of course, I would repay a loan later with good interest. . . ."

"There can be no question of interest, but for the moment I'm rather short of money. Just wait until my people arrive from Huchow with the silk transport; then we'll talk it over."

The actual truth was that Friend Chang was some months behind with his rent, and was being hard pressed by his landlord. He was therefore by no means cheered by Hsi Men's inconclusive answer, and was rather cast down when he left with Beggar Ying.

The days went by, but he heard nothing from Hsi Men. He kept on suggesting to Beggar Ying that the latter might intercede for him. Beggar Ying was agreeable, and on several occasions he set out with Chang in order to speak to his friend, but they were always informed at the gate that the master was not at home.

Poor Chang was quite accustomed to being pestered by his landlord, but that he should constantly have to listen to the reproaches and upbraidings of his wife seemed to him utterly intolerable.

"A nice husband, who can't even provide a home for his family!" she cried scornfully. "You've been a friend of the rich Hsi Men for goodness knows how long, but when it comes to making use of the connection for once, you come home with a jug of bad water instead of good wine."

For ten days he had listened to this sort of thing, and had held his peace, gazing dully into vacancy. But now he could bear it no longer, and he made up his mind to take action. On the morning of the eleventh day after his vain appeal for help he rose early from his bed and hurried off to Beggar Ying. Dragging him into a tavern, he treated him to a hot breakfast and a bottle of wine. After a few beakers had been emptied he began:

"In the matter you know of I have heard nothing from Hsi Men since our last conversation. By day I have to endure being pestered and admonished by my landlord, and at night my wife overwhelms me with reproaches and robs me of quiet sleep. I can bear it no longer. Do me the favor of once more accompanying me to Hsi Men's house, while it is still so early that he will not have gone to the court. I absolutely must speak to him."

"Your confidence honors me," the other replied. "Good, I will see what can be done for you."

They quickly finished their breakfast and hurried off to their friend's house.

It was then that delicious season at the beginning of autumn when men are refreshed by the clear atmosphere and the cool golden wind, and are doubly inclined to drink. Hsi Men, in short, for many successive days had been constantly feasting in the houses of others or entertaining guests in his own house, and since he urgently needed a little rest and relaxation he had appointed this particular day as a day of rest, and had even declined an invitation from the River Prefect Chow. Since breakfast he had been strolling along the wide and beautiful promenades of the park with his merrily chattering wives, Moon Lady, Jade Fountain, Gold Lotus, and Mistress Ping.

Ying and Chang thanked heaven that they had at last the good fortune to find him at home. They were shown into the reception hall. While they sat there waiting they saw outside the two men-servants, Shu Tung and Hua Tung, crossing the courtyard, carrying on staves a great box full of silken garments. They were panting under their heavy load, and they set it down just in front of the hall door, in order to recover their breath.

"Where is your master, then?" Ying called to them.

"At the back, in the park."

"Be so good as to announce us."

They nodded, and disappeared with their burden. At last Shu Tung returned and informed them that his master would be with them directly.

"Since your last visit my whole time has been taken up with invitations and social obligations," said Hsi Men, in apology. "It's terrible; one has simply no time to become sober. I am feeling quite run down, and I've already declined an invitation for today from the River Prefect Chow. I must take it easy for a while."

"There was a chest full of clothes carried past here just now. What was the meaning of that?" asked Ying.

"Oh, now that autumn is coming on one has to get more clothes for the women. The chest contained a few new, unfinished dresses for my First."

Chang looked quite taken aback. "What, all those dresses were merely for your First!" he burst out. "According to that you need six chests of clothes for your six wives! You must be a wealthy fellow! People like us can hardly afford a few rags of plain calico!" He concluded his mournful reflection with a sigh that drew a hearty laugh from the other two.

459

"Haven't your people returned from Huchow yet with their cargo of silk?" asked Ying, coming to the point.

"No. I really don't know where they are delaying so long. I haven't even had news of them by letter; I am getting quite uneasy."

"Seriously, dear friend," continued Ying, moving closer to him, "our good Chang is somewhat embarrassed. His landlord is pressing him, and besides that, his wife constantly overwhelms him with reproaches. He is quite distracted because he hasn't heard from you since the other day. Now, when the cold season is approaching, he and his wife have nothing to spare for autumn clothes. They have pawned all their warm things. Prompt help is doubly helpful. If you are really prepared to come to his aid you should do so at once, and save him from listening any longer to his wife's nagging. I have come here today at his urgent desire in order to beg you to come to his assistance."

"Well, of course, I have promised to help him. But just now . . . you will understand, that expensive journey to Kai fong fu . . . I really wanted to wait until the silk convoy arrived. Then, of course, I can get money. Is Chang so very hard pressed?"

"I should think he is! But above all, he can't stand his wife's jabber any longer."

Hsi Men reflected awhile.

"How many rooms does he want in his new house?"

"Well, a sitting room, a reception room, a bedroom, and a kitchen; he needs at least four rooms, for himself and his wife. He'll hardly get them for less than three or four ounces."

"Then I'll make the following proposal. I'll give him for the time being a few ounces of broken silver which I happen to have by me. With that he can manage the necessary outlay on clothes and household expenses. As soon as he has found a suitable house I'll advance the rent."

He beckoned Shu Tung.

"Ask the First mistress to give you the package containing the broken silver from my leather-covered money chest!"

Shu Tung brought the required package.

"Here, this is a gift packet I had left from my recent visit to the Chancellor's palace," said Hsi Men, spreading out the contents before his two friends. "There are twelve ounces of broken silver."

With burning eyes Chang devoured the heap of white metal fragments. Quickly he packed them up again, and beaming with delight, hid the package in his sleeve pocket. Then he rose to his feet and bowed his thanks to the giver; after which the friends passed on to a brief philosophical consideration as to values, and the best way of utilizing the money.

"How many cases are known to history," said Beggar Ying, thoughtfully, "of people who could not keep their money, but threw it away with both hands, yet were blessed in their sons and grandsons, who increased the reputation and prosperity of the family, and in the end multiplied many times over their legacy from their father. On the other hand, we have many examples of wealthy misers who thought only of saving and heaping up their money, but were cursed with such unprofitable descendants that in the end they had nothing left for the upkeep of the family tombs. From this we can perceive how just is the retribution of Heaven."

"To be sure," said Hsi Men, pointing to the package of broken silver, "this stuff likes movement and circulation and hates lying still! It is a natural product intended by Heaven to be equally useful to all men. If there is a superfluous accumulation of it in one place there is elsewhere a lack of it. This heaping up of treasure in one place is decidedly a crime against the community."

So they theorized a little longer, and then Chang took his leave and returned, in high spirits, to his cold dwelling.

He had barely set foot over the threshold when his wife greeted him with loud abuse.

"You good-for-nothing, you empty-pate, loafing about the streets all day and leaving your wife at home to starve! Aren't you ashamed to go running after your pleasures without a care while we don't know where we shall find a roof to cover us next week?

You live for your pleasure, and leave it to your wife to swallow all the bad sour breath that hateful people breathe out at us!"

Friend Chang did not open his mouth, but cheerfully allowed her to scold herself out. When at last she was silent he casually drew the bag of silver from his sleeve and carelessly let it fall, chinking, on the table. Then he opened it, peeped inside, and said, in affected surprise:

"Hey, what do I see shining, what do I hear chinking? A treasure! I am paralyzed with amazement! Why didn't you present yourself a little earlier, dear treasure? Then I should have been spared the raving of this wicked woman!"

Staring with widely-opened eyes at the glittering heap, she tenderly nestled against him and greedily extended her hand. But he gently pushed her aside, covered the silver again, and spoke: "At other times you have only abuse for me; now at the sight of silver you suddenly become affectionate. But as a punishment for your unloving behavior you will receive none of it. Tomorrow I shall separate from you and leave you alone. I have had enough of allowing you to make my life a burden."

She forced herself to smile an embarrassed smile. "Oh, you are only joking. Tell me seriously where the money comes from."

And as he was silent, she continued uncertainly:

"You are not really angry with me? I meant it for the best, and wanted only to put some energy into you. Now that there's money in the house we can quietly discuss what to do with it. How can you be so resentful to your faithful wife, who has always been true to you? You are really unjust to me."

As he still said nothing, she played the part of a much-injured person, and began to shed a few tears. At this he gave a long sigh, and in order to crush her more effectually he quoted the lines:

> "She weaves no linen,
> She tills no soil,
> But scolds her husband,
> His life to spoil."

462

For a long while they sat side by side in silence. He was thinking to himself: "It will serve her right if I make her atone for her wickedness. But people would call me heartless, and perhaps I should lessen Hsi Men's good opinion of me."

"Yes, it's only my joke!" he cried suddenly, and he burst out laughing. "Who would think of being angry with you? Now I'll explain how I came by the money. Because I couldn't bear to listen to your reproaches any longer, I went this morning to Hsi Men in company with Friend Ying. We were fortunate; he happened to be at home, and he lent me these twelve ounces. With this we can meet the most necessary expenses. As soon as we have found the new house we can have more."

"So the money comes from Master Hsi Men? You must be sparing of it, then! The most necessary thing is that we should get some warm clothes for the winter."

"That is just what I think."

"Have you had anything to eat?"

"I have, but you haven't. I'll go and get something for you."

"Well, only rice."

He tucked the wicker basket under his arm and disappeared. When on his return she noticed a piece of mutton in the basket as well as rice, she at once began to scold him again, and blame him for his extravagance.

"But I must make up to you for hurting your feelings as I did just now," he said gallantly. "Really a roast ox would hardly suffice to atone for my injustice."

Reconciled, the husband and wife jested and teased each other until the wife disappeared into the kitchen to prepare their midday dinner.

Chang spent the afternoon in High Street, inspecting with the comfortable assurance of the solvent customer the goods exposed by the various clothiers. In the end he chose, for his wife, one plain blue silk overcoat, and another long, wadded coat of flowered red silk, a short green taffeta skirt and another of white taffeta, and a white taffeta petticoat; in all, five garments. For himself he purchased a long wadded overcoat in cockatoo yellow and a few plain coats of calico and grass linen. Altogether he spent six ounces and five bits. He had everything made up into a large bundle, lifted it on to his back, and went home with it. His wife's first question was: "How much?"

"Six ounces and five bits."

Of course, she thought that much too dear, but she was quickly appeased by the sight of the fine new things; she packed them all carefully in a trunk, and the rest of the day she was contented and happy as she had not been for a very long time. All her resentment was sunk in the deepest depth of the Eastern Sea.

After Chang had taken his leave of Hsi Men that morning Beggar Ying had continued for some time in conversation with his friend.

"Although I have only a modest official position," Hsi Men began, "my connections with all classes of mandarins in the capital and the provinces are always becoming more extensive, and since I have had the honor of being received by the Chancellor I cannot cope with the flood of letters and petitions which I receive. I simply must have a scholarly writer to take this burden off my shoulders, who could also act as tutor to my little son. Can you by any chance recommend a suitable person?"

"That is not so simple. If the person in question is to live in the house, then apart from his other qualities he must be a man of reliable character. I do, however, know of someone. He is an old friend of mine; he is called Water, and is a doctor of the third degree, a man of quite exceptional ability. And as for his character, he is steeped through and through in the moral principles of the venerable Kung tse and Mong tse. Moreover, he used to possess a hundred acres of land and three dwelling houses."

"But then he apparently has enough to live on and would hardly wish to accept employment."

"Unfortunately he had to sell his land and his houses long ago, and today he owns nothing but his naked skin—little enough for a family of four. For he has a charming young wife of twenty and two pretty little children. . . ."

"Well, if he has such a charming young wife," said Hsi Men, interrupting his friend again, "he will hardly wish to leave her in the lurch in order to accept a situation among strangers."

"It is a fortunate fact," continued Beggar Ying, as solemnly as ever, "that two years ago his wife eloped with a lover to the Eastern Capital, and his two little children died of smallpox. For he could not really support them. So today he is quite alone and would be glad to accept employment."

"You crazy fellow, stop your joking and tell me seriously if you think him a suitable person."

"Indeed, I do! As far as his abilities go, he is simply incomparable. He will draw up documents for you which will positively be poems! He will carry on your correspondence so brilliantly that people will never cease to marvel at your high culture!"

"Well, there is something in what you say. However, I should like to be convinced by a little example of his literary style before I engage him. Since he is alone he can very well live in the house, and he shall be made comfortable."

"An example of his style? There I can help you. He wrote me a letter quite recently, in which he begged me to find a suitable situation for him. I know his letter by heart. Listen. . . ."

And he recited from memory the ten sentences of the letter in question. When he had finished Hsi Men burst out laughing.

"But that's a poem, not a letter! It talks about a yellow cockatoo, about rafters and clouds and smoke and all sorts of things! Where is there a single word about a situation? He must have a very confused mind!"

"Dear friend, you don't understand," said Beggar Ying, reprovingly. "That is precisely the art of the higher style, to disguise sober and commonplace things in flowery phrases. For the connoisseur, especially among friends and close acquaintances, it is most enjoyable to read the concealed meaning of the characters of such a manuscript. It is an intellectual treat, a mental tonic. This letter is a masterpiece of the higher style."

"Well, as far as I'm concerned. . . . And what about his character?"

"Oh, as regards his character, that is perhaps even more distinguished than his intellectual faculties. He was once four years a tutor in the family of the Minister Li. The house was simply swarming with dozens of pretty young maids. Believe me, he never looked at one of them, though they all positively ran after him! Like a saint, he just sat over his books. So for your household, in which there are so many women, he ought to be the very man. You could let him sleep in the same room as your wives, and I warrant you he'd never touch them."

"Oh, you accursed joker, there's no talking seriously with you!" said Hsi Men, laughing, as he broke off the conversation. "I'll stick to Master Warm, who was recently recommended to me by my colleague Hsia."

CHAPTER THIRTY: *Mistress Ping mourns for her dead Child. In the Night she is terrified by evil Dreams*

GOLD LOTUS kept in her pavilion a large and handsome ram cat. Because his silky fur, apart from an oval black mark on the forehead, was a pure snowy white all over his body, she used to call him by the pet names of "Snow Lion" and "Snowball." She had come to regard this animal as a good friend, and when Hsi Men was not paying her a visit she even took him to bed with her; for he was a well behaved and cleanly cat. He was also an obedient animal. A call, and he came leaping towards her; a wave of the hand, and he trotted off. Gold Lotus had taken especial pains to train him to bring her her fans and her handkerchiefs. As a reward, she pampered him with good food. Every day he had an abundant meal, not of bad stockfish, but of fresh meat, either stewed or roasted. It was no wonder that he became fatter and more vigorous every day, and his white fur was so thick and so long that one could have hidden a hen's egg in it. Recently Gold Lotus had been teaching him to scramble for bits of meat wrapped in a red cloth, and to extract the toothsome contents from its silken wrapping with his claws.

One day Mistress Ping had laid her child, wrapped in his little red silk dress, on a low divan on the open veranda of her pavilion, leaving him in the charge of the maid Pear Blossom. She herself had left the pavilion for the great house, and the nurse, Ju I, was seated in the adjoining room, eating her dinner. In an unguarded moment, when the maid Pear Blossom had just turned her back, and had begun a little chat with the nurse, Sister Fifth's white cat suddenly appeared on the rail of the veranda. When he saw the child lying before him in his red silk dress, the cat may well have taken him for a large piece of meat wrapped in a red cloth. In short, he sprang upon the divan with one mighty leap, and as his mistress had long trained him to do, he began vigorously to work at the red bundle with his claws, scratching and scrabbling in order to tear the covering from the soft contents.

In a few moments the whole of the poor child's body was covered with bleeding scratches. Rushing on to the veranda as they heard his pitiful cries of distress, the maid and nurse gazed with horror upon the injuries which had been inflicted. The poor little creature was crying no longer. He lay there mute, his silken dress half torn from his body, his tiny arms and legs shaken by convulsive spasms, his eyes turned fixedly upwards, so that only the whites were visible.

While the nurse quickly seized him in her arms, the impudent cat continued to leap and claw at his prey, until the maid, by violently striking at him, scared him away. She then ran to the women's quarters, and in a tone of consternation informed her mistress: "The child has had an accident. He is in convulsions."

Beside herself with horror, Mistress Ping hurried back to the pavilion. When she realized the pitiful condition of the child she felt as though a dagger were lacerating her bowels. His eyes were still turned up, and his limbs were shaken with convulsive terror. Froth was dropping from the corners of his mouth, and moaning cries issued from his closed lips. She quickly pillowed the child on her bosom, pressed his little head tenderly to her cheek, and spoke to him in a soothing tone. Then she asked to be told what had happened.

In the meantime Moon Lady had arrived. When she understood what had been happening she sent for Gold Lotus. The nurse and the maid insisted that it was Sister Fifth's white cat which had attacked the child. Gold Lotus, being questioned, placidly inquired:

"Who insists that it was my Snowball?"

Moon Lady pointed to the nurse and the maid.

"They can both bear witness to it."

468

"Now look at those two lying wenches!" said Gold Lotus, coolly "At that time my Snowball was lying quietly on my bed."

Moon Lady did not know what to think.

"How could the Fifth's cat have got in here at all?" she asked, turning to the two witnesses.

"He has often jumped into the veranda before," replied Pear Blossom.

"Then why did he never touch the child before?" said Gold Lotus, triumphantly. "You see by that how ridiculous your assertions are."

And she angrily turned her back and retired to her pavilion.

Worthy Reader, this was, of course, a secret blow of Gold Lotus's. With increasing fury she had been forced to realize how Hsi Men, for the sake of the child, favored the Sixth in a hundred ways, and if she expressed a desire for anything he gave her ten times what she asked. Gold Lotus was convinced that it was only on account of the child that Hsi Men preferred her rival, and that he would favor her as of old if the child were no longer there. It must therefore be removed. The training of her cat had been a coldly calculated scheme. The child, who was timid by nature, was to be frightened to death by the beast.

While the usual domestic remedy, a hot infusion of ginger, was being prepared for the child, old Liu made her appearance in response to a hasty summons. Her face betrayed her consternation when she had felt the child's pulse and listened to his breathing.

"This time he has had a serious shock," she said. "If only he gets over it!"

She quickly cooked a "gold and silver soup" of rushes and lotus leaves and dissolved a "gold-leaf pill" in it. Only by the use of force, and with the help of a brooch which Moon Lady pushed between the child's convulsively clenched teeth, was it possible to open his mouth and give him a little of the liquid. Old Liu was not satisfied with the effect of her soup.

"The best thing would really be to cauterize his body in a few places with burning wormwood," she now suggested.

"But only with his father's consent. Otherwise he might be angry," objected Moon Lady.

But the anxious mother felt that there was no time to be lost.

"It's a matter of life and death," she said. "If we waited until he comes home it will be too late. I shall be the one he will reproach."

"Very well, as you wish. After all, he is your child."

Thereupon old Liu cauterized the child in five places: between the eyebrows, beneath the larynx, on the back of each hand, and on the pit of the stomach, after which he fell into a deep sleep. When Hsi Men came home in the evening Moon Lady pressed five bits into the old woman's hand and spirited her away. She told her husband merely that the child had had an attack of convulsions and was not quite recovered. Hsi Men had a foreboding of ill when he noted the tear-reddened eyes of his Sixth, and his suspicions were increased when neither the maid nor the nurse would say a word in reply to his questions. Now he discovered the fresh burns on various parts of the sleeping child's body. Panting with excitement, he ran to find Moon Lady again, and cross-examined her; and now he had to be told how the child, having been frightened by the cat Snowball, had fallen into convulsions, and had been treated by old Liu with burning wormwood.

"His mother wanted to have him treated at once, without waiting until you returned, because she feared for his life. Old Liu cauterized him in five places. Fortunately he has been sleeping soundly ever since."

Hsi Men was beside himself. His three souls gave one mighty leap, his five entrails clashed together, and evil bubbles of wrath rose from his gall. Straightway he ran to the pavilion of the Fifth, seized the cat Snowball by the hind legs, carried him in silence into the courtyard, and swinging his body in a wide semi-circle, dashed his head against the stone steps of the entrance, so that his brains were scattered in all directions, and his teeth were loosened from his jaws.

With a darkly-knitted brow, sitting motionless on the divan, Gold Lotus had watched him from her room.

"Pah, how brutal," she said, quietly, between her angrily compressed lips. "What harm did the poor creature do him? Before the Judge of the Realm of Shades he will one day call him to account!"

Hsi Men, having revenged himself upon Snowball, withdrew to the neighboring pavilion.

"How could you let old Liu try her quackery on the child?" he said, reproving Mistress Ping. "If the treatment results in a cure, I'll say no more this time. But if any harm comes to the child I shall have the woman up before my court, and she shall have a taste of the finger press."

"Oh, come! She meant well, and she's a good, faithful soul," said Mistress Ping, in defense of the old quack. But her hopes of an improvement were delusive. In the night a violent wound fever set in, followed by collapse, and by the morning the child was so exhausted that he refused his nurse's breast. In their consternation, without Hsi Men's knowledge, his mother and Moon Lady once more sent for old Liu, and allowed her to bring her blind husband, the astrologer, who once more had to exorcize the demons by his magical conjurations. As even this did no good a children's doctor was summoned, who blew rice powder into the child's nostrils. If the powder made the nose run there would be some prospect of recovery. But not a drop would appear; and the medicine which the child was given was thrown up again. In vain did Mistress Ping sacrifice a fee of forty silver ingots to the nuns Pi and Wang, for the reading of fifteen hundred passages from the holy sutras; in vain did she spend another twelve ingots for burnt sacrifices and incense in the "Temple of the Five Sacred Mountains." The child's condition grew worse from day to day; and Mistress Ping, who was accustomed to have the child beside her at night, and to attend to him herself, fell into a state of nervous irritability as a result of the exhausting night watches and her constant anxiety. On a fine night, when the moon was full, in the last third of the eighth month, she had fallen into a brief, restless sleep, when she was startled by a vision which appeared to her in a dream. It seemed to her that she saw her dead husband, Hua Tze Hsu, wearing a long, white

471

mourning robe, advance with slow steps into the room, and that she heard him speak to her in hollow tones:

"Faithless one! For the sake of your paramour you cheated me of my property. The hour of judgment has come!"

He turned to go, but she seized him by the sleeve and held him fast. "Dear brother, forgive me!" she pleaded. But he tore himself away and vanished. Terrified, she started up in bed. It seemed to her that she could still feel the folds of the dead man's robe in her hand, but it was only the sleeve of her child's nightgown, which her fingers were convulsively grasping. Outside the third watch of the night, the hour of midnight, had just been sounded. A shudder passed over her; her hair stood on end, a cold sweat covered her body, and overcome with terror, she crept under the blankets. Next morning she told Hsi Men of her dreams.

"Dead men do not rise from the grave," he said, with a laugh, seeking to reassure her. "You are overwrought, and you have been dreaming of the past. I will send for Little Silver and your old Fong to keep you company, and help you to think of other things."

That evening the child was attacked by convulsions while feeding at his nurse's breast. His eyes turned up in his head, so that only the whites were visible, and his breathing stopped; he breathed out only, but not in. Terrified, Mistress Ping laid him against her own breast, and hastily sent for Hsi Men.

Hsi Men had a caller just then: Friend Chang Shih Kia, who had come to borrow the money for the new four-roomed house, which he had now succeeded in finding, and which would cost five and thirty ounces. In the midst of their conversation came the alarming news of the child's fresh attack of convulsions. Hsi Men sprang to his feet and rushed off to the pavilion of his Sixth.

"Come back again, and I'll give you the money I promised," he cried hastily, as he deserted his friend, who dejectedly took his departure with empty hands.

Hsi Men arrived just in time to see his child draw its last breath of life. It died on the afternoon of the twenty-third day of the eighth month at the hour of the Monkey. It had lived exactly one year and two months, for it was born on the twenty-third day of the sixth month, and at the hour of the Monkey.

Mistress Ping lost all control of herself. She tore at her hair, wrenched at her ears, and with her pointed fingernails plowed bleeding furrows in her cheeks; then she flung herself down and beat her head upon the floor until she lost consciousness. When she came to herself again she pressed the little body to her breast and mourned aloud.

"Poor unfortunate child!" she cried. "Why have you left me so soon? Now I wish to live no longer! Yes, I will gladly follow you in death! My heart, my liver, why have you caused me such suffering?"

The nurse and the maid sat beside her, sobbing quietly to themselves, while Moon Lady sought to console them with gentle words. Hsi Men had already gone to the front of the house, in order to make arrangements for the lying-in-state in the reception hall. When on his return he found the unhappy mother completely beside herself, with wildly disheveled hair, scratched cheeks, and reddened eyes, he spoke gently to her, concealing his own pain:

"My dear, you must not give way quite so desperately to your grief; have a little thought for your own health! By weeping and wailing you won't bring the child to life again. You must try to imagine that it was not our flesh and blood, but rather a strange child, which we had adopted for a time as our own. Even in grief one must contrive to observe moderation."

And he gave a sign to the servants, meaning that they should lay the little body on cushions and cover it with blankets and carry it into the hall. But Mistress Ping absolutely refused to surrender the dead child.

"Why this brutal haste, sister?" she pleaded, turning to Moon Lady. "Feel for yourself, his whole body is still warm!"

And once more grief overwhelmed her; she broke down utterly, and again beat her head violently upon the floor. The servants, taking this opportunity, gently removed the dead child from her

473

embrace and carried it into the western wing of the front reception hall where it was to lie in state.

Now Tai A was sent to notify Neighbor Kiao of the child's death, for he, as the prospective father-in-law, was the person most intimately concerned. And further, the District Necromancer Master Hsue was summoned, in order that he might draw up the announcement of the death; while Hsi Men's business manager, Pen Se, was given ten ounces with which to buy planks of the best fig wood and pay the coffin makers who were to make the child's coffin.

Before long Mistress Kiao arrived, who paid the first visit of condolence. She had the whole story told her from head to tail, and then the early decease of the little son-in-law was vigorously bewailed, as was only proper, Hsi Men's wives joining with a will in the lamentations. And presently Master Hsue, the District Necromancer, appeared. Having noted the remarkable agreement between the date of the child's birth and the date of his death, and the cause of that death, he drew up the prescribed announcement of death. Then he pored awhile over the "Black Mystery Book" of prognostications, after which he announced:

"In his former existence the deceased belonged, as son of the house, to the Tsai family in Yao chow. He was a deplorable drunkard, who respected neither heaven nor earth, nor regarded the six degrees of relationship, and was guilty of criminally defrauding a fellow creature, one of his most intimate friends, of his property. This guilt he has purged in his second existence by his premature death. By transmigration of the soul he will be born again in a third existence as a son of the Wang family in Chong chow; he will achieve office and dignities, and will attain to the age of sixty."

Master Hsue closed his book of oracles with a snap. "Is the dead child to be burned or buried tomorrow?" he asked of Hsi Men.

"There is no question of tomorrow," that latter told him. "He is to lie in state in the house for four days. On the third day the soul mass will be read, and on the fifth day he will be laid in our ancestral burial place outside the Southern gate."

Two days later eight bonzes came from the "Cloister of Gracious Recompense" and held a solemn soul mass. On the same day Neighbor Kiao and various friends of the family and relatives appeared, in order to mark their sympathy before the soul tablet of the child by burning the usual paper spirit money and making the customary threefold offering to the dead, consisting of fish, pork, and fowls.

Since the death of her child Mistress Ping had not taken a mouthful of food. She was inconsolable. Distressed by her appearance, Hsi Men took means to ensure that in the daytime, when he himself was engaged in official or other business, she should not be left alone for a moment. Moon Lady, the maids, the nurse, Little Silver, and the nun Pi had to take turns sitting with her, and they all did their best to console her. Sister Pi was especially ingenious in thinking out serious reasons for consolation. One evening she read a long passage from the famous Langkavatara Sutra, which sought to prove the unreality of apparent reality.

"You must console yourself with the thought," she said, as she concluded her long sermon, "that the dead child was not your beloved child at all, but some creature who was ill-disposed to you, and who wished to revenge himself upon you for a wrong inflicted upon him in a former existence. Hear what is written in the *Sutra of Incantations:*

" 'There was once a woman, who three times in succession bore a child, who each time died after two years of life. She was inconsolable, and would by no means part with the third child after it was dead. One day, as she was wandering along the river bank, weeping and wailing, with the dead child in her arms, the holy Mother Kwan Yin took pity on her, and appeared to her in the form of a nun, and spoke to her as follows: "Weep not, for behold, this child is not thy child, but thine enemy from a former life, who was three times born, in order three times to attempt thy life!" And as the woman did not credit her words, she stretched forth her hand, and lo, the dead child was changed into an evil nightmare, which hovered over the river and also spoke to her: "Thou didst murder me in a former existence, for which reason I have three times returned to revenge myself upon thee. But because thou hast always been steadfast in thy faith in Buddha and his holy doctrine, good spirits have protected thee day and night, so that I could do thee no harm. And today the holy Mother Kwan Yin has commanded me from now onwards to leave thee in peace." After these words the specter plunged into the river and was seen no more.'

"It is certain," the nun continued, "that your dead child came into the world only to revenge himself upon you for some wrong which you had done him in a former existence. But because you have a pure and credulous heart, and have assured yourself of the protection of good spirits by such pious works as having fifteen hundred chapters of the Holy Scriptures read aloud, it has realized that it can do you no harm, and has therefore left you in good time. Only the next child that you bear will really be your child."

So ran the wisdom of the nun Pi. But with all her eloquence she could not convince poor Mistress Ping, or check the flood of her tears.

On the twenty-seventh day, at an early hour of the morning, eight blue-clad, white-bonneted coffin bearers appeared, who lifted the coffin, covered with a white pall, on to their shoulders, and carried it out to the gate. Before them went men with red death banners, pennants, and feather fans, while twelve Taoist priests from the Jade Emperor's Temple took up their position to the right and left of the coffin, providing the funeral music and murmuring from time to time their formal conjurations of the spirits. Behind the coffin came Hsi Men and some of his friends, who followed it for some distance on foot, mounting their horses at the eastern end of the High Street. A dozen women's palanquins brought up the rear.

The child's mother had remained at home, at Hsi Men's express desire, for he did not wish to expose her to the emotional strain of the last solemnities. Snowblossom, Little Silver, and the two nuns had to keep her company. But she could not be prevented from at least accompanying the coffin to the gate, and gazing after it until it had disappeared from view.

476

Utterly broken in spirit, she returned to her bedroom, where she was overcome by a fresh outburst of grief at the sight of the child's rattle, hanging at the head of the bed. In despair she hammered on the table with her fists, and beat her head upon the floor so violently that she made her forehead bleed and lost all the ornaments from her hair.

"The child is gone forever, and you will not call it back with tears and sighs," said Little Silver, gently raising her from the floor.

And Snowblossom interposed: "You are still young; why shouldn't you have more children later?" And in order to divert her thoughts, and at the same time to incite her against an adversary whom they all hated, she continued, in a whisper: "I will name no name, for the walls have ears and the doors have eyes. But it must of course be obvious to you that a certain person has your child's death on her conscience. Now, the hour will come, sooner or later, when the dead child will call his tormentor to account before the Judge of the Underworld. We have both of us, you as well as I, often traced the poisonous hand of this certain person, who would like, if she could, to see us buried in the earth alive. And what is the explanation? She is crazy for men. She cannot endure that the man whom she would like to keep for herself should ever enter our bedrooms. Then she begins at once to gnash her teeth and wag her wicked tongue. We have to weigh every word spoken in her presence, and wash our eyes every day, and be on our guard before her. But she will assuredly come to a bad end one day."

"I know, I know!" said Mistress Ping, waving her away. "Her behavior has already made me quite ill. But since I shall die, as it were, today or tomorrow, I don't want to begin fighting with her now. Let her do what she will!"

During these last words the nurse Ju I had entered with hesitating steps. Then she flung herself on the floor before Mistress Ping. "The death of the child is a grievous misfortune for this despicable maid also," she said. "She is afraid that you will need her no longer now, that you will discharge her. Where will the despicable maid drag out her life?"

"The child is dead, it is true, but you can stay so long as I am here," said her mistress, consoling her. "And if I should die, sooner or later, at all events the First could make use of you, for she is expecting a child. So you need not be anxious as regards your future."

When the nurse had left the room Snowblossom and Little Silver begged Mistress Ping that she would at last take a little food. Protestingly she dipped her chopsticks into a bowl of rice, only to lay them aside after a few mouthfuls with a gesture of aversion.

Towards evening Hsi Men returned from the funeral, after entertaining those who had attended it at a solemn funeral banquet in the belvedere. His wives were accompanied by Mistress Kiao, since she felt the need of saying a few words of cordial sympathy to Mistress Ping.

"I am so sorry that your expectations of relationship have been thus disappointed," said Mistress Ping with a painful smile. "You will assuredly have nothing but disdain for the mother of so short-lived a son-in-law."

"But, my dear friend, who would reproach you on that account?" replied Mistress Kiao consolingly. "For every human being the duration of life is predetermined by Fate. Who can look into the future? Do not grieve too sorely! You are still young: why should not more children be vouchsafed to you?"

Hsi Men spent this night, like the foregoing nights, as a considerate husband, with his Sixth. With mild and affectionate words he sought in a hundred ways to console her. Above all, he saw to it that all the child's clothes and playthings, which had remained in her pavilion, and the sight of which must always be a cause of grief, were put out of sight and removed to the apartments of his First.

After a silent week of mourning the red of festival once more glowed upon the walls of the "Hall of the Assembled Horizon," and cheerful music echoed across the autumnal park. This was on the occasion of the opening of Hsi Men's new silk mercery. Lai Pao and Han Tao Kwo had completed their mission to the salt works of Yangchow, and had resold the consignments of salt allotted to them at great profit to the retail traders. Their ways had then parted. One journeyed on to Nanking, the other to Hangchow, in order to buy, in each city, a ship's cargo of silk, of the value of ten thousand ounces. Since the silk shop in Lion Street had no accommodation for such a huge consignment, Hsi Men had acquired a one-storied house in close proximity to his estate, in which he intended to open a second shop. As business manager of the new shop he had engaged an experienced man of forty, one Kan, recommended by Beggar Ying. The rooms behind the shop, which were divided from it by a courtyard, served as a dwelling house for Master Warm, whom Judge Hsia had engaged as secretary, and his wife.

After the twenty-eighth of the seventh month, on Hsi Men's birthday, Han Tao Kwo's junk with its cargo of Hangchow silk had safely entered the harbor of Tsing ho hsien. Four weeks later Lai Pao too arrived with his cargo of Nanking silk. The fourth day of the ninth month, the day when the new shop was opened, was celebrated by Hsi Men by a great banquet in the belvedere pavilion, his guests being his partner Kiao, his business managers, and numerous friends and acquaintances. The sales were most gratifying from the very outset; on the day of opening there was a turnover of five hundred ounces. The profits of the two silk merceries in which Hsi Men and Kiao were partners were divided into five parts: three-tenths going to each partner, while the other four-tenths were divided among Hsi Men's three managers, Han and Kan and Lai Pao, and Master Kiao's manager Tsai Pen.

The cunning Han, of course, contrived on this occasion to secure various pickings for himself, over and above his considerable share in the profits. On the evening of his return from Nanking, when he was back in his home in Lion Street, and his wife was helping him to unpack, she discovered, to her surprise, that his small leather handbag was filled to the top with silver money.

"These two hundred ounces," he explained with a smirk, "I have put aside for us. They are the profit on a little consignment of goods which I sold outside the city on my own account."

. . . . . .

The mental shock of the last few weeks had gravely aggravated the old trouble from which Mistress Ping had suffered since the birth of the child. Doctor Yen's medicine proved to be as ineffectual as a stone dropped into deep water. In consequence of the constant loss of blood her emaciated cheeks assumed a pale and sickly hue, her body lost the soft curves of earlier years, and her one-time beauty faded from day to day.

One night, in the first third of the ninth month, as she lay tossing restlessly, half asleep, on her moonlit bed, she was once more tormented by a dream vision. It suddenly seemed to her that someone was rapping outside on the windowsill. Hastily she rose, put on her slippers and her dressing gown, and called the maid and the nurse. But she could get no answer; they were fast asleep. So she herself crept out of doors, to see who was there. And in the moonlight she saw her former husband, Hua Tze Hsu, standing before her. He had her child in his arms, and he beckoned to her. "The new home for the three of us is ready. Come with me!" he whispered. She shuddered. She did not want to leave Hsi Men, yet she longed to be with her child. She tried to seize it and wrest it away from her former husband. But he pushed her back so violently that she staggered, and then he disappeared, with the child.

Terrified, and bathed in cold perspiration, she started up in bed. She had been dreaming.

> *The moon is new; its silver rays*
> *Fall on the shrine above the bed.*
> *Freed from the body in amaze*
> *The soul is hovering overhead.*
> *Alas, remorse has come too late!*
> *Alas, delight is all too brief!*
> *It is of old the lover's fate*
> *That love must pay its toll with grief!*

480

CHAPTER THIRTY-ONE: *The Magician Pan seeks to banish the Ghost of the deceased Hua. Hsi Men bewails the Loss of his Sixth*

SOONER THAN THOSE about her, Mistress Ping felt that her life was nearing its close. To what end should she embitter the brief interval that remained to her by contending with such a dangerous rival as Gold Lotus? One evening in the first third of the ninth month, as Hsi Men returned home from one of his secret meetings with the Sixth Wang, to spend the night in her apartments, she herself sent him to her neighbor's pavilion.

"There you are eagerly awaited," she said. "In a sense, it only means suffering for me if you continue to stay with me. Every minute which you spend with me your Fifth reckons against me. I would rather avoid needless annoyance."

"But my heart, my liver, I can't do without you!"

"You will soon have to accustom yourself to doing so, once I am dead," she replied, with a painful smile. "Go now, go! I feel unwell, and must not waste my strength."

With a sigh he rose and went to the neighboring pavilion.

"What fortunate breeze has blown you here to me?" asked Gold Lotus, who had just composed herself to sleep. She was both surprised and delighted to see him, since his visits had been rare of late. Then, with a searching glance at his wine-reddened face, she inquired: "But where have you been drinking again today?"

"My business manager Han invited me," he replied, with an innocent expression. "He meant it well; he wanted to offer me a little distraction in this time of mourning, and he had engaged a blind singing-girl who often visits Yo San's, the house next door. A really admirable artist! I shall ask her to come to us for a couple of days at the Feast of Chrysanthemums. You will be delighted with her singing. She knows a hundred and twenty songs by heart. . . ."

"That's all very well, but no evasions!" she impatiently interrupted him. "All you went for was the Sixth Wang."

"But, I beg you! . . . The wife of my business manager! How could I . . . ?"

"Oh, you could very well! How long do you hope to make fools of us? No, this time your lies won't help you. Who was it crept into the bedroom of your Sixth not long ago, secretly and quietly as a cat, when she happened to be out, and took one of her golden brooches in the form of the character Shou? How did the Sixth Wang come by this brooch? And why did she blush so red with embarrassment when she called on us lately, and we asked her where her handsome brooch had come from? As far as that goes, I don't understand your taste. What on earth can you see in that gushing, painted creature, with her commonplace, hackneyed, water-brushed mop of hair? And don't you feel ashamed in the presence of her cuckold of a husband, who encourages her to go with you, and then makes her tell him everything you have said to her?"

Hsi Men realized that his clever Fifth had seen through him again, but would not admit it.

"You are dreaming!" he said, with a forced laugh. "Her husband didn't leave my side this evening. She herself never put in an appearance."

"That may deceive others, but not me! Don't you see, you silly fool, that he's merely using his wife as a means of making money out of you? For him you're the lamb that he's pasturing, in order to kill it later on. The tree which he's tending, and will one day use as firewood!"

He was stubbornly silent; he swallowed a restorative pill, washing it down with a little warm wine, preferring once more to drown by the wild intoxication of the senses the tiresome voice of clearer insight which under the influence of her words had timidly made itself heard in his inmost heart.

482

On the day of the Feast of Chrysanthemums, on the ninth of the ninth month, Hsi Men sat down with his six wives at a great octagonal table in the "Hall of the Assembled Horizon," in order to listen to the recitatives of the blind singing-girl, whom Moon Lady, at his request, had invited to the house for a couple of days. Protesting, but making a supreme effort, Mistress Ping had managed to reach the table. Suffering as she was, she would far rather have remained in bed, but she did not wish to hurt her husband's feelings by her absence, as he had really devised the concert as a mark of attention and a means of diverting her thoughts. Accordingly she rose from her bed and painfully dragged herself up to the belvedere, like a withered leaf blown in at the door by the wind. Hsi Men was startled to see how ill she was looking.

"My love, you must forget for a time what is depressing you," he said gently, "and allow yourself to be cheered a little by the art of the blind singer!"

"She is here in your honor," Jade Fountain interposed. "You must say what you would like her to sing to us."

But Mistress Ping was incapable of speech. Wearily she sank into a chair, and responded, as though in a dream, by a silent nod of the head. As the feast was beginning Beggar Ying and Friend Chang were announced.

"Take them for the moment to the Malachite Veranda and tell them I'll be with them directly," said Hsi Men, who was rather annoyed by this interruption.

"Uncle Chang," said the servant who had announced them, "is accompanied by a porter with two boxes of presents."

"Probably he wants to show his gratitude for the fifty ounces which I recently placed at his disposal for the new house," said Hsi Men turning to Moon Lady. "He ought to keep what is left over, and open a shop, which would enable him to earn a modest living."

"Then you ought to receive them both properly and keep them company," said Moon Lady. "I'll send word to the kitchen so that one can put something before them."

Accordingly Hsi Men rose and went to greet the two visitors.

"Give your very best performance in honor of my Sixth!" he admonished the singer, as he left the pavilion.

"You must suggest something that you would like her to sing," Gold Lotus urged Mistress Ping, when Hsi Men had gone. "She is here only on your account."

"Very well, let her sing the song of 'Red Dust in the Purple Lane,'" said Mistress Ping at last, speaking with difficulty.

The singer took up her twelve-stringed lute and broke into the desired song. When she had ended Moon Lady pushed a goblet of wine toward the Sixth.

"Drink, Sister, the sweet wine will do you good," she said encouragingly.

But Mistress Ping had hardly taken a sip from the goblet when she felt a wave of heat invading her body. A sudden dizziness overcame her, so that she was near fainting. She rose and left the table without a word, leaning heavily on the shoulders of the two maids, to return with dragging feet to her pavilion.

In the meantime Hsi Men had greeted his two visitors. He found them in front of the Malachite Veranda, absorbed in the contemplation of the chrysanthemums, which flaunted their manifold hues to the right and left of the screen of fig trees. As he approached them, Chang gave a sign to his porter, and the two large boxes which the man was carrying were set down at Hsi Men's feet.

"What can this be?" asked Hsi Men.

"Friend Chang would like to convince you of his gratitude for your friendly and generous service to him," said Beggar Ying, speaking for his companion. "He cannot manage a regular banquet, so he begs that you will graciously accept these trifling gifts. In the one box there are boiled crabs; in the other, two roast ducks, prepared by his wife's own hands."

"But, Brother Chang, how could you go to such trouble?" said Hsi Men, thanking him. Then he had the two boxes opened by his servants. Seductive odors issued from them. In one was a brimming dish containing forty crabs, carefully shelled, garnished with paprika and rice, and swimming in a thick, piquant fennel sauce, of which the other ingredients were ginger, garlic, oil, and vinegar. In the other were two crisply roasted ducks. Hsi Men gave the porter half a bit as drink money, and had the boxes with their savory contents carried to the kitchen by his servants. Then he ushered his two friends into the Malachite Veranda. They were still quite engrossed in the spectacle of his chrysanthemum beds.

"Where did you get these magnificent specimens?" they asked.

"A present from my good friend, the Head Eunuch and steward of the Imperial Domains, Liu!" he explained, in a gratified tone. "He sent me twenty boxes of young plants from the estates outside the city, and in every box there was a different variety! They are the rarest and loveliest chrysanthemums in existence."

They gazed in admiration at the friend who could boast of such distinguished connections.

"Are you now comfortably settled in your new home?" inquired Hsi Men, turning to Friend Chang.

"Thanks for your kind inquiry!" replied Chang. "We moved in three days ago, and yesterday we opened the shop in front. I have engaged my wife's young brother as salesman."

"The event must really be celebrated by a house-warming feast in the new house," Hsi Men proposed, who felt a renewed longing to carouse with the jolly drinking companions of his former care-free days. "We'll invite Friend Hsia also, so that there'll be four of us. That will be enough. Each must contribute a trifle. But you, Chang, must not involve yourself in any expense on their account. I will have the meal prepared here and sent to your house. I'll engage two nice little singing-girls, too, and we'll just make a really jolly, comfortable day of it. What do you think?"

His proposal was of course greeted with enthusiasm.

"I had already thought of it," said Chang, shyly, "but I did not feel that I could invite you to my poor, restricted apartments. I was afraid you would feel affronted by such presumption."

"That's all right!" Hsi Men reassured him, laughing. "You really needn't apologize. I will let Friend Hsia know at once. He can come over here, too, at once, and help us to dispose of your crabs and ducks!"

So after a while Hsia Hsi Ta appeared.

"Friend Chang has secretly and surreptitiously moved into a fine new house," Hsi Men explained. "Of course we must celebrate the occasion properly with a house-warming banquet. I'm having the food prepared here and sent over. Friend Chang is not to go to any expense or trouble. The rest of us will contribute according to our abilities."

Laughing and gayly conversing, they sat down to eat, and thoroughly enjoyed the delicious crabs and the crisply-roasted ducks. Brother-in-law Wu presented himself just in time to share in the feast.

While they were all talking Hsi Men quietly directed his servant Shu Tung to hurry over to the belvedere and ask the singer to favor them with a song.

"Who is that singing there?" asked Beggar Ying, suddenly pricking up his ears as the sound of music was wafted from the belvedere. "Is that by any chance Cinnamon Bud?"

"You've guessed wrong."

"Then it must surely be Little Silver."

"Nonsense. It's a blind woman, a young teacher of singing."

"Why can't we have a look at her, then?"

"She is giving my wives a concert up there, in connection with the Feast of Chrysanthemums. Her singing wouldn't be good enough for your sharp dog's ears!"

"Please, please, don't insult my refined ears! They can hear a bee coughing at forty miles' distance!"

At the general request, Hsi Men at last sent for the singer, and asked her to give a few examples of her art for the benefit of his jolly guests. He had apparently quite forgotten that one of his household was seriously ill.

When Mistress Ping returned to her bedroom and attempted to undress she was overcome by a sudden vertigo, and fell on her face, striking her forehead upon the floor. Fortunately her fall was

486

broken to some extent by the intervention of Pear Blossom, who sprang forward just in time to catch her, so that she escaped with a slight cut on the forehead. The maid and the nurse lifted her on to the bed, where she lay motionless for a long while before she awakened from her swoon. This was of course the end of the celebrations in the belvedere. At the news of this misfortune the wives left the banquet table in consternation, and hastened to the bedside of the Sixth. They poured a hot infusion of ginger into the mouth of the unconscious woman, and waited, in tense anxiety, until she at last opened her eyes. Then they assailed her with questions.

"I don't know how it happened," she said, in a subdued voice. "Everything suddenly turned black before my eyes, heaven and earth seemed to be spinning in front of me, then I fell down and lost consciousness."

"I will send Tai A to inform your husband," said Moon Lady. "He must send for Doctor Yen at once."

"Oh, we won't disturb him unnecessarily; he's enjoying himself just now with his friends on the Malachite Veranda. I should be sorry if his pleasant afternoon were spoilt."

Moon Lady complied with her thoughtful request, so that Hsi Men did not hear what had happened until the evening, after he had bidden his guests farewell. In great consternation he hurried to the sick woman's bedside. His heart contracted when he saw her lying there feeble and exhausted, her face yellow as wax, and noted the plaster over the wound on her forehead. She affectionately grasped his sleeve, and with tears in her eyes told him once more what had happened.

He had a bed made up against her own, and faithfully kept watch beside her all night, without closing his eyes. Next morning he led Doctor Yen to her bedside and made him examine her pulse and her breathing. The physician's expression was doubtful.

"Her condition is definitely worse than it was a little while ago," he said. "The seven passions have overtaxed her liver. There is too much heat in her lungs. The flow of her blood is unchecked and unruly as mountain torrents after a landslip. If the medicine which I shall prescribe does not stop this abnormal bleeding there will be little hope."

In vain did Hsi Men implore him to employ the whole of his medical art, and hinted at the most extravagant reward if he could heal the patient. The prescribed remedy, which the patient had to swallow, proved to be quite ineffectual, and the hemorrhage continued unchecked. At this Hsi Men sent for Doctor Hu in the High Street. He considered that the immoderate bleeding was due to the fact that air and heat had penetrated certain veins and caused them to burst, and he prescribed another remedy, which proved to be as ineffective as that of his colleague Yen.

On Han Tao Kwo's recommendation a third doctor was called in, Doctor Tao, the specialist in women's diseases, who lived outside the city, by the Eastern Gate.

While two of Hsi Men's servants hurried off to the Eastern Gate, Neighbor Kiao, who had called out of sympathy with his friend, proposed to call in a fourth physician, Doctor How, who was eighty-one years of age, and lived quite close at hand, not far from the district yamen.

"The best thing, dear cousin," suggested Kiao, "would be if you were to call in both doctors and ask them to consult together. Let them first come to an agreement as to the nature of the malady, and they will surely find the right remedy."

Hsi Men followed his advice, and promptly sent for Doctor How, who proved to be a lively old gentleman. One after the other they examined the patient, each in accordance with his own method, and then they entered upon a long medical argument, and the upshot of this was that old Doctor How flatly declared that the medicine which his voluble, self-satisfied junior had prescribed was poison. Hsi Men angrily dismissed the latter, after paying him two bits as his fee, and agreed with old How and Neighbor Kiao that he was a puffed-up ignoramus and a charlatan.

"I did not like to say it in his presence," old How observed, when his rival had gone, "but where he lives, by the Eastern Gate, he is generally known as the 'Ghost-knocker.' He runs about the streets with his jingling staff and peddles his prescriptions. What does such a crank and quacksalver know of the scientific diagnosis of pulse and breathing?"

He tucked away his fee—a silver ingot—and took his leave. But the two alleged styptics which he prescribed did the poor patient as little good as the other medicines. Her condition grew worse from day to day; in her weakness she could no longer rise from her bed, and every day she was more like a fading flower, a withering leaf. Hsi Men was inconsolable. He now went only every other day to the yamen; the alternate days he spent at her bedside, weeping and wailing. It saddened her to see him suffering so, and although she was perfectly well aware of the hopelessness of her condition, she tried, in her tender consideration, to persuade him that she would soon be well again.

"You mustn't neglect your official duties on my account," she gently admonished him. "Things are not quite so bad with me as that. When once this bleeding stops my appetite will return, and all will be well again."

"Dear Sister, I cannot let you leave me!" he groaned.

"Only one thing disturbs me," she continued softly, looking anxiously round the room. "Lately his ghost has again appeared to me in a dream. He was holding our child in his arms, and he gnashed his teeth at me so horribly. He had found a new home for the three of us, he said, and I must go with him. And when I tried to take the child away from him he gave me such a push that I fell to the ground. I dread the night. I am so terribly afraid he will appear to me again."

"But, my dear child, he has been dead for two years now! When we die it is as though a lamp goes out. It is all over with us then. There are no ghosts. Your nerves are overexcited on account of your illness. What you think you saw was not reality, but only imagination. Yet if it will make you easier I will send to the High Priest Wu at the Jade Emperor's Temple. He can send a few formulae of exorcism which we can hang up in your bedroom to protect you.

Then the spirit of the dead man will no longer have any desire to return and frighten you."

And he immediately sent his servant Tai A to the Jade Emperor's Temple. On the way Tai A met Beggar Ying and Hsia Hsi Ta. He jumped from the saddle and greeted them.

"Where are you going? Is your master at home?" asked Beggar Ying.

"The master is at home. He has just sent me to the Jade Emperor's Temple. I have to ask the High Priest Wu for formulae of exorcism against evil spirits."

The two friends were startled to hear such a bad account of Mistress Ping, and, greatly concerned, they hastened to call at their friend's house.

"We met your groom Tai A on the way," they told the despairing Hsi Men. "What is he going to do in the Jade Emperor's Temple?"

"My Sixth is tormented by bad dreams. The spirit of her deceased husband has twice appeared to her at night. To calm her I am having formulae of exorcism hung up in her bedroom."

"If she is alarmed by ghostly apparitions, then I can recommend the Taoist priest Pan at the 'Temple of the Five Sacred Mountains,'" said Beggar Ying: "He has tremendous magical powers; he can conjure up thunder and lightning and banish any specter. For that reason he is known as 'Pan the Devil-catcher.' You must get him to come. He has already helped many people with his spells of exorcism and holy water."

"Thanks for the information. I will get him to come tomorrow. Today I will see what the texts of High Priest Wu will do."

Presently Tai A returned from the Jade Emperor's Temple. He brought a number of spells with him, written in flourishing characters on red paper. These Hsi Men fastened on the doors and walls of the bedroom. He was very soon to have striking evidence of their wonderful magic power. As he entered the room late that evening the sick woman suddenly woke from an uneasy doze.

"The dead man has just appeared to me again!" she gasped, still trembling with terror in every limb. "He had two men with him, who wanted to drag me away. You were just in time; they disappeared when you came."

"My dear, don't distress yourself!" he said, endeavoring to soothe her. "Tomorrow I will get the Taoist priest Pan from the 'Temple of the Five Sacred Mountains' to come here and protect you. Friend Ying has warmly recommended him. He has tremendous magical powers, and with his spells and his holy water he can scare away every specter and cure every sickness."

"Oh, Brother, let him come soon!" she pleaded, gazing at him with eyes dilated with terror. "I am so afraid of the night. The dead man gave me such a terribly menacing stare before he disappeared."

"Shall I ask Mother Fong to lie down here and keep you company for a time?"

She nodded in assent; so that same evening he sent his servant Lai An to bring old Fong from Lion Street. But when Lai An knocked at the door of her house Mistress I Chang Tsing opened it and informed him that old Fong had gone out. He charged her to ask Mother Fong, when she returned, to come as quickly as possible to see his Sixth mistress, who was dangerously ill.

Next morning, even before Mother Fong arrived, the nun Wang came to visit the Sixth. She was carrying two boxes under her arm, in which she had packed twenty curd cakes and a dozen egg melons. The sick woman was evidently glad to see her. She made Pear Blossom prop her up on her pillows, and told the visitor to sit beside her bed.

"You have neglected me shamefully, my dear!" she said, reproachfully. "Since you read prayers for me with Sister Pi you haven't given me a thought! And I have been so ill in the meantime!"

"It was only yesterday that I heard of your illness," said the nun in apology. "The servants whom your First sent to our convent told me about it. And now that you have mentioned prayers, I will just tell you that since then I have had a proper quarrel with Sister Pi, that deceitful woman. The truth is that she overreached me in

491

dividing the fee which you then so kindly paid us. Five ounces too little she paid me, the swindler! She will be punished for it in Hell! You will understand that I've been so upset that I haven't called here since then, not even on the birthday of your First."

"It would be better if each of you were to hold services independently, instead of working in partnership. Then there would be no danger of such unpleasantness. Moon Lady was quite annoyed with you for overlooking her birthday. She had reckoned on your holding family prayers."

"My dear Bodhisattva, I am indeed sorry! I have just come from her now, and I have already apologized to her. But I really had no time, for I was busy a whole month with house prayers for another family. Yesterday the month was up, so I came straight here today to see how you were getting on. I hope you will not disdain the little gift which I have brought you."

"How thoughtful of you! Many thanks!"

"Sister," said the nun, turning to the maid Pear Blossom, "be so kind as to have these two slices of curd cake heated up in the kitchen. I should like to see for myself if our dear mistress can enjoy them."

Presently the maid returned with the freshly-baked cake and with tea for the visitor. Unwilling to hurt the giver's feelings, Mistress Ping, to please her, allowed her maid to push a piece of the cake into her mouth with the chopsticks. But she had hardly taken a mouthful when she mournfully shook her head, and complained that unfortunately she could eat nothing at all. It was only then that the simple-minded nun understood how ill the poor woman was.

Soon after this the maid Pear Blossom entered the room again and informed her mistress that the elder Hua, the brother of her deceased husband, had called and was anxious to see her. Sister Wang rose and hurried away.

"Come back later! There is something I want to discuss with you," said Mistress Ping, beseechingly.

"Very well, I'll come back."

The elder Hua apologized for having only just heard of his sister-

492

in-law's illness, and announced that his wife would presently be calling on her. She breathed a few words of greeting; then she turned her head aside and buried her face in her pillows. The presence of a kinsman of the husband who terrified her in her dreams at night made her uneasy. However, he went away again almost immediately.

"Old Kung Kung, in his day, brought a number of powerful remedies from Kwang tung," he told Hsi Men, whom he found outside the pavilion. "Among them is a remedy for hemorrhage such as that from which my sister-in-law is suffering. It has to be taken in five doses, mixed with wine. Has my sister-in-law tried it?"

"She has taken several remedies of that sort which have been prescribed by the doctors, but unhappily always without result."

"That is bad indeed. Then there is only one last expedient, to place a coffin in her room, which perhaps will banish the evil influences."

The elder Hua had only just gone when old Fong appeared, coughing and snuffling. "You're a fine one, to neglect your good mistress like this!" said the maid, reproachfully. "Where were you hiding yesterday evening when Lai An was sent to fetch you?"

"The way I'm hunted about!" she groaned. "The whole blessed day one never has any rest. But what won't one do for one's soul's salvation! Early in the morning one runs off to the temple to pray and burn incense; and when one comes home in the evening one is pestered for alms. One no sooner gets rid of Brother Chang than Brother Wang and Brother Li turn up, and so it goes on."

This flood of words from the fussy old woman elicited a faint smile from Mistress Ping. "She can never stop trying to humbug one, the old windbag!" she thought with amusement.

"It is wonderful what you can do, Mother Fong!" cried the maid, joyfully. "For days our mistress hasn't eaten a mouthful, and she's looked wretched all the time. And as soon as you are here she laughs. Now you must just stay here a couple of days, and I'm sure she'll be well again."

"That's agreed; I'll attend your mistress for a time as professor of exorcisms!" said the old woman, in her jesting manner. While she was making further inquires of Pear Blossom as regards the condition of the sick woman, Hsi Men entered the room, and Mother Fong whisked out of the door.

He sat on the edge of the bed. "How is your mistress feeling today?" he asked the maid. "Did she take her rice soup this morning?"

"No. Nor the curd cake that the nun Wang brought with her today; she only nibbled at it out of politeness. She could hardly swallow a couple of mouthfuls."

"Have patience until tomorrow, darling; then the great magician will come from the 'Temple of the Five Sacred Mountains,' and he will make you well again."

"Oh, if he would only come soon! That horrible ghost gives me no peace. But he'll probably come too late. I feel plainly that I am going to die. It was so lovely to think of living a long and happy life by your side! And now, unhappy woman, I have to leave you when I am only twenty-seven! And we shall meet again only at the gates of the realm of shades! There I shall stand and wait for you."

Her voice failed her; she tenderly clasped his hand and burst into violent sobs. He too was overcome by unutterable grief.

"How can you speak so!" he at last managed to say, in a choking voice.

Just then the servant Kiu Tung entered, and announced that Judge Hsia had sent to inquire whether Hsi Men would be present on the morrow—the fifteenth—at the customary rites of homage before the name tablet of the Son of Heaven.

"No, I shall not be going to the court tomorrow," he told the servant. "I must ask Master Hsia to perform the ceremony without me."

"I think you ought to go," Mistress Ping advised him, when the servant had left the room. "You mustn't neglect your official duties on my account. And my hour has not yet come. But it will come soon. You ought to be thinking about my coffin."

"So your brother-in-law, the elder Hua, has already told me. I will have one brought to the house as quickly as possible. Perhaps it will frighten away the evil influences which are threatening your life, and its presence will make you well again."

She nodded her head in agreement.

"Send for it. But don't spend an unreasonable amount of money on it. A few simple planks, costing ten ounces, will do. And when I am dead I should like to be buried by your deceased First. I don't want to be cremated."

Her words pierced through his heart and liver like a dagger.

"Dear sister, how can you speak so!" he cried, miserably. "I feel that I want to die myself!"

Moon Lady entered the room, bringing a basket of fresh apples.

"These are sent you by your sister-in-law Hua," she said, and she told the maid Pear Blossom to wash and peel a few apples and cut them into small pieces.

"I must thank her for her kindness," said Mistress Ping, and she allowed a slice of apple to be placed between her lips. But no sooner did she take a bite of it than she brought it up again. Moon Lady settled her comfortably on her pillows and quietly withdrew into the next room with Hsi Men. "Her condition is very grave. You ought to think about the coffin in good time."

"So Brother-in-law Hua has told me already. Just now, when I spoke of the coffin to her, she begged me earnestly not to give too much for it. I had so many mouths to feed, all of whom wanted to live. Isn't that touching? This kindly soul . . . it's a knife in my heart and liver. But I should like to wait and see what the magician Pan can do. Perhaps he will make her well, and there will be no need for a coffin."

"I should advise you rather to see about getting a good coffin in time. You have seen for yourself that she's only the shadow of a human being. She can't take even a drop of water now. There is no hope. But if, against all expectation, the magician did effect a cure, we can always sell the coffin to someone else."

"You are right," he agreed, and he went to the front of the house, in order to consult with Pen Se.

"I want you," he said, "to go out at once with my son-in-law and see that a good coffin is sent to the house today."

Provided with five large bars of silver, the two men set out immediately. When they returned in the afternoon they announced that they had met Neighbor Kiao in the street, and he had sent them to Shang, a doctor of the third grade.

"His father brought from Chong ta, in the province of Sze-ch'uen, where he was prefect of police, two fine unfinished coffins, one of which is still available. There are five planks of the very best quality, the very thing to make a pleasant resting place for a dead person, a 'Peach Blossom Grotto.' Actually Doctor Shang wanted three hundred ounces for them, but after a long discussion with us and with Neighbor Kiao he finally agreed to take fifty ounces. It so happens that he needs money for his examination next year in the capital, or he would not have thought of selling."

"Neighbor Kiao's recommendation is enough for me. I agree to the price. Let the coffin be made quickly, but without beating of drums and banging of gongs."

Towards evening half a dozen coolies appeared, who silently carried the coffin boards, draped with a great red cloth, through the door of the front reception hall. Then the coffin joiners arrived, and proceeded to turn the costly, fragrant planks into a strong, handsome coffin. All night long they were heard busily sawing and hammering, for Hsi Men had promised them the generous wage of five ounces if they had finished their task by the morning.

Meanwhile Mother Fong and Sister Wang sat with Mistress Ping and faithfully kept her company. Hsi Men had really wished to watch through the night at her bedside, but in view of the presence of her two visitors Mistress Ping would not allow this, and asked him to spend the night in the adjacent pavilion.

When he had gone her maids had to lock the door, light the lamps, and open her wardrobes and her jewel cases. First she called

496

the nun to her bedside, and bade her take out a silver bar, five ounces in weight, and a bolt of plain silk.

"Be so kind as to read, after my death, with some of your sisters of the cloister, a solemn mass for the repose of my soul!" she begged.

"With all my heart," said the recipient of these gifts, with emotion. "But you are too humble, dear mistress; Heaven will have compassion on you without any masses for your soul."

"And one thing more. Don't mention to the First that I have given you money."

Now old Fong was called to the bedside. She received four ounces in bullion, a long white silk coat, a short coat of yellow silk, and a silver hair comb.

"Dear old Fong! You have served me faithfully since my earliest childhood. Take these trifles in memory of me. Use the money to pay for your own coffin, when you yourself come to die. For the rest, don't worry about your future. I shall ask my husband to let you go on living after my death in my Lion Street house. You mustn't be afraid that you will be turned adrift."

Old Fong, hastily reaching for her presents, flopped down on the floor and gave a loud sob.

"Dearest, kindest of mistresses, it seems to me only a short day since I began to serve you, and now you already wish to leave us! Where will this old person find her refuge when you are dead?"

Now it was the turn of the nurse, Ju I. She received two coats of purple silk, one closed and one slit open, a short coat of blue silk, two gold brooches, and a silver-embroidered hood.

"I had hoped to make use of your services for a second child, after the first had died. Now, alas, I myself must die. But do not be anxious as to your future. I shall speak to my husband and his First, and arrange for you to stay on here. The First is expecting a child also, whose nurse you shall be. Don't grieve too much, and accept these things in memory of me!"

"This despicable maid had hoped that she would be able to serve you for many long years," said the nurse, between her sobs.

"But Fate has not willed it. First the little one dies, and now you yourself are snatched away by illness. You were always so kind to me, you have never spoken an angry word to me. Where shall I go, poor forsaken creature, when you are dead? Oh, say a good word for me, so that I can stay here, please, please!"

Mistress Ping beckoned to the two maids. They knelt at her bedside.

"You have always served me well and faithfully. Take these two gold flowers in memory of me! You, Pear Blossom, have already been possessed by your master, so it is better for you that you should stay here. I will arrange for you to serve the First in future. You, Apricot Blossom, must marry. I will ask the First to find another situation for you. What could you do after my death in these forsaken rooms? They would regard you as a superfluous, unemployed servant, and would treat you with contempt. I should wish to save you from that."

"But I don't want to go away from here," wailed the younger maid, weeping.

"Foolish thing, do just think! What will you do here when I am here no longer?"

Next morning, when Hsi Men paid his morning visit to the sick woman, her first question related to the coffin.

"It stands ready in the front hall," he replied. "It is to be hoped that it will frighten away the evil influences which are threatening you, and enable you to get well again. Then I shall be glad to send it out of the house."

Soon after Hsi Men had left the room, Moon Lady and Sunflower entered.

"How are you feeling today?" asked Moon Lady, sympathetically.

"Very ill, dear big sister," replied the sick woman, grasping her hand and bursting into tears.

Moon Lady too could not repress her sobs.

"My dear, have you anything further to ask of us?" she inquired softly.

"Alas, those few years of our life together as sisters are over now! I had hoped that they would continue until we were all white-haired. But my evil fate has ordained otherwise. I am concerned about the future of my two maids. The elder has already been possessed by her master; I should like you to take her into your service after my death. As for the younger, in case you yourself do not want her, I beg that you will find her a suitable husband and marry her to him, or that you will obtain for her a position as help in the household of a widower or a widow. I should like to save her from being slighted as a masterless, unwanted maid. And then there is the question of my nurse, Ju I; she has begged me to arrange that she can remain here. Perhaps you can make use of her, if sooner or later you bring a little son into the world."

"You may trust me entirely, dear sister! Your wishes shall be faithfully respected. I will take Pear Blossom for myself, and the younger maid can serve Sister Sunflower. As for your nurse, who, as you tell me, has no home and no kinsfolk, I will give her in marriage to one of our servants, whether I have a child or not."

Mistress Ping nodded her head in approval, and the two maids, at a sign from her, performed a kowtow before Moon Lady and Sunflower, their future mistresses. And now Jade Fountain, Snowblossom, and Gold Lotus entered the room. For each of them the sick woman had a kindly word of farewell. At last, when the other visitors had gone, she was left alone for a time with Moon Lady.

"If you should be blessed with offspring," she said, speaking softly but urgently to Moon Lady, "I advise you to be on your guard in respect of a certain person, lest you, like myself, should be the victim of underhand attacks."

"Sister, I understand you," said Moon Lady, whose sobs were choking her. She had then to leave the room, for the servant Kiu Tung appeared, and announced the arrival of the anxiously awaited magician Pan from the 'Temple of the Five Sacred Mountains.' The sickroom was hastily cleared and fumigated, while all the women crept into the next room, in order to peep at the magician and listen to his words.

Now they could see the magician, accompanied by Hsi Men, approaching the pavilion. He was clad in a short black horsehair gown, tied about the waist with a rope girdle of many colors. On his head he wore a tall black magician's hat, on which five mountains were depicted, surrounded by reddish clouds. At his back, thrust into the many-colored rope girdle, he carried an ancient bronze sword with diagonal wavelike markings. His feet were thrust into coarse, down-trodden bast sandals. In his right hand he held a five-colored exorcist's fan. Above his black, piercing eyes, round as apricots, his curving eyebrows swept steeply upwards. From the corners of his square-cut mouth hung a pair of long, gray, ragged whiskers. His expression was intimidating, and men trembled in his presence. If he had not been a cloud-wandering disciple of Tao one might have taken him for a supernatural being, who had just arrived from the Isles of the Blessed.

Now he had entered through the gate and had turned the corner of the spirit wall. But before he set foot on the steps of the corridor which led to Mistress Ping's bedroom he took two steps backward, as though an invisible apparition had barred his progress, and he murmured, under his breath, a few magic formulae. Then he continued on his way, and entered the sickroom, where he took a seat on a chair by the head of the bed.

Motionless he stared at the sick woman with his mysteriously penetrating eyes. Then he stood up, drew his sword from behind his back, and brandished it in the air for a time, while his feet made curious striding movements and his mouth uttered mystic sentences. Now he went with Hsi Men into the adjacent veranda room. At his request a small incense table was placed in the open veranda. First Hsi Men had to ignite a bundle of incense sticks; then he himself burned a number of strips of paper inscribed with magical formulae, and sprinkled the ashes with holy water from a flask which he had brought with him. Then, turning towards the park, he cried with a loud voice: "Lord of the Spirits, appear!"

At the foot of the steps leading up to the veranda a little whirl-wind suddenly sprang up, which gradually grew denser and assumed the form of a spectral apparition. The magician raised his hands in conjuration, and stretched them out towards the apparition, crying: "Hear me, O Lord of the Spirits! She who was born a Li of the household of Hsi Men has called upon me to help her in her need. A specter prowls about here at night and terrifies her in her sleep. Send me six of thy protective spirits, that I may catch this specter!"

He closed his eyes and waited awhile in a posture of convulsive ecstasy. As he awakened from his trance the apparition dissolved and disappeared. Hsi Men now accompanied him to the belvedere, and there the magician spoke to him: "The poor lady has done someone a wrong in a former life, on account of some sort of love affair, and now, as a punishment, she is visited by the ghost of the wronged man."

"Cannot one appease the offended spirit by sacrifices?"

"No. And since his cause is just, not even the Judge of the Under-world has power over him," replied the magician. Then noticing Hsi Men's dejected bearing, he continued: "What is the age of your Sixth?"

"Seven and twenty."

"I will sacrifice to her star of destiny and make the test of the life lamps."

"When and where will you offer the sacrifice, and what prep-arations must I make?"

"This night, at midnight, is the right time, and this is the right place. I need a circular altar hill of white ashes on which to place the seven and twenty life lamps.

"Around the altar of ashes the ground must be covered with a wide border of yellow silk. For the sacrifice neither flesh nor wine is required, but merely a broth of rice, barley, wheaten meal, beans, olives, and dates. The lamps have to be roofed over by an honorific umbrella. Prepare yourself worthily for the sacrifice by fasting and earnest recollection, and clothe yourself in a simple dark blue gown.

While I offer the sacrifice you will kneel in silence at the edge of the altar and gaze with humility upon the ground. And you will see to it that we are absolutely undisturbed. Let any dogs or other domestic animals be carefully confined!"

Hsi Men gave the necessary directions and spent the rest of the day quietly in his library, in the company of Beggar Ying. After he had taken a bath, changed his linen, and donned a clean, simple blue gown, he partook of a frugal supper with the magician and Friend Ying, and at the hour of the third drum beat he and the magician went alone to the place where the altar had been prepared in the shadowy park. First of all, the seven and twenty life lamps, under the threefold shelter of an honorific umbrella, were kindled on the white bed of ashes. While the magician seated himself on a high chair, Hsi Men, with his eyes on the ground, knelt humbly at the edge of the altar. All was absolutely silent. No human being or animal was near them.

With his long beard flowing downwards from his chin, his gaze directed towards the constellation of the Great Bear, and swinging his bare sword, the magician sat awhile on his high chair, uttering unintelligible rhythmical phrases, in the intervals between which he inhaled the air into his lungs with all his might. Now he rose from his seat and slowly paced three times round the altar, lighting an incense stick as he began each circuit. Returning to his chair, he threw up his arms and uttered a loud incantation.

Suddenly a clap of thunder was heard; and although overhead a bright moon was shining in the starry sky, an absolute darkness enveloped the neighborhood of the altar, while the air was filled with a mysterious roaring. It was like the howling of tigers, the snorting of dragons. It was a roaring that forced its way through doors and windows, that bowed the flowers and leaves, that scattered flocks of birds, so that the wild goose cried for her lost mate, while the gulls and herons in the tree tops took to flight, and the moon fairy fearfully closed the portals of the moon-palace. So must it have sounded when the great magician Lia tse rode upon the winds and the air resounded with his mighty voice.

The stormy wind swept by in three tremendous blasts; then it crept like an icy breath across the altar and with a single puff extinguished all the twenty-seven life lamps.

Hastily the magician leaped down from his high chair and cried to Hsi Men, who was cowering on the ground: "Stand up! Our prayer has not found hearing. The Lord of the Spirits refuses his aid to your sinful Sixth. All her life lamps are extinguished. Between morning and evening she must die."

Hsi Men bowed his head in grief. "And I had counted ten-thousandfold on your help, Master," he said, in a hollow tone.

"The number of our years is predetermined. We cannot escape our destiny. Farewell, I must go."

"What, so late in the night? Will you not be my guest until the morning?"

"I have renounced the world and all its ways. I am accustomed to making my bed on the dewy grass, to dwelling in the woods and hills, to resting in temples and cloisters. My way lies where chance leads me."

While Hsi Men escorted his strange guest to the gate, he privately told his servants to bring him a bolt of dark sackcloth and three ounces of silver. "Here, Master, is a trifling recompense for your trouble," he said to the magician. But the man shook his head.

"I follow the exalted Tao which is prescribed by highest Heaven, and have taken the solemn vow to renounce earthly treasures. I must not break my vow."

After repeated urging he finally consented to accept the bolt of cloth, which would provide him with a new gown, and allowed the lay brother who had accompanied him to carry it for him.

"Do not forget that your fast must be continued until tomorrow morning!" he reminded Hsi Men as he was leaving him. "And refrain from entering the sickroom tonight, for otherwise evil influences might be transferred to your person."

He crossed his arms over his breast in greeting, and disappeared into the darkness of the night.

In downcast mood Hsi Men repaired to the library, where Beggar

Ying was waiting for him. He sadly informed him of the unfavorable result of the rite of the life lamps.

"You must resign yourself: for the number of our years is predetermined by Fate," his friend advised him. "One can do nothing against the powers of Destiny." Outside the fourfold drum beat of the night watch announced the second hour of the morning.

"You are tired and disturbed, dear friend, do at last allow yourself some sleep!" he continued. "As for me, it is time I went home."

"The servant, Lai An, will light you on your way. Farewell!"

For some time after Beggar Ying had gone Hsi Men sat alone in his library, which was dimly lit by a single wax candle. But his heart was so heavy that solitude oppressed him.

"It is true that he bade me remain in solitude until the morning," he told himself, "but I can't endure this sitting in silence. If I die of my punishment it is all one to me—but I must see her and speak to her!"

And disregarding the magician's instructions, he made his way to Mistress Ping's bedroom. She was lying awake, her head buried in the pillows, and as he entered she turned her pale face towards him. "My Ko ko, why have you left me alone all the afternoon and evening?" she asked reproachfully.

"Master Pan bade me observe the strictest solitude."

"And what of his rite of the lamps?"

"The result was excellent."

"Dear Ko ko, don't try to deceive me. I know how it is with me. Just now his ghost appeared to me again. He was accompanied by two other men, and he threatened that next time he would take me away with him. 'Your magician has no power over me,' he said, scornfully. 'The Judge of the Realm of Shades has heard my complaint against you. Tomorrow I am to come again and execute his judgment.'"

Hsi Men was overcome by violent emotion.

"Dear sister, don't allow yourself to be disquieted by the ghost. I hope you will remain with me for some time yet. But if against expectation you have suddenly to leave me, then I myself will close my eyes and will breathe no more, and will gladly follow you in death, as truly as my name is Hsi Men."

She tenderly encircled his neck with her two hands and replied, shaken with sobs:

"My Ko ko, I too had hoped to live beside you until the snow of age had bleached our hair. But it was not to be. Let me profit by the brief span of time during which my eyes are still open to say, in these last hours of all, a few last words. You have a great household under you, you have extensive business dealings, and you fill a responsible position in public life. Yet you lack a truly reliable friend, a loyal and helping hand. Therefore be cautious in all your doings, and beware of overhasty or capricious resolves. Treat your First with particular care and consideration, for she is shortly expecting a child. Think, too, what you owe to your office, and in future do not so often indulge in drink. Hitherto I have loyally done my best to advise you when in many important matters you have not known what course to take. Who will replace me as an honest counsellor when I am dead? That is my only anxiety."

At these words Hsi Men felt as though his bowels were being cut to pieces with sharp daggers.

"I know, I know, dear sister," he sobbed. "But don't worry too much about me. Best of all I should like to die with you; I cannot endure that you should leave me so soon."

He had to promise her that the two maids and the nurse, as she had already arranged with Moon Lady, should still be employed in the household. Then, at her urgent request, he left her and went to Moon Lady. He told her of the result of the midnight lamp rite in the park, and described, with profound emotion, his parting from the dying woman.

"She has just charged me with her dying wishes. And she was still quite clear in her mind when I was talking to her. May Heaven grant her a merciful end! She was always such a kind creature; she never wronged any member of this household by a single word. Tell me, how shall I live without her?"

He was so shaken that he could speak no longer; and Moon Lady too was overcome with emotion.

In her own pavilion the sick woman had given her last orders. The maid Pear Blossom and the nurse, Ju I, had made up her bed for the last time and had laid her back in a more comfortable position.

"How late is it?" were her last words.

"The fourth watch of the night is almost over. But the cock has not yet crowed," the nurse had replied.

Then she fell asleep. Mother Fong and the nun Wang had fallen asleep long ago. Now the maid and the nurse also were overcome with weariness, and slept. Pear Blossom may have been lying for half an hour in a profound slumber, when she dreamed that her sick mistress had descended from her bed, had shaken her by the shoulder, and with the words: "Take good care of the house! Now I must go!" had left the room.

In bewilderment, Pear Blossom woke with a start. The silver lamp was still burning on the table. She rose, went over to the sick woman's bed, and bent over her, closely examining her face. Alas, no breath was passing her lips! A lovely woman had dreamed out her dream of springtide!

The horrified maid shook the other inmates of the pavilion out of their sleep, and when these had confirmed the sad fact they hastened to inform Hsi Men and Moon Lady, who rapidly dressed themselves and hurried off to the deathbed, taking two steps at a stride. They lifted the bedclothes, and there, in truth, lay the poor Sixth in her short pink nightgown, stiff and still, never to move again. Her features were quite unchanged, and her body was even now warm to the touch.

In despair Hsi Men flung himself upon the lifeless form, pressed the soft cheeks between his hands, and began to lament aloud: "Sixth, my dear, kind, unhappy sister! Why have you left me? Now I too wish to live no longer! What is life to me without you?"

Moon Lady, the maids, the nurse, and Hsi Men's four other wives, who had hastened thither in the meantime, joined in his cries of woe, in a sobbing chorus, and soon the room was echoing with their loud weeping and lamentation. Moon Lady, who was the first to recover her calm, proposed to dress the corpse immediately, while it was still warm and unchanged. But for the moment Hsi Men held it fast in his embrace, and would not make way for them. Incessantly stroking the dead face, he now began to make despairing accusations against himself:

"May the punishment of Heaven fall upon me! Have you ever, dear sister, in the three years which you have spent with me, had a single happy day? I, I alone am guilty of your early death! I was luring you into a disastrous pitfall when I took you to myself!"

Moon Lady could not continue to listen to these exaggerated self-reproaches. "Whoever did have a happy day beside you, if not she?" she demanded. "We must all go the same way soon or late, when the count of years which Fate has allotted to us is full. You go too far in your grief. And now you must leave the dead. One should deal with a corpse at a respectful distance. If you bend so close above her face, noxious influences may be transferred to you."

She turned to Sunflower and Jade Fountain.

"Here is the key of her clothes press. Go and bring some of her clothes so that we may dress her together as is seemly."

"Let them choose really beautiful clothes, those that she liked best to wear," added Hsi Men, who under the influence of Moon Lady's sensible words was gradually recovering his sober senses.

Moon Lady described to them in detail some recently completed articles of clothing which the dead woman had worn with especial pleasure, and presently Sunflower and Jade Fountain returned with a complete outfit, consisting of a chemise, stockings, trousers, a tunic, a skirt, three upper garments, and a crimson mantle. First the dead woman's hair was dressed, and adorned with four golden brooches, and a blue silk kerchief was placed in her hand.

"Which were her favorite shoes?" asked Sunflower.

"The flame-colored ones with the golden heels," said Gold Lotus. "She wore them only twice."

"No, that pair would not be a good choice for her entry into the

Realm of Shades," objected Moon Lady. "With them she might fall into one of the fiery pits. Bring rather the other pair, which she wore recently when she visited her sister-in-law. The brown silk shoes with the golden heels."

Obediently they brought the desired pair, and then, with seven hands and eight feet, they busied themselves with clothing the body from head to foot. After this the corpse was lifted onto a bier, and this was carried into the front reception rooms, Hsi Men leading the way. In the central hall it was gently laid to rest upon blankets and pillows, and surrounded with a curtain. At the head of the bier was placed a small table for offerings of food, an incense table was set up, and a death lamp was lighted. To the right and left of the bier two servants had to take up their positions. One had to strike upon a chink-stone of jade, in the form of two sides of a triangle, which hung from a double ring under a turretlike stand. The other had to burn incense and paper spirit money.

After the body had been carried out the women returned to their apartments, and Moon Lady locked the death chamber. The maids and the nurse, who remained in the pavilion, had thoroughly to fumigate the other rooms, while old Fong, loudly wailing and snuffling, lamented her dead mistress, and the nun Wang recited sutra after sutra and implored the "Bodhisattva of Paths and Stairs" to provide a kindly escort for the departed.

In the gray dawn, just as the crowing of the first cock was heard, the hastily-summoned District Necromancer Hsue arrived. He noted the time of decease and made out the prescribed certificate of death. Then he opened the *Black Mystery Book* of prognostications and announced:

"In her former life the deceased was the son of a certain Wang family in Pinchow. At that time she incurred the guilt of slaughtering a lambing ewe. For this wrong, although she was rich and happily married, she has had to atone by deadly sickness. In her future existence she will be a daughter of a certain Yuen family in Kai fong fu in the province of Honan; in her youth she will be ailing, but at twenty she will marry a rich man, and she will die, after a happy marriage, at the age of forty-two, in consequence of emotional excitement."

Questioned by Hsi Men as to a suitable day for the funeral, he turned over the leaves of the calendar and decided that the eighth of the tenth month would be a fitting day for the opening of the grave, and that the twelfth of the tenth month would be a suitable day for the funeral. Since Mistress Ping had died on the seventeenth of the ninth month, the burial would take place in the fourth week after her decease.

The sky was red in the east when Hsi Men escorted the District Necromancer to the gate. He was tired and unnerved, but sleep was not to be thought of that day. There were many other arrangements to be made. Servants must be dispatched in all directions, to notify friends and relations of the death. Tai A was sent to the Lion Street shop, and Pen Se to another shop outside the city wall, with instructions to order an enormous quantity of white mourning for the household. Another messenger had to hurry off to Master Chow, and ask him to come to the house with a dozen journeymen. A third messenger was sent to the yamen, to announce that on account of a death in the family his master would not be able to attend the court that day.

In the midst of all this bustle it suddenly occurred to Hsi Men that he had quite forgotten to procure a portrait of the dead woman. He summoned his confidential agent Lai Pao.

"Do you know a capable master who could paint a truthful portrait of my Sixth?" he asked.

"I should recommend Master Han, who has already supplied us with various wall paintings. He was formerly in the Imperial service and is an excellent portrait painter."

"Good, then be off and bring him here quickly!"

As a result of all the various fatigues and excitements of this sleepless night Hsi Men was in a bad temper. He scolded the maids and kicked the menservants. And when he had no excuse for giving orders or awarding blame, he knelt beside the corpse upon its bier and gave himself up without restraint to bewailing his loss. He looked worn out, was unwashed and uncombed, and had as yet eaten no breakfast. Moon Lady could not bear to see him like this.

"He is absolutely wearing himself out," she told the other wives. "The dead are dead, and will not be brought back to life by lamenting. This wailing and lamenting is in his case like an endless thread, which will not break. Three nights in succession he has not closed his eyes; he is uncombed and unwashed; he has not touched his morning soup, and if to this we add all the agitations of the night, no man could stand it, even if his nerves were of iron. If he goes on like this he will collapse with exhaustion."

As she was speaking these last words young Chen entered the room. He was carrying a bolt of white silk under his arm.

"Here is the stuff for mourning robes and mourning handkerchiefs," he told Moon Lady. "Each of you can cut off as much as she needs."

Moon Lady saw that he was relieved of his burden; then she said: "Be so good as to ask him to take something to eat here! It will soon be dinnertime, and he hasn't had a bite of food or a mouthful of tea."

"Oh, I would rather not irritate him," young Chen replied. "The servant who wanted to know if he wouldn't take some breakfast was almost kicked to death."

"If you won't ask him I must send someone else," said Moon Lady, and she summoned Tai A.

"Your master has had nothing in his stomach since yesterday. You must take him some breakfast, and you must absolutely force him to take something at last."

"He won't be able to do that unhelped. But if you would get his friends Uncle Ying and Uncle Hsia Hsi Ta to come, and would have a breakfast set before them, I will wager that our master would keep them company at table," said the shrewd young man.

"Well, of course, you ought to know!" said Moon Lady, smiling. "You, who are lodged like a worm in his bowels, understand his peculiarities better than all of us put together! But how do you arrive at this presumption of yours?"

"It is not difficult to understand. Those two are his best friends, who must never be absent on any festive occasion, whether great or small. And they always put him in a good humor, no matter how out of temper he may have been before their arrival."

Moon Lady accordingly took his advice and hastily sent the lad Kiu Tung to fetch the two friends. Very soon they appeared, and were ushered into the front reception hall, where they fell on their knees before the soul tablet of the deceased, and uttered, as was seemly, a short cry of lamentation, constantly repeating the words: "O, our dear, kind, gentle sister-in-law!"

"These accursed oily-mouths!" hissed Gold Lotus, listening behind the curtain, to the Third, who was standing beside her. "Aren't we by any chance dear and kind and gentle?"

The two friends, having risen to their feet, were greeted by Hsi Men, and led into an adjacent room, where they were joined by Master Warm.

"When did she actually die?" inquired Beggar Ying.

"At the time of the fourth night watch, about the second hour of the morning."

"Strange! About that time I had a singular dream. I dreamt that you sent a messenger to me, inviting me to a banquet. I hurried off to join you. You were dressed in festive red and you showed me two brooches, which looked exactly alike. 'A pity that one is broken in two,' you said. I examined them closely for quite a long while. Then I said to you: 'And what is especially regrettable is that the jade one is broken. The unbroken one is not of jade at all, as you believe, but of ordinary soapstone.' I awoke, and at once I thought to myself that the dream had an unfavorable interpretation. My wife wanted to know why I had been sighing in my sleep. I replied that she must wait until the morning; then she would know. And then, when I saw your servant in white mourning, it was clear to me at once what the dream had meant."

Hsi Men had listened pensively.

"Strange, but this night I had an exactly similar dream," he said. "Friend Ti had sent me six brooches from the Eastern Capital and the finest of all was broken in two. When I woke, and began to tell Moon Lady of my dream, Pear Blossom came to tell me that my poor Sixth had just died."

He was once again overcome by a violent outburst of grief, and began to indulge in dismal reflections concerning the aimlessness of his future existence.

"What wrong have I committed that Heaven should chastise me so?" he cried despairingly. "First it takes my child, and then my beloved wife. What does it mean to me even if I can fill the Great Scales in the heavens with my gold? That is no substitute for lost happiness. No, I have no desire to go on living!"

"Dear friend, I understand your grief," said Beggar Ying, consolingly, "but you must think a little of the obligations which life imposes upon you. You have a large family. You fill an important office, you have a future before you, and many people look up to you as to the summit of Tai shan. You are their stay and their support. What would become of your wives if you were suddenly to die? But you are generally so sensible, you really don't need advice from another. It is right that you should bewail the loss of your Sixth, who has left this life so long before her time, and that you should have a solemn soul mass read, and prepare a burial place that will be worthy of her; but when that is done let there be an end of mourning: then, find your way back to life!"

His words were not without effect. Hsi Men wiped the last tears from his cheeks and reached for the tea bowl. Then he bade Tai A order from the kitchen a sufficient breakfast for himself, Beggar Ying, Hsia Hsi Ta, and Master Warm.

CHAPTER THIRTY-TWO: *Master Han makes the Dead live again in his Picture. The Groom Shu Tung secretly departs with swelling Sails*

WHILE HSI MEN was still sitting over breakfast at the octagonal table in the western wing—the original company having been increased to eight persons by the addition of young Chen, the business manager Han Tao Kwo, and the two brothers of Moon Lady, who had come to offer their condolences—the painter Han appeared, accompanied by Lai Pao. Hsi Men led him, followed by the whole company, to the curtained enclosure in the great hall where the deceased was lying in state. The artist raised the "Banner of the Thousand Autumns" that veiled her face, and remained for a time absorbed in the attentive consideration of her features. Despite the fact that the dead woman had suffered from protracted illness, they were in no way disfigured; indeed, apart from their waxen paleness they still appeared so instinct with life and so worthy of love that at the sight of them Hsi Men was once more seized with emotion.

Master Han now drew his brush from his sleeve pocket, opened his color box, and set to work, while Lai Pao and Kiu Tung held outstretched before him the silk-covered scroll which he had brought with him.

In reverent silence the others stood round him and followed with eager attention the swift movements of the artist's hand.

"Master," said Beggar Ying, "the face you see before you is the face of an invalid. In former days it was fuller and even lovelier."

"I know," replied the artist. "If I mistake not, I have already seen her. On the first of the fifth month did she not visit the 'Temple of the Five Sacred Mountains' in order to sacrifice and burn incense?"

"That is so," replied Hsi Men. "Then she was still strong and well. Exercise your utmost skill, Master! I want two portraits of her; one half-length and one full-length. As your fee you shall have ten ounces of silver and a bale of silk."

"I hear your command. You may rely upon me," replied Master Han, and he resumed his work with redoubled zeal. First he finished the half-length portrait, which was greeted with general admiration. What jade-smooth delicacy, what flowerlike loveliness in the features, what natural freshness in the coloring! Hsi Men was greatly pleased with the result, and he immediately bade Tai A to carry the picture to the back apartments, and show it to Moon Lady and the other wives.

"The master is asking for the ladies' judgment on the picture," said Tai A. "If they see any fault in the likeness, will they kindly mention it, so that the artist can improve it."

"Extremely flattering!" said Gold Lotus, disapprovingly. "She may perhaps have looked like that as a young girl, but not as his wife. Well, let him make his kowtow to the picture. But I'd like to know if he'll have the rest of us painted when we are dead? We've just as good a claim."

"Of course, it was only in her best days that she looked so well," said Sunflower and Jade Fountain, simultaneously. "Besides, her lips were not so full; they were thinner."

"And her left eyebrow was higher and both were more curved," said Moon Lady. "Nevertheless, it's amazing how well the painter has caught her likeness."

"He saw her once in the 'Temple of the Five Sacred Mountains,' burning incense," Tai A explained. "He remembered her features as he saw them then."

A servant entered and requested that the picture should be taken back. Neighbor Kiao had come, and wished to see it. So Tai A carried it back to the front of the house.

"The ladies think that her lips were really thinner, that her left eyebrow was higher, and that both eyebrows were more curved," he informed the artist.

"That is easily altered," replied the latter, and taking up his brush, with a few strokes he had made the desired improvements.

"As natural as though it were living!" said Neighbor Kiao, in commendation. "It has only to breathe!"

Hsi Men gladly paid the master the promised fee, and as further reward he had a sumptuous meal set before him, at which he three times offered him a brimming beaker with his own hands. He begged that he would first of all put the finishing touches to the half-length portrait, so that it might as soon as possible be hung above the soul tablet of the dead in the great hall. The full-length portrait he could finish at home at his leisure. It must show the dead woman in her finest array, and at the funeral it would be carried in front of the coffin.

That evening Hsi Men made his bed on a simple couch of bast mats, enclosed by screens in a corner of the great hall. Not until the morrow did he repair to Moon Lady's apartments to wash and dress his hair.

On the third day, before a great throng of relatives and acquaintances, and in the presence of the District Necromancer Hsue, the solemn ceremony of laying the body in the coffin was performed. A troop of bonzes from the "Cloister of Gracious Recompense" accompanied the ceremony with their prayers and hymns, and performed the funeral music. A picture of the Buddha was set up, and a sacrificial mass was read, while incense and paper spirit money was burned. After the body, now in full dress, had been bedded in the coffin, four further dresses were laid in the latter. In the mouth of the corpse was placed a large pearl, and in each corner a packet of small silver coins was laid on the floor of the coffin. Hsi Men had insisted on this, although the elder Hua had sought to dissuade him, saying that sooner or later the valuables would be stolen. Then the coffin lid was nailed down with the "Nails of Eternal Life," and the ceremony reached its close, to the accompaniment of sobs and lamentations in which all the witnesses joined.

On the last day of the first week of mourning sixteen bonzes from the "Cloister of Gracious Recompense" came to the house and held a solemn mass for the dead in the Buddhist manner. On the same day the High Priest Wu from the Jade Emperor's Temple came to offer his condolences, and obtained for his Taoist temple the privilege of continuing the family services during the second week in the Taoist manner. Such family services meant a handsome profit for the officiating priests, so that it was important that he should be on the spot and safeguard his interests.

Night after night, during the four weeks that preceded the funeral, Hsi Men continued to sleep on his draughty bed of mats beside the coffin, retiring in the morning to the bedroom of his First. At night, and until he rose, he had always young Shu Tung, his favorite body servant, beside him, while it was the office of the maid Jade Flute to clear away the bed of mats in the morning. For some little time, therefore, the two servants had come to know each other better, and every morning, when Hsi Men rose from his couch and withdrew to the rear apartments, they indulged in a little gossip and some amorous skirmishing.

One day in the second week of mourning Hsi Men rose very early. The other inmates of the house were still asleep. The maid and the young manservant took this opportunity of visiting the library pavilion in the park, and indulging in a brief hour of secret, and, so they hoped, undisturbed lovemaking. But this same morning, unhappily, Gold Lotus also had risen early, and had gone to the reception hall in the hope of finding Hsi Men alone. To her astonishment she found that he had left his bed, though it had not been cleared away, and the hall was forsaken. She went out again, making for the women's apartments, and on the way thither she met the boy Hua Tung, who had just been sweeping one of the courtyards.

"Hey, boy, just put your broom aside for a moment and run an errand for me!" she said. "Go to the son-in-law of the house and ask him to give you a little white silk to make a mourning skirt;

my mother is still without one. She would like to take the silk with her when she goes home today."

"He will probably be asleep still, but I'll go to him at once," replied the servant, obediently propping his broom in a corner. When he returned a little later he informed her:

"Master Chen says the distribution of material is not in his department. You should apply to Pen Se or Shu Tung, who have charge of the stock. At this early hour Pen Se won't be here, so only Shu Tung is available."

"Well, where is the fellow? Go and find him!"

"He's just gone by. He was making for the park. I expect he was going to the library pavilion, where the mourning material is kept."

"Oh, then I'll go and look for him myself. I was thinking of going that way. You can go back to your work."

And she hurried off to the park. When she came to the library pavilion she could hear, from inside, the sound of happy chuckling and laughter. She quickly flung the door open, to find the maid and the manservant closely embraced on the divan.

"This is a pretty way to behave here!" she scolded the surprised pair, who started apart in alarm, and fell trembling at her feet. Gold Lotus gazed at them awhile in silence, with a cold, mocking smile on her lips.

"Run and bring me a piece of white silk for a mourning skirt, and some white linen for a mourning hood!" she bade the manservant, speaking harshly. Obediently he disappeared into the store room and brought her what she desired. In the meantime she had not vouchsafed a word or a glance to the kneeling maid. And now, as she walked towards her pavilion, with the material over her arm, she took not the slightest notice of the girl, who was anxiously trotting behind her. The culprit did not leave her side until they had reached the pavilion; there she flung herself on the floor and implored Gold Lotus not to report her to Hsi Men.

"First of all, out with the truth, you wretched bit of catsmeat!" Gold Lotus snorted at her. "How often have you been with him?"

And after the maid had assured her that this was the first time, and that she had come into closer contact with Shu Tung during the recent period of mourning because they both had duties in the reception hall, she continued:

"You want me to forgive you and not report you. Well, I will do as you wish, but only on three conditions."

"Ask what you like! I will do anything for you, mistress!" said the maid, beseechingly.

"Then in the first place: In future you will tell me exactly what has happened during the day in your mistress's rooms. If I should hear of anything that you have not told me I shall report you after all. Secondly: If I ask you to do me any service, you must obey me. Thirdly: You must tell me how it is that your mistress is pregnant again after long years of unfruitfulness."

Jade Flute, thus driven into a corner, could not refuse to divulge the secret of Sister Pi's magic potion, even to the last details. Gold Lotus impressed these on her memory and released the maid. Jade Flute herself said nothing of what had happened. But young Shu Tung, feeling that the icy smile with which the dreaded Fifth had regarded him could bode nothing good, preferred to slip away that very day. He was convinced that his career in Hsi Men's household was ended, as a result of that morning's exposure, so he preferred to avoid the thrashing which he felt was to be expected by a timely flight. But first he appropriated various articles of clothing from the laundry, to which he had access. He had already saved ten ounces in bullion, but this was not enough for the journey which he had in mind. He therefore hit upon the reprehensible plan of getting a further twenty ounces out of the cashier, Fu, by asserting that Hsi Men had told him to draw this sum in order to buy a further consignment of white material for mourning garments at a draper's outside the city wall. Since he, as well as Pen Se, had been entrusted with the purchase of material, the cashier did not hesitate to pay him the required twenty ounces. Thus abundantly furnished with cash, he went straight to the harbor and booked a passage on a passenger junk which was sailing for his native city of Suchow.

518

A few hours later his disappearance was already commented upon. The two Head Eunuchs, Pi and Liu, who were friends of Hsi Men's, sent him that morning a tray full of sacrificial food, sacrificial wine, and spirit money, announcing that they proposed to visit him in a day or two. In order to save them the expense of having white garments made for them, which as a matter of form should be worn by the visitors to a house of mourning, Hsi Men decided to send them, with a courteous message, some white material from his own stock. But the key to the store room had last been in the possession of Shu Tung. He accordingly sent for Shu Tung, but the man was nowhere to be found. Then Fu the cashier came forward and reported that Shu Tung had come to him early that morning, and had drawn twenty ounces on Hsi Men's behalf, in order to buy mourning material outside the city wall.

Hsi Men, of course, knew nothing of any such purchase, and sent to all the drapers outside the wall, asking for news of the missing man. But his messengers came back without the required information. Then Moon Lady became suspicious, and spoke to Hsi Men: "There is something wrong. Probably the man has done something stupid and has run off in secret with the twenty ounces. Let someone have a look in the laundry! Perhaps he has taken something else."

Her suspicion was confirmed when Hsi Men sent a messenger to the laundry. The key of the store room, which had last been in the fugitive's keeping, was hanging peacefully on the wall by the door. When the door was opened and the linen in the great linen press was counted, it was seen that a whole consignment of washing was missing. Hsi Men therefore denounced the man to the city sheriff, and obtained a warrant of arrest against the dishonest servant. The incident had greatly disturbed him. Shu Tung had been his favorite servant, and had possessed his full confidence.

Apart from this, he was greatly overcome by the confusion and the fatigues of this time of mourning, and was feeling excessively irritable. Day after day, early and late, the many visits of condolence continued; he had to show himself, entertain the callers, and drink with them, and so many times a day he had to change his clothes, and attend the solemn sacrifices and soul masses, and the performances of funeral plays. And on the top of all there was this trouble in his household!

At last the eighth day of the tenth month had arrived, when Hsi Men had to go to his family burying ground outside the walls, to be present at the opening of the grave, at which the District Necromancer presided. At his house, in the meantime, the assembled priests of the "Cloister of Delightful Prosperity" read the nth Buddhistic soul mass.

On the following day a beginning was made with the erection at the burial ground of the tents of matting, in which the many guests to be expected on the day of the funeral would be received and given refreshment. Enormous quantities of food and wine were sent out, and other preparations were made.

The day before the interment was devoted to the performance of a series of suitable plays which had reference to the ultimate problems of human life: for example, the drama of "The Butterfly Dream of the Wise Chuang tse," the drama of "Plum blossoms in the Snow," the drama of the wise "Lao tse, how riding on a black Ox he disappeared through the Han ku Pass," the drama of "The Hero in the Cave, who with his Magic Sword slew the Yellow Dragon," and other mystery plays besides.

And then came the twelfth of the tenth month, the great day of the interment. For this day Hsi Men had asked his friend the River Prefect Chow to place fifty men-at-arms at his disposal, ten of whom were told off to guard the house, while the other forty, on horseback, and armed with bows and lances, would escort the coffin out of the city, riding in two files, on either side. He had also been granted twenty guards from the District Yamen, who would march beside the coffin and clear the way. Twenty more were on guard at the entrance to the burial ground.

From an early hour of the morning the streets and lanes of the neighborhood echoed with the neighing of horses and the rattling of carriages, which were bringing, from far and near, mandarins of every grade, relations, friends, acquaintances, and neighbors, to take part in the funeral procession. There were more than a hundred palanquins, in which the women of the household, and of Hsi Men's kinsmen and acquaintances, took their seats, and there were also dozens of little palanquins containing the maids and the inmates of the various flower gardens. All Hsi Men's wives and all his people took part in the procession; only Snowblossom was left behind, in the company of the nuns Wang and Pi, in order to look after the house, while Ping An, with ten men-at-arms, had to guard the gate.

On his lofty wooden platform, at the eighth hour of the morning, the leader of the funeral procession, with eight blows of his mallet, gave the signal for the sixty-four bearers to lift the coffin. And the endless procession began its deliberate progress.

In front went a long row of inscribed banners and honorific pennants, and the innumerable figures and objects of gilt and silvered papier-mâché which were destined to be burned. Before the coffin strode a troop of bonzes from the "Cloister of Gracious Recompense," who provided the funeral music. Immediately behind the coffin came the palanquins of Moon Lady and Hsi Men's other wives, and then followed, in an endless train, the rest of the participants. Young Chen, who during the whole period of mourning had to represent the son of the house, walked beside the coffin with one hand resting on the bier, as though he were helping to carry it, as befitted a pious son.

It was a clear, sunny day of autumn. No wonder the streets through which the procession passed were thronged with spectators. And all these people sighed with admiration, and were unanimous in the verdict that it was long since they had seen such a handsome "corpse."

On turning out of East Street the procession came to a standstill at a signal from the leader. High Priest Wu of the Jade Emperor's Temple, wearing over his dark red priestly robe a mantle of crane's feathers of five colors, and on his head the nine-storied thunder-and-lightning tiara, and on his feet double-soled shoes of cinnabar red with upturned toes, while in his hand he held his ivory writing tablets, was carried aloft in a chair, on the shoulders of four power-ful bearers, swaying high above the heads of the other participants. Now he turned a little to one side, and at a sign from Hsi Men he suddenly unrolled the full-length portrait of the deceased which had been painted by Master Han. And then, while the person representing the son, young Chen, had to kneel before the portrait in the dusty street, he delivered, in a loud, sonorous voice, which was plainly heard by the near relatives in his more immediate neighborhood, a long encomium to the memory of the deceased.

". . . Her breath of life, indeed, is exhaled into the limpid ether of Heaven, and her body returns to the earth, but in this, her faith-ful likeness, she will continue to live for this and for future genera-tions." So he concluded his long address, swinging the scroll above the heads of the crowd.

While he was descending from his lofty seat and resuming his place in his palanquin the musicians struck up with a mighty clashing and booming, and from the whole procession rose a loud weeping and wailing that echoed to the clouds and shook the earth. At the same time the procession began slowly to move again. From the Southern Gate of the city Hsi Men and the other male mourn-ers, who had hitherto gone on foot, proceeded on their way in the saddle or in their carriages. Only young Chen, as representing the son, had to continue on foot, his hand resting on the bier, until the end of the journey.

Before the entrance to the burial ground Hsi Men's friend, the Camp Commandant Chang, had posted a guard of honor two hundred strong, whose musicians received the approaching proces-sion with the dull thudding of drums and the booming clamor of gongs.

At the hour of noon, after a sacrifice had been offered to Mother Earth, the coffin was slowly lowered into the "Grotto of Desire," and the ceremony without the walls was concluded with a huge, noisy mass banquet under the tents of matting. But at home, after the return from the funeral, the soul tablet, which had hitherto been placed in the front reception hall, had to be removed into the thoroughly cleansed and fumigated bedchamber of the dead woman, and there given a place of honor. Last of all it was the duty of the District Necromancer Hsue to sacrifice to the tutelary spirits of the household, and to purge the house of any evil influences that might still be present by sweeping the ground outside the doors and affixing exorcismal charms to the sills and lintels. Rewarded with a fee of five ounces and a bolt of cloth, he was the last to leave the house of the innumerable persons whose services had been required for the dignified conduct of the funeral. And with this a ceremonial which had lasted four weeks, and had absorbed enormous sums of money, was finally accomplished.

Towards evening, when the last mourners had left and quiet had returned to the house, Hsi Men felt an irresistible urge to visit the pavilion of his dead wife. He wished to pass the night in her bedchamber, in the presence of her soul tablet, which had been set up on the wall facing the window.

Beneath the tablet, leaning against the edge of the frame, was the half-length portrait of the dead woman, drawn on cardboard, while beside it, on the wall, hung the scroll on which her full-length and life-size portrait had been painted. The room was arranged precisely as when it was inhabited; the bed was newly made, with the same bedclothes and pillows as before. Over the backs of chairs hung garments which she had once worn; on the toilet table were all the accessories which she had once employed in dressing her hair, in powdering and painting her face; and a pair of those slender satin slippers peeped out which had formerly enclosed her delicate "golden lilies." On the table, beside the silver lamp, stood her favorite vase, filled with freshly-cut flowers. And there, at the edge of the bed, was the low bed table with its silver fruit and cake dishes, and the two golden goblets, from which she had so often taken yet another sip of sweet wine before falling asleep.

The sight of all these familiar objects filled him with infinite melancholy and drew the hot tears from his eyes. Sighing, he stretched himself out on the bed which Pear Blossom—for Apricot Blossom, the second maid, had already been taken into service by

Sunflower—had made up for him on the low divan against the wall facing the soul tablet. For a long while he lay there, restlessly tossing to and fro, his eyes fixed upon the portrait, which the rays of the moon that slanted into the room illumined with a spectral radiance; until at last beneficent sleep released him from his mournful reflections.

In the morning, when breakfast was served, he had a second place laid for the invisible beloved, and just as he had been wont to do of old, he offered her a little of each dish on the unused plate, and addressing her vacant place, uttered such words as "Please, do begin!" just as though a living woman had been at his side. With astonishment and sympathy the nurse and the maid surreptitiously observed his strange behavior. Next morning it was the same. Three nights in succession he spent in this manner, in the bedchamber of his dead Sixth.

On the third night he felt a longing at a late hour for a bowl of cold tea. He had been entertaining guests all the afternoon, and had gone to bed in a somewhat intoxicated condition. His burning gums were thirsting for a cool drink. Since the maid Pear Blossom had long been fast asleep, and did not hear him call, the young nurse Ju I got up to bring him the desired refreshment. And while she knelt beside him and held the tea bowl to his lips with the one hand, it so chanced that her other hand smoothed the bedclothes over his body. The light touch was enough to bring his blood instantly to boiling point, and to kindle his sensual desires. He drew her to himself, flung his arm around her neck, and pressed his lips upon her mouth. She remained quite motionless, responding in silence to his silent caress, inasmuch as she gently sucked at his tongue, which was playing between his lips, in this manner confessing to him her secret understanding of his need. Without a word he stripped off her thin nightdress and drew her to himself under the blankets. After weeks of voluntary abstinence Nature claimed her rights again.

Presently Ju I ventured for the first time to open her mouth.

"Master, you have honored this despicable maid with your regard," she said softly; "may she hope that she will remain in your household? She will joyfully do everything to serve you."

"You have only to be very nice to me, child, and you shall be happy with me; you shall lack for nothing," he replied, kissing her.

This she heard with delight, and with great good will she joined him, amidst the pillows and blankets, in the wanton frolics of an amorous pair of phœnixes.

Next morning she helped him to dress, and he in return bestowed upon her four golden brooches which had been among the possessions of her dead mistress. The maid, Pear Blossom, realized at once, from the altered bearing of the nurse, what had occurred. While hitherto she had shyly and helplessly trotted at the heels of the maid, who had experience of intercourse with Hsi Men, and had barely ventured to utter half a word in his presence, now all her shyness had suddenly fallen from her, and she exhibited a self-assurance that no longer sought for alien assistance. The maid understood very well that the hitherto clumsy girl had contrived to win her master's favor, and Pear Blossom must silently accustom herself to acknowledging her, from now onwards, as a person equally privileged with herself.

Moreover, the young woman now decked herself out in such a conspicuous style that those in the world outside the pavilion began to notice her and to draw the inevitable conclusion. And presently a general and knowing whispering and giggling went the rounds of the maids and menservants.

CHAPTER THIRTY-THREE: *Mistress Lin receives Hsi Men for the first Time. Young Wang runs in Terror from the Flower Garden*

THE CHANGE WHICH had recently been perceptible in the nurse Ju I, not only in her behavior, but also in her external appearance, naturally did not escape the keen eyes of the Fifth, and a little reflection enabled her to understand the cause of this transformation.

"This must not go on, sister; you positively must speak out!" she said one day to Moon Lady. "It is shameless, the way he carries on with her behind our backs. It began just in the same way with that servant's wife, Lotus Petal. Do you want that scandal repeated to-day? If this vulgar maid has a child by him, how shall we be able to face her? Why, she would laugh at us!"

But Moon Lady was deaf to all her whisperings. She remembered the warning that the Sixth had given her on her deathbed.

"I shall take good care not to interfere in this matter," she replied, coldly. "You always want me to be the spokeswoman, and when the storm breaks the rest of you take shelter, while I am left sitting in the puddle. No, I have learned wisdom from experience. If you don't like it, kindly speak to him yourself."

At which Gold Lotus retired without a word. But at the next opportunity, when the nun Pi was visiting the household, she secretly invited her into her pavilion, gave her an ounce of silver, and ordered from her the same magic potion which she had previously prepared for Moon Lady.

Although Hsi Men had recovered nine-tenths of his spirits, under the healing influence of time, and thanks to the vigorous embraces of his newly-won darling, yet his thoughts often lingered with his departed Sixth.

On one of the last days of the tenth month, while he was lying on the divan in the garden library and taking his siesta, she appeared to him in a dream. It seemed to him that he suddenly heard the faint jingle of the bead curtain as the strings were parted, and saw her enter the room. She was wearing a long, flowing purple shift, with a white, slashed petticoat over it. Her waxen face, around which hung her wildly disordered locks, wore an anxious expression. She floated up to his couch and spoke to him:

"My Ko ko, I have longed to see you again, and to tell you how it has been with me. It is true that I am liberated from my sufferings, but my adversary had me dragged before the Judgment bar of the Realm of Shades, and now I have to do penance for my guilt. Yet thanks to your intercession my punishment is mitigated by three degrees. But my adversary is not yet contented. Now he wishes to retaliate upon you also, and to come for you. That is why I have come, to warn you. Sooner or later you will feel his venomous hand! Be on your guard! Do not go abroad so much, and never drink far into the night. A thousand and ten thousand times, remember my words!"

They embraced, and he burst into tears.

"Where are you going now? Where?" he insisted, sobbing, but she silently withdrew herself from his arms and dissolved into nothingness.

When he woke he was aware of a shadow behind the strings of the bead curtain; and a moment later Gold Lotus entered. She made herself comfortable beside him on the divan.

"So here is the long-sought sleeper!" she said, with a sidelong glance at him. "Do you know your eyelids are quite red?"

"Perhaps I've been sleeping the wrong side up."

"It seems to me the redness is due to tears."

"Why should I have been weeping?"

"Perhaps because you were thinking of someone whom you cherish especially in your heart."

"Nonsense. I don't know whom I cherish especially in or on my heart."

"Then I'll tell you. You cherish the Sixth in your heart; the nurse Ju I lies on your heart; and all the rest of us are long ago turned out of your heart."

"What crazy notions you get!" he cried, with an embarrassed laugh. "But, to speak sensibly: do you by any chance remember what the Sixth was wearing next to her skin when she lay in her coffin?"

"Why do you ask that?"

"I want to know."

"I knew at once that you were with her again in your thoughts. Well, she was wearing a long purple lawn chemise and a slashed petticoat of white silk over it."

Lost in thought, Hsi Men nodded as though in agreement, "Then it was really she," he told himself. And then, aloud: "She has just appeared to me in a dream."

"Then I guessed rightly. With dreams it's just as it is with a cold. What lies deepest in your heart you sneeze out in a dream. Will you think as constantly of the rest of us when we are dead?"

Hsi Men, smiling, drew her to him and pressed a kiss upon her lips. The nearness of her well-tended, musk- and orchid-scented body had an automatic effect on his readily inflammable senses.

Only too willingly she responded. It had long been her secret endeavor to rekindle his old, long-cooled affection. All the greater was her annoyance when they were disturbed by the arrival of Beggar Ying.

"Let him come in!" Hsi Men told the servant who had announced the visitor. The cheerful society of his friend was always a welcome diversion.

"Let him kindly wait until I've gone!" Gold Lotus called angrily after the servant. She had just time to arrange her clothes and slip out of the back door before Beggar Ying entered.

"You've been invisible these last few days!" was Hsi Men's greeting.

"One has one's troubles," sighed the other. "Any visits were out of the question."

"What sort of troubles have you?"

"That a poor rapscallion like myself should be superfluously blessed with a child! If at least it had arrived in the daytime! But no, its mother was taken with her pains in the middle of the night, and out of bed I had to jump and run off for the midwife! And when I came racing back with her, I found in the meantime the child had arrived!"

"A boy or a girl?"

"A boy."

"You silly fellow, then one can only congratulate you! And you speak of trouble! Who is the mother, then? Of course, your Second, little Chun Hua?"

"You've guessed it."

"Well, it serves you right. Who put it into your head to take that wanton little woman into your house? Your First will be properly angry!"

"Won't she! And now, in the middle of winter, such an increase is doubly disastrous. With a rich man like you, of course, it doesn't matter. Such a new-born child is merely another ornament on the Damascus carpet of prosperity! But how can people like us feed and clothe such a little creature? Where is the money for the midwife to come from, and for the banquet which one has to give to one's friends and relations—on the third day to celebrate the washing of the child, and on the thirtieth day as a matter of form? It's enough to send one crazy. I shall just leave my family in the lurch and hide myself in a monastery."

"You a monk! A splendid notion!" cried Hsi Men laughing uproariously. "You'd soon be longing for your warm bed, on your hard monastic bench!"

Beggar Ying took refuge in a dejected silence.

"Come, out with it—how much do you need?" said Hsi Men, in an encouraging tone. "Perhaps I can manage it."

"Oh, if you really would—twenty ounces would do me; of course, against a note of hand. I've brought it with me; here it is."

Hsi Men laughingly waved it away. "Between good friends one needs no note of hand. Hey, just go to your First mistress," he said, turning to the servant who was then bringing them tea," and ask her to give you one of the two packages of silver that are lying in the cupboard behind her bed."

Presently the servant returned with the required package.

"Here, take it! There ought to be fifty ounces there," said Hsi Men, handing the package to Beggar Ying. "It comes, together with the other package, from Censor Sung; they are contributions which he collected for the great banquet which I recently had to give here, at the general request of the provincial bureaucracy, in honor of the Imperial Legate, the High Eunuch Huang. Count it, please, to see if there are really fifty ounces."

Beggar Ying hastily opened the package and counted. "Rather more than fifty," he announced.

"Well, take it all. And what you don't need now, put aside as 'future provision' for your 'reigning darling.'"

Beaming with delight, Beggar Ying thanked his friend in exaggerated terms. "But don't you really want my note of hand?" he asked again.

"Nonsense! I look upon you and your dependents almost as members of my own family. I regard your child as mine no less than yours. We'll educate him at our joint expense. At most, you might make this return: when you are safely past the bothers of the thirtieth day you can lend me your little Chun Hua for a few days."

"Woe and alas!" cried Beggar Ying, in feigned consternation. "Now I have walked into a fine trap!" And laughing, he ran off with his booty.

Since Hsi Men had lost, by the death of his Sixth, that one of his wives for whom he had cherished a genuine, deep, and enduring love, and the only one who could long keep him at home, his old restlessness had revived, urging him once more to visit the flower gardens in search of fresh adventures and experiences. For the embraces of a simple, uneducated maid like Ju I could not in the long run satisfy his pampered and exacting taste.

So he readily agreed when his business friend Huang Se, to whom he had often lent money on interest, and to whom he had secretly granted a special favor, invited him, in recognition of his kindness, to a joyful drinking bout in the flower garden of Mother Chong, to be held on the sixth day of the eleventh month. Besides the host and his partner, Beggar Ying and Master Warm would be of the company.

The guests were entertained by Mother Chong's two daughters, Favorite Perfume and Little Moon, of whom the latter and younger enjoyed Hsi Men's particular favor. And further, four young singing-girls were engaged, who performed scenes from the "Story of the Western Pavilion" and other dramas, with such art and such moving delivery that "the clouds burst and the stones broke loose." Later on they were joined by Little Silver from the neighboring establishment of Mother Wu. And Beggar Ying, with his never-failing humor, saw to it that the mood of the party was joyous and carefree.

At a late hour Hsi Men stole away from the riotous company and withdrew with Little Moon to the quiet, comfortably furnished "Spring Grotto," which was fragrant with musk and orchid. And it was there, between the blankets and pillows of her downy couch, that Little Moon told him something that inflamed his desirous senses and held out a promise of new and exquisite delights.

"Have you seen Cinnamon Bud lately?" she suddenly asked him, as they were conversing.

"Not since her visit of condolence."

"Oh, I know something I could tell you about that."

"And that is?"

She was silent for a time. Then she continued: "After all, I would rather not tell you. She might reproach me for telling tales behind her back."

"My dear child, you can count on my discretion. I shouldn't be so foolish as to betray you."

"Well, you remember the scandal in which she was involved on account of young Wang? You helped her out of a difficult position. Well, recently she has once more had relations with that frivolous young man. For some days past he has been a constant guest in her house, together with a gang of seven boon companions, among whom are your friends Chu Shih Nien and Sun Tien. He has once more let her relieve him of an enormous sum of money, and recently, when he was hard up, he gave Mother Li a fur cloak in pledge, and a pair of golden bracelets of his young wife's."

"That is inexcusable of Cinnamon Bud!" exclaimed Hsi Men. "When I helped her on that occasion she had to give me her express and solemn promise that she would never again get entangled with young Wang. And that's how she keeps her word!"

"Now don't get excited! I haven't done yet. Perhaps you can get something for yourself out of the business!"

"Get what?"

"But you mustn't tell anyone anything about it—not even Beggar Ying!"

"Nonsense! As though I should!"

"Well, listen. Young Wang's mother, who was born a Lin, is a widow, and although she's thirty-five she is still a handsome and graceful woman, a regular seductive vixen. While her son is knocking about in the flower gardens she herself indulges in adventures on the quiet. As a rule she pretends that she is going to this or that convent, in order to fast and pray, so that she can leave the house without exciting remark. In reality she is carried to Mother Wen's, the marriage broker, and old Wen takes her to her lover.

"And further, there's young Wang's little wife, who is only nineteen. She is, as you know, a niece of the High Eunuch Huang of the Imperial Court, and you must already have heard of her incomparable beauty and her culture. Of course, the poor thing takes the dissolute behavior of her miserable husband very greatly to heart, and they have three times cut the cord from her throat with which she has tried to hang herself. To my simple mind, it seems that you ought not to find it difficult, first to win the mother, and then to possess the lovely daughter-in-law."

Aha! this tickled Hsi Men's lustful ears, and his heart swelled with rapture and desire.

"My Tjin tjin," he said, tenderly pressing to his bosom the little powder-face beside him, "you have thought that out magnificently. But how is it that you know all these details?"

"I'll explain. At one time I was often invited to her house, as a singer, and in that way one learns all sorts of things. And then someone told me about it who has himself been introduced to Mistress Lin by old Mother Wen."

"And who is this someone?"

"My first love, who deflowered me, a young merchant from the Southern Provinces. He comes here only now and then, as he prefers hazardous adventures. He has made Mistress Lin's acquaintance."

"My dear child, if in future you'll continue to be sweet and affectionate I'll pay you an allowance of thirty ounces a month. But you mustn't belong to anyone else."

"For thirty, or even for twenty ounces I'd gladly belong only to you."

"It shall be thirty."

Since they were still fully dressed, they gradually began to feel rather hot under the foot-high layer of blankets and cushions.

"Won't you undress and spend the night with me?" she asked.

"I should very much like to. But they'll miss us in front, and recently, in a dream, my Sixth warned me so urgently not to spend the nights in flower gardens. After all, I can come to see you in the daytime."

He threw the heavy bedclothes aside, and bade her quickly undress. Oh, how young and tender she was!

> *Slender as a willow wand*
> *As her chalice half uncloses,*
> *Just to cool her blood, the maid*
> *In the vernal breeze reposes.*

After the clouds had shed their contents they quickly dressed and returned hand in hand to the front of the house. Remembering the warning of the dead, he presently took his leave of the riotous company and had himself carried home.

On the following day he ordered Tai A to discover the address of the marriage broker Wen and to see that she called on him as soon as possible. Since old Wen had formerly acted for Hsi Men's own son-in-law, young Chen would know something about her. So it was to him that Tai A applied.

"You must first go along East Street," young Chen told him, "And then turn southwards toward the Pailou by the 'Bridge of Philanthropy'; then you turn eastward into Wang Lane, and just halfway down the lane you come to a police station. Just opposite this you cross a ruined stone bridge, and then you pass a convent. Then you turn to the west, up a steep lane, and in the third house is a shop where they sell bean curd. Mother Wen lives next door, in the house with a double gate, painted red."

"Oh, please, won't you just repeat all that once more? I've forgotten it already!" said Tai A.

Young Chen did as he wished. Tai A thanked him for the information, saddled his gray horse, and trotted off in the direction indicated.

Turning to the east into Wang Lane at the Pailou by the "Bridge of Philanthropy," he did actually find a tumbledown stone bridge, opposite a police station, halfway down the lane. Crossing this, and proceeding westwards past the "Cloister of Great Compassion," he found that the thoroughfare led into a steep lane, where a sign was suspended in front of the third house, advertising "Fine Bean Curds." In front of this house a woman was spreading asses' dung to dry in the sun.

"Hi, where does the marriage broker Wen live?" he cried to her.

The woman pointed to the house next door, which stood a little higher, and had a double gate, painted red. Tai A sprang quickly from the saddle and tied his horse to a tree. Then he beat a few times with his whipstock on the red gate. A young lad opened it and asked him peevishly what he wanted.

"I come from His Excellency, the District Judge Hsi Men," Tai A explained. "He wishes to speak to Mother Wen without delay."

On hearing Hsi Men's name the lad's features immediately assumed an amiable grin. He introduced himself as the son of the house, and pressing Tai A to enter, he made him take a seat and offered him tea.

"My mother has gone out," he said. "I'll tell her to come and see your master early tomorrow morning."

Tai A did not believe him. "Her donkey is there in the courtyard: I think she must be at home," he said, and he coolly walked past the youth, making straight for the rear apartments. And there, sure enough, was Mother Wen, together with her daughter-in-law and a few nuns, eagerly chattering and drinking tea.

"There you are, Mother Wen!" he cried, taking her by surprise. "Why do you deny that you're at home?"

Mother Wen laughed in embarrassment and murmured a *Wan fu* in greeting.

"It's very kind of you to trouble to come and see me. But today I happen to have guests and can't get away. I'll come early tomorrow. What does your master want of me?"

"That I don't know. He simply ordered me to fetch you as quickly as possible."

She made an obsequious kowtow.

"How do I come to be honored? All these years he has sent for his old Fong and Sisters-in-law Pi and Wang when there was any work for a go-between. How strange that he should suddenly want me! Well, he must have a little patience. He can't expect a dish of beans all in a moment from a cold cookpot! I suppose he wants a new wife for the empty nest of his late Sixth?"

"That I don't know. You'll learn that from him."

"Good. I'll come with you."

Having bidden her son saddle the donkey, she donned a mask,

535

and at a jogging trot she followed the nimble gray to Hsi Men's residence.

The gatekeeper Ping An directed them to the house on the opposite side of the road, for at that moment Hsi Men was in Master Warm's study. He admitted old Wen immediately.

"A long time since I've seen you, Mother Wen!" he said.

At a sign from him his secretary went out, leaving him alone with old Wen. Only Tai A remained standing like a shadow behind the curtain, in order to listen.

"You have to do with noble houses from time to time," said Hsi Men, as he opened the conversation.

"To be sure. Among my clients are the Imperial Prince Yuen, the River Prefect Chow, the Emperor's son-in-law, Master Kiao, Judge Hsia, and many other noble gentlemen."

"Are you by any chance known in the house of the former Minister Wang?"

"Why, certainly! Lady Lin and her lovely daughter-in-law are my especial patronesses."

"Quite so. Then I have a little commission for you. First, accept this!"

He pushed towards her a silver bar of five ounces in weight. Then he spoke for some time in a confidential tone.

"So I rely on you," he concluded, "to arrange for me to meet the Lady Lin as soon as possible. You may be sure of my enduring gratitude."

"Ha, ha!" the old woman laughed; "how do you come to know so much about the noble lady?"

"Oh, one just hears things. As the tree has its shadow, so every woman has her reputation."

"And the Lady Lin has every right to hers. She is really a woman of class, and with her five and thirty years she looks barely thirty. And how cleverly and deliberately she goes to work! Whenever she goes out she's accompanied there and back with a great retinue, so that no one would ever imagine that she could be slipping up a secret path! And she never dreams of setting foot in a lover's house; no, when her son is away she contrives, with the greatest ingenuity, to smuggle him unnoticed into her own home. Naturally there could be no question of her choosing my little rooms for her interviews. So I can't accept your kind present. But simply to oblige you I'd gladly speak a word to her."

"No, keep it; you would seriously offend me by your refusal. Later on you shall have some fine material for a few new dresses."

The old woman kowtowed her thanks.

"Well, if you are so insistent there's nothing for it but to accept. I'll go to Lady Lin at once and watch for your lucky star."

"Do so at once, and then come back to me! I shall wait here for your news. I'd rather not send a messenger to you again, as it might attract attention."

"Good; I'll come back as soon as possible, but it may not be until tomorrow or the day after."

She took her leave of him and hurried out.

First of all she rode home and dismissed her guests. Then she called on Lady Lin.

"Is my lord your son at home?" she asked, coming straight to the point, after a few introductory phrases.

"For some days now he's been gadding about the city," Lady Lin replied, with a sigh. "Unfortunately he has fallen into bad company again; he spends his nights among flowers and willow trees, and he leaves his young wife, who is lovely as a spray of blossoms, deserted at home. She is so worried that she no longer shows herself; she lies in bed all day, weeping."

Mother Wen was relieved to hear this; she would not be disturbed in her interview with Lady Lin.

"Well, I know who could rid your son of his bad companions and lead him back to domestic life," she said, in a confidential tone. "But I don't know if I may speak with perfect frankness?"

"You know that I always value your advice. Tell me just what is in your mind."

"Then I'll tell you his name: it's our District Judge, His Excellency Hsi Men. You will of course have heard of his great wealth;

all our officials are more or less in his debt. Besides his great drug store and dispensary he has four prosperous silk mercer's shops: his trading junks go into the provinces, he does a big salt business with Yangchow, and in Tung ping fu he carries on a roaring trade in incense and wax candles; he has dozens of business managers and agents; you could lose yourself for ever in his fields, and the superfluous grain lies rotting in his granaries. The Chancellor Tsai King in the Eastern Capital is his adoptive father, the Intendant Ti his cousin; Governors and Censors are his intimate friends, to say nothing of lesser mandarins. As well as his chief wife, a Wu by birth, daughter of the Left City Commandant Wu of Tsing ho hsien, he has four or five secondary wives, and the dancing and singing girls and the various maidservants whom he favors are numbered by the dozen. He is just five and thirty, and in every way a fine, handsome gentleman. You simply cannot imagine his efficiency in love; and as though his vigor were not already more than sufficient, he stimulates it with miraculous pills of quite peculiar power. For the rest, he is a delightful talker, and has had the most refined and many-sided education; he is not only an expert in knucklebones, chess, football, and all the other social games, but he is also thoroughly well-read, and as familiar with the writing of the hundred philosophers as with those of our poets. Really, wherever one sounds him, one comes upon veins of gold and precious jade.

"He has long cherished the desire to enjoy closer intercourse with your highborn family, which has stood for generations on its firm and sufficient foundations, and as a friend to promote the interests of your son, who is devoting himself to the military profession, and whose career he is watching with the keenest interest. He would much like to pay his respects to you on your coming birthday. On the other hand, he does not feel that it would be seemly to appear thus suddenly and unannounced, so he has instructed me to ask you beforehand whether his visit would be agreeable to you. I would urgently advise you to gratify his desire, for it is not only a question of agreeable intercourse between the two houses, but you could also depend on his good services, and by means of his intervention you could get your son away from his bad companions and save the good fame of your household from further defilement."

The Lady Lin was quite impressed by the old woman's volubility, and in her heart she was already won.

"But I cannot invite him without some good and adequate reason," was her only objection.

"Oh, there is no difficulty about that. I shall say that you wish him to proceed officially against the seducer of your son, and that you would like a personal interview first. That is a sufficient reason."

"Very well," Lady Lin agreed, eagerly. "Then kindly ask him to come here the day after tomorrow."

On the following day old Wen called on Hsi Men. He received her again behind drawn blinds, in Master Warm's study.

"I have sung your praises in tremendous tones," she reported. "My conversation was simply one hymn of praise—praise of your person, your wealth, your aristocratic connections, your noble and generous nature, your social talents, and not least of all, your astonishing mastery in matters of love. She was quite swept off her feet, and is burning to make your acquaintance. She wishes to receive you secretly tomorrow evening."

Hsi Men was delighted; he rewarded her then and there with two pieces of fine flowered satin for a new dress.

"But don't arrive too early tomorrow!" she continued. "Wait for the hour when one carries a lantern and the streets are empty. Then make your way to the back entrance to the house of Wang in Piecrust Lane. I shall wait for you there in the porter's lodge. The gatekeeper, Mother Tuan, is a good friend of mine; it was I who got her the place; so she is under an obligation to me, and she opens and shuts the back gate just as I ask her. Let your groom knock three times on the door of the porter's lodge; I shall know you are there, and then I will open the gate and pilot you into harbor safe and unseen."

She made her bow and hurried away with her bundle of satin, in order to warn Lady Lin.

On the following day, at the hour of twilight, Hsi Men, wearing a mask to avoid recognition, mounted his horse and made his way, accompanied by Tai A and Kiu Tung, to the silent Piecrust Lane. On reaching the back entrance to the house of Wang he reined in his horse and bade Tai A to knock three times, as agreed, on the door of the porter's lodge.

The door immediately opened, and Mother Wen appeared, cautiously peering about her. At a signal which she gave to someone behind her the park gates opened; Hsi Men leaped from his horse and allowed Mother Wen to lead him in, upon which the gates immediately closed again. Kiu Tung remained waiting in the lane with his horse, while Tai A disappeared into the porter's lodge.

Along the winding alleys of the park the old woman led Hsi Men to a one-storied building. It was the pavilion of the Lady Lin, a dwelling house of five rooms. The door of the pavilion was closed, and there was no one to be seen in the neighborhood. Mother Wen raised the bronze knocker and struck one light blow upon the door. A maid opened it, admitted the two visitors, and led Hsi Men into a reception room which was illumined with lamps and candles.

As he entered the room his gaze fell upon a great ancestral portrait on the wall facing the door. It portrayed the famous ancestor who centuries before had been a powerful governor, and the brother-in-law of the Son of Heaven. Clad in a red Court robe, on which a design of serpents was embroidered, his waist encircled with a jade girdle, he sat, a massive, broad-shouldered figure, in an armchair covered with a tiger skin, gazing into the room with such a grim and intimidating expression that one might have taken him for the War God Kwan Ti if his beard had been a little longer. Above the door was a vermilion tablet on which was inscribed, in three golden characters, "Hall of Continence and Widowly Virtue." While Hsi Men was engaged in deciphering the wise aphorisms displayed to the right and left of him on long wall scrolls, the faint tinkle of a bead curtain fell upon his ear. Mother Wen came in, bringing him tea.

"Can I greet the lady of the house?" he asked.

"She will receive you directly. First refresh yourself a little," replied the old woman, and she flitted out again.

In the meantime the Lady Lin, from her adjacent sitting room, had secretly peeped through the curtain, closely examining her visitor. His dignified person and his well-groomed, virile appearance had not failed to impress her. This was a genuine charmer, a real voluptuary! His mourning bonnet of white satin excited her peculiar interest.

"For whom is he in mourning, then?" she inquired of old Wen.

"For his Sixth. She died recently, in the ninth month. Now he is off catching quails again. Take care you don't find yourself in his cage unawares! He has a dexterous hand!"

Lady Lin heard this with secret joy. But for the sake of appearances she continued to affect reluctance for a time, before she at last made up her mind and sent the old woman to invite him into her room. Hsi Men found himself in a comfortable sitting room, which was furnished with the most exquisite taste. Thick carpets covered the floor, embroidered cushions, like clouds of many colors, were heaped upon the capacious divan, the windows were hung with rose-pink muslin curtains, and a silk screen barred the doorway leading to the moonlit terrace, while wafts of orchid perfume filled the pleasantly warmed room, simulating the balmy, aromatic breath of Spring.

And there he saw her standing before him. The coif upon her head was embroidered with gold and enriched with tiny leaves of kingfisher-blue enamel. Above her long white silk robe she wore a slashed tunic of a deep red, and over her shoulders a mantle of golden-yellow satin trimmed with heron's feathers. What a noble, dignified bearing! The woman was a beauty; moreover, one could see at a glance that she was of good family, and that she had been reared in the strict seclusion of the women's apartments of an aristocratic household. She was a silently ruling Bodhisattva of the house; a lady.

Hsi Men could but do homage to her, falling on his knees and twice beating his forehead on the floor. He then had to sit in an armchair while she sank on to the edge of the divan beside him. The maid Waterlily brought tea, and Mother Wen, modestly standing at the door, assumed the task of stimulating the flow of conversation.

"The Tai tai was anxious to claim your judicial protection, and she commissioned me to invite you here for a preliminary interview," she explained, by way of introduction.

"In what connection can I be of service to the Tai tai?" he asked.

"It is about my son," interposed Lady Lin. "He is the only son, and therefore rather spoiled. My husband, unhappily, died early, and so from childhood he has lacked the strict discipline of a father, and has hitherto shown himself by no means worthy of his famous ancestors. He would like, as a matter of inclination, to devote himself to a military career, but he has not really studied very seriously as yet. He has fallen into bad company. A gang of irresponsible people are constantly luring him from his home and his studies and carousing with him by day and night in the flower gardens, and they encourage him to expend enormous sums of money. Hitherto I have been afraid to bring a formal accusation against the seducers of my son, because I should not wish to see the good name of our family dragged into the open. It is for this reason that I have invited you to my cold home, and I hope you will be able, without a formal indictment, to rescue my son from his bad companions and lead him back to a more enlightened way of life, worthy of his ancestors. I should be infinitely grateful if you would do so."

"Noble lady, I think one must make some allowance for your son's youth. Assuredly he will one day do all honor to his highly-respected house, which for generations has supplied the realm with meritorious dignitaries and famous generals. But at your behest I will gladly take the requisite steps to rescue him once and for all from his bad companions. I shall do what is necessary no later than tomorrow."

She rose, and bowing slightly, breathed a grateful *Wan fu*.

Even during this formal conversation glances had been exchanged between the two which expressed something more than mere conventional respect and politeness. Now she invited him to take his place at the ready-laid table, an invitation which he did not accept without a little courteous resistance.

"I have today had the honor of being received by the Tai tai for the first time. How can I, who have not paid her the smallest civility, now, without further ceremony, pretend to any claim to enjoy the sumptuous hospitality of the lady?" he objected.

"Alas, at such short notice it was not possible to make worthy preparations for your visit. The beaker of watery wine which is all that my cold home can offer you is only a pitiful means of expressing my true sentiments," she said, in apology.

Well; the "beaker of watery wine" constituted, at all events, a magnificent feast of sixteen choice dishes. Moreover, the maid Waterlily poured from a golden ewer an extremely strong liqueur, which was drunk from jade goblets. Rising to her feet, Lady Lin herself presented the first bowl to her guest. Hsi Men modestly refused to accept it, but rising in his turn, wished to offer the first bowl to her.

"No, on this occasion it is for the Tai tai to offer you the first bowl," said Mother Wen, deciding the contest in politeness. "But on the fifteenth of the eleventh month, your birthday, it will be your turn to do her that honor."

With joyous satisfaction, Hsi Men surrendered himself to the stimulating charm of a meal at which he was the only guest. The tapers flickering in the tall silver candelabra, together with the glowing red of the newly-replenished golden braziers, filled the room with a delicious warmth. The delicacies comprised in the sixteen courses, and the generously appreciated contents of the golden ewer, warmed the hearts of those who partook of them. As bowl followed bowl and course followed course his boldness increased and her reserve disappeared. Jesting words were spoken, laughter shook the air, and soon their converse sounded like the morning antiphony of an amorous pair of song birds.

543

Wine increased the courage of the senses.
The two hearts were long ago entangled;
Now their longing was inflamed.

Already the water clock announced the beginning of night, and from the terrace the moonlight fell slanting on the carpet. Mother Wen and the maid Waterlily had withdrawn after the sixteenth course was cleared, and they did not appear again. So the Lady Lin was compliant when Hsi Men, growing even bolder, moved closer to her side, grasping her wrist, stroking her shoulder, touching her hips. She did not repulse him even when as though in jest he laid his arm about her neck and pressed his mouth against her cinnabar-red lips. For a while only the sound of passionate lips and tongues was to be heard; then a few words, uttered in a whisper, spoke of a secret understanding.

She rose and quietly locked the doors. Then she loosed her girdle; her clothes fell to the ground, and she stretched herself out on the divan amidst the musk-scented, embroidered silken cushions. Hsi Men, by way of precaution, had already swallowed one of Father Fan's invigorating pills. What with this and with that, the flames of hot desire were mutually kindled. With truly simian lust he flung his arms about her; he was utterly beside himself, like a butterfly madly intoxicated with the fragrance of rare flowers. When at last they parted, after a long and ardent contest, they were both completely exhausted. Her coiffure was displaced, her hairpins were protruding in all directions, and a beneficent languor possessed her limbs. For a while they rested side by side, head to head, thigh to thigh. At last they rose, washed, and dressed themselves. Three more farewell goblets, then she escorted him to the door. He bent his body in a deep bow, assured her of his gratitude and his devotion, and allowed Mother Wen to lead him back by the way he had come to the postern gate of the park. It was late when he rode homewards. In the empty streets lay a damp autumnal mist. Apart from the gong signals and passwords of the night patrols as they met each other there was not a sound to be heard.

In accordance with his promise to Lady Lin, the very next morning, after the Court had risen, Hsi Men instructed some of the yamen bailiffs to ascertain the present whereabouts of young Wang of the house of Wang Chow Hsuen and the names of his seducers and bottle companions. A few hours later the bailiffs were able to inform him that they had traced the person in question to the flower garden of Mother Li. They had drawn up a list of his companions; it consisted of seven names, and among them were the names of Hsi Men's sworn confederates, Chu Shih Nien and Sun Tien Hua. Included as accessories were the two flower girls, Cinnamon Bud from the house of Li and Mushroom from the house of Tsin.

Hsi Men first of all drew a broad brush stroke through the names of the two girls and his two friends; then he ordered the bailiffs to arrest the five other roisterers and to bring them before his Court next morning. The bailiffs accordingly surrounded Mother Li's establishment and arrested the five as they unsuspectingly left the house late that afternoon. Young Wang, who at the first alarm had crept into Cinnamon Bud's bed, was not discovered, but was able to return home during the night.

Next morning, when he was sitting on the bench with Judge Hsia, Hsi Men had the five prisoners brought before him, and after a brief hearing he condemned them each to twenty blows with the heavy bamboo. After this painful business was over, he addressed a few severe words of warning to the culprits. "Today," he said, "you have got off lightly. But if I ever catch you accursed blackguards again, leading youthful strangers of good family astray with your whoring and debauchery, then I shall have each of you put into the heavy wooden collar and pilloried all day outside the gates of the flower garden."

With this he released them.

The five blackguards were delighted to have recovered their liberty so soon, but on the other hand it annoyed them to think that in this case justice had not been fully satisfied. No sooner had they left the yamen than they began to give utterance to their discontent, and to guess at the probable identity of the contriver of this raid upon them.

"Probably old Huang in the Eastern Capital has been set on to us again by his niece, young Mistress Wang," one of them suggested.

"I doubt it. If the old High Eunuch Huang in Kai fong fu had been responsible for the raid, we should hardly have got off so quickly. I should rather assume that the trouble was due to some jealous singing-girl," said a second.

"You've both missed the mark," a third interposed. "I'll tell you who it was. Judge Hsi Men and no one else was at the bottom of it. He evidently wanted to have a smack at young Wang, because he was angry with him for snatching away his darling, Cinnamon Bud. But as he didn't dare to go for the aristocratic young Wang himself, he vented his hatred on us lesser folk. It's always the same; the innocent deer has to pay when the dragon comes to blows with the tiger."

"After all, it really doesn't matter whom we have to thank for what happened," said the fourth. "But why did Sun Tien Hua and Chu Shih Nien, who had just as much to do with the affair, get off without punishment? Where's the justice of that?"

"It's precisely that which proves that Hsi Men is at the back of it," the fifth interposed. "Those two are his intimate friends; he won't want to sentence them!"

"That's so," the first began again. "And that, moreover, is why nothing happened to the two girls."

"Of course!" echoed the second. "One of them, Cinnamon Bud, is an old flame of his, and if he didn't want anything to happen to her he had, of course, to let the other one go too."

"Instead of which he netted us five," added the third indignantly. "Now one understands why during the hearing he wouldn't let his colleague, Judge Hsia, have anything to say."

"An unheard-of instance of partiality!" agreed the fourth. "We must at least make young Wang indemnify us all, since it's for him that we had our backsides castigated! He'll have to come out with a few ounces as compensation, or our wives at home will laugh us out of countenance!"

"Agreed! Come along to Mother Li's!" cried the whole gang, in chorus, and they promptly rushed off to Mother Li's establishment, thinking that at that time of day young Wang would still be there. But Mother Li's gates were barred, and the house was silent and inaccessible as an iron barrel; it gave no sign of life, despite their shouting and raving. At last they were told, by someone in the adjacent house, that young Wang was no longer there; he had made his way home the previous night. So they rushed off to the house of Wang, and settled like a swarm of blue-bottles in the reception hall.

Young Wang was actually at home, but he lay hid in the women's apartments, and had the intruders informed that he was out. But the gang refused to believe his servant, and insisted, with a great deal of shouting and uproar, that his master must come out and show himself. "Do you think you can deceive us, you scoundrel?" their spokesman roared at the flabbergasted servant. "Here, look at our flayed limbs! Go in and tell your master how ill we've been used on his account! By rights exactly the same thing ought to be done to your master. Either he indemnifies us, or we bring him too before the judge!"

In order to lend greater emphasis to his words the whole company rocked themselves to and fro on the chairs and benches and filled the air with their groans and their cries of lamentation.

Young Wang, completely dismayed and intimidated, began to realize that he would never dare to show himself. Now there were angry cries for his mother; they insisted upon speaking to her. Lady Lin told herself, wisely, that before all things she must gain time. "My son has been away at our country seat since early this morning. I will send for him at once. In the meantime the gentlemen must make themselves comfortable." She spoke soothingly to the excited gang, addressing them from behind the screen.

"Very well, if the Tai tai will send for him we'll wait patiently for a while. But he must come as quickly as possible or the abscess will burst," replied the spokesman, in an impudent, menacing tone. "We've had a thrashing in court on his account. If he doesn't show himself soon and compensate us I can't answer for anything."

Lady Lin hastily sent to the kitchen in order to stop their mouths, for the time being, with a cup of tea and a few cakes. Then she took counsel with her son.

"We ought to send old Wen to Judge Hsi Men," she said, after some reflection. "She has been known to him for some time, for she acted as go-between when his daughter was betrothed."

"Excellent. Then let's ask her to come with all speed," said young Wang, urgently.

"As far as that goes, it is questionable whether she will come," his mother continued, with adroit hypocrisy. "Since you annoyed her recently she is angry with us, and doesn't come here any longer."

"I'll conciliate her with a present. We simply must get her here."

Seeming to yield unwillingly to his urging, Lady Lin sent a servant with a message to old Wen, and he soon returned with her. The crafty old woman, exchanging a swift glance of understanding with Lady Lin, began by raising objections to young Wang's proposal.

"It is true that I did formerly serve him as go-between at the time of his daughter's betrothal, but that is a long while ago," she said. "For years now I have been quite out of touch with him. How can I suddenly and without preliminaries force myself on so exalted a gentleman?"

Only when young Wang besought her on his knees to help him, and held out the promise of a generous reward, did she consent, and then it was in response to Lady Lin's persuasion.

"But I can't very well undertake to call on him alone," she added. "The young gentleman must come with me and make his request to Master Hsi Men in person. Otherwise it can't be done."

"But I've already said that I'm not at home. If those fellows were now to see me going out of the gate with you, what then?" the young man objected.

"Don't be afraid. We'll slip away unseen through the gate at the back of the park. Besides, I'll speak a few soothing words to them before we go, to lull their suspicions."

While young Wang was hastily changing his clothes, Mother Wen, unaccompanied and unafraid, entered the reception hall.

"I come on behalf of the Tai tai," she began her address, after greeting those present with two ceremonious bows. "She wishes to thank the gentlemen for their friendly visit and regrets that at the moment her son is not present. He is out of town, at her country seat. But a messenger has already been sent after him, and he will soon be here. In the meantime the gentlemen must please make themselves comfortable and be patient a little longer. She is infinitely sorry to hear that the gentlemen have suffered such unpleasantness, and will see to it that her son gives the gentlemen satisfaction. Moreover, should the yamen desire him to appear before the court he will of course present himself at any time and will do his utmost to ensure that the affair is satisfactorily settled."

Her speech had the desired anodyne effect upon the gang.

"Mother Wen, why didn't you speak to us at once as sensibly as you are speaking now?" came the chorus of applause. "Then all this excitement would have been unnecessary. But as you will unstand, it annoyed us extremely that we alone had to endure a thrashing. Now, since you are so understanding and sympathetic, you might do one thing more for us, and contrive that in the meantime something decent to eat and drink is put before us. After all, we have only just been released from the yamen, and haven't yet even a drop of morning soup in our stomachs."

"Patience, gentlemen; I'll speak to the Tai tai at once and see that you have a good breakfast," the old woman promised, and she hurried off to the back of the house. And truly enough, there presently arrived from the kitchen a number of steaming dishes of boiled meat and roast, with hors d'œuvres and dessert, and there was not lacking a mighty jug of wine.

While the savage horde was thus tamed and appeased by cunning, young Wang had dressed himself and was in readiness. He crammed the scholar's black biretta on to his head, tucked away

549

his visiting card and a hastily-written petition, and put on his mask, and then, quietly and secretly, he slipped out of the postern gate with Mother Wen.

When Hsi Men examined the red visiting card which was brought to him by the gatekeeper Ping An, and read on it the words: "The late-born of the house of Wang bows his head in greeting," he immediately understood what had happened. He first had a private conversation with old Wen, and then received his visitor in the front reception hall. After a formal and ceremonious greeting, and a preliminary sip of tea, young Wang began, in a hesitating voice: "The unworthy nephew is in a difficult position. He does not know whether he ought to trouble the venerable and austere uncle with the circumstance."

With these words he drew his petition from his sleeve and offered it to Hsi Men. At the same time he rose from his chair and fell on his knees.

"Tell me confidently what oppresses you, my dear young friend!" said Hsi Men, amiably, raising young Wang from his kneeling position.

"Your culpable little nephew has revealed neither merit nor capacity. Merely for the sake of the honor of his famous ancestors he hopes that the venerable and austere uncle will have consideration for him and will spare him the shame of appearing before his tribunal. For the despicable nephew it would be equivalent to a rising from the dead. Trembling and with chattering teeth he awaits your decision."

In the meantime Hsi Men had unfolded the petition.

"Here I actually read the names of the five blackguards whom I urgently warned only this morning, and released after a mild punishment!" he cried. "What are the scoundrels doing in your house?"

"They threatened me, raving and shouting, saying that they would cite me too before your Court if I did not compensate them, by a large money payment, for the thrashing which they suffered on my account. Driven to desperation by their blackmail, I have

550

fled hither to implore the protection of the venerable and venerated uncle."

In support of his appeal he laid before Hsi Men a list of presents.

"These accursed blackguards!" cried Hsi Men, after he had read the petition to the end. "First, treat them with clemency; and then they repay my consideration by such abhorrent and extortionate behavior as this!"

He returned the list of presents to young Wang.

"Of course there can be no talk of presents, my dear young friend. Nor will any sort of proceedings be taken against you. Be quite easy in your mind! But I'll have these five blackguards arrested at once."

"A thousand, ten thousand thanks!" stammered the delighted young Wang. "Never will the despicable nephew forget that the kind and venerable uncle did not leave him in the lurch! On some later occasion he earnestly hopes that he may give some further and particular proof of his gratitude."

Hsi Men accompanied him to the secret gate.

"Excuse me if I bid you good by here," he said. "I am in my house gown; it would be unseemly to escort you through the gate in such an inadequate garment."

He once more took old Wen aside.

"The youngster needn't worry any longer. Nothing will happen to him. I shall send my people immediately, who will clear the house of these insolent intruders."

Not long after old Wen and her charge had secretly slipped into the house by way of the postern gate, five guards from the yamen forced their way unheralded into the reception hall and without more ado arrested the five blackguards. These fellows, who with noisy satisfaction had just been eating and drinking their own health, were not a little dismayed when they suddenly felt the cold iron of the handcuffs on their wrists. Their faces assumed an earthen pallor. Then they cackled and shrieked with indignation: "There, Friend Wang has sold us nicely! What baseness! He has led us into the trap with bread and wine!"

"Shut your mouths!" the guards harshly ordered them. "If you've any complaint to make be pleased to make it before the Ancient Commander!"

And with a few violent pushes they forced their prisoners into a rapid trot. They had been ordered not to take them straight to the yamen, but to bring them to their master's house. In the front reception hall Hsi Men conducted a brief, improvised trial.

"Accursed rascals!" he cried, enthroned above them on the dais, to the men kneeling before him. "What possessed you to force your way into a strange house and intimidate the innocent son of the house by factitious references to my judicial office, and with insolent threats to demand the payment of money? How much did you extort from him? Speak out, now! Or I'll have all your knuckles cracked in the finger press!"

At a sign from him five fine new finger presses were set down before the eyes of the men kneeling in front of the dais.

"We didn't squeeze a single copper cash out of him!" the five prisoners declared, with innocent faces. "We simply called on him to tell him of our morning's experience in court. He was not at home; we were asked to wait until he returned, and in the meantime we were entertained with food and drink. That is all."

"How dare you, accursed rapscallions, be so impudent as to force your way uninvited into a strange house?" cried Hsi Men, angrily reproving them. "Of course you meant to squeeze money out of him! But you won't confess. The proper place for you is jail, for the whole stubborn crew! And you'll have to wear the heavy wooden collar as a public warning!"

A loud and pitiful lamentation rose from the five prisoners.

"Oh, Advocate of Heaven, great and exalted Commander, spare us the shame of the wooden collar! Save us from the dungeon! It would mean our certain death in this cold winter weather. We promise never again to trouble young Wang and his house!"

"Well, if you give me your firm and solemn promise I will once more show you consideration," said Hsi Men, in a milder tone. "Go cleanse your hearts, and begin a new life! But if you are ever caught

552

again at your game of luring young strangers into the flower gardens and swindling them out of their money, I'll have you put behind the bars and flogged to death without mercy! Now go!"

He had their fetters removed, when his servants drove them out of the gate. Then he repaired to the rear apartments.

"What Master Wang was that who called on you today?" asked Moon Lady.

"The son of the later Minister Wang Chow Hsuen; the young man who was recently involved in Cinnamon Bud's scandal. You remember? Cinnamon Bud herself, when we gave her shelter here, solemnly vowed that she would never have relations with the young man again. And now the irresponsible creature has shamefully deceived us. She has been allowing him to keep her all this time, for thirty ounces a month; he has plunged into debt on her account, and has pledged his wife's fur cloak and her gold bracelets with Cinnamon Bud's mother. By chance I heard the whole story from a friend of Cinnamon Bud's. In order to save the young man from further trouble, I had the five companions who had enticed and seduced him arrested, and awarded them a bit of a thrashing. Who could have imagined that as soon as they were set at liberty they would have invaded young Wang's house like a swarm of blow-flies, attempting, by means of insolent threats, to extort money from him? In his distress, through the mediation of old Wen, he turned to me for protection, and even tried to force me to accept a present of fifty ounces, which I of course refused, while thanking him. Well, I had the impudent rascals arrested anew and have taken means to see that they never molest the heedless young man again. As for him, I have made an urgent appeal to his conscience. As I have told him, he must have regard for the good fame of his ancient family, and it would be as well if he would pay rather more attention to his studies, so that he may one day be worthy of his famous ancestors. It is an irresponsible way of behaving for a young man barely twenty years of age to go racketing about the back streets and the flower gardens, leaving his young wife, who is pure and lovely as a freshly-plucked bough of blossom, to sit forsaken at home."

During this long speech he had spoken with increasing vigor, in the convinced accents of moral indignation. Moon Lady could not refrain from smiling. Had he not been holding up a mirror to himself?

"It seems to be that young chickens and the old drake drink out of the same muddy puddle!" she remarked, in airy mockery.

He gazed at her blankly, and withdrew, without a word, to his library.

CHAPTER THIRTY-FOUR: *Gold Lotus chastises the Nurse Ju I. Young Wang honors Hsi Men as his Mentor*

HSI MEN would only too willingly have accepted the invitation which young Wang sent him a few days later, in order to fan the freshly-kindled fire of his new and seductive liaison. To his regret, however, he had to decline the invitation, for on the tenth of the eleventh month, simultaneously with Wang's invitation, arrived instructions from the Eastern Capital, to the effect that all those higher officials who had received preferment about this time were without fail to attend the customary audience of thanks and congratulation in Kai fong fu. And Hsi Men was among those thus favored. He was promoted First District Judge of Tsing ho hsien in the place of his colleague Hsia, and at the same time his rank was increased by one degree of precedence, while Judge Hsia was given a command in the Imperial Bodyguard. A young nephew of the High Eunuch Hou I had been chosen to succeed Hsi Men in his former office.

He had therefore to pack his trunks with all possible speed and prepare himself for the journey. On the twelfth day of the month Hsi Men and his colleague Hsia, with a retinue of twenty men, began the march to the Eastern Capital.

During his fortnight's absence Moon Lady insisted upon strict order being kept in the house. The gatekeeper Ping An was allowed to open the main gate only in the case of the most urgent necessity, and with her express permission, and the entrance to the women's apartments was securely locked and bolted from sunset until the following dawn. During the daytime Moon Lady kept a sharper watch than usual over everything that happened in the house, and would not allow young Chen to enter the remoter regions of the park unaccompanied, as he did at other times, in order to remove pledges from the store room in the pavilion of the Sixth, or to place fresh pledges in safety. A servant always had to walk beside him. So this time Gold Lotus contrived no opportunities of keeping secret trysts with her adorer, but had to accustom herself, like the other four wives, to sitting quietly and discreetly in her apartments, and keeping ennui at bay, as far as possible, with needlework and lute playing and other domestic occupations. However, she consoled herself by frequent quarrels with her detested new adversary, the nurse Ju I.

One day the practical Moon Lady, taking advantage of her husband's absence, ordained a great, general washing day. All the servants' wives and the maids had to do their share, working in shifts. Now it so happened that in the pavilion of the Fifth, where Spring Plum and Autumn Aster were toiling at the washtub, there was no wooden dolly. Spring Plum sent Autumn Aster to the neighboring pavilion in order to borrow a dolly. But in the neighboring pavilion the nurse Ju I, with the maid Pear Blossom, and the Sixth Wang, who happened to be calling, were themselves busily engaged in batting the washing.

"What do you suppose?—we need our dolly ourselves!" the nurse curtly informed Autumn Aster. "Why didn't you make your arrangements earlier? We are just doing Master Hsi Men's shirts and drawers. We can't have our work upset by you."

Autumn Aster returned from her fruitless errand in a bad temper. "They refuse to give it to us," she reported. "Pear Blossom was ready to do so, but the nurse wouldn't let her."

"That disobliging lump!" hissed Spring Plum, in a fury. "She'd refuse to give one an empty lamp in broad daylight if she could! But we can't get on without a dolly. Go to the First and see if you can get one there."

Gold Lotus had overheard this dialogue from the next room. "Go across yourself, and if the woman refuses again, give it her properly!" she said, inciting Spring Plum to hostilities.

Like a gust of wind the angry little maid swept down upon the neighboring pavilion.

"That person there doesn't belong to the household at all," she burst out, pointing at the Sixth Wang. "How comes she to lay hands on other people's property? Let her give up our dolly at once!"

"Now, now, gently!" the nurse retorted. "We've got the say here! Cousin Wang is helping us with the washing at the express wish of the First. Besides, she's just doing the master's shirts and drawers; one can't disturb her in the middle of her work. I've already told Autumn Aster she must just wait patiently till we've finished batting, then she can come again and fetch her dolly. Swooping down on one like this is no way to behave!"

Unnoticed, Gold Lotus had crept up behind her maid.

"What does this mean?" she cried, suddenly interrupting the argument. "I suppose you imagine that because they allow you to wash the master's body linen you can give yourself airs and crow over the rest of us? But I happen to be here! And I tell you, you aren't going to intimidate me and play the tyrant over me! Not by a long way!"

"But, my dear Fifth mistress, no one meant to do anything of the kind," said the nurse. "It was only at the express wish of the First mistress. . . ."

"You needn't trouble to make excuses, you wretched, misbegotten harlot!" cried Gold Lotus, furiously interrupting her. "Who forced her way in here in the middle of the night, offered him tea, and then stroked him through the bedclothes, eh? Who helped him to dress in the morning? Do you imagine I don't know all about your scandalous doings? But I'm not afraid, not I, of the secret bastard in your belly!"

"You needn't be! When lawfully born children are murdered a servant's child isn't likely even to be born!" interjected the nurse, venomously.

At this the fire in Gold Lotus's heart burst into flame, and she flushed crimson with fury. With a sudden leap she fell upon her enemy, and while she clutched at the nurse's hair with her left hand,

557

with her clenched right she dealt her several violent blows in the abdomen. It was all that the Sixth Wang could do, as she rushed forward, to part the combatants.

"Insolent, shameless seducer and harlot!" panted Gold Lotus, who was quite out of breath. "What business have you here at all? But if you tried a thousand times over to play the designing Lotus Petal risen from the dead I'd be a match for you!"

The maltreated nurse howled aloud. "What do I know of any designing Lotus Petal and her doings? That was before my time," she replied in her simplicity. "I have merely done my job here as nurse."

"As nurse, indeed! If you'd only confined yourself to your job as nurse! But you've crept into a stolen tiger skin, you miserable vixen, and allowed yourself to take insolent liberties!"

The arrival of Jade Fountain prevented further speech from Gold Lotus. "Sister, I thought we were going to play a game of chess! Why have you kept me waiting so long?" said the phlegmatic Third, taking Gold Lotus by the hand and leading her away at a leisurely pace to her own pavilion. Then she thrust her into a chair and gave her a bowl of tea to calm her nerves.

"What was the matter just now?" she then inquired.

"Oh, that accursed wench of a nurse! Just look, Sister, how my hand is shaking with excitement! I can hardly hold the tea bowl. Now listen! When you sent your Little Phœnix to me some time ago and asked me to come here and play chess with you, I was just lying down for a little siesta. My Spring Plum was in the next room with Autumn Aster, busy with the washing. They wanted a dolly, and Spring Plum sent Autumn Aster to the pavilion of the Sixth to borrow one, as they had one there. I heard the little thing come back in a state of excitement, saying that they had refused to give her the dolly, and the nurse had called out a few impudent remarks after her. So then I sent my Spring Plum across, and I myself slipped after her on the quiet, just to hear what was being said over there.

"Well, that insolent creature spoke to my Spring Plum as though she were the mistress of the house and all the rest of us had to sing small to her. Naturally I was furious, and I told her just what I thought of her. And then, as she dared to make a few shameless remarks to me, I seized her and gave her a few blows on the body. If the Sixth Wang hadn't pulled us apart with all her might I believe I would have torn the shameless creature's heart from her body, I was so furious!

"But the First is not without blame; she has let matters go altogether too far. She must surely see that the affair with Hui Lien is being repeated. I had given them fair warning of the intrigues of their servant's wife, and the plotting of her husband, that dangerous drunkard Lai Wang, and instead of thanking me the First reproached me. Today just the same thing is beginning over again. And even if the First is blind, nor a grain of sand will escape my keen sight. I have seen exactly how this shameless and designing wench, who was engaged merely as wet-nurse, has been making up to him. At first she hovered about him as timid and silent as her shadow. Then one night when he asked for tea she pressed herself against his bed, and while she was holding out the bowl she stroked him, with lustful intent, through the bedclothes. And at that he took her into bed with him. Next morning she helped him to dress. How did she come to offer him tea and help him to dress? The maids are there for that, not the wet-nurse.

"Since that time he had told us, I don't know how often, that he wanted to burn incense and sacrificial money in the bedroom of his deceased Sixth, and that out of piety he was going to sleep beside her soul tablet, but in reality he went there simply to make love to the nurse without being disturbed. Once I surprised them; they were finely startled, and so confused that they couldn't speak a word! But Moon Lady sits in her room and sees and hears nothing of all this, and if one opens one's mouth she simply makes reproachful remarks."

Jade Fountain had listened with increasing astonishment.

"But where do you get all these details from?" she asked at length.

"Oh, one just learns them. As a tree has its shadow, so human beings have their reputations. A grave in the snow isn't hidden for long; one day the snow melts and the corpse appears. The schemes that she concealed under a thin cover of deceit and simulation could not long remain hidden from my watchful eye."

"But has she really any charm—I mean, can she influence a man?"

"At first, when she came to us, she certainly didn't look like it. She was pale and emaciated then, a mere lump of misery. But during the two years of her time here she has stuffed herself nicely, and now you can see the lust and depravity sparkling in her round, rolling eyes. If we don't call a halt to her doings in time she'll be foisting a lively little bastard on us one of these days."

"You think of everything," Jade Fountain commented, laughing. "Well, do whatever you think fit."

And she unconcernedly began her game of chess with her companion.

One day towards the end of the eleventh month Hsi Men returned home. The first thing he did, after he had washed and changed his clothes, was to have an incense bowl placed in the courtyard, where on a fasting stomach he prostrated himself and thanked Heaven and Earth for his safe arrival home.

"What does this mean?" asked Moon Lady, in astonishment.

"Oh, don't ask! The return journey was terrible. It wasn't bad on the outward journey: I had fine, warm weather, and was able to get a little exercise in the saddle from time to time. But on the way back the frost was so cruel that I never left the cushions of my palanquin, and my limbs are still quite stiff with lying down so long. To make it worse, the day before yesterday we had hardly crossed the Yellow River when we were involved in a frightful sandstorm. In a moment all the seven openings of our bodies were choked with sand. The whole caravan got into a tangle; the pack animals tried to bolt, the porters and caravan leaders were in a panic. What's more, it was already evening, and there was no human settlement within a hundred *li!* Also the neighborhood is infested with bands of robbers. So our situation was desperate. At last we found shelter for the night in a little tumble-down Buddhist temple—it was called the 'Temple of the Yellow Dragon.' But what a miserable lodging! The few poverty-stricken bonzes who lived there had neither oil for their lamps nor a grain of corn for the cooking pot. An icy wind blew most uncomfortably through the cracked walls and broken windows. Yet we were glad that we had at least a roof over our heads, and were able to refresh ourselves, by the dim light of candles, with weak tea and a bad bean soup. That night I made a vow. On the first of the coming month a pig and a sheep are to be killed, and sacrificed to Heaven and Earth as a thank-offering for my safe return. If the sandstorm had caught us two hours earlier, just as we were crossing the Hoang ho, or if we hadn't by chance discovered the 'Temple of the Yellow Dragon,' we should hardly have escaped alive."

"Did you come straight home, or did you go to the yamen first?"

"I went first to the yamen, and for the present I have found accommodation there for my new young colleague. His uncle, the Intendant for the Palace buildings, the High Eunuch Hou I, overwhelmed me with amiability at Kai fong fu, and put me up as his guest in his town house. He was very anxious that I should do my best for his nephew. The young man is barely twenty years old; he owes his appointment to the exalted protection of the Princess Ma, Imperial Concubine of the first rank and mistress of the 'Palace of Continued Well-Being.' His uncle is employed more especially in her household. He is quite inexperienced, without a notion of the laws and official regulations, so that I shall have to lead him and support him at every step. For the rest, he will move into the house of my late colleague Hsia. His uncle has bought it for him for twelve hundred ounces; I negotiated the sale. Directly Hsia's furniture has been removed he will take possession. In the meantime he is putting up with a few rooms in the yamen which I have had furnished for him. Hsia has already entered upon his new post in the Imperial Bodyguard; he won't be coming back here. He has particularly asked me to look after his house and his family a little until the removal. We ought to pay his wife some little attention; you must call on her as soon as possible."

"There, you have once more let yourself in for all sorts of obligations!" said Moon Lady, reprovingly. "You are much too good-natured. One shouldn't always give one's whole heart away on meeting strangers. However, apart from all this it is Mistress Hsia's birthday on the second of next month. It will be quite enough if I pay her a formal visit then and take a few trifles with me."

Meanwhile the other wives had gradually assembled to greet their husband. Involuntarily he reflected that in the summer, when he had last returned from a journey to the Eastern Capital, all his six wives had been there to welcome him. This time the beloved Sixth was absent. Possessed by this sad memory, he could not refrain from paying a visit to her forsaken pavilion and lingering for a quarter of an hour in silent devotion before her soul tablet. Then the duties and obligations of everyday life reasserted their claim. So that same day he had half a pig, half a sheep, two smoked hams, two ducks, ten chickens, and a good supply of rice, noodles, herbs, and other ingredients sent to young Hou's lodgings in the yamen; nor did he forget to place a good cook at his disposal.

The first night at home Hsi Men spent with his Fifth. It is needless to say that after a fortnight's continence their longing for love was insatiable and unbounded. Gold Lotus, still endeavoring to recover his old favor, exhausted herself by a hundred caresses and a thousand endearments, and only regretted that in her sheer devotion and submissiveness she could not creep into his body and lose herself there. That night there was little thought of sleep; he had so much to tell her of his traveling experiences, and she, for her part, had all sorts of things to tell him of what had been happening at home in his absence.

"Have you missed me just a little?" he asked her suddenly.

"Oh, this whole fortnight, all the time you have been away, your slave has not had a peaceful hour," she declared passionately. "My sleepless, lonely nights were the worst; they seemed to creep past me endlessly. At first I found it intolerable that I should lie abed in soft silk and yielding down while I knew that you were exposed out yonder to the cold of winter and the rude shelter of inhospitable inns. So I threw the warm bedclothes aside and covered myself with a thin traveling rug. In the early mornings I awoke with my limbs frozen stiff and could hardly move. At last it distressed my little Spring Plum to see me sitting so desolately on the edge of the bed and weeping half the night. She helped me to while away the long afternoons with gossip and games of chess, and at night she crept into bed with me. So, my Ko ko, now you know what I feel for you in my heart. But now I should like to know what you feel for me in *your* heart."

"But, my darling, everyone in the house knows that none of my wives is as dear to me as you."

"Oh, come, you are trying to fool me! While you are tasting one dish you are already looking for the next out of the corner of your eye. How was it when you were running after that servant's wife, Lotus Petal? You never looked at me; and later, when the Sixth had had her child? Like a haughty cockerel you avoided me, your truest hen! But in spite of all, I have been faithful to you as the flowering catkin of the trembling aspen, which joins in every leap of the twig. And now once more you have got involved with a miserable wench, with a common wet-nurse. Doesn't it ever occur to you that her husband is still alive, and may give you trouble one of these days, after letting his flock graze on your meadow? Haven't you the very least regard for what is due to your office, your social position? The woman is already beginning to be insolent and to crow over us, your lawful wives. While you were away there was a fine rumpus here between her and my Spring Plum, on account of a washing dolly. She was insolent even to me, she would hardly let me speak a word."

"Let well alone, my dear child! What harm can she do to you? You are the mistress here, and she's the maid. She would need seven foreheads and eight galls to deal with you. Why, you have only to hold up your hand, and she must crouch before you."

"Yes, yes, that sounds very fine. But what is the actual state of affairs? Hasn't she already made herself comfortable in the empty nest of your Sixth? Hasn't she already got round you so far that you once promised her that you'd give her all that your Sixth had possessed if she would only love you faithfully?"

"That's nonsense. I never promised anything of the kind. You're imagining all this. I beg of you to make it up with her. I'll tell her she must make her kowtow to you and ask you nicely to forgive her."

"But I don't in the least want her to ask me to forgive her. Above all I don't want you to go on spending the night in the next pavilion."

"Don't worry your head about that: it's simply an insuperable longing for my Sixth that drives me to her pavilion from time to time, and makes me spend the night beside her soul tablet. It is merely piety. You surely are not jealous of her soul tablet?"

"I tell you, I don't trust you. When anyone has been dead a hundred days it is usual to clear away the soul tablet and burn it. I don't see the point of this exaggerated and continued worship of her soul tablet. You are behaving just as though you were night watchman of a valuable granary which you had to guard! But I know perfectly well, you can't leave the woman alone. Well, go to her! But tell me honestly beforehand, and tell me what she wants you to give her. I simply can't stand all this secrecy!"

"Dear little oily-mouth!" he said, in a flattering tone; and he stifled any further speech with his kisses and embraces.

Among the many invitations by which Hsi Men was overwhelmed immediately after his return, not one, as may be imagined, was so welcome as that of young Wang. After all, he might hope, on this occasion, to see the Lady Lin again. The dinner in the house of Wang was given on the third afternoon following his return. His young host received him before the threshold and led him, with elaborate courtesy, into the front reception hall.

Above the entrance to the hall he read, in letters of gold, formed by the Imperial brush, the inscription: "Hall of Long-Inherited Loyalty." After the introductory formalities, and during the course of the meal, Hsi Men begged for permission to greet the Lady Lin, and a little while later he was invited to enter the central reception hall. Lady Lin was there awaiting him. She was wearing a dark red robe, clasped about her waist by a jeweled golden girdle. Over this she wore a short, open tunic of black satin, embroidered with a hundred flowers. Her tresses were weighted with great pearls, golden brooches, and blue-green kingfisher feathers of enamel. She stood there like a precious statue of cast silver. Hsi Men offered his apologies, explaining that on account of his official journey to the Eastern Capital he had been unable to wait upon her punctually on her birthday; and he gracefully presented her with a congratulatory beaker, which Mother Wen, standing in the background, placed in his hand. He then beckoned to his servant, Tai A, who offered to Lady Lin the present which his master had brought with him—a robe of glittering gold brocade, lying on a red lacquer tray. The lady thanked him, visibly delighted, and in return she welcomed him with a brimming golden beaker, which Mother Wen offered on a silver tray.

Now they sat down, and young Wang really wanted to bring in the four singing-boys, whom he had engaged for the evening to entertain his guest. But his mother protested.

"Let them display their art later on, in the front of the house; they would disturb us here now," she decided. And she continued, turning to Hsi Men: "May I beg the noble gentleman to rise to his feet? My child wishes to honor you by his filial reverence. Hitherto the young man has neglected his studies and has frequented bad company. If in your kindness you will condescend to allow him, in future, to profit a little by your wisdom and your advice, he begs that he may greet you in my presence as his moral father."

Hsi Men, who of course was perfectly conscious of the secret intention behind her proposal, protested at first, merely out of politeness.

"Noble Tai tai, my young friend, your son, is by nature endowed with remarkable talents. One must make allowances for his verdant youth if hitherto his impetuous foot has not been wholly able to accustom itself to the exalted path of the true Way, the Tao. But be assured that his own nature will sooner or later lead him towards the inner transformation, and open wide the portals of his heart to all things good and beautiful. Your fears are groundless."

"If you decline to acknowledge him as your moral son, then I must repudiate responsibility for his further misdemeanors."

Hereupon Hsi Men resigned himself to mounting the dais, and in that exalted position he accepted the fourfold filial kowtow of young Wang, and the brimming beaker which the latter offered him once and twice and thrice. Then, descending from the dais, he bowed before Lady Lin with his hands clenched before his breast, in the easy greeting which is customary between husband and wife. Radiant with delight she responded with a gentle *Wan fu*.

"Now lead the noble gentleman to the front of the house again, and see that he makes himself comfortable and is well entertained," she bade her son.

Hsi Men therefore took his leave of her and allowed his host to escort him back to the front reception hall, where the interrupted meal was resumed. The four young musicians, with voice and lute, provided the table music.

From this hour the relation between Hsi Men and young Wang was like that of father and son. Henceforth Hsi Men no longer needed to creep secretly into the house, entering by the postern gate of the park; he could enter openly, holding up his head, through the main portal. And so a worthy institution was made the means of opening a convenient path to wanton intercourse.

CHAPTER THIRTY-FIVE: *Gold Lotus is put out of Humor by a Mourning Custom. Jade Fountain feels herself cast aside and falls ill*

AMONG THE CONGRATULANTS who fore-gathered in Hsi Men's house on the day before Jade Fountain's birthday, which was on the twenty-sixth day of the eleventh month, and who, in accordance with ancient custom, would remain his guests for a few days, were the two nuns Pi and Wang. Nun Pi had kept her promise, and had brought with her the magic potion which Gold Lotus had ordered. She took advantage of a convenient moment to slip away unnoticed from the general company, which had seated itself beside Moon Lady, in order secretly to visit Gold Lotus in her pavilion.

"Here is what I promised you," she said, when she found herself alone with Gold Lotus, giving her the little flask which contained the magic drops. "On the seven-times-seventh day of the sixty-day cycle, to be mixed with a little wine and taken on a fasting stomach! If you sleep with your husband that same night you may rely on it that you will conceive and in due time bear a son. The great Bodhisattva in the rear apartments became pregnant after she had employed my prescription. To increase its effect I have brought you this little red powder. Keep it safe in your perfume sachet and on every night of love use it as I shall tell you. Then it will certainly be a male child."

Greatly delighted, Gold Lotus thanked her and hid the little flask and the powder in her secret drawer. Then she opened the calendar. The seven-times-seventh day of the sixty-day cycle fell on the twenty-ninth day of that month.

She weighed out three scanty bits of silver and gave them to the nun. "Take this as a small payment for your trouble. If your prescription should take effect and enable me to become pregnant, you shall have also a length of material for a new gown."

"Oh, pray don't go to any expense on account of such a trifling service!" said the nun, with a rather sour expression. "I am not so set on gain as Sister Wang. Only think how she haggled and squabbled with me over the few ounces of our fee when we had to recite the household prayers for your recently departed Bodhisattva! I do such things entirely without any selfish intentions, merely because it rejoices me to do good to a fellow creature."

At the common supper on the eve of Jade Fountain's birthday Hsi Men's thoughts dwelt once more, in melancholy recollection, on his Sixth, whose place was today unoccupied; and he could not repress a few tears of emotion. Gold Lotus observed them with chagrin. And when he bade the two singing-boys, who had been engaged to entertain the company, to intone in honor of the dead the mournful hymn that begins with the lines:

> *This solemn feast to hold again*
> *Full many a noble guest is here:*
> *To sobbing flutes the lyres complain:*
> *Where art thou, best beloved, O where?*

—then she could no longer control herself. Nervously rocking to and fro on her chair, as though in burlesque agony, she burst out, in the middle of the performance:

"Children, that sounds as solemn and desolate as if we were pledging ourselves to the ten penances in a cold place of worship! After all, the Sixth had already been married a long while; she didn't enter the household as an untouched virgin!"

"Pst!" Hsi Men protested, with a reproving glance. "One can't appreciate a note if you chatter like that. Do please allow them to sing it through!"

And long after the mournful hymn was ended he sat in silence with bowed head. But Gold Lotus rattled on all the more persistently, teasing the two singing-boys with derisive and disapproving comments on their performance. At last Moon Lady lost patience: "Sister Five, kindly control yourself and leave the boys alone!" she cried, in a tone of severe reproof. "As a matter of fact, you might go and keep Aunt Yang and Sister-in-law Wu company for a little while. They are sitting all alone in their room, and must find it tedious. Sister Sunflower will go with you."

In this way Gold Lotus found herself politely dismissed.

Hsi Men rose from the table not long afterwards, in order to continue the feast in the front of the house with Beggar Ying, Master Warm, and Brother-in-law Wu. Gold Lotus had made up her mind, since his return, that she would not let him out of her sight. When the company assembled in Moon Lady's room had broken up late that evening she made as though to go to her pavilion, but immediately afterwards she crept back again and lay in wait in the shadow of the wall not far from the inner gate that led to the women's apartments.

She had not long to wait before she saw Hsi Men approaching. He had just bidden his guests farewell, and was now on his way through the inner gate to Moon Lady's apartments. She cautiously crept after him and crouched, listening, under the window of the still brightly-lighted sitting room. She could distinguish the voices of Moon Lady and Jade Fountain, and a little later the accents of Hsi Men. They were discussing the two new singing-boys, who had visited the house for the first time that night, and were definitely not appreciated by the ladies. "Perfect little tortoises, who can't sing, but simply play the fool!" said Moon Lady, disapprovingly; while Jade Fountain thought their program unsuitable.

Moved by one of her sudden whims, Gold Lotus had crept silently into the room and was hiding by the door behind the hangings of the divan.

"You are perfectly right; the little tortoises ought to have sung for the living, not for a dead person!" she suddenly exclaimed from her hiding place, repeating the very words which had just been used. Startled, the others turned round.

"Sister Five, how do you come to be here of a sudden?" cried Jade Fountain in astonishment. "You gave me a nice fright! You creep about just like a ghost!"

Gold Lotus, ignoring her, turned to Hsi Men, and continued, raising her voice: "Was the Sixth in any way better than the rest of us? Was she an untouched virgin when she entered this household? What was the sense of that preposterous glorification of her by a sentimental song which didn't in the least fit her case? But it's true, isn't it?—now she's dead your food means nothing to you, and you can't digest it properly? Aren't those your own words? We other women, including your First, this pattern of a wife, simply don't count. Only one woman, the Sixth, means anything to you! The rest of us can do what we will to please you, it leaves you cold! But one has only to mention your Sixth, and your heart brims over with emotion!"

"My dear Sister Five, do drop the subject!" said Moon Lady, resignedly. "After all, it is usually the best who die young. We others are just a little behind our time. But do let him say what he wishes!"

"No, I won't have him speak so unjustly!"

"This is all so much nonsense," growled Hsi Men, who in his intoxicated condition had some difficulty in following the rapid dialogue of the two women. "When am I supposed to have spoken unjustly?"

"Just think a moment! Your friend Ying and Master Warm could bear witness that you once complained in their presence that since the death of your Sixth nothing goes right in the kitchen, or indeed in the whole household. You can't expect that it will until all the rest of us are dead, and have made way for the new wife, Ju I, whom you find so exactly like the Sixth, so precisely what you want! Poof, you heartless scoundrel!"

But this was too much even for the good-natured Hsi Men. Like an enraged animal he leapt at Gold Lotus and aimed a furious kick at her. But Gold Lotus was quicker; like a breath of vapor she had fled from the room. He tried to overtake her, but outside the door he collided with her maid, Spring Plum. He checked himself for a moment, laid his arm heavily on the girl's shoulders, and dragged her with him to her mistress's pavilion. Moon Lady was thankful to be rid of him, as he was badly intoxicated, and she particularly wished to be undisturbed that evening, so that she could give her mind to spiritual things in the society of the two nuns.

Gold Lotus had fled into the protecting darkness of the promenade, where the maid Jade Flute joined her. Hsi Men, supported by Spring Plum, had just gone by without seeing her.

"I wager he means to sleep with you tonight," said Jade Flute, softly.

"He must sleep off his drink first, then!" replied Gold Lotus, disdainfully. "I can't stand him in that condition."

She followed the two at a distance, and after she had convinced herself, from outside the pavilion, that Spring Plum was helping him to undress, she returned at a leisurely pace to Moon Lady's sitting room. There all were gathered round the nun Pi, who, with her feet tucked under her, and a low incense table beside her, was sitting on the comfortably heated kang, where she was about to preach a sermon on the doctrine of the Buddha. Pushing the curtain aside with a smile, Gold Lotus suddenly appeared amidst the devout assembly.

"Where have you suddenly reappeared from?" asked Moon Lady, in surprise. "I thought you would have put him to bed. You angered him dreadfully just now. You won't get off this time without a beating."

"Ha, ha! Just ask him," said Gold Lotus, with a careless laugh, "whether he would dare to beat me!"

"I am surprised at your impudence. Sister Three and I sweated two handfuls of anxiety while you were talking. I pity the poor dog who'll have to bear his anger in your place!"

"Let him rage! I am not afraid of him. It does him no harm to listen to the truth for once. Wasn't it infuriating? To have a dismal hymn of farewell sung on Jade Fountain's auspicious day! Besides, all this pious fuss isn't even genuine; it's common hypocrisy!"

"It would have been wiser to let him have his way and be silent," Aunt Yang suggested. "After all, one can sympathize with him; it must have grieved him to think of other such occasions, when the circle was complete, whereas today he saw the place of his Sixth empty."

"We others, after all, shouldn't have said anything, and we should probably have thought no more of his want of tact. But our Fifth," Jade Fountain continued, "who always immediately grasps the inner meaning of every song, discovered instantly that for him the song was a eulogy of the deceased. Since he had always in some ways preferred the Sixth, and has really been insufferable with his worship of her, Sister Five was quick to take this opportunity of telling him the truth for once!"

"She's so clever, your Fifth!" cried Aunt Yang, admiringly.

"Very clever; you have only to give her the beginning of a song, and she'll tell you at once how it continues!" Moon Lady added. "She knows the words of every song by heart, and she notices every little fault in its performance."

The conversation halted. Moon Lady washed her hands and rekindled the censer; whereupon Sister Pi related one of her legends of the saints. After this the company refreshed themselves with tea, cakes, and candied fruits. Then they proceeded to play round games. At last Gold Lotus took her leave of them and returned to her pavilion; and there, late at night, she took her place on the couch beside Hsi Men. In the meantime he had slept off his intoxication, and the little quarrel was soon forgotten in the usual sport of love.

On the following morning, as they lay in bed, and the conversation turned on the feast of the thirtieth day, which was to be held on the morrow, when Beggar Ying, to celebrate the birth of his child, had invited all Hsi Men's wives to his house, Gold Lotus suddenly declared, in a stubborn tone, "I'm not going."

"But why not, my dear child?"

"I've no furs to wear, and I don't want to catch cold on the way back, when we shall be overheated with wine. All the other wives have their fine furs, but I have none. You must give me the fur cloak the Sixth used to wear, or I shall stay at home."

"We have many good furs among our pledges in the store room. You could borrow one of those."

"Thanks, I don't wear pawned articles. I want to wear the cloak I spoke of; no other. I have only to put on a white silk gown, with a dark red tunic over it, embroidered with cranes, and I look just like your Sixth."

Next moment, completely conquered by her passionate caresses, he had given the desired consent.

After dressing, since Gold Lotus did not feel inclined to get up yet, he went across to the neighboring pavilion, in order to breakfast there. The nurse Ju I waited on him, a challenging smile on her over-powdered and painted face, for the maid Pear Blossom had to run to Moon Lady and fetch the key of the bedroom.

"Why is the bedroom to be opened?" asked the nurse inquisitively.

"I want to find a fur cloak for my Fifth."

"The sable, I suppose?"

"Yes, that's the one."

Since they were alone in the room, he seized the opportunity to pull her towards him and press her buxom bosom.

"How firm your breasts are! Yet you weaned the child months ago."

He affectionately pressed his face to her cheek and his mouth to her lips. And then she began: "Master, I see you spending so much time with your Fifth. I don't want to say anything about your other wives, but I do find the Fifth so unbearable. Recently, when you were traveling, she made a frightful scene over a washing dolly, and actually flew at me. I don't know what would have happened if the Sixth Wang hadn't separated us and if the Third mistress hadn't happened to come up. I don't know what mischief your Fifth may have made because you like me. Has she said anything to you about it?"

"Yes, she has. The best thing for you to do is to make a nice kowtow of apology to her on the next opportunity, and the thing will be forgotten. My Fifth is a rather difficult person. One can't do anything once she begins to talk."

"On the day after the quarrel she was quite friendly again. She told me that I must put up with the fact that she holds a privileged position. As far as that went, she didn't want to get in my way. A harbor has room for many vessels. All she wanted from me was frankness."

"Is that so? Then you've as good as made it up already. All the better. Now, be ready for my visit each evening!" he said eagerly.

Their conversation was interrupted by the entrance of the maid Pear Blossom. Hsi Men made her unlock the bedroom door and fetch the sable cloak from the wardrobe. She had to shake it thoroughly outside and then wrap it in a cloth. In the meantime Ju I took advantage of this favorable opportunity. "I have absolutely nothing to wear. Won't you find something for me in the wardrobe?" she begged.

At this he crossed the room, and laid out before her, with his own hands, the following garments from his late wife's richly-furnished wardrobe: a long, kingfisher-blue satin gown, a short yellow silk petticoat, a pair of long, blue, wadded trousers, and two pairs of drawers of flowered rose-pink silk. Beaming with satisfaction, and thanking him with a curtsy, Ju I gathered up these brightly-colored treasures. Hsi Men locked the bedroom door and sent the nurse to the neighboring pavilion with the sable cloak.

Gold Lotus, of course, understood immediately why he had chosen the nurse as his messenger.

"Has he been giving you some clothes too?" she wanted to know.

"Yes, two dresses! Also, I've got to ask you to forgive me."

She knelt and performed four kowtows. Gold Lotus was satisfied.

"Good, Sister. Always be perfectly honest. I know your master likes you, and I've nothing against that. As I have told you already, a harbor has room for many vessels. But I won't tolerate any opposition."

"I recognize you as my only mistress. Early and late I will try to win your favor."

"The First will probably want to know where you got the new clothes. What will you tell her?"

"I had already asked her consent. She gave it."

"Then that is all right. Now you can go."

When the nurse returned, Hsi Men had already left the pavilion. She asked the maid: "Did the First say anything when you went for the key?"

"Yes, she wished to know why the master wanted it. I told her he wanted to get a fur cloak out of the wardrobe for the Fifth. She said nothing to that."

In the meantime Hsi Men had gone to Moon Lady in order to return the key in person.

"Why did you want it?" she asked.

"The Fifth complained that she would have no fur to wear tomorrow, when she went to the celebration of the thirtieth day at the Yings'. She was afraid of catching cold on the way home. At her request I gave her the sable cloak the Sixth used to wear."

Moon Lady looked at him reprovingly.

"I think you are strangely inconsistent. When in accordance with the last wishes of the deceased I wanted to take the maid Apricot Blossom from the pavilion and allow her to wait on Sister Sunflower, you were angry, and reproached us bitterly, because you said we were in such a hurry to break up the household of the Sixth. And now you yourself are dispersing it and frittering it away."

Hsi Men did not know what to say to this.

That afternoon, while in the women's apartments Jade Fountain's birthday was being duly celebrated, Hsi Men was once more the host at a subscription dinner, which at the request of a number of high mandarins he was giving in honor of the Prefect of Kiu kiang, a son of the Chancellor Tsai King, then passing through the city, in the apartments which were so famed for their hospitality. Towards evening, when this official banquet was over, and the noble guests had taken their departure, he refreshed himself by an hour of jolly carousing with Beggar Ying and Master Warm. At last this session also was ended. Weary, and more than a little intoxicated, leaning heavily on the shoulders of his servant Lai An, he made his way, with reeling steps, to the pavilion of the Sixth. It had not occurred to him to honor his Third on her birthday with a brief hour of his society.

On hearing that he was about to go to bed Gold Lotus had hastily forsaken the feminine society assembled in Moon Lady's sitting room, and standing at the door of her pavilion, which he would be obliged to pass, she waited for him. And then he came with his escort, staggering past her with dragging feet. Without further ceremony she seized him by the hand and drew him into the pavilion, giving the servant to understand that his presence was no longer required. Lai An accordingly went to the women's apartments, where he helped to wait upon the guests.

"Where is your master, then?" asked Moon Lady.

"He is with the Fifth mistress," he replied. Moon Lady was indignant.

"It's unheard-of!" she said, turning to Jade Fountain. "I expressly told him that as it was your birthday it was only proper to spend the night with you. He's forgotten it already, and now he's carrying on with the Fifth. Since his return home it has been the same night after night. She has positively monopolized him."

"Never mind, Sister," said Jade Fountain, wearily. "You meant it kindly, but you shouldn't have spoken to her first. It looks as though I wanted to compete with her. If he doesn't come of himself. . . . To compel love . . . no, I couldn't do it."

With a sigh, Moon Lady changed the subject, washed her hands, and rekindled the censer. All gathered about the nun Pi, who had once more taken her place on the kang, with her feet tucked under her. Opening the roll of the Holy Scriptures which she had brought with her, in a soporific voice she began to read the wonderful legend of the pious virgin Huang.

With a few songs, contributed by Cinnamon Bud and the blind

singing-girl, Shen, and the consumption of enormous quantities of tea and sweetmeats, the birthday celebrations reached their close at a late hour of the night, without the assistance of Hsi Men.

Hsi Men did not remain long with Gold Lotus. When she asked him why he did not undress he confessed, with a smile, that he intended to spend the night in the neighboring pavilion. Still smiling at her reproaches, he stumbled out of the door.

Next morning Jade Flute came to Gold Lotus, faithful to the secret agreement between the two, in order to tell her what had happened the day before in Moon Lady's apartments.

"Why didn't you remain with the others last night?" Jade Flute began. "My mistress went for you finely after you had rushed off so suddenly. She said it was unjust and tactless of you to monopolize Master Hsi Men on the Third mistress's birthday. And then the Third said you had no sense of decency, and that you were trying to play the mistress of the household, but that she refused to compete with you."

"Just wait a bit! They shall have something to complain of when I come to reckon with them!" said Gold Lotus, gnashing her teeth with rage. "But how did your mistress know that he spent last night with me?"

"Oh, well, in that connection you are the only person who counts now that the Sixth is dead."

"Really? So her empty nest has not been occupied in the meantime?"

"My mistress was annoyed, moreover, because you had taken the sable cloak of the Sixth to wear without saying a word to her first. When Master Hsi Men brought the key back to her she told him he was inconsistent, and that he himself was now squandering and frittering away the effects of his Sixth."

"Absurd. He is master in the house, and it's for him to decide what he will and won't do."

The feeling of resentment against Gold Lotus which had for some time been accumulating in Moon Lady's heart, was given further nourishment this day by two fresh incidents. While Hsi

577

Men's five wives were being entertained in Friend Ying's house, where they were celebrating, together with a dozen wives of relatives and neighbors, the day on which Ying's offspring had safely completed his first month, another company had assembled for a joyful banquet in the pavilion of the Sixth. The nurse Ju I had invited the maids Apricot Blossom, Pear Blossom, and Spring Plum, and also Hsi Men's daughter, Sister-in-law Wu, and Gold Lotus's mother, to help her to dispose of the abundant remains of the previous night's supper. Thanks to their consumption of a very heady wine, they were soon in uproarious spirits, and little Spring Plum conceived the notion of inviting the blind singing-girl, Shen, to spice the conversation by singing a few songs. But the singer would not take orders from a maid; she proudly refused to come. And then the hot-tempered little Spring Plum made so violent a scene that the singer took offense, packed her things, weeping as she did so, and left the house.

In the evening, on her return from the house of Ying, Moon Lady found that the singer, who had been her guest, was gone, and learned that she had been intimidated by Spring Plum. This filled her with anger, and she felt obliged to blame Gold Lotus for the unbecoming behavior of her maid. Gold Lotus, of course, took her maid's part, and retorted with scornful personalities. Hsi Men refused to take the matter tragically: he thought the singer would soon be conciliated if on the morrow Spring Plum were to take her an ounce of silver and a few delicacies. Moon Lady, however, was not to be appeased; losing her temper, she retired, with Hsi Men, to her bedroom.

As a result of the uncomfortable atmosphere the rest of the women silently retired to their own apartments. Gold Lotus alone, still decked in all her splendor, and wearing the sable cloak, just as she had stepped out of her palanquin, remained in the sitting room, nervously waiting for Hsi Men to appear again and accompany her to her pavilion. For this was the seven-times-seventh day of the sixty-day cycle; tonight, at all costs, she must share her couch with him and test the efficacy of Sister Pi's magic potion.

But she waited in vain. Hsi Men did not appear. At last she lost patience. She simply opened the door of the adjoining room, and called out: "I can't wait for you any longer. I am going."

"Yes, you go on ahead; I shall just finish my drink and will follow you at once," he cried good-naturedly; at which she rustled away.

"You are not going to her! I won't have it!" said Moon Lady, interrupting him sternly. "For once, I must speak to you very seriously. I know, of course, that you eat out of the same platter. All the same, it is an unheard-of piece of insolence that she should actually force her way into my bedroom and call to you. She behaves here as though you were her wife, and had to obey her orders, and as though the rest of us didn't exist. Since you returned from your journey we others have barely seen the edge of your shadow, she has monopolized you so completely. Not a single night have you had to spare for the rest of us. That of course, doesn't matter as far as I am concerned, but I do know of someone who is suffering greatly from this behavior of yours, even though she says nothing. Sister Jade Fountain couldn't swallow a mouthful at the party today, she was so full of suppressed emotion. Her sister-in-law Ying forced a beaker of wine on her; she drank it out of politeness, but she brought it up again immediately. You owe it to her to go to her now and ask her how she is feeling."

"I don't want any more to drink. I don't feel like it," Hsi Men declared, peevishly. He rose to his feet and went off to find Jade Fountain.

She had already undressed herself and put aside her hair ornaments; she was lying face downwards across the bed, dressed only in her nightgown, vomiting into a pail. Hsi Men was greatly shocked by her pitiful appearance.

"My dear, what is the matter with you? Tell me! I'll send for the doctor as soon as it's day," he said, in consternation.

She made no reply, but was sick again. He picked her up and sat down beside her.

"My stomach's upset," she said at last, speaking with difficulty, pressing her hand to the pit of her stomach. "But why do you ask? What's the use? Go away and amuse yourself!"

"My darling, I had no idea that you were unwell! I have only just learned of it."

"That just shows me that for you I simply don't exist! Go away, do, go to your beloved!"

He laid his arm about her neck and kissed her. Then he called the maid Fragrant Orchid.

"Quick, some bitter tea!"

"I've just made it."

"Give it to me! And then take away the pail!"

He took the bowl of bitter, steaming tea in his hand and carefully held it to the sick woman's lips.

"Thanks, but I can manage it myself," she said, as she took the bowl from his hand. "Why do you trouble about me? For you to come here is as unnatural as though the sun were to rise in the West. I know Moon Lady persuaded you to come. I don't want you in the least."

"I really couldn't come to see you any earlier," he said in apology. "I've been so occupied all day."

"I know your heart was occupied all day!"

"You must be hungry," he said, changing the subject. "I too have had no supper. We'll have something together."

"No thanks. You have something yourself. I'm not in the mood for eating."

"Then I won't have anything. Tomorrow I'll send for Doctor Yen. And now we'll lie down and go to sleep."

"Please spare me your doctors. Old Liu is just as good."

"Wait a minute—I'll doctor you myself. An acquaintance of mine brought me recently ten pills of the best Kwang tung ox-gall. An excellent remedy for stomach troubles. Just go quickly to my First," he said, turning to Fragrant Orchid, "and ask her to give you two of the Kwang tung ox-gall pills. They are in a small agate bowl on the ledge of the mirror in her bedroom. And bring a flask of hot wine at the same time."

580

"I am really curious to see what sort of a doctor you are!" said Jade Fountain, who was already in a more conciliatory mood. "But as for wine, I have some here."

Presently the maid returned with the required remedy. Hsi Men peeled off the wax covering of the pills, which had a golden luster, and dissolved them in a beaker of hot wine. After Jade Fountain had drunk the contents he asked for a second beaker for himself.

"I want to take some medicine too," he added.

Jade Fountain knew what medicine he intended to take.

"Hadn't you better go somewhere else to do that?" she asked with a searching glance. "It seems to me that this is hardly the right place for such stupid tricks."

"Very well, I won't take it." He undressed and lay down beside her. For some little while he gently stroked her breasts and her body.

"Do you feel any better yet?"

"Thanks, the pain has gone. I still feel a certain amount of commotion in my body."

"That's not a bad sign, and it will soon quiet down. Do you realize that while you were out today I had to discuss the whole menu of the dinner which I am giving here the day after tomorrow, at the request of my colleagues, in honor of the Censor Sung. I had to go through it all with Lai Hsing. Fifty ounces that little junketing will cost me. And then on the first I have to go to the temple, where I must offer a sacrifice and burn incense in fulfillment of a vow I made in respect of my safe return home. On the third I have to give another dinner, and so it goes on. You wouldn't believe how all these social obligations take up my time; and then there are my official duties, so that I really have hardly any time left for domestic affairs."

As he spoke he gently drew one of her legs towards him, until it lay across his chest. How smooth and white her thigh was! And how charming the red satin slipper looked on her slender foot!

"Do you know, I think your smooth white legs are your greatest charm," he said, in a flattering tone. "In the whole world there is no one to compare with you in that respect!"

"You deceiver! Do you suppose I take any notice of your flattery? What you really mean, of course, is that there's no one in the whole world with such great legs and such a muddy skin as mine. One knows well enough that you mean right when you say left!"

"My heart, my liver, may I die here and now if I am lying!"

"Better not challenge destiny!"

He had been nestling closer and closer; and now he had found his way.

"I did beg you not to bother me with your nonsense!" she said, still feigning to resist him. But very soon her mouth was making those quivering, snapping motions which one may observe in a dog that is snapping at flies, and her lips without ceasing, uttered their tender cry of *"Ta ta."* With redoubled efforts Hsi Men endeavored that night to atone for the injustice with which he had treated his Third. But Gold Lotus sought her lonely couch with a heart full of bitter resentment. She had been shamefully cheated of her hope of testing the nun's magic potion on this seven-times-seventh day of the sixty-day cycle.

Next morning, at the family breakfast table, Moon Lady, turning to Jade Fountain, asked whether the wax pills had benefited her.

"I was sick twice more early this morning, but now I feel quite well again."

Gold Lotus did not appear at breakfast. Moon Lady wanted to send Little Jewel for her.

"Little Jewel is in the kitchen, baking the cakes; I'll go instead," said Jade Flute; and off she went.

"I must tell you what happened last night," she said to Gold Lotus. "When you had gone my mistress said just what she thought about you. She said you were shameless, that you ruined the peace of the household, and that you and Master Hsi Men ate out of one platter. You had completely monopolized him; you ordered him about as if he had been your wife, and never let him show himself in the women's apartments. And then she sent him to the Third.

He spent the night with her. What's more, she told her sister-in-law and the two nuns that you had ruined Spring Plum, and it was your fault that she had no manners. Master Hsi Men wanted to send Spring Plum to the blind singer; she was to apologize to her and take her an ounce of silver as compensation."

Gold Lotus made no reply, but what she had heard she stored up in her heart.

"Where is the Fifth?" asked Moon Lady, as Jade Flute returned.

"The Fifth mistress will be here directly."

"You see," said Moon Lady, turning to Sister-in-law Wu, "one said barely two words to her yesterday, and she's behaving as though she had been insulted. I expect there'll be another scene today."

"Who dares to say that I've monopolized him?" suddenly cried Gold Lotus's voice, from behind the curtain of the veranda door. She had crept up to the door unnoticed.

"Do you wish to deny it?" cried Moon Lady, angrily. "Day after day, since his return, you have seized upon him and kept him for yourself. The rest of us barely see the edge of his shadow. You behave as though you were his only wife, as though the rest of us didn't exist. Yes, that was exactly what I said."

"And it's a pack of lies! He wasn't with me yesterday, nor the day before."

"*You* are lying! Hadn't you the insolence to come in here last night, when he was quietly sitting with me, and order him to come to you, as though it were a matter of course that he would do so? He is man enough to know what he ought to do and leave undone. How do you contrive to fetter him with cords of pig's hair and rob him of his freedom of movement? You are always running after him and trying to catch him for yourself. Is that seemly? Is it the reserve that one expects of a decent woman? Moreover, you appropriated the sable cloak of the Sixth behind my back. Couldn't you have spoken to me about it first? And what of the unmannerly way in which your maid behaved to the singing-girl, who was my guest, who frequents a hundred houses, and will of course gossip about us and bring us into disrepute? Can't you teach her better manners?"

"Well, chastise her yourself! She's as much your maid as mine. I've nothing to say to that. As for the fur, I didn't appropriate it; it was given to me. As far as that goes, on the same occasion he presented somebody else with various articles from the Sixth wife's wardrobe. Why do you blame only me for unseemly conduct?"

Moon Lady mistakenly believed that this last remark was aimed at her, though it actually referred to the nurse Ju I and her secret relations with her master. Angered beyond all control, her cheeks crimson with fury, she burst into voluble speech: "I suppose that means that I myself am guilty of unseemly behavior? No, I at all events know what is right and proper. I was decently brought up in an honorable family, and I was lawfully married to him; I am an honest and respectable wife, not a shameless harlot like yourself, who runs after every man she sees!"

"Big Sister, don't be so angry!" said Jade Fountain, seeking to appease her. "In your excitement you quite overlook the fact that you are hitting us with the same club!" And turning to Gold Lotus: "Sister Five," she said, "do let there be an end of all this controversy! Must you always have the last word?"

"This dispute is not exactly pleasant for your guests," added Sister-in-law Wu. "If it continues perhaps one had better get into one's palanquin and leave the house."

Gold Lotus, who was beside herself with rage at these rebukes, threw herself down at full length. Her hair became unfastened, tears of rage flooded her cheeks, and like a madwoman she struck herself and beat her head upon the floor.

"I will endure this aimless life no longer! I would rather die!" she cried in despair. "I am supposed to have run after him when he took me into his household! Very well, as soon as he comes home I shall ask him for a letter of divorce, and go. Then no one can ever say again that I ran after him."

Jade Fountain could endure this squabbling no longer. She took

584

Gold Lotus by the hand and tried to lead her away to her own pavilion.

"You really ought to control yourself better! We are making ourselves a laughing stock to our guests! Come! Stand up!" And with the help of Jade Flute she pulled the resisting woman to her feet and escorted her to her pavilion.

"One always enjoys one's visits to you when everyone is cheerful and contented," said Sister-in-law Wu, when Gold Lotus had gone. "But under these circumstances one loses all desire to remain any longer."

The two nuns had already made their preparations for departure, and now came to make their farewells, carrying food boxes in their hands.

"This has been very painful," said Moon Lady, in an apologetic tone. "I do hope you won't think us too ridiculous."

"My dear Bodhisattva, you needn't apologize!" replied Sister Pi. "In every household it sometimes happens that the chimney smokes. But the dusting of a soul tablet is a work pleasing to the gods. You should just try to be a little more indulgent to each other. One must contrive to master whatever monkey feelings and horse thoughts one may harbor. And now, dear Bodhisattva, many thanks for all your kindness! The simple nun takes her leave of you."

Moon Lady responded with a double *Wan fu,* sending Hsi Men's daughter and Sunflower to see her to the gate, so that she would not be molested by the watchdog.

"See how my shoulders are twitching with excitement, and my hands are icy cold," said Moon Lady to her Sister-in-law Wu. "The cup of tea which I drank before this unpleasantness is splashing about inside me undigested."

"I have always warned you against excitement, but you wouldn't obey me. You ought to have more consideration for your state of advanced pregnancy."

"Sister-in-law, you have been visiting this house for years. Have you ever seen me quarrel with her before? But this time I was in the right, and she behaved like a nocturnal brawler who storms at the night watchman when the latter bids him be quiet. I am certainly a tolerant person, but she is really intolerable. We are five women to one man, but she wants him for herself alone. Instead of taking the lamp and turning it upon herself she dares to accuse other people of invented improprieties. When the Sixth was alive she made things difficult for her, and did everything possible to humiliate her. Now I shall have to wash my eyes and take care that she does not bring me to the grave. She has the face of a human being, but the heart of a beast. Everything about her is false. She herself doesn't believe in her declamations and her oaths; she is only trying to impress people. With the best of intentions I invited her to breakfast this morning with her mother. Who could have guessed that she had already sent her mother home? She had made up her mind beforehand to have a quarrel with me. And think how she suddenly came creeping in, after listening outside on the veranda! She's really becoming quite gruesome! I am only concerned with what she may tell him when he comes home. Probably it will come to this, that he will give the letter of divorce not to her, but to me!"

"Jade Flute and I were in the room, attending to the stove, when the Fifth mistress suddenly came in," Little Jewel interposed. "Neither of us saw her or heard her outside on the veranda."

"She creeps about as silently as a ghost," said Snowblossom. "No wonder; she has felt soles to her slippers. She once forced such a quarrel on me, and abused me so to the master that he struck me."

"Truly," agreed Moon Lady, "none of us is safe from her attacks. Who knows what I have to expect? Did you see how she beat her head upon the floor? Of course she's reckoning that when he sees her bruises he'll pity her and be furious with me."

"But that would be turning the world upside down!" cried Snowblossom.

"You don't know her. She's a nine-tailed vixen. She's capable of any sort of witchcraft. Think of her insolence last night, when she came into my room and called out to him that she couldn't wait any longer for him, and was going on ahead! As though he were her sole possession! Not for a single night does she allow us to have him; she has no respect even for a birthday! Surely as a child she must have put all ten fingers in her mouth in her gluttony!"

"My dear, you shouldn't take the matter to heart so; you must put it out of your mind, or you'll be quite ill!" said Sister-in-law Wu. "What good will it do you to quarrel with her? Show more pride, and ignore her!"

Moon Lady, complaining of pain in her head and her body, retired to her bedroom, in order to lie down for a brief rest. Hsi Men was not a little surprised to find her lying tired and languid on the kang when he returned from the yamen at noon. When he asked her what had happened she did not reply; nor were her maids more communicative. His surprise increased when he found Gold Lotus lying on her bed. She seemed to be quite distracted; she had a headache, her eyes were red with weeping, and she too was dumb when he questioned her.

It was from Jade Fountain that he at last learned what had been happening. In consternation he hurried back to Moon Lady.

"You must have regard for your condition," he said, gently raising her. "How could you allow yourself to be involved in a quarrel with that silly woman?"

"It was not my fault; it was she who forced the quarrel on me. Ask the others if I am not speaking the truth. I am terribly anxious about the little one I am carrying under my heart. For there is a commotion in my body as though a great toad were kicking and struggling there. My head pains me and my shoulders are quite limp and lifeless, and I cannot digest my food. What I should like to do more than anything else today is to take a cord and hang myself."

Shocked by her words, Hsi Men pressed her to his breast. "Dear big sister, don't take the thing to heart so! You mustn't pay any serious attention to the irresponsible chatter of this uncultivated person, who can't tell high from low, or stench from perfume. I'll go straight to her now and call her to account."

"It's no use doing that. She'll simply entangle you in a hog's-hair string of lies until you don't know which way to turn."

"She had better not anger me, or I'll give her such a kicking.... Do you feel a little better now?"

"I don't know. Although I've had only a cup of tea today, there's such a commotion in my body, the pain in my head hasn't stopped, and my limbs are numb and heavy. If you don't believe me, feel my cold, trembling hands and see for yourself. . . . I haven't been able to take hold of anything since."

"Then I'll send for Doctor Yen at once."

"He can't help me. If it comes to that, it simply depends on fate whether one lives or dies. And why so much fuss about me? A humble grave by the city wall; I don't ask for more."

"But my love, what a way to talk! Don't worry about the mud that miserable woman throws at you! The doctor must certainly come. I want to know whether the fruit of your body is unharmed."

"Then let old Liu come. A few of her drops and two pricks of her cauterizing needle in my head; that's all I need."

"Nonsense! What does that old quack know of diagnosis and midwifery? You must have the doctor."

And he then and there bade his groom Kiu Tung saddle a horse and ride off to fetch Doctor Yen. But he came back without the doctor, who was that day the guest of the prefect. However, his wife would send him early in the morning. At first Hsi Men absolutely refused to leave his first wife's side, although Neighbor Kiao had repeatedly sent for him; for Kiao had invited him to his house that afternoon. Moon Lady persuaded him that he ought not to ignore this invitation.

At last he gave way to her, and left the house. Early that evening he was back again. The first thing he did was to visit Moon Lady. She had already left her bed. Sister-in-law Wu, Sunflower, and Jade Fountain were keeping her company.

"Well, are you better?" he asked sympathetically.

"Thanks, I have managed to take a little rice soup. My body has quieted down pretty well, only I still have rather a headache."

"And tomorrow you will be quite well again, when the doctor has given you something."

"Please don't have him! I feel so awkward in his presence. I won't in any circumstances show myself to a strange man."

But next morning, when Doctor Yen came, she did, after persistent refusal, show herself to him, to please her husband. With her hair carefully arranged, and fully dressed, she agreed to a short, ceremonious interview in the veranda room. He could not, of course, enter her bedroom; her strict views on such matters as good form and decency made this impossible. Sitting stiffly and demurely in her chair, she laid her right hand, which was hidden in the wide sleeve, on the damask cloth of the table which divided her from the doctor, and timidly allowed her delicate bamboo-shoot fingertips and her jade knuckles to peep forth beyond the hem of her sleeve. After Doctor Yen had felt her pulse for some time he thanked her with a bow, whereupon she rose, breathed a second *Wan fu,* and withdrew with measured step to her bedchamber.

While the doctor was refreshing himself with a cup of tea, the lad Kiu Tung appeared, having been sent by Moon Lady to facilitate his diagnosis by explaining in detail just how his mistress was feeling, and the nature of her various troubles.

"All that I knew beforehand," said the doctor pompously.

"My great and honorable First is pregnant and near delivery," Hsi Men added by way of further explanation. "Her troubles are due to the annoyance and excitement which she suffered yesterday. I have confidence in your supramundane power of intellect; you will surely take measures for her quick recovery. You may count on a generous reward."

"This tyro," said the physician, "gives ear to your instructions and will not fail to do the utmost that is in his power to restore to her womb the necessary peace and to her breath the accustomed harmony."

He thereupon launched into a learned and long-winded description of the case, in which he spoke of "too little blood," "too much air," "fire in the liver," and "impeded flow in the veins." He then wrote his prescription, and he had also to prescribe a remedy for the Third wife's stomach trouble. This done, he pocketed his fee and took his leave.

In the meantime Jade Fountain had paid a visit to Gold Lotus, when she tried to bring about a reconciliation between the Fifth and Moon Lady. She found Gold Lotus undressed and unkempt, sitting on the edge of her bed. She was pale, and looked as though she had had a sleepless night.

"Why, Sister Five, not dressed yet?" she began. "Today is Moon Lady's birthday; you surely won't be missing from the table! Do at last bury your resentment and wear a cheerful face again! She is quite ready to make it up. Just go to her room, make a kowtow of apology, and add a few friendly words. Then the whole thing will be dead and buried. A kind word in winter makes us forget the cold, an angry word makes us-shiver on a midsummer day. So the proverb tells us. You have both spoken your minds; now you must make it up again. Otherwise you will let yourself in for further trouble, if Hsi Men comes to see you and wants to discuss the affair."

"How can I ever show myself to her again?" Gold Lotus objected. "After she has said that she is a respectable and lawfully married wife, not such a creature as you or I, who had to run after our husband, and who before that used to sleep in the grass and the dew. . . . No, after such words as those, women like you and me can't venture within reach of her highly respectable toes!"

"I know, I know. But I've already answered that on behalf of the rest of us: don't you remember? I told her that she was beating us all with the same stick, for we were all of us married later than Moon Lady. But after all, our entry into this household was made in a perfectly respectable fashion. Weren't the matchmakers employed, weren't witnesses summoned, in the proper manner? No, there can be no question of our having run after anybody. There she is quite in the wrong, and she really sees it herself. It only needs a little tolerance on either side, and all will be forgotten. What will our guests and acquaintances be thinking if they find such discord prevailing in the household? So dress yourself quickly and come with me."

Gold Lotus pondered awhile; then she made up her mind. She would control herself, and swallow the words that were on her tongue. So she sat down to the mirror and put up her hair and dressed herself. Jade Fountain took her by the hand and led her to Moon Lady's apartments.

"I have brought her!" she cried, raising the curtain and triumphantly dragging her hesitating captive into the room. Gold Lotus went humbly up to Moon Lady, raised her eyes from the ground, and said in a low voice: "Cousin, I have come to apologize. In my youthful lack of thought I have annoyed you. I beg that you will this time overlook it. If I am ever so ill-mannered again your hand may chastise me as it will; I shall not move."

She knelt and performed four kowtows before Moon Lady. No sooner had she risen to her feet than she nimbly sprang at Jade Fountain and gave her a gentle slap, crying, in a jesting tone: "Wicked woman, through your fault yet another 'New One' has entered the household!"

At this all the wives, including the dignified Moon Lady, burst out laughing. With two words Gold Lotus had contrived to change the painful solemnity of the moment into merriment.

"When you are all so happy and cheerful it is pleasant to be with you," said Sister-in-law Wu, in a gratified tone. "If you would always be so friendly and peaceable! A peony blossom is a very lovely thing, but it is seen at its best only in the green wreath of its foliage."

"One must admit that there is no one like our Fifth for speaking the right word at the right time," added Moon Lady, with a smile.

And so peace was restored in the women's apartments.

CHAPTER THIRTY-SIX: *Spring Plum has a Fit of the Sulks and pretends to be injured. Hua Tung flees from Master Warm*

THAT EVENING, when Hsi Men had bidden his First good night, and had already left the room in order to join Gold Lotus, Moon Lady called him back.

"Don't go to her tonight," she begged. "After she has just had to apologize to me she had better be left alone for a while to think things over. Your visit might bring her too quickly to another frame of mind."

"But I wasn't going to her."

"Also, please, avoid the pavilion of the Sixth. I shouldn't like you immediately to give her another excuse for complaining that I am intolerant only where she is concerned, but indulgent when you amuse yourself with a certain other person."

"Oh, don't worry so much about her opinion."

"Do oblige me, and at least for today avoid both pavilions. I don't ask you to remain with me. Go to Sister Sunflower. You have neglected her for a long while. From tomorrow you can do what you like again."

Yielding to persuasion, he spent that night with Sunflower. It was late the next evening before he visited Gold Lotus, for all day long he was fully occupied by his official duties and a protracted banquet. Before he set foot across her threshold she had quickly undressed herself, deliberately disordered her hair, turned out the lamp, and thrown herself across the bed, clad only in a nightgown.

On entering the pavilion he called for the maid Spring Plum. There was no answer. In the darkened bedroom he found her mistress lying across the bed, her face buried in the pillows, as though fast asleep. She did not move when he called her name. He sat on the edge of the bed and carefully lifted her in his arms.

"What does this mean? Why don't you answer? Are you out of your mind?" he asked, anxiously, already prepared for more bad news.

Instead of replying to his questions she burst into such a violent and piteous fit of sobbing that only if he had been made of stone and iron could he have failed to be completely softened and subdued.

"My darling, do be calm! Everything is all right again!" he assured her, tenderly embracing her. "How could you involve yourself in this unnecessary squabble?"

"I didn't do anything," she burst out violently. "She picked a quarrel with me in order to humiliate me before everybody. She said I had monopolized you and wouldn't let anyone else have you, and I ran after you until you took me into your house. She was a respectable and reliable person, and a lawfully married wife, but I was a thoroughly perverted creature, no better than a common harlot.

"Why do you trouble to come here—why don't you stay with her? You'll only be monopolized and tied hand and foot with cords of hog's hair. I've unlawfully appropriated the fur cloak that belonged to the Sixth, and I've taught my maid bad manners—I had to endure all this! And in the end I had to give in; I was made to go to her and kneel down before her like a common maidservant and whine for her forgiveness. And all these humiliations on account of a blind singing-girl! It would never have come to this if you were a real man—if you didn't let yourself be ordered about. Have you got to ask for permission beforehand if you want to give anyone a fur coat? But of course, women like us don't count. What one buys dear one holds dear; what one gets easily one parts with easily, says the proverb. There is no relying on you at all!

"Who wouldn't venture to come here yesterday for fear of arousing her displeasure? Who was so anxious about her health that he sent for the doctor? A fuss is made about her, but I live on the shady side of the mountain. Not a ray of sunlight warms me; I can grieve and pine, I can die in my solitude, and no one asks what I am suffering. And then I am persuaded to violate my feelings, to stifle my tears; I must go running to her and beg her forgiveness! Oh, it's unbearable!"

While she poured forth her troubles the pearly tears never ceased to roll down her peachlike cheeks. Now, loudly sobbing, she laid herself upon his breast.

He stifled her further complaints with his kisses. Then he called for tea. Autumn Aster, who had some time ago returned to Gold Lotus's service, appeared with the lamp and a tea tray.

"Oh, but I don't want my tea served by this girl's grubby hands," he said, peevishly pushing the tray aside. "Where is Spring Plum?"

"Do you ask me that? She might very well have starved to death by now," Gold Lotus informed him. "She's lying there next door; for three days she hasn't touched a grain of rice, a drop of tea; her only desire is to die. She can't forget how your First humiliated and shamed her before everybody."

"Really?" he said, doubtfully.

"If you don't believe me go and see for yourself."

Greatly perturbed, Hsi Men rose and went into the next room. There he found the little maid just as he had found her mistress; lying across the kang with loosened hair and disheveled clothing.

"Well, little one, why don't you get up when your master has come?"

She did not move, but pretended to be asleep. He seized her by the waist and attempted to lift her, but she leaped into the air like a carp in the net, so that she would have given him a thumping blow on the nose if he had not started back in time. He seized her firmly by the hands and forced her down upon the kang, so that she could not escape him again.

"Ta, ta, please let me go!" she begged. "And anyhow, what do you want with your unworthy slave? You only soil your hands when you touch her."

"Crazy little oily-mouth, how can you make such a grievance of two words from your First mistress? Have you really eaten nothing for days?"

"Whether I have eaten or not doesn't matter in the least; I am only a miserable slave. What does it matter if I die? But I have always done my work faithfully, and now I am to allow myself to be shamed and chastised on account of any chance-come blind ballad singer. She has brought only misfortune to the house, and if ever the Sixth Wang, who sent her, shows herself here again she shall learn something!"

"Now won't you be so kind as to bring me a bowl of tea? I don't care to accept anything from the grubby hands of Autumn Aster."

"What if I were dead? Then you'd have to!"

"What is this talk of dying? Now, be reasonable and pull yourself together! The three of us will have a nice little supper together. Autumn Aster can run to the kitchen and bring something good to eat and drink."

He took the stubborn little creature by the hand and led her into the next room, where she had to lay two tables, a larger one for him and her mistress and a smaller one for herself.

Autumn Aster presently returned from the kitchen with a huge food basket, which contained all sorts of choice dishes and a jug of strong wine; and with a jolly feast the storm of the last few days reached a peaceful conclusion in the pavilion of the Fifth.

On the following day, the second of the twelfth month, both Hsi Men and Moon Lady were away from home. Hsi Men, who the day before had been entertaining the Governor of Shantung, escorted his departing guest to the gates of the city with the usual guard of honor; while Moon Lady had arranged to pay a birthday visit to the wife of the former District Judge Hsia. While both were absent Mother Wang, the proprietress of the tea house, made an unexpected appearance. Accompanying her was the District Inspector Hu Kiu, who, as the reader will remember, once laid Hsi Men under an obligation to him by helping him to hush up the murder of Wu Ta. Mother Wang would not at first venture to enter the gate, but asked to see Tai A. "Is your master at home?" she asked.

595

"Ha, what rare visitor has blown this way? No, the master isn't at home; he had to escort the Governor of Shantung, and the First has gone to pay a birthday visit," replied Tai A. "I'll tell the Fifth you are here."

Gold Lotus received her immediately. Quite overcome by her brilliant appearance, and the aristocratic setting in which she found her, Mother Wang was on the point of prostrating herself in a formal reverence. But Gold Lotus checked her with a laugh, dispensing with all ceremony. She was delighted to see a good old friend of earlier days, and invited her, without formalities, to sit beside her on the divan.

"Why haven't you shown yourself all this time, Mother Wang?"

"In my thoughts I have often been with you, but I have not ventured to cross your noble threshold. Has any little one arrived in the meantime?"

"Twice already. But the one child didn't live and the other was prematurely born. Has your son married in the meantime?"

"Not yet. He has been home a year now, and he brought some savings back with him, so that he was able to buy a donkey and set himself up in a little business; he sells noodles. Is Master Hsi Men at home?"

"No, he's escorting the Governor of Shantung to the city gate. The First is out also. What's the matter, then, Mother Wang?"

"I've brought District Inspector Hu Kiu with me. He wanted to make a petition to Master Hsi Men. It concerns his younger brother, who has unjustly been arrested on a charge of banditry. Here is the petition. Would you be so kind as to hand it to Master Hsi Men? It is to be hoped that he will be merciful. Master Hu Kiu would show his gratitude by a handsome present."

"Good, I'll see to it."

"Many thanks."

The old woman refreshed herself with a cup of tea, and during a pause in the conversation she examined her magnificent surroundings. "How fortunate you have been!" she sighed in admiration.

"What does fortunate mean? If only there were not so many

vexations it would be better. But day after day one has one's troubles."

"Dear mistress, you have so much to eat that your hands are hardly dry from washing them after meals, you dress in silks and satins, your hair is full of gold and silver ornaments, you have only to call for maids and servants. How can you speak of trouble and vexation?"

"When several eat out of the same dish there is bound to be trouble and strife. It isn't easy to get on with so many wives."

"But you will hold your own with the rest of them! Take advantage of the hour of his favor."

The old woman rose to take her leave.

How important an insignificant chance may sometimes be! That evening Moon Lady, Jade Fountain, and Gold Lotus were accompanying Sister-in-law Wu, who was returning to her own home, as far as her palanquin, when they found the youngest servant of the household, the pretty little Hua Yung, standing in the gateway and weeping, while he put up a desperate defense against the gatekeeper Ping An, who had seized him and was trying to throw him into the street. Moon Lady first bade her sister-in-law farewell; then she spoke severely to Ping An, and asked him why he was attacking the boy.

"Because he's so obstinate," replied Ping An. "Master Warm has sent for him to go over to his house, and he just won't go."

"If the Master sends for you, you must obey. Why do you stand there weeping?"

The lad apparently did not hear her question; he kept on shouting at the gatekeeper: "Let me go! Let me go! What does it matter to you whether I go to him or not?"

"But do at least explain why you don't want to go," said Moon Lady, impatiently. But the lad absolutely refused to speak.

"You ill mannered boy, you must answer when your mistress questions you!" Gold Lotus interposed.

But the boy remained obstinate, and he merely howled the louder when Ping An gave him yet another sounding smack across the mouth.

"But how can you strike him like that!" said Moon Lady, reprovingly. "You won't make him speak by violence."

At this moment Tai A came riding into the gateway. Hsi Men, who had accepted an invitation to dine in the city, had sent him to fetch some outdoor clothes. When he became aware of the howling Hua Tung he dismounted and asked him what was the matter.

"Master Warm has sent for him and he simply won't go," replied Ping An, speaking for him.

"Oh, I can understand that!" said Tai A, with a meaning laugh. "He has a good enough reason for not wanting to go! It isn't for nothing that Master Warm has earned a certain nickname!"

"And what is that?" asked Moon Lady innocently.

"Mistress, I really can't tell you. You must ask him that yourself," said Tai A, in embarrassment.

The more experienced Gold Lotus told herself that where there was wind there must be rain, and she resolved to look into the matter more closely. She drew the boy a little to one side and subjected him to a searching cross-examination. "Speak quite frankly to me. What has he been up to with you? If you are stubborn and won't speak you'll be beaten; d'you understand?"

Thus intimidated by the dreaded Fifth, the boy stammered out the truth.

"He wants to misuse me. First he gets me over there, and gives me wine, and then. . . . Today he wanted to do it again, so I ran away. Now he's sent for me again, but I'm not going."

Moon Lady, inquisitively listening, had heard only half. She was distinctly annoyed.

"Couldn't you have whispered that to me just as well, you little simpleton?" she said, scolding him. "Why do you have to be cross-examined by the Fifth before you speak? However, I still don't altogether understand your story. This man, this Southern rascal, isn't by any chance one of those who avoid women and secretly carry on with boys?"

"You can rely on it that he is," Gold Lotus assured her. "He is one of those hypocritical ascetics who pretend they mortify the flesh by sleeping on cold mats, and in that way avoid suspicion."

"But I thought he had a wife?" Jade Fountain interposed. "So how does he come to behave in such a shameless way?"

"Have any of us ever seen his wife since he has been living here?" inquired Gold Lotus.

"It isn't possible to get a sight of her," Ping An declared. "She lives entirely behind locked doors. In the six months they've been living here I have once seen her leave the house in her litter about noon and return towards evening. She had gone to see her mother. Apart from that she has been absolutely invisible."

"She was very foolish to marry him. It must be terrible to sit imprisoned in a room all day and never to see the sun or the sky," said Gold Lotus thoughtfully. Then they all returned together to Moon Lady's apartments.

When Hsi Men came home that evening and mentioned, in the course of conversation, that he intended to present an acquaintance with two wall scrolls which he would commission Master Warm to paint for him, Moon Lady interrupted him, saying: "Master Warm? You surely won't have anything more to do with that shameless fellow? If his scandalous doings became known our own good name might very possibly be involved!"

"What do you mean?" he asked, in a puzzled tone.

"Don't ask me, please, for any further explanation! Ask Hua Tung!"

"We had just escorted Sister-in-law Wu to her palanquin," Gold Lotus interposed, "and we found the boy howling in the gateway. Ping An had got hold of him and wanted to push him out into the street. The boy was resisting and couldn't be persuaded to go. When we questioned him he wouldn't speak at first. Finally I cross-examined him, and then it came out that he had been sent for by Master Warm, but he refused to go because the Master has often made him drunk and misused him."

Hsi Men would not at first believe this, and examined the boy himself.

"Out with it now, or it's the finger press!" he said, sternly.

Thus intimidated the boy knelt down and confirmed what Gold Lotus had just said.

"And besides that he asked me all sorts of questions about what went on in the house," he added. "But I held my tongue. What's more, he ordered me to steal gold and silver dishes for him when I had the opportunity. And he has often taken letters and documents from the office and has given them secretly to Judge Hsia to read." Hsi Men was beside himself.

"To think one can be so deceived in a man!" he cried. "I took him for a decent fellow, and now it turns out that his human exterior concealed the nature of a dog! Of course, he must go at once. Stand up, my boy, and henceforth you will take no notice if he sends for you!"

"Now I understand," he said, when the boy had gone, turning to Moon Lady, "why Uncle Ti in the Eastern Capital warned me expressly to observe greater official secrecy. He reproved me because Judge Hsia had obtained knowledge of the content of his private correspondence with me. I couldn't then explain how Judge Hsia had come by such knowledge. Now I know that this scoundrel had been playing the spy for him. Am I to tolerate such a fellow any longer in my house?"

"Of whom do you ask that? I am entirely of your opinion; he must go," Moon Lady insisted. "We have no son for whom we need a master, and we are not dependent on a man like that, who betrays heaven and earth, just because of the visiting cards he writes from time to time."

"Good; he shall go tomorrow."

The gatekeeper Ping An was accordingly told to refuse Master Warm admittance, and to inform him that his present dwelling was required as a storeroom; so that he must look for other quarters at once.

Master Warm felt that he had fallen from the clouds on the following day, when he crossed the road to speak to Hsi Men, and was told by the gatekeeper Ping An that the master was not at home, and had left word that he must find other accommodation at once. It was clear to him that Hua Tung had been talking. He hurried away in the greatest consternation, to return a little later, dressed in his best clothes. He positively must speak to Hsi Men. But again the gatekeeper told him that the master was not at home. He ran back to his house and wrote a long letter; he then stationed himself outside the entrance to Hsi Men's establishment until he managed to get hold of the servant Kiu Tung. Stopping the man, he begged him to deliver the letter to his master. But the servant refused to do so. He now realized that he would have to go.

Sadly he packed his things, and that very day he returned ignominiously to his former dwelling.

> *The brand of shame upon his brow will stay:*
> *No Western flood can wash the mark away.*

The septennial Governmental epoch, Chong ho, "Harmonious Government," had now expired, to be succeeded by the new epoch, Chung ho, "Harmonious Renewal." In the household of Hsi Men the New Year brought with it the usual festive commotion, which on this occasion was to find its climax on the twelfth of the first month, the eve of the Feast of Lanterns, in the shape of a great banquet. In the meantime Gold Lotus's birthday was celebrated on the ninth. On this occasion a little incident occurred which plainly revealed the pettiness and the heartlessness of the Fifth. On the day before the celebration her mother had come to stay with her as usual. She had expected to be received as a guest of honor, and did not think it necessary to provide herself with money. She had not even brought a bit of silver for her litter bearers, for she took it as a matter of course that the noble and wealthy Hsi Men would defray the expenses of her visit.

For some time past Gold Lotus, as the successor of Jade Fountain, had been in charge of the household cashbox. Her manner of administering the household finances was very different from that of her generous predecessor; she insisted on the most painful exactitude in all items of expenditure. She herself had procured a new pair of scales, on which she personally checked the weight of all goods purchased for domestic consumption. She insisted on a full accounting for every copper cash expended, and was generally feared by the servants by reason of her strict conscientiousness. In short, on the morning of her aged mother's arrival, when she was told that the bearers had not been paid, and were waiting outside for their fare, she declared that she was very sorry, but that expenditure for the fares of visitors from outside was not provided for in the household finances.

"Well, never mind," said Moon Lady; "pay the men their bits of silver and write a receipt for the amount."

"I shall do nothing of the kind," she insisted, obstinately. "The housekeeping money which is entrusted to me is intended simply to provide for household necessaries. Those who have no money to pay their bearers would do better to stay at home."

The old lady, who had to listen to all this in front of the other wives, could have sunk into the earth for shame. Her daughter, however, cared nothing for that; she sat unmoved, staring coldly at her mother. Finally the good-natured Jade Fountain brought the painful scene to an end by taking the necessary bits of silver from her own pocket and sending the already impatient and importunate litter bearers on their way.

But for Mother Pan this was by no means the end of the unpleasantness. In her daughter's pavilion she had to listen to the most vehement reproaches.

"What possessed you to come here at all if you had no money for the litter? You disgrace me before other people."

"But, my child, for you in particular this trifling expenditure was really not worth talking about! If I can't rely on you, on whom can I rely?"

"If you by any chance imagine that you can come cadging money here you are much mistaken. The smallest deficiency in the cash box is investigated by envious eyes. I tell you once for all, if you have no money to pay your bearers you mustn't come to see me in future. I don't care to disgrace myself here by parading my poor relations. I have only just had an unpleasant dispute with the First on your account. You have no idea of the difficulties of my situation here. You see only the brilliant exterior. Horse dung looks quite pretty when one sees the outside, but it's still dung."

Naturally enough, Mother Pan was completely disconcerted by this inconsiderate speech. She burst into loud sobs, and had to go to bed for several hours in order to recover, in some degree, her mental equilibrium.

As Hsi Men was spending the night with his Fifth, Mother Pan was given accommodation in the neighboring pavilion. The maid Spring Plum and the nurse Ju I amiably pressed her to take a seat on the heated kang, and offered her cakes and sweet wine. Mention was made of the deceased Sixth, and Mother Pan could not refrain from airing her troubles.

"It is well with the good creature now, for she has gone to Heaven," she sighed. "And how she was honored after death! But she deserved it; she was kindness and goodness itself. How sweetly she always behaved to me, as though I had been her own mother! She would keep me company and sit talking with me far into the night. And how careful she always was to see that I had plenty to eat and drink; and when I bade her good-by she had always packed up something good for me to take with me. Even the coat I am now wearing was a present from her. My own daughter, on the other hand, hasn't so much as a broken needle to spare for her old mother! May my eyes fall out of my head if ever I've had as much as a single bit of silver from her! Why, today she wouldn't even pay the litter bearers for me, and she coolly told me that if I hadn't the money for a litter I needn't come here at all! Did one ever hear of such wicked lack of affection, such wolfish cruelty? I am still feeling quite beside myself. One brings her up with a mother's love and care; one has waited on her hand and foot since her seventh year, when her father died; one denies oneself in every way in order that she may have a good education, and this is her gratitude!"

"Then she has actually had the opportunity of learning the written language?" inquired the nurse.

"Of course she has. From her seventh year she was instructed by Master Yu in all the higher branches of a young lady's education. She was by nature a quick and talented child, so that by the time she was ten years old she had not only mastered the difficulties of the literary language, but she actually knew, character by character, all the famous songs and rhyming stanzas and the tales in literary prose."

Ju I gave Mother Pan's hand a gentle squeeze as a hint that she should say no more. The outer door was heard to close, and immediately afterwards the maid Apricot Blossom announced that Spring Plum was approaching the pavilion.

"I understand!" said Mother Pan. "She's been sent over here to spy on me."

Spring Plum entered the room and sat down on the kang beside Mother Pan. "I wanted to see how you were," she said, turning to the old lady. "I have prepared some supper for you over there —Apricot Blossom, just run across and bring it here!"

Presently Apricot Blossom returned with a can of "Gold-blossom" wine and various plates of roast duck, smoked ham, baked fish, and other delicacies, the sight of which immediately transformed Mother Pan's distrust of Spring Plum into the contrary attitude.

"My dear child," she said, "I see from this that you are a good soul, who has a little sympathy for a forsaken old mother. Heaven will reward you with prosperity. I certainly haven't received so much kindness and attention from my own heartless daughter, your mistress," she added bitterly.

"You see only one side of the matter, Mother Pan, and you overlook the other side," said Spring Plum, in defense of her mistress. "It is true that your daughter is living in a wealthy household, but very little of Hsi Men's wealth ever comes her way. She has to give an account of the smallest expenditure. Do you imagine that she can get as much as a handkerchief or a flower for her hair without previous permission? You are really unjust to her."

"Yes. I think so too," Ju I interposed, eagerly. "If your daughter had money at her disposal she would surely give you plenty, for she has no other relatives. You just have patience; one day there'll be heaps and heaps of gold in her chests, and she'll be as wealthy as my late mistress."

"Oh, holy Amida Buddha, I shall hardly live to see that!" sighed Mother Pan. "My old days are numbered. But I should be only too glad to think that I have been unjust to her."

With this the discussion of that morning's disagreeable incident was closed, and under the consoling influence of an abundant meal and a sufficiency of wine Mother Pan soon recovered her spirits.

CHAPTER THIRTY-SEVEN: *Hsi Men pays for his Debauchery with his Life. In the same Hour Moon Lady becomes Mother and Widow*

SINCE HSI MEN had realized that his supply of invigorating pills was steadily diminishing a strange uneasiness had overcome him. His thirst for fresh amorous adventures had become incessant and immoderate; his desires were so precipitate that even while he was with one mistress he lusted for the embrace of another; he wished that he could have duplicated himself, in order to satisfy his insatiable craving. Even apart from his five wives—and the duty visits which he paid them in more or less regular alternation had long ceased to excite him—no one had been able to captivate him permanently and completely as his late Sixth had done for a time.

The nurse Ju I had long ago been succeeded in his affections by the smart young wife of his new servant, Lai Kue, who was ten years her junior; and the charms of the Sixth Wang no longer moved him deeply since he had discovered the merits of the wife of his business manager, Pen Se. When his other manager, Tsin Pen, on returning from the salt works of Yangchow, spoke with enthusiasm of the crisp freshness of the sixteen-year-old girl whom his protégé Miao Tsing had selected for him, as a mark of gratitude, and was sending to him on the next opportunity, Hsi Men wished that he had wings, so that he might instantly fly to Yangchow, then and there to taste the new delicacy. Again, he was ashamed to think that when Little Moon, his favorite among the flower-girls, asked him whether he had yet possessed the lovely wife of young Wang, he had to reply with a pitiful "No." Hitherto his conquests in the home of Wang Chow Hsuen had not extended beyond the bedchamber of Lady Lin. And when the quiet, level-headed Moon Lady, on returning from her first visit to the house of Assistant Judge Hou, positively went into raptures in describing the incomparable beauty of the eighteen-year-old wife of his colleague, a niece of the High Eunuch Lan, he told himself that he must at all costs win this treasure for himself.

Now he was feverishly awaiting the twelfth day of the month. On this day—that is, on the eve of the Feast of Lanterns—there was to be a double banquet in his house. In the belvedere he and a few of his intimates would carouse at their ease, while in the reception hall at the back of the house his wives would sit down to dinner with a number of noble and high-born mandarins' wives. On this occasion he hoped to have the satisfaction of seeing, for the first time, not only the young Mistress Wang, but also the wife of his colleague Hou. For recently, when between his tender embraces he had whispered into the ear of Lady Lin that he hoped to see her at his home on the twelfth, together with her son and her daughter-in-law, she had not refused the invitation, and Moon Lady, who had at first objected to his inviting two ladies who were complete strangers to her, finally, though under protest, agreed to receive them. From the Hou household a formal acceptance had been received.

On the twelfth Hsi Men did not begin the day by going to the yamen. He was on his feet at an early hour, for he wished to supervise in person the preparations for the banquet in the rear reception hall. His lovely guests must receive a favorable impression of his household. During the morning the princely company of actors whom he had engaged for the occasion arrived, their theatrical properties bestowed in a number of boxes. It was one of their duties to station themselves at the inner gate and greet the arrival of each lady guest with a festive clamor of gongs and drums. Then came the four flower-girls and the three boy singers, who were engaged to make music and to wait on the guests.

By noon the ladies had one by one arrived; only the chief guests, Lady Lin, with her daughter-in-law, and the wife of young Hou, had still to make their appearance. Hsi Men was already feeling nervous. Twice and thrice he sent his servants to the Wang and Hou households, to repeat his invitation. At last, punctually at noon, Lady Lin appeared. To his great disappointment Hsi Men was informed that young Wang was still absent in the Eastern Capital, where he was paying a New Year's visit to his uncle by marriage, the High Eunuch Huang, for which reason his bashful wife would not leave the house. Well, the arrival of the eagerly expected Mistress Hou would presently reconcile him to her absence.

Peeping from behind the curtains of a room in the western wing, Hsi Men, trembling with excitement, watched his lovely guest as she alighted from her great upholstered palanquin as its four bearers set it down, whereupon his wives led her into the reception hall. She could have been barely eighteen. She was wearing a robe of heavy, deep red silk damask, embroidered in five colors with a design of the four spirit animals—unicorns, dragons, tortoises, and phœnixes—and her tall, rather full, yet slender figure was clasped about the waist by a green jade girdle, inlaid with gold. Over this she wore a short slit tunic of blue silk, the two panels of which grazed her knees, as she walked, with a slight flapping sound, as though seeking to impede her steps. A maid, who had accompanied her in a litter, walked beside her, supporting her with a hand under each elbow. Other servants followed her, carrying a chest which contained her fur cloak.

What charm, what roguishness were expressed by her flower-like face! How bold yet graceful the upward sweep of the tresses above her temples! They were so curved that their line, if it had been prolonged, would have coincided exactly with the curves of her "butterfly antennae." How vivacious and urgent the speech of her phœnix-eye, gleaming with the moist radiance of the autumn wave! How supple that waist, like a pliant young osier in the playful embrace of the breeze! And that voice! It sounded like the sweet fluting of a golden oriole rejoicing in the sunshine of a spring morning. How light and graceful the gait of her lily feet! She was like a fairy lightly hovering in the moonlight over a flowery knoll, sparkling with pearls of dew. She was more than a flower, for flowers are mute. She was more than a gem, for gems have no fragrance.

The sight of her, the sound of her voice, thrilled Hsi Men to the marrow. His soul was rent into its two halves. His spiritual soul floated away into the ninth sphere of heaven; but his bodily soul instantly entered the body of the lovely stranger. It was only with an effort that he managed to collect himself in some degree when Moon Lady presently called him into the hall and introduced him to Mistress Hou. While he bent his head in reverence, bowing as deeply as possible, his heart was thumping against his ribs, and his eyes dazzled. Alas, that good form prescribed that he must withdraw directly after the introduction! His peace of mind was destroyed. Indifferent and distracted, as he sat with his friends in the belvedere he spoke barely a word. At frequent intervals he contrived to slip away from the table. On these occasions he hurried off to the reception hall, where he stared with hungry eyes, through the openwork of a screen, at his colleague's wife.

"What's the matter with you, brother?" Beggar Ying asked him once. "Don't you feel in a festive mood today?"

"I have been sleeping badly the last few nights, and I feel rather tired," he said, feigning a yawn.

Valued reader, a full moon does not remain full for ever, the lovely tints of a cloud do not long endure. When good fortune has reached its highest point, it is the rule that misfortune has its beginning, and conversely. Hsi Men thought fit to exploit his name and his position in ways that made it easier for him to indulge his lusts. He did not reflect that the Devil is wont to present his account to his debtors precisely when they are most prosperous.

Towards evening, when his lady guests were about to take their leave, Hsi Men, having received a timely warning from Tai A, once more deserted the table. He sought his former hiding place in the western wing, where he watched unseen as the guests, after the usual fireworks had been ignited in the inner courtyard, entered their palanquins one by one, and were carried out through the gateway. The white figure in the magnificent mantle of ermine was Lady Lin; the figure in the cloak of golden sable, flung open in front, was his latest object of adoration, the wife of his colleague Hou. With burning eyes he gazed after them until the last inch of their litters was swallowed up in the darkness of the gateway. Unseen by his own wives, he crept away, sighing, and returned, pondering deeply, to the company in the belvedere, whom he had once more left in the lurch. It so happened that on the way thither he collided, in the dark, with Hui Yuen, the young wife of the servant Lai Kue; and this encounter occurred just outside the door of her room. She had come from the reception hall, where she had been helping to wait on the guests. To his intensely stimulated senses she constituted, at this moment, a heaven-sent occasion of diversion and relief. There was no one to be seen, and her husband was busy elsewhere. This, he felt, was not the time to be backward. Without a word he drew her into her room and repaid himself, in her arms, for the loss of other delights, which were for the moment unattainable.

> *Whether the emerald moon is bright*
> *Or some red lantern dimly gleams,*
> *Light for the bowl of jade is light:*
> *Or green or red, still bright it seems.*

Comfortably refreshed and relaxed, he returned some time later to the festive company in the belvedere. His friends soon realized that there was nothing to be got out of him for that day, and since there were to be more New Year's banquets on the following days, they broke up at an earlier hour than usual, long before midnight. Hsi Men, who seemed to feel the languor of early spring in his limbs, was conscious of an overpowering need of rest, so he avoided for the night the stimulating society of Gold Lotus, preferring to enjoy a sound sleep for once in the peaceful and sedative atmosphere of Moon Lady's bedchamber.

Next morning Moon Lady told him of a dream which she had dreamed in the night.

"Yesterday at our party Mistress Lin was wearing a dress of dark red satin. Well, I dreamed that Sister Six was still living, and that she had in her chest just such a dress of dark red satin. She took it out and wanted to give it to me. Sister Five, who was standing beside me, snatched it out of her hand, and put it on herself. I was annoyed by this, and I said to her: 'First you steal the sable cloak, and now you snatch the red dress away from me.' She was angered, and in her rage she tore a great hole in the dress. We had a violent altercation, and that woke me."

"Dreams betray our secret thoughts and wishes," he said, knowingly. "Don't be afraid, I'll have just such a dress made for you as the one Lady Lin was wearing."

Although he had slept soundly, he still felt timid and languid, and had no appetite, so he decided that he would not go to the yamen that day, but would take things easy.

He dressed and went to the library. But he was incapable of any sort of mental effort, so he stretched himself out on a divan and got his boy Wang Tsing to massage his legs. While the servant was massaging him the maid Jade Flute came in, bringing him, on behalf of the nurse Ju I, a bottle half filled with milk from her own breast. With the milk was mixed a strengthening medicine. By this he was to realize how tenderly Ju I was watching over his health. He sent Wang Tsing away, and casually enough drank the half-bottle of medicinal milk. Then he handed to Jade Flute two golden hair clasps and four silver finger rings. These presents, however, were not given in recognition of the nurse's touching attention; they were intended for his new favorite, the wife of his servant, Hui Yuen. Of course, Jade Flute saw a way of profiting by the incident. Here was another exciting bit of news to report to Gold Lotus.

Wang Tsing, a younger brother of the Sixth Wang, when he found himself alone with his master after the maid's departure, quickly handed him a small packet.

"My sister sends you this, and hopes you will soon visit her," he said softly.

Hsi Men opened the packet and took from the paper covering, firstly a "willow leaf" of long, lustrous, blue-black woman's hair, which was bound with woolen threads of five colors, and interlaced with two brightly-colored satin ribbons, so that the whole made an artistic suspensory bandage, and secondly, a pouch for the girdle, filled with melon seeds, whose double opening was in the shape of a pair of mandarin ducks.

Hsi Men was quite touched by the sight of this tasteful bandage. He quickly hid the pouch in the drawer of a bookcase, and had just time to slip the bandage into his sleeve pocket when the curtain was drawn aside and Moon Lady entered unannounced.

"Where are you, then?" she asked. "I have a good strengthening soup waiting for you. Are you still feeling unwell?"

"I have such a painful twitching in my legs."

"Probably it's the spring air in your limbs. Come along, my soup will do you good."

He rose, followed her to her sitting room, and sat down to his invalid soup.

"Apparently all the New Year festivities have been too much for your strength," she suggested. "You ought to take more care of yourself; you shouldn't so constantly allow your friends to persuade you to drink."

There was really no escaping the love and care which surrounded Hsi Men on every hand. And this confirms the aphorism already cited, that the Devil is wont to present his account to his debtors precisely when they are most prosperous.

"You are right," he replied. "I must keep these drinking companions at arm's length for a bit. But one can't very well avoid an official dinner. And today, at noon, I have to pay a birthday visit to Brother-in-law Hua. Towards evening I shall go for a stroll through the Lantern Market, and I shall take the opportunity of looking in at the Lion Street shop, where I can eat a simple supper with my two managers."

But, of course, he was thinking of another house in Lion Street. After he had paid his duty visit to Brother-in-law Hua, and had

had his fill of watching the festive activities of the Lantern Market, he called, for the sake of appearances, at the silk shop in Lion Street. He listened to a report on recent business from Pen Se and the younger Brother-in-law Wu, who for the time being was filling the place of Han Tao Kwo, the latter having gone on another journey for his employer; then he sat down to supper with them. Moon Lady had thoughtfully sent a basket of food and a jug of wine. As usual, they went out after supper and for some time enjoyed the spectacle of the Lantern Market, now gay with a thousand lights. Then he took his leave of his companions; not in order to go home, but to visit the Sixth Wang, who lived a little further along the street. She had already been warned of his advent, and had made preparations to receive him. As always, he himself had taken care to provide some good wine.

"Why is it so long since you last came to see us? My First has invited you twice," he said as he greeted her.

"I have been rather tired lately; I didn't feel in the mood."

"Longing for your husband, of course?"

"No, indeed! But your visits have been so few and far between of late, it seemed to me that you were getting tired of me. Isn't there someone else . . . ?"

"Oh, nonsense! All this New Year commotion has taken up so much of my time."

"Yesterday was the great banquet at your house, wasn't it?"

"Yes. My First had to do something in return for various invitations. It was nothing special: just a matter of form."

She made him describe the banquet in further detail. Who had been present, what the women had worn, what they had to eat, what drama was performed by the players—she wanted to know everything.

"Of course, only aristocratic guests would be invited to your house for such a fine banquet. People like us would be out of the question," she said, in a tone of resignation.

"Nothing of the kind; on the sixteenth it will be the turn of my business managers' wives, and you will be among them," he said, quickly consoling her.

"Well, if your First should really think me worthy of a card of invitation, I shouldn't refuse to come," she replied, in a gratified tone. "I thought perhaps she would have been vexed with me on account of the unpleasant incident when your Spring Plum had such a quarrel with the blind singer. After all, it was through me that the singer had entered your house. The poor creature came back quite overcome, and I had to listen to all her grievances. She was simply inconsolable. It was only when you sent my brother Wang to her the other day, with a basket of food and an ounce of silver, that she calmed down again."

"Yes, my little Spring Plum is rather hot-tempered," Hsi Men agreed, laughing. "She is given to sulking. On that occasion she would gladly have scratched my eyes out. But why did the blind woman irritate her needlessly? She might have obliged her with a song. However, the incident is closed."

They sat down to table. Old Fong, as always, waited on them at first, afterwards leaving them to themselves. The copious draughts of strong wine soon warmed their hearts, although there had been a certain coolness in their attitude.

"Did you get my little package?" the Sixth Wang inquired, giving him a hurried, sidelong glance from between her half-closed eyelids. "How did you like my bandage? I sacrificed a thick lock of hair for you. Wasn't that generous?"

"Your two presents were really very cleverly designed. Many thanks!" he said.

He settled himself comfortably on the kang, swallowed one of Father Fan's magic pills in a little wine, and joined her in the usual sport of love. But although the magic pill had its wonted effect, and the Sixth Wang did all that could be expected of her, he did not really put his heart into the business. His thoughts were centered upon Mistress Hou.

"Do you still really love me?" he asked, apropos of nothing in particular, during a pause in the contest.

"Do you ask me that still, Ta ta? I only wish that the springtide vigor of your loins would last a little longer. Without you life has no meaning for me. I am already dreading my husband's return from his journey. I find it hateful even to have to speak to him."

Her devotion, which he believed to be genuine, flattered him.

"What if on his return I were simply to give him another wife?" Hsi Men suggested, after a few moments' reflection.

"Yes, Ta ta, do, find him another wife!" she cried, passionately. "Whether you prefer that I should live by myself, or whether you would rather take me into your household, my body ought to belong to you alone!"

He took a crumpled bill from his sleeve pocket. "Here, take this bill!" he said. "You can choose a new dress—whatever you fancy— from my second silk shop."

She thanked him delightedly with a *Wan fu*. Secretly rejoicing, she saw herself already promoted to be his new Sixth, and sunning herself in the glory of his aristocratic household. And with redoubled joy and devotion she applied herself to the resumption of the interrupted contest.

It was midnight when Hsi Men, very drunk and half asleep, was helped into the saddle by his escort, which consisted of Tai A and Kiu Tung and Wang Tsing, and proceeded to make his way home.

Slowly he rode along Lion Street in a westerly direction. The street, which was silent and deserted, was lit by a cloud-encircled moon. Kiu Tung and Tai A walked beside him, holding the bridle of his horse on either hand, constantly on the alert to catch their master if he should tumble sideways from the saddle. Wang Tsing, who carried a lantern on a stick, went before them to light the way. So they came to the western exit from Lion Street, opposite the marble bridge that crossed the canal. Suddenly Hsi Men was aware of an icy breath, and from underneath the bridge a spectral form, like a gray swirl of mist, swept by close in front of him. His terrified horse reared up, and then, thoroughly frightened by a cut of the whip, proceeded to run away with him. Like a flying cloud it raced home, where it stopped with a jerk before the gate, with

615

foaming mouth and quivering flanks. Bathed in icy perspiration, Hsi Men, during this mad ride, had lain prostrate on his horse's neck, clutching convulsively at its mane. Now, quite exhausted, he slid off its back into the arms of the gatekeeper, who sprang forward to help him. Following far behind, his escort of three arrived exhausted and breathless. There was no doubt about the matter: they had encountered the "Lord of the Five Ways." And as a rule such a meeting announced a death in the immediate future.

With faltering step, leaning heavily on his servants' shoulders, Hsi Men allowed them to lead him to Gold Lotus's pavilion. She was waiting for him, and had not retired for the night. She helped him to undress and put him to bed. He was so overcome by drink and weariness that he could not even cover himself without help. He fell asleep immediately, and presently the sound of his snores filled the room like the rumble of distant thunder.

Gold Lotus lay down beside him. Instead of allowing him to rest, she began, impelled by her insatiable lust, to caress him as usual. But he lay like a man dead. Then she lost patience: she shook him until he woke.

"Where have you put Father Fan's pills?" she asked.

"Oh, do let me sleep! I'm tired; I don't want to do anything more tonight," he grumbled. "But if you really must know, the pills are in my sleeve pocket, in the gold box with the openwork lid."

She rose at once and went through his sleeve pockets. Yes, there was the gold box with the openwork heart in the center of the lid. There were just four pills in the box. She took one out and washed it down with a beaker of mulled wine. Then she filled a second beaker for him, and since she considered that in view of his exhausted condition a single pill might not be sufficiently effective she dropped all the three remaining pills into the beaker.

Now she held the beaker to his mouth, and he, drowsy and intoxicated as he was, swallowed the contents unthinkingly without opening his eyes. Hardly so much time had elapsed as one needs to sip a bowl of hot tea when to her great satisfaction the triple dose began to work with threefold efficiency. But only for a time; and then she wondered why he lay there so motionless and breathless. He had fainted. It was long before he recovered consciousness.

"Ko ko, how do you feel now?" she asked anxiously.

"I feel so strangely dizzy," he said, faintly.

She did not tell him that she had disregarded Father Fan's warning and had given him three pills instead of one.

Valued reader, even lechery has its limits, and the store of virility is not inexhaustible. When the oil gives out the lamp expires, and when no marrow is left in the spine the man dies.

> *Young woman, how thy body allures!*
> *Yet that soft body conceals*
> *A deadly invisible sword.*
>
> *But it threatens none with a bloody death;*
> *No: when his loins are drained of life*
> *The libertine meets his pitiful end.*

No sooner had Hsi Men got out of bed next morning to dress himself than a dizziness once more overcame him and he collapsed unconscious. It was only because Gold Lotus and Spring Plum sprang forward that he did not strike his forehead against the edge of the bed. When he came to himself again he crept across to an armchair and sank upon the cushioned seat, helpless as an old man. For a long while he sat there, his head resting wearily against the back of the chair. Gold Lotus tried to persuade him and herself that his weakness was due to an empty stomach, and she sent Autumn Aster to the kitchen for a strengthening soup. Of course, the maid gossiped in the kitchen, and from the kitchen the news had soon reached the women's apartments, that Hsi Men had been overcome by a fit of dizziness that morning, and had fallen unconscious. Moon Lady, in great distress, hurried off to the pavilion of the Fifth. There she found him still sitting limp and apathetic in the armchair.

"Where did you go last night?" was her first question. "Of course, you had too much to drink again."

He did not answer.

"He came home very late, and was very drunk," said Gold Lotus, under her breath. "Who knows where he may have been racketing about?"

"He was going to have supper with his two managers in the Lion Street silk shop," replied Moon Lady. "I had to send a simple meal for three persons and a modest jug of wine to the shop. I don't in the least understand how he managed to get drunk. He expressly assured me yesterday that he was anxious to have done with this eternal feasting and carousing."

In the meantime a steaming bowl of appetizing soup, which had arrived from the kitchen, was set before him. But he had barely tasted it when he began to retch, and he could not take it. Moon Lady noted his lack of appetite with anxiety.

"How are you really feeling?" she asked him.

"I don't know; I feel such an emptiness in my brain, and everything is going round before my eyes."

"Of course, there can't be any question of your going to the yamen today."

"It's not to be thought of. I shall be satisfied if I can drag myself as far as the library. My son-in-law must write a few cards of invitation for the fifteenth."

"But you must at least drink a little invalid milk first."

Spring Plum had to run and ask the nurse Ju I to fill a bottle of milk from her breast.

Hsi Men obediently drank the milk, into which some medicine had been stirred. Then he rose to his feet, and began to totter across to the library, supported by Spring Plum. But he did not get so far. On reaching the garden gate he felt so giddy that he returned as quickly as possible.

"You positively must have two days' complete rest, and you must give up all thought of invitations for the present," said Moon Lady, emphatically, and she insisted that he should go to bed again immediately. Then she took Gold Lotus aside. She intended to find out what had happened the day before.

"Was he very drunk last night when he came home? And what did you do with him?" she asked, sternly.

"Nothing, nothing whatever!" Gold Lotus declared eagerly; she only regretted that there were not a number of witnesses to absolve her of any suspicion of guilt. "He was so drunk when he came to me last night that he was incapable even of giving me an ordinary polite greeting. He asked me to give him some punch. In order not to make him still more intoxicated I gave him some hot tea instead of punch. And then I put him to bed immediately. But who knows what on earth he had been doing outside the house? That's not for me to say," she added, shrugging her shoulders.

Since there was nothing to be got out of her, Moon Lady decided to examine Tai A and Kiu Tung, who had escorted Hsi Men on his yesterday's outing.

"Where was your master drinking last night?" she inquired.

"He simply had supper with the two managers at the Lion Street shop. He didn't go anywhere else," Tai A untruthfully replied. But his statement did not tally with that of his younger brother, whom she questioned a little later.

"He had supper with me and Pen Se," said the younger Wu, "but he left us very early and went on somewhere else."

"But where?"

Angered by the dishonesty of the groom Tai A, she sent for him again and subjected him to a drastic examination. In order to escape the thrashing with which she threatened him, he resigned himself to confessing that Hsi Men had visited the Sixth Wang.

"Now the truth is coming out!" cried Gold Lotus, turning triumphantly to Moon Lady. "But of course I had to be suspected first! Now you might also ask the boy where his master went recently when he was supposed to be paying a New Year's call on his colleague Hou. Such New Year's calls don't usually last until late in the night."

Tai A, now that he was driven into a corner, continued his confession: "That time the Master called on the Lady Lin also." This was a fresh surprise for Moon Lady.

"Now," she said, "I understand why he was so insistent lately that I must send her an invitation. I objected that I didn't know her at all, and that she was hardly likely to accept the invitation. But he dispelled my scruples, and to please him I did as he asked. That painted old coquette! Who would have thought it!"

"Why, she has a grown-up son! And still has love affairs! She ought to be ashamed of herself!" cried Jade Fountain indignantly.

"That old thing!" Gold Lotus exclaimed contemptuously. "I am only thankful that you too are convinced now that her honorable matron's bearing was only whitewash, hiding the blackest corruption! You were so attracted by her at first. Now, I hope, I shall not be rebuked when I make fun of her. I saw through her from the very first, the lustful old woman!"

"Well, you ought to know her, since you were once, as I am told, a servant in her house!" said Moon Lady, with a touch of irony. She was not sorry to humiliate Gold Lotus by referring to her youth, when she had spent some years in a menial situation in the family of Wang Chow Hsuen. Her remark had the intended effect. A burning blush spread over the face of the Fifth, from her temples to her neck and throat.

"A servant? Did she dare to say that?" she cried in a rage. "My aunt was living next door, and was on neighborly terms with her, and when as a child I was staying with my aunt she sometimes took me with her to play in her neighbor's garden. That was how it was. And of course I was able to observe her, to see what sort of woman she was, and what eyes she made."

"You can tell her that yourself when you meet her again," said Moon Lady coldly. It was obvious to her that Gold Lotus was merely trying to deny the fact of her servile origin. She left her embarrassed and speechless, and went to the kitchen, where she ordered some light pastry for Hsi Men. Then she turned back to the park, to visit the invalid. On the way she met the gatekeeper Ping An, who was going in the same direction.

"Where are you going?" she asked him.

"To the master. The singing-boy Li Ming is waiting outside, and he wants to know about the banquet on the fifteenth. The master told him recently to engage four singing-girls for the day."

"Nonsense! there can be no talk of a banquet and singing-girls!" said Moon Lady, crossly. "Go and tell the little tortoise to take himself off at once."

While the abashed gatekeeper hurried back to the gate she continued on her way to the pavilion of the Fifth. She went to the sick man's bedside and told him that she had just sent Li Ming away. There could of course be no question of the entertainment planned for the fifteenth. He agreed resignedly, nodding in silence.

His original expectation, that he would be on his feet again after a few hours' rest in bed, was to prove illusory. On the following day a feverish inflammation of the testicles declared itself, with painful urinary colic. There could be no thought of getting up. Moon Lady now insisted that Doctor Yen should be called in. When he had examined the patient his expression was grave. He murmured something about exhausted nervous energy, inflammation, and void in the brain, and prescribed a medicine which certainly did something to relieve the vertigo, but did not otherwise improve the patient's condition.

Through Li Ming the news of Hsi Men's illness reached the outer world. In the afternoon Cinnamon Bud and Little Silver came to his bedside, and a little later, Beggar Ying called with two other friends. Each of these visitors gave his or her opinion, together with well-meant but useless advice. Now the spring air was to blame, now the immoderate drinking during the New Year celebrations. The arrival of his three friends cheered the sick man a little. He had the pillows packed at his back so that he was able to sit up, and at their request he attempted to take a little food with them.

But he had barely tasted the rice soup when he felt sick again, and sank back exhausted. With silent consternation his friends noted the change in his appearance, the suspicious glitter of his eyes, the flush on his cheeks; and they thought it better to take an early leave of him. On leaving the pavilion Beggar Ying took Tai A aside. "Tell your First Mistress from me that I was very anxious about your master. I advise her urgently to send for Doctor Hu, in the High Street. But at once, before it's too late."

Tai A delivered his message, and Moon Lady told Hsi Men what he had said. But Hsi Men would have nothing to do with Doctor Hu. He had done no good when the Sixth had fallen ill. But Moon Lady considered that the Sixth was, in a way, doomed to die, while this time it was only a question of curing a slight illness, and it could do no harm to try Doctor Hu's medicine. So Doctor Hu had to come. His diagnosis was one of contagious intestinal poisoning; but the medicine which he prescribed had as much effect as a stone cast into the deep ocean.

Now, in her anxiety, Moon Lady sent for the eldest of the city physicians; Doctor Hou, who was eighty-two years of age, lived not far from the District Yamen. This active old gentleman recognized quite correctly that this was a case of orchitis and urinary colic, but his medicine had as little effect as the others; it merely caused a painful, iron-hard stiffening of the affected part of the body, which continued all night. Gold Lotus, who slept beside the sick man, was stupid enough, in her unrestrained lustfulness, to interpret this as the re-awakening of his virile power, and she sought to behave accordingly. Naturally this did nothing to improve his health, and on the following day he felt more wretchedly ill than ever. In vain did Little Moon, who came to see him during the day, fill the sick-room with her amorous twittering, while she tried with her own hand to feed him with the savory pigeon broth which she had brought with her. After a few mouthfuls he had to refuse it with a painful smile. His stomach was refusing its duty.

On the advice of his colleague Hou, who also came to see the invalid this day, a foreign physician of his acquaintance, a specialist in cases of intestinal poisoning, who happened to be paying him a visit, was called in consultation. Twice during the day Hsi Men credulously swallowed the bitter infusion prescribed for him, with the result that his condition was further aggravated, and all night long he was unable to sleep for pain. What had been red, inflamed swellings had become open, festering, and bleeding wounds.

After all the arts of the physicians had thus lamentably failed, Moon Lady resolved, as a last resource, to see what magical conjurations would do. Once again the blind husband of old Mother Liu—the astrologer Liu—had to make his appearance and perform, behind the belvedere, his devil-exorcizing dance. The Master of the Tao, High Priest Wu of the Jade Emperor's Temple, was then called in. When he noted Hsi Men's alarmingly disfigured and wasted appearance, he declared, with merciless candor: "There is here no possibility of recovery. Wine and women have drained, wasted, and exhausted your virile powers. Your bowels are consumed by the sinful fire of lust. The sickness is too deeply rooted in the body for human art to do anything." And he refused to apply the magic of his art of exorcism.

At Moon Lady's desire, however, he was persuaded to draw the patient's horoscope. Its findings were bad enough. In the first month of the current year his destiny would be fulfilled. Now it was clear to Hsi Men and his wives that there was no more hope, and that it was time to make the final dispositions. For hitherto Hsi Men had never remotely considered the necessity of making a written will.

"Ko ko, have you anything else to say to me?" the tearful Moon Lady asked him that evening, when she and all the other wives, and his daughter, and young Chen were gathered about his bed.

It was some time before he could control his emotion. Then he began:

"Yes, I have a few last words to say. If after my death you should bring a son into the world, then I should wish that all my wives would still live together as sisters, and look after the child in common. In this case I should not like you to expose yourselves to the mockery of the people. Sister Five"—he indicated Gold Lotus— "must at last overcome and forget her former dissensions."

When he had proceeded so far Moon Lady was overcome by emotion and burst into loud sobs. He waited until she was calmer; then he continued:

"Son-in-law, since I have no son, you must bear me to the grave in the place of a son, and afterwards, in good days and bad, you must be the comfort and support of my wives. I hope you will worthily accomplish your task.

"In my silk shops fifty thousand ounces of capital are invested, half of which was furnished by myself and half by Neighbor Kiao. Let the goods be sold off by the manager Fu, and pay Neighbor Kiao the capital and interest due to him. The business is not to be continued. In the satin and yarn business which is managed by Pen Se six thousand five hundred ounces are invested; in the wool and embroidery shop under Brother-in-law Wu's management, five thousand ounces. Both these businesses are run exclusively on my account. They too are not to be continued. See to the selling of the goods and apply the proceeds of the sale to the upkeep of the household. I want you to continue only the apothecary's shop in conjunction with Dispenser Fu, and the pawnshop. Five thousand ounces are invested in the apothecary's shop; twenty thousand in the pawnshop.

"You must auction the cargo of silk and cotton goods which Han Tao Kwo and Lai Pao will bring from the Southern Provinces, and divide the proceeds in equal shares between my wives and my daughter. At the same time you can sell the other two shops, the one opposite the apothecary's shop and the one in Lion Street. Besides these, I have a number of sums of money out on loan. There is written record of these. See that the loans are punctually repaid."

"Father-in-law, I note your instructions and I will obey them faithfully," young Chen declared, with a choking voice.

Then the business managers were called in. Dispenser Fu, Pen Se, Kan, Brother-in-law Wu, and Tsui Pen—all were present with the exception of Han Tao Kwo, who was still on his travels. Hsi Men repeated his last wishes in their presence, whereupon they solemnly promised to respect and obey them.

Hsi Men was vouchsafed yet one more day of life. On this day many friends and acquaintances came hurrying to his deathbed in order to take farewell of him. Then his destiny was fulfilled. After a difficult death struggle, which continued for many hours, beginning at midnight, and which now and again made him roar like a bull, he breathed out his life in the early hours of the twenty-first day of the month. He had not passed his forty-fourth year.

> *It is vouchsafed us in a thousand ways*
> *Our span of life breath to expend,*
> *And yet for each there comes the day of days*
> *When all our plans and schemes must end.*

After Hsi Men had closed his eyes it was Moon Lady's first care to entrust her younger brother and Pen Se with the duty of procuring a coffin. She hastened to her bedchamber, opened her treasure chest, and took out of it four heavy bars of silver. Hardly had she sent them off with the silver when she felt a violent pang in her pregnant body, and fell into a deep swoon.

Sunflower, Jade Fountain, Snowblossom, and Gold Lotus had remained by the deathbed, and were busily engaged, with seven hands and eight feet, in clothing Hsi Men's body. Now, as Little Jewel brought the news that Moon Lady had fallen in a swoon, Sunflower and Jade Fountain at once rushed off to help her. In the meantime Moon Lady had recovered her senses; she was holding her hands pressed against her body and writhing with pain. It was clear to the three women that she was in labor. While Jade Fountain hurried off to send one of the servants for the midwife Tsai, Sunflower and the maid Jade Flute remained with Moon Lady. Directly she entered the room Sunflower had noticed the open chest, which she saw was full of glittering white and yellow metal. Now, as Moon Lady fell into another swoon, her mind was made up. She sent Jade Flute out of the room on the pretext that she wished her to fetch the nurse Ju I. Directly she found herself alone with Moon Lady she bent over the open chest and quickly removed five of the glittering bars. She concealed her booty as well as she could in the fullness above her girdle, between her gown and her shift, and hurried away to her own room.

Now Jade Fountain returned. She was surprised to find neither

Sunflower nor Jade Flute in the room. But Sunflower returned almost immediately.

"Where were you, then?" asked Jade Fountain.

Sunflower pointed to the bundle of bast paper which she was holding. "In case of emergency," she said indifferently. "I could see no bast paper here, so I fetched some from my room. I sent Jade Flute for the nurse."

Jade Fountain was quite satisfied with this reply, and in view of Moon Lady's critical state this was no time to concern herself with trifles. Now the midwife Tsai made her appearance. And while the mournful lament for the dead sounded from the room in which Hsi Men's still warm body was lying, here there was presently heard the lively squalling of a healthy newborn man-child. Almost in the same hour Moon Lady had become both widow and mother.

Moon Lady made an excellent recovery from childbirth. This was evident from the vigorous manner in which she haggled with the midwife over the amount of that worthy's fee. The midwife, since the child was a boy, had counted on receiving at least five ounces. But Moon Lady was willing to give her only three, on the grounds that it was a fatherless child. Also the maid Jade Flute was soundly reprimanded for leaving the treasure chest open all the time. Under these circumstances Jade Fountain felt that her continued presence beside the invalid was not required, and she returned to Hsi Men's deathbed. She took Gold Lotus aside and related the details of the successful confinement.

"It's all very well," she added quietly. "He has barely closed his eyes when the First begins to show, by her haggling and scolding, that she is now the head of the household."

That Sunflower had taken a favorable opportunity of abstracting five bars of silver had not yet been discovered.

On the evening of this day Hsi Men's body was borne to the great reception hall on the shoulders of the assembled menservants, and solemnly laid in state. Then the District Necromancer Hsue appeared, made out the certificate of death, and fixed the dates for the various funeral rites. For the day of the burial the thirtieth day of the second month was appointed. The five weeks which preceded that date filled the house with the usual commotion of innumerable visits of condolence, sacrifices to the dead, soul masses, and mourning banquets. In the meantime there came the Feast of Washing the Child, which brought a further host of congratulatory visitors to the house. A curious blending of solemnity and merriment, of mourning and joy, filled the rooms of Hsi Men's house during this period. The friends and neighbors could not get over the fact that almost in the same hour a master of the house had died and a master of the house had been born. This was generally regarded as a case so unusual as to verge upon the miraculous.

One day there appeared among the other mourners Cinnamon Bud and her sister, from the house of Mother Li, in order to pay their tribute of mourning and to burn their spirit money and incense before the soul tablet of the dead. This was in the second week of mourning. Moon Lady, since her time of lying-in was not over, did not yet show herself to her guests, but still kept to her "secret chamber." The two girls were received and entertained by their Aunt Sunflower and Jade Fountain. At a convenient moment, when Jade Fountain had left the room, they quietly told their aunt that they had a message from their mother.

"Mother considers that you are free now that he is dead, and that you now by rights belong to our flower garden once more. You needn't keep to the stupid rules that apply to widows, and forbid them to remarry. Also, with the help of Brother Li Ming you ought to put by as much money and valuables as you can lay your hands on. After all, you mustn't be foolish; you ought to think of your old age."

Sunflower cherished their words in her heart, and promised to act accordingly.

On this day it also happened that the Sixth Wang had called. She was not a little surprised to find that none of Hsi Men's wives appeared to greet her. After she had sacrificed to the soul tablet she stood lonely and forsaken in the great hall, and no one paid any attention to her. She did not know that Tai A had told of her secret relations with Hsi Men, and that no one belonging to the household was willing to speak to her, since it was suspected that she was directly responsible for his death. After all, she was the person with whom he had spent the last night before his collapse. Her brother Wang Tsing had already been dismissed on this account, and no servant would venture to announce her to Moon Lady.

It offended Moon Lady's elder brother to see her thus treated in defiance of all the prescriptions of good form, so that he finally bade the servant Tai A announce her presence to his sister. But Tai A met with a lively reception.

"You accursed fellow, I've heard enough of your Sixth Wang!" she angrily rebuked him. "What have I to do with this adulterous bitch, who plays the harlot with other women's husbands and destroys them with her embraces? What has she come to this house for? Let her kindly take herself off!"

In consternation Tai A ran off and told the elder Wu how ill the mistress had received him. At this the elder Wu himself went to Moon Lady.

"You really should control yourself a little more," he told her. "Even in dealing with an enemy one should observe the external rules of good form; that is a time-honored maxim. After all, my late brother-in-law appointed her husband, Han Tao Kwo, to a confidential post of great commercial importance, and a considerable proportion of the family property is in his hands. What if his wife tells him how you have treated her here? He could take a very unpleasant revenge. If you yourself won't receive her, do at least allow the Second or Third to greet her."

Moon Lady pondered for some time. She could not deny that her brother was right. This Han Tao Kwo had charge of a great cargo of silk. She therefore mastered her feelings and asked Jade Fountain to give the hated visitor a formal greeting. Jade Fountain thereupon went into the great reception hall, made the Sixth Wang take a seat in front of the soul tablet, and drank a bowl of tea with her. But the Sixth Wang was inwardly so exasperated by the way in which she had been treated that she could hardly drink a single bowl, and after exchanging a few words with her hostess she rose to take her leave. And she left the house with the firm resolution to revenge herself on the first opportunity for the insult which had been offered her.

Since Hsi Men's death not a day had passed upon which Gold Lotus and young Chen failed to find opportunity for brief encounters and secret dalliance. The fact that Moon Lady, the strict guardian of domestic propriety, was confined to her "secret chamber," during her period of lying-in, so that she could not exercise her accustomed supervision, together with the general confusion that naturally results from a death in the family, made it very much easier for the two to meet. Neither of them, apparently, was mourning very profoundly. They did not scruple to hold clandestine interviews and commit their amorous misdemeanors even in front of Hsi Men's soul tablet. And one evening, after one of those theatrical performances with which the household cheered its spirits from time to time during the first four weeks of mourning, when the great hall was again empty, Gold Lotus slipped out from behind the curtain enclosing the seats of the female spectators, and told him: "My dear, today I will be wholly yours. This is a favorable opportunity. Your wife and the other women are with the First, and they will have to entertain their guests. We shall be undisturbed. Come, take me to your room!"

Silently he took her by the hand and led her across the pitch-dark courtyard to his apartments in the eastern wing. A feeling of unspeakable pride and happiness made his heart beat until its beating was audible, and his spirits rose to the clouds. Today, at last, after prowling hungrily around her for two long years, enveloping her in his longing, he was to enjoy complete fulfillment!

Such was the piety practiced, only a few days after Hsi Men's decease, by his favorite wife and his nearest male relative! But strictly speaking, even the correct Moon Lady deserves the reproach of impiety. For it was one of her first orders that the soul tablet of the Sixth, together with her portraits, should be destroyed by burning. All the dead woman's chests and coffers were brought to her own apartments. The nurse Ju I and the maid Pear Blossom had to take service under her, while Apricot Blossom was allotted to the Second. Lastly, the rooms which the Sixth had inhabited were locked, and the key given to Moon Lady for safe keeping. In this way the household of the Sixth was completely broken up, and nothing was left to remind people of the wife who had once held the foremost rank in Hsi Men's household, and whom he had loved and respected above all the rest.

Day after day the obsequious Li Ming, feigning sincere attachment and willing devotion, made his way to the house of mourning. His frequent appearance no longer aroused comment, for he contrived to make himself invaluable in connection with the many theatrical performances and pantomimes, now as director, now as actor and singer, now as a dexterous prompter. Why should it attract attention if he now and then disappeared into the apartments of his aunt Sunflower? If only it had been realized that he always returned home after these innocent visits to his aunt with remarkably heavy-laden pockets!

So the secret collaboration between aunt and nephew, to the detriment of Hsi Men's household, continued undisturbed during the four weeks of mourning, up to the day of the interment. But at last a whiff of smoke betrayed the fact that there was somewhere a fire. On the day of the interment at the family place of burial outside the gates Cinnamon Bud had again a secret conversation with her Aunt Sunflower. "Mother asked me to tell you that you had better pack your things in good time, and take advantage of your next difference with the First to leave the house and come back to us. You had no children by Hsi Men, and are therefore under no obligation to waste the best years of your life as a mourning widow. You should remember the time-honored motto of the flower garden:

"Why mourn for the clients
Who left us of late
When others, warm-hearted,
Are thronging the gate?
No, let us not mourn
Dead days of the past:
To the living Today
Let us gayly hold fast!

"Beggar Ying came to see us recently, and he gave us reason to believe that the rich young Chang from the High Street—you know, the second son of the Provincial Governor—would gladly make you his Second for five hundred ounces. So don't waste time considering, but act!"

Her whispering aroused the suspicions of the ever-watchful Gold Lotus, and these suspicions were confirmed when Spring Plum shortly afterwards informed her mistress that she had recently seen Sunflower passing out from behind the curtain in the great hall various articles of gold and silver, which her nephew promptly hid under his cloak. Gold Lotus reported this to Moon Lady, and the gatekeeper Ping An was given strict orders to refuse admittance to Li Ming in future. His absence made Sunflower suspicious. She discovered that her doings were known, and she now waited for a plausible occasion for leaving the house in a seemly manner. She was soon to have such an opportunity. Moon Lady naturally had the gravest suspicions of her honesty, and she made this clear to Sunflower by her cool treatment of her, and by intentionally ignoring her. In short, a day came when Sunflower happened to enter the room as her sister-in-law and Jade Fountain were taking tea together. They deliberately omitted to invite Sunflower to take her place at the tea table, whereupon she declared that she had been insulted, flew at Hsi Men's soul tablet, which since his burial had been placed in Moon Lady's room, belabored it with her fists, and behaved like a madwoman. Indeed, that night, for the sake of appearances, she made an unskillful attempt to hang herself. At this Moon Lady sent for Mother Li and requested her to take her sister back to the flower garden. This was just what Mother Li wanted. But in order to derive as much profit as possible from the removal she pretended at first to refuse, and then demanded that her sister should be paid a cash indemnity of some dozens of ounces, in order to "cover the shame" of her expulsion from the household. The frugal Moon Lady was of course unwilling to sacrifice a single ounce of bullion, so there was at first a good deal of ceremonious bargaining. At last it was agreed that Sunflower should take with her, on leaving the house, her jewels and ornaments, her clothes and linen, her bedding, and other personal property. But when Mother Li tried also to claim her sister's two maids Moon Lady bluntly refused, and declared angrily that she would on no account allow two respectable maids to be initiated into vicious ways in the flower garden and turned into harlots. In order that the negotiations should not break down altogether on this point, Mother Li at last declared, with a sigh, that she was prepared to withdraw her claim to the two maids, and so that very day Sunflower stepped into her palanquin and was carried back to the flower garden from which she had come.

Respected reader, for these people of the flower garden the body is merely merchandise and love a trade. Let a noble cavalier take pains to bind such a person to himself in a hundred different ways, and to accustom her to the cage of his respectable household, he will never succeed in curing her of feeling like a monkey and thinking like a horse. Such a person is accustomed to receiving Master Li in the morning and Master Chang in the evening. The old clients are let out at the back door, the new ones admitted by the front gate. For a time such a woman will adapt herself to a respectable household and do her best to restrain herself, but no sooner is the master of the house dead than she feels herself liberated from all her fetters, and is glad to ladle her soup out of the old pot.

CHAPTER THIRTY-EIGHT: *Han Tao Kwo steals from his Master and runs away. Lai Pao repays former Benefits with Disloyalty*

IN THE PREVIOUS autumn Lai Pao and Han Tao Kwo had been furnished with two thousand ounces and sent into the silk country of Kiang nan in order to purchase fresh goods. Once more the goal of their journey was Yangchow, where they were to be the guests of Hsi Men's protégé Miao Tsing. After devoting a few weeks to a thorough study, at their employer's expense, of the night life of Yangchow, they set out on their homeward journey, with their cargo of silk and cotton goods, at the beginning of the New Year. The young maid whom Miao Tsing, in his gratitude, had selected for his patron, as some return for saving him from the headsman's ax, had fallen ill a little while before this, so that she would have to be forwarded later.

Shortly before they arrived in their home port, Han Tao Kwo passed an acquaintance from Tsing ho hsien, a man he knew well, who was traveling upstream, and who shouted, from the deck of his junk: "Hi, have you heard the news? Your master has died recently."

At this moment Han Tao Kwo was standing quite alone in the bows of the vessel. Neither Lai Pao, who was sitting in the cabin, nor any of the crew, who were engaged in navigating the ship, had heard the man hailing him. And Han Tao Kwo decided that for the present he would keep his knowledge to himself.

Now, during the last few years the two provinces of Honan and Shantung had been visited by a terrible drought. For thousands of *li* wide stretches of land on which cotton was usually cultivated, and where the silkworm found its nourishment, had become a sterile wilderness. Naturally, in this region the price of silk and cotton had risen by leaps and bounds, until it stood at three times the usual figure. And speculators came from afar, pouring into the great ports, in order to buy from the ships the goods arriving from the more distant provinces. And among such ports was the harbor of Tsing ho hsien. Under these circumstances Han Tao Kwo had long ago laid his plans. On the day of their arrival he said to Lai Pao:

"We have about four thousand ounces' worth of goods on board. At the moment the state of the market is extraordinarily favorable: three times the usual price is being paid for silk and cotton cloth. I propose that we sell half the cargo at once, on board ship. This would have the further advantage that we should have to pay only half the import duty, since only half the cargo would pass the city limits. It would be a sad pity if we were to allow this favorable conjuncture to escape us."

"There is much to be said for your proposal," was Lai Pao's opinion. "But I'm afraid Master Hsi Men will be angry with us if we sell the goods here on our own account."

"You leave that to me. I take the whole responsibility on myself."

"Very well, then."

After Han Tao Kwo had sold a thousand ounces' worth of goods that day he spoke to Lai Pao again: "You stay here with your man Hu Hsien, to guard the cargo and settle the customs formalities on board. In the meantime I'll hurry on ahead, notify Master Hsi Men of our arrival, and give him the thousand ounces we have taken."

"Agreed. And don't forget to ask Master Hsi Men to give you the usual letter of recommendation to the customs inspector, as it will save time and we shall have less to pay."

Han Tao Kwo accordingly went ashore with his own man, Wang Han, hired two mules and a baggage donkey to carry his personal baggage and the cashbox, and hastened along the highway to the Southern gate, inwardly rejoicing over his successful trick. It was twilight when he reached the city wall. He was about to enter the gate when he saw Chang An, the overseer of Hsi Men's family burial ground, who was just coming out. He was pushing a little cart in front of him, which was laden with baskets of food and jugs of wine. When he caught sight of the manager he stopped.

"Hi, you're home again!" he cried.

"Just come in. Why are you wearing white mourning?" asked Han Tao Kwo. He wanted to make sure that Hsi Men was really dead.

"Haven't you heard yet? The master died quite recently. Tomorrow, on the ninth of the third month, is the end of the seventh week of mourning. I have to take out some sacrificial food. The First is coming out tomorrow to offer sacrifices."

Han Tao Kwo pretended to be painfully surprised. He then continued on his way. The busy traffic at the gate, which was choked with carts and pedestrians, made further conversation impossible. He now considered whether he should make directly for Hsi Men's house, or whether it would be better to go home first. Since it had now grown dark he decided on the latter course. Before anything else he wished to consult his wife. Having reached the house in Lion Street he had his baggage unloaded and taken indoors; then he paid the drivers and sent them on their way with the hired animals. The Sixth Wang welcomed him and set a generous supper before him. Then he told her his story. And when he had done so he proceeded to unpack. First the handsome clothes and the fine linen which he had brought with him from Kiang nan were produced, and then came the turn of the money chest with its thousand ounces. The Sixth Wang could hardly trust her eyes when she saw bar upon bar piled up on the kang.

"Where does that come from?" she asked, quite dazed by the silvery radiance which suddenly filled her humble living room.

He gave a cunning laugh, and told her how by chance he had learned of Hsi Men's death on his homeward voyage; and of his clever notion of profiting by Lai Pao's ignorance of the event, and the favorable state of the market, to sell a consignment of goods on board for his own benefit. Then he produced a leather pouch containing a further hundred ounces, which he had previously put aside as his commission on profitable purchases. The Sixth Wang could but admire his business efficiency, and for the moment she was able to forget that she really abhorred him.

"Has he been taking any notice of you?" he inquired.

"From time to time. That's over now. What are you going to do with all this money?"

"That's just what I wanted to discuss with you. Shall I keep half for ourselves and hand over only the other half? What do you think?"

"Bah, you won't be so foolish! Such an opportunity won't come again. He is dead, and we are not in any way bound to consider those he has left behind. If you were so foolish as to hand over half the money you would only expose yourself to awkward discussions, and questions as to what had become of the other half. No, don't go to the house at all; pack the thousand ounces on a donkey, and we'll ride at all possible speed to the Eastern Capital. We have a splendid refuge there with our daughter in the Chancellor's palace, and shall be safe from all pursuit."

"Excellent. But what is to become of our house here? We can hardly get rid of it at a day's notice."

"Stupid fellow, what is the use of having a younger brother? Give him a few ounces and let him look after the house for the time being. And if they ask after you in Hsi Men's house, he can simply tell them that our daughter sent an urgent message begging us to go to the capital. We shall see then who it is that has seven foreheads and eight gall bladders, and would be so bold as to attempt to drag us from the inaccessible region of a Chancellor's palace."

Han Tao Kwo had actually been of her opinion for some time past, but in order to quiet his conscience he felt it necessary to express a last moral scruple.

"I have received many benefits from Hsi Men. Would it not be rather ungrateful to do as you suggest, and against the heavenly laws?"

"Nonsense. Those who haven't the courage to break the heavenly laws are likely to starve as the result of their cowardice. It has always been so. He amused himself many a time with me when he was alive. His pleasure isn't bought too dearly with these few ounces. At the same time, the money is just compensation for the indignity I have suffered recently in Hsi Men's house." And she told him how she had fared there.

He had to agree with her, and after this explanation his moral scruples were completely dispelled. That same evening he came to an understanding with his younger brother. Next morning he and his wife hastily packed their belongings. Two large, comfortable traveling carriages were hired, and then, accompanied by his wife, two maids, and a manservant, he passed through the Western gate on his journey to Kai fong fu.

On this same day, early in the morning, Moon Lady, accompanied by Jade Fountain, Gold Lotus, Hsi Men's daughter, and young Chen, and also by the nurse Ju I, who had to carry the seven weeks' child, proceeded to the ancestral burial ground, in order to offer the customary sacrifices. There the overseer Chang An told Moon Lady that he had encountered the manager Han Tao Kwo on the previous day.

"Then why hasn't he come to see me yet?" said Moon Lady, in surprise.

"Perhaps he thought it too late to call on you last night."

Moon Lady took it for granted that he would appear that day, and since she was anxious not to miss him, and to learn of the bestowal of the valuable cargo, she did not remain very long at the burial ground, but was ready to return to the house early in the afternoon. Strangely enough, Han Tao Kwo had not called. She therefore sent young Chen to his house in Lion Street. After repeated knocking the door was opened, and young Chen found himself confronted by one of the manager's brothers.

"My brother and his wife have gone away," young Han explained, calmly. "They received a pressing invitation from my niece in the Eastern Capital.

"And where is the junk with the cargo of goods?"

"That I don't know."

The extraordinary news which young Chen brought home with him made Moon Lady extremely uneasy. She sent him off again at once, this time to the harbor. He must make inquiries there as to the whereabouts of the silk junk. After a long search he discovered it amidst the throng of vessels lying at moorings off the quay.

"Han Tao Kwo has already sold a thousand ounces' worth of goods," Lai Pao informed him. "He left for the city yesterday; he was going to deliver the money in person."

"He didn't come to us, either yesterday or today," replied young Chen, who was taken aback by the news. "The overseer Chang An saw him yesterday evening at the Southern gate, but since then he has disappeared, with his wife, two maids, and a groom. When I went to Lion Street to inquire for him a brother of his opened the door. I was told that he had left for Kai fong fu with his wife and servants. Presumably he has stolen the thousand ounces and taken it with him."

Lai Pao gaped: he was speechless. But he thought, privately: "This accursed fellow has diddled me nicely! Of course, he intended from the first to embezzle the money, and I, like an ass, was taken in by his talk of the favorable state of the market!" And he decided that he would do as the cunning Han Tao Kwo had done; he too would take care to profit by Hsi Men's death. And accordingly he set to work at once.

He was able to lead the weak and compliant young Chen to a neighboring flower garden, where wine and women detained him until the following morning. At the same time he generously gave his man leave to spend a long holiday in his country home. In the meantime he had goods of the value of a thousand ounces quietly unloaded and taken to a distant quayside tavern to which he often resorted. Two days later, relieved of a considerable part of her freight, the junk, after the necessary customs formalities had been complied with, entered the municipal area of Tsing ho hsien. The remaining cargo was warehoused in the eastern wing of Hsi Men's house, for the two retail businesses had in the meantime been discontinued and the premises closed. When on counting the bales it was discovered that two thousand ounces' worth of goods was missing, it was easy for Lai Pao to persuade Moon Lady that the absconding Han Tao Kwo had purloined not one but two thousand ounces' worth of silk and cotton goods. But when Moon Lady wanted to send him immediately to Kai fong fu, in order to demand the embezzled money from Han Tao Kwo, he contrived by skillful argument to persuade her against this course.

"It is a ticklish business to force one's way rudely into a Chancellor's palace and attempt to make a disturbance there. Instead of obtaining one's rights one is in danger of putting oneself in the wrong. It would cause displeasure in high places, and sooner or later that would have disagreeable consequences. No, that would be an undertaking to make a madman scratch his head in amazement."

"Then I'll apply to Intendant Ti in writing," said Moon Lady, dejectedly. "After all, he is under an obligation to our household, since my dead husband obtained for him the concubine whom he values above all things."

"That's just where the difficulty lies. What Darling says means more than anything to him, and she will naturally influence him in favor of her parents, and not in your favor. No, take my advice, Mistress: regard the few ounces as irrevocably lost, and don't moan any longer for them!"

Moon Lady did as he advised; sighing, she resigned herself to the loss of the money. In order that she should not again be cheated by dishonest managers, she resolved to sell the rest of the cargo personally through young Chen. But young Chen had no experience of this branch of commerce and was unable to effect a sale. This was the opportunity for which Lai Pao had been hoping; now he could show that he was indispensable.

"Young man, you don't yet understand the sweets and bitters of trade," he told young Chen. "I, on the other hand, have knocked about the world, and I know how to get round the buyers. You just leave the business to me!"

And without waiting for Moon Lady to give him a definite commission, he got into touch with a few well-known dealers, and had very soon sold all the rest of the cargo for something over two thousand ounces in bullion. This amount he immediately delivered, down to the last bit, to young Chen. Moon Lady herself controlled the delivery of the goods and the payment of the money, and convinced herself that on this occasion there had been no irregularity.

In recognition of his efficiency she wanted to give him a commission of thirty ounces. But this he declined.

"Keep the money!" he told Moon Lady. "You can make use of it yourself. Now that your husband is dead you are a lake of still water, without a constant fresh supply. You must keep what you have."

This, of course, was merely a calculated gesture. Moon Lady would attribute his refusal to his honesty and unselfishness, and would have increased confidence in him. He had already embezzled a thousand ounces; he could now permit himself the luxury of declining a mere trifle of thirty ounces. And very soon his foresight was to be rewarded.

One day a letter arrived from the Indendant Ti in Kai fong fu. He had learned from Han Tao Kwo and his wife, who had reached the capital in safety, of the death of Hsi Men; and he had also heard of the household orchestra, consisting of four delicious young maids, for whom there would really be no further occupation, and whom he, in return for an adequate consideration, would only too gladly receive into his own household. He knew that he could absolutely rely on Hsi Men's taste. Once more it was the experienced and far-traveled Lai Pao on whose advice Moon Lady relied in this case. She herself had no notion of what she should do. She did not, however, feel inclined to comply with the Intendant's request.

"You women understand nothing of such affairs," Lai Pao told her impudently. He thought that as the confidential adviser of a helpless widow he could venture on this disrespectful mode of address. "You would give Master Ti great offense if you refused to comply with his wish. That such an unreasonable request has been made at all is due, of course, to the fact that your late husband was much too generous in his entertainment of his friends and acquaintances. All these feasts and receptions! No wonder that people outside talk of the treasures and the rarities to be found here! Of course the Hans and their daughter will have talked, and exaggerated everything. You must just put up with it. Do what he asks willingly; that's better than displeasing him by a refusal, when he might quite possibly subject you to unpleasant means of compulsion. But you needn't, of course, send him all four maids at once. Two will suffice for the present. Then at least you will not have lost face."

Moon Lady considered the matter. Jade Fountain would not be willing to give up Fragrant Orchid, and Gold Lotus would certainly refuse to part with Spring Plum. Apricot Blossom she wanted to keep herself; she had proved herself so valuable as the little boy's nurse. She therefore asked Jade Flute and Pear Blossom if they felt inclined to go to the capital. They were both pleased with the prospect; they liked the notion of a change. Of course, Lai Pao would have to accompany them, since owing to his former missions he was well acquainted with Kai fong fu and the Chancellor's palace.

The rascal was able to derive a threefold profit from this commission. To begin with, he could not refrain from nibbling a little, during the journey, at the sweetness of the two young creatures who had been entrusted to his care, before delivering them to their new lover. Then, he contrived to place Han Tao Kwo under a lasting obligation to him, by explaining how badly things might have gone with him had Moon Lady written to the Intendant, as she had originally proposed, in connection with the embezzled thousand ounces. It was thanks entirely to his adroit and friendly intervention that she had abandoned this intention, and had resigned herself to losing the money. Thirdly, it went without saying that on his return Moon Lady would receive only one of the two heavy silver bars, each weighing a hundred ounces, which the Intendant Ti had paid him as the purchase price of the two delicious young girls of seventeen; the other bar would go into his own pocket. Moreover, in his report he could make out that it was due solely to him that such a good price had been paid. Further, he made it clear to her that Han Tao Kwo's family enjoyed the greatest respect and favor in the household of the Intendant. How wise it had been, therefore, to refrain from annoying such important people in respect of such a trifle as a little embezzlement!

"He simply overwhelms the two Hans with all manner of considerations and attentions. A handsome dwelling house, the finest clothes, choice food, attentive servants—everything is at their disposal," said Lai Pao. "He affectionately addresses Han Tao Kwo as 'dear old Father-in-law.' And as for Darling, their daughter! It is past all belief, how beloved she is, how highly she is regarded. Every day, every hour she is in the company of his principal wife; the two of them are positively inseparable. If she expresses one wish, ten are fulfilled. And how she has blossomed forth! She has grown a little taller, and she is really dazzling. Her jewels, her clothes! She shines and glitters through the rooms like a costly gem. She greeted me in the pleasantest fashion. 'Uncle Pao,' she called me. We mustn't under any circumstances get on the wrong side of these influential people. They hold us in their hand like a needle and thread."

Moon Lady allowed herself a be deluded by his description, and she felt that she must reward him for his services in a special manner. First she had food set before him; then she attempted to make him a present of money, but as he modestly declined to accept it she gave him dress material for his wife.

Lai Pao was secretly delighted. All was going just as he wished. The next thing to be done was quietly to dispose of the stolen bales which were still warehoused in the quayside tavern. His brother-in-law Liu Tsang, who figured as the vendor, obtained a thousand ounces for the goods. Lai Pao bought himself a house, next door to the home of his brother-in-law. This he furnished as a comfortable dwelling house, with a shop in front, which dealt in an assortment of goods; both being held in his brother-in-law's name.

From this time onwards he and his wife lived a double life. In Hsi Men's house they played, as of old, the part of humble and obsequious servants. In the city they were an independent, well-to-do, comfortable citizen and his wife. The wife, who did not find it so natural as did her husband that both master and mistress should leave the house for half the day, generally explained her frequent absences by stating that she was going to visit her sister-in-law. As a plainly dressed servant, she would often disappear from her brother's house, to emerge into the street from her own house next door as a richly dressed citizen's wife, when she would proudly take her place in the palanquin which bore her to the house of one of her many acquaintances. When the palanquin set her down again at her own door her jewels and her silks were quietly laid aside, and in a shabby blue cotton gown the servant appeared as usual from the house next door.

Of course, such doings could not be permanently concealed. The conscious wind bore the news to the house of Hsi Men, first into the kitchen and the servants' bedrooms, and then into the wives' apartments; Lai Pao's wife had been seen here and there, carefully painted and laden with jewels; and what a dissipated life Lai Pao himself was leading when he was not at home! There were heated explanations and altercations. The wife excused herself by saying that the jewels were only borrowed, and the fine clothes had been bought out of her earlier savings; and the man declared that his skin was immaculate and transparent as limpid water; he had nothing to hide under it; on the contrary, it was thanks to his loyal behavior that Han Tao Kwo had not run away to Kai fong fu with the whole cargo. But the suspicion once expressed continued to lie upon them, and when Lai Pao, in moments of intoxication, had repeatedly ventured to press his attentions on Moon Lady, she resolutely put an end to the situation and turned the obnoxious couple out of the house.

CHAPTER THIRTY-NINE: *The fortunate Chen wins Two Darlings instead of One. Gold Lotus hides the Fire in her Heart under a frozen Exterior*

WHEN GOLD LOTUS and young Chen had at last known nights in which they enjoyed to the full the sweets of their passion, they could not bear to be apart. Morning and evening they contrived to indulge themselves in the warmth of secret meetings, and to mitigate the chill of solitary tedium. From day to day their intercourse became more daring. If they knew that they were unobserved they stood or sat shoulder to shoulder, billing and cooing like a newly-mated pair of mandarin ducks. If others were near, so that speech was impossible, they resorted to written notes, which one would secretly slip into the other's hand, or drop on the ground as though by chance. Now she gave him an appointment, now he had something to say to her. More than once they were nearly detected by Moon Lady.

One day in the fourth month Gold Lotus, during his absence, had once more thrown such a written message through the open window of his workroom. He found the note, with a strand of her hair and a few cypress kernels, wrapped in a silver-embroidered handkerchief which was thrust into a red silk perfume sachet. He read:

"This silver-embroidered handkerchief with its contents is sent to you by your loyal slave. Take the strand of my hair as a token that my body is wholly yours. May our love ever remain green as the cypress whose kernels you will find in the handkerchief. In the solitary night, by the light of the lamp, I write these lines, bedewed with my tears. Expect me tonight in the Crayfish Arbor. Do not fail to profit by the favorable hour!"

He could hardly wait until nightfall; then he made for the Crayfish Arbor. But he waited in vain; she did not come. Then he lost patience and went straight to her pavilion. He had no idea that Moon Lady was paying her a chance visit. He stood at the door and called into the house: "Darling, where are you?"

Gold Lotus, recognizing his voice, rose quickly to her feet, ran out into the courtyard, and gave him by signs to understand that caution was imperative. Then she said aloud, so that Moon Lady could hear her indoors: "Is that you, Daughter's Husband? Your wife is no longer here. She went out into the park some time ago, to pick some flowers."

Young Chen understood by this that she had a visitor, and therefore could not come to meet him. Quickly he thrust into her hand the fan which he had brought with him, and as quickly withdrew. Gold Lotus hid the fan in her sleeve and returned unconcernedly to Moon Lady.

"What did he want with you?" asked Moon Lady suspiciously.

"He was looking for his wife," replied Gold Lotus innocently. "But she went away some time ago; she wanted to pick some flowers in the park."

Once again by her presence of mind she had averted the danger of discovery. When Moon Lady had gone she drew the fan from her sleeve. It was carved out of that gold-besprinkled bamboo that grows along the Hsiang River, and of which it is related that the sprinkling of gold is due to the tears with which the faithful widows O Huang and Nue Ying, on the death of their joint husband, the Emperor Shun, once bedewed the banks of the river. On the fan, in pregnant allusion, was painted a full bunch of grapes from which the juice was dripping, and beside it she read the words, written by his hand:

"Between brown, gold-bedewed bamboo sticks white silk is spread to form a fan. Greenish-blue shimmers the miracle of growth, the delicious, inestimable grape. On your leisurely wanderings may the fan afford you shelter from the scorching heat and bring you cooling breezes. But when others are about hide it carefully in your sleeve. Beware lest any unlicensed hand should find it."

She had read this with secret gratification. How enticing was this warm summer night! The moon had just risen. Its mild radiance fell through the half-open window of her bedroom on to the couch, which was ready to receive an occupant. Both maids were already asleep. She had prudently given them plenty of wine that evening. Quickly she washed herself with warm, perfumed water; then she hurried out into the shadowy park. She would wait for him under the Kashmir Thistle Arbor.

Young Chen, after his first unsuccessful attempt, had withdrawn dejectedly to his apartments in the Eastern wing. As luck would have it, the nun Wang was paying Moon Lady a visit that day, and Moon Lady had invited his wife to be present at one of her favorite Buddhistic household services. These family devotions were as a rule very long-drawn-out, so that he might well venture to make a second attempt. He gave Yuen Hsiao, his wife's maid, an embroidered kerchief, and bade her guard the premises.

"I am going to play just one more game of chess with the Fifth. Directly your mistress returns, call me."

He hurried off to the Privet Arbor. He swept the park with an attentive gaze. Yes, there she was, by the Kashmir Thistle Arbor. How the moonlight glistened on her glossy head! Tonight she had let down her hair, and it fell over her shoulders in long, rippling tresses. She was like a lovely flower fairy, hovering in a ghostly landscape. Quietly he crept towards her through the shrubbery, and coming up behind her, he suddenly clasped her in a tender embrace.

"You rascal, to startle me so!" she cried, scolding him and laughingly releasing herself.

She took him by the hand, and together they strolled across the flower-enameled grass to her pavilion.

In her bedroom they sat themselves down at the ready-laid table to eat a cold supper by candlelight. Wine, that ancient procuress, had soon attuned them to the appropriate mood. Before long their cheeks were flushed with the peach-blossom flush of sensual excitement. As the lampshade sinks over the lamp, so cheek to cheek, mouth to mouth, they sank into the pillows.

The cloud had just had time to shed its refreshing moisture when the maid Yuen Hsiao came, as agreed, to the outer door, and announced that her mistress had returned. Regretfully young Chen was obliged to break off his "game of chess." But he had had the satisfaction of playing at least one successful gambit.

Gold Lotus's pavilion possessed, as has already been mentioned, an upper floor, which consisted of three rooms. In the central room she practiced her devotions from time to time: here was a picture of the Buddha, and a statue of the Compassionate Mother Kwan Yin. The two lateral rooms were utilized as a storeroom and a warehouse respectively. One morning Gold Lotus decided to go upstairs in order to burn incense before the statue of Kwan Yin. It so happened that young Chen had just come to fetch certain drugs from the warehouse. In short, they met in the upper rooms. Young Chen immediately put down his parcels of drugs, and Gold Lotus thought no more about her solitary devotions. Closely embraced, they sank upon a divan, and took advantage of this fortunate encounter to practice morning devotions of another kind.

But they were disturbed in these devotions by the sudden appearance of Spring Plum, who all unsuspecting had come upstairs with a tea canister in her hand, in order to fetch some fresh tea leaves. The startled lovers freed themselves from their close embrace, while Spring Plum was tactful enough to turn round immediately, and hurry down the stairs. Moved by a sudden inspiration, Gold Lotus called her back. "Little sister, dear kind little sister, do just come up here! I have something to say to you!" Obediently Spring Plum reascended the stairs.

"You needn't stand on ceremony before our Daughter's Husband, dear little sister," Gold Lotus continued. "After all, he is no stranger in this house. I want to confess to you, quite frankly, that he and I love each other and are inextricably bound to each other.

647

I can say this to you. For I can depend on your discretion, can't I?"

"Dearest mistress, you really don't need to ask me that. You know that for years I have been your faithful slave," declared Spring Plum, eagerly. "How then should I gossip about your doings?"

"Good; you shall be rewarded for your discretion; and at the same time I will put you to the test, to make sure that you honestly mean what you say. Now that our Daughter's Husband is here I permit and order you to lie down beside him here and now. If you refuse I shall take it as a sign that you don't mean honestly by me and mean to betray me."

Little Spring Plum blushed and paled by turns. She saw herself lured into a trap from which there was no escape. Should she lose her mistress's favor by refusing? She obeyed; she took off her coat and her petticoat, and silently lay down on the divan beside young Chen. He naturally did not intend to behave like a fool and a spoil-sport; he entered with enthusiasm into his part of this favorable bargain. He thought himself lucky indeed to have won two precious pearls at one and the same time. By a clever trick Gold Lotus had made sure of her maid's discretion. From this time onwards the three were like one family. Whether he kept tryst or diverted himself with one or the other, it was all in the family.

It was an oppressively hot evening. The heavens were overcast; neither moon nor stars were visible. Gold Lotus had a hot bath prepared. She bathed, and lazily clipped her toenails; then she slipped under the mosquito net, lay down on her bed, fanned herself with Chen's fan, and waited.

"One can tell that the dog days begin today," said Spring Plum, groaning in the heat. "Wouldn't you like to polish your nails with a little phœnix-herb juice? Shall I pick you a few stalks?"

"Is there any phœnix-herb here?"

"Oh, yes, I know a few places in the great courtyard where it grows."

"Good. In the meantime Autumn Aster can go to the kitchen and crush garlic."

She signed to Spring Plum to come nearer, when she added under her breath: "Since you are going into the courtyard you might just tell the Daughter's Husband that I want him to slip across here."

After some little time Spring Plum returned with a bundle of phœnix-herb. She squeezed the sap out of the stalks, and poured it into a bowl, and Gold Lotus whiled away the time of waiting by meticulously polishing her toenails. But on such a day it was intolerably hot on the bed. She made Spring Plum place a divan in the courtyard, and exchanged the hot cushions of the bed for an airy couch under the open sky. This was a pleasanter resting place. From time to time she could feel a gentle breeze, bringing wafts of spicy fragrance from the adjacent park. And from time to time an inquisitive firefly ventured through the half-open gates and circled round the fair sleeper.

At last there was a rustling in the lilac bush at the side of the path outside the gate. It was not the wind that shook the boughs so violently to and fro. This was the appointed signal that young Chen had come. She answered the signal with a gentle whisper. Immediately afterwards he opened the half-closed gate and fell into her arms. She stripped herself naked, and that night, on her outdoor couch, she tasted the joys of love under the open heavens.

A few days later they kept another tryst. This time she wanted to visit him in his room at night. For the nun Pi was once more a guest in Moon Lady's apartments; there would be endless family devotions, and his wife, as usual, would take part in them. Gold Lotus could therefore visit him in safety. But it so happened, and he had forgotten to warn her beforehand, that he was invited that afternoon to the house of the former manager, Tsui Pen. A jolly company was assembled, and the fun was fast and furious. He was quite drunk when he returned home that evening; he could no longer stand upright, and he fell on his bed like a sack of flour. In short, when Gold Lotus entered his room a little later, as was agreed, she found him lying across the bed fast asleep. She shook him vigorously, but could not wake him. She understood that he must have got drunk somewhere, and she at once concluded that he must have been with a woman. Perhaps she would find something to confirm her suspicion. Yes, in his left-hand sleeve pocket she came upon a gold hair clasp. And the two-line inscription showed that it belonged to Jade Fountain. Now she no longer doubted that behind her back he was carrying on an intrigue with the Third. How otherwise should the clasp have come into his possession? "The faithless fellow!" she thought, indignantly. "Who knows how often he has betrayed me?" And she resolved to let him know that she had been there by a few lines which she would leave in the room. She went to his writing table and dipped the brush in the ink, and with flying strokes she wrote upon the wall. The lines which she improvised were as follows:

> *He sleeps, and vainly from the clouds above*
> *The fairy to the magic mountain flies.*
> *Faithless King Hsing speaks no word of love,*
> *For still his weary eyelids veil his eyes.*

Disappointed, she returned to her pavilion. When some time later young Chen awoke from his intoxicated sleep he at once, to his dismay, remembered his tryst with Gold Lotus, and he could not blame himself sufficiently for being asleep at the time of his mistress's visit. That she had been in the room he knew at once from her fresh handwriting on the wall. Since the night had only begun, and he knew that his wife and her maid were attending the service in Moon Lady's apartments, he resolved to atone for his remissness by paying Gold Lotus a return visit. So he slipped across to the pavilion of the Fifth, and made his presence known, as usual, by shaking the boughs of the lilac bush beside the entrance gate. But this time he heard no answering signal. He went to the gate: he found it locked. With sudden resolution he climbed over the whitewashed wall at a point where the stone of the adjacent outlook platform facilitated this proceeding, and swung himself down into the courtyard.

The two maids were already asleep, but Gold Lotus herself was lying awake, gazing dejectedly at the silver disc of the moon, whose slanting rays fell through the open window on to her bed. Then, in the silence of the night, she suddenly heard someone climb the wall and leap down into the courtyard. "That can only be he," she thought, and she silently rejoiced. In order to make sure of the intruder's identity she crept quietly to her bedroom door and looked down into the courtyard. Yes, it was really he. She left the door ajar and slipped into bed again. Now he cautiously opened the door and entered the room.

"Darling!" he cried softly. "Don't be angry with me! I had quite forgotten to tell you that I had to accept an invitation this afternoon. Tsui Pen had invited me and a number of friends to his country house outside the city for an archery contest. There was rather a lot of drinking, and so, unfortunately, I was asleep when you came. Forgive me, please! I am so sorry!"

She made no reply at first, but remained lying with her face to the wall. Perturbed by her silence, he knelt at the bedside and attempted, while he continued to speak to her, to take her gently by the shoulders and turn her to face him. But no sooner had he touched her than she fiercely twisted herself round, and the next moment she had boxed his ears.

"You scoundrel! Can't you at least be quiet?" she hissed. "If the maids were to hear you! I know you have someone else, and all your talk was just lies."

"Darling, I was truly with Tsui Pen at the archery contest. In my drunkenness I quite forgot our appointment. Your lines on the wall told me that you were angry, which is why I have come to you so late at night."

"It's idle to talk! How did this clasp come to be in your sleeve?"

"I found it in the park the day before yesterday."

"Found it indeed! You want me to believe that? Find another, and then I'll believe you. I know the clasp well enough; it belongs to the Third. And recently, when I was not at home, you had supper with her. The case is perfectly clear: you are convicted. Probably you have blabbed to her about our relations. She has laughed at me in such an equivocal way just lately. But I tell you one thing: from

now on it's all over between us. You go your way, and I go mine!
And now have the goodness to clear out!"

But he remained, begging and imploring her to relent.

"If there is the slightest, dirtiest hempen thread of a connection
between the Third and myself, may I die before my thirtieth year,
and may I first be plagued for five years with the jaundice, and
afflicted with ulcers as big as plates!"

Nevertheless, she did not believe him, but silently turned a stubborn back upon him. He crept into bed beside her, but when he
came too near she angrily pushed him back. In this way he spent a
most unrestful night beside her, and was really thankful when he
saw at last that the dawn was at hand. Then he rose from the chilly
couch, slipped out into the courtyard, and hurried back to his room
as he had come. Gold Lotus, however, when she suddenly found
that the place by her side was empty, felt something like remorse.
Perhaps she ought not to have treated him so cruelly. By chance she
met him next morning by the pavilion of the Sixth, where he had
just been removing some pledges from the storeroom on the upper
floor. She stopped him.

"You really needn't have been so touchy about the few words I
spoke to you yesterday—and as for simply running away in the
early morning . . . ! We'll let it be forgotten."

She had spoken these words in the gentlest of tones.

"I wonder you speak to me at all," he retorted coldly. "Who
turned her back to me all night, and punched me and boxed my
ears?"

"Silly fellow! If there's nothing between you and the Third you
needn't have run away like a coward."

"It was almost broad daylight. I didn't want to be found by the
maids."

"Very well, come back this evening!"

"I expect I shall be too tired. I had no sleep last night. Well, I'll
try to make up for it during the day."

"Listen: if you don't come I shall be angry!"

And reconciled again, they parted. He really spent only a little time in the shop that day. As soon as he could get away he crept to his room and threw himself, completely tired out, on his bed. He wanted to be rested for the night.

Towards evening there was an unexpected thunder storm, and just as he wanted to go to Gold Lotus it began to rain in torrents. Since it continued to pour he suddenly picked up a red felt blanket, threw it over his shoulders, and hastened along miry paths and through puddles to his beloved. He knew that his wife and her maid were once more in Moon Lady's apartments.

Gold Lotus, in anticipation of his visit, had once more taken the precaution of making Autumn Aster drowsy with several beakers of wine, and allowing her to go to bed early. Spring Plum, in any case, had to lie beside her, in order to make it less likely that the girl would spy upon her mistress. He was therefore able to enter Gold Lotus's room unannounced, for the doors were unlocked. She was now gentle and affectionate. After he had sworn several times that he had not been given the hair clasp, but had actually found it in the park near the Privet Arbor, she entertained him for a time with wine and a game of chess. But it was still early when she drew him onto the bed. That night she introduced him to all the many amorous tricks which she had formerly practiced with Hsi Men. Like a wanton pair of phœnixes they romped half the night, and made up by their diligence what they had missed the night before.

It was not surprising that Autumn Aster, who had gone to bed slightly intoxicated the previous afternoon, should have been very wide awake quite early the next morning. The day was only beginning to dawn, and the cock had just begun to crow.

As she stretched herself, yawning, and gazed with blinking eyes at the gray dawn, she suddenly heard from her mistress's bedchamber the muffled sounds of a conversation; indeed, she could distinguish, beside her mistress's voice, the deeper tones of a masculine voice. Now she heard the bedroom door open and close, and then light footsteps groping along the corridor. Quickly she sprang to the window and looked out into the courtyard. She was just in time to see a strange man with a dark red blanket over his shoulders rapidly cross the courtyard and slip through the gate, which stood ajar. She had seen only his back, but she knew, from his height and his walk, that he could be none other than young Chen.

"So she plays the wanton at night with the Daughter's Husband!" she said to herself. "And with that she pretends to watch over the virtue of others! The hypocrite!"

And directly after breakfast she ran off to the big kitchen, and imparted her discovery to Little Jewel. Now Little Jewel was a bosom friend of Spring Plum, and before she did anything else she ran off to Spring Plum and told her what she had just heard from Autumn Aster. And Spring Plum told her mistress, Gold Lotus.

"You ought to give the chatterbox a good thrashing, or she'll ruin you with her chattering," she advised her.

Gold Lotus followed her advice. She made Autumn Aster come in and kneel before her.

"It's a long time since you had a beating, you miserable piece!" Gold Lotus angrily shouted. "And now your backside is itching for the stick again, isn't it? You just wait!"

And seizing the stick, she dealt the girl thirty blows with her own hand, striking her with all her might. Spring Plum looked on with malicious glee, and helped her mistress by scolding the victim soundly.

"Be thankful you are getting off so lightly! Really your mistress ought to get the menservants to give you thirty with the heavy bamboo, so as to drive out your monkey's feelings and your horse's thoughts. Discretion is part of a servant's duty! You ought to understand that by now, you accursed chatterbox!"

And she herself gave the girl another dozen blows. After that Autumn Aster was allowed to go. Groaning and weeping, she dragged herself off to the great kitchen. She swore that sooner or later she would obtain satisfaction for such treatment.

One evening in the eighth month young Chen had once more a secret tryst with Gold Lotus. This time they lay long awake; they had rejoiced in the beauty of the full autumn moon, had played a three-handed game of chess with Spring Plum, and had drunk more than enough. In short, next morning young Chen slept through the dawn twilight, at which time he generally disappeared, and was discovered by Autumn Aster. She immediately hurried off to the women's quarters. Today she would tell her story to Moon Lady herself. As she was entering Moon Lady's apartments she ran into the arms of Little Jewel. She drew her aside.

"He is with her again," she said breathlessly. "He has slept with her all night. I had a beating recently because I told you what I saw. At that time I had no proof of my suspicion. But today your mistress can convince herself with her own eyes for he is lying in bed with her now. Tell your mistress; she ought to go across at once."

But she had chosen the wrong confidant. "Pah, you old sneak!" Little Jewel scolded her. "Do you want to ruin your mistress altogether with your chatter? The First has something better to do; she's just dressing. Clear off!"

Moon Lady became aware of the excited whispering outside the door.

"What is it?" she asked Little Jewel.

"The Fifth has sent Autumn Aster here. She wanted to speak to you," said Little Jewel in her embarrassment. She would say nothing more.

Moon Lady put up her hair and betook herself to the pavilion of the Fifth. Gold Lotus and young Chen were still lying in bed, when Spring Plum suddenly rushed into the room, excitedly announcing: "The First mistress is coming!"

The two lovers had a terrible fright, but Gold Lotus immediately recovered her wonted composure. She sprang out of bed, flung on her clothes, and told her lover to remain where he was and lie perfectly still. At the same time she piled the blankets and pillows over him until every inch of his body was covered. Now she went into the adjacent sitting room, and sat down before a small table on which Spring Plum had to pile as many jewels as she could lay her hands on at a moment's notice.

When Moon Lady entered the room a moment later she saw

Gold Lotus, carefree and innocent, pondering over her treasures. She was sitting there as though she had been there for who knows how long, and as though she had not a thought in her mind unconnected with trying on her jewels.

"You sent for me. Did you want to ask me anything?" Moon Lady inquired, sitting down beside her. "Did you get up so early to look at your pearls and enamel flowers?"

Gold Lotus realized the situation immediately.

"Yes, I've been trying a new arrangement, and I wanted your opinion as to whether it was becoming," she replied eagerly, holding various ornaments against her hair as though to test their effect.

"That looks quite delightful," said Moon Lady. "The sesame flowers in front, the jagged wings in gold filigree on either side, and in the middle the chrysanthemum with the sucking bee: really quite a charming combination. I'll wear it myself at the next opportunity, and you must help me to arrange it."

This sounded harmless enough, and Gold Lotus gave an inaudible sigh of relief. Her heart was no longer leaping wildly as a roebuck. Spring Plum brought some tea, and after discussing the jewels a little longer Moon Lady rose to go; but not before Gold Lotus had amiably invited her to breakfast with her. After she had gone Gold Lotus and Spring Plum broke out into a cold perspiration. This time all had gone well. Young Chen could leave his stifling retreat and return unseen to his own room.

"I should just like to know what brought the First to me so early," said Gold Lotus, thoughtfully, turning to Spring Plum. "She must have had some reason for coming."

"Perhaps Autumn Aster has been chattering again," Spring Plum suggested.

Her suspicion was soon to be confirmed. Little Jewel appeared, breathless. She informed them that Autumn Aster had recently come to the house and had let out this and that.

"Fortunately she ran into my arms, or the First would have learned everything. I've told the disloyal creature exactly what I think of her. But you must be more on your guard in future."

But in Moon Lady's mind certain doubts had subsequently arisen. It seemed to her very curious that the Fifth, with whom she was, after all, on the very coolest of terms, should have sent for her at such an unwonted hour, and on such a trivial pretext, merely to look at some jewels. And she quietly took Autumn Aster aside. From her she learned the true state of affairs. But she was not willing to believe all that she was told, and it was very difficult to obtain evidence after the fact. On the other hand, she did not refuse to admit that a lonely, amorously inclined woman like Gold Lotus might very well fall into such reprehensible ways. And in order that the good name of the household should not suffer, she decided to take certain counter-measures. So Hsi Men's daughter was given a friendly hint that it would be well not to leave her husband alone so often. Further, the young couple had to change their quarters, and move into the empty rooms which had formerly been inhabited by Sunflower. She would then have young Chen close beside her, and would find it easier to keep a watch over him. She also gave orders that whenever young Chen had to go to the dispensary stores in the pavilion of the Fifth or the room in which the pledges were kept, in the pavilion of the Sixth, the boy Tai A must accompany him. All the gates of the park and the courtyard were henceforth locked punctually at twilight. And only on pretexts of importance would the maids be allowed in future to visit other parts of the establishment than those to which they were attached as servants. Thanks to these strict measures young Chen and Gold Lotus had no further opportunities of meeting.

Since then a month had gone by. Not once had the lovers been able to meet alone. Gold Lotus was suffering more from day to day under the enforced loneliness of her life; she was chilled by her cheerless situation. She lost her appetite and her high spirits. Her girdle grew even looser about her emaciated loins. She began to neglect her clothes and her general appearance. The park had no further charm for her since she could no longer expect to meet a lover there; she spent her days, for the most part, lying on her bed and brooding. It grieved little Spring Plum to see her vivacious mistress so sadly altered. One day she spoke to her thus:

"Dearest mistress, what is the use of abandoning yourself to dismal thoughts? Since yesterday the two nuns are staying here. This evening there is going to be a long service again. Why don't you profit by the opportunity of meeting him? Towards evening, when the gate to the rear apartments is locked, I shall slip out to the stables on the pretext of getting some hay to stuff a cushion. From the stables it isn't far to the shop. I shall just run quickly into the shop and tell him he is to visit you tonight at all costs. What do you think?"

"Dear little sister, if you would really do that for me I should be eternally grateful."

"But, dear mistress, how can you doubt that I mean it seriously? Now Master Hsi Men is dead I belong to you wholly and absolutely and I will follow you wherever you go."

"Very well, then. I agree."

That afternoon Gold Lotus showed herself at the family tea in Moon Lady's apartments; then she played the trick of the cricket that frees itself from its own husk, and withdrew early on the pretext that her stomach was upset. When the gate of the rear apartments was locked at twilight all the wives and maids had assembled in Moon Lady's rooms to take part in the household devotions. The way lay open for Spring Plum.

"Little sister, be quick and bring him here!" Gold Lotus urged the maid.

"Patience. I'll make Autumn Aster drunk first, the stupid thing, so that she will go to sleep early and not disturb us."

After she had seen to this, and when Autumn Aster had laid herself down to sleep on the kang in the kitchen, she picked up a basket and hurried off to the stables. She filled the basket with hay; then she cautiously crept towards the back door of the pawnshop. Dispenser Fu had already gone home; only young Chen remained in the shop. Now he suddenly heard his name softly called from the courtyard. It was surely Spring Plum's voice. He opened the door.

It was really she. "It's you, little sister!" he cried, beaming all over his face. "Come in, there's no one here but me."

She entered quickly and cautiously closed the door.

"Where are the servants this evening?" she asked.

"Tai A and Ping An are busy in the dispensary. The others are all in their rooms."

"My poor mistress is quite ill and wretched with longing for you. She has sent me here today to say that you simply must visit her."

"How sweet of her! Good, I'll come. Walk a few paces in front of me. I have just got to clear away something here; I'll follow you at once."

He took a white silk kerchief and a silver comb from a drawer and gave them to her. Then he drew her down beside him on the kang, and embraced her closely for a while. Presently he gently pushed her toward the door. With her basket full of hay, she returned safely to Gold Lotus.

"He's coming!" she announced. "And how delighted he was to get your message! He gave me this white kerchief and this silver comb."

That night—it was the beginning of the ninth month—a full round autumn moon shone down from the clear sky. Young Chen summoned Ping An from the dispensary and asked him to take charge of the pawnshop in his place. He himself, he explained, wanted to take part in the household service, to which Moon Lady had invited him. He then departed, and disappeared into the park through a small side gate which Spring Plum had left open. Avoiding the moonlit path, he crept cautiously under the trees and through the shrubberies to Gold Lotus's pavilion. Now Spring Plum, pressed close against the shadowy side of the wall, heard the well-known signal; there was a rustling in the lilac bush on the other side of the wall. Quickly she opened the gate and let him in.

Smiling, Gold Lotus greeted him on the threshold of her bedroom.

They sat down, and were happy, after so long an interval, to drink once more from the same side of the same beaker, and to lean cheek upon cheek, thigh against thigh. Spring Plum was allowed to drink with them that day, in return for her loyal service to her mistress. Indeed, she was further rewarded. After they had drunk themselves into the mood, Gold Lotus removed all her clothes, young Chen and the maid followed her example, and all three rejoiced in their rosy nudity, unimpaired by a thread of clothing. Now Gold Lotus took her place in one of those comfortable armchairs which were designed especially for drunken old gentlemen. Then she ordered Spring Plum to bring the silver lamp nearer, and to take from the picture chest that silken frieze which had once adorned the chamber of an Emperor's wife, and which had passed from the possession of old Kung Kung into that of the Sixth, and had finally been given by Hsi Men to Gold Lotus.

Snuggling close together, they examined, by the light of the lamp, the four and twenty sections of the frieze, in which were depicted, with perfect art, the most varied modes and phases of the sport of love. After they had gazed their fill they left the armchair for the wide cushions of the couch, in order to rehearse the pictorial lessons on their own persons. And the three abandoned themselves to the unutterable blisses of their passionate reunion.

It was nearly midnight when Autumn Aster woke on her hard kang in the kitchen, and felt the need of relieving herself. She got up, in order to go out into the courtyard. Spring Plum had prudently bolted the gate from outside, but Autumn Aster, who by this time was sober, succeeded in squeezing her hand between the bars of the grille and pushing back the bolt. After she had done what she wanted she took a little moonlit stroll round the pavilion. Curiosity urged her to stop and listen outside the window of her mistress's bedroom.

To her surprise, she saw that there was a light in the room, and she could distinguish voices; and as she now cautiously spied through the peephole of the window she saw her mistress tumbling on the couch with young Chen and Spring Plum. All three were stripped from head to foot, and they seemed to have been drinking immoderately.

"So that's what their virtue is like!" she thought, resentfully. "Before other people they are marvels of respectability, and they punish me if I dare to speak a word! But this time I've seen their scandalous doings with my own eyes. Tomorrow I'll go to the First and tell her everything. That'll spoil their pleasure!"

She turned and crept back into the kitchen. Spring Plum was the first to wake next morning. She quickly roused young Chen and let him out of the pavilion. Then she went into the kitchen.

"Why is the kitchen door open?" she asked Autumn Aster. "I bolted it last night."

"I had to go out into the courtyard during the night. So I pushed back the bolt from inside."

"Couldn't you have managed it in the kitchen? There's the tub. You silly creature, why did you have to go running out into the courtyard for that?"

"I didn't think about it."

The altercation continued for a time; then Spring Plum returned to her mistress.

"What was the matter in the kitchen?" Gold Lotus inquired.

Spring Plum informed her, with some uneasiness, that Autumn Aster had gone out into the courtyard during the night. Presumably she had been spying again. This information enraged Gold Lotus beyond measure. She wanted to punish the girl by beating her then and there. But it was too late: Autumn Aster was already off and away to Moon Lady.

Autumn Aster did not on this occasion find the way to Moon Lady barred by Little Jewel, but she received as little credit as on her former visit. Indeed, she had to endure Moon Lady's violent reproaches. The First had had enough of these constant upsets; she wanted to be left in peace.

"You worthless creature, you simply want to throw suspicion on your mistress and ruin her by this tale-bearing, which is quite unjustified!" she cried. "Last time you came rushing over here for no reason at all. Didn't you then declare that young Chen was in bed with the Fifth? I went straight across to her pavilion, so that I must

661

have found him there. He was nowhere to be seen. Kindly spare me your gossip in future!"

Disillusioned by the ungracious reception of what she regarded as her loyalty to the First, Autumn Aster withdrew dejectedly. After this she no longer carried news to the women's apartments, but kept her observations to herself. Gold Lotus, however, who was informed by Little Jewel of the rebuff which the scandalmongering Autumn Aster had received, was triumphant, and felt securer than ever.

CHAPTER FORTY: *Moon Lady clamors for Help in the "Palace of Sunrise and Sunset." Spring Plum bids a tearless Farewell to the Household of Hsi Men*

DURING THE NEXT FORTNIGHT the absence of Moon Lady allowed the two lovers to meet daily. Moon Lady had undertaken a long-planned pilgrimage to the Tai shan, in order to offer a sacrifice on the summit to Niang Niang the "Heavenly First Mother." At the same time she wished to absolve a vow which she had taken during Hsi Men's illness. These cool, clear autumn days were just the right weather for traveling, so she hesitated no longer. One morning about the middle of the ninth month, after bidding a solemn farewell to Hsi Men's soul tablet, she stepped into her large, comfortably-upholstered palanquin, and set out upon the journey to the holy mountain of Shantung. Her elder brother and the servants Lai An and Tai A, riding on muleback, formed her escort. She intended to return by the end of the month.

After a few short days' marches the district capital of Tai an chow was reached, and the towering majesty of the Tai shan rose before the wondering eyes of the travelers. It was already late in the afternoon when they arrived. They therefore contented themselves for the time being with the sight of the mountain, and sought shelter betimes in a hostelry. Well rested, they began the ascent early next morning. First they offered sacrifice and broke their fast in the ancient and renowned temple of Tai yo, dedicated to the divinity of the mountain, which lies at the foot of the Tai shan. Then began the ascent of the forty-nine stations of the mountain.

So steep was the path at times that the bearers of the mountain litters had to clutch at the bushes and creepers growing at the side of the track in order to haul themselves up.

Fifty *li* measures the distance from the mountain temple at the foot to the summit. They left the temple at the eighth hour of the morning; by the fifth hour of the afternoon they found themselves before the "Palace of Sunrise and Sunset," which towered high above the level of the clouds. They were now at a height from which they could look down upon thunder and lightning, wind and rain. Now they entered the temple gates, above which, on a cinnabar-red background, shone the inscription in three great golden characters: *Pi hsia kung,* "Palace of Sunrise and Sunset;" and then at last they stood before the magnificent golden statue of the Niang Niang, the "Heavenly First Mother."

Reverently Moon Lady prostrated herself before the goddess, while a boy, a servant of the temple, laid at her feet the bowls containing the sacrificial food which the pilgrims had brought with them, and the High Priest ignited the incense in the golden censer, and read aloud a document in which it was solemnly recorded that Moon Lady had now absolved her pious vow.

There was something peculiar about this priest. About forty years of age, he was short and sprightly, with a long, triple-pointed beard. He was wearing a dark red cassock, and his priestly bonnet was coquettishly adorned with an ornate golden brooch. Shi Po Tsia, as he was called, was despite his ecclesiastical rank a very worldly-minded and frivolous fellow, under whose cassock lust and avarice were concealed. He had a secret understanding with a man who was known and dreaded throughout the countryside: a wealthy libertine by the name of Yin, a brother-in-law of the Prefect of the Tai shan district.

This Yin was not only a passionate hunter of wild animals, who was constantly roaming the plain with a rout of dissolute companions of his own sort, indulging in his favorite sport with the help of the longbow and crossbow; he was also a notorious woman hunter, and was particularly fond of loafing about the two temples in alternation—that at the foot of the Tai shan, and that on the summit. For there were, of course, divers beauties to be seen among the many women visitors to the temples, who year in, year out, came hither on pilgrimage from all quarters of the Empire, in order to pay their solemn devotions. And often enough he was not content with merely looking at them. His accomplice, the High Priest Shi Po Tsai, made it his special task to induce suitable visitors to pass the night in the cells of the temple, and to see that they were disposed to welcome the delights of love.

Now, this Shi Po Tsai immediately conceived that Moon Lady was a suitable victim for his patron Yin. His experienced eye told him that this cultivated lady, who had arrived in the company of a dignified old gentleman and two servants, must surely be a member of some very aristocratic family. There was about her that certain something which would have a quite peculiar charm for a pampered libertine like his patron. Accordingly his approach to her was marked by the most winning and plausible courtesy.

"May I now invite the valued patron and the noble patroness of our temple to take a modest sip of tea in the guest cells?" he said, with a sanctimonious grin, when the ceremony of sacrifice was completed.

"Master, we should not like to put you to any trouble. We really want to start on the way down immediately," said the elder Wu, in a deprecating tone.

"Oh, there is still plenty of time to get down," replied the priest, smiling, and he pressed Master Wu and Moon Lady to accompany him to the reception hall.

In the comfortably furnished room, with its snowy, white-washed walls, a wide and handsome divan invited the travelers to rest. Its lacquered framework displayed a tasteful design of sesame flowers, while the silken hangings were embroidered with a pattern of willow leaves. Above an incense table hung a painting which showed a hermit seated before his cave, feasting his eyes upon a cluster of peonies. To the right and the left of this two texts were painted on the wall. One of these texts ran as follows: "A holy man with nothing but empty air in both sleeves makes wild cranes dance"; and the other: "A holy man on the moonlit balcony recites pious texts to the night."

Now two pretty, neatly-dressed little temple boys appeared, bringing tea. But more than a "sip of tea" was offered: here was a sumptuous meal, with roast meat and boiled, with preliminary snacks and dessert, and every desirable condiment. This did not seem like frugal temple fare. There were even silver-rimmed amber beakers, filled with delicious "Golden Billow" wine.

But of this Moon Lady refused to partake. It seemed to her a sin to drink wine in this holy place. She rose and beckoned her servant Tai A. At her bidding he handed the priest, on a red lacquer tray, a bale of cotton cloth and two ounces of white metal.

"A small token of our recognition of the trouble you have taken," said the elder Wu, to the obsequiously bowing priest. "But please, Master, spare yourself further inconvenience. There can be no question of drinking wine. It is already late in the day. We must now think of taking our departure."

"Why these sumptuous gifts? To accept them embarrasses me; to refuse them would be unmannerly. The trifling hospitality which the simple disciple of the Tao has to offer you is truly not worthy of mention," replied the priest earnestly. "The grace of the heavenly First Mother, who has placed me here as the guardian of the 'Temple of Sunrise and Sunset,' provides our temple more than abundantly with presents from all four quarters of the land. Why should I not apply the surplus to the entertainment of our noble patrons and patronesses? Stay, I beg you, just a little longer, and at least drink these little cups with the simple disciple of the Tao."

Willy-nilly his guests resumed their seats, and to please him drank the wine he offered them.

"Ugh, this thin stuff is no good. Bring instead of this a jug of the good 'Lotus-flower' wine that was given us recently by Master Hsue, the Prefect of Tsingchow," said the priest, turning to the two little boys. And now, with both hands, he offered his guests two brimming beakers of the better wine. Moon Lady protested.

"My sister cannot stand so much wine," the elder Wu explained.

"Please, please take it!" the priest urged. "It will do you good before the return journey through frost and autumn mist."

And yielding to his urgency, the elder Wu consented to drain the beaker offered him, while Moon Lady drank only half hers.

"Well, how does it taste?" inquired the priest eagerly.

"Most excellent," the elder Wu had to admit.

"That was a fine present from my old patron, the Prefect Hsue," said the priest, proudly. "With his wife, son and daughter he comes here every year. We are good friends, and I have had many proofs of his favor. Really half the income of all temples has to be paid into the public treasury. That our two temples here on the Tai shan have of recent years been relieved of this tribute is due entirely to the kindly recommendation of the Prefect to the Throne. Hence it comes that we need not stint our worthy guests, and have no occasion to be parsimonious."

By such diplomatic speeches the priest cleverly insinuated himself into the confidence of his guests, and before they knew it the one beaker had become two and more. And when at last they wished to take their leave the crafty disciple of the Tao declared in a positive tone:

"There can no longer be any question of going down today. It is much too late now. If you do not disdain our humble cells, you had better spend the night here. Starting early tomorrow, you can take more time over the descent."

The elder Wu submitted to the inevitable. But he would not drink any more. He had already sufficiently convinced himself of the potent effects of the strong wine. When his host offered him yet another full beaker he refused it on the pretext that he must disappear for a moment, and he betook himself to the back of the temple premises, in order to feast his eyes on the glorious panorama. This was just what the crafty priest wanted. Moon Lady must be left alone.

She was feeling very tired. The early start, the wearisome ascent of the mountain, the solemn sacrificial ceremony, the sumptuous meal, the strong wine—all co-operated to induce an imperative need for rest. So she gave the priest to understand that she wished to lie down for a little while, whereupon he promptly disappeared. He did not forget to lock the door quietly behind him. He was hardly out of the room before Moon Lady sleepily threw herself on to the sesame-flower divan, under the willow-leaf hangings.

She had not been lying there long when she heard a faint creaking. It came from the wall behind the divan. A secret door had opened there, and suddenly a strange man stood before the startled Moon Lady. He was a desperate-looking fellow, about thirty years of age. He was wearing a light purple silk dressing gown, and a dark green turban was wound about his head. In three narrow "willow leaves" a thin moustache and beard hung from the corners of his mouth and his chin. There was a lustful glitter in his eyes, and his cheeks were flushed with excitement. Before Moon Lady could prevent it he had swiftly seated himself beside her and flung his arms about her.

"Noble lady, do not be frightened!" he panted softly. "I am Yin, the brother-in-law of Prefect Kao of Tai an chow. Long ago the fame of your beauty and virtue and noble origin reached my foolish ear. Oh, heavenly ornament of the land, as the thirsting man yearns for cold water, so have I longed for you! To possess your jasper body would for me be the supremest happiness of all my three existences. Oh, listen to me, have pity upon me! And in life and death I shall eternally be your debtor!"

He had nestled close against her. But now Moon Lady, having recovered from her first terror, sprang wildly to her feet.

"What does this mean?" she cried aloud, in a voice trembling with indignation. "Here, in this holy place, without warning, to insult heaven and earth and attack a respectable woman of honorable family! Leave me alone!"

She tore herself loose and rushed to the door, in order to escape into the open air. But she did not get so far. Her assailant hung on to her and embraced her, while he slowly sank down at her feet.

"Noble lady, don't scream like that!" he pleaded. "Have mercy on your devoted slave!"

But Moon Lady, desperately defending herself, raised her voice louder than ever. Her cries for help had already been heard by the two servants, Tai A and Lai An, who were eating their supper not far away. They hastily warned the elder Wu that apparently something had befallen their mistress, and the three of them now tried to force their way into the reception cell. But the locked door opposed their efforts. With swift resolution the elder Wu seized a heavy stone and dashed it against the thin carved framework, so that a gaping hole appeared.

"Don't be afraid, sister, I am here!" he cried encouragingly. With hands and feet the hole was enlarged at top and bottom until the aperture was large enough for a man to squeeze through. But when they at last entered the room the libertine Yin had already fled like a wreath of smoke through the secret door.

"Has anyone done violence to you sister?" the elder Wu anxiously inquired of the trembling Moon Lady.

"I didn't let it come to that. The fellow came in through the wall behind the divan. There is a secret door. And he slipped out again by the same way."

Now the elder Wu wanted to cross-examine the High Priest. But the scoundrel was nowhere to be found. In vain his assistants endeavored to appease the infuriated Wu. He would not rest until with the help of Tai A and Lai An he had smashed the door and window and all the furniture of the scoundrelly priest's cell to splinters. Then they entered their litters, and descended the mountainside with all possible speed.

Twilight was falling as they turned their backs on the "Palace of Sunrise and Sunset," and it was already pitch dark when at last they reached their hostelry. The host betrayed no little consternation when he heard what had happened on the mountain.

"Alas, this is a bad business!" he said, scratching his head in embarrassment. "This Yin is the brother-in-law of our Prefect and a most powerful lord. Who would care to get on the wrong side of him? If he heard that I had given you shelter here he would make me pay for it heavily. I am sorry, but after this incident I must ask you to continue on your way. I cannot possibly keep you here overnight."

Whether she liked it or not, Moon Lady, tired and shaken as she was, had to enter her traveling palanquin and resign herself to a hurried march that was more like a flight. There was no time to be lost, for infuriated by his ill-success, the libertine Yin, at the head of a band of thirty confederates, armed with daggers and cudgels, had set off in pursuit of the fugitives. In order to escape their pursuers, whose menacing cries they already heard behind them, the little company turned aside from the highway, and were soon lost in the trackless thickets of a wild mountain ravine, where it was difficult to make any progress.

It was about the third watch of the night when they saw, in the distance, through the pitchy darkness of the wood, a faint gleam of light. On drawing nearer they found themselves at the entrance of a rocky cave, in which sat an ancient hermit, who was reading a roll of the sacred scriptures by the light of an oil lamp. The elder Wu went forward and greeted him, told him of their adventure on the Tai shan, and their nocturnal flight, and asked him the way to Tsing ho hsien. They had lost themselves in the wood.

"You are on the eastern slope of the Tai shan," the old man told him. "I am the hermit Pu Tsing and have already lived for thirty years in this cave. Not chance, but predestination has brought you to me. That you will recognize later. But I do not advise you to continue your march tonight. It is not safe in this neighborhood and at this hour; robbers and wild beasts are prowling about. You can spend the night with me. I will show you the way tomorrow."

"Many thanks, Master! But pursuers are behind us. They will find us here."

"Have no fear; they have already turned back," the old man placidly declared. "Who is the lady?"

"My sister, the widow of the former District Judge of Tsing ho hsien. She has been offering a sacrifice on the mountain in order to absolve a pious vow, and now she has had to endure this un-righteous behavior. She will be grateful to you all her life for sheltering her so kindly during her flight in the darkness."

The hermit examined Moon Lady with a searching gaze. Then he showed his guests to their sleeping places in his cave. Next morning, when they were leaving, Moon Lady wished to present him with a bale of cloth in recognition of his hospitality. But the hermit shook his head in refusal. "I ask you for your little son in recompense. He shall be my future assistant, and one day he will continue my holy work," he said, quietly and positively.

Taken aback by this extraordinary demand, Moon Lady looked inquiringly at her brother.

"It is true that my sister has a son, but he is an only child," the elder Wu replied. "Later on he will be the heir to the family property, and will continue his father's line. Under these circum-stances you will hardly insist upon your demand. If she had several sons she would naturally be glad to fulfill your wish."

"My son, too, is so small—he is barely one year old—that he could hardly be of any use to you," added Moon Lady.

"I can wait," the old man insisted. "In fifteen years I shall repeat my request. Will you let me have him then?"

Moon Lady reflected. She did not wish to offend the strange old man who had sheltered and protected her by a flat refusal. Fifteen years was a long time; anything might happen in that time; the old man might die, or the whole affair be forgotten.

"Very well, I agree. In fifteen years' time you shall have my son," she promised him lightly.

The old man nodded, and pointed silently in the direction of Tsing ho hsien.

A few days after Moon Lady had set out on her pilgrimage Gold Lotus again sent for young Chen to come to her pavilion.

"There is something I must tell you," she said. "For some time I have noticed certain changes in myself; I feel weak and exhausted, my limbs are tired and heavy, and my girdle has grown too tight for my swollen body. When Hsi Men was still living I once made use of a conceptive medicine which the nun Pi prepared for me. But however much I had to do with Hsi Men, there were never any results. But now, since I have had to do with you, my body has suddenly begun to swell. And you are the only man by whom I could be pregnant. It is six months now since I have had intercourse with you, so that the fruit of our relations must be pretty well developed. Now, please, don't be a sleeper and a dreamer! Take advantage of the First's absence! The fruit absolutely must be disposed of before it is too late. Do we want people to mock at us? For me the scandal would mean death. So please look about for a doctor and procure some means of abortion for me!"

He reflected.

"We ourselves have a great number of medicines in the dispensary, but I don't really understand them. Wait a minute: I'll go to Doctor Hu, the woman's doctor in High Street; he is sure to know of a suitable drug."

"Dear Brother, go," she urged, "and lose no time!" He provided himself with a few silver bits and went immediately to Doctor Hu.

"What are your esteemed commands?" inquired the doctor, who had immediately recognized in his visitor the son-in-law of the wealthy Hsi Men.

Young Chen laid three bits on the table. "I should be obliged if you could prepare for me an efficient means of abortion!"

"My dear sir, other people rejoice when they have offspring, and you are thinking of abortion! No, I am sorry."

Young Chen rightly concluded that this refusal meant that he wanted a higher fee. He laid two more bits on the table.

"I grant that the blessing of children is generally to be desired; but this is a case of a young woman who would be in a painful predicament if she gave birth to a child."

The doctor pocketed his five bits.

"Very well, I will prescribe a 'red flower medicine' which will thoroughly clear the body. She must move about a little after taking it; then it will soon take effect."

672

That evening Gold Lotus swallowed the prescribed liquid mixed with a little hot soup. She then moved about as ordered, pacing up and down her room. She might have covered a distance of perhaps five *li* when she began to feel a twitching and a commotion in her body. She lay down: Spring Plum helped her by stroking and kneading her body, and a little while later the desired result of an easy abortion was obtained. It was a well-developed, fair-skinned embryo of the male sex. Gold Lotus had it wrapped in bast paper, and Autumn Aster threw it into the garbage pit. Next day the scavengers removed it with other household garbage.

It is an old story that good works most frequently remain hidden, while evil deeds become known at a distance of a thousand *li*. Within a few days the rumor was going the rounds of the household that the intercourse between Gold Lotus and the Daughter's Husband had not been without consequence, and that Gold Lotus had secretly made away with the result.

At the beginning of the tenth month Moon Lady returned from her Tai shan pilgrimage, and was greeted on every hand with wondering reverence, as though she had come straight from heaven. After she had thanked heaven and earth and Buddha for her safe return by an offering of incense, and had prostrated herself before Hsi Men's soul tablet, she diverted herself for a time in the company of her little boy, and in the evening she joined the other wives in a general dinner of greeting, when she related her experiences of travel. She felt somewhat overcome by the hardship of the return journey, which was spoilt by cold winds and autumn fogs, and she decided that for once she would allow herself two or three days' rest in bed. She was therefore still in bed on the morning after her return when Autumn Aster appeared and insisted upon speaking to her. This gossiping creature could not wait to unburden her heart, which was once more overflowing with indignation; she must run to the mistress of the household with the latest scandalous news. But once again she was unlucky. Little Jewel barred her way on the threshold and received her with a ringing box on the ears.

"Accursed scandalmonger!" she cried. "Have you come again with your tale-bearing? Can't you have any consideration for the fact that my mistress is worn out by her journey and in need of rest? Get out!"

Autumn Aster sulkily retired. But she refused to be intimidated, and a few days later, when she again surprised Gold Lotus and young Chen secretly billing and cooing in the balcony room upstairs, she once more ran off to the women's apartments, and this time she made her way into Moon Lady's presence unhindered.

"Twice and three times I have called your attention to their doings in vain, and you would never believe me," she burst out. "During your absence they have often slept whole days and nights together, and Spring Plum has joined them. Moreover, the Fifth had a child in secret recently, and dropped it into the garbage pit. At this very moment she is playing the harlot with him upstairs in the balcony room. If you won't believe me, come and convince yourself."

Moon Lady hurriedly rose and followed her into the park. Gold Lotus and young Chen were just in the act when Spring Plum came running up the stairs, and shouted into the balcony room: "Beware, the First is coming!"

The startled lovers broke their embrace. Hastily gathering up the goods which he had previously taken out of store, young Chen rushed down the stairs and into the park. Just before the entrance gate of the pavilion he ran against Moon Lady.

"Why in such a hurry?" she cried to him.

"The customers are waiting in the shop. I had no one to send."

Moon Lady assumed a severe expression.

"Haven't I expressly forbidden you to go to the store room unless you are accompanied by a servant?" she said in a tone of rebuke. "How can you do such a thing as to come here alone and boldly force your way into the house?"

He hardly listened, but fled from the spot, pursued by a bad conscience. Then it was Gold Lotus's turn. It was some time before she had recovered herself sufficiently to come downstairs and face Moon Lady.

"You ought to have a little more regard for good form and discretion!" said Moon Lady, in a tone of quiet reproof. "You should take me as an example of how one should conduct oneself as a widow. The time for foolish dalliance is past. It was different when the house was still filled with the odor of man. Aren't you ashamed in front of the servants? You are getting yourself talked about. I tried at first not to believe your Autumn Aster, but now I have convinced myself that she is speaking the truth. And now I have told you my opinion. Please act accordingly!"

During this speech Gold Lotus turned white and red alternately. As always in a ticklish position, she took refuge in lying.

"But not a word of all this is true!" she declared. "I have simply been burning incense upstairs, and he had something to do in the store room. We didn't exchange a word."

Moon Lady turned away in displeasure and left her. This day there was a violent altercation between young Chen and his wife. He could endure that she should accuse him of unfaithfulness. But that she should also permit herself to remark that he was living the life of a lazy parasite in his father-in-law's house offended him sorely.

"Didn't I put down five hundred ounces when we came here? Am I to be called a parasite after that?" he cried, and he ran off in a rage.

From this time onwards he avoided the rear apartments. If someone had to go to the dispensary stores or fetch a pledge he sent Tai A and Ping An together. He was too proud to go on accepting food from the kitchen, so he fed himself at his own expense, buying food from the street vendors, or now and again eating a meal in his parents' house, which his father, when he so precipitately left the city, had entrusted to the care of his uncle on his mother's side, whose name was Chang. All intercourse between him and his beloved was now, of course, at an end. Moon Lady exercised the strictest supervision: she had the gates and the doors locked in the afternoon, and went the rounds herself in the evening, lantern in hand, to make sure that all was in order. In the secret battle for power between herself and Gold Lotus young Chen became the chief sufferer, and the truth of the old saying was once more confirmed:

When tiger and dragon quarrel
Then the young stag has to suffer.

The lovers had endured a month of complete and miserable separation when one day young Chen saw the matchmaker Pi passing the shop. Afterwards it occurred to him that she was the very person to take his beloved a message. And that same day, under the pretext of collecting some customers' accounts in the city, he called on Mother Pi. He had the good fortune to find her at home.

"What wind blows you hither?" she asked.

Without much circumlocution, he proceeded to speak of the object of his visit. He had for a long while carried on a love affair with the Fifth, which for a month past, thanks to the gossiping Autumn Aster, had been completely broken off. He was very anxious to send his beloved a sign that he was still living, and it had occurred to him that she might be kind enough to help him. In confirmation of what he had said he handed her an ounce of "tea money."

Mother Pi clapped her hands in amazement. "Oh, you rascal! To take up with the concubine of your own father-in-law! That's an offense against all the good principles of the social order! Well, fire away! What can I do in the matter?"

"Be so kind as to take her this letter!"

"Very well. I will run this errand in connection with a visit I was thinking of paying to the First."

"Shall I then hear from you?"

"I'll see you in the shop afterwards."

On the following day Mother Pi made her way to Hsi Men's house. First she called on Moon Lady, offering for sale various enamel ornaments for the hair, in order to provide a plausible

676

pretext for her appearance. After she had passed the time of day with the Third and the Fourth it would have been positively ill-mannered if she had not paid a visit to the Fifth. Gold Lotus had just allowed Spring Plum to persuade her to wash down her melancholy with a little wine.

"Don't droop your head!" the maid had advised her mistress. "Think rather how you can improve your situation! The First is fully occupied with her child. She can't pay much attention to what we do on the quiet. You are still beloved, and you have friends who would storm heaven for you. Enjoy your life and drink! Today is today!"

She pointed to a couple of dogs which were behaving in the manner of dogs in front of the terrace steps.

"See how delightfully the animals enjoy their lives! Why shouldn't we human beings do the same? Drink!"

So Mother Pi found the two in the right mood as she came panting up the steps.

"Well, I call that a diverting spectacle, and a lucky omen too!" she said, laughing, with a wily glance at the two dogs, who did not allow her arrival to disturb them in their strenuous occupation. Her appearance was joyfully greeted as a welcome diversion; Gold Lotus and the maid invited her to sit down and drink with them. After a few preliminary phrases Mother Pi began to approach the object of her visit.

"Since Master Hsi Men's death you have found it very quiet and dull, haven't you?"

"Oh, there are no words to express what I suffer in this solitude! And then, this constant espionage! There's no concealing the fact, unhappily, that the First is quite a different person now that the child is there. The pleasant sisterly relation that used to exist between us is out of the question now. There has been an upset again quite recently; for days now I haven't entered the rear apartments, and I am living a life of absolute retirement."

"The last upset was the fault of that miserable Autumn Aster," Spring Plum interposed. "She had nothing better to do than to spy on her own mistress and tell tales about her. And this dragged me into it too. There was a fine to-do recently."

"What, a servant betray her own mistress? That's unheard-of!"

"Hush! Spring Plum, be so good as to see what she's doing. It's quite possible that she's eavesdropping again."

"She's sitting in the kitchen husking rice," Spring Plum reported, as she presently returned. "She's a regular water tap. Everything that happens here trickles into the outer world through her mouth!"

"Well, for the moment we shan't be disturbed, so I can speak," Mother Pi began. "Yesterday the Daughter's Husband came to see me, and he too complained of how strictly the First is supervising the household; how she has all the gates and doors bolted early, and makes it impossible for him to slip into either of the store rooms unobserved. He told me, too, that he has had a violent scene with his wife; she reproached him with living the life of an idle parasite in his father-in-law's house; and since then he never has a bite from the kitchen, but lives at his own expense on food which he brings in from the street, or he has a meal with his uncle and aunt, instead of supporting the old people, in accordance with the rules of piety. He regrets infinitely that he has been compelled to neglect you so long, and he begged me to bring you this letter, so that you may know that now, as of old, he is true to you in his thoughts. You must not despair, or lose faith in your final reunion."

Gold Lotus ran through the short letter, in which the writer had expressed himself in deliberately obscure phrases, which any other member of the household would hardly have been able to decipher. He assured her of his devotion, and hoped confidently for the day when despite all machinations, despite all opposition, he would cross the "blue bridge" with her to the long-desired goal of marriage. Much gratified, she tucked the letter into her sleeve. It had quite restored her spirits.

"He begs you to send him a few lines, or at least a little token to remember you by," Mother Pi added.

Gold Lotus disappeared into her bedroom, where she took a

white silk kerchief and a golden ring from a drawer. On the kerchief she hastily wrote a few lines in which she assured her lover of her fidelity and her longing for him. Then she hid both in an envelope and returned to Mother Pi.

"Take him, please, this message, and my greetings! He had better not eat with his relations and be a burden to them; it would only be held against him. He had better show pride and have his meals quietly with Dispenser Fu in the shop."

Mother Pi tucked away the letter and her fee of five bits, and hurried off to the shop. After she had delivered her message and had already taken leave of young Chen she turned back again.

"I had almost forgotten something important," she told him. "The First called me indoors just now. I am to come back this evening and take the maid Spring Plum away with me, and sell her to someone else. Now that the girl has collaborated in your secret intercourse with the Fifth and has even had relations with you herself, she can't be tolerated here any longer."

"Oh, that is excellent! Then I can see the child and speak to her at your place very shortly."

Mother Pi did actually return to Moon Lady that evening.

"I bought her from you for sixteen ounces," Moon Lady told the go-between. "I am asking you just the same price in return."

Then she turned to her maid Little Jewel.

"Take Mother Pi to her. She is to pack her things and get ready to go. But all her clothes and her jewels are to remain here."

Gold Lotus was as though menumbed when Mother Pi appeared once more and explained that she had been instructed to take Spring Plum away with her that evening. She was to lose her only confidant, her loyal companion!

"We have been such good comrades," she told the go-between, in a voice that was choked with tears. "Since his death we have borne many troubles together, and now she is to be taken from me! That is heartless, that is vile of the First! Because she has brought a dirty brat into the world she thinks she can trample us underfoot! But the brat has got to go through scarlet fever yet, and measles, and other childish illness. The Sixth had a child, but it didn't live a year. Who knows what punishment Heaven will send her?"

"Was Master Hsi Men very fond of the little maid?"

"Wasn't he just! He treasured her like a piece of his own self. Every wish of hers he granted ten times over. He loved and valued her as though she had been a real wife."

"Then undoubtedly the First is not doing as he would have wished, when she harshly drives such a nice, pretty creature out of the house. She may not even take her clothes and her jewels with her. It is very wrong of her to expose the poor creature so before the neighbors."

"What? She can't even take her clothes and her jewels?" cried Gold Lotus, angrily.

"She expressly forbade her to do so," said Little Jewel, in confirmation.

Spring Plum, who as the person chiefly concerned had received the news of her sudden expulsion quite unmoved, and with dry eyes, tried to console her mistress.

"Dear mistress, don't take the matter too much to heart! It will only injure your health if you excite yourself. Wait until I'm outside, then you will be able to find a way. The little bit of clothing and jewelry—bah, what do I care for that! An old proverb says:

> *"A true man makes his way*
> *irrespective of time and circumstance.*
> *The honest woman first proves herself*
> *in a simple every-day gown."*

"She can safely take two good dresses." Little Jewel interposed, moved by compassion. "Mother Pi can carry the bundles, so that it won't attract attention. I'll close my eyes."

"That I call sisterly and compassionate behavior!" said Gold Lotus. "Many thanks!"

"Dear mistress, which of us all is safe against unforseen changes of fortune?" said Little Jewel, modestly. "Frog or cricket, both are exposed to the same cruel mattock. The fox mourns the death of the hare. You today, I tomorrow!"

Gold Lotus quickly chose two handsome dresses from her maid's chest, and added a pair of satin slippers and various hair clasps, earrings, and finger rings, and she packed the whole in a bundle which Mother Pi was to carry. But all the rest of Spring Plum's splendid possessions, the well-stocked wardrobe and the beautiful jewels, were left untouched. Then Gold Lotus, together with Little Jewel and Mother Pi, accompanied her maid to the gate. Spring Plum had really wished to take leave of Moon Lady and the rest of the household. But Little Jewel advised her not to do so; Moon Lady did not wish it. One last clasp of the hand, and Spring Plum walked out of the gate behind Mother Pi, calm and cheerful, without once turning her head. Gold Lotus returned sadly to her pavilion. Now that she had lost her only companion, she became fully conscious of her disconsolate solitude, her forsaken state. Sobbing aloud, she flung herself on her couch and without restraint abandoned herself to her grief.

> *Still in the room there lingered*
> *The voice she knew so well,*
> *Then all was gloom and sadness:*
> *Silence fell.*

CHAPTER FORTY-ONE: *Mother Wang falls a Victim to her Avarice. Wu Sung takes Revenge upon Gold Lotus and sacrifices to his dead Brother*

O<small>N THE VERY</small> next day young Chen realized his intention, and hurried off to Mother Pi's in order to speak to Spring Plum. But Mother Pi was not inclined to make things too easy for him; she wanted to profit by the situation.

"What are you thinking of, my dear Daughter's Husband?" she asked. "Your mother-in-law has expressly forbidden me to let you meet the young person. At any moment she may be sending one of her servants here, and if you are caught here then I have to bear the consequences. So just you be off."

Young Chen smilingly pressed a shining ounce into her hand.

"Here is a little tea money. Later on I will show that I am more than ordinarily grateful."

"Well, if you mean that you can redeem the enamel flower ornament and the cushions which I recently pledged at your pawn shop, the sum lent, with interest, comes to just upon an ounce."

"Good. You shall have your pledges tomorrow."

With a gratified air she accepted the ounce; then she took him to the sitting room, where he found Spring Plum. Mother Pi also provided them with tea, pastries, wine, meat, and fish.

"You are a nice sort!" Spring Plum greeted him reproachfully. "You and my mistress have delivered me to the executioner's knife!"

"Little Sister," he assured her tenderly, "now that you have gone I can't endure it any longer at home. I have made up my mind to divorce my wife and marry your mistress. But first I must go to the

682

Eastern Capital and consult my parents. As for you, I hope with all my heart that with Mother Pi's help you will make a thoroughly good match."

It relieved them to unburden their hearts, which were bursting with indignation at Moon Lady's outrageous behavior. Then they cheerfully ate and drank, and after that there was plenty of kissing and caressing. The time to say farewell came only too soon. Mother Pi, in constant anxiety lest some messenger should come from the suspicious Moon Lady, urged the young man to leave early.

Next afternoon, as he had promised, he appeared with the redeemed pledges. He also brought a jug of wine and two gold-bordered kerchiefs and two pairs of lawn drawers for Spring Plum. And once more old Pi granted them an hour of undisturbed converse. But this time their meeting did not remain a secret. Suddenly Lai An appeared, having been sent by Moon Lady to ask whether Spring Plum had been sold yet, and the horse outside the gate told him that young Chen was there. Of course, the first thing he did was to inform Moon Lady that the Daughter's Husband was secretly meeting Spring Plum at Mother Pi's. Moon Lady was furious, and immediately sent for the old woman.

"Did I entrust the maid to you in order that you should let her play the harlot in your den of vice?" she began, angrily. "Why do you put me off from day to day? I want to see my money. If you don't sell her at once I'll take her away from you and apply to Mother Fong. And in that case you shall never cross my threshold again!"

"By Heaven, you do me injustice!" the old woman exclaimed. "I have already applied to two or three households, but no one would pay the price you are asking. Am I, a poor go-between, to add something out of my own pocket?"

"I am not asking that at all. But today you allowed the Daughter's Husband to drink with the wench and make love to her!"

"Heaven forbid! He simply brought me some things which I had pawned with him and wanted to redeem. Out of mere politeness I offered him a cup of tea. He didn't touch it; he rode off again almost immediately, he was in such a hurry. Your Lai An happened to come while he was with me. Presumably he has told you something."

"This savage, this Daughter's Husband, is capable of anything," Moon Lady grumbled. She had already beaten a retreat before the talkative and plausible matchmaker.

"My dear mistress, am I a three-year-old child? How could I allow such unseemliness? My daughter-in-law too was present; she can bear witness that nothing happened. Moreover, the River Prefect Chow wants to acquire the young person as his concubine. He has no one to continue his line, and hopes to get a son by her. But we haven't yet agreed upon the price. He wants to give only twelve ounces," she said, boldly lying. "And since you press me so hard I have decided to let him have her for thirteen. You must reduce your price by three ounces. After all, the girl is no longer an untouched virgin."

After some desperate haggling between the two women Moon Lady declared that she would agree to reduce the original price to thirteen ounces, and Mother Pi took her leave, promising to conclude the sale at once.

The very next day she took Spring Plum, in her litter, carefully dressed and painted, to the house of the River Prefect Chow and smilingly accepted the fifty ounces which Master Chow gave her without demur for the pretty young creature. She secretly kept thirty-seven ounces of the purchase price for herself, while she dutifully delivered the rest to Moon Lady.

"And this one ounce he gave me as my hard-earned 'joy-money,'" she said with a sigh. "It is all I am making out of the business, for I don't imagine that I can expect any commission from you."

Moon Lady could not avoid complying with the gentle hint that lay concealed in these words; with her own hands she weighed out another half ounce on the money scales. So the business brought old Pi the magnificent profit of thirty-seven and a half ounces.

Since all young Chen's comings and goings had been supervised by Moon Lady, and all intercourse with Gold Lotus had been discontinued, his life in his father-in-law's house was daily becoming more intolerable. He felt that he was being deliberately wronged and slighted, and he had only one wish: to escape. But although he was constantly threatening his wife that he would go away and divorce her, hitherto he had done no more than threaten, for no decisive step followed his threats. It was a twofold accident that finally brought about the inevitable breach.

On the seventh day of the eleventh month Jade Fountain was celebrating her birthday. With the kindest intentions she sent various savory dishes and a jug of wine to the shop for young Chen, so that he could enjoy a good feast in company with Dispenser Fu. Moon Lady had raised objections, saying that the Daughter's Husband was an ill-conditioned fellow who did not deserve such kindness. And when young Chen, who was in the mood for drinking that day, asked for more wine she strictly forbade the servants to comply with his wish. At this young Chen was filled with the liveliest indignation, which he vented by violently upbraiding Lai An, whom he had vainly sent for more wine: "You too are one of these false rascals on whom there's no relying! I am the son-in-law in this household, and I have just as much claim as those women to decent fare. If my father-in-law were still alive you would have jumped to another tune! Now that he's dead all the servants have lost their senses, and are taking my mother-in-law's part against me. But I'm not going to be intimidated by her!"

"Dear Daughter's Husband, you exaggerate," Dispenser Fu interposed, endeavoring to appease him. "We respect and honor you just as before. How is Lai An responsible if the First won't give you any more wine? I understand your displeasure. But do express yourself more cautiously! The walls have cracks and the partitions ears. It seems to me that you are six-tenths no longer sober."

Immediately young Chen's anger was diverted to Dispenser Fu.

"Stupid fellow, even though my belly may be full of wine I've enough sense left in my head to understand the intrigue that is being carried on against me. But you wait, I'll bring this deceitful woman before the judge's bench one of these days. And this time she'll look

685

in vain for help from the Chancellor's palace. If you imagine that she can embezzle the chests and boxes full of gold and silver which I brought with me when I came, and which contained the property of my uncle, Marshal Yung, without being punished, you are quite mistaken. The whole place shall be distrained upon, and they themselves shall be put up to public auction. I shan't be content to catch a single fish; no, I'll stir up the whole pond! I'll insist on my old rights of possession and become the master of the household!"

Dispenser Fu had listened to this with increasing consternation.

"Don't take it amiss, dear Daughter's Husband, but it seems to me that you are ten-tenths no longer sober. What you are saying is all sheer nonsense."

Young Chen looked at him angrily. "You damned old yapper, I've seen through you long ago! First you enriched and fattened yourself at the expense of my father-in-law, and now you'd like to help to drive me out, so as to have the whole business to yourself. But you just wait, you'll be in the indictment as well!"

His words gave the honest but rather timorous Dispenser Fu a terrible fright. Next morning he ran off to Moon Lady in the greatest consternation, told her of the dismal threats which the Daughter's Husband had made the night before, and begged her to dismiss him immediately.

"There can be no question of dismissing you," said Moon Lady, briefly and authoritatively. "You will continue to be my business manager. You needn't worry yourself in the least about the nonsense which this naughty fellow has been talking. I know nothing of the chests of treasure which he is supposed to have brought with him when he came here asking for shelter. There can be no question of anything but a little jewelry and his wife's property. And as for the few hundred ounces which his father gave him in addition, it was expressly agreed that my late husband was to use it as he thought fit, in order to avoid any possible trouble with the authorities. The fellow was barely seventeen then, a mere chicken in yellow down. During the years he has lived here he has acquired, thanks to my husband, all sorts of

686

business knowledge, and now that his wings are grown he repays the kindness that was shown him by ingratitude, and offends against all the heavenly laws of morality and filial love. Heaven will chastise him yet for his scandalous behavior. Don't allow yourself to be disconcerted, but carry on quietly with my business as usual."

A few days later the pawnshop was very busy; Dispenser Fu and young Chen had as much as they could do to cope with all the clients, when the nurse Ju I came in, bringing the dispenser a jug of tea. On her left arm she was carrying Moon Lady's child, which began to scream and whimper at the sight of all the strange people.

"Be quiet at once, you naughty child!" said young Chen, threatening the child with his finger. And the child immediately stopped his whimpering and screaming. Proud of his success, young Chen observed to the admiring customers: "You see, he obeys his father at a word. I am his father, of course."

This was naturally intended as a jest, but the nurse took it otherwise, and said, reprovingly: "That's a nice sort of thing to say before these people here! You just wait. I'll repeat that to my mistress!"

"You dare, and you'll get a kick on the behind!" he said, threatening her, and still in jest, he twice made as though to kick her.

The nurse was in no mood for jesting, and ran off raging to Moon Lady. "Just think, the Daughter's Husband declared in front of all the people that he was the father of your child!" she cried, excitedly.

This was altogether too much for Moon Lady, who was likewise in no mood for jesting. She, the paragon of all virtue, to be held up before the people as an adultress! It was unheard-of. She swooned immediately, falling at full length on the floor.

The entire household came hurrying up in response to Little Jewel's terrified cry for help. With seven hands and eight feet they lifted her on to her bed and administered the usual hot infusion of ginger. When at last she recovered consciousness it was some considerable time before she could utter a word, so great was her emotion. The other wives departed one by one, after making the nurse repeat her exhaustive description of the incident in the pawnshop. Only Snowblossom remained. This seemed a good opportunity to incite Moon Lady against her old adversary, the Fifth.

"The fellow is annoyed because you won't allow him to go with the Fifth any longer, and also because you have sent Spring Plum away. He wanted to pay you out. In your place I shouldn't allow myself to get worked up; I should act. You'll never have any peace until you are rid of the whole troublesome set. The only difficulty is that one must consider Hsi Men's daughter. But she has already more or less separated from the family by her marriage. No one can expect you to keep her and her impudent husband here for ever. I should see that he is given a sound thrashing, and then I should turn him out. And I should send for old Wang and arrange for her to remove the Fifth and settle her elsewhere. With that woman, that eternal mischief maker, one ought not to stand on ceremony. She's no better than so much filth and rubbish. Away with her! Why should she stay here now?"

Moon Lady nodded in agreement, and began to discuss with Snowblossom the steps to be taken in detail. On the following day they proceeded to carry out their plan. On the pretext of a business consultation young Chen was enticed into Moon Lady's sitting room. No sooner did he enter than she ordered him to kneel.

"Do you confess to your offense?" she asked harshly.

And as he obstinately refused to kneel and assumed an innocent expression, she gave a signal, whereupon seven or eight powerful maids and servants' wives, who had been hiding behind the curtains, rushed at him, surrounded him, and began to belabor him furiously with short cudgels and with long. Taken by surprise, he already lay on the ground when a saving thought occurred to him in his distress; and in an instant he had divested himself of his trousers. Appalled by such a terrible sight, the women hastily dispersed, escaping behind the curtain into the adjoining room. It was all that the Moon Lady could do to preserve her austere bearing instead of bursting into laughter. She had just time to fling an indignant "Shameless tortoise!" at his head before he scrambled to his feet and fled from the room without a word.

"That was a good idea of mine!" he told himself. "Otherwise it would have gone ill with me!"

Moon Lady sent the servant Lai An after him. She wished him to make up his accounts at once and hand over the business to Fu. It was clear to him that he could not remain, so he packed his things and removed that same day, without saying farewell, to his parents' house, where his Uncle and Aunt Chang were living.

A few days after Moon Lady had thus got rid of the troublesome Daughter's Husband she sent Tai A to Mother Wang. Old Wang had before this given up her tea house. Her son, who had recently returned from the Hudi province, had managed to make a hundred ounces by various kinds of sharp practice, and with this useful bit of money he had bought a couple of donkeys and fitted up a little flour mill in the courtyard, which was worked by the donkeys, and was considerably more profitable than the sale of tea.

"It's a long time since I've had the pleasure," she said, in greeting to Tai A. "Of course, you come on behalf of your Fifth mistress. Perhaps she is expecting a little something and wants my help?"

"Not a bit of it. It's the First who has sent me here. She wants you to take the Fifth away again and find her a husband elsewhere. She's had an affair with our Daughter's Husband!"

"Good heavens, that's a nice story! Well, I told myself at once that she wouldn't hold out long without a husband once Master Hsi Men was dead. When Master Hsi Men was still living and I went to see her once—it was on account of that affair of the District Inspector Hu Kiu—she was as proud as anything and would hardly know me. She offered me a miserable cup of tea, and when I left she gave me a broken brooch. And now it's all up with her magnificence!"

"She has been on bad terms with the First, and she has often been the cause of unpleasant scenes. Just lately there was an upset again that might almost have cost the First her life. She wants peace and quiet, and she has already turned the Daughter's Husband out of the house. And now she wants to be rid of the Fifth at last, and asks you to fetch her as soon as possible."

"In her day she made her entry into Master Hsi Men's household with all ceremony. They can't refuse to allow her to make a dignified departure; that is, to place a litter at her disposal, and let her take all her possessions with her."

"I have no doubt the First will agree to that. You'd better arrange the details with her personally."

Mother Wang got ready to go and accompanied Tai A to Moon Lady's apartments. Moon Lady once more gave a full explanation of the motives of her decision.

"It is all one to me, old Mother Wang, whether you find a husband for her elsewhere or whether you arrange for her to live alone. You will understand that the death of my husband has involved me in considerable expense and loss. I have to reduce my household, and I can no longer feed so many people. Whatever you require to meet the cost of negotiations I will of course repay you. To make up for it I will have one soul mass the less read for my late husband."

Old Wang, who scented a profitable stroke of business, did not hesitate to agree to this proposal.

"You can rely on me. I understand: you don't care about the cost so long as you cleanse your home of filth. As for that, this is an auspicious day in the calendar. I could take her with me today. There is just one point. She came here in her palanquin and brought a full chest with her. You will of course allow her to leave under the same conditions?"

"She can take a chest with her. She doesn't need a palanquin," replied Moon Lady harshly. But Little Jewel interceded for Gold Lotus.

"Dear mistress, in this point you ought not to let yourself be influenced by your feelings," she said. "Think of the reputation of the house! The neighbors would mock and stretch their necks finely if she was allowed to leave without a palanquin."

To this Moon Lady did not know what to reply. Now Gold Lotus was called in and informed of the decision which had been taken. The change was really welcome to her, for since Spring Plum and young Chen had gone she was finding her life in the household of Hsi Men more wretched and unendurable every day. Yet in order to obtain better conditions on her departure she behaved as though she was the victim of intolerable injustice. In the course of the years Hsi Men had given her many presents of clothing and jewelry. She could not possibly find room for all these in a single chest.

"What have I really done that they should wish to send me away so suddenly?" she said defiantly.

"Dear little woman, don't pretend to be so innocent!" Mother Wang advised her solemnly. "When a number of snakes live in one and the same hole none of them is a stranger to the rest. Where the behavior of a human being shows the tiniest flaw, there comes the blue blowfly of gossip and lays its eggs. After all, an adulterous love affair isn't an everyday matter like eating and drinking. No, long speeches are out of place here. Everybody in the house knows. But be comforted; even the finest feast comes to an end sometime. And now be reasonable and get ready to go with me!"

Gold Lotus turned to Moon Lady. "It really is not right that you should listen to the scandal of maids and servants and turn me out so unfeelingly and heartlessly after I have lived beside you for years as a sister. Yet as far as I am concerned, I bow my head to superior might. But one should not exert one's power to the limit; and if one wants to strike one's fellow creature one need not strike her full in the face. If I go I should like at least to go in a dignified manner."

Moon Lady understood the meaning of her words, and allowed her to take the litter and a second chest, and also her toilet table. She herself went with her to the pavilion and chose the four dresses, the ornaments, the linen, and the shoes which she was to take with her. After both the chests were packed and Gold Lotus had got ready to go Autumn Aster had to lock the pavilion and give the keys to Moon Lady.

Gold Lotus took her leave of Moon Lady, prostrated herself, weeping, before Hsi Men's soul tablet, and last of all bade farewell to Jade Fountain, from whom she was sorry to part. For she had always agreed well with Jade Fountain, who was like a sister, and Jade Fountain herself was sorry to lose her. She gave her, secretly, a pair of gold brooches, a long blue satin robe, and a short red petticoat.

"I hope that you will marry again very happily," she said in farewell. "And when you have found a new home let me know, so that I can come to see you. We will keep up our sisterly relations."

Of all the members of the household, only Little Jewel joined Jade Fountain when the latter escorted Gold Lotus to the gate. She too was sorry to see the vivacious Fifth leave them, and showed her affection by quickly giving her two gold hairpins as they reached the gate.

"Thank you, sister, you still have a human heart!" said Gold Lotus, who was touched by the gift. Then she entered the palanquin. A few coolies, whom Mother Wang had engaged, carried her two chests and the toilet table after her.

At Mother Wang's Gold Lotus was given a sitting room of her own, but at night she slept in the same room as the old woman. She whiled away the time by dressing her hair elaborately and painting her face, and standing under the eaves of the doorway, as of old, and watching the passers-by; or she sat in her room and strummed on her *pi pa,* or if old Wang was out she played cards or chess with her son Chow. Hungry for love as she was, she had soon made friends with the handsome young fellow, and at night, when old Wang was lying fast asleep, she often crept quietly into his room, to repay herself for the deprivations of the last few months.

One day it came to young Chen's ears that Gold Lotus was no longer living in the household of Hsi Men, but was lodging with Mother Wang, while waiting for a suitable opportunity to remarry. He quickly made his way to Mother Wang's. He did not forget to take with him, hung round his body under his tunic, two strings of copper cash. The old woman, who was occupied in sweeping away the asses' dung in front of the house, asked him inside at his own request.

"How can I serve the gentleman?"

"Is Mistress Pan from the house of Hsi Men living with you?" he began.

"May I first ask who you are?"

"I am her younger brother."

The old woman stared at him from head to foot.

"Brother? I didn't know she ever had a brother. Speak out frankly, young man; aren't you the Daughter's Husband from the house of Hsi Men? But I tell you this at the outset, I don't open my hand and let the fly go as easily as that."

"Here, take this for the present as a trifling payment and let me have an interview with her. Later on you shall have more."

"Oh, what are you thinking of!" the old woman began. "Master Hsi Men's First has strictly forbidden me to allow just anyone to see her. If you positively must speak to her—five ounces for each visit! If you want to marry her—a hundred ounces! My matchmaker's fee of ten ounces not included. With these miserable coppers you won't set the water flowing."

Young Chen had not been prepared for such obstinacy. Since he had no more cash with him he took two silver hair clasps with golden knobs from his hair—they weighed five ounces—and laid them beside the copper cash. Then he fell at the old woman's feet, embraced her knees, and began to cackle, in a piteous voice, like that of a hen about to be killed: "Dear Mother Wang, be satisfied with that for the moment! Later I will add a silver ingot to it, I promise; you can rely on that! Only let me have a little talk with her now! I simply must see her and speak to her!"

The old woman at last allowed herself to be softened. She took the brooches and the copper cash and led him to Gold Lotus's room. Gold Lotus, as he entered, laid aside the *pi pa* on which she had been strumming, rose from the kang, and slowly moved a step nearer.

"You're a nice fellow!" she said reproachfully. "Letting me lie helpless in the middle of the highway! And it is on your account that I have suffered all this! Why didn't you at least think of me a little?" Her words were followed by passionate weeping.

"Dear sister, you know I'd let myself be hacked into pieces for you!" he declared. "But how could I do anything for you? It was only yesterday that I learned by chance from Mother Pi what has been happening since I saw you. And today I've come to discuss our future with you. I can't, whatever happens, part with you; I am firmly resolved to marry you. But how? My plan is as follows. I will simply write my wife a letter of divorce and demand the return of the treasure chest which I brought to my father-in-law's house. It contained the reserves in gold and silver bullion which my uncle, Marshal Yung, had saved against his retirement. If they refuse to surrender it I shall go to Kai fong fu and lay the matter personally before the Chancellor Tsai. As one who was formerly a good friend of my uncle's he will no doubt help me to obtain my rights, and this infernal Moon Lady will sooner or later pay heavily for her obstinacy. Then I'll send the palanquin for you and take you home as my new wife. And nothing in the world shall ever tear us apart. What do you say?"

"Can you produce the hundred ounces that Mother Wang demands for my purchase price?"

"Oh, well, I dare say one can discuss the price with her," he said.

But the avaricious old woman was not of this opinion. She hastily interrupted him. "Your mother-in-law expressly told me that Master Hsi Men had spent so much money on Gold Lotus during his lifetime that one could have cast a life-sized silver statue with it. Now she wants a hundred ounces of that back, and not a copper less."

"Dear Mother Wang, don't be so hard!" he pleaded. "You will surely be content with fifty or sixty ounces, for it is a question of our life's happiness."

"There can be no question of that; not even eighty," the old woman insisted. "I have already refused a silk dealer from Huchow, who offered me seventy. And recently the new District Judge, young Master Chang in the High Street, sent two of his secretaries here as his agents and offered me eighty. They had brought the money with them; nevertheless, I refused his offer. They were all serious clients. But you, a young nobody who has nothing to show, who would like to put me off with empty phrases, you simply don't come into question!"

And she ran straight out into the street, in front of the house, and there she began to call and shout in a voice so loud that all the neighborhood was bound to hear her: "Hey, people, neighbors, did you ever hear of a man wanting to marry his own mother-in-law? And he dares to come into my house and kick up a row in my honorable sitting room!"

In the greatest consternation young Chen ran after her, and with all his might he dragged her back into the house. Once indoors he fell on his knees before her and pleaded with her: "Dear Mother Wang, please, please no public scandal! I agree, and I'll pay you the hundred you ask. Only have just a little patience. Tomorrow I shall leave for the Eastern Capital, where I shall see my father. I shall certainly be able to get the money."

"You must be very quick, then, or she'll have sold me to someone else by the time you return!" Gold Lotus warned him.

"Rely on me! I'll ride day and night, and take no rest. At the latest I'll be back in half a month: at the soonest, in ten days."

"Who delivers his rice first gets his dinner first," said the old woman dryly. "That's my principle. And don't forget: I want my matchmaker's fee of ten ounces as well as the hundred. I should like that to be clearly understood beforehand."

"I know, I know," he assured her. Hastily taking his leave, he rushed home in order to make the necessary preparations for his journey. Early the next morning, accompanied by a servant, he set off for the Eastern Capital.

While the fate of Gold Lotus was thus still in the balance, her maid Spring Plum, who, as we have seen, had passed as concubine into the possession of the River Prefect Chow, had settled down very happily in her new surroundings. Master Chow was delighted with her from the first, and after her arrival he spent three successive nights in her chamber, from which it may be concluded that his choice had been a right one. He placed three rooms in the eastern wing and a couple of maids at her disposal, and saw to it that she lacked for nothing in the way of food and clothing. Since his childless wife was confined to her room by an affection of the eyes, and was also completely engrossed in the service of Buddha, and neglected the affairs of the household, while his Second wife, who lived in the eastern wing, had recently borne a daughter, he entrusted all the keys and the management of the household to Spring Plum, so that she was actually playing the part not of a Third wife, but of a First.

One day the go-between Mother Pi came to see her, and from her she learned that her late mistress Gold Lotus had also been turned away by Moon Lady, and was now with Mother Wang, facing an uncertain future. Moved by longing and painful sympathy, she spoke to her husband through her tears: "We have both lived together for years in the most cordial agreement, and have known joy and sorrow together. Even in her greatest anger she has never spoken an ungentle word to me. She always treated me as though I had been her actual sister. Won't you take her yourself, so that we can be united again, and continue to live happily together?" And she entered into a detailed description of all Gold Lotus's charms and qualities: how she was now thirty-two years of age, and born at the hour of the Dragon; how clever and cultivated she was, how admirably she could play the *pi pa* and handle the writing brush, and how thorough was her knowledge of the works of the poets and philosophers.

"I will gladly give up my rank to her if you should take her into your household, and content myself with the position of a Fourth," she concluded her long and persuasive speech.

And her words were not without effect upon Master Chow. He at once sent two of his confidential servants to Mother Wang with a few little presents, empowering them to open negotiations if they should find that Spring Plum's description of Gold Lotus was justified. Now, their eyes convinced them that Spring Plum had not exaggerated, so they began to bargain with Mother Wang. They were empowered to offer anything up to eighty ounces, but Mother Wang would on no account agree to this, and insisted on the price of a hundred ounces which Moon Lady was supposed to be demanding. After protracted haggling the negotiations were broken off, and the two messengers returned to their employer with nothing done.

Moved by their favorable description, Master Chow raised his offer by five ounces, and the two servants went to Mother Wang once more. But again she took refuge behind the express orders which her patroness was alleged to have given, and refused under any circumstances to take less than a hundred. On the other hand, she generously declared that if the worst came to the worst she would be willing to renounce her matchmaker's fee. After the negotiations had again fallen through, Master Chow had no intention of taking any further steps. But during the next few days Spring Plum besieged him so with her tears and her plaintive requests that he finally gave way and sent his servants a third time to Mother Wang. There were three of them on this occasion, for Master Chow, by way of reinforcement, had sent his house steward with the others, and this time they took with them ninety ounces, carefully packed in a leather pouch. But again the avaricious old woman was immovable.

"What do you want now? I'm not dependent on your ninety ounces!" she said, boastfully. "I've had inquiries from other directions, and I can sell her without more ado to District Judge Chang for a hundred ounces."

At this the steward lost patience. "Woman, you are the three-legged money-toad incarnate! Do you suppose we are dependent on you, and can't find a suitable woman elsewhere? If the master's little New One hadn't pleaded so, it would never have entered his head to waste this unreasonable sum on the person you have to sell. And that's the end of it!" He bade the two servants repack the bars of bullion which were already on the table, and left the house with them.

"You just take care my master doesn't have you locked up to-morrow and give you a taste of the finger press!" he cried threat-eningly.

Old Wang let them go. She was thinking of the ten ounces more which she hoped to get from young Chen. She knew what she was doing.

When the River Prefect had heard the report of his servants, he said, irritably: "As far as I'm concerned she shall have the hundred. Go again tomorrow and take the litter with you!" He wanted to have a little peace; he was tired of being importuned by Spring Plum.

"Even if we lay the hundred on the table this avaricious woman will still make difficulties and bargain for five ounces more as her matchmaker's fee," objected the exasperated steward. "I should suggest that you keep her in suspense for a few days and give her a taste of the finger press in prison to make her more docile."

But there was no occasion to utilize either of these methods. It was now too late. The destiny of Gold Lotus and Mother Wang was to be accomplished before they could be applied.

One day Wu Sung returned from the place to which he had been banished. He had been pardoned on the occasion of an Imperial amnesty, and could now resume his old post as Captain of the Guard at the District Yamen. He moved into the little house in Purple Stone Street which had belonged to his dead brother Wu Ta, and took his niece, the seventeen-year-old Ying, to live with him and keep house for him. When he fetched her from the house of the Yao family, the neighbors to whom he had entrusted her, he heard various items of town gossip; he learned also that his enemy Hsi Men had died during his absence, and that his sister-in-law Gold Lotus was now living with Mother Wang, and was on the point of marrying again. When he heard this the old resentment blazed up within him, and he resolved that he would now perform the long-delayed act of vengeance.

On the following day he dressed himself carefully and called on Mother Wang. Gold Lotus, who was standing as usual under the eaves of the doorway, recognized him immediately, and terrified by his approach, she fled into the sitting room. He greeted old Wang, who was in the courtyard at her treadmill, busily sifting flour, with a polite *Wan fu,* and made her show him into the sitting room.

She opened the conversation in a somewhat embarrassed manner. "So you are safe home again, Master Captain of the Guard!" She was not feeling at all comfortable.

"Yes, I've been pardoned, and I've been back for some days. I wanted to thank you for being so kind as to look after the house a little during my absence."

She sighed with relief. "How you have improved! You are much handsomer and more powerful than you used to be. And how well the beard suits you!" she flattered him. "And one really must remark that life abroad has given you polish and refinement!"

She made him sit down and gave him tea.

After a pause he began: "There is another reason for my coming here. I am told that Master Hsi Men has died during my absence. That my sister-in-law has left his house and is now staying with you. Also that it is her intention to marry again. Would you be so kind as to ask her whether she would be willing to become my wife? I should like to feel that my niece Ying was no longer motherless. She is now of a marriageable age, and I should wish my sister-in-law to see to her education a little, and help her to make a good marriage. Also, on account of what people may say, I don't want to live alone under the same roof with the young woman."

Mother Wang reflected awhile. "It is true that she is living with me. But I don't know how far she has decided otherwise. At all events, I'll ask her what she thinks of your proposal."

"I thank you."

Their conversation had been overheard from beginning to end by Gold Lotus in the next room. Her feelings for her handsome brother-in-law were at heart what they had always been, and they were fanned into a blaze by his sudden reappearance. This was a man—a very different person from that whimpering young Chen! "So Fate has destined us for each other after all!" she thought, rejoicing, and she could not wait until Mother Wang called her into the other room. With a smile full of promise she went up to her brother-in-law, and put into her clear *Wan fu* all the music and all the intimate warmth of which her voice was capable.

"With all my heart, my dear brother-in-law, I will do what you wish and look after little Ying most faithfully," she continued.

"But there's just one point!" interposed the matter-of-fact voice of old Wang, in grating tones. "Master Hsi Men's First won't let her go under a hundred ounces."

"Why is she asking so much?" inquired Wu Sung.

"She declared to me that Master Hsi Men lavished so much money on the Fifth that one could cast a life-sized silver statue with it. So she naturally wants a certain amount of compensation."

"Very well. I will pay the hundred, and also five ounces as the matchmaker's fee, in order to show my gratitude."

The old woman's face expanded in a wide, comfortable grin. "That, of course, must be left to you; I am sure you know what is proper. These few years in foreign parts have made a real fine gentleman of you."

Gold Lotus went to the kitchen, and in her joy she brewed for her guest a pot of extra-fine tea, with infusion of melon seeds.

"I have already had three or four inquiries, very serious inquiries, all from great and aristocratic houses," Mother Wang assured the visitor in a boastful tone. "I should advise you to pay the money as promptly as possible, for my principle is: He who delivers his rice

700

first gets his dinner first. You wouldn't like her to slip out of your hand again."

"Yes, dear brother-in-law, if you really want to marry me please lose no time!" said Gold Lotus, in support of Mother Wang.

"Don't be uneasy, Sister-in-law. Payment will be made tomorrow, and in the evening I'll take you home."

Mother Wang ventured to doubt whether a mere captain of the guard could really produce the large sum of a hundred ounces, and she believed Wu Sung's assertion to be empty boasting. But he did actually reappear on the following afternoon, when he quietly laid the agreed sum upon the table. He took it from a leather money bag which his camp commandant in Mongchow on the Great Wall had entrusted to him on his departure for delivery to an acquaintance of his.

Oh, how Mother Wang rejoiced in the sight of the glistening heap of silver! Reverently she weighed bar after bar on the scales, and convinced herself that not the smallest fraction of the agreed sum was lacking.

"I call that a prompt and proper transaction!" she said, in a gratified tone, honoring Wu Sung with an obsequious bow.

"Now I should like to take my sister-in-law home at once," Wu Sung responded quietly.

"Why in such a hurry? The evening will be time enough for that. I should just like to deliver the money to my patroness, then I'll bring her across to you. In the meantime you get everything ready for her reception! So important a matter ought to be treated with proper ceremony."

With feigned indifference he complied with her wish and took his leave. When he had gone, she reflected: "What the First wanted more than anything else was to be rid of an obnoxious housemate. She didn't insist on any definite price. If I give her twenty ounces she'll be satisfied." So she weighed out twenty ounces and repaired to Hsi Men's house. Moon Lady was satisfied with the twenty ounces. She was thankful that the matter was disposed of as far as she was concerned.

"Who is the man in question?" she inquired.

"No matter how boldly the hare wanders, he returns in the end to the old burrow. In short, she is going to ladle her soup out of the old pot and marry her brother-in-law Wu Sung."

"Well, so long as that turns out successfully!" said Moon Lady to Jade Fountain; but she had a presentiment of evil.

Once home again, Mother Wang bade her son carry Gold Lotus's two chests and her toilet table into the next house; then, towards evening, she offered her arm to Gold Lotus, who, carefully groomed and adorned, was wearing a dress of a joyous red color, and led her across the threshold of her new home. Wu Sung ushered them into the inner veranda room, which was festively lit with candles. The two women stopped short: there, in the middle of the wall facing the door, they saw an incense table, and above it, solemn and austere, the soul tablet of the deceased Wu Ta. A feeling of discomfort overcame them. It was as though invisible hands were clutching at their hair, as though iron hooks were entering their bosoms.

In the meantime, at a sign from Wu Sung, Ying locked and bolted the front door. This did not escape Mother Wang. Foreboding nothing good, she wanted to leave at once. But Wu Sung detained her.

"But Mother Wang, you will surely drink a beaker of bridal wine with us?" he said, with a jovial laugh.

There was nothing for it but that Mother Wang must at once take her place at the ready-laid table and partake of the dishes that little Ying brought in. With increasing discomfort she noted that Wu Sung, without paying attention to his guests, or drinking to them, was silently gulping down beaker after beaker.

"But now I must really go," she said, when she had eaten and drunk with the others for the sake of appearances. "I am sure you young people will want to be alone."

"Nonsense, old woman, you stay here!" Wu Sung replied, with a growl. "I have still a word or two to say to you."

At the same time she heard a faint metallic vibration, and behold, he had drawn from under his tunic a gleaming knife, full two feet in length. His eyes, uncannily rolling, suddenly fixed themselves upon her, and he continued, in a menacing tone: "Old woman, don't pretend you are asleep and dreaming! No debts without creditors, no hatred without cause: that's an old proverb. You have my dead brother on your conscience!"

"Master Captain, it is late, and you are no longer sober; in your condition you shouldn't play with such dangerous toys!"

"Silence! I'll deal with the other one first. Then it will be your turn, old sow! And don't you move a step from where you are! Otherwise. . . ."

With an unmistakable gesture he held the bright blade close before her eyes. Then he turned to Gold Lotus.

"Listen to me, woman! How did my brother come by his death? Speak the truth, and I will spare you!"

But Gold Lotus preferred, on this occasion, as in other desperate passes, to seek refuge in lies.

"Your brother died of heart failure. I can't tell you more. I had nothing to do with his death," she replied calmly.

Angrily Wu Sung struck at the table with his knife, so that it remained sticking into the wood, quivering. Then he seized her hair with his left hand, and with his right hand at her breast he shook her furiously to and fro, upsetting the table, which was in his way, with a mighty kick, so that plates and dishes and beakers rolled on to the floor, and flew into shards with a loud clatter.

Old Wang profited by this moment to spring to her feet and rush to the front door. But she found it locked. And now Wu Sung, moving with long strides, came up behind her. He forced her to the ground, and with his girdle he lashed her hands behind her back, fastening them to her ankles, so that she cowered there like a monkey picking up beechmast with backward-curving hands, and could not move from the spot.

"Let me go, Master Captain!" she shrieked in desperation. "What have I to do with your sister-in-law's affairs? I am innocent!"

"Shut your mouth, old sow! I know all about it. Your lies won't help you. Just you wait, it'll be your turn directly! First I'll finish with the other!"

He carried her back into the sitting room like a bundle of rags, to drop her on the floor in front of his brother's soul tablet. Then he picked up his knife and turned to Gold Lotus, who was standing terrified in a corner.

"Brother-in-law, spare me!" she pleaded. He flung her with a jerk across the room, so that she faced the soul tablet, and then he bade her kneel.

"And now out with it!" he ordered harshly. Completely cowed, Gold Lotus began to relate the history of her relations with Hsi Men, and to explain in detail how Wu Ta came by his death; how first of all Hsi Men had injured him by a kick in the stomach, and how she had then killed him with poison, on the advice of old Wang, and finally, how she had not buried the corpse, but had reduced it to ashes, in order to destroy all traces of her crime.

"The stupid creature!" thought Mother Wang, as she angrily listened to Gold Lotus's narration. "Now she has blabbed the whole story, it's all up with me too!"

In silence, and breathing deeply, Wu Sung had listened to Gold Lotus's confession. Now he prostrated himself before the soul tablet, sprinkled sacrificial wine on the floor, and set light to some spirit money. Then he solemnly lifted up his voice and spoke, raising his eyes to the soul tablet. "Hear me, Brother! I know your spirit is close at hand. The hour of vengeance has come, and I, Wu Sung, will be your avenger!"

In her deadly terror Gold Lotus now began to shriek for help. But in a moment he had silenced her by filling her mouth with a handful of ashes from the incense bowl. Then he violently pressed her head against the floor in a forced kowtow. In an access of rage, by a violent exertion of strength, she escaped for a moment from the pressure of his hand, and tore all the jewels and ornaments from her body, so that brooches and pins, enamel flowers and pearls and rings fell in confusion to the floor, and faintly tinkling, rolled hither and thither. A furious kick caught her in the loins and threw her over on her side. Then a hard boot crushed her tender bosom, robbing it of breath, and a voice like the pealing of thunder fell upon her ears: "Woman, it has always been said that you were wise and clever. Now I will see for myself whether your heart has the seven portals of the hearts of the wise!"

With these words he plunged the knife deep into her body, under the breastbone, enlarging the narrow gash until it was a bloody, yawning orifice, from which a crimson fountain gushed forth. A brief twitching and stamping of the legs, and her two souls had escaped from her flesh. Now he withdrew the knife, thrust the blade between his teeth, and dragged her warm heart from the cavity of her body. Laying it in a dish, with a ceremonious bow he set it down before his brother's soul tablet, a sacrifice to the dead.

Now he turned to old Wang, who began in a loud voice to shriek, "Help! Murder!" Without further circumstance he severed her head from her trunk.

"Uncle, I am afraid!" A tremulous voice broke the sudden uncanny silence that had fallen in the room. It was Ying, who, shuddering, with her hands pressed to her face, was leaning against the wall.

"Child, I cannot attend to you now," he replied curtly, and he rushed past her into the courtyard behind the house. There he swung himself over the wall into the courtyard of old Wang's house. For he had it in his mind to kill her son also. But he found that he was no longer in the house. Wang Chow had heard the screams for help from next door: and when he hurried to the house, and could get no answer to his knocking, he suspected the worst, and alarmed the neighborhood. But the neighbors had a great respect for the mighty Captain of the Guard. Who would have dared to interfere in his family affairs?

So Wu Sung had time to turn everything upside down in Mother Wang's house, to take the eighty ounces which were still left of his hundred, as well as various trinkets, and then, under cover of the darkness, to escape unseen over the back wall of the courtyard. Early next morning, as soon as the city gates were opened, he left the city unhindered and made his way to the forests of the Liang Mountains, where he joined the robbers.

CHAPTER FORTY-TWO: *Young Chen honors his dead Beloved by a Sacrifice. In the Yung fu se Temple Spring Plum meets her former Mistress*

WU SUNG had long left the city behind him when next morning the neighbors and the local authorities at last ventured to force the locked doors of his house and to enter. Then they found the forsaken and hopelessly distracted Ying, and lying in a great pool of blood, the corpses of the two murdered women. The yamen was notified, and the District Mandarin sent his officers to draw up a written report, while he issued a public placard accusing the fugitive Wu Sung, for whose arrest a reward of fifty ounces was offered.

That morning the messengers of the River Prefect once more knocked at the door of Mother Wang. They had, of course, no suspicion that anything out of the way had occurred. They had brought the required hundred ounces, and a litter, and they had been told that this time they were not to return without Gold Lotus. Now, alas, it was too late, and they had to turn back with their commission unfulfilled. Spring Plum was absolutely heartbroken. For three days she refused all food, and surrendered herself to her grief without restraint, so that Master Chow, in his anxiety, sent for a troupe of jugglers who were giving performances in the city just then, in order to cheer her up a little. But all the arts of the jugglers were incapable of making her smile. It was weeks before she was her cheerful self again. Day after day, at her request, Master Chow had to send to the District Yamen and ask whether they had at last arrested the murderer of her beloved mistress.

In the meantime young Chen, inspired by the one idea of buying his beloved's freedom as promptly as possible, was riding at express speed toward the Eastern Capital. Halfway there he met an old servant of his parents, who was coming to bring him the news of his father's mortal illness. His father wanted to see him once more as he lay on his deathbed, and to communicate his last wishes to his son. With redoubled zeal young Chen continued his ride, but when the exhausted rider reached the capital, and the house of his other Wang aunt, with whom his parents had been living, it was only to learn that his father was already dead; by ill fortune, just as he was about to be reinstated in his former offices and dignities in accordance with the recently proclaimed Imperial amnesty. This was a disastrous turn of events, for the observances of the complicated mourning rites, at which he must play the principal part as the only son of the house, and the leisurely conveyance of the coffin to the dead man's house, would detain him for weeks, and in the meantime Gold Lotus might pass into the possession of another man. So he said to his mother:

"In these winter months the highways are made most unsafe by famishing bands of robbers. Such an imposing funeral convoy would naturally attract considerable attention everywhere, and we should undoubtedly excite the appetite of the robbers if the coffin were followed by a number of heavily-laden carts full of household goods and valuable property. We might very possibly lose all that we possess in that way. I would therefore rather propose that for the present you allow me to go on ahead with two cartloads of valuable goods. You, when the New Year is past, can follow with the coffin, and the rest of the things, and the servants. In the meantime, on arriving home, I will get the house ready for you. The masses for the dead can be read and the rest of the mourning ceremonial observed later on in Tsing ho hsien."

His mother agreed to his proposal, and two days later—it was the first day of the twelfth month—she allowed him to start on the return journey with two heavily-laden carts. He arrived in Tsing ho hsien safely and in good health, and to his great satisfaction his

Uncle and Aunt Chang, on hearing that his father was dead, and that his mother was returning to the ancestral home, in which they had been living as caretakers, immediately vacated the house. Now he was the master of the house; he had brought with him several chests of money, part of the dead man's estate, and there was now nothing to prevent his bringing Gold Lotus home. Later on he would settle affairs with the wife he no longer loved, and the avaricious Moon Lady, who had detained Uncle Yang's savings.

This was his intention. But

'Tis Heaven disposes in the end
Whatever human minds intend.

On the day after his return he made his way to Purple Stone Street with the required purchase price of a hundred ounces. He had decided to give Mother Wang not five ounces only, but ten as her matchmaker's fee. He could now afford to be generous. In the highest spirits, and hurrying on winged feet, he approached her house. Then he suddenly stopped. Before the door, at the side of the street, in an open trench, two scantily-covered corpses were lying. At their heads dangled a lantern, suspended between two poles. Above the door a placard was affixed, and on it he read, in large and conspicuous characters:

MURDER

For the capture of Wu Sung, guilty of the murder of Mistress Pan and the Widow Wang, a reward of fifty silver ounces is hereby offered.

The District Mandarin of
Tsing ho hsien.

Stricken to the heart, young Chen, absorbed in thought, gazed unmoving at the placard. Then two watchmen appeared from a guardhouse, which had been set up in the neighborhood, calling to him in a loud voice: "Hey, who are you and what do you want here? The murderer hasn't been found yet. But you look as though you know something about him."

They were walking slowly toward him. Then he suddenly felt afraid, and fled in haste, running along Purple Stone Street to the stone bridge that crosses the canal. There he was overtaken by an old friend of his, one Yang, who lived in the neighborhood, and had been running after him all down the street.

"Hey, Brother Chen, what possessed you to stand still in front of a house where such a murder has been committed? Of course it arouses suspicion!" said Yang. "But where have you been these last weeks? One has seen nothing of you."

Young Chen, concealing his inward emotion as well as he could, told him briefly that he had just returned from Kai fong fu, and had happened to notice the placard as he was passing the house. Its contents had interested him because he had known one of the two victims, Mistress Pan. She was the fifth wife of his late father-in-law Hsi Men.

"The murderer is her own brother-in-law," the young man told him eagerly; "the Captain of the Guard, Wu Sung, who was banished some years ago to Mongchow on the Great Wall, and was recently enabled to return in accordance with the amnesty. No one knows why he did it, or why he refused to spare old Wang. However, he has left a young niece behind him, Ying by name. During his banishment he gave her into the charge of my Aunt Yao. My aunt has just taken her into her home again, and wants to marry her to someone outside the city. Poor women, I suppose they will lie in the street unburied until they have caught the murderer. But enough of that dismal story; after all, it doesn't concern us. Now we'll speak of other things and drink to our meeting. I will be host."

He had, of course, no suspicion that the story very intimately concerned his friend. Young Chen, accepting his invitation, followed him into the wineshop near the stone bridge, but he was so dejected that at the third beaker he took his leave. A broken man, he crept home and flung himself weeping on his bed.

In the evening, however, when darkness had fallen, he repaired once more to Purple Stone Street, and found a quiet corner on the bank of the canal, under the stone bridge. There, crouching on the ground, he burned spirit money and incense in honor of the dead.

"Dear Sister, through my fault and my remissness you have lost your life," was his lament. "Torn by remorse, I bring you today a little spirit money, which may lighten your journey to the realm of shades. But I beg that your spirit will help me to find your murderer and revenge you. I shall not rest until he has received his reward on the scaffold."

That night Gold Lotus appeared to him in a dream. Her dress was steeped in blood, and her damp hair hung in tangled strands over her pale face.

"Brother, I have come to a sorry end," she said. "I waited for you in vain. I was fated to die a miserable death at the hands of Wu Sung. Now I cannot win my way into the realm of shades, but must haunt the neighborhood night and day, a poor wandering ghost. By our past love I implore you to have this kindness, to provide for a coffin and an honorable burial, so that my poor body need no longer lie in the street, exposed to wind and weather."

"Beloved Sister, I hear you and I wish I could do as you desire," young Chen replied, through his tears. "But I cannot, on account of the heartless Moon Lady. But go to Spring Plum! She will gladly help you."

"I have already tried to approach her. But the gate spirits in the house of the River Prefect hold me off and will not let me enter. Now I will try again."

He stretched his hand toward her and sought to embrace her, but she faded away and was gone. This was only a midnight vision.

It was now a month since the murder. It was learned that Wu Sung had fled to the wilderness of the Liang Mountains, where he had joined the robbers; and since the District Mandarin of Tsing ho hsien now considered that there was no possibility of arresting him he at last released the two bodies for burial. Old Wang was buried by her son, but poor Gold Lotus was still left lying forsaken by the roadside. No one had pity on her. Spring Plum had sent to the yamen every second or third day, to ask whether the murderer had been caught yet. But her messenger had always returned with the information that he was still at large. The body of her beloved mistress was still lying unburied at the roadside, under the eyes of the police.

Then one night, shortly after the New Year, Gold Lotus appeared to her also in a dream, and she plainly heard her dead mistress say:

"Sister, dear sister, today at last I am able to reach you. Hitherto the spirit guardians of the gate have harshly forbidden me to enter. Now I implore you, have pity and remove my poor body! Do not let it still lie unburied at the roadside, ruffled by the winds, drenched by the rain and snow, defiled by dogs and birds. Think of our old friendship and give me at last a seemly burial, or I cannot find entrance to the realm of shades, but must continue to wander here, restless and unquiet, a homeless ghost."

Spring Plum was about to reply when she woke. Her cheeks were wet with tears, and she could not sleep again that night. When day had come she again sent the confidential servants Chang Shong and Li An to the yamen.

"What has happened to the two bodies?" she asked them anxiously on their return.

"The murderer has escaped; he has fled to the wilderness of the Liang Mountains and has joined the robbers. He will hardly be arrested now," they reported. "The District Mandarin has therefore decided that the two corpses need no longer be exposed to wind and weather, and has released them for burial. Old Wang has already been buried by her son, but the other woman is still lying at the roadside."

"Listen, I have a request to make of you. Of course, I shall reward you generously."

The two servants fell on their knees before her. "But dear little mistress, there can be no talk of reward. We are contented if from time to time someone praises us before our Ancient Commander. We would go through fire and water for you."

Spring Plum disappeared into her bedroom and returned with

ten ounces and two bales of cloth. "You must know that the dead woman was my sister. Formerly we lived together in the household of Hsi Men, and I loved her dearly. Now I want to ask you—but you must say nothing of this to the Ancient Commander—with these ten ounces to buy a coffin, to wrap her body in this cloth, and lay her to rest in some quiet nook outside the city walls. Will you do this for me?"

They nodded eagerly. Then one of them said: "It would be as well if we could show one of the Ancient Commander's cards. Otherwise the District Yamen may make difficulties over the delivery of the body."

"That is not necessary," said the other. "If we say that we have come on behalf of the wife of the River Prefect and that the dead woman is her sister, they are hardly likely to make any difficulties."

They took the money and the bales of cloth and went to the servants' room. On the way they exchanged opinions: "Our little mistress must have been very fond of the dead woman, to have taken the matter so much to heart. When she heard the news of her death she was quite disconsolate, and three days long she would eat nothing, but only cried. The jugglers whom the Ancient Commander sent for to cheer her up didn't make the least impression on her. It shows great humanity in her that she should care for the forsaken corpse. We will do all we can to oblige her, and make a thoroughly good job of it. Since she was so fond of the dead woman she will be grateful to us and will recommend us to the Ancient Commander, which won't do us any harm. He thinks a great deal of her, fulfills her every wish, and treats her as though she were his chief wife. Yes, and he even hopes to get an heir by her, who will continue his line."

They went to the District Yamen, and on stating that they came on behalf of the River Prefect's Third wife, and that the dead woman was her sister, they were given the necessary order of delivery without demur. Then, for six ounces, they bought a simple coffin, washed and cleaned the dead body, carefully sewing up the wounds, clothed it in the cloth which they had brought with them,

713

and had it carried by two coffin bearers to the Yung fu se Temple outside the Southern Gate, not far from the burial ground of the River Prefect's family.

"We bring here the sister of our little mistress, the Third Wife of the Ancient Commander, and we beg you to grant her a little bit of earth in which we can lay her to rest," they told the Prior.

How should the Prior refuse such a request from one of the wives of his noble patron? He led his visitors to a quiet spot behind the actual temple buildings. There, at the foot of an old hollow aspen tree, he showed them the place of burial which they desired.

A grave was dug, and after the coffin had been lowered into the ground the two servants went back to their little mistress, reported that their commission had been faithfully accomplished, and conscientiously returned the remaining four ounces.

Spring Plum thanked them and rewarded each of them with an ounce, a great jug of wine, a ham, and a leg of veal. On the following day, at her request, they had to give five ounces to the Prior, with the request that he would read a solemn soul mass for the dead woman. She also spent half an ounce on spirit money and incense. The two servants faithfully carried out these further instructions, and they never wearied of praising the good heart of their little mistress.

About this time young Chen's mother arrived in Tsing ho hsien with the servants, the rest of the household goods, and the coffin of her late husband. Until the funeral the coffin was placed in the same Yung fu se Temple in which Gold Lotus had found her last resting place. On the day after her return Chen's mother sent him to the temple in order to pay the Prior a fee of five ounces for the soul mass which was to be read on the morrow, to mark the expiration of the seventh week of mourning. On the way to the temple young Chen again met his friend Yang from Purple Stone Street.

"When were the two dead bodies removed?" he asked incidentally. "I saw that they were no longer there when I passed old Wang's house yesterday."

"Haven't you heard? The District Mandarin released them for

burial half a month ago, after it came out that the murderer had escaped to the inaccessible Liang Mountains and joined the robbers. Mother Wang was thereupon buried by her son, and Mistress Pan was fetched away yesterday by some people from the household of the River Prefect, and buried outside the city in the grounds of the Yung fu see Temple."

"Spring Plum's doing," young Chen told himself. "In which Yung fu se Temple?" he asked. "There are various temples of that name."

"I mean, of course, the temple outside the Southern Gate, whose patron is the River Prefect."

"That fits in well; I can visit her grave at once," thought young Chen, and he hurriedly took leave of his friend. Having reached the Yung fu se Temple he hastily asked the Prior, before executing his actual commission: "Where is the grave of the young woman who was buried here recently?"

The Prior showed him the way to the old aspen tree behind the temple wall. There, at the edge of the freshly-dug grave, he knelt down, burned spirit money and incense, set out wine and sacrificial food, and uttered several loud and plaintive lamentations for the dead. After he had thus done his duty by his dead mistress he returned, with conscience appeased, to the Prior, gave him the five ounces, and discussed with him all the details of the soul mass to be said for his father. A few days later his father's coffin was conveyed to the hereditary burial ground of the Chen family.

One day Hsi Men's wives learned from Mother Pi the most recent item of personal news: that old Chen was dead and had just been buried, that his widow had left the capital to settle down in Tsing ho hsien, and further, that Spring Plum, at her own expense, had laid Gold Lotus to rest in a seemly burial place in the temple of Yung fu se.

"But such a coffin is a costly thing, and such a soul mass is not to be had for nothing," said Snowblossom in amazement. "How does the little girl contrive to do such things? Surely her husband, the River Prefect, must have reproached her severely?"

"You simply can't imagine it!" exclaimed Mother Pi, laughing.

"He is absolutely crazy over her, and says 'yes' to everything she does. She has him completely in her power. He has furnished three fine rooms in the eastern wing for her, has placed two maids at her disposal, and immediately after her arrival he had clothes for all four seasons of the year made for her. His First doesn't count at all. She is in the fifties, and half blind, sits all day in her room, eats only vegetable food, and cares for nothing but Buddha and his holy doctrine; she pays no attention to household affairs. But his Second, who lives in the east wing, has lately borne him a daughter, and is still in bed. So he has handed over all the keys to Spring Plum; she has entire charge of the household, the kitchen and the store rooms are under her control, and she decides what is to be bought and what is to be spent, as though she were not the Third, but the First. And she too is expecting a little one."

Moon Lady and Snowblossom exchanged a silent glance and made no response. But in private they marveled at the curious ways of destiny, and thought with a mixture of envy and shame of the brilliant career which had been allotted to little Spring Plum, who had recently been expelled with ignominy from the household.

"One can't get out of a visit of condolence to the house of Chen," said Moon Lady at last. "I myself, of course, should not care to go; I shall ask to be excused for reasons of ill health. But Hsi Men's daughter can go, and you, Mother Pi, will perhaps be so good as to accompany her."

Mother Pi agreed, and it was decided that the visit should be paid on the following afternoon.

Young Chen happened to be standing at the door and looking down the street when a palanquin was set down before his house, from which Mother Pi alighted.

"What brings you here?" he asked Mother Pi.

"Don't pretend you don't know, Master Daughter's Husband! As you may imagine, your mother-in-law sent me. I was to express her sympathy and bring you various sacrificial gifts. She herself begs you to excuse her, as she is not well. But she sends in her place Master Hsi Men's daughter. Her palanquin will be here directly."

"What's that! My mother-in-law! I refuse!" he burst out angrily. "And as for her sacrificial gifts, they ought to have been sent a fortnight earlier. My father has been long under ground."

"Dear Daughter's Husband, she regrets extremely that she should be a step behind the event. But you will understand, as a lonely widow her feet are as lame as a crab, and she does not leave the four walls of her house. In short, it was only yesterday that she heard of the death in your family. You must have a little consideration."

In the meantime the palanquin of Hsi Men's daughter had arrived.

"Who is that coming?" he asked.

"Why, I have told you already, your mother-in-law is not feeling quite well today, and she is sending Master Hsi Men's daughter, so that she can pay due reverence to the soul tablet of your deceased father in her place."

"What's that? What's that? May she rot! Let her clear out again as quickly as possible!"

He made a sign to the bearers that they were to go away, and as they did not at once understand him he ran angrily out into the road and got them going with a few kicks.

"March! Off with you, or I'll break your bones and tear the accursed woman's hair out, a hair at a time!" he shouted at the terrified bearers. At this they hastily lifted the palanquin and went off at a trot. And there was nothing left for Mother Pi to do but return to her own palanquin. She had at least taken the opportunity of handing to Chen's mother, who had appeared in the meantime, the boxes of sacrificial gifts which she had brought with her.

Moon Lady was beside herself with wrath, and she actually fell into a momentary swoon when she was told of the caller's unfriendly reception at the house of Chen.

"This undutiful creature! this pattern of wickedness!" she cried, when she came to herself again. "When he was in trouble he found a refuge and hospitality here, and this is his gratitude for all our kindness! He sets himself above all heavenly commandments and treats his mother-in-law as if she were a filthy old rat!"

Turning to Hsi Men's daughter, she continued:

"All the same, while you live you are his wife, and after death you will continue to live in his family as a household spirit. I cannot keep you here permanently. Don't let him intimidate you, but go to him again tomorrow! You belong to his household. If he goes too far with his insolence we shall see whether there are not laws which will give you your rights."

And next day she sent Hsi Men's daughter again to the house of Chen, this time under the escort of Tai A. Young Chen was not at home. He was at the ancestral burial ground, where he was performing the rite of heaping earth upon the grave. His mother received her daughter-in-law in the friendliest manner, and begged her to excuse the events of the previous day.

"He was drunk, and did not know what he was doing. I will speak to him, and little by little I shall bring him to see reason. Give Moon Lady many greetings from me, and my cordial thanks for her kindly sympathy!"

When young Chen came home towards evening and found his wife in the house he again flew into a rage. He struck her, kicked her, and shouted at her: "What are you doing here again? Give me my property and Uncle Yang's treasure chest, which I brought to the house with me! I won't have it said any longer that I am living like an idle parasite in my father-in-law's house! For all I care you can rot! I want nothing more to do with you!"

Then she too lost patience and retorted passionately: "Scoundrel! Aren't you ashamed to trample on the heavenly commandments like this? Is it my fault if the Fifth was killed by her brother-in-law? You have no right to treat me so basely!"

Her words made him rave with fury. He tore at her hair and struck her in the face with his clenched fist; and as his mother came to the rescue of the maltreated woman by placing herself in front of her he even roughly thrust his own mother aside. At last the ugly scene came to an end, and the young woman returned to her palanquin, weeping.

It was the middle of the third month. Tsing ming, the delectable festival, had come. On this "Day of Bright Clarity," dedicated to the memory of the dead, Moon Lady paid a visit to Hsi Men's grave, accompanied by Jade Fountain, the maid Little Jewel, the nurse Ju I, and her child. Moon Lady's elder brother, with his wife, brought up the rear. As they emerged from the narrow streets of the city, field and meadow lay outspread before their delighted eyes, clad in fresh and luxuriant green; flowers of every color shone resplendent, and on every side, on the paths and byways, were gay parties of men and women enjoying the vernal radiance of the morning. What season of the whole year is so delicious as the Spring? It was one of those days on which one sees Nature and the world and all things in a glamorous light: on which the sun not only shines, but "laughs"; the wind becomes a "zephyr," the sorry jade a "noble steed," the dust on the highway a "fragrant powder"; it was the day of which the poet sings:

> Tsing ming! the air is incense
> That bathes the fields and trees.
> Shreds of spirit gold
> Float upon the breeze.
> The quivering grass is gay
> With laughter, song, and flowers;
> The blue and smiling heavens
> Spill their passing showers.
> On the boughs the colored
> Birds rejoice and sing;
> Over drowsy temples
> The leafy willows swing.
> Fair as any picture
> The maidens go their ways,
> And the young men's eyes
> In rapture gaze and gaze.

After the burial ground was reached—it lay at some five *li* from the city wall—and the company had taken some refreshment, Tai

A was bidden to set up the sacrificial altar before Hsi Men's grave, when they all came forward one by one, each carrying a burning incense taper, and honored the dead with a ceremonious kowtow. Moon Lady was the first to advance. She swept the area surrounding the sepulchral mound, sprinkled it with sacrificial wine, burned incense and spirit money, performed her kowtow, and addressed a few words to the dead man.

"My brother, you who once lived as a man amongst us, and who now dwell among the spirits, today, on the day of Tsing ming, your mourning wife, she who was a Wu by birth, together with your Third wife and your little son, who is now one year old, have gathered at your tomb in order to sacrifice to you with due reverence. Vouchsafe your blessing and your protection, that your son may live a hundred years, so that you may have someone to cherish your memory and to protect your grave from neglect when I am no more. Full of grief and sadness I remember the time when we were still happily united; I remember your nature and your words."

Her speech ended in a loud cry of lamentation. Then she returned to her place. After her, in order of precedence, came Jade Fountain, then the nurse with the child in her arms, Brother Wu, and Sister-in-law Wu, all of whom honored the dead with a kowtow and the burning of incense.

Almost at the same hour, in the temple of Yung fu se, at the foot of the old hollow aspen tree, Spring Plum was performing the same loving service in honor of her dead mistress, Gold Lotus. During the night she had dreamed an uneasy dream as she lay at Master Chow's side, and when he questioned her she explained, through her tears, that the dead woman had just appeared to her in her sleep, and had urgently besought her not to forget her on the day of Tsing ming.

"Well, if one knew where she was buried," said Master Chow.

"She is buried in the Yung fu se Temple, outside the Southern Gate," Spring Plum quickly replied.

"Well, that will just fit in. Not far away is the hereditary burial ground of my family. We will all set out together tomorrow morning, and while the rest of us are sacrificing to my dead kinsfolk you can hurry off to the grave of your former mistress."

So, traveling in four palanquins, Master Chow, his three wives, and a numerous retinue set out on this same morning for the Southern Gate. Shortly before reaching the Yung fu se temple he parted from Spring Plum, continuing on his way, with his two other wives, to his country estate, where his family burial ground lay.

But now we will return to Moon Lady and her company. Having performed their obligations, they resolved to take advantage of the smiling spring day and to make an excursion as far as the "Apricot-blossom village" of Hsing hua, which lay at a distance of some five *li*. There, at a very popular tavern, poetically situated in an undulating landscape, they decided to rest themselves and enjoy the wide and beautiful prospect. In view of the glorious weather they would go thither on foot. The elder Wu, holding his mule by the bridle, led the way, followed by the flock of women. The servants brought up the rear with the food baskets and palanquins.

They had gone perhaps three-fourths of the way when Moon Lady noticed a splendid temple, set within spacious grounds, which appeared not far away amidst the luxuriant green of an acacia grove. What with the luminous red of its enclosing walls, the glistening emerald green of its glazed, five-fold, "dragon-scale" roofs, the sturdy mass of its bell towers and kettle-drum towers, and the springing grace of its pagoda, that seemed to be striving to reach the clouds, it constituted a magnificent adornment of the landscape.

"What kind of temple is that?" Moon Lady asked her brother.

"It is the Yung fu se Temple, the 'Temple of Eternal Blessedness,' dedicated to the service of Buddha. Its patron is Master Chow, the River Prefect; but Brother-in-law Hsi Men, shortly before his death, also gave it an endowment of a mule load of silver. One of the five halls in which the statue of Buddha stands was recently built at his expense. You can tell it by the fresh, glittering glaze of its 'dragon scales.'"

"Oh, then we really must have a look at it," Moon Lady proposed, and the whole company turned aside into the little acacia grove. Asking that they might be presented to the Prior, they introduced themselves. Of course, Chang lao, the "Tall Ancient One," most readily gave the widow and relatives of a benefactor to whom the temple owed so much his permission to view the interior of the hall which had been founded by Hsi Men. After they had inspected the hall he politely invited the company to take a dish of tea and a monastic meal of vegetable food in the reception hall. While talking of this and that, they were told that the monastery then contained a hundred and ten Brothers, and that the "Hall of Meditation" at the back of the temple always harbored a flock of "cloud-wandering" mendicant monks.

While they were talking and eating two servants, dressed in blue, suddenly rushed into the cell, and informed Chang lao, panting as they spoke: "The little Nai nai is here. Why don't you come out and greet her?"

Quickly the "Tall Ancient One" slipped into his ceremonial cassock, thrust his priest's bonnet on his head, and hurried out to the gate.

"May I beg the worthy Bodhisattvas to excuse me, and will they for the time being sit in the next room? I must receive the little wife of our patron. She wanted to sacrifice here today. As soon as she has gone I shall again be at the disposal of the worthy Bodhisattvas," he cried to his guests, as he left the room.

Immediately the dull booming from the bell tower and kettledrum tower announced that an honored guest had arrived, and borne at the double by six sweating bearers, in the midst of a crowd of blue-robed yamen retainers, the palanquin of the little Nai nai entered the forecourt of the temple through the "Mountain Portal." There it was set down. Before Spring Plum had time to step out on to the flagstones of the forecourt the "Tall Ancient One" was beside the palanquin, making his apology with reverently bent back. For he really ought to have received such an important visitor outside the "Mountain Portal."

"The simple monk was unaware that the little Nai nai would do his negligible monastery the honor of a visit today. He begs her a

722

thousand times to excuse his remissness," he murmured in dismay.

"That is all right," came the gracious answer from within the palanquin, and with measured and dignified step Spring Plum, the simple maid of yesterday, the noble lady of today, allowed herself to be escorted to the modest grave at the foot of the old hollow aspen tree in the furthest corner of the temple precincts.

Meanwhile, in the reception cell next to that in which they had been first received, the assembled women were burning with curiosity, eager to catch a glimpse of the important visitor whose arrival had set the whole monastery in a turmoil.

"Why doesn't the 'Tall Ancient One' return?" they asked the young bonze who was waiting on them.

"He has to accompany the little Nai nai to the wall at the back of the temple grounds. There she will find the freshly-dug grave of her recently deceased sister, to whom she wishes to sacrifice on this day of Tsing ming."

"Will that by any chance be Spring Plum?" Jade Fountain suddenly inquired.

"Nonsense! Since when has she had a sister?" said Moon Lady. Then she turned to the young bonze: "What is the name of the little Nai nai?"

"Her family name is Lung. She recently contributed five ounces to the cloister, in order that we might facilitate her poor sister's entry into heaven by saying masses for her soul."

"As far as I can remember, Spring Plum's family name is Lung. No doubt it is she," said Jade Fountain once more.

Now they heard without the trampling of many feet; then the Prior rushed into the neighboring reception cell, and shouted excitedly for tea of the very best quality, and immediately afterwards the palanquin, with the guest of honor, was lifted across the threshold. In tense expectation the five women, huddled together behind the dividing curtain, peeped into the adjacent room. Jade Fountain had guessed correctly. The person who stepped out of the palanquin was none other than Spring Plum, once their little maid. But how she had improved since her departure from the house of Hsi Men!

723

She seemed to have grown much taller and handsomer, and her face was round and symmetrical as the disc of the full moon. And how elegantly and tastefully she was dressed! And her jewels—how costly, how abundant! And this assured and aristocratic bearing! The observers behind the curtain were overcome with amazement.

The assiduous Prior made her sit in the high-backed, comfortable chair of honor which was the most ornate and conspicuous object in the room. He had tea brought in and set before her, and he never ceased explaining how infinitely he regretted that he had been too late to welcome her before she entered the forecourt.

"Then I can count on your occasionally reading a soul mass for my dear dead sister?" said Spring Plum, interrupting his flood of verbiage.

"The little Nai nai may be quite easy in her mind! After your great generosity to us we shall take all imaginable pains to satisfy you with a dignified celebration. You shall be notified in good time."

Spring Plum seemed to be in no hurry to leave; she sipped her tea in the most leisurely manner. Moon Lady, however, on account of the child, was anxious to return betimes, and therefore sent the young bonze to ask the Prior if he would kindly come to them in order that they might take their leave of him. At his request, however, she consented to stay a little longer. When the Prior went back to Spring Plum he informed her that he had other lady visitors, who had come to see the temple, and were now anxious to leave; and he asked her, diffidently, if she would pardon the interruption and permit him to escort his other visitors to the gate.

"But my dear Chang lao, why stand on ceremony? Why did you not bring them in here long ago and mutually introduce us?" Spring Plum inquired.

The "Tall Ancient One" hurried back to Moon Lady and begged her to come into the next room. At first Moon Lady refused, for she felt that it would be painful to meet her former maid, whom she had treated so badly. But she finally gave in, and with all her company followed the Prior into the adjoining room.

"Oh, it's you!" cried Spring Plum, in astonishment. Rising from her seat of honor, she approached the newcomers with a modest and friendly bearing, first greeting them in the order of precedence as politely and prettily as though she were still the maid, and not a lady of equal rank. Moon Lady and her companions were completely shamed by her noble behavior, which betrayed no trace of the ill humor and susceptibility which would have been quite justified, and they responded to her greetings with a friendly courtesy not inferior to her own, addressing her as "Sister." And when Spring Plum took a golden arrow from her hair, and fastened it upon the child's little cap, as the nurse Ju I held him in her arms, and the boy, at Moon Lady's bidding, wished the giver "good day" in his pretty little childish voice, which made them all burst into a hearty laugh, the spell was broken, and the embarrassment of the first moment was followed by a mood of cheerful unconstraint.

"Sister, who knows whether we should ever have met again in this life if chance had not brought us together here today!" said Jade Fountain, thoughtfully.

"I came to do homage to one who was to me as my nearest relative, who was recently laid in her last resting place here," replied Spring Plum earnestly.

"But as far as I remember your mother has been many years under ground? I didn't know she was buried here," Moon Lady interposed.

"You have not understood her," said Jade Fountain, now herself speaking earnestly. "By 'nearest relative' she meant Gold Lotus."

There was a moment of embarrassed silence.

Then, deeply moved, Sister-in-law Wu ventured to say:

"Sister Lung, such touching loyalty, such goodness of heart as you have revealed in this case are not often to be seen. You give her burial, you honor her this day of Tsing ming with sacrifices and incense, and you also make provision for a dignified soul mass. You are a noble woman."

"What I have done I have done as a matter of course," replied Spring Plum simply. "She was always so good to me! Her terrible end has caused me such infinite grief, and to think that her poor body would still be exposed to wind and weather—no, I simply couldn't bear it."

Jade Fountain had silently risen to her feet. She too, under the impression of Spring Plum's words, was filled with a great sense of compassion. Now she would atone for her remissness. She went out of the room, bought from the Prior incense and spirit money, both silver and gold, and asked to be shown the way to Gold Lotus's grave. And presently Little Jewel and the nurse Ju I, with the child in her arms, followed her example. Only Moon Lady remained where she was.

Having reached the grave at the foot of the old hollow aspen tree, amidst the green young willows, Jade Fountain lit an incense-taper and set light to the spirit money which she had brought. Then she bowed in greeting to the narrow, brown mound of earth, and said: "Sister Five, do not be angry with me if I have not thought of you sooner, and accept these little gifts from me, which may make it easier for you to enter Heaven."

After she had mourned a little longer, uttering a loud cry of lamentation, she returned to the rest of the company with Little Jewel and Ju I. In the meantime a large table had been laid for the women. The elder Wu was served with food in a separate cell. The Prior had all the good things which his monastic kitchen was capable of producing brought up for the visitors; Spring Plum contributed to the feast the plentiful provisions which she had brought with her; and there was no lack of meat and wine and cakes and sweetmeats, nor yet of silver goblets and ivory chopsticks.

During the meal two express messengers from the River Prefect appeared, knelt before their little Nai nai, and begged her to proceed to the Prefect's country seat, where a troupe of jugglers had just begun their performance, and all was prepared for her coming. The company broke up, and all were on the best of good terms when Moon Lady's party bade farewell to Spring Plum outside the gate of the temple: not without exacting the promise of an early visit. Spring Plum, with her blue-coated retinue, turned into the lateral path which led to the estate of "New Court." Moon Lady with her company set off along the highway for the "Apricot-blossom village" of Hsing hua tsun.

Tai A had long ago ridden ahead, and had been in time to reserve, on the outlook hill in front of the tavern, a good table, "with the heavens for roof and the earth for carpet." At last, after a long delay, the rest of the company appeared, riding in palanquins or on mule back. They took their seats at the table, and applied themselves with renewed appetite to the rustic meal, to provide which Tai A and the host had done their best. At their feet passed the waves and streams of traffic; excursionists in festive mood, whom the delicious spring weather had enticed from the city in swarms, were surging to and fro. How entertaining it was to look down upon this ever-moving multitude from above!

At one point the crowd was jammed together like a wall. Here there were feats of horsemanship and gymnastic performances to wonder at, organized by the athletic trainer of young Master Li, the son of the District Mandarin Li of Tsing ho hsien. With a troop of some thirty friends, all strong and nimble young fellows, young Master Li had today come to the village of Hsing hua tsun in order to wrestle with them in the spring sunshine on the green turf, and to enjoy all sorts of joyous athletic pastimes, what with longbows and crossbows, blowpipes and footballs, lances and singlesticks. For the vivacious, well-built son of District Mandarin Li, now thirty years of age, was no friend of Shi King and Shu King, no bookworm and scholar; he preferred to bestir himself in the open air, to go hunting with hound and hawk, to ride and fence, to play football, and to stroll along the highways. Among the people he was generally known as "the Madcap."

Now the young men had broken off their games for a while, and had joined the throng of spectators who with tense interest and cries of applause were following the hazardous feats of the dauntless trainer, who leapt into the saddle of a galloping horse, rode standing on his head, and performed the most incredible contortions and tricks of fence.

While young Li was standing there and idly watching the performance, his gaze happened to fall upon the knoll in front of the tavern, where it fixed itself upon a group of feminine guests who were sitting round a table and sipping their wine. It was the tallest of them who particularly attracted his attention, and to whom his gaze returned again and again. He felt that he positively must know to what family she belonged, and whether she was already married or still accessible.

"Go up and inquire who are those three ladies in mourning white at the central table in front," he quietly bade his body servant, who was standing beside him.

After a time the boy returned, and whispered into his ear. "They belong to the household of the late District Judge Hsi Men. The little one, the eldest, is his sister-in-law, Wu by name. The middle-sized one is his former First wife, a Wu by birth, Moon Lady by name. The tall full-figured one, with the faint freckles, was his Third, and her name is Jade Fountain. She, like the other, hasn't yet married again."

"Good; thanks."

And wholly absorbed in his thoughts, young Li continued to stare at the tall full-figured woman in mourning white, until he saw her rise indolently from the table, until the soft curves of her back disappeared into a palanquin.

CHAPTER FORTY-THREE: *Lai Wang elopes with Snowblossom. Jade Fountain marries for Love*

THAT SAME AFTERNOON, while the other ladies were enjoying themselves in the country on the outlook hill of Hsing hua tsun, Snowblossom and Hsi Men's daughter, who had to look after the house in their absence, were standing outside the gate and watching the passers-by in the street.

While they were standing thus and looking on, predestination willed it that a street peddler should go by, offering in a loud voice, while violently ringing his bell, such requisites of the "inner chamber" as powder and paint, combs and hairpins, and the like. Hsi Men's daughter sent the gatekeeper Ping An after him, to ask whether he had any polish for metal mirrors. The peddler replied in the negative. But instead of passing on he stood still, set down his pack, and stared fixedly at Snowblossom.

"Well, man, why do you stand and stare at me?" cried Snowblossom.

"Don't you remember me? I am Lai Wang, Master Hsi Men's former servant Lai Wang."

"What, you are Lai Wang?" cried Snowblossom, in surprise. "I shouldn't have known you again, you have grown so fat since then. Where have you been hiding all these years?"

"After Master Hsi Men had driven me out of the house I returned, at first, to my native city of Hsue chow. For a long while I was unemployed and couldn't find anything to do. Then I obtained a situation as servant to another gentleman, whom I had to accompany to Kai fong fu, where he was to take up an official post. But while we were on the road his father died, so he had to turn back, on account of the mourning rites, and I was dismissed. Then, as I wasn't very far away from Tsing ho hsien, I came here and obtained a situation in a silversmith's house. With him I learned all sorts of silversmith's work. During the last few days he has sent me out with a pack, in order to get rid of a consignment of remainder stock as a street dealer. When I passed you just now I saw you, of course, but I didn't venture to introduce myself. If you hadn't called me over I should have gone on."

"You needn't be afraid of us. What have you got in your box there? Come in and let us see!" said Snowblossom, invitingly, in whom the old affection had instantly revived.

He gladly accepted her invitation, and on entering the inner courtyard he displayed all sorts of pretty trifles. Hsi Men's daughter chose a pair of brightly-colored enamel flowers for her sidelocks, while Snowblossom decided upon four enamel brooches in the shape of a pair of phœnixes and a pair of fish, which was, of course, a gentle hint to Lai Wang. While Hsi Men's daughter paid him for her purchases on the spot, Snowblossom declared that she must owe him her ounce and two bits for the moment; he must come again on the following day. This was, of course, only an excuse for meeting him again.

"Moon Lady is out at the burial ground today, with the Third and the child," she explained. "I must just wait until she returns."

The servant Lai Chow came forward now, and bade his former colleague a friendly good day, while his wife I Chang Tsing even brought him a dish of tea.

"Come again when you like, and show yourself to the First!" said Lai Chow, as he took his departure.

In the evening, when Moon Lady's party had returned, there was much to tell. Moon Lady described the strange encounter with Spring Plum, and the accidental discovery of Gold Lotus's grave, and Snowblossom told of the unexpected reappearance of Lai Wang. What a remarkable coincidence! A threefold encounter with three former housemates on the same day!

730

"Why didn't you keep Lai Wang? I should have liked to speak to him," said Moon Lady.

"He's coming again tomorrow."

And sure enough, on the following day Lai Wang again presented himself with his pack, and was most amiably received by Moon Lady.

"Why haven't you given us a glimpse of you all this time?" she asked.

"After all that had happened I didn't dare to come here."

"Oh, nonsense! Your master has been dead for some time now, and you used to be like one of the family; you could have come whenever you liked. It was that woman, the Fifth, who was responsible for the whole unfortunate story. It was she who always stirred up the fire and squirted cold water. She had your wife, the kindly Lotus Petal, on her conscience; she harassed her until she hanged herself in despair. And then she gave Master Hsi Men no peace until he sent you away. But now Heaven has punished her for her evil deeds.

"It does me good to hear you speak like that."

"What fine things have you there in your pack? Open it and let me see!"

And she bought freely of his wares, to the value of three ounces and two bits. Then she entertained him with wine and cakes. And Snowblossom sent him from the kitchen some very special titbits, prepared with loving hands. After he had taken his leave of Moon Lady, Jade Fountain, and Hsi Men's daughter with grateful and obsequious kowtows, Snowblossom contrived to speak to him alone. "Do come oftener!" she begged him softly. "You needn't hesitate. I have still such a lot to tell you. If you like I'll wait for you tomorrow evening in the unoccupied room over by the red wall."

He understood what she meant.

"But can I get in here in the evening? I expect the inner gate is closed pretty early?"

"Wait in Lai Chow's lodge until it's dark. When I give you a

731

sign, set a ladder against the wall and climb over. I'll be there to help you down."

A beaming smile of delighted anticipation spread over his face, starting from the corners of his eyes, and lifting his pack he hurried away with a joyful heart.

Next afternoon he made his way to Lai Chow's lodge, as agreed. This time he was not burdened and hampered with a pack. I Chang Tsing was not present, as she was busy in the kitchen. He gave Lai Chow a glittering ounce.

"Here, you and your wife can get a jug of wine with that. I have a little money coming to me from Snowblossom, for the bits of jewelry she bought of me yesterday. I was to fetch the money this evening, and until then I should like to wait here."

With an understanding grin the other pocketed the silver ingot. That was more than enough for a jug of wine! He understood; and so did his wife, I Chang Tsing, when she arrived from the kitchen and he showed her the good money.

"No present without a consideration, of course," she said, with a knowing wink. "For that matter, Mistress Snowblossom has told me already. You can rely on us entirely."

And in a joyous mood they sat down to the supper and the jug of wine which the boy Iron Bolt had bought at a moderate price, and toasted their old friendship.

"In confidence, we should much like to see you steer into the desired harbor," said Mistress I Chang Tsing. "But if you should have an opportunity of making off with a few of the treasures of the house, please don't forget us; let us too taste a little of the forbidden nectar!"

Lai Wang dropped a jesting curtsy.

"How should I ever forget my benefactors!" he exclaimed.

I Chang Tsing accepted his assurance contentedly, and ran off to the women's apartments, in order to warn Snowblossom that her friend was waiting.

About the hour of the second watch of the night, when all the members of the household had gone to bed, Lai Wang, equipped with a ladder, took up his position at the point indicated, in the shadow of the inner wall. Now a stifled cough was heard on the other side of the wall: this was the agreed signal. Lai Wang leaned the ladder against the wall and quickly scrambled on to the coping. On the further side of the wall he descended another ladder, which Snowblossom had thoughtfully placed there for him. At the foot of this ladder he found her waiting for him. They embraced in silence and disappeared into the unused room, which was close at hand. Before they parted Snowblossom gave her lover a heavy parcel of gold and silver ornaments and some broken silver. It contained also two satin dresses. She had learned wisdom from previous experiences, and she knew that Moon Lady liked to see her poorer housemates leave the household with completely empty hands.

"Come again tomorrow evening!" she whispered. "I have still quite a lot of things to give you. And please, look about in the city for a nice house. For you can hardly make these secret visits over the wall a permanent habit. The only sensible thing is for you to carry me off one night, and then we shall be man and wife. Now, since you have a situation with a silversmith and have found a way to earn your living, we needn't be afraid of the future."

"I know of a suitable house outside the city, by the eastern gate. I have an old aunt there, who lives in Rice Lane. It's a crooked little lane, quite out of the way; no one ever goes there. We could very well live there for the present. Later on, provided Moon Lady lets the matter rest and doesn't make inquiries for us, we can go to my native city, Hsue chow. Then I will buy a few acres of land and till the soil; that will pay us better than working with the silversmith."

After they had made plans in this fashion for the remote future, Lai Wang took his departure, climbed back over the wall, and spent the rest of the night in Lai Chow's quarters. Next morning, as soon as the gate was open, he went off to his own house.

Next evening they repeated their sport, and so on for quite a number of days. On each of these nocturnal visits to the house of Hsi Men he carried away a heavy bundle. A quantity of jewelry, clothing, linen, silver plates, golden beakers, and other household goods disappeared unnoticed, Lai Chow and his wife receiving their share of the fat booty.

One night they decided that it was time to elope as they had planned. Snowblossom sent her maid early to bed—she was, fortunately, a rather simple creature—made up a great bundle of clothes and stolen articles, and followed Lai Wang over the wall at midnight. They went first of all to the quarters of Lai Chow and his wife, in order to thank them for their loyal co-operation and to hearten themselves for their bold undertaking with a farewell drink. Lai Chow advised them to escape over the roofs and not through the gate.

"After all, I am partly responsible for the gate. How should I clear myself afterwards if the First were to reproach me for letting the fat ducks out through the gate?"

And he advised them, further, to loosen a few shingles, as they made their way over the roofs, for then visible traces of their flight would remain, and he would be cleared of any suspicion of complicity. They both agreed to do as he suggested, and at the hour of the fifth drum beat, each holding an incense taper to scare obtrusive spirits, they climbed on to the roof with the help of a ladder, and crept from roof to roof until they had reached the edge of the last of all, which projected over the outer wall, overhanging the street. On the way they did not forget to loosen a shingle here and there. Luck was with them. In the east the dawn was already gray, but the street was still absolutely empty. From the distance echoed the challenge of a patrol.

Lai Wang was the first to jump down into the street. Then he helped his companion to descend, offering his shoulder as a support. Sighing with relief, they ran quickly from the house and made for Lai Wang's quarters. Then, at a crossroads, a night watchman barred their way and bade them halt.

"Who goes there? And whither?" asked a hoarse voice.

Mistress Snowblossom's knees began to wobble with fright. But Lai Wang succeeded in keeping his head. He calmly exhibited the bundle of incense tapers which he held in his hand. "We are man and wife, and we are going to burn incense and pray in the 'Temple of the Five Sacred Mountains' outside the walls. We are starting rather early in order to get back in good time."

"What's in the bundle you are carrying on your back?"

"All sorts of incense and spirit money."

"All right. Off you go!"

Lai Wang, without a word, took his companion's arm and dragged her quickly along with him. With flying steps they came to the eastern gate just as it was being opened, and drawing long breaths they set foot outside the walls. There was already a great deal of traffic outside the gate; they were no longer conspicuous, and could moderate their pace. Through a maze of streets and crooked lanes they came to the short, twisting Rice Lane, which contained only a few houses, and they stood at length before the goal of their journey, the squalid little house of Aunt Kue. It was really in a quiet, out-of-the way corner.

After long knocking the door was opened, and Aunt Kue appeared.

"Good day, Aunt, I am bringing my New One," said Lai Wang, as he pressed three ounces into her hand. "I suppose we could live in one of your rooms until we have found a house of our own?"

In view of the weighty argument which she felt in her hand, Aunt Kue did not deny him, but cleared a little room for the pair.

Now Aunt Kue had an ill-conditioned son living with her. It could not escape the lustful eyes of this young man, living at such close quarters with the newcomers, that they had a considerable quantity of gold and silver jewelry in their room; in short, he took advantage of their occasional absence to enter the room and appropriate this and that piece of jewelry. His booty was drunk and gambled away at night. One night, on the occasion of a raid, he fell into the hands of the police, and since the poor devil was found to be in the possession of valuable jewels and ornaments, he was arrested as a suspected thief. Under the torture of the finger press he confessed to everything.

Now not only his mother, but Lai Wang and the terrified Snow-blossom were arrested, and dragged off to the yamen. Naturally their arrest was the cause of great excitement in the neighborhood, where the people lived close together, and where everybody knew everyone else. The lanes through which they had to pass were filled with a gaping crowd.

"That is a concubine of the late District Judge Hsi Men," said someone who had known Snowblossom in the old days. "The fellow next to her is a former servant, now her lover; he eloped with her, and with her assistance he got away with a vast amount of plunder, mostly gold and silver. And the son of old Kue has been helping himself to their loot. That is how matters stand."

In a trice the story had made the rounds of the city, where an ounce became ten or even ten hundred.

Moon Lady was like one fallen out of the ninth heaven when the morning after Snowblossom's elopement the maid came running to her and excitedly announced that Snowblossom had disappeared, and with her all her gold and silver ornaments and a quantity of clothes, linen, and household goods; she had left only three old dresses behind.

"But didn't you see any sign of her going away?" asked Moon Lady.

"Lately she used to leave the house in secret every night, but she always came back some time later. So I didn't think anything of it when she went out this last time," replied the simple-minded maid.

Now Moon Lady questioned the servant Lai Chow.

"You were in charge of the gate that night? How could she have gone out unnoticed?"

"The gate was safely locked and barred that night as usual," replied Lai Chow, shrugging his shoulders. "If she didn't fly, she probably got away across the roofs. I'll have a look at once. Perhaps there are traces there."

After a while he came back and reported: "There are some displaced and splintered shingles to be seen on the roofs of the eastern wing; indeed, one can make out a definite track as far as the edge of the roof overhanging the street."

It was then obvious to Moon Lady that Snowblossom must have escaped over the roofs, and she made no further inquiry. She suspected neither Lai Chow nor Lai Wang, until one day she received further information from the District Yamen.

The official investigation, which was facilitated by the generous application of gentle pressure, had elicited a confession from the four prisoners, and had led to the discovery of a great quantity of loot: gold and silver hair ornaments, gold finger rings and bracelets, a golden statuette of a god, silver lamps, and the like, and altogether sixty ounces of bullion in bars and broken silver. The District Mandarin found Lai Wang, Snowblossom, and young Kue guilty of theft, and old Kue of receiving stolen goods, and he sentenced Lai Wang and young Kue to five years' banishment and hard labor, while Snowblossom and old Kue were condemned to immediate corporal punishment with the finger press. The loot was confiscated. Old Kue, after she had received her punishment, was allowed to return home. As regards Snowblossom, the mandarin sent to Moon Lady and privately requested her to send for her and take her back into the house. In this way Moon Lady learned the whole story of the elopement, including the fact of Lai Chow's complicity.

Moon Lady consulted with her elder brother and came to the conclusion that she would not on any account take Snowblossom back into the house; that by her behavior she had smirched the honor of the household. So the mandarin was obliged to have her put up to public auction by an officially appointed go-between.

Naturally, the news of the scandal found its way into the household of the River Prefect. When Spring Plum heard that Snowblossom was to be offered for sale in public she remembered the old enmity that had existed between the Fourth and her mistress Gold Lotus, and the shame which she herself had once suffered in the kitchen, thanks to the hostility of the Fourth; and she resolved to pay the woman in her own coin.

"She can cook admirably; she would be a real treasure in the kitchen," she told her husband.

And Master Chow did as she asked: he sent to the district yamen and acquired Snowblossom for the modest price of eight ounces. With whatever ornaments and other finery she still possessed she was brought to the house of the River Prefect, where she had to make her preliminary kowtow to his wives, in order of their rank. She was finally introduced to his Third. Snowblossom started violently when she recognized in the Third the former maid, the Spring Plum whom she had once despised and tormented. Spring Plum, negligently outstretched under the silken sheets of her magnificent bed, which was adorned with gilt carvings, hardly vouchsafed a glance at the new servant, who stood before her so humbly, her eyes timidly fixed upon the floor. There was no help for it: Snowblossom had to bend her knees and make the fourfold introductory kowtow before the former maid, now her mistress.

"Take that finery off this wretched maid, put her into a plain cook's dress, and then away with her to the kitchen, where she belongs! She can light the fire and get me some breakfast!" Such were Spring Plum's curt orders to her maids.

Deeply ashamed, Snowblossom had to submit to being led out and transformed into a common kitchenmaid. At the sooty hearth she had time to meditate on the bitter truth of the old proverb:

> Life is a seesaw: low it swings and high.
> Today a feast, tomorrow scanty fare:
> The slave today who gleans the fallen rye
> Tomorrow may have granaries in his care.

When young Chen heard from Mother Pi of the scandal in Hsi Men's house he told himself that the time had come for him to make a vigorous protest to Moon Lady in respect of his old claim; for Moon Lady would hardly wish to expose herself to the unpleasantness of yet another family scandal. So one day Mother Pi called on Moon Lady on his behalf, when she spoke to her as follows:

"The Daughter's Husband is spreading it about the city that he wants to be divorced from his wife, and also that he intends to lodge a complaint against you with the Provincial Governor and the Provincial Censor. He declares that you refused to surrender certain chests of money, which he brought to the house on his arrival here years ago, and which were formerly the property of his late uncle, the Marshal Yang."

Moon Lady, who had not yet recovered from her recent emotions, fell into the greatest consternation. She hastily summoned a palanquin, and sent Hsi Men's daughter, escorted by Tai A, to young Chen's house. In order to appease the contumacious son-in-law, some porters were engaged to carry a number of chests and boxes containing various articles belonging to his marriage portion, or that of his wife.

But young Chen was by no means satisfied, and he explained to Mother Pi: "These are all part of our marriage portions. I am asking for my money chests. And besides them I want the maid, Yuen Hsiao."

"Your mother-in-law sends word that this is all you brought to the house with you. She knows nothing about any alleged money chests," Mother Pi informed him. At his request she once more went to Moon Lady. But Moon Lady persisted in her repudiation of her son-in-law's claim, and she refused to part with the pretty maid, whom she herself needed as her child's day nurse. Now Chen's mother took a hand. She sent for Tai A, and spoke to him. "Give your mistress a courteous greeting from me, and tell her that she ought not to refuse my son's request in respect of the maid Yuen Hsiao. She has hitherto served his wife as maid, and also my son has already physically possessed her."

This last argument of Lady Chen's hit the mark; it was one that Moon Lady could not very well disregard; so she at last consented to surrender the maid. And young Chen was glad to have achieved something of what he intended, if not all, and to have obtained a substitute for Gold Lotus. And he told himself triumphantly: "Now I'm on the way to get the better of her!

"You may fight like a devil, but still, I think,
The slops of my footbath shall be your drink!"

This time he did not send Hsi Men's daughter, his wife, away.

But now let us speak of the young Master Li, the noble offspring of the District Mandarin Li. Since he had seen, on the day of Tsing ming, while standing before the outlook hill of Hsing hua tsun, the melon face and the generous charms of Jade Fountain, he had been firm in the resolve to lead her home as his wife. He had lost his first wife some considerable time before this date, and was more than weary of the life of a lonely pike. Various go-betweens had received instructions to look about for a new consort, but they had never found anyone suitable. But now Jade Fountain had fairly bewitched him.

He considerately waited until the waves of emotion in respect of the latest scandal had somewhat abated; then he commissioned the official matchmaker Tao to take the necessary steps. So one day the matchmaker Tao entered her litter and was carried to the gate of Hsi Men's house.

"Am I right—is this the house of Hsi Men?" she asked the gate-keeper, Lai Chow.

"Yes, but Master Hsi Men is no longer among the living. Who are you, and what do you want?"

"I am the officially appointed matchmaker Tao, and I come on behalf of the young and highborn Master Li, the son of our District Mandarin," she replied with dignity. "He wishes to pay court to a certain lady who belongs to the household."

"I suppose you aren't quite in your right senses? Our master has been barely six months dead. His two widows would hardly be thinking of remarrying so soon; you don't know them. The best thing you can do is to trot off, and be quick about it. Otherwise I shall risk a thrashing, if the ladies hear that I've even discussed your absurd nonsense."

"Brother House-steward, can one blame the servant for the master's fault?" said the old woman, smiling. "I have only to carry out my instructions. Nothing else can have any significance for me. So just go and announce me!"

"Well, it's all one to me. But I don't yet know to which of the two I am to announce your arrival. The one with the child or the one without?"

"My patron is thinking of the one he saw on Tsing ming day, on the outlook hill at Hsing hua tsun. A tall plump lady with light freckles on her face."

"Oh, I know whom you mean!" Lai Chow nodded, and vanished into the house.

Worthy reader, it cannot be denied that Jade Fountain also, on that afternoon of Tsing ming, had remarked young Li from where she was sitting, and had secretly taken pleasure in his dashing, audacious virility. In the matter of age they were well-enough matched, and the way in which he sat in the saddle and wielded the longbow filled her with silent admiration. So the attraction was not one-sided, but was confessed, alternately, by two pairs of eyes. She had spoken to no one of her feelings, but she had thought in her heart: "Hsi Men is dead; all the sympathies of the household are now for Moon Lady's offspring; I have become entirely superfluous. Moon Lady, since her child was born, is no longer the old Moon Lady; she has become quite unsociable. Is it not foolish of me to sit here alone, waiting for nothing and wasting the springtide of my life? Why shouldn't I take a step forwards and seek a new spot in which to strike root?"

It was by these and other such thoughts that she was moved as the days went by. So when Moon Lady came to her and announced that there was someone waiting without, one of those whose calling it is to bring mountains together, that she came on behalf of young Master Li, and that she wished to speak to her, Jade Fountain— then it seemed to her that she was receiving an inevitable and long-expected message, so completely was her heart already prepared to receive it.

"Oh, I don't believe such nonsense!" she said; outwardly cool, and concealing her secret satisfaction from Moon Lady. Nevertheless, she could not prevent a fiery blush from flooding her cheeks, and she agreed that Lai Chow should bring the matchmaker in.

"Well, what is it?" said Moon Lady, who opened the negotiations in her own room, without the presence of Jade Fountain.

The matchmaker made her proposal.

"How does your patron come to know anything about us? We hardly ever set foot outside the gate."

"He had an opportunity of admiring the ladies recently on the day of Tsing ming, when they were on the outlook hill at Hsing hua tsun. He was chiefly interested in the tall, plump lady with the light freckles on her melon face."

Moon Lady introduced her visitor to Jade Fountain, who in the meantime had quickly thrown on her finest clothes.

"This and no other is the one he means!" said the matchmaker, after she had uttered her *Wan fu* and had closely and complacently examined the object of her patron's desires. "And one must admit that his description wasn't exaggerated. You are really a most unusual and quite individual beauty, and well worthy of becoming the First Wife of the noble son of our District Mandarin."

Jade Fountain smiled at this pleasant flattery.

"You are romancing, my dear woman. Let us now talk seriously and to the point. How old is the young gentleman? Has he already been married? Has he concubines? What is his name? Does he fill any office? Please, answer strictly to the point."

Mother Tao drew a deep breath.

"Good heavens, but how distrustful you are! I am, you must know, an officially appointed matchmaker, not one of the other sort, who just make up lies, and for whom two is the same as one. Now listen to me: He is the only son of our District Mandarin. His father is fifty years old; he himself is thirty-one, and he was born on the twenty-third day of the first month, at the hour of the Dragon. He studied at the Imperial Princes' Academy, and he expects before long to take his doctor's degree. His belly is full of learning, and he has mastered the writings of all the hundred sages, but he is just as great a master of the longbow and the noble art of riding. Two years ago he lost his first wife, and she left behind her a passable chambermaid, whom she brought with her when she married. He has no concubines."

"Has he any children? Where did his family originally come from? I am asking that in case his father's or his own office should one day be terminated, when he might want to drag me off, who knows where, over a thousand swamps, and a thousand hills. My own relatives all come from hereabouts."

"Neither sons nor daughters have sprung from his loins. He comes from the district of Tsao kiang hsien in the prefecture of Chen ting fu, not far from the Northern Capital of Peking. That is not so very far from here; at most six or seven hundred *li* to the north, reckoning from the Yellow River. There his family has a country seat with extensive fields and meadows, great herds of cattle, and innumerable servants. The region is under the special protection of the Emperor, as the honorary arches of marble on the highway proclaim. Later, when he has become a mandarin, you will naturally be granted a corresponding rank and an honorary title. Well, doesn't that sound enticing in your ears?"

Did it not? Jade Fountain sent for the maid Fragrant Orchid, and had tea and cakes set before the woman who brought mountains together.

"Don't take it amiss that I should have questioned you so closely," she said to her guest, "but with you professional matchmakers one never knows. . . ."

"Dear lady, I am not one of that sort! With me one is one, dark is dark, light is light. Now, if you are disposed to accept my proposal, then be so kind as to write the card with the eight signs of your date of birth, so that Master Li has your consent in writing."

Jade Fountain selected a strip of red satin, and got Dispenser Fu to paint the desired eight characters in a skillful and artistic manner.

"At your last marriage Mother Pi acted as your go-between. Won't you employ her in this case also, and allow Mother Tao to

743

second her in the further negotiations?" suggested the prudent Moon Lady.

So Mother Pi also was sent for, and the two matchmakers set off together for the District Yamen. On the way thither Mistress Tao listened to all her colleague had to tell her about Jade Fountain; after which she remarked: "According to her birth card she is now thirty-seven. My young master is six years younger. It's to be hoped the difference of ages isn't too great for him."

"You are right, colleague. But the fault can easily be remedied. We will simply ask the first scholar we come across who understands the calendar to make a little correction."

Sure enough, they presently found themselves passing the booth of a public scribe, all hung with blue cloth, in which sat a scholar learned in the calendar, waiting to supply passers-by, for a trifling fee, with his interpretations of the calendar and prognostications of fortune. For half a bit of "destiny money" he was quite willing to make Jade Fountain three years younger, altering the number thirty-seven on her birth card to thirty-four. He first assured himself, by referring to the calendar, that the new combination of the eight characters would harmonize with the relevant planet of destiny, and would not unfavorably distort the formation of the astral constellation.

Despite the correction which had just been made, Mother Tao felt that she was in duty bound to call her patron's attention to the still considerable difference in the age of the two parties. "As far as physical advantages go she is, of course, incomparable," she told him; "still, she is somewhat advanced in years. So I don't wish to employ actual persuasion; I would rather leave the decision entirely to your own judgment."

But the enamored wooer paid no further heed to her objection.

"Two or three years more or less are of no importance," he decided, briefly. "Say no more!"

"I must praise your insight," ventured Mother Pi, taking her turn. "There is an old saying that runs:

> *She may a few years older be*
> *But they bring gold and prosperity.*

"In other respects her physical qualities are beyond criticism. And then, her compliant nature, her gentle character, her education . . . !"

"I know, I know," said Master Li, interrupting her volubility with a smile. "I have already convinced myself of that with my own eyes. Now the only thing to be done is to find two suitable days for sending the betrothal presents and bringing the bride home."

"And when would the gentleman wish us to inform her of his decision?"

"As soon as possible: tomorrow. Here is your ounce of 'errand money.' Each of you will receive five ounces more on the night of her entering my home."

The two matchmakers curtsied, well satisfied, and on the following day they hastened to apprise Jade Fountain of the fateful decision. The eighth day of the fourth month saw them again in Hsi Men's house. In their train was a long column of bearers, bringing twenty loads of betrothal presents; among which were twenty dishes of various kinds of food, a gold-embroidered head-dress, a cornelian girdle, a pair of musically-tinkling, jeweled earrings, a number of gold and silver bracelets, half a dozen dresses, thirty silver ounces in cash, and many other fine things.

On the evening of the fifteenth day of the same month the bride was ceremoniously carried to her new home, her furniture and her many boxes having been removed in the morning. Jade Fountain was allowed to take all her personal possessions and all her furniture with her. She left behind her only the gayly-lacquered bed, which she presented to Hsi Men's daughter. In place of it Moon Lady gave her as a wedding present the magnificent bed with the shell pattern which had once belonged to Gold Lotus. She also allowed the bride to take both her maids, Fragrant Orchid and Little Phœnix.

Jade Fountain, clad in bridal red, her head covered with pearls and golden ornaments, above which rested the gold-embroidered coif, bowed in greeting for the last time before the soul tablet of the late Hsi Men. Then she bade farewell to Moon Lady, to whom it came hard to lose her sister.

"Sister Three, it is really not nice of you to leave us. Now I am quite alone and have no one to keep me company," she said, in an unsteady voice.

They lingered for a time hand in hand, shedding tears of farewell. Then the bride was brought by the assembled members of the household to the festal palanquin at the gate. Sister-in-law Mong and the two matchmakers escorted her to her new home. A further escort of eight men bearing lanterns of red gauze suspended on poles walked beside the great palanquin with its red hangings, which was carried by four bearers. The street was thronged with curious onlookers.

"Look, that's the former Third of the late Hsi Men. The most noble son of our District Mandarin is leading her home today!" So the news ran from mouth to mouth, and words of praise and of blame were uttered. Those who praised said: "It's very sensible of Master Hsi Men's widow to reduce the household and not to prevent the other women from seeking their happiness elsewhere. What would all those people do in the house when the son is grown up?"

Those who spoke words of blame said: "Well, the fidelity of Master Hsi Men's wives doesn't seem to amount to much. No sooner is he dead than they marry again. But it serves the fellow right. The way he went racketing about and wenching when he was alive, hoarding money and seducing other men's wives and daughters, affronting Heaven and disdaining all the laws of human reason! It serves him quite right if his house is being plundered and if one hen after another is running away!"

Such, were the differing opinions of the people. When, on the evening of the third day after the bride was brought home, Moon Lady returned from the usual banquet given by the newly-married pair to the lonely silence of her widow's home, a certain melancholy took possession of her heart, and involuntarily she recalled the bygone time when Hsi Men was still alive and the house full of life and merriment. In those days, when she returned from such visits, she was welcomed by a little flock of companions, and there was no end to the joyous chatter and gossip and carousing. Now all was silent and lonely. A painful sense of desolation overcame her, and sobbing aloud she flung herself upon the floor in front of Hsi Men's soul tablet.

> *In silence must she bear*
> *The pain that makes her quail.*
> *Only the moon would hear*
> *Did she her woe bewail.*

CHAPTER FORTY-FOUR: *Young Chen allows Jade Fountain to lure him into a Trap. The Apricot Anchorite takes Pity on him*

AT YOUNG CHEN'S urgent request his mother placed two hundred ounces of his father's estate at his disposal, and allowed him to open a draper's shop in the front of her house. As his business manager she appointed the old servant Chen Ting. But the frivolous young man used the money less for buying goods than for carousing and gambling in the society of a few dissolute boon companions. And when the money was gone he put the blame on the worthy manager, whom he described to his mother as a dishonest fellow, so that he induced her to turn this inconvenient spectator and monitor out of the house, together with his wife. He was allowed to appoint his friend Yang as manager in the place of Chen Ting. He was simple enough to place confidence in this cunning, conscienceless fellow, and the day came when he bitterly rued his folly.

First of all, he borrowed a further three hundred ounces from his mother, and set out with his friend Yang for the river port of Lin tsing, ostensibly in order to buy cloth. Now this Lin tsing was not only an important and much frequented trading center, where the merchants of all the provinces were wont to meet, and where the streets echoed with the incessant rumble of heavily-laden wagons: it also boasted a number of "flower and willow lanes," where by day and by night no fewer than seventy-two houses of pleasure enticed the passer-by with flute and fiddle, competing eagerly for the privilege of lightening the heavy purses of the strangers who came thronging through their gates.

This joyous traffic was entirely to the taste of the frivolous young

Chen. In short, he invested only the smaller portion of his good money in goods; the rest he squandered with his boon companions in frequent voyages of discovery through the port of Lin tsing. And when a few days later he returned to Tsing ho hsien, he brought with him, in addition to a scanty cargo of bales of cloth, a pretty little "powder-face" of eighteen, Golden Jewel by name. He had paid for her no less than a hundred ounces. His old, invalid mother, who had found it hard to bear the loss of the first two hundred ounces, took this new prank of her son's to heart so sorely that ere long she died of it. Having become, through her death, the sole possessor of his father's house and fortune, he now for the first time began to squander it wholesale, and to give full rein to his inclinations. The best rooms in the house, which had hitherto been occupied by his mother, he now gave to his darling Golden Jewel. He bought her a maid, and overwhelmed her with costly attentions. His lawful wife, Hsi Men's daughter, was modestly installed in the side wing of the house, where she led a neglected and joyless existence.

The life of pleasure which he now led day after day, sometimes in the company of his mistress, sometimes in the society of dissolute boon companions, made serious inroads upon his stock of bullion, and forced him to consider how he could unlock new sources of income. Now his perverted mind evolved an audacious scheme.

He still possessed the brooch which Jade Fountain had lost, and which he had one day happened to find in Hsi Men's park. What if he used this brooch in order to subject the original owner to a little blackmail? He knew that she was now in easy circumstances. Apart from the fact that she had married into the aristocratic family of the District Mandarin Li, she herself came of well-to-do people. What if he now simply confronted her and boldly asserted that she had received as her marriage portion the money chests of his late uncle, Marshal Yang, which Moon Lady had hitherto detained, and the restitution of which he now demanded from her, Jade Fountain? And what if he threatened, in the event of refusal, to show her father-in-law the lost brooch as evidence that there had been an affair between her and himself? She would surely be terrified, and willing to pay any price in order to prevent the destruction of her new married happiness. If she were not he would carry out his threat, and he did not doubt that the correct old Li would annul the new marriage in consequence of his revelation, and surrender Jade Fountain, together with her dowry to him, young Chen, her former suitor. Then he could bring home the wealthy Jade Fountain as his new wife. That would be no small achievement! So ran his audacious plan.

> *From the Moon he would snatch the Jasper Hare,*
> *And in the Sun the Fire-bird snare!*

But it was all to turn out quite otherwise.

District Mandarin Li, after the conclusion of his three-years' period of office in Tsing ho hsien, had in the meantime been appointed Sub-Prefect of Yen chow fu in the province of Che kiang, and some little time before this he had already removed, with his dependents, to his new sphere of office. Since Yen chow lay in the midst of the most important of the silk-producing areas, young Chen decided to combine his intended visit to Jade Fountain with a business expedition. And so one day in the eighth month, accompanied by his friend and manager Yang, and equipped with a thousand ounces, he set out for the well-known silk market of Hu chow on the Yangtse river, which was on the road to Yen chow; and here he bought half a ship's lading of silk. Then, proceeding a little farther, he cast anchor in Tsing kiang, the nearest river port to Yen chow. Here he went ashore with his friend Yang, invited him to a sumptuous dinner in a good hostelry, and spoke to him as follows:

"From here I want to make a little excursion to the neighboring city of Yen chow, in order to visit my sister. She is married to the son of the sub-prefect there. In the meantime be so good as to look after the ship and the cargo. You can stay at the inn here at my expense and enjoy yourself. I shall be back in five days at latest."

Friend Yang assured him that he could rely upon him absolutely;

and accompanied by the servant Chen An, who had to carry the few presents intended for Jade Fountain and her husband, young Chen, provided with only a few ounces of bullion, made his way to Yen chow fu, the capital of the prefecture. There he took up his quarters in a temple, and began by making inquiries. He learned that the new sub-prefect, Master Li, had entered upon his new office a month earlier, and that his family, together with his household goods, had arrived a few days previously.

On the following day young Chen dressed himself in his best, and went to the prefecture with his servant and the presents.

"I am the younger brother of the new wife of the son of your sub-prefect, and I wish to wait upon their lordships," he told the doorkeeper.

Young Li was sitting in the library, poring over his books, when his alleged brother-in-law was announced.

"Master Brother-in-law, why did I not have the honor of greeting you recently on the occasion of my wedding?" he asked his visitor.

"I was on a business journey just then, which took me to Sze ch'uen and Kwangtung, so that I was a whole year away from home," said the young liar. "It was only after my return home that I learned of the recent remarriage of my sister, and I could not fail to bring her my belated congratulations, together with a few trifling wedding presents. I beg that you will excuse my remissness."

Master Li now sent word to his wife that her younger brother had come to visit her.

"Younger brother? That can only be Mong Jui. Extraordinary: what can have brought him here across a hundred mountains and a thousand waters?" So Jade Fountain said to herself.

But it was he; she read the name Mong Jui on the list of presents which was now laid before her.

"Bring him in," she told the maid Fragrant Orchid, and she disappeared into her bedchamber, in order to prepare herself for his visit.

How great was her surprise when, on looking through the curtain, she recognized, in the visitor whom her husband had just

751

introduced into the sitting room, none other than young Chen! What could this mean? However, the Daughter's Husband was no stranger: she was glad that he had come, and in any case she would go in and greet him. So she quickly gave orders for something good to eat and drink.

> *Kinsman or stranger though the man may be,*
> *Home through the native speaks with accents clear.*
> *Though bright or foul it journeys to the sea,*
> *The river of our home is always dear.*

It so happened that Master Li, just as she entered the room, was called away by a servant, as another visitor had arrived. She was therefore left alone with young Chen, a circumstance which he welcomed with secret satisfaction. He could now come to the point without circumlocution. After a few questions of a personal and domestic category had been asked and answered, and several beakers of wine filled and emptied, he began: "Sister, all this time I have longed for you as the man dying of thirst longs for a drink of cold water. Do you ever think of the happy hours we spent together in my father-in-law's house, when we sat knee to knee at the chessboard or the card table? How sad that all this is past, and that destiny has so cruelly torn us apart!"

"One must put up with the inevitable," she said, consolingly, with a smile.

He took from his sleeve a pouch filled with scented tea paste. The pouch was worked in the form of two closely-embraced lovers. He offered it to her with a curtsy.

"Sister, if you still have any feeling for me take this and taste it!" he pleaded.

She blushed all over her body; then she controlled herself, and let the pouch drop to the floor. "Please, no folly!" she said quietly. "I wish you well, and I have received you as a friend. Please don't abuse my kindness, or I must go."

He saw that he must alter his tactics.

Calmly he picked up the rejected pouch and continued in a different tone: "I too wished you well, but I see you don't mean to understand me. So I suppose I must make myself plainer." He held out the brooch which she had once lost in the park. "Do you recognize that? Even your name is engraved upon it. Will you perhaps deny that you did me the honor to give it me as a pledge of your love, after you had already given me yourself? Later on you allowed yourself to be turned against me by Moon Lady, and you married young Li instead of me. Well, I don't care. But you will kindly hand over my property—I mean the various chests of treasure which you brought away from Hsi Men's house, and which originally belonged to my late uncle, Marshal Yang."

And he stood up as though he were about to leave the room.

Jade Fountain examined the brooch more closely. There was no doubt about it; this silver trinket in the form of a lotus stalk, with a golden head, was one which she had been accustomed to wear, and which she lost one day in the park. How had it come into young Chen's possession? What he was attempting was the most impudent blackmail. But appearances were against her. It would do her no good to make a scene. She decided to employ cunning. And concealing her indignation, she replied, softly, smiling, and taking him by the hand: "Stay, my dear, I still feel just what I used to feel for you!" And snuggling close against him, she allowed him to embrace and kiss her, when he made his protruded tongue play like a supple snake in and out of her mouth.

"Say, 'dear Tjin tjin!'" he begged her. "Then I'll believe that you honestly mean this."

"Quietly! We might be overheard!"

"Listen, off Tsing kiang I have a trading junk with half a cargo. I shall expect you tonight outside the gate. Disguise yourself as a doorkeeper and fly with me!"

"I'll do all you ask of me. But first of all—let me say, precisely at midnight—wait for me behind the garden wall. I must in any case pack up some gold and silver, and throw the package over the wall to you. It might attract attention if I were to take it out with me."

753

"Good, I'll cough to let you know I'm there." He swallowed down a few more beakers of wine, and left her. Master Li escorted him to the gate.

Worthy reader, when a woman in love means to have her way no wall is too high for her—she will reach her goal in spite of it. But when the man in the case is indifferent to her, she can sit beside him and yet be miles away from him. If Jade Fountain had happened to marry a fool she would doubtless have run away with young Chen. But she was now the wife of a young, handsome, and vigorous husband, who had a future to offer her, and not only did she love him, but he was worthy of being loved. What reasonable excuse would she have had to exchange him for an old admirer?

When young Chen had gone and the unsuspecting Master Li asked his wife: "Where exactly is your brother staying? I should like to pay him a return call tomorrow," she suddenly burst out:

"Brother, indeed! That was the Daughter's Husband from the house of Hsi Men! And he wants to elope with me, the impudent fellow! I pretended to agree to his proposal, in order to get rid of him without a scandal. I have told him to be behind the garden wall at midnight, in order to take charge of a package of gold and silver which I pretended that I should give him. We must arrange matters so that he seems to be a thief; then he'll take care to leave us alone in future."

Master Li was furious. "The scoundrel! He wants to poison our married happiness? He shall pay for that! And he can thank himself for the consequences. I didn't ask him to come here. He has come to his own funeral uninvited!"

Punctually at midnight young Chen, behind the garden wall, made his presence known, as agreed, by clearing his throat. Jade Fountain replied from within by softly calling his name. Immediately afterwards a rope wriggled over the wall to his feet. At the end of the rope a heavy package was suspended. It contained two hundred ounces from the yamen treasury, which had previously been made to look as though it had been broken open. Young Chen had just untied the package and handed it to his servant Chen An when suddenly, out of the darkness, four men rushed upon them, brandishing cudgels and loudly shouting: "Robbers! Robbers!" Before they realized what was happening they were thrown to the ground and bound with cords. In the yamen jail they spent the rest of the night meditating upon this unexpected turn of events.

Next morning they were brought before the tribunal of Prefect Hsue. Old Li appeared as prosecutor. He had no suspicion that the whole story of the burglary had been fabricated by his son and daughter-in-law.

"Last night, at midnight, these two rascals broke into the treasury of my yamen and stole two hundred ounces from it. They were caught just as they were escaping over the garden wall. I demand that they shall be severely punished."

The prefect signed to the prisoners to come nearer and made them kneel. With astonishment he noted the aristocratic appearance of the younger culprit, who seemed to be a man of education and of good family.

"How came you to force your way into the yamen by night and commit a vulgar theft?" he inquired.

But young Chen could not be induced to speak. He simply performed innumerable kowtows and cried, "Injustice!"

Old Li bent over the Prefect and whispered in his ear: "Examination would be superfluous. After all, they were caught in the act. The two hundred ounces of official money which were found upon them are sufficient evidence. And here is a sketch of the treasury door, which was broken open. Severe corporal punishment would be in order."

The Prefect signed to his beadles and ordered them to give the two men twenty blows apiece. But young Chen kept on shrieking: "Injustice! Injustice!" and at intervals, as though to himself, he brought out the words: "She led me into the trap, this woman!"

This utterance of his did not escape the Prefect, and after the tenth blow he told the beadles to stop. He was one of the just and thoughtful mandarins, and he told himself that there was something queer about the case. Disregarding the description of his sub-prefect, he decided to get to the bottom of this mysterious affair.

"Take them away! The case is adjourned until tomorrow," he said.

"Why such consideration?" whispered old Li. "The hearts of criminals are hard as iron: one softens them only in the crucible of stern punishment. The fellows will try to lie their way out of it all tomorrow if you give them a whole day to think things over."

"I have my reasons," the Prefect informed him, coldly. That night he sent a confidential agent of his, under the mask of a prisoner, into the cell in which young Chen and his companion had been thrown. It was his business to overhear what the two prisoners said without attracting attention to himself. The man succeeded in entering into conversation with young Chen, and he shared his mat that night.

"Hey, young friend, you don't seem to me a regular member of the craft," he said to his fellow prisoner. "Perhaps you've only been popped in here through some misunderstanding?"

"Just how it happened it's difficult to explain in a word," replied young Chen, for it eased his mind to confide in a fellow sufferer. "I am the Daughter's Husband from the household of Hsi Men in Tsing ho hsien, and I had an affair there formerly with a woman, a Mong by birth, who recently married the son of the local Sub-Prefect Li. She brought into her new marriage, from Hsi Men's house, ten treasure chests, which had really belonged to my late uncle, Marshal Yang, and which after his death became my property. I wanted to claim their return from this Mong; that was why I came here. But she made a fool of me and with the help of her present husband she pretended that I had stolen two hundred ounces, in order to be conveniently rid of me. And now I'm in a trap."

Early next morning the Prefect's confidential agent was released. He told his master exactly what young Chen had confided to him. Old Li fell from the ninth heaven when at the public hearing of the trial of Chen and his companion on a charge of larceny the Prefect declared: "The two accused will now be released. The warrant of arrest is cancelled."

"But why? Their guilt is proven!" old Li insisted. The Prefect drew himself up, gazed reprovingly at the Sub-Prefect, and gave him a thorough dressing-down, before all the assembled officials and subordinate officers, beadles, servants of the yamen, and members of the public:

"My office is a public office; I have not been appointed Prefect in order to help you, in a partial manner, by the exercise of my official powers to assist you in settling your domestic disputes and differences. The young man was quite justified in demanding the return by your daughter-in-law of the treasure-chests which had been the property of his late uncle Marshal Yang and which have since then been illegally detained. How came you without reason to accuse him of burglary? Your behavior accords but poorly with the good principles which all who fill a public office ought to follow."

His face covered with shame, old Li had to swallow this public reproof in silence. But after the session was over he vented his rage all the more violently upon his family. "This is a fine, good-for-nothing son that we have reared!" he cried, raging against his wife. "He's been fooling me—he has simply fabricated the whole story of a burglary! And I had to suffer the Prefect to rebuke me in public session, before all my colleagues and the public! I could expire with rage!"

Then it was his son's turn. He was given thirty strokes, put into irons, and imprisoned in an empty room. There, he was resolved, he would leave the culprit to die of starvation. As for his daughter-in-law, he had really intended to turn her out of the house then and there. In the end, the heartfelt pleading of his wife softened him so far that he allowed the young people to retire to the family estate of Tsao kiang hsien, near Peking. Within three days they were to pack their boxes and leave the parental roof.

With smarting limbs, and completely exhausted, young Chen

757

returned to the river port of Tsing kiang. The little money which he had taken with him he had expended during the journey, or while he was in prison. The first thing he did was to go to the inn where he had parted from his friend Yang. But Yang was no longer there.

"He left the day before yesterday," the innkeeper declared. "He told me that you had written to say that you couldn't come, and that he needn't wait any longer. So he set off on the voyage home with your junk."

Young Chen was beside himself. He ran off to the harbor, and truly enough, the berth at which the junk had lain was empty. Without means as he was, he must find some way of getting home as quickly as possible. There was nothing for it but to sell all the jewelry he was wearing, and even his fine silken outer garment. The price he received was just enough to pay for a bad place on board a passenger junk which took him to Tsing ho hsien. Hungry and bitterly cold and ragged as a vagabond, he at last reached home on a chilly autumn day. What a pitiful outcome of a proud undertaking!

It will be understood that his temper was none too sweet on his return home, and it was not improved when the messenger whom he sent to his friend Yang's house came back without an answer. This faithless fellow, who had so vilely betrayed his confidence, had disappeared without leaving a trace, together with the valuable ship's cargo. A domestic quarrel made his ill temper boil over completely.

During his absence there had often been squabbles between his wife and his darling Golden Jewel. The two rivals were on such terms that each invariably turned her back upon the other. In short, no sooner was young Chen at home again than he was besieged on either hand by complaints and accusations. "This person has used all the housekeeping money for herself alone," Hsi Men's daughter complained. "She has continually had a fellow from her flower garden here; she has given him heaven knows how much money for her flower garden mother, and she was for ever getting him to bring her wine and all sorts of expensive luxuries for her own use, while absolute necessities were lacking in the house. She sleeps until late in the day, and she has never stirred a finger to help in the housework."

"She doesn't do a hand's turn of work all day, and everything's all at sixes and sevens in the house," Golden Jewel complained in return. "For herself and her maid she had boiled meat and roast, and all sorts of pickles and preserves and cakes prepared; while I had to be thankful if I could get a little thin rice soup."

Naturally, he took sides against his unloved wife. "You'll die of colic yet, you idle, gluttonous woman!" he railed at her, and he kicked both her and the maid.

"And I suppose all that you've secretly taken to your flower garden counts for nothing, you impudent harlot?" Hsi Men's daughter angrily shrieked the words into the other's face. "It's unheard of, the way you turn everything upside down! It's just as if the midnight brawler wanted to arrest the night watchman! You simply want to thrust me aside and make yourself look important. But I'd rather die than put myself on a level with you!"

"Be silent!" young Chen ordered her harshly. "You can't put yourself on a level with her—you aren't worth the nail on her little toe!"

And brutally dragging at her hair, he struck her several blows in the face with his clenched fist, so that the blood spurted from her nose and she fell senseless.

That night, while he lay asleep beside Golden Jewel, his unhappy wife made an end of her melancholy life by hanging herself on the bedpost. The poor creature was only twenty-four years of age.

Through Chen Ting, the old servant of the Chen family, Moon Lady learned on the following day of the melancholy end of Hsi Men's daughter. Now, the ice that lay over her relations with the Daughter's Husband was not a matter of yesterday only; indeed, one may say that it had long been a full yard in thickness. Without taking overlong to reflect, she assembled eight powerful servants from her domestic staff—some of them men and some of them maids—and with this formidable retinue she proceeded to her son-in-law's house. First she asked to be shown the corpse, and she mourned it for a while, as was proper, with loud cries of lamentation. Then she give a signal to her people, and suddenly the whole troop fell upon the unsuspecting Daughter's Husband, who was standing beside her. In a moment he was lying on the floor, and was thrashed by the united energies of the whole party, the men kicking and punching him, the women stabbing him with needles and brooch pins. After they had sufficiently thrashed and pricked him, they let him lie and directed their attention to his mistress.

First of all, Golden Jewel had to be pulled out from under her bed, where she had taken refuge. She too received a proper share of thumps and pricks, so that when all was over she felt more dead than alive. When this treatment was ended the party proceeded to smash all the furniture in the house, beating in the doors and windows, overthrowing the tables, shattering the crockery, tearing down the curtains, and slitting the cushions and bedclothes. This done, Moon Lady contentedly retired with her fighting escort.

But the revenge which she had sworn to take on her hated son-in-law was not yet complete. Once home again she summoned her two brothers to a family council.

"He has driven his wife to kill herself, and has therefore put himself in the wrong before the eyes of the world. Take this opportunity of making him innocuous once for all. Bring him before the judge's bench!" the elder brother advised her. "Otherwise, if you let the matter lie you will be continually subjected to his nagging and pestering in respect of the treasure chests. You must somehow prevent that."

"You are right," Moon Lady agreed, and that very day, with her brother's help, she drew up an indictment against her son-in-law. Next morning she went to the District Yamen and submitted her plea in person. Master Huo, the new District Mandarin, broke the seals of the document and read the following:

"Complaint of the born Wu, four and thirty years of age, widow of the late District Judge Hsi Men Ch'ing,

against

her son-in-law Chen Tsing Ki.

"My son-in-law, at one time, on account of the opening of disciplinary proceedings against his father Chen Hung, took refuge in my husband's house. During the years of his residence with us he proved himself to be a drunkard and an immoral destroyer of domestic peace. In order to prevent more serious and punishable excesses I turned him out of the house. In his vexation at being thus ejected he subjected his wife, my husband's daughter by a former marriage, to constant maltreatment. Recently he took a public harlot by the name of Golden Jewel into his house and illegally gave her precedence before his lawful wife. Yielding to the instigations of this harlot, he again insulted his wife in the most brutal manner, and physically maltreated her, tearing her hair and kicking her, and finally, on the night of the twenty-third of this month, he strangled her. He has also uttered threats of murder against myself. I beg for protection, and ask you to have him arrested and to try him on a charge of murder, so that justice may be done in accordance with the laws of the land, so that the wicked may be warned, so that the virtuous may live in peace, and so that the dead, his victim, may not have to complain of injustice.

To the Venerable Commander and Celestial Governor in the District of Tsing ho hsien."

The decided tone of this indictment, together with the impression of trustworthiness created by the aristocratic plaintiff, who knelt before him clad in mourning white, wearing the girdle that distinguished her as the wife of a mandarin of the fifth grade, did not fail to influence the Celestial Governor. Rising from his chair with a slight bow, he addressed her thus: "Stand up, noble lady, I am already aware of the facts of the case. You can go home, and need not trouble to come here again. It will suffice that at the next

761

session you send one of your people as your representative. The accused shall be arrested and brought up for trial immediately, as you have desired."

At this Moon Lady thanked the judge with a bow and returned to her palanquin. She entrusted the servant Lai Chow with the duty of representing her in court. Young Chen and Golden Jewel were that same day dragged out of the house by the District Mandarin's bailiffs and thrown into jail.

"How did you come to ill-treat your wife and actually to strangle her?" Master Huo asked young Chen when he was brought up for trial next morning.

"I had returned from a business journey, and I was rather ill-tempered, because while I was away I had been cheated by a dishonest manager and had suffered a serious loss. I asked my wife for something to eat, and as she did not comply with my wish I became angry, and in temper I gave her a few kicks. That is all. I did not strangle her. She hanged herself."

"Why did you need to trouble your wife? Could you not allow your concubine to prepare your food? But apart from this, it is stated clearly and positively in the indictment submitted by the born Wu that you beat your wife almost to death and finally strangled her."

"The born Wu has long hated me. She is trying to strike at me by means of a false accusation."

"Nonsense! The dead woman is evidence enough against you. I'll soon drive your obstinacy out of you!"

And Master Huo sentenced the accused to twenty blows, while the co-accused, Golden Jewel, was at the same time subjected to the finger press. Then he had the prisoners removed. Next, he sent a commission to Chen's house, which had to view the corpse on the scene of the crime. The commission came to the conclusion that the deceased had committed suicide by hanging in a state of mental distress due to the bodily ill-treatment which she had previously suffered. This deviation from the description of the incident in the indictment, which spoke of murder, was at least one point in the prisoner's favor. And when, on top of this, young Chen contrived, in the course of the day, to send the District Mandarin a hundred ounces, having written to his servant Chen Ting, who just managed to scrape the amount together from the till of the shop and young Chen's private purse, Master Huo mitigated his original severity and allowed the charge of murder to drop.

In pronouncing sentence he referred only to bodily injury, and after ordering young Chen ten more strokes and a few days' imprisonment, and incidentally giving him some good advice, he discharged him. He also bade him see to it that the dead woman had proper burial, and forbade him to trouble his mother-in-law with any future visits or complaints. Golden Jewel was sent back to her flower garden in the river port of Lin tsing. She was never again to enter Chen's house.

Actually, young Chen could not have kept her any longer. He was so impoverished by the repeated blows of fate and the cost of his wife's funeral that he could hardly feed himself. Indeed, he had to resign himself to selling, first the smaller of the two houses which he had inherited as family property, and then, piece by piece, the furniture of the larger house, in which he was still living, in order to exist at all. Instead of taking any practical steps, he sat brooding in the empty rooms, clutching desperately at the hope that he might yet recover the valuable cargo of which his faithless friend Yang had robbed him. It was no wonder that he was steadily going downhill.

Day after day he knocked at the door of his friend Yang, only to be told that his whereabouts were unknown. Friend Yang, after liquidating the stolen cargo of silk, had sojourned now in this city, now in that, for his bad conscience would not allow him to venture on returning to Tsing ho hsien. But when he heard that young Chen had been subjected to painful legal proceedings in respect of his wife's sudden death, and had even spent half a month in jail, he felt that he need no longer be afraid of him, and one day he reappeared in Tsing ho hsien. He had an understanding with the other inmates of his house, to the effect that if young Chen should inquire for him they would deny that he was there, saying, as before, that he was away on his travels.

One day when young Chen was again knocking at his friend's door, a younger brother of Yang's opened it.

"Is your elder brother back yet?" young Chen asked politely. "I should like at least to recover the cargo of silk which he made off with."

"Oh, stop bothering us about your cargo of silk!" the other shouted angrily. "It would be more to the point if you would produce our brother! He disappeared months ago. Probably you have him as well as your wife on your conscience. Who knows where you may have thrown him overboard and drowned him? A human life is of greater value than your filthy goods!"

Now, this younger Yang was well known as a gambler, a drunkard, and a dangerous rowdy, so that as he slowly approached young Chen with clenched fists and a threatening mien, the latter was overcome with terror, and he ran away as fast as he could. The other, shouting insults after him, followed him at a little distance. Now he picked up a broken, sharp-edged tile, and flung it at the fugitive, striking him on the back of the head, so that the blood ran down his neck.

"Don't you take it into your head to trouble us again, you fellow, or you'll get a very different reception!" young Yang shouted after him.

Gasping for breath, young Chen reached his own house just in time to bolt the door behind him, for at that very moment the stones and bricks which his pursuer had hurled at him crashed against it. Completely distracted, he locked himself in his room, where he hardly dared to breathe. Having just suffered the terror of a criminal prosecution, he was so cowed that he saw a venomous viper in a harmless bit of rope. After this incident he did not dare to approach brother Yang's house again.

> *The hoar frost breaks the tender stalks,*
> *But hoar frost fears the shining sun.*

Each rogue and malefactor walks
In terror of a stronger one.

It was not long before young Chen's money was again exhausted, and he had to resign himself to selling his second house, after which he rented a miserable dwelling in an out-of-the-way lane. He had been there hardly a fortnight when the maid Yuen Hsiao died —the only one of his servants whom he had retained. Now he was quite alone, and his life became daily more dissolute and melancholy. The last, indispensable articles of furniture disappeared, and one day he could no longer scrape the rent together, and had to leave the house. Poor and homeless, he was turned into the street. He had become a beggar, and with other beggars he must spend the night in the "cold shed," the asylum for the homeless.

However, his fellow-beggars were friendly to him. They willingly gave him a special corner on the warm kang, and shared their best scraps of food with him. They were sorry for the newcomer, with his refined and handsome face and his good manners, for it was obvious that he had seen better days. On the other hand, as he was young and able-bodied, he was often roused from the most delicious sleep and dragged off to perform some public service: he might have to accompany a night patrol as drummer and bell ringer, or give a hand in extinguishing a nocturnal conflagration. That was a miserable job at this time of the year, for it was now the twelfth month; the very middle of a bitterly cold winter. Such work meant tramping up and down the streets all night with the biting north wind whistling in his ears, and often enough, when he returned to the asylum from such nocturnal expeditions, he was bent double and his shoulders were stiff and numb with cold.

One night he was out even longer than usual. His patrol, in the course of its rounds, had found a half-frozen beggar sleeping against a wall, and in order to save the poor fellow from being frozen to death young Chen collected all the straw and dead leaves that he could find in the neighborhood, made a warm bed of them, and watched over the man until help arrived. The cock was already

765

crowing when he was at last able to seek shelter after this night of self-sacrifice. Tired to death, he sank on to his own bed beside the heated kang, and immediately fell fast asleep. On that dark winter morning he dreamed that he was back again in his comfortable home in Hsi Men's house, lapped in the old brilliance and luxury, and he knew the inspiriting embraces of a Gold Lotus. He woke from his beautiful dream with a start, and a deep sigh. Asked by the other beggars why he was so depressed, he could only reply:

"Oh, brother, if you knew!"

O bitter my grief
And hard my bed!
No friend, no father,
My dear one dead!

No roof of my own,
No goods or gear,
My back grows cold
And my belly is lear.

Lonely I wander
Up and down;
With rattle and staff
I beg thro' the town.

I wait at doors
For my daily crust;
I sleep on stones
As a beggar must.

In wind and rain
Thro' street upon street:
That is the beggar's
Daily beat.

At this time there was living in Tsing ho hsien a wealthy man of sixty, by name Wang Ting Yang. He was known throughout the city both for his piety and for his benevolence. In the front of his house was a pawnbroker's establishment from which he derived a handsome income. This, however, was in the charge of a manager, for he himself spent his time in zealously serving Buddha, by prayers and sacrifices, by preaching sermons and expounding the sutras. From time to time he would manifest his piety by good works; standing before the door of his house and distributing alms to passing beggars, or medicines to poor sick persons. At such times his fingers incessantly busied over the rosary with the hundred and eight beads, while his lips murmured the name of Buddha. In respect of such piety, and also in allusion to certain apricot trees which were growing in his garden, his house was generally known as "the Apricot Cloister," and he himself as "the Apricot Anchorite."

On one of these cold winter days he was standing on the threshold of his hermitage, his fur bonnet, with its ear flaps, pulled down over his face, muffled up in a thick waterproof cloak, telling his beads as he kept a lookout for beggars and others in need of assistance. And then, as chance would have it, young Chen came that way.

In the kindly old man he recognized an intimate friend of his late father's, and he hastened to greet him with a kowtow on his bended knees. The Apricot Anchorite replied to his greeting with courtesy.

"Who are you, young friend?" he inquired. "My foolish eyes have grown dim with age, and do not recognize you."

"I am the son of the late Chen Hung," said young Chen, trembling with cold, and also with shame.

In mute astonishment the old man ran his eyes over the ragged figure before him, over the miserable face with its hollow cheeks.

"Worthy nephew, how have you come to this sorry pass?" he asked finally. "How are your parents?"

"Both are dead."

"Are you no longer living in your father-in-law's house?"

"My father-in-law is dead. My mother-in law has driven me from the house, and she even took legal proceedings against me when my wife died not long afterwards. Through a dishonest marriage I have suffered great losses, and am absolutely destitute. I had to sell my house and all that I possessed. Now I have nothing left; I have no occupation, and no roof over my head. I have to go begging."

The old man sighed. "And where are you living at present?"

"In the 'cold shed.'"

"That is deplorable! When I think of the days when my good friend, your father, was still living here, and you were still a little boy! How highly respected, how firmly established was your family then! And now it has come to this! That is really terrible! Have you no other relations who would look after you?"

"No one. I have long been on bad terms with the one uncle who lives here."

The Apricot Anchorite kindly bade him enter, led him into the warm living room, and began by making him eat his fill for once. Then he provided young Chen with some warm clothing. He gave him a wadded overcoat of blue cotton cloth, a felt bonnet, thick woolen socks, and a pair of comfortable felt boots. When he had dressed him in these clothes he gave him a string of five hundred copper cash and a fine bright silver ounce.

"But use the money wisely!" he urged his visitor. "With the copper cash rent a modest little room, and use the silver ingot as working capital in some kind of petty trade; no matter what, so long as it brings you in something to eat. That is better than begging and living in the asylum for the homeless. What you need for your monthly rent I will gladly advance."

Young Chen fell on his knees again and thanked the old man with a kowtow. "The unworthy nephew hears your advice and will follow it faithfully," he promised.

And he cheerfully pocketed the money and went his way. But as soon as he was in the street the little room which he was to rent and the petty trade which he was to follow were already forgotten. The first thing he did was to go to a good tavern, where he did himself well with roast meat and savories and the best wine. The rest of his money he lost at play, gambling with his comrades, and barely two days later he had gambled away his fine warm clothes. He was just as poor as ever, and had to go begging again.

And one day he was again passing the Apricot Cloister. Again the kindly old man was standing in the gateway, and again young Chen made his respectful kowtow. Full of astonishment, the old gentleman observed his destitute appearance. The blue wadded overcoat, the warm woolen socks had disappeared; only the felt bonnet and the felt boots were left.

"Well, worthy nephew, how is business?" he inquired. At first young Chen was unable to speak for shame; but at last, after much hesitation, he confessed that he had been foolish and had squandered the money.

"Ei ei!" said the old man, reprovingly. "How can anyone be so unreasonable! Why did you not obey me and set yourself up in some petty trade? After all, that would be better than this vagabond's life. For by that you dishonor the good name of your ancestors and expose yourself to the mockery and contempt of the people."

He once more invited him into the warm living room, had food set before him, and gave him a pair of wadded trousers, a white linen shirt, a pair of woolen puttees, a string of five hundred copper cash, and a bushel of rice.

"Once more let me advise you, worthy nephew, to take up some petty trade, such as selling firewood or beans or melon seeds, or what not; that is better than begging," he admonished his departing visitor.

Young Chen promised obedience with his lips, but no sooner was he out of the house than he had forgotten his resolution. A few days of easy living, and again his money was gone, and his new trousers gambled away, and he stood once more in his beggar's rags. For a long while he was too ashamed to enter the street where his benefactor lived. But one day in the first month he again made his way to the Apricot Cloister.

The old hermit was standing as usual before the gate, sunning himself in the already warm rays of the January sun. At first he deliberately ignored the young man who approached his threshold in the same ragged guise as on two former occasions, looking past him with cold eyes; but when young Chen threw himself down at his feet, looking up at him with a pitiful, pleading gaze, his human feelings once more got the better of him.

"I am afraid you are incorrigible, worthy nephew," he said, reproachfully shaking his head. "Your gullet seems to be unfathomable as the sea. Do you never give a little thought to your future? How will you ever escape from the bottomless abyss into which you have fallen? Well, come in, come in; I will give you one more trial. I know of yet another way in which you could obtain a quiet and secure livelihood. But indeed I do not know whether it is really of any use to advise you."

"Oh, kind old uncle, if you will once more have pity on me and help me to live a better life, this time I positively will not be disobedient," young Chen pleaded.

"Outside the city, not far from the harbor of Lin tsing, lies a small Taoist temple, dedicated to the 'Prince of Ethereal Radiance,' Yen Kung Miao," said the old man as they sat in the warm living room. "It lies in a blessed region, where the cultivation of rice and the breeding of fish flourish, and because of the nearness of the port, with its trade and its traffic, there is much money in circulation. I am on terms of friendship with the Prior of the temple, Master Yen. What if we were to go thither and persuade him to accept you as a novice? Of course, you would have to familiarize yourself with the various duties of a temple servant, but on the whole it would represent an honorable and sufficient livelihood."

"I most gladly agree."

"Good, then we'll go there tomorrow. So come to me again early tomorrow morning."

During the afternoon the kindly old man sent for a tailor and had two Taoist cassocks made for his protégé; he also provided him with a priest's cap, and all the other items of a Taoist priest's equipment. Next morning he made him take a hot bath, dressed him in new clothes from head to foot, gave him an ample breakfast, and set out beside him for the "Temple of the Prince of Ethereal Radiance"; he riding on horseback, while young Chen mounted a mule. Behind them two servants carried a number of presents for the Prior. After a march of seventy *li* they reached the temple as twilight was falling. The old man first asked to see the Prior alone.

"It is a special pretext that brings me here today," he began, after a few preliminary phrases. "I come to plead for the son of my dear old friend, the respected Chen Hung, now dead. The young man is now four and twenty years of age, and is a nice, amiable, talented fellow. But in former years, unhappily, he neglected his studies, and owing to the premature death of both his parents he lacked wise guidance. To this one must add that fate has dealt him a series of blows, by which he has lost the whole of his considerable fortune. In short, he is today absolutely destitute, and without a roof to shelter him. The memory of the old friendship which formerly bound me to his father has induced me to intercede for him, and to appear before your Reverence today with a request that comes from my heart. Would you be disposed to accept the young man as a novice in your temple?"

"Worthy and venerable lay brother, I am of course only too glad to be of service to you. But is the young man in question willing and good-tempered? I have unfortunately had very great trouble with my latest novices, and have often been regrettably angry with them."

"You may be quite easy, Master; he is amiability and good nature incarnate. And then he is so clever and wide-awake. Truly, you will find him a useful assistant."

"Good. When do you think of bringing him here?"

"I have brought him with me now. He is waiting outside the 'Mountain Portal,' guarding a few little presents which I have chosen for you, and which I hope you will accept with a smile of approval."

"But, my honored and reverend lay brother, why this ceremony?"

The Prior sent word for young Chen and the two servants with their load of presents to enter. He read the list of presents: "The old friend Wang Ting Yang bows his head in greeting and at the same time offers, with a heart full of devotion, a bale of coarse satin, a jug of ordinary wine, a couple of hams, two roast ducks, two baskets of fruit, and five silver ounces." His face lit up and he quickly made a profound obeisance.

"Highly respected old lay brother, what superfluously rich presents! Truly, you embarrass me. On the other hand, it would be uncouth to affront you by a refusal."

Meanwhile his eyes rested with satisfaction on the smart and pleasing appearance of the faultlessly dressed novice whom the Apricot Anchorite now introduced to him, and he willingly accepted his graceful, eightfold bow of installation.

"What is the number of your springs?" he inquired.

"Four and twenty."

"Good. I bid you welcome as novice and my new assistant. As your temple name you shall henceforth bear the name of Tsung Mei, 'Offspring of Beauty.'"

He called him thus to match the temple names of his two other assistants, one of whom was called Tsung Ming, "Offspring of Enlightenment," and the other Tsung Shun, "Offspring of Humility."

The ceremony of installation concluded with a substantial feast. Since it was late when they rose from the table, the Apricot Anchorite spent the night in the temple. Next morning, with his two servants, he set out on his homeward journey.

"Now do you behave well, and always obey your master, and be diligent in familiarizing yourself with the temple regulations!" he urged young Chen when he bade him good-by. "I shall come here now and again and ask how you are progressing. Every quarter I will bring you a little clothing and body linen and shoes." And he added, under his breath, "From now on look into yourself, cleanse your heart, and improve yourself! If once again you fail to follow my advice, and commit fresh follies, I shall not trouble to help you in future."

The Prior, despite his spiritual office, was a very worldly gentleman. That he was not averse from the delights of the table, and a drop of good wine, was manifest from his generous girth and the toper's nose that shone red above the thicket of his long gray beard. Yes, he loved a social gathering, and he liked to lead a jolly drinking catch with his jovial, booming bass. So there was a continual coming and going of guests and strangers in his temple. For the recent opening of the Imperial Canal, the "Tribute River," which crossed the River Tsing from north to south with a double lock near the port of Lin tsing, had very considerably augmented the already great water-borne traffic at this point, and the passengers and the crews of the many mandarins' junks and trading vessels which in uninterrupted sequence passed through the locks of Lin tsing rarely failed to take this opportunity of visiting the adjacent "Temple of the Prince of Ethereal Radiance," either that they might sacrifice to the gods and pray for a fortunate voyage, or in order to absolve a pious vow, or because they had good works of some sort in mind.

The visitors belonged to every class of society, from the pampered, aristocratic mandarin to the simple deck hand whose ordinary bed was a rush mat. And none came with empty hands. All brought their tribute of money or victuals. For endless receptions and banquets were given in the temple; the victuals accumulated in the larders, and the silver ingots in the treasury.

Rather than allow his surplus wealth to lie idle, the Prior had opened a rice shop and a money changer's office in the port of Lin tsing; both prosperous businesses which brought him in a very pretty revenue. They were under the supervision of his eldest assistant, the "Offspring of Enlightenment," to whom all the business affairs of the monastery were confided. This assistant, a man of thirty, was apart from his commercial ability a most unprofitable fellow, who preferred to spend his leisure in wineshops and flower gardens. Two neat, clean little temple boys were allotted to him as his personal servants, and with them he was accustomed to share his bed. But now the new novice, with his red lips, his white teeth, his girlishly smooth cheeks, and his well-built figure had impressed him. In short, he so contrived matters that one night he shared his couch with young Chen, after dosing him thoroughly with wine.

773

And young Chen was experienced and crafty enough to exploit the situation to the utmost. First he assumed the defensive, and began to shout. And when the elder man, in alarm, pressed his hand upon his mouth, he said: "I see that you take pleasure in me. Good, you shall have your will. But in return I demand three things."

"If you ask for ten you shall have them all," said the "Offspring of Enlightenment" eagerly.

"Firstly, no one else is to share your bed. Secondly, I want the keys of the temple gate and the larders. Thirdly, I want to go in and out as I please."

"If that's all! You shall have what you want."

With that the pact was concluded. The "Offspring of Enlightenment" did actually give him the keys for which he had asked, and closed his eyes when it pleased young Chen to make a raid on the larders or visit the neighboring city. And he was by no means behind the Prior in his praise of the new novice. In short, before long young Chen had a priest's patent in his pocket, and within the limits of the strict monastic discipline he was able to allow himself all sorts of liberties and lead a most agreeable life. He was on his feet again.

One day he met in Lin tsing an acquaintance who was able to give him news of an old love—of Golden Jewel. After the death of her former mistress she had originally passed into the possession of Mother Cheng's flower garden in Tsing ho hsien, but now she was in Lin tsing, and might be met any day in a large and aristocratic wineshop. Did he want to see her again? Of course he did. Young Chen was still fond of Golden Jewel. So, on the following afternoon, having provided himself with plenty of money from the temple till, he repaired to the wineshop in question, accompanied by his friend. It would have been better for him had he never gone there. For there he was to encounter a cruel adversary, whom he must, one supposes, have wronged in another existence, five centuries ago, and who was now to be his bane.

The wineshop in question was the largest establishment of the kind in Lin tsing. It was pleasantly situated on the side of a hill, and each of its hundred and ten drinking rooms had its own veranda, with a pretty green-lacquered balustrade of carved wood. From these verandas one had a delightful view over the busy Imperial Canal, and the mountain landscape beyond it, fading away into the blue distance.

Young Chen and his companion were in one of the upper rooms when the door opened and Golden Jewel entered, with a small copper gong in her hand. No sooner had she pronounced her *Wan fu* than the tears rose to her eyes, for the sight of young Chen had greatly moved her, and he himself was equally disturbed. He took her by the hand and made her sit down beside him.

"Sister, how have things been going with you since we last saw each other?"

"My flower-garden mother was terribly shocked when I was taken back to her from the District Yamen. She died soon afterwards, and I went to Mother Cheng in Tsing ho hsien. But as there had been too few customers of late she sent me back to Lin tsing, and hired me out by the day to this winehouse. Yesterday I heard from your friend that you had been working here lately in a rice shop and a money changer's office, and that you would be coming here today. So I have reserved my time for you. Oh, how glad I am to see you again!"

Sobbing aloud, she leaned her little head upon his shoulder. He drew a handkerchief from his sleeve and carefully dried her tears. "Dear little sister, all is well now, and I am with you again!" he said consolingly. "Things have gone very badly indeed with me in the meantime, and I have lost the whole of my inheritance. But now, by a stroke of good luck, I have been received into the 'Temple of the Prince of Ethereal Radiance,' and have become a priest of the Tao. I have nothing to complain of nowadays. My Prior gives me his confidence, and I enjoy all sorts of liberties and advantages. I can often come here and be with you. Where do you sleep at night?"

"I have, as I told you, only to wait on the guests here in the daytime. I sleep in the house of the rich alehouse keeper Liu to the west of the canal bridge. A few other singing-girls and flower-maidens who are let out on hire are living there with me."

She was calmer now, and what with the presence of her lover, and the influence of good wine and choice food, with which he generously plied her, she soon became more cheerful. Taking up her *pi pa,* she sang him a little song which she called "Happiness exulting to Heaven." It ran thus:

> *Tears start from the eyes,*
> *From the eyes start tears.*
> *Fill with noble juice three beakers!*
> *Three beakers fill with noble juice!*
> *A phœnix pair must suffer a cruel parting,*
> *A cruel parting must suffer a phœnix pair.*
> *See the slanting rays behind yonder mountain!*
> *Behind yonder mountain see the slanting rays!*
> *Twilight falls over the earth,*
> *Over the earth falls twilight.*
> *Alas, I dread a fresh parting!*
> *A fresh parting I dread, alas!*

Young Chen's companion had quietly crept away. Now Golden Jewel lay upon one couch with her lover, and with him she surrendered herself to the delights of reunion.

CHAPTER FORTY-FIVE: *In the Wine house Master Liu, the "Local Tiger," raves with Anger. Snowblossom, whom Spring Plum finds in the Way, becomes a Singing-girl*

FROM THIS TIME onwards young Chen betook himself every third day to the wine house on the Imperial Canal, in order to be with Golden Jewel. And she counted on his punctual visits. If for once in a way he was unable to come he might be sure that she would immediately send him a love letter, which usually expressed a practical desire of some kind: as that she wanted some firewood, or some rice, or an ounce of pocket money, or money for the rent.

When after such visits he returned to the temple in the evening with wine-flushed cheeks, and the Prior wanted to know where he had been drinking again, he usually alleged that he had emptied a few beakers in the rice shop, in the company of the manager, in order to sweeten the bitterness of destiny. And the "Offspring of Enlightenment" would do his best to protect young Chen and conceal his activities from the Prior. The worthy Prior had no suspicion that in the meantime the hole in the Temple treasury was constantly growing bigger. So far all was well. But one day young Chen was to hasten to his doom.

The aleshop keeper and brothel master Liu, in whose house Golden Jewel was living, and by whom she was hired out, was a brother-in-law of Chang Shong, already known to the worthy reader as a confidential servant in the household of the River Prefect. He had heard, by devious ways, that his pretty tenant, Golden Jewel, had formed a secret and permanent connection with a certain temple priest. This "Local Tiger" was not unjustly so named. He was generally dreaded on account of his brutality, not only by the poor girls who were his tenants, whom he avariciously exploited and maltreated in the most unscrupulous manner, but also by the guests in the wine rooms and flower gardens, with whom he loved to wrangle and brawl on the slightest pretext. He was the true chieftain of all rowdy pimps, the leader of all roisterers and swash-bucklers, and all were most careful to avoid giving him offense. Young Chen knew nothing of all this.

On a certain afternoon he was once more sitting in the wine house on the Imperial Canal, carelessly and merrily drinking and dallying with Golden Jewel, when suddenly the Local Tiger, with rolling eyes and fists as big as plates, came pelting up the stairs and thundered on the locked door of Drinking-room No. 2. As it was not immediately opened he tore down the curtain, and with a few powerful kicks he smashed the panels of the door into splinters. While young Chen was so terrified that he barely ventured to draw a breath through his nostrils, Golden Jewel had so far pulled her-self together that she was able to go up to the infuriated man with a smile, and ask him, gently: "What's the matter, dear Uncle?"

"What are you playing at here?" he snorted. "You damned trol-lop, you owe me three months' rent already! Out with it!"

"Mother Cheng will send you the money today. Please be patient, just a little while, dear Uncle," said Golden Jewel, still concealing her fear beneath an innocent smile.

But at this he seized her by the waist and flung her on the floor so violently that she struck the back of her head heavily against the edge of the step leading up to the veranda, sustaining a wound which began to bleed profusely.

"No more waiting! I'll have my money today, you accursed bag-gage!" he shouted at the girl as she lay on the floor. He then turned to young Chen with a menacing stare. One kick, and the table which stood between them toppled over on its side, while the plates and beakers fell clattering to the floor.

Young Chen felt that he must now or never show his manhood.

"Hey, just who are you that you insolently force your way in here and rave like a savage?" he cried. The words escaped him before he had time to consider what he was saying.

"What! An accursed priest like you dares to crow? I'll teach you to go whoring with women here!" retorted the Local Tiger, foaming with rage.

And already he had seized the other by the topknot, and had thrown him down; and he then began to belabor him with kicks and punches until young Chen lost consciousness. In the meantime the noise had brought the landlord and a number of guests on the scene, who squeezed themselves into the doorway and followed the proceedings, from a safe distance, with a timid gaze. No one ventured to interfere. Only the landlord ventured rather faintly to address the raving man, who was obviously drunk: "Honored Uncle Liu, do not be so angry! The guest didn't know who you were. If he had known whom he had to deal with he would surely have refrained from irritating you with thoughtless words. Please have a little regard for the good name of my house and leave him alone!"

At these words the Local Tiger at last turned away from his victim. Then the police appeared, having in the meantime been informed of what was happening, and led the two sufferers away, bound with the same cord.

Since the incident had occurred in the river and port area, the case came within the competence of the River Prefect Chow. Thus, in the course of the following day young Chen was transferred, together with his fellow prisoner, to the River Prefect's yamen in Tsing ho hsien, on the charge of grossly infringing the sacred rule of the religious order by tippling and whoring. Once again he had to make painful acquaintance with an inhospitable prison cell.

Before he was brought up before the River Prefect the yamen beadles and prison warders paid him a visit, endeavoring, as was their custom when a new prisoner was brought in, to squeeze a little tribute out of him.

"See here, we'd advise you to stand well with us," they told him. "There are twelve of us, and during the trial we have the

pleasant job of applying the torture to you malefactors. You understand? And the two master jailers, Chang Shong and Li An, have
a good deal to say in the matter. You mustn't forget them."

"I understand," young Chen replied, dejectedly. "And I had
money on me, but it was taken from me during the scuffle. And my
coat is torn in two, so that won't be of any use to you. This one
silver brooch is all I have left. Here, take it and give it to the two
master jailers!"

Greatly disappointed, the beadles and warders took the brooch
and went to find the two master jailers. "Here, this is all that he
shelled out. He hasn't a single bit on him," they reported.

"Bring him here!" Chang Shong commanded. "I'll question him."

Young Chen was accordingly dragged along to the master jailers.

"How long have you been in your temple? And what is your lay
name?" Chang Shong inquired.

"My real name is Chen Tsing Ki and I come of an honorable
house. I have only recently been admitted to the temple."

"And how comes it that you, as a member of the priesthood, go
tippling and wenching in wine houses, and creating disorder? Don't
you know the rule of your Order? This will be a bad business for
you. Or do you imagine that our yamen is a thing to play with?
If only you had enough money to improve your position! This
worthless, silver-plated thing here won't set the streams running.
You can keep it."

And turning to the warders, he continued: "Stick the thing in his
topknot again and bring up his case before the Ancient Commander at the very beginning of the session. This scabby dog of a
priest shall learn a lesson! They know how to beg aloud from all
four quarters of the heavens; they know all about fleecing their
benefactors; they know how to gorge and tipple and wench! That's
what their spiritual office amounts to! You just wait, my man, you'll
get a taste of the bamboo rod and the finger press!"

Young Chen's prospects were gloomy in the extreme. For Golden
Jewel matters were much less serious. Mother Cheng had hastily sent
someone from her flower garden, who distributed four ounces be-

tween the master jailers and the beadles. The tone in which Chang Shong now addressed Golden Jewel was much more amiable:

"Your case is less serious; you belong to the class of flower-girls, and are naturally obliged to earn your living in the wine houses. No one can hold that against you. In your case it all depends on the temper of the Ancient Commander. If he's in a bad temper then there'll be a bit of finger squashing. If he's in a good temper he'll let you off altogether."

Soon after this the booming strokes of the cloud gong announced the approach of the Prefect. The higher and lower officials of the yamen quickly took up their position in two rows to the right and the left of the judge's desk, and the session was opened.

There is no true fairy story without a miracle, and no meeting without predestination. Here it must be said in parenthesis that in the eighth month of the previous year Spring Plum had presented her husband the River Prefect with a lively little boy. He was now six months old, and was such a pretty, well-grown child that the River Prefect treasured him as a jewel of inestimable value. In the meantime his First Wife had departed from this world, and in her place Spring Plum was promoted to the rank of principal consort. She had now a handsome suite of five rooms at her disposal, and her domestic staff had been increased by two nurses, two young maids, and two musically trained companions, aged sixteen and seventeen respectively. The favor which she already enjoyed from her husband was greatly increased by the birth of a male child, if such increase indeed was possible. In all things the River Prefect was subservient to her will.

The child had a special affection for the servant and master jailer, Chang Shong, and was enraptured when the latter picked him up in his arms and played with him. Even when the River Prefect was holding a public session, at which Chang Shong's presence was always required, he often took the child with him. Indeed, this had now become a regular habit. On the occasion of the present session too the child was present, nestling quietly and prettily against Chang Shong's breast.

The first case to come up for hearing was that against young Chen and Golden Jewel. The River Prefect's judgment was very quickly delivered.

"Fellow," he said, to the "Offspring of Beauty," who was kneeling before him, "you are, as I perceive from the indictment of the spiritual estate, a member of the Taoist priesthood. You have offended grievously against the discipline of your Order, inasmuch as you are guilty of drinking and wenching and creating an uproar in a public place. I sentence you to twenty strokes, also to the cancelling of your patent of priesthood, and retrogression to the lay status."

Then he turned to Golden Jewel: "In your case I have decided to let you off with fifty squeezes of the finger press. Also you must not return to Lin tsing, but to your original flower garden, which is your proper place."

Sentence was carried out forthwith. While some of the beadles applied the finger press to Golden Jewel as mercifully as possible, others dealt less considerately with young Chen. Laying him with his face to the floor and pulling down his trousers, they bound him, and brought the bamboos whistling down upon him with all their might, uttering savage cries as they did so.

But then—O miracle indeed!—when they had barely started upon their work, suddenly the child in Chang Shong's arms began to whimper loudly, trampling its feet and stretching its little arms towards young Chen as though it was determined to make its way to him. Lest he should draw down upon his head the wrath of the Ancient Commander by allowing a solemn session to be so vexatiously disturbed, Chang Shong hastily slipped out of the session hall with the little cry-baby, and carried him back to his mother in the rear apartments. But the child would not be quieted; he cried louder than ever.

"What is the matter with the child?" inquired Spring Plum in astonishment.

"I took him across to the session hall, where a case was up for hearing. He was perfectly quiet at first, and behaved as nicely as ever. But when sentence was executed on Brother Chen of the 'Temple of the Prince of Ethereal Radiance,' almost before the first blow was struck he began, for no reason at all, to cry and trample with his feet and stretch out his little arms to the condemned man as though he wanted to get away from me and go to him. And even now there's no quieting him."

"Chen?"

Without taking much time to think, Spring Plum rose and hurried away to the openwork screen in the session hall, where she could watch the proceedings in court without being observed. One glance, and in the young priest who writhed groaning on the floor she had indeed recognized the Daughter's Husband. She thereupon sent Chang Shong to the River Prefect, asking him to come to her immediately. The River Prefect, without hesitation, complied with her wish and adjourned the session. The beadles, who had already given young Chen ten strokes, had to hold their hands for the time being.

"What's the matter?" he asked his wife.

"That priest is a cousin of mine on my mother's side. For my sake spare him, I beg you! And I should like to speak to him," she pleaded.

"Why didn't you tell me sooner? Now he's already had half his punishment."

He returned to the session hall and announced briefly: "The prisoner will not be required to undergo the rest of his punishment. The woman is to be taken back to her flower garden."

"Don't let the priest go just yet!" he added quietly, turning to Chang Shong. "My wife wants to speak to him. He is a cousin of hers."

Spring Plum was excitedly waiting in her apartments for the still beloved Son-in-law to appear. Suddenly she sighed profoundly. Snowblossom! She had not at first thought of her. Snowblossom would recognize young Chen and betray the truth to the River Prefect—that he was no cousin of hers, but a former lover. No, it would not do. She must countermand the order which she had just given.

"Tell my cousin I don't find it quite convenient to receive him at the moment," she told Chang Shong. "I will ask him to come and see me later."

Now, however much young Chen might regret that he must for the time being abandon the hope of meeting Spring Plum again, he was thankful to have got off so lightly. His back was already feeling better. The main thing was that they had left him his priest's patent. Cheerful

> *As the fish that escapes the net again,*
> *As the watchdog scouring the open plain,*

he turned his back upon the yamen of the River Prefect and hurried off to his temple.

In the meantime the Prior had already heard of the disagreeable incident which had occurred in the wine house on the Imperial Canal, and had been informed of the consequent imprisonment of the "Offspring of Beauty." The news had shocked the old man profoundly: for one thing, because he found himself so rudely disabused of the limitless confidence which he had reposed in the well-recommended young man, and for another, because he feared that he himself might be dragged into court on a charge of grossly neglecting his duties of supervision. On top of this came the horrid discovery that the temple treasury had been shamefully robbed by his assistants. On account of his corpulence his heart was rather weak. In short, he was not equal to all this excitement; he suffered an apoplectic stroke from which he did not recover. That very night he died, in his sixty-fourth year.

Before the unsuspecting young Chen had reached the temple next day he had already heard of the Prior's death from the inhabitants of the immediate neighborhood.

"It was through you that he met his death," he was told reproachfully. "And in spite of that you will dare to return to the temple? It would be wiser if you were to disappear from this neighborhood altogether."

Young Chen, thoroughly frightened, and burdened with a bad

conscience, followed this advice; he turned about immediately, and hurried off to Tsing ho hsien. Now he was safely back on the old spot.

When Spring Plum resolved to abandon the idea of meeting the friend and comrade of the happy days of old, and to let him go his way, she was obeying the voice of reason, but not the voice of her heart, which grieved over this decision. Unable to suppress her emotion, she sought her bedchamber and flung herself half naked across her bed, where she surrendered herself to her passionate grief, sobbing aloud and clutching convulsively at the bedclothes, or wildly beating her breast. She was still in this condition when the River Prefect found her on returning from the session hall some time later. Greatly perturbed, he begged her to tell him what was the matter, and whether anyone had annoyed her; and as she was obstinately silent he concluded that it must be her sympathy for her cousin that had so excited her; and he blamed himself for the ten strokes to which he had sentenced the poor fellow. Then his wrath was diverted to the master jailers, Chang Shong and Li An.

"Why didn't you tell me in time?" he demanded. "You must be aware that the young priest is a cousin of my wife's! She is quite beside herself at the thought of the cruel treatment which he received. And why did you let him run away? I expressly told you that my wife was most anxious to speak to him."

"By your leave, Ancient Commander," Chang Shong interposed, timidly, "we wanted to take him to the Nai nai, but afterwards the Nai nai countermanded her orders, and told us to send him away after all."

Master Chow did not know what to think. But the two master jailers now went to Spring Plum, and complained that they were in disgrace with the Ancient Commander, simply because they had faithfully carried out her orders, and they implored her to intercede for them with their angry lord.

In the meantime Spring Plum had once more become capable of cool reflection. She meant, in spite of everything, to have her desire, and bring her beloved back. But first one obstacle must be removed: namely, Snowblossom. She had long ago made up her mind. This undesired confidant must under one pretext or another be sent out of the house. She was sorry for the two reprimanded servants, who had to suffer on account of a contradictory order whose motive no one in the house could understand—except Snowblossom. She sent for her husband.

"I suddenly felt ill a little while ago; that is why I said after all that I would not receive my cousin," she quietly explained. "But you mustn't be angry with the two servants on that account; it was not their fault that I was ill. Besides, as a priest my cousin has behaved badly: he may regard it as a punishment if I keep him waiting awhile."

This explanation sounded quite convincing. The River Prefect was relieved, and he was no longer angry with his servants. On the other hand, he sent for a physician, who had to examine the alleged patient.

"She is suffering from a morbid irritability of the six lusts and seven passions and a consequent immoderate pressure on the stomach," was the physician's verdict, and he prescribed a bitter medicine, which Spring Plum naturally did not touch, but angrily threw into the face of the maid who was attending on her. This day she deliberately played the part of the irritable, difficult invalid, sending away whatever food was put before her as unsuitable and badly prepared, and making this the pretext for violent outbursts of anger. In this way she would bring about the desired quarrel with Snowblossom, who was responsible for the kitchen. Late at night she suddenly asked for a savory chicken broth.

"I have quite an appetite for chicken broth," she told the maid Orchid Bud. "Go to the kitchen and tell the person there what I want! But please, it must be highly seasoned, and she mustn't forget the marinated bamboo shoots. And she will kindly wash her paws first, the wretch!"

The maid hurried off to the kitchen and repeated the order to Snowblossom. Snowblossom washed her hands, cleansed her fingernails, and killed two young pullets. She severed the wings, plucked them carefully, and removed the meat, which she cut into small pieces. In making this chicken broth, as her mistress liked it, only the tender meat of the wings of quite young birds could be used. Then she proceeded to boil the meat. As flavoring she poured into the boiling broth two small cupfuls of a sauce consisting of oil, vinegar, salt, and pepper, in which were floating not only the required bamboo shoots, but also onion scales and coriander leaves.

Spring Plum looked at the steaming, aromatic broth which her maid Orchid Bud had served in a handsome red lacquer tureen. She examined it with a distrustful and scrutinizing gaze, holding it close to the lamp. Then she tasted it cautiously, but after the first mouthful she immediately put down her spoon, angrily wrinkling her forehead.

"Poof! This is mere watery soup!" she cried, wrathfully. "The idea of daring to set such insipid stuff in front of me! I suppose you are doing this today with the deliberate intention of annoying me? Take it away!"

The maid hastily carried the tureen back to the kitchen.

"The Nai nai finds that the broth is too flavorless," she told Snowblossom. "She gave me a fine talking-to. Quick, put in some more flavoring!"

Snowblossom imperturbably stirred another cupful of the piquant sauce into the broth. It was now so strong and spicy that even a distant sniff of it tickled the nose. But once again the delicious product of Mistress Snowblossom's kitchen found no favor on the palate of her exacting mistress.

"It's pure brine!" was the indignant verdict; and Spring Plum angrily turned the tureen over, so that the contents fell with a splash on the floor, and the frightened maid received several drops of the hot liquid on her face.

"Go and tell that crazy person that I am most displeased with her, and she must apologize for her miserable cooking," was Spring Plum's order to her maid.

When Mistress Snowblossom learned that she had again failed

to satisfy her mistress she turned sulky, and could not refrain from muttering: "Who on earth does she think she is? No sooner has she jumped up a little than she scolds and pesters her servants to her heart's content!"

Of course, the maid could find nothing better to do than to repeat these words immediately to her mistress, who was already in a sufficiently bad temper. It only wanted this: almost before Spring Plum had heard her to the end her eyebrows went up, her pupils dilated, she gnashed her silvery little teeth as though she would break them, and a dark red flush rose into her cheeks.

"Bring her here, the wretch!" she cried hoarsely.

Three or four maids ran to the kitchen and dragged Snowblossom into her mistress's bedroom. Spring Plum tore the coif from her hair and trampled it underfoot.

"So I've just jumped up a little, have I, you wretched creature? I suppose I counted for nothing in Master Hsi Men's house, eh? I have treated you kindly here, and you repay my kindness by scamping your work and negligence. The broth I ask you to prepare is either too inspid or too salt. And on top of that you take the liberty of making insolent remarks. I can't keep such a cook in my household."

She sent for her husband, and asked him to have Snowblossom taken into the courtyard. There she must be made to kneel; her clothes must be torn from her body, and she must be given thirty strokes on the naked body. At a sign from the River Prefect, Chang Shong and Li An seized the unfortunate woman and dragged her out into the dark courtyard, where she was forced to kneel. The thrashing was to be administered by the light of lanterns. The heavy bamboo cudgels were on the point of swishing down upon their victim. But Snowblossom, moved by a sense of modesty, protested against baring her body, and the servants could not at first bring themselves to undress her by force. Master Chow's Second Wife took advantage of this hesitation: moved by compassion, she addressed the infuriated First Wife in a conciliatory tone:

"Big Nai nai, you can chastise her as much as you like, but do spare her the shame of having to undress before the servants," she pleaded urgently. "You go too far in your severity. And it isn't like the Ancient Commander's way."

It was the fact that Master Chow also felt that Spring Plum's orders were unpleasantly harsh, but he did not dare to oppose them openly lest he should still further irritate her.

"What, are you too siding against me now?" shouted Spring Plum, to the consternation of the Second. "Do you want to drive me absolutely frantic? I'll dash the child to the ground and hang myself!"

And in order to show that her threat was serious, she flung herself down and banged her head upon the floor until she fell unconscious. Master Chow sprang forward in dismay and carefully lifted her in his arms.

"You shall have your way," he told her when she had recovered consciousness. And so poor Snowblossom had to suffer herself to be stripped by the hands of the servants, who laid her face downwards on the ground, and brought the heavy bamboo cudgel smacking down on her buttocks thirty times in succession. In the meantime the go-between Mother Pi had been sent for. Wretched and exhausted as she was, the pitiful victim was taken away by Mother Pi that very night.

"I am asking only eight ounces for this wretched creature," Spring Plum had secretly whispered to Mother Pi. "But do this to please me—sell her, whatever happens, to a public establishment! If you should oppose my wishes and find her a husband, you are done with as far as I am concerned; you needn't show yourself here again!"

"How should I wish to quarrel with my Nai nai! You can rely on me!" Mother Pi had promised. So that night Snowblossom enjoyed Mother Pi's hospitality.

"Dry your tears and make up your mind to put up with this little misfortune!" said the go-between consolingly. "The Ancient Commander has nothing whatever against you. It's only the Nai nai who seems to harbor some old grudge against you. And he's too weak to oppose her now that she has given him an heir. But all will be well yet."

Snowblossom wiped her tears away. "Thank you, Mother Pi. I hope you will find me a nice home where I shall get enough to eat."

"Don't you worry. It's true she wanted me to sell you to a place of public resort. But how could I be so unscrupulous? I'll see that you go to a respectable widower, or a widow of independent means, so that your livelihood will be assured."

"A thousand thanks!"

Two days later Mother Pi's neighbor, Mistress Chang, called upon her.

"Sister-in-law, what sort of a woman is this who is living with you now?" she asked. "She must be very unhappy. I can hear her through the wall at night, sobbing in the most heart-rending manner."

"She has cause to weep. Hitherto she has lived a sheltered life in a large, aristocratic household, and she has recently had to leave it in disgrace on account of a quarrel with her mistress. I have been commissioned to find a home for her elsewhere. She would like to go to the house of a nice widower."

"Indeed? Then I know of someone. He is a cotton dealer of my acquaintance from the provinces, who always comes to see me when he is passing through here on the way to Lin tsing with his wagons of cotton. He is thirty-seven years of age. As a matter of fact, he is here again today. And he told me recently that he lost his wife six months ago, and is very anxious to marry again, so that his old mother, who is seventy, shall not be without help. As far as I can see, the little woman who is staying with you now would suit him in respect of age."

"Why, yes, she is just thirty-five. And she comes of very good family, and is excellent at all kinds of housework, especially cooking. I ought not to let her go under thirty ounces."

"Has she any sort of dowry?"

"Only her dress, her underclothing, and the ornaments which she is now wearing; she wasn't allowed to take more with her."

"Indeed! Well, I'll speak to the gentleman—Fan, he's called. He can look at her for himself; perhaps she'll suit him."

On the following afternoon Neighbor Chang called again upon Mother Pi, accompanied by the alleged cotton dealer Fan. He was satisfied with Snowblossom, and acquired her, after a little haggling, for the price of twenty-five ounces, not including the go-between's fee of one ounce, which he agreed to pay Mother Pi. Next morning Mother Pi went to Spring Plum and paid her the eight ounces which the latter had asked, showing her the written agreement of sale, having first got a scribe to alter the figures accordingly.

"She is entering a house of public resort," Mother Pi added. The whole story of the alleged widower and cotton dealer was in truth a mere trick which she had devised in collusion with Neighbor Chang. The Master Fan in question was a common procurer. That very day Snowblossom was removed by her pretended wooer, who took her, first of all, to the house next door, where at night a mock marriage was celebrated. At early dawn she was ruthlessly dragged out of bed, bundled into a cart, and taken to the port of Lin tsing. It was nearly dark when they got there, and the cart stopped before a handsome house not far from the Imperial Canal.

When Snowblossom was received, in the room to which she was taken, by a dubious-looking old man of sixty, and a conspicuously painted and powdered young person who greeted her—as did her companion—with a curtsy; and when she saw, hanging on the wall beside the kang, a flute, a little gong, and a *pi pa,* and heard the music and the laughter proceeding from all the neighboring rooms, she realized, to her terror, that she was the victim of a treacherous trick, and that she had been conveyed by a procurer to a house of public resort. And the proprietor of this house was the alehouse keeper and whoremaster Liu, the "Local Tiger."

Now, Snowblossom was given little time to bewail her situation or indulge in fruitless reflection. By a few brutal cuffs her seducer recalled her to the crude reality, and she had to school her fingers, which had hitherto dealt only with cooking pots and kitchen knives, to spread themselves nimbly across the catgut strings and feel their way up and down the slender shaft of the flute. After a few days of scanty rations, plentiful blows, and strenuous music lessons, the old man dressed her in fine clothes, when she was exhibited outside the front door and in the street, and required to entice the male passers-by, as a flower-girl must, with wooing glances and inviting smiles.

One day the brother-in-law of the Local Tiger, the River Prefect's servant and master jailer, came to the house as a customer. He had been sent to Lin tsing by his master to buy a bushel of barm, to be used for the making of homemade wine. The Local Tiger, out of compliment to his brother-in-law, had a sumptuous meal served to him in the best room in the house.

"And which girls would the gentleman desire for the entertainment of his guest?" the manager asked the Local Tiger.

The Local Tiger named four girls, among them "Diamond Daughter." This was Snowblossom's flower-garden name. Chang Shong could not believe his eyes when amidst the powdered, giggling company that entered the room he discovered Snowblossom, his master's late cook, who had recently been turned out of the house. Snowblossom, too, had recognized him, but like himself, she gave no sign of recognition. Not until all were slightly intoxicated did he manage, without attracting attention, to draw her into conversation.

"Aren't you Snowblossom? How do you come to be here?" he asked her quietly.

Her eyes filled with tears. "Mother Pi betrayed me; sne pretended she was going to marry me to a widower, but in reality he was a procurer, who bought me for twenty-five ounces and dragged me here. Now I have to wait on the guests and laugh and sing for money, even when in my heart I am nearer weeping."

Chang Shong had always felt a liking for Snowblossom. Now he refused to let her leave him. She had to sing a little song for him, accompanying herself on her *pi pa,* and help him to empty beaker upon beaker, and at night, after the rest of the company had withdrawn, she shared her couch with him.

> *Wine, Women, Gold: three things are they*
> *On which the judgment goes astray.*

That night the two tumbled upon their couch as happily as little fishes in the water, and swore inviolable oaths of mutual love and fidelity. Next morning, when he left her, he gave her three ounces, promising to come again before long. He earnestly enjoined the Local Tiger that Snowblossom was to be treated with special consideration, and shielded from all disgrace. After this Snowblossom enjoyed a position of privilege; she had to pay no tithes, and in return for a fixed monthly payment of a few ounces, which Chang Shong punctually remitted, she was not required to surrender herself to any other man.

CHAPTER FORTY-SIX: *Spring Plum returns to her old Home. A faithless Friend shows his wolfish Face*

ONE DAY ABOUT the middle of the twelfth month Spring Plum said to her husband: "It will soon be the third anniversary of the day on which Hsi Men died and his little boy was born. In commemoration of the day I should like to send a few trifles to Moon Lady's house, so that she will not think me lacking in piety."

The River Prefect agreed that she should do so, and sent a servant to Hsi Men's house with a jug of good wine and a tray of sacrificial viands. In response Tai A brought a card of invitation for Spring Plum. It read:

"To the noble and virtuous wife of the River Prefect Chow. With sincere gratitude I acknowledge the receipt of your generous present. I have taken the liberty of preparing a sorry dish of turnips in order to show my appreciation of the attention, far beyond my deserts, which you have shown me. I should think myself happy if my heart-felt hope were fulfilled, and if your lofty palanquin of state did not disdain to call a halt at my humble threshold.

"Greeting you in due respect
Hsi Men's widow, born Wu."

Spring Plum, on her visit to Hsi Men's house, found many changes. The veteran servant Lai Chow was dead; his wife, I Chang Tsing, had gone away with her boy Iron Bolt and had married again. The maid Apricot Blossom had been received as a novice in Sister Wang's convent. The servant Lai Hsing had been left a widower, and had been obliged to marry the nurse Ju I. And the maid Little Jewel had become the wife of the groom Tai A. The gatekeeper Ping An, however, when his colleague Tai A, who was two years his junior, not only married a pretty little wife, but gained a handsome dowry, felt that he had been badly treated, and in his chagrin he stole a valuable gold ornament from the pawnshop, and made off with it. When the owner of the ornament wanted to redeem it, and it came out that the thing had disappeared, there was a scandal and a lawsuit, and in order to avoid any further unpleasantness, Moon Lady had closed the pawnshop. Of Hsi Men's many enterprises only the dispensary survived.

Spring Plum felt very melancholy when she saw the old familiar places after so long an absence; and when she entered Moon Lady's warm, comfortable apartments, and found herself confronted by Hsi Men's soul tablet, she could not repress a few tears. Reverently she bowed before the tablet, burned a little spirit money, and stood there awhile, absorbed in silent memories of the dead.

After she had enjoyed the "sorry dish of turnips" in company with Moon Lady and her sister-in-law Wu—the "dish" was in reality a banquet of sixteen choice courses—she felt a longing to visit the pavilion in which she had shared the joys and griefs of so many years with Gold Lotus. "Nai nai," she begged, "be so kind as to let me see the park once more, and the belvedere, and the home of my dead mistress."

It was evident that Moon Lady was embarrassed by her request.

"Sister, do you really want to go there? It looks wretched and desolate now. Since Hsi Men's death no gardener has set foot in it, to keep it in order. It has all run wild, and everything is dilapidated. I had so many other things to think about."

"It doesn't matter. It is just that I must see the dear old places once more."

Moon Lady finally yielded to her urging. She gave the maid Little Jewel the keys of the park gates, and the three of them—for Sister-in-law Wu joined them—entered the park. But how its appearance had changed in the interval! On the walls and buildings the many-colored stucco had faded, and in some places had fallen away, so that the bare stone was uncovered, overgrown here and there with moss. The marble flags and blocks of the steps and terraces had become displaced, and had sunk unevenly into the ground, so that gaping crevices were formed, in which the weeds were flourishing. On the roofs the shingles had split or become dislodged, making way for a vigorous green growth. The precious stones and minerals on the banks of the lake were overcast with a crust of dirt, and had lost their luster. The woven cane of the wicker furniture in the pavilions was torn and hanging in shreds. The entrance of the grotto was overhung with dense gray cobwebs. The fishponds had become the abode of frogs. The "Pavilion of Cloudy Repose," was now the lair of foxes. The "Grotto of Hidden Spring" was swarming with philoprogenitive rats.

Spring Plum beheld all this with silent grief. Now they had reached the pavilion of the Sixth. Here too was decay wherever the eye turned. Upstairs was some broken lumber; downstairs the emptiness of dusty rooms. The forecourt was full of weeds and thistles. A few steps further, and with a sigh Spring Plum entered what had once been her home. In the store room upstairs there were still a few forgotten boxes containing drugs. On the ground floor nothing remained but a couple of old chests of drawers.

"Where is the bed with the snail-pattern decorations that the Fifth admired so?" asked Spring Plum.

"It was given to Jade Fountain as a wedding present," she was told.

"A pity. I would gladly have given thirty or forty ounces for it, as a souvenir of my former mistress."

"If I had only known . . ." said Moon Lady, in a tone of slightly embarrassed apology.

"And the bed of the Sixth? It was just like the other."

"Sold."

"A pity."

"Yes, since Hsi Men's death I have, unfortunately, to think of money. The household hasn't the income it formerly enjoyed."

A shadow had fallen upon Spring Plum's mood. And later on,

when the meal was continued, and the two singing-girls whom Moon Lady had engaged to entertain them had sung their songs to the accompaniment of their lutes, her cheerful spirits did not revive. She returned home from this visit in a mood of dejection. And she was tormented by her anxiety in respect of the son-in-law. Where could he be, the man whom her child, at the time of the trial, had seemed, by instinct, to recognize as his father?"

"Darling, I am sure you are worrying about your cousin," said the River Prefect, who noticed her depression. "I will have another search made for him."

And he sent for his two confidential servants, Chang Shong and Li An.

"I told you to bring your Nai nai's cousin here. Why have you not obeyed?" he asked, in an angry tone.

"We have made inquiries for him in vain. He did not return to his temple. No one knows where he is."

"Bring him here within five days, or it will go ill with you!"

In dismay they heard this stern command, and resumed the search with redoubled zeal.

Young Chen, who on receiving the dreadful news of his Prior's sudden death had not dared to return to the temple, wandered aimlessly for a time about the streets and lanes of Tsing ho hsien, and finally landed once more in the asylum for the homeless, resuming his old life as a beggar.

In the street one day he ran across his disloyal friend and former manager Yang. Dressed like a coxcomb, he was sitting, with a puffed-up look, on the saddle of a mule whose bridle was heavy with silver. A groom followed him. "At last I've caught you!" thought young Chen, and quickly snatching at the cheekstrap of the mule he brought it to a standstill.

"Hey, Brother Yang, where have you been all this time?" he cried to his false friend. "And what has become of my shipload of silk that you robbed me of in Tsing kiang? Not long ago, when I innocently knocked at your door and asked for news of you, your brother raged at me finely; he threw stones at me and threatened me with violence. What does this mean? Don't you see to what I have been reduced by your guilt—how I stand here naked and unwashed for very poverty?"

Yang, inspecting the ragged fellow before him with disdainful eyes, gave a mocking laugh.

"May the plague take you, you damned, starveling specter!" he shouted. "What are you dreaming of, to bar my way like this, and what is this fairy tale of a stolen cargo of silk? Make way at once, or you'll have a taste of my whip!"

"Have you no compassion on me, then?" cried young Chen, despairingly. "If you won't surrender any of your wealth to me, let us at least go somewhere where we can talk undisturbed!"

"What is this nonsense?" shouted the other, angrily, as he leaped from the saddle and dealt poor Chen a few slashing blows with his whip. Then he cried to his groom. "Hey, clear this damned beggar out of the way!" At this the groom struck young Chen such a violent blow in the chest that he had to release the cheek-strap, staggering away with a groan, while Yang helped him on with a kick. Yang was about to remount when there emerged from the crowd of onlookers, which had rapidly assembled, a homely-looking man, who placed himself, broad and powerful, in his way. He was a tall, strong fellow. As headgear he wore a piece of blue sackcloth wound about his topknot. He was wearing a coarse brown smock and dirty, light-colored drill trousers; on his feet he had plain bast shoes. An untended, three-pointed beard hung over his mighty chest. From the red, weather-beaten, four-square face a pair of bright, dauntless eyes looked out from beneath bushy eyebrows. His fists, on which the swollen veins stood out, were clenched in menace, and advancing them towards the dismayed Yang in a manner not to be misunderstood, he spoke as follows: "Hey, my friend, why do you ill-treat the poor young fellow? He has done nothing to you. That is not decent behavior! Give him some money rather! After all, you used to know him. But even if you don't want to give him anything, you needn't on that account strike him."

798

"You don't know the facts of the case," Yang protested. "He accuses me falsely of stealing a shipload of silk from him. Just look at him! How could such a poor devil come by a shipload of silk?"

"Why not? He looks to me quite as if he had seen better days and was a man of good family. Who knows how he came to be a beggar? One can't look into that just now. At all events, you're a wealthy fellow, and if you take my advice you won't delay any longer—you'll shell out a few bits so that he can get a bite of food!"

The intimidated Yang decided to take his advice. Muttering, he pulled out a five-bit piece, which he gave young Chen. He even went so far as to raise his hands and vouchsafe the unknown stranger a cursory greeting; then he regained the saddle unhindered and went his way. When he had gone young Chen hastened to thank this valiant helper in his need. He had recognized him as a former comrade of the asylum, known as the "Flying Devil," a foreman mason by trade, who during a period of unemployment had shared a mat with him in the "cold shed." Recently things had been going well with the "Flying Devil"; he was in charge of the erection of a large new building in the "Water-Moon Temple" outside the Southern Gate, where he had to act as overseer to fifty workmen. With a jovial laugh he shook young Chen by the hand.

"Well, brother, that came off all right! But if I hadn't spoken my mind to the fellow you would hardly have got your half-ounce! What a rascal! Well, he showed sense in the end. That was just as well for him, or he would have learned something about the strength of a workman's fists! But now we'll drink to our reunion!"

He led the way to a little tavern, smelling gloriously of garlic and onions, where he ordered two jugs of wine, four plates of meat and vegetables, and a huge dish of noodles boiled in stock. His famishing guest ate with relish, and they drank their wine, not out of the usual small beakers, but out of large porcelain bowls.

"I have a proposal to make to you, brother," said the "Flying Devil" as they sat talking. "You needn't go back to your 'cold shed.' Tonight I'll take you to my inn, and tomorrow you'll come out to the building. I've got a big contract from the 'Water-Moon Temple' outside the Southern Gate; I have a gang of fifty men under me. We are to build a hall of meditation and two side wings with monastic cells. A fine job. I can make use of you there. Of course, I shan't expect you to do heavy work, but you can very well carry a little earth and sand, and by that you can earn your half-bit daily. At night I can put you up out there in my barrack. Well, does my proposal suit you? Isn't it better than begging and sleeping in the asylum?"

"Big brother, if you will really take me on I will willingly set to work. How long will the job last?"

"Probably ten months yet. We began only a month ago."

"Then I should be out of the reach of poverty for some time to come. I can't tell you how grateful I am."

Smiling, the older man pressed his hand; then he paid the account for both, and took his protégé to his inn.

Early next morning they passed through the gate. First of all young Chen was taken to see the barrack in front of the temple, where he was to live in future. It was rather close quarters, but otherwise quite habitable; it had a heated kang, a brazier, a hearth, cooking utensils, and a well-stocked larder. Then the "Flying Devil" led young Chen to the site of the building in the temple precincts, and introduced him to his workmen as a new colleague. At first, of course, the workmen could not refrain from making fun of the "pretty little fellow" with the refined, girlish face, who did not look in the least capable of heavy manual labor, and some of their jests were coarse enough; but after the "Flying Devil" had given them a dressing-down they held their tongues, and went quietly about their work as before: one excavating soil, another carrying burdens, a third stirring mortar, and a fourth chiseling at a block of stone and rough-hewing the figures of gods.

A month had gone by. Young Chen had long grown used to his new environment, and his fellow-workmen had become accustomed to regarding him as one of themselves. One morning he was at work as usual, carrying excavated soil to a dump outside the temple precincts. Tired with all the running about and carrying he was indulging in a brief rest, squatting down in a sunny corner by the outer wall, not far from the temple gate, where the sun shone warmly on his naked torso. To pass the time he hunted the fleas which had made themselves at home on his body. While he was thus sitting comfortably in the sun and catching fleas, he noticed a single rider traveling along the highway. He was dressed in a tight-fitting blue tunic; a red sash was wound about his hips, and the swastika sign on his cap showed that he belonged to some yamen. In his hand he was holding a bunch of freshly-plucked begonias. He was about to ride past, but on catching sight of the half-naked, flea-catching coolie squatting by the wall he suddenly reined in his mount. With one leap he was out of the saddle, and with a profound and polite obeisance he approached the astonished young Chen.

"So one finds you here!" he cried, and his face was beaming with delight. "What a hunt we've had—we've been looking for you everywhere!"

Young Chen politely responded to his greeting. "May I ask who you are and where you come from?"

"But Master Brother-in-law, I am the master jailer Chang Shong from the yamen of the River Prefect Chow! Don't you remember me from the time when you had that stupid trouble on account of which you had to come to us in the yamen? You are the worthy cousin of our Nai nai! The Nai nai was quite inconsolable when you disappeared; she has had search made for you everywhere. We have to take you to her directly we find you. Today, so it happened, I had to go at her request to the Prefect's country seat, which is not far from here, in order to bring her some fresh begonias. What a lucky chance that I have found you here! But now, be quick, there's no time for hesitating! Please ride my horse; I'll walk beside you."

Young Chen had hardly time to bid farewell to the "Flying Devil" and his fellow workmen, who crowded about him, gaping, before his captor had lifted him into the saddle, when he made off with long strides, leading the horse by the bridle. The workmen stretched their necks and opened their mouths; they were beside themselves with astonishment on discovering that "the little fellow" had such exalted connections.

> *The foulest grit may hide the finest jade;*
> *In mud a golden nugget may be laid;*
> *A noble youth is hid where none would heed him,*
> *Yet Heaven's envoys to the ninth sphere lead him.*

CHAPTER FORTY-SEVEN: *The false Cousins now secretly resume the old Phœnix Relation. In Lin tsing young Chen meets Acquaintances of former Days*

O N ARRIVING at the yamen of the River Prefect young Chen, at Spring Plum's request, had to get into a tub of scented water and undergo a thorough cleansing. He was then clad from top to toe in clean underlinen and new clothes. After his outer man had thus been given a seemly appearance, he was led into the presence of the mistress of the household. It was early as yet, and the Prefect was still presiding in court. Spring Plum had made a careful toilet in her visitor's honor. Although their greeting was restricted to the prescribed ceremonial forms, while their conversation began in a quite conventional manner, touching upon the weather and other general topics, each was conscious of the other's repressed emotion, and there was a gleam of tears in the eyes of each.

Spring Plum, who feared that she might at any moment be surprised by her husband, thought it better to break the bonds of convention without delay, and to take certain measures of precaution.

"If he comes to you afterwards and questions you, tell him you are a cousin of mine on the mother's side," she hastily whispered. "I am a year older than you; that is, five and twenty, born on the twenty-fifth day of the fourth month, at the hour of the Bull. Do you understand?"

"I understand."

"When I told my husband that you were my cousin he was terribly sorry that you were so badly treated. We would so gladly have had you to stay with us then, but it wasn't possible while that wretched maid Snowblossom was in the house. Do you understand? Well, I managed to get her out of the house soon after that, but in the meantime you had disappeared, no one knew where. What trouble my husband has taken to find you! Who would ever have imagined that you were hiding among the builder's workmen in a temple outside the city? And however did you manage to become a priest?"

Young Chen told her all that had happened to him, concluding with the words: "Well, that is my long story. And it is you I have to thank, beloved sister, for the fact that I have at last escaped from my misery! Oh, if you only knew how the dear sight of you comforts me! It is as though I had risen from the dead: that is how I feel!"

Overcome by emotion, they both broke into loud sobs. But they soon had to recover their composure, for a maid appeared, announcing that the session was ended and that the River Prefect might appear at any moment. Some time later the curtain was pushed aside and the Prefect entered. He greeted young Chen with exquisite courtesy and amiability.

"Noble Cousin, it pains me infinitely to think that recently, in consequence of the heedlessness of my stupid subordinates, you should have suffered such grossly inequitable treatment! I beg that you will not be angry with me on that account!" he began.

"The wrong was entirely on my side," young Chen replied, with a bow. "I had shown myself unworthy of my priestly office, and had brought shame upon the rules of the Holy Order. Now that I am so happy as to meet you face to face I beg for your kindly consideration."

He prostrated himself on the floor and performed a kowtow. The River Prefect gently raised him to his feet, and begged him to take a seat; which young Chen, after protracted refusal, such as courtesy prescribed, very willingly did.

"May I inquire as to your respected age? How comes it that I have not hitherto had the pleasure of making your acquaintance?

And what induced you to renounce the world and become a priest?" the River Prefect inquired, after the first bowl of tea had been emptied.

"I have uselessly squandered four and twenty years, and am a year younger than my cousin," his guest declared, following the instructions which Spring Plum had given him. "She, of course, was born on the twenty-fifth day of the fourth month at the hour of the Bull. Since both my parents were dead, as well as my wife, and since I had lost my whole inheritance by a stroke of ill fortune, I decided to renounce the world and seek admission to the 'Temple of the Prince of Ethereal Radiance.' I did not then know that my cousin was married, and I therefore have to beg that you will excuse me in that I have not hitherto waited upon you."

"Since your sudden departure your cousin has been worrying about you day and night," the River Prefect continued, in a gratified tone. "She never had a peaceful hour. All search for you was in vain. That one of my people should by chance have found you today means indeed that a lucky star has shone upon us, for which we cannot be sufficiently thankful."

Valued reader, you will wonder how it came about that young Chen, since the River Prefect had so often been a guest in the house of his father-in-law Hsi Men, should have remained a complete stranger to him, and should not have been immediately recognized by him.

The fact was that Master Chow had always been to Hsi Men's house in company with other dignitaries, so that although he must have heard of the Son-in-law he had never met him face to face. This explains how it was that he could be deceived by the two lovers, and could really believe his guest to be his wife's cousin, whose acquaintance he had only now made, since he had left the family circle and had become a priest.

In short, the deception was successful. A sumptuous dinner of welcome was given in honor of the young kinsman, and then the kindly Master Chow had a comfortable living room furnished for him in the library of the west wing, for he was to remain as a new member of the household. Spring Plum saw to it herself that he was given a really handsome and comfortable bed with soft pillows and fine sheets, and that he had a sufficient choice of good silk coats, fine body linen, and footwear and so forth. Further, a young lad was to act as his body servant. His meals he was to take in the rear apartments, with his so-called cousin. Young Chen had now bobbed up again, and he felt as happy and secure as in the good old days when he was living in the house of his father-in-law, Hsi Men.

On Spring Plum's birthday, which fell on the twenty-fifth day of the fourth month, Moon Lady did not fail to send her congratulations, together with a few little presents, in charge of her servant Tai A. On the list of presents which Tai A handed to him as he knelt before him the River Prefect read: Two roast geese, four young pullets, a bowl of life noodles, a dish of life peaches, two bowls of fruits and preserves, and a jug of Southern wine. After the Prefect had read the list, Tai A heard him tell one of his servants: "Take this list to my brother-in-law! He must write a letter of thanks, and look out a nice piece of linen and put three silver bits into it, and also divide a hundred copper ingots among the bearers of the gift boxes."

Tai A, having been graciously dismissed, waited awhile in the forecourt for the letter of thanks and his messenger's fee. After some little time he saw a richly-dressed young man come out of a door in the side wing of the house. The young man beckoned to a servant, gave him a letter and a parcel of money, and turned back towards the women's apartments.

"Great heavens!" said Tai A to himself. "Wasn't that our Daughter's Husband? How does he come to be here?"

And still quite dazed with astonishment, he took the letter and the packet of money from the servant and allowed himself to be escorted to the gate.

"Did you see Spring Plum?" asked Moon Lady, on his return.

"I didn't see her, but I saw the Daughter's Husband," he replied.

Moon Lady burst out laughing. "You comical fellow, how can

you call the River Prefect 'the Daughter's Husband?' He is a middle-aged, dignified gentleman! Such a title is no longer suitable in his case."

"I don't mean the Prefect, I mean our Daughter's Husband young Chen," Tai A declared quietly. "When the Prefect had dismissed me, and I was waiting outside in the forecourt for the letter of thanks and my messenger's fee, he came out of a side door in the west wing, gave a servant the letter and the money, and went off in the direction of the women's apartments. Any mistake is out of the question."

"Come, come, you are talking nonsense!" cried Moon Lady, incredulously. "That strayed sheep has long ago sunk into poverty and perished. What would that useless fellow, that beggar, be doing in the house of the River Prefect? How could the River Prefect bear such a man near him? Or can it be that Spring Plum . . . ? No, it's quite unthinkable!"

"If the Nai nai will make a wager with me, I am ready to take it. I'll be burned to ashes on the spot if I didn't really and truly see him!"

"How was he dressed?"

"Irreproachably, from head to foot. Even to the gold brooch in his topknot. And he looked very cheerful and well-fed!"

"I can't believe it."

Tai A's eyes had not deceived him. It was really young Chen whom he saw, who was going to the women's apartments in order to show Spring Plum the list of presents. He found her sitting before the mirror, engaged in powdering her face and painting her eyebrows.

"How comes it that Moon Lady sends you presents?" he inquired.

Spring Plum told him in detail how they had met by chance on Tsing ming day, in the Yung fu se Temple, and how this meeting had brought them closer together; how her husband had subsequently been of service to Moon Lady when she was subjected to unpleasantness in connection with the gold ornament which Ping An had stolen from the pawnshop, and how Spring Plum had been invited by her, Moon Lady, on the anniversary of Hsi Men's death and the birth of his little son, on which occasion she had given the child a ring, and how in this way a friendlier relation had gradually sprung up between the two women.

Her story seemed to displease him.

"Sister, it seems to me that you have a bad memory," he said, as he considered her with a penetrating gaze. "Don't you remember how cruelly this woman tore us three apart—you, me, and Gold Lotus—chased us one after the other out of the house, and drove Sister Five to her death? Never in a thousand years ought you to meet her again! She isn't worthy that you should exchange a word with her. And you have even met her on friendly terms! I don't understand you. If I had been here earlier you would never have acted thus. She is our common enemy. What can Sister Five in the realm of shades be thinking of you?"

Spring Plum was silent awhile. She was embarrassed.

"Let the past be!" she said at last. "I don't want to rake up all these old stories. One must accept her presents today for the sake of appearance. Now she will be expecting that I shall return the compliment and invite her here!"

"That you mustn't do under any circumstances, nor must you visit her again in future!"

"It would be very ill-mannered of me if I didn't. For decency's sake I really must send her an invitation. Whether she comes is her business. If she comes, then you must remain in the library while she is here; of course, you mustn't show yourself. But in order to reassure you, I won't ask her here again in the future."

Young Chen made no reply; he was greatly annoyed. He went back to the front of the house. Spring Plum, however, sent a message to Moon Lady, inviting her to attend her birthday celebrations that day. Moon Lady accepted her invitation, and made her appearance that afternoon, accompanied by her little son, the nurse Ju I, and the groom Tai A.

While the women were sitting over tea and cakes in Spring Plum's apartments, and listening to the performances of a couple of singing-girls, Tai A was enjoying a good meal in a room of the east wing. While he sat feasting there, and looking out of the window from time to time, he noticed a servant, laden with plates and dishes of cakes, crossing the courtyard to the door of the opposite wing. He quickly rose and ran after him.

"For whom are those nice mouthfuls that you are carrying intended?" he asked innocently.

"For our Master Brother-in-law."

"What is your Master Brother-in-law's family name?"

"Chen."

"So I was right!" Tai A told himself, triumphantly. He allowed the servant to proceed, but slowly followed him at a little distance. When the servant had disappeared into the house he quickly crept under the window that was next to the door, and cautiously peeped in through the gauze curtain. Yes, it was really young Chen that he saw, lying on a divan and reading a book. Now he sat up and took his place at the table, on which the servant had placed the dishes and plates that he had brought.

Tai A had seen enough. He left his observation post and hurried back across the courtyard to the servant's room in the opposite wing. On the way home he told Moon Lady what he had seen. She was now convinced, and this was the end of any intercourse between the two houses.

But Spring Plum and young Chen were able, now in her apartments, and now in his room, to go on meeting openly or secretly, and to play undisturbed the part of the amorous phœnix and his mate. The River Prefect's day was largely occupied by his manifold official duties, and he had little time to spare for his family; so the two had many opportunities of engaging in a game of chess, or dining together, or indulging in amorous dalliance, and every kind of pleasurable intercourse. But the much-occupied master of the house must have done a little quiet thinking. One day in the fifth month he spoke to Spring Plum:

"In obedience to the command of the Throne, I have shortly to take the field, with the Prefect of Tsi nan fu, against the rebels of the Liang shan mountain. This business will take me away from home for several months. Do me the kindness of arranging, as quickly as possible, a suitable match for your cousin, so that he no longer remains unmarried. Besides this, I will provide for his advancement, inasmuch as I will include his name in the list of my personal retinue. If the punitive expedition against the rebels meets with success the Throne will not be sparing of acknowledgments and promotions, and then your cousin will probably be granted a title and a little benefice. That will reflect credit upon your family."

Spring Plum acquiesced in his proposal, and soon after he had marched away she sent for the matchmaker Pi. With the assistance of Mother Pi she brought about the desired marriage. Her choice fell on the twenty-year-old daughter of the wealthy silk merchant Lo in the High Street, who met with her approval in every respect, and on the eighth of the sixth month, provided with a marriage portion befitting her position, she made her ceremonial entry into the west wing of the Chow mansion. Spring Plum had shrunk from no expense that would give the wedding a dignity and brilliance corresponding with the high rank of her husband, and she also bought the young couple a little chambermaid. And young Chen had no reason to complain of the pretty, intelligent, and cultivated Tsui Ping, who had now become his "New One." He felt that he was once more raised to the summit of good fortune.

However, his marriage did not in any way interrupt his intimate relations with Spring Plum. She quickly made a friend of the New One; she formed a habit of dining every day in company with her and her husband, and whiling away the time with games and conversation. But apart from this, she was always finding opportunities for being alone and undisturbed with her "Cousin." For in addition to three living rooms in the west wing young Chen had at his disposal a garden pavilion which served him as office. Here, as private secretary, he undertook all sorts of literary work for the River Prefect, and here he was often surprised by her secret visits.

One day at the beginning of the eleventh month the River Prefect returned from his punitive expedition against the Liang shan rebels. The expedition had been successful, the distressed province was liberated, and the Throne had been lavish of its rewards and promotions to higher rank. Among other officers promoted, the River Prefect was created Marshal of the Province of Shantung; while young Chen, his alleged retainer, received the title of Intendant's Secretary, to which a modest but permanent monthly salary was attached. Of course, there were great rejoicings in the house of Chow, and the return of the victor was celebrated by a magnificent banquet. Master Chow was further rejoiced by the attractive addition which his household had received in the person of the young Tsui Ping, and he gave her a handsome dress and ten ounces to buy a piece of jewelry.

"It was rather a costly affair, this marriage," said Spring Plum, reflectively, when she found herself alone with her husband on the evening of his return home, and proceeded to discuss the various household events which had taken place in his absence.

"Oh, the spending of a few ounces will soon be forgotten. After all, he is no stranger to us, but your only near relative. We must put ourselves out a little for your cousin."

"It was very nice of you to help him to obtain a title which will win people's respect. Of course, the income attached to it is a very small one; he and his wife will hardly be able to live on it."

"You are right. I can't really do very much for him just now, for sometime during the next few days I must set out for Tsi nan fu, in order to enter upon my new office there. One had better place a little capital at his disposal, and leave it to him to find a capable manager for some sort of commercial enterprise. After all, he could then pay me a trifle, every fifth day, out of the takings of the business, by way of interest on the loan and amortization. Then there would be some purpose and interest in his life."

Spring Plum quite agreed with him. She waited a few days, until the River Prefect had made the necessary preparations for his removal to Tsi nan fu, and had left the house. Then, when all the household was quiet again, she sent for young Chen, in order that she might consult with him.

"I have been speaking to my husband recently about your future career. He thinks it best that you should enter upon some independent business undertaking, which will bring in enough to provide you and your wife with a livelihood. We are prepared to place the necessary capital at your disposal. You must then find something suitable outside the city, near the port, where there is plenty of money changing hands."

Young Chen delightedly agreed, and immediately began to look about for a manager. One day, as he was scouring the streets of the city on this quest, he happened to meet his good old school friend Lu.

"Where have you been hiding all this time?" his friend inquired, and he made young Chen relate in detail all that had befallen him since their last meeting. With amazement he learned of the various vicissitudes of his lot, which had now flung him to the heights.

"Well, and now you are looking for a manager and a lucrative undertaking? Now, I have a likely proposal to make to you. Look at this Yang, by whom you were so vilely cheated! Today he is the fortunate possessor of a great wine house in the port of Lin tsing. He has an extraordinarily capable manager, Hsia by name. I can tell you, this Yang is making his pile out of it! And that's not wonderful, what with the situation, the crowds of customers, the demand for entertainment and singing-girls! He is making so much that he is able to loan his superfluous money at usurious interest. You have no idea what a magnificent appearance he makes. He wouldn't even recognize fellows like us, his old friends. And his swashbuckling brother, what a dissolute life he leads! Drinking, gambling, getting up cockfights, going out hunting—it's all he does."

"Don't talk to me about that scoundrel! Last year I had the doubtful pleasure of making his acquaintance. I knocked quite inoffensively at his front door and inquired for his elder brother. He bellowed at me and threatened me with violence; indeed, he actually threw stones at me. I can tell you this: I hate them both! I hate them with a hatred that goes to the very marrow of my bones!"

"Come with me to the wineshop over there, and we'll discuss this further," the other proposed, and he led young Chen into a neighboring tavern.

"I understand your justified hatred, and there's an old proverb that says:

> *"Him do I call a proper man*
> *Who hates at times as hate we can.*

"But I'll tell you how you can obtain satisfaction. This incorrigible scoundrel, this Yang, is a fellow to whom you can't talk peaceably. He's the sort of fellow you must threaten with his coffin, or there's nothing to be got out of him. My plan is this: You needn't spend time looking for another concern; you must simply take possession of his business. Present an indictment against him to our District Judge, claiming the value of the cargo which he misappropriated. A claim coming from the yamen of the River Prefect will be sure to produce an impression. He won't be able to pay the amount in cash, so he'll have to surrender his wine house in order to satisfy your claim. In this way you will become the proprietor of a splendid business, which may very well yield even larger profits if you invest a little money in it for purposes of renovation, repainting, refurnishing, and so on. As far as that goes, you'll take over the present manager, Hsia, for he understands his job, and if you make me his assistant you'll have someone you can trust who will keep an eye on him and look after your interests. You need only come every fifth day and examine the books; that's all you will have to do, and I wager you'll pocket your hundred ounces of profit monthly. Well, what do you say?"

"Splendid! It shall be done."

They drank up, and young Chen hurried home in order to discuss the matter immediately with Spring Plum. She too thought the plan a good one, though she doubted whether it were wise to carry it out in the absence of the River Prefect, and whether an indictment would be effective if it were advanced not by the Prefect, but only by young Chen. But the old servant Chow Chung, whom the River Prefect had left behind him as steward—for he had taken the two master jailers, Chang Shong and Li An, to Tsi nan fu—and who was present at the consultation, knew how they should set about the matter.

"The Master Brother-in-law need only write out the text of the indictment; we shall attach to it a card of the Ancient Commander's, and I, his proxy and steward, will bring it before the court. It then looks exactly as though the indictment were issued by the Ancient Commander himself, and there is no doubt that it will make the desired impression."

So it was done, and next morning the steward Chow Chung, in the public session of District Judge Hou's tribunal, entered complaint against the Brothers Yang. The great red card of the mighty River Prefect and Marshal Chow, which accompanied the indictment, did not fail to make its impression on the District Judge. The claim, which was for nine hundred ounces, was therefore admitted, and the immediate execution of judgment was decreed. Master Hou handed his own card to the plaintiff's representative, and graciously requested him to convey his respects to the Nai nai. The case was settled as Chen had hoped, and the money had to be raised immediately.

Not two days had passed before the wine-house proprietor Yang was arrested and imprisoned by the beadles of the District Judge on a charge of fraud, and his brother on a charge of causing bodily injury. To say nothing of the thrashing which they received, they had to surrender all the cash in their possession, which amounted to three hundred and fifty ounces, and to cover the rest of the debt they had to give up the wine house, and their dwelling house in the city, together with all furniture and equipment. At one stroke they were reduced to poverty. Young Chen, on the other hand, had sated his thirst for revenge, and had become the fortunate proprietor of a wine house. He put a little capital into the new undertaking, and had various necessary repairs carried out. The house front was freshly white-washed, the walls were handsomely painted, and the rooms were equipped with new furniture; in short, he did not rest until the whole building, from top to bottom, outside and in, was as good as new. The result was a noble and dignified guest house, of which one could justly say:

Here, when the pitchers are opened, the wine so abundantly flows
That all are drunk in a trice, in the next door houses as well;
When the big tureens are uncovered the savor tickles the nose
So that people for miles around go sniffing the spicy smell.
Here is the place where noble lords of a highborn house
Loosen their girdles of jade and joyfully limber their knees;
Chancellor here and Minister love to sit and carouse,
Discarding their golden sables and draining their cups at ease.

Young Chen, according to his agreement, entrusted the management of the house to his friend Lu and the former manager, Hsia, who had experience of the trade. He himself rode over to Lin tsing only once in five days, to inspect the books and accounts and to draw his profits. The daily turnover reached the more than respectable sum of thirty to fifty ounces. At each of his visits, of course, a sumptuous banquet was given in his honor, and since there were never fewer than four singing-girls engaged, who were chosen for their beauty, it is needless to say who defrayed the cost of the entertainment.

One fine spring day, in the third month, young Chen had once more repaired to his wine house in Lin tsing. The business part of his visit was concluded, and he applied himself to the enjoyment of an excellent meal, feasting his eyes, between the courses, as he leaned against the green-lacquered rail of the veranda, on the magnificent prospect of the smiling spring landscape. As he stood there gazing his eyes lighted by chance on two shabby, insignificant-looking junks which had made fast to the hither bank of the river. He noticed, on the decks, a great quantity of chests and boxes and household gear, which was then being unloaded. Five coolies were unloading the cargoes, and they were actually bringing their burdens into Chen's wine house. The astonished young Chen hurried off to find the manager, Hsia, of whom he demanded, in an angry tone:

"What does this mean? Here are strangers who come and stack their rubbish in my wine house without so much as by your leave—without permission from either you or me!"

"I was just coming to find you, to explain how the matter stands. You anticipated me," the manager replied. "It's a married couple, with their daughter, who have just arrived from the Eastern Capital. Since they have no relations in the place they wanted to stop here for two or three days. The rooms to which their baggage has been taken have very kindly been placed at their disposal by their present tenant, Neighbor Fan. The matter is quite in order."

The two ladies were now approaching. The elder was perhaps thirty-five, the younger might have been twenty. The younger lady came forward and bowed slightly in greeting to Chen, lifting her two wide sleeves to the level of her bosom, grasping the end of the left sleeve in the right hand, and whispering a faint *Wan fu*. Then she spoke. "The gentleman must pardon us for being so bold as to intrude here. There was nothing else to be done. We ought to have given proper notice of our arrival. The oversight is entirely on our part. Your people are not to blame. Pray do not be angry with them! We think of staying here only from three to five days."

Young Chen listened to her apology in silence, staring at the lovely speaker and examining her from head to foot. If he could only remember where he had met her! This voice, this figure was so familiar to him! In the meantime the elder lady had approached him.

"Sir, are you not the Daughter's Husband from the house of Hsi Men?" she inquired, with a scrutinizing gaze.

"I certainly am. But how . . . " he began, in astonishment.

"Don't you recognize us? I am the Sixth Wang, and this is my daughter Darling."

"What brings the ladies here from the Eastern Capital? And where is Han Tao Kwo, your husband?"

"On board one of the junks, where he is supervising the unloading."

Young Chen immediately sent for him, asking him to come ashore. He did so at once. He had aged greatly; his hair and beard were quite gray.

"There have been great changes in the capital," he began, excitedly, after a brief greeting. "On the complaint of Chen Tung, the Chief Secretary and President of the Imperial Princes' Academy, the government has fallen, and both Chancellors, with all their dependents, are in disgrace. They were brought up before the Supreme Court and banished to a pestilential neighborhood; the son of the Left Chancellor, the Minister of Public Worship and Instruction, was beheaded; and all their property was confiscated. Our Intendant Ti was of course involved in his Ancient Commander's disgrace. The three of us escaped just in time, or we too should have been sent into exile. We really meant to go to my younger brother, in Tsing ho hsien, whom I left in charge of my house there. But when we got there he had gone, we don't know where, and the house had been sold. So we decided to turn back and go to some relatives of ours in the South, breaking our journey for a few days only. What a lucky chance, Master Daughter's Husband, that we have met you here! Are you still living in Hsi Men's house?"

Young Chen shook his head.

"No, I left it long ago. I am now living in the house of the River Prefect Chow. I have recently been appointed his Commissariat Secretary. But that is more or less an honorary post. In order to earn a little money I engaged, at his request, a couple of managers, and opened this wine house. Good old acquaintances like yourself are of course heartily welcome. Make yourself thoroughly at home! You are welcome to stay here as long as you please."

The three travelers bowed gratefully. Young Chen thoughtfully provided them with tea and a snack, and also placed a couple of lads at their disposal, who were to help with the unloading of the household gear. Then he took his leave of them, for it was already afternoon, and if he wished to reach the walls of Tsing ho hsien before the gates were shut, he would have to make haste. He did not forget to recommend the travelers to the special care of his manager. But during the homeward ride, and throughout the night, he could think of nothing but the lovely young woman who so justly bore the name of Darling.

Two days later he again made his way to his wine house in Lin tsing. Having concluded his business consultation with his managers, he was just about to inquire after his guests when Han Tao Kwo's old servant Pa Lao appeared, inviting him on behalf of his employers to join them over a cup of tea. He gladly accepted the invitation, and he found it very pleasant to linger awhile with his three guests, talking over the good old days when Hsi Men was still alive. During this conversation glances of silent understanding were constantly exchanged between young Chen and Darling. Then Han Tao Kwo left the room.

"How many springs have you seen?" Darling inquired of young Chen.

"Six and twenty. And you, Sister?"

"Just so many," she replied, with a smile. "Cannot we speak of a miraculous dispensation, that we should meet again here, over a distance of a thousand *li,* after that one brief meeting, years ago, in your father-in-law's house?"

"Ah, yes, I remember, it was when you came to see us with your mother before you left for Kai fong fu."

Now the Sixth Wang also rose to her feet. She felt that the conversation between the two young people was on the point of taking the right turn, and she did not wish to prevent it from doing so. Now they were alone. Young Chen, after all, was no fool, and he had many years' experience of the arts of love, and the right interpretation of mysterious allusions and ambiguous phrases. Presently they were no longer sitting stiffly facing each other, but close together, knee pressed against knee.

"Please," she suddenly begged, "let me just have a look at that fine gold brooch in your topknot."

He was about to remove it, but she, restraining his hand, had herself withdrawn it from his hair.

"Shall we continue our conversation upstairs, in my room, which has a fine veranda?" she asked, with a smile that was full of promise. "I have so many things I want to say to you."

"I shall be delighted."

They went upstairs and into her comfortably furnished room.

"What is it that you want to tell me, Sister?"

"Why, that destiny has made it clear that we are intended for each other. I am longing to taste with you the fleeting delights of a common bed."

"Oh, you darling!"

Nestling closely together, they sank on to the soft divan, and in each of the lovers the flame of passionate desire blazed up. Then she took off her cloths and stretched herself out. After the cloud had poured forth its content, she sat up and returned the brooch to its old place. She became quite matter-of-fact.

"By reason of the overthrow of the government, and our hasty flight, my parents are in some financial difficulty. At the moment five ounces would be a convenience to them. Perhaps you could advance this sum to them?"

"Why, gladly. It shall be done immediately. If you need anything you have only to speak the word."

He drank another bowl of tea with her, then, making the excuse that he had business to attend to, he took his leave.

"And we can count on you this afternoon, quite definitely, can't we?"

He kept his word, and that afternoon he joined the others at the dinner which Han Tao Kwo had ordered in his honor. They dined in the room upstairs with the fine outlook, which was now Darling's room. The two managers, out of politeness, remained only for a little while, and soon after their departure Darling's parents also withdrew to their rooms downstairs. When he was alone with her he gave her the promised five ounces.

"You'll stay the night with me?" she pleaded.

"Yes, I think I will ride home early tomorrow morning. I am not accustomed to drinking so much wine, and I feel rather tired."

She quickly ran downstairs and gave her parents the money. That evening, and half through the night, Darling's room was full of the twittering of swallows and the cries of the golden oriole; oaths high as the mountains and vows deep as the ocean were exchanged, and a bond established indissoluble as that between size and lacquer. While living in the capital, in the house of the Intendant Ti, Darling had had opportunities of completing her education, and of learning to play the *pi pa*. So young Chen's delight and satisfaction knew no bounds. It was as though he had won Gold Lotus over again.

Thoroughly exhausted by the exertions of this night of love, he returned home on the following day. On his tearful departure from Darling he had to promise that he would come again not more than three days later, or at most five. Of course, the marks of a dissipated night did not escape the perspicacious gaze of his wife, and after he had presented his accounts to Spring Plum, and had paid her thirty ounces as interest, he had to listen to a little lecture from his wife. She had no intention of letting him escape again in five days' time, much less in three, but kept him at home for eighteen consecutive days. During this period a servant was sent to Lin tsing in his place, to see how business was progressing, and to receive the cash surplus.

Young Chen's protracted absence caused the Hans no little embarrassment. The five ounces which he had given them were soon spent, and it was necessary to obtain further funds. Now, as luck would have it Han Tao Kwo possessed in the person of his wife a still effective lure for those who were hungry for love. What her ripe beauty might lack in natural charm she was able to make good by art and coquetry. In short, it was not long before she had formed a lasting friendship with one who was truly devoted to her—the wealthy silk merchant Hou from Hu chow—thanks to the kindly intervention of the head waiter. Master Hou was a superior sort of a person, a man in the late 'fifties. He had with him a cargo of silken goods of the value of a thousand ounces, which he wanted to sell in Lin tsing. At first it was thought that Darling would suit him, but Darling, whose thoughts were fixed exclusively on young Chen, could not be persuaded to leave her room upstairs and show herself to the stranger. So the Sixth Wang took the superior Master Hou for herself, and once he had tasted the ripe sweetness of her embraces, he could not tear himself away from her. He made his appearance punctually every other day, and since this had been happening the Hans were always in funds. In the meantime Darling sat in her balcony room and pined with longing for the Daughter's Husband. The days crept by like months, and each of her lonely nights was as long as half a summer. Since her lover would not show himself, she resolved at length to send old Pa Lao to Tsing ho hsien. Pa Lao succeeded in getting hold of young Chen's body servant just as he was leaving the River Prefect's yamen.

"What is your master doing?" he asked, softly. "Why doesn't he come out to Lin tsing any longer?"

"He hasn't been very well lately; that's why he couldn't come." This was all that Pa Lao could elicit from him. On hearing that the Daughter's Husband was unwell Darling decided to remind him of her existence by a little attention. Pa Lao was once more sent into the city; this time he had to take a gift basket with him, whose contents consisted of two hams, two roast ducks, two stewed carp, and various kinds of pastry. The basket was accompanied by a perfume sachet and a letter written by Darling's own hand. But she had impressed it on the old man that he was to give the perfume sachet and the letter only to the Daughter's Husband in person.

So Pa Lao once more took up his seat on the stone bench opposite the gate of the River Prefect's yamen, and waited. At last he saw Chen's body servant come out into the street. He called him and led him to the market street corner.

"I was to bring your master this basket of gifts, and to give him a verbal message. Could you perhaps ask him to come here?"

The lad did as he was asked, and he presently returned, accompanied by the Daughter's Husband.

"Darling sent me here," the messenger told young Chen. "She is anxious about your health, and begs that you will kindly accept these trifles as a token of her thought for you. And she gave me this letter for you."

"How is she?"

"Since you have stopped coming she cannot rest. She sends you many greetings. You are to visit her as soon as possible."

Young Chen opened the letter, and read:

"This insignificant girl, born Han, whose personal name is Darling, lifts her sleeves in greeting and bows before the beloved, the worthy and noble Master Chen.

"Since this girl has no longer been permitted to see your beloved face she has never ceased to think of you and she longs for you incessantly. Remembering your oaths and promises, she leans hopefully against the doorpost and looks for your appearance as though frozen to a block of ice. With great concern she heard from the messenger whom she vainly sent to you yesterday that your precious health was not all that it might be. Since then she has been oppressed by tormenting anxieties; she feels a hopeless void in her bosom, she finds no rest, whether sitting or lying, and she avoids all company. She tells herself that of course her lord has in his own home a beautiful and lovable wife. Why should he waste thought upon this insignificant girl? In sign of her loyal thoughts she sends him these few trifles and hopes that he will receive them with a kindly smile. What she feels for him she cannot, of course, express in words, but the accompanying perfume sachet embroidered with a pair of mandarin ducks, and the inscription worked on the lining, with her own hand, in dark green silk, will give some indication of that feeling.

"Written on the twentieth of the midsummer month by the insignificant girl, who once more sends her greetings,

born Han with the personal name of Darling."

Young Chen opened the red satin pouch and read on the lining, embroidered in threads of dark green silk, the inscription: "Laid at the feet of her beloved, the noble young Master Chen." Touched by the message, he slipped the pouch and the letter into his sleeve pocket. He bade his servant take the messenger to a neighboring tavern and see that he had a snack and a drop of wine. In the meantime he would write a few lines in reply.

"And afterwards, when you take the basket into the house, if my wife asks where it comes from, tell her simply that my business manager in Lin tsing wished to show me a little attention."

He hurried indoors, and presently returned with a letter of reply. This he gave to the messenger, together with a package containing five ounces.

"Here, this is for your little mistress. And give her many greetings. I shall be coming out myself in three days' time, or five at most."

His answering letter, which Darling read that evening by the light of her lamp, ran as follows:

"The loving younger brother
Chen Tsing Ki
bows his head in greeting.

"Beloved!

"You have been so kind as to inquire after me repeatedly and to assure me of your tender cloud-and-rain feelings. I should have hastened to greet you long ago, but alas, I was compelled, as a result of the indisposition of my despicable body, to disappoint your expectation. Now you have today sent me such a generous present. You cannot think how it has rejoiced me, particularly the fine red perfume pouch. In two or three days I hope I shall once more feast upon the sight of you. In the meantime I send you as a small token of my thoughts of you while we are apart an embroidered kerchief and five ounces of white metal.

"Wishing you happiness ten thousand times,
in greeting,
Chen Tsing Ki."

Darling, delighted with this letter, ran off to the Sixth Wang and gave her the five ounces. All her ill-humor had evaporated; and as so often happens when a beloved visitor is expected, joyful anticipation found relief in exhilarating conversation, which continued until late into the night.

CHAPTER FORTY-EIGHT: *The "Local Tiger" raves in his Drunkenness against the Sixth Wang. Chang Shong overhears an insidious Conversation*

YOUNG CHEN had to possess himself in patience for three days longer before he could pay his intended visit. For before he could do so he had to take part in the celebration of Spring Plum's birthday, on the twenty-fifth of the fourth month. But then he said to her: "It is a long while since I have been out to Lin tsing. I feel that I personally ought to take a look at the progress of business. Besides, in this torrid heat it will do me good to cool off a little on the banks of the river."

So early next morning he stepped into the light summer palanquin, since it was too hot for riding, and made his way to Lin tsing, accompanied by his body servant and two of the yamen guards. It was afternoon when he arrived. After a brief consultation with his managers he went straight to his beloved. He found her sitting in her veranda, in the company of the Sixth Wang, writing brush in hand, in the very act of putting on paper a draft version of a love poem.

"What rare guest has the wind wafted hither?" cried the Sixth Wang, greeting him with a smile, but in her words there was a faint undertone of reproach. Before long she rose and left the lovers alone together. It is needless to say that these two young people were as wanton with joy at meeting again as two little fishes merrily splashing in the water, and the amalgamation of size and lacquer could be no more intimate than their tender embraces.

Now Darling drew from under the stone ink palette that lay on the writing table a sheet of flowered paper covered with written characters, which she handed to him that he might read it.

"My work!" she declared proudly. "I wanted to shorten the time of waiting a little. It is to be hoped that it does not offend the critical eye of the noble gentleman!"

He read:

> *Faint I sink upon my bed,*
> *The curtain I can hardly drop,*
> *My hand's too tired to reach my head*
> *And loose the hair knot—let it stop.*
>
> *Why does he send me, waiting here,*
> *Never a word, so quick to say,*
> *When I must think upon my dear*
> *Every hour of night and day?*

A long, tender kiss was his acknowledgment. And now each had much to tell. In the meantime they turned their attention to the wine and the pleasures of a richly supplied table. Ere long the flames of passion were kindled, and equally overcome by the languors of intoxication and by mutual desire, they sank upon the couch in each other's arms. During the days which he had spent at home he had avoided all intercourse with his wife, advancing the pretext of ill-health, so that he had saved all his energies for his beloved. And she, again, had for his sake repressed her womanly desires, and in the long interval of waiting had refrained from male intercourse. Thus their union today was like the refreshing summer rainstorm that patters down upon the thirsting plain. They could not have enough, but continued their amorous play until they were completely exhausted. Since it was a day of scorching heat, it is not surprising that Chen presently fell into a deathlike sleep.

Chance or destiny willed it that at the very time when the two young people upstairs were tasting to the full the delights of reunion, the Sixth Wang, downstairs, was visited by her gentlemanly old lover, the wealthy silk merchant, Hou, from Hu Chow. Han Tao Kwo, having drained a beaker in their company, discreetly withdrew and set out upon an evening stroll through the city. The Sixth Wang was enjoying a most confidential *tête-à-tête* with her friend when all of a sudden the Local Tiger came wildly leaping and storming into young Chen's wine house. He was extremely drunk. For the sake of greater comfort in the prevailing heat he had flung open his tunic, so that his bare brown chest enhanced the savage aspect of his outer man. With rolling eyes and clenched fists he raved like a furious western hurricane through the corridor of the wine house, roaring so loudly that his cries echoed from the walls: "Where is the Southern rascal, that Hou? Out with the fellow!" The two startled managers came running up, seeking by their eager obsequiousness to appease the dreaded Tiger.

"Uncle Liu, Master Hou is not here today," they lied.

Growling, he pushed them away. He knew that he could rely on his eyes and ears which watched and listened for him in every wine house. He was not to be misled; he went raging along the corridor, searching room after room. Now he had come to the living room of Master Han and his wife. Tearing the curtain half aside, he stared with bloodshot eyes through the openwork carving of the door panel. Now he had found the man he wanted. Master Hou was sitting very peacefully shoulder to shoulder with the Sixth Wang, and he was in the act of holding a brimming beaker to her lips.

"Yes," he roared, wrenching the door open, "there they are, the damned dog and his bitch! Hey, my venerable friend, you owe me two months' rent and the money for the two powder-faces you spent the night with in my wine house not so long ago! Instead of whoring here with new women you'd better pay your old debts!"

"Don't excite yourself, Friend Liu!" said Master Hou, seeking to appease him. "The matter shall be settled tomorrow, but please don't disturb me now!" And he attempted to push the Tiger gently through the door. But he had mistaken his man.

"You old liar, now you shall learn what a proper stinger is like!" the Tiger roared, and biff! the other received, full in the face, so violent a blow that the left cheek turned green and blue under the eye. Completely bewildered, he rushed from the room.

Now the Local Tiger turned to his second victim. One kick, and the loaded dinner table overturned on the floor. At this the Sixth Wang could contain herself no longer.

"Hey, who are you, anyhow, you accursed rascal, that you impudently force your way in here and go rampaging about without a shadow of excuse?" she shouted angrily at the Local Tiger. "But you don't know me. I'm not one to be intimidated by a damned blackguard like yourself!"

He straddled before her with a mocking grin.

"And who are you, woman without name, to run a brothel here on your own account? I tell you what, I feel quite an appetite for you! I give you the choice: either you come to me of your own free will, or I denounce you for earning your living by immoral means without a license. Then you'd have the authorities to deal with, and you'll get a thrashing from me as well."

"Who are you, anyhow?" the Sixth Wang retorted angrily. "Who are you, you accursed vagabond and thug, that you should dare to subject a respectable woman to your coarse insults? I am living here with my husband, because we have no relatives in the city. We are respectable citizens, don't forget that!"

And she began to shriek and wail at the top of her voice.

"Take care, you old whore, if you don't want your guts kicked out!" he shouted contemptuously. "It seems you don't realize whom you are dealing with!"

By this time, attracted by the noise, a crowd of guests and passers-by had assembled.

"Mistress Wang, you are a stranger here, so you naturally couldn't know him," someone told her, quietly, with the best intentions. "He's the Local Tiger, the rich wine-house proprietor Liu, the brother-in-law of the master jailer Chang Shong in the yamen of the River Prefect! Be sensible, and don't anger him! He's well known as a woman beater and the terror of the wineshops! Who was so foolish as to get on the wrong side of him?"

828

"You pack of cowards!" she cried, defiantly. "Surely there are still men who are men enough to tackle this accursed rascal!"

Fortunately for her, the two managers had pushed themselves between her and the Local Tiger, and they now gently advised her to make her retreat. But the Sixth Wang could not calmly swallow the Tiger's insults. She suddenly felt that her husband should be at hand to protect her. But Han Tao Kwo was nowhere to be seen. He was amusing himself in the city. Then she felt that she must at all events speak her mind to her daughter and young Chen. So, quite unstrung, and with a face in which the tears that she had shed so abundantly had left little watercourses in its coating of paint and powder, she suddenly appeared in the upstairs balcony room. The lovers, startled out of their sleep by the uproar in the house, had quickly dressed themselves.

"Just think!" she began, in a trembling voice, for she was still gasping for breath, "only this minute some rude fellow, some accursed procurer, forced his way into my room and insulted me in the most unheard-of way, and actually threatened me! People tell me his name is Liu, and he's known as the Local Tiger, and he's a brothel keeper and a brother-in-law of the master jailer Chang Shong in the yamen of the River Prefect. He comes in without the slightest excuse, insults me, throws the table over, and smashes the furniture! What do you think of that? I'm beside myself with anger!"

"Liu the Local Tiger?" Young Chen started as though bitten by a venomous viper. He hastily sent for his managers, and made them tell him exactly what had happened, when he learned of the presence of the silk merchant Hou, which the Sixth Wang had modestly passed over in silence.

"Master Hou owed the Local Tiger a little rent and money for flower-girls. That was what it was about," he was told. "He gave poor Hou a regular stinger. And at that he ran away. The rest you've heard from the lady herself."

"Strange!" thought young Chen. "I myself had a terrible encounter with this fellow, this Local Tiger, when I was still a priest.

It is like a doom; as though a malignant enemy had followed me here, whom I somehow injured during a former existence, and who now means to avenge himself."

It was obvious that this encounter had left him with a considerable respect for his cruel adversary. In a very dejected tone, and not at all as the indignant Sixth Wang had expected, he cautiously inquired whether the fellow was still in the house.

"No. Thanks to our persuasion he has gone away." Young Chen drew a sigh of relief. Now, with a clear conscience, he could play the manly comforter to these terrified women.

"Calm yourselves, good ladies!" he said, turning to the Sixth Wang. "You are perfectly safe in my house. I will take good care that nothing of the kind ever happens again."

This was, of course, the end of their confidential *tête-à-tête*. They were no longer in the mood for such intimacies. Young Chen quickly went through the accounts with his managers, made his farewells, and stepped into his palanquin. He reached Tsing ho hsien as darkness was falling. After he had made a brief report to Spring Plum and paid her the interest on his loan, he laid himself down on his bed, for he was utterly exhausted. But the thought of the malignant enemy from a former life, the brawler who had today crossed his path for the second time, would not leave him and robbed him of his sleep.

After a night of troubled meditation he really felt inclined to go straight to Spring Plum next morning, to tell her the truth and ask her advice. But he decided that he would do so another time. He wanted to take purposeful action, to obtain information which would incriminate both the Local Tiger and his brother-in-law Chang Shong, so that he could give Spring Plum and the River Prefect solid grounds for taking proceedings against them. For he must get them both out of the way. If he were to put only the Local Tiger out of action, he would still have a dangerous enemy in Chang Shong, who one day, perhaps, in order to avenge his brother-in-law, might betray Chen's real origin to the River Prefect.

That would mean the end of his position in the River Prefect's house, and his easy and prosperous life.

Next time he went to Lin tsing he took his two managers and his head waiter aside and pumped them a little. "Has that fellow, the Local Tiger, been here again?" he inquired.

"No, not since the recent incident."

"Do you know anything of an incriminating nature concerning him and his brother-in-law Chang Shong?"

"Well, the Local Tiger is known to everyone as a disreputable bawd and blackmailer. As regards his brother-in-law, he has a permanent affair with Snowblossom, who was his master's cook, and who was dismissed under ignominious circumstances, which isn't, of course, exactly loyal to his employer. At all events, they neither of them do much credit to the River Prefect."

"Good. Thanks."

Young Chen took these statements to heart. Now he had a conclusive reason for taking action against the two men. Spring Plum would be infuriated on learning that Chang Shong was carrying on behind her back with the hated and rejected Snowblossom. Calm and assured, he set off on the homeward journey.

But a doom once predetermined by destiny cannot be delayed by human calculations, however ingenious. In the days of which we write the invasion of the "Golden Horde," the Kin Tartars, had assumed alarming proportions. These wild bands of horsemen were no longer content with raids upon the frontier regions; no, they had recently pushed forward far into the bowels of the Empire. In its consternation the Throne had acquiesced in a shameful peace, and had promised the enemy a yearly tribute of some millions of ounces in gold and silver and silk. Then the reigning Son of Heaven abdicated in favor of his son, who was to reign as the Emperor Kin Tsung. He himself had discarded the title of "Exalted Emperor and Lord of the Great and Noble Way," and had withdrawn to the "Dragon-Energy Palace." His successor summoned to the Court, as the savior of the country in time of need, the valiant Censor, Li Kang, the man whose memorial, written in blood, he had to thank for his accession to the throne, and him he appointed Marshal of the Empire. Li Kang at once took energetic measures of defense against the Tartars, and made warlike preparations in all parts of the Empire.

Among other things, the veteran River Prefect and Provincial Marshal Chow was ordered to secure the Northwestern frontier at Tung chang fu with all available troops against the further advance of the Golden Horde. This meant that Master Chow must hastily break up his establishment in Tsi nan fu and remove to the new headquarters in Tung chang fu. He had sent his two confidential servants and master jailers, Li An and Chang Shong, ahead of him with his personal baggage. They took with them, in a number of carts, in addition to his household gear, a great treasure in gold and silver, which he had amassed during his year's service in Tsi nan fu, and which he did not wish to take with him to the frontier, preferring to leave it in security in Tsing ho hsien.

So one day the two servants, with the transport entrusted to them, arrived at the yamen of the Prefecture in Tsing ho hsien. Here they were to await the arrival of their master, who would follow some days later with his troops, and in the meantime they were to guard the house and courtyard both day and night. For the times were unquiet, and the full treasury might very well attract thieves and robbers.

Young Chen had returned from his last visit to Lin tsing with the firm intention of taking decisive action, in conjunction with Spring Plum, against the two enemies who stood in the way of his happiness. On his return he found that both Li An and Chang Shong had reached the yamen, and that the River Prefect would shortly arrive. So he would not delay action any longer.

It happened that on the following day his wife, Tsui Ping, was visiting her mother, with whom she had intended to stay for several days. That night, therefore, he was alone in his bedroom in the western wing. Spring Plum took this opportunity of stealing off to his room during the night, once again, after long abstention, to share his couch. Young Chen felt that the moment had come when at last, in the silence of the night, he could speak of the matter which he had been pondering for weeks.

"This fellow, this Chang Shong, is becoming more and more intolerable," he said, in the course of conversation with Spring Plum. "That he is always boasting to people that I am in his debt, because it was he who discovered me at the Water-Moon Temple and took me to his mistress, and that he should therefore give himself airs in front of me—that, after all, one could put up with. But he has a most horrible fellow for his brother-in-law—Liu, the Local Tiger he is called—who is a brothel keeper and a bawd and a blackmailer of the very worst kind, and is a positive danger in all the wine houses. He brags of his connection with your husband's yamen, and he recently molested some guests of mine and actually brawled in my own rooms in the most scandalous manner. And the worst of it is that this Chang Shong, as I have learned, has a permanent affair with Snowblossom, that dangerous, intriguing person of whom we have only just managed to rid ourselves.

"I have wanted for a long time to talk this over with you. Hitherto I could never find a convenient opportunity. But now, since your husband will very soon be home, we positively must take action. You must speak to him and see to it that these two pestilent fellows disappear. Otherwise I shan't, in future, dare to enter my own wine house, and shall have to abandon that excellent business. And it is not only my own position that is imperiled; no, but your own also, for you can imagine that you can't expect any kindness from Snowblossom. It is an intolerable thought, that your husband should continue to give his confidence to a man who has a secret relation with your worst enemy."

His allusion to Snowblossom had the anticipated effect.

"As soon as my husband comes home I will speak to him, and that will be the end of these two fellows," she declared, briefly and positively.

Unfortunately, in their zeal the two lovers had forgotten that sometimes walls have ears. They had no suspicion that anyone was listening to them. Chang Shong, on his nightly patrol round the courtyards, was passing, just about this time, that portion of the west wing which was inhabited by young Chen. Suddenly he heard from indoors the unmistakable sounds of a lively dialogue, and creeping under the window in question on his silent felt soles, he plainly distinguished the voices of his mistress and her reputed cousin. At first with superficial curiosity, then with ever-increasing attention and excitement, he listened to every word, and realized what a deadly attack was being hatched against his brother-in-law and himself.

"You wait—I'll steal a march on your nice little plan!" he told himself furiously, as he hurried off to his servant's room. There was no time to be lost. He opened a drawer, took out a dagger, whetted the steel blade, which was slightly rusty, until it was bright and keen, and then, gripping the hilt of the dagger firmly in his right hand, he crept back to the west wing.

Providence willed it that once again Spring Plum should escape death. In the meantime the maid Orchid Bud had hurried to her mistress and had called her to the bedside of her child, who had suddenly become feverish, and could not sleep. So when Chang Shong, with the glittering steel in his hand, forced his way into young Chen's bedroom, he found him alone. Young Chen, at his sudden appearance, threw back the bedclothes in terror.

"Hey, what does this mean?" he shouted at the intruder.

"That I am going to kill you!" came the reply, in a hollow tone. "I heard what you and that woman were saying. You thought to destroy me; now I will destroy you. You owe it to me that I picked you out of the gutter and pulled you out of the mire. And this is how you repay my benefits, you thankless rascal! Once again one sees the truth of the old adage:

"Seek not to save the adder: let it die,
Or it will slay its savior by and by.

And now your last hour has come!"

With menacing tread he approached young Chen's bed, tore the bedclothes, under which his victim had crept in terror, from his naked body, and with all his might he drove the dagger between his ribs. And when he saw that his victim still lived, and writhed in desperation, he drew the dagger out and drove it in again, this time just where the heart lay. Then he cut off the dead man's head. And then all was still on the bloody couch.

> *It is vouchsafed us in a thousand ways*
> *Our span of life breath to expend.*
> *And yet for each there comes the day of days*
> *When all our plans and schemes must end.*

Young Chen was barely six and twenty years of age when he breathed out his young life under the hand of Chang Shong.

Now the murderer wished to deal with Spring Plum also. But in vain he crept behind the bed and searched the neighboring rooms for her. He could not find her. Then he told himself that she must, in the meantime, have gone to her own rooms. And with long strides he went storming along to the women's apartments. There, before the inner gate, he came upon Li An, whose duty it was to guard the gates at night.

"Hey, where are you going?" cried Li An, barring his progress. From his sinister expression, and the thing that he saw glittering in his right hand, Li An foreboded nothing good. Angered by the other's interference, and without deigning to answer him, Chang Shong attempted to proceed. But Li An did not move aside. Then Chang Shong, in a fury, lifted his arm to stab him. But before he could do so Li An, with a kick swift as a lightning flash, and exactly aimed, had struck his right hand. The dagger fell tinkling on the stone flags. Next moment a heavy boot had covered it.

"Old friend, now you see that it was not for nothing that I had the famous fencing master Li Kwei for my uncle!" said Li An, with a cold, mocking smile, to his disarmed opponent. There was a brief and violent struggle. And then Li An, deftly crooking his leg, brought the other to the ground, where he trussed him up with his own rope girdle and rendered him harmless.

The sound of the nocturnal struggle had aroused the rear apartments. Spring Plum came running out, pale and distracted. There was a terrified question in her gaze as it swept over the man lying bound at her feet, and then crept upwards to rest on Li An, who was sullenly standing on guard above him.

"He meant to murder the Nai nai. I was able to catch him just in time," the good man explained, simply. "There is the weapon he was going to kill you with."

Her gaze fastened itself upon the dagger, glittering at her feet in the green moonlight.

"But there's blood on it!" she cried in horror.

Silently Li An pointed to the west wing. Filled with a fore-boding of evil, she hastened thither on winged feet. There she found young Chen lying cold and stiff beside the bed, in a pool of blood. With a shriek she sank on the disheveled couch.

A few days later the River Prefect, on his march to the North-western frontier, paid a short visit to his house. He made short work of the unfaithful servant to whom his wife, beloved above all things, had so nearly fallen a victim. He sentenced him to a hundred blows of the heavy bamboo cudgel. After the hundredth blow the malefactor breathed his last. Then bailiffs were sent to Lin tsing, who arrested the Local Tiger and brought him in chains to the tribunal of the River Prefect. He too was beaten to death. Snowblossom, however, who must have feared lest she might be dragged into court on a charge of aiding and abetting the murderer, put an end to her own life by hanging herself.

The incident caused a great sensation, both in the city and in the surrounding country. The population of Lin tsing sighed with relief, and gave praise to Heaven, through whose mercy they were at last freed from a wicked malefactor and a veritable public nuisance.

The River Prefect attended to various domestic affairs, including the sale of the wine house in Lin tsing and the burial of young Chen in the Yung fu se temple; then he could no longer delay his march to the frontier. For the news from the Northwest sounded more and more menacing; the appeals for help from the frontier were becoming more urgent. On the evening before his departure he once more joined his First and his Second in a solemn toast of farewell. Spring Plum could not utter a single cheerful word. She was disturbed by premonitions of evil.

"Dearest, when shall I see you again?" she asked through her tears. "I don't know why I find it so difficult this time to let you go into battle. Do promise, for my sake, not to imperil yourself too much! These Barbarians, one knows, are like savage beasts."

"Don't worry about me, my dear, and take good care of our child for me!" he said earnestly. "Duty calls me. I must serve the Throne to whom I owe my office and my income. Whether ill hap or good awaits me, whether I live or die; that I leave with confidence to Heaven."

Early next morning he made his farewells and returned to his troops, who lay encamped outside the city walls. And then they were off, by forced marches, to Tung chang fu and the threatened frontier passes.

But now we will speak of Darling. She was completely shattered by the sudden death of young Chen. Her tears flowed both day and night. Now she had only the desire just once to behold his corpse. She insisted that she must go to Tsing ho hsien, to the yamen of the River Prefect. In vain did her parents endeavor to talk her out of this notion. In order to calm her somewhat they sent the servant Pa Lao in her place. He returned with the news that the dead man was already buried, and this in the Yung fu se Temple. Now she insisted upon visiting his grave in the Yung fu se Temple. At last her parents gave way, and in three small palanquins they all set out together one day for the temple of Yung fu se.

The grave was in the further portion of the temple precincts, not far from the spot where Gold Lotus lay buried. Darling threw herself down upon the mound of freshly-turned earth, burned spirit money, and uttered loud cries of mourning for the dead.

"Beloved, I had hoped to grow old and gray beside you, and now you have left me before your time!"

So she cried through her sobs, and in her grief she wept ever more violently, and beat her head so long and so fiercely upon the ground that at last she sank unconscious. While her terrified parents were busy about her, two ladies, with their women servants, had approached the grave unnoticed, for this was the third day after the interment, and Spring Plum had come, together with Chen's young widow, in order to make, according to rite and custom, an offering of fish, pork, and game, and to burn the wonted incense.

With astonishment they noted the group beside the burial mound, in whose midst was a young woman in white mourning. Now the gray-headed man, then the middle-aged woman, turned about and bowed themselves in greeting before Spring Plum. There was a mutual recognition.

"And who is this?" asked Spring Plum, pointing to the younger woman in white mourning who had just opened her eyes.

"Our daughter Darling," Han Tao Kwo explained.

Spring Plum reflected. Of course, she had once seen Darling, years before, in the house of Hsi Men. Now she listened to the older people's story: of the revolution in the Eastern Capital, of their flight back to their home, of their encounter with the Daughter's Husband in Lin tsing, and of his relations with Darling.

"She insisted on visiting his grave and burning a little spirit money for him," Han concluded. In the meantime Darling had recovered. Bowing herself in greeting before the newcomer, she continued her father's narrative.

"Although our relation was ratified by no civil ceremony, yet it was that of husband and wife, as we had sworn unchanging fidelity in oaths high as the mountains and deep as the ocean. In token of which he gave me this kerchief of Suchow lawn and wrote this verse upon it with his own hand. Pray read it, noble lady, lest you should doubt my words."

She spread out the fine lawn kerchief that she had drawn from her sleeve, and handed it to Spring Plum. This is what Spring Plum read:

> *"Kerchief of Suchow lawn, so smooth and fine,*
> *Moist from the brush, this message take for me:*
> *Tell her, Han's little daughter, Darling mine,*
> *A phœnix pair we shall forever be!"*

"There is also a second pledge of our union," Darling continued: "A little perfume pouch, wrought in the shape of a pair of mandarin ducks. He always carried it about with him. On the lining of the pouch the inscription is embroidered: 'Laid at the feet of her beloved, the noble young Master Chen.' "

"Have you seen anything of a perfume pouch?" asked Spring Plum, turning to the young widow Tsui Ping.

"Yes, I found it fastened to the belt of his trousers. I laid it in the coffin with him."

Spring Plum no longer doubted the truth of Darling's statement. She kindly invited her, with her parents, to take some refreshment in the temple. But when the Sixth Wang rose to her feet, saying that it was time to be gone, Darling absolutely refused to accompany her.

"No, I want to stay with you!" she pleaded urgently, falling on her knees before Spring Plum and Tsui Ping. I don't want to go back to Lin tsing with my parents! My place is in the house of my dead beloved; there I will live and mourn him, as befits a faithful widow! And when I die I want to be buried at his side!"

She spoke these words with the utmost passion, and the fountain of her tears gushed forth anew. While Tsui Ping preserved an embarrassed silence, Spring Plum, seized with compassion, gently objected: "Sister, you are still in the green springtide of your life. You will find it hard to endure the strict seclusion of a widow's joyless existence. Do you really wish to renounce the brightness of a new future?"

"Dearest Nai nai, I belong once and for all to him! And though they should tear out my eyes and cut off my nose, I have solemnly promised that I will not belong to any other man."

And turning to her parents: "Go now, go!" she said. "I am remaining with the Nai nai."

"Dear child, your parents had hoped that you would be the comfort of their old age," said the Sixth Wang, reproachfully. "We have saved you from the tiger's lair and the dragon's pool. In return for that will you leave us in the lurch?"

But Darling would not give way.

"I stay!" she declared, positively. "I would rather die than be unfaithful to the dead."

Since her parents realized that further persuasion was useless, they tearfully bade her farewell and entered their palanquins, in which they were carried back to Lin tsing. But Darling followed Spring Plum and Tsui Ping to the yamen of the River Prefect.

CHAPTER FORTY-NINE: *On her wanderings Darling meets her Uncle. A Magician takes Possession of Hsi Men's son*

WHEN HAN TAO KWO and the Sixth Wang returned to Lin tsing without their daughter, they felt as though a mountain on which they had just established themselves had suddenly collapsed beneath them. But what was to be gained by lamentation? They had to live. So it was an occasion for rejoicing when the kindly silk merchant Hou, once he had no longer reason to fear the Local Tiger, immediately reappeared and resumed the old relation with the Sixth Wang. The three lived together so harmoniously that one day Master Hou said to Han Tao Kwo:

"I shall soon have disposed of the rest of my goods, when I shall collect payment. How would this be? Would you two care to follow me to my home in Hu chow? Wouldn't that be better than remaining here and facing an uncertain future?"

Han Tao Kwo joyfully agreed, and a few days later they packed their boxes and boarded a hired junk, and the three of them set out upon their voyage to the South. Darling, on the other hand, had attached herself to Spring Plum, and was now her indispensable companion. Each called the other "Sister." But while Darling had reconciled herself to the widow's life of renunciation, and had no desire for anything else, Spring Plum was consumed by an ever-increasing unrest, by a longing for life. It was not enough that she possessed a surplus of all other earthly blessings, that she feasted every day on the most delectable dishes, that she wore the most costly garments, and could, if she chose, load her tresses with gold and silver and sparkling jewels; all these things did not make her happy. When evening came, when the night fell upon her lonely

pillow, her nature cried aloud for love, and her heart was hot with passionate desire.

Her husband was still campaigning, and young Chen was dead. Now her eyes rested on the faithful Li An. He was a good-looking fellow, and besides, he had saved her life; and how faithfully, by day and night, he guarded the house and its inmates! Did he not deserve her affection?

Late one evening in the eleventh month, when Li An, outstretched on the heated kang in his room, was allowing himself a brief hour's rest from his exacting service as guardian of the house, he heard a faint rapping at the door. He rose and opened it. When he lifted his lamp to light the face of his late visitor he saw that it was the nurse Kin Kwei.

"Well, what brings you here so late?" he asked in surprise.

"I haven't exactly come on my own account. The Nai nai sent me."

"Come in. What does the Nai nai want, then?"

"I was just to see whether you were already asleep. And then"—and she produced a bundle from behind her back—"here, she sends you these two dresses as a present for your mother. She feels that she owes you thanks, because you so faithfully brought the Ancient Commander's treasure chests from Tsi nan fu, and also because you saved the Nai nai from Chang Shong's murderous attack. That's all I was to do."

She was already leaving the room, when in the doorway she turned round again.

"There was something else, something important, which I almost forgot. Here, this pretty silver bar, weighing fifty ounces, is for you yourself! Take it!"

And she was gone. Moved by conflicting emotions, Li An could not sleep that night. Next morning he made the dresses into a bundle and went to see his mother. The silver he left lying in his chest.

As a good, conscientious son he told his mother what had happened overnight, and he begged her to advise him.

"Ei, ei!" sighed the old woman, disapprovingly. "I see nothing good behind this. Such extreme amiability is a momentary whim. You would be setting foot on a perilous path. What if the day came when she found you inconvenient and a burden? Think of Chang Shong, what happened to him? Think a little too of your good old mother, who is already over sixty, and hopes that you will one day be the support of her age! My advice to you would be: don't go back there at all!"

"Well, but if she sends for me?"

"Then you must pretend that you have an illness of some kind: a chill, or influenza."

"But if I don't go back at all I shall be acting unfairly to the Ancient Commander."

"Go to Tsing chow fu and hide for a time with your Uncle Li Kwei! After a few months there you can decide what to do."

Now, Li An, as we have said, was a good, obedient son. He did not return to the yamen of the River Prefect, but packed his bundle and went straight to Tsing chow fu, to his Uncle Li Kwei.

Spring Plum was not a little surprised when Li An failed to return. Three times, five times she sent for him. First she was told that he had the influenza and could not leave his bed. Then, when the messenger asked for ocular evidence, and wanted to see him, he was told that urgent family affairs had compelled Li An to leave for his native place. It may be imagined that his disappearance caused Spring Plum no little vexation.

Light and shade come in swift alternation; days and months flash by quick as a weaver's shuttle. Once again it was the New Year. Marshal Chow felt a longing to have his family beside him, in his headquarters at Tung chang fu, during the New Year festival. He therefore sent a messenger to Tsing ho hsien, who was to escort his First and Second Wives, his two children, their nurses, and the maids, to Tung chang fu. The house was left in the care of his younger brother Chow Hsuen, who generally lived at the country seat, not far from the city. Safe and sound the wives and

843

children and their great baggage train reached the Marshal's head-quarters.

"Why don't I see Li An?" asked the Marshal, in surprise.

"Oh, why do you speak of that useless fellow at all?" said Spring Plum, disparagingly. "I meant to please him, because he had saved me from Chang Shong, so I gave him a few clothes for his mother. For all thanks, while he was guarding the house at night, he made off with a bar of fifty ounces of silver from the inner hall. It was part of the proceeds of the harvest on our estate. I had forgotten to take it to the treasury, and had stupidly left it lying about. Next day, without saying a word, he ran off, and he never came back. When I sent to his mother's house I was first of all told that he was ill and couldn't come, and then that he had been obliged to go to his home on account of urgent family affairs. In the mean-time the stolen money was found in his room. Probably he didn't dare to come back, on account of his guilty conscience."

"How utterly one may be deceived by a man's character!" sighed Master Chow. "This is his gratitude for all the benefits he has re-ceived. Well, I'll get hold of him; I'll send at once to Tsing chow fu and have him arrested."

Spring Plum said nothing about Darling and the meeting at young Chen's grave in the precincts of the Yung fu se temple. Unfortunately the Marshal could devote only a couple of days to his family; then military matters demanded his whole attention. He had to hold a council of war, to inspect the troops, to draw up reports to the Throne, to dispatch couriers—in fact, the Marshal was so overworked that he had barely time to eat, and at night he had time only for sleep, but none for the delights of the curtained bed. In short, Spring Plum was disappointed, and felt that she was being neglected.

In her long hours of leisure she obtained relief in the companion-ship of Chow I, the smart, nineteen-year-old son of the veteran servant Chow Chung. It began with her asking him to do her trifling services, or to chat with her; then she invited him to a game of chess or dominoes, or to take tea or wine with her; and finally he became her secret lover. The much-occupied Master Chow noted nothing of all this. His attention was wholly taken up with war and politics.

These were the stirring days when the Golden Horde was over-running and devastating the Liao Empire on the Northern frontier, and was once more threatening the "Middle Plain." In two columns they came pouring southwards. Chamuho, with a hundred thousand horsemen, thrust across Tai yuen against the Eastern Capital, while a second host, under Kanlipu, made an assault upon the Kao yang Pass on the Northwest frontier of Shantung. The Imperial Marshal Li Kang thereupon sent his "fire alarms" and his "winged messages" to all four quarters of the heavens, summoning the six Northern Provinces of Shantung, Shansi, Honan, Hopei, Kwantung, and Shensi to offer armed resistance to the invader. Marshal Chow was entrusted with the defense of the province of Shantung. He had immediately to break up his camp in Tung chang fu and occupy the threatened Kao yang Pass with all available troops.

Alas, Spring Plum's forebodings of evil were fulfilled.

On a hot day in the first decade of the fifth month, in the midst of a frightful sandstorm, whose yellow swathes concealed the horizon and clouded the vision, the valiant champion engaged in a hand-to-hand contest with the enemy leader Kanlipu. A treacherous arrow, loosed as his enemy lay hidden behind his horse's neck, struck him in the throat, and he fell dead from his horse. Fortunately his followers were at all events able to bring his body out of the melee and bear it to a place of safety. The enemy were already attempting to drag it into their own lines by means of hooks and nooses. He fell in the bloody lists at the age of forty-seven. To him the lines apply:

> *A valiant hero, ever staunch and true,*
> *Selfless he served his Emperor and the land:*
> *Cunning or simple was he? Ask not, you!*
> *With his heart's blood he drenched the desert sand.*

The cries of lamentation rose to the skies from the women's

apartments when the body of the fallen Marshal entered the yamen of Tung chang fu. Spring Plum procured a great double coffin and returned to Tsing ho hsien with the Second and her servants, in order to lay the dead man to rest in the family burial place.

In the meantime, during Spring Plum's absence, Darling and Tsui Ping had been living at home, in strict seclusion, on weak tea and scanty meals, as becomes respectable widows, whiling away their lonely days by diligently plying their needles as they sat in their living room, heedlessly letting the beautiful spring go by. But one fine summer evening they could bear their confinement no longer; so they strolled out into the park, delighting in the flowers and listening to the melodious call of the golden oriole and the twittering of the swallows. The magic of the glorious summer evening had a very different effect on the two young women; while Tsui Ping became perceptibly more cheerful, Darling's spirits, as she thought of her dead lover, sank ever lower and lower, and a feeling of infinite grief and sadness overcame her. The chance appearance of the River Prefect's brother roused her from her melancholy thoughts.

"You ought not to surrender yourself too completely to your grief; you should try to find courage to face life again," he told her, kindly and gently. "But to change the subject, what do you make of the dream which I have now dreamed on several successive nights? I saw a color staff, from the point of which a bow was hanging. Suddenly the staff broke in two across the middle, and the bow fell to the ground. Now, has that a good or an evil significance?"

"Alas, I hope it means nothing bad!" said Darling, full of foreboding. "Perhaps something has befallen your brother on the frontier?"

She had hardly spoken when she saw a man of the Marshal's retinue, dripping with sweat and covered with dust, hastily striding towards her through the park. He was dressed in mourning white!

"Ill tidings!" he cried from afar off. "The Marshal—dead!" And coming nearer, he reported how the hero had fallen in battle in the

Kao yang Pass, on the seventh day of the fifth month. "I have ridden ahead to announce the arrival of the Nai nai. She is bringing the coffin with her."

Presently Spring Plum arrived with her retinue and the coffin, and during the next few days the house was full of the turmoil accompanying the performance of the traditional rites of mourning. It was incumbent upon the dead man's brother to apprise the Throne in person of the heroic death of the head of the family, whereupon the Throne, in a gracious proclamation, bestowed upon the Marshal, in consideration of his self-sacrificing loyalty and devotion, the honor of a State sacrifice, and the posthumous title of Grand Marshal, while his little son received a splendid appanage.

Spring Plum, alas, now showed that she was little worthy of the glory that had fallen upon her house. Her reason quite unsettled by the superfluous wealth in which she was lapped, and which was now at her sole disposal, she began, even during the period of mourning, to lead a life of immoderate luxury and sensuality. By day and by night her favorite, Chow I, the son of old Chow Chung, had to help her to satisfy her prodigious appetite for love, and to forget that her youth was passing. Living such a dissolute life, it was no wonder that she fell a victim to spinal consumption. So rapidly did she waste away that before long she was like a thin, powerless slip of firewood. No wine, no medicine was of any avail. One morning of the sixth month, in a last ecstasy of lust, she breathed out the feeble remnant of her life-breath in the arms of her lover. She was nine and twenty years of age.

When her lover realized that she was no longer breathing he bent greedily over her chests, and with both hands he stuffed into his pockets as much gold and silver and jewelry as he could rake together. Then he sought to escape. It was not long, however, before he was discovered by the servants of the late Marshal's brother in the house of an aunt who lived outside the city. He was brought back under arrest. The younger Chow would not make the matter public, lest it should injure the good name of his house; so he himself punished the unfaithful servant, inasmuch as he had him beaten to death in the front hall with forty blows of the heavy cudgel. Spring Plum, however, was buried with due solemnity in the ancestral burial ground, beside the River Prefect.

Then came the day of shame when the horsemen of the Golden Horde stormed Kai fong fu, the Eastern Capital of the Empire, and carried off as prisoners to their northern realm the two Emperors—both Hui Tsung, who had abdicated, and his son Kin Tsung—with all the princes and princesses, and the entire Court. The "Middle Plain" was without a ruler; on every side there was confusion and revolution; all the bonds of public order were dissolved; the population left their houses and began to flee; the black-haired mob wailed aloud as they saw houses and byres sink into dust and ashes; and the hundred families mourned beloved kinsfolk, who had hanged themselves, or remained lying where they fell by the roadside during the exodus. Parents were separated from children, husbands tore themselves away from their wives; ghosts shrieked and specters howled.

The general panic had seized upon the population of the province of Shantung among others, and even the people of Tsing ho hsien were swept away by the southward-moving waves of the mass exodus. Tsui Ping and all the other inmates of the house of Chow had long ago made their escape. Only Darling had remained. But at last she too decided to tie up her bundle and to set forth, clad in a simple cotton gown, on her journey into the unknown.

First she turned her steps towards the port of Lin tsing. There she hoped to find her parents. But when she came to the wine house which had once belonged to her lover she found it silent, and all the doors were locked. Of managers and waiters not an inch of a shadow was visible. All had fled. But by chance she met a neighbor and former acquaintance of her father's, and from him she learned that her parents had left months ago for Hu chow, in company with the silk merchant Hou. Now she resolved to make the long journey thither on foot. Valiant and full of quiet self-confidence, now and again plucking at the lute which she carried tucked under her arm, and singing a little song to it, she wandered patiently from place to place, from village to village, from city to city, always keeping to the highway that ran beside the great canal that led to her distant goal. She was quite cheerful and confident; she would not starve, for she had a little money, and at night she always found shelter among kindly people. If only her pretty little shoes had not pinched her so!

After many days of wandering she came one evening to a lonely little village not far from the city of Hsue chow fu, the capital of a prefecture. Since it was already late she knocked at the first little house she came to, in order to beg shelter for the night. An active old woman of seventy opened the door. She came from stirring a pot of soup that was steaming on the hearth.

"*Wan fu!*" said Darling, in greeting. "On account of the unsettled state of Tsing ho hsien I am on my way to Hu chow, where I hope to find my parents. It is already dark outside. Might I perhaps spend the night in your house? I could go on early tomorrow. I would pay you well for your kindness."

"Why, come in and rest yourself on the kang," said the old woman kindly, who saw at a glance that she had to deal with no beggar. "Excuse me for a little while, I must get the supper ready, as I am expecting some canal workers who generally take their meals here."

She once more approached the mighty caldron on the hearth, in which a thick rice and bean soup was simmering, and continued to stir it vigorously with the laddle. Then she poured two more platefuls of fresh vegetables into it, adding a handful of salt. Now the door opened, and six rough, sunburnt fellows, whose hair was tousled and uncombed, and who were dressed in patched sweatstained blouses and short, close-fitting breeches, while their naked feet were thickly crusted with yellow mud, came pounding into the room with their heavy spades and mattocks. They stood their implements in a corner and sat themselves on the benches round the table, which sounded as though they would crack under the weight.

"Well, mother, is there anything good to eat?" they cried impatiently.

"You just wait! There'll be enough for every mouth."

"Who's the little woman on the kang?" asked one of the five, gazing over the edge of his brimming bowl of soup. His hair, hanging in tangled strands over his deeply sunburned face, was still quite yellow with dried clay.

"A fugitive from Tsing ho hsien," the old woman told him. "She is on her way south, to look for her parents, and she wants to spend the night here."

"May I ask your name?" inquired the man who had spoken, turning to the stranger.

"I was born a Han, the daughter of Han Tao Kwo."

"What? Then you are my niece Darling!"

"Uncle, it's you! I didn't recognize you at first!" she cried, joyfully. He quickly put his bowl aside, went up to her, and clasped her tenderly in his arms, and they both shed tears of joy and emotion.

"How did you get separated from your parents, then?" he asked. "I thought you were all three living together in the Eastern Capital?"

Darling told him in detail all that had happened since then, and how she came to be separated from her parents.

"They have joined themselves with a certain silk merchant Hou from Hu chow, and I am now making my way thither all alone, in order to find them again. I have my lute with me, and if my money should give out I shall get through somehow by singing and playing. And now tell me your story!"

"When your parents went to live with you in Kai fong fu they left their little house in Tsing ho hsien in my charge. But in the long run just loafing about didn't suit me. So I sold the little house and went off on my wanderings, and here, on the excavations for the new canal, I have found employment and am earning money. I have at least as much as I can eat every day. But now, after destiny has miraculously brought us together, I shall naturally stay with you and accompany you to your parents."

"Oh, that's fine, Uncle! Then I shan't feel so forsaken!"

"Won't you take your drop of soup, little lady? You'll be hungry," the old woman interposed, as she handed her guest a full bowl.

Darling thanked her and set to. But she could manage only half the bowl. She was too unaccustomed to this coarse fare. Next morning, in the company of her uncle, she resumed her journey towards the South. But it was a long, long way. Her narrow shoes pinched her feet, her slender ankles ached. In short, she decided to sacrifice some of the jewelry which she had with her, and at Huai an she and her companion boarded a passenger junk, which took them in comfort and security to Hu chow.

There, after a little searching, she succeeded in finding her parents. They were living in the pleasant little house of Master Hou. For Master Hou, who had recently died, had bequeathed to the Hans the whole of his property, together with his six-year-old daughter. With the house went several acres of well-watered rice-fields, whose yield provided them with a sufficient livelihood. Before a year had passed Han Tao Kwo also was dead, and now the Sixth Wang married her brother-in-law. The two had been fond of each other for years. The Sixth Wang was anxious that Darling too should marry again. Her unusual beauty had not failed to attract attention in her new environment, and she had no lack of attractive offers. But Darling obstinately refused to remarry; she remained faithful to her oath, and in order to avoid further importunity she had her beautiful cloudy hair cut short, and her "butterfly antennae" shaved off, and entered a convent.

The savage horsemen of the Golden Horde, after seizing the Kao yang Pass, poured into the province of Shantung, and stormed and captured the fortified city of Tung chang. They were now advancing upon Tsing ho hsien. A new tide of refugees flowed over Tsing ho hsien, and washed away with it all who still remained and were able to escape. The masses of fugitives blocked the city gates as they made for the open country. Women shrieked, children wailed, and all fought despairingly for their lives; family ties were broken, differences of class forgotten; each found that his own life meant most to him; the stronger trampled on the weaker, tigers wrestled with dragons, lizards and serpents devoured one another. But far in the Northwest the horizon was smoking with monstrous clouds of dust that veiled the sun. The teeming enemies crept on like advancing armies of ants, like swarms of wasps, a wandering bamboo forest of bristling spears and lances. Smoking heaps of ruins and bleaching bones by the roadside marked the path of the Golden Horde.

In the city of Tsing ho hsien, of ten houses nine stood empty and forsaken. Even Moon Lady hesitated no longer to join the general mass exodus. After carefully locking all the gates of the spacious premises, and having got together a quantity of bullion and various kinds of valuables, she left the house one afternoon in the company of her brother, the younger Wu, her fifteen-year-old son, the groom Tai A, and the maid Little Jewel. Of carts or palanquins there could, of course, be no question. They had to resign themselves to traveling afoot. At the cost of hours of unspeakable effort they at last fought their way into the open through the southern gate of the city.

Moon Lady had decided to make for Tsi nan fu. There she would seek refuge with Yuen Li Shou. This Yuen Li Shou was one of the old circle of Hsi Men's friends, a member of the league of the ten sworn Brothers. On him, she believed, she could place all the more reliance inasmuch as he owed his present high position as City Commandant entirely to the friendship and protection of Hsi Men. Moreover, the children on either side, her son and Yuen's daughter, had for years been promised to each other in marriage. Under his roof she hoped to find shelter.

Twilight was already falling when the five fugitives, at a crossroads in the open country, met a strange-looking old man. The long, reddish-brown cassock which fluttered round his emaciated form revealed him as a servant of Buddha. In his hand he was holding a sacred Khakkharama staff, with the usual nine loosely-swinging, jingling metal rings upon the shaft. His feet were thrust into bast sandals, and a knapsack was strapped upon his shoulders, which was filled with sutras and prayer rolls.

He appeared quite suddenly, walking with long strides. Now he halted before the little company of five fugitives.

"Whither now, Lady Wu?" he cried to Moon Lady in a loud voice. "Where is the young assistant whom you once promised me?"

Moon Lady looked about her in dismay. Then she suddenly turned pale.

"Master, of what assistant are you speaking?"

"Don't pretend to be asleep and dreaming, noble lady. Don't you remember the hermit Pu Tsing, who once offered you the hospitality of his cave, when you had lost your way in the woods by night on descending from the summit of Tai shan? It is just fifteen years ago. And now the hour has come when you must keep your word."

Moon Lady reflected. It was true. Fifteen years earlier, when she had made the pilgrimage to the summit of Tai shan, when her little son was barely one year of age, she had lost her way, on descending from the peak, in the dense underwoods of the eastern slope, and at last, in the pitchy darkness, she had come to the cave of the hermit Pu Tsing, who had given her and her companions a hospitable reception. Next morning, when in return for his hospitality she had offered him money and a present of cloth, he had refused both, declaring that it was pre-ordained that she should find her way to his grotto, and it was also pre-ordained that she should abandon her little son to him, so that he might have a disciple who would one day continue his holy work. In vain she had pointed out that the child was her only son and heir, whom she could never give up to another. He had persisted in his monstrous demand. Then she had objected that the child was barely a year old, so that he would be of no use as an assistant. To which the hermit had replied: "Very well. Today I will not insist further. But in fifteen years' time I shall repeat my request." She had thought: "Fifteen years is a long time. Before then he may have died or forgotten the matter." And in order to get away from him she had seemed to promise that in fifteen years' time she would grant his request. How could she guess that fifteen years later this strange hermit would once more cross her path, and would actually insist that she must keep her promise?

While these thoughts flashed through her mind, the younger Wu had intervened in the strange conversation.

"Master," he said, "bethink you that this boy is her only child, the support of her old age, the heir of the house, who must one day continue the name and the line of his father, and offer pious sacrifices to his soul in the realm of shadow? How could you imagine that the boy would be willing to tear himself away from his mother, to renounce the world, and follow you as your assistant?"

"So you do not wish to give him to me?"

"Good Master, what idle talk this is! Do not delay us longer. We must hurry on! The enemy is pressing close behind us. One is no longer sure of life from one day to the next. Let us go our way!"

"Well, I will not urge you further. But it is now already late. You cannot go far in this darkness; you will lose your way. Follow me! I know of a temple near by where you will be in good hands for the night and safe from the enemy."

Moon Lady agreed, so they joined the old man. Now he turned off to the right, following a narrow path which led through a small, pitch-dark wood. They then found themselves confronted by the high, red-painted walls of an enclosure. They had come to the Yung fu se Temple.

Within all was profoundly silent. The "Tall Old Man" and the majority of the brothers had left long ago, joining the general flight to the South. Only in the great Hall of Buddha a few "cloud-wandering monks" still lingered. They were reverently kneeling beneath the tall, glazed standard lamp, beside the great bronze statue of the Buddha, burning incense and zealously murmuring prayers.

The five fugitives installed themselves for the night in two adjacent cells at the back of the monastery, not far from the "Hall of Meditation." A temple boy, whom Moon Lady remembered to have seen at the time of her earlier visit, brought them tea and a frugal dish of rice. After the scanty meal had been consumed in silence, the fugitives lay down to rest, for it was already late at night, and they were tired out by their long and exhausting march. Moon Lady, her son, and Little Jewel shared one cell, the younger Wu and Tai A the other. It was not long before they were all sunk into a profound slumber. Only Little Jewel was unable to sleep.

Moved by an inexplicable urge, she quietly rose from her couch and crept into the adjacent "Hall of Meditation." Cautiously she opened the door an inch or two, and peeped into the hall. There, in the dim light of the oil lamp that stood before the statue of Buddha, the strange old man, the hermit Pu Tsing, was huddled cross-legged and motionless on a prayer bench. He was apparently in a state of meditation, lost to the outside world. His right hand was grasping the wooden fish, the symbol of sleeplessness, and his lips were incessantly and mechanically murmuring mysterious formulae and passages from the sutras. The faint green moonlight fell slanting through a window into the dark hall, producing, in combination with the dull reddish glimmer of the half-extinguished lamp, a vague twilight, against which the crouching form and the figure of Buddha stood out in spectral unreality. No sound was audible from without. It was the hour of midnight.

The listener was able vaguely to distinguish, from the murmured speech of the old hermit, that he was appealing, moved as he was by the terror and misery of the times, to the compassion of the Buddha, and praying for the deliverance of erring humanity, for the salvation and rebirth of the souls of the damned. Dazed by the mystic twilight of the hall, lulled by the monotonous murmur, she was gradually slipping over the threshold of clear consciousness into a dream state of clairvoyant trance, in which the unreal became actual and the unseen visible.

Now it seemed to her that an icy draught was blowing through the hall, and as though a mysterious, rustling, moaning sound was heard. And before her entranced eyes there emerged outlines and shadows, which took form as specters, drifting in a long procession past the nocturnal necromancer on the prayer bench. Baleful figures they were, with bloody foreheads and calcined limbs, with severed,

855

mud-bespattered heads, with lopped arms and limping legs, with slit bellies and strangled throats. And all floated silently past him, drawn thither by the mighty spell of the necromancer, in order to hear from his lips the saving formula of conjuration which was to bring them deliverance and rebirth. So, in an endless procession, the damned souls, the victims of a bloody and lawless present, drifted past their deliverer, in order to bow before him in gratitude, and then to flee.

Hitherto the listener had been able to discover no familiar face in that procession of ghosts. But now her pupils dilated. A mighty, mail-clad form was approaching, an arrow fixed in his throat. This figure was not unknown to her.

"I am the Marshal Chow, slain by an arrow in single combat with the general of the Tartars," she heard it say to the crouching necromancer. "By the power of your spell I am permitted rebirth as a son in the house of Chen Chen, in the Eastern Capital."

The figure melted away. Another specter was approaching, well formed, but with common and ignoble features.

"I am the wealthy Hsi Men from Tsing ho hsien, and the drunkenness of lust was my ruin and my death," said the specter, "and now, through the magic spell of the Master, I am recalled to life as a son in the house of the wealthy Tan Tung in the Eastern Capital."

A third specter appeared; one who bore his severed head beneath his arm.

"I am Chen Tsing Ki, murdered by Chang Shong, but by the mercy of the Master I am born again as a son in the house of Wang in the Eastern Capital," said the head.

A woman's form followed. Her bosom revealed a gaping wound.

"I who was born a Pan, and was known as Gold Lotus, the wife of Wu Ta, the mistress of Hsi Men, was murdered by Wu Sung; but thanks to your words of deliverance I am called back to life as a daughter in the house of Li in the Eastern Capital."

Hardly had she vanished when there appeared a dwarfish cripple with a wrinkled skin.

"I am Wu Ta, poisoned by my wife, by birth a Pan, at the instigation of the tea-house woman Wang; now, by your magic power, delivered and born again as a son in the house of Fan in Chen fu."

"And I was by birth a Li, with the personal name of Ping," said a thin, female form with pale, bloodless cheeks. "The wife of Hua Tze Hsu, the mistress of Hsi Men, by the mercy of the Master I am called back to life as a daughter in the house of Yuen in the Eastern Capital."

"And I," said the following specter, "am Hua Tze Hsu, brought to my grave before my time by my hateful wife. Now, thanks to your merciful magic, I am born again as a son in the house of Chong in the Eastern Capital."

A woman with a strangled throat appeared.

"I am the wife of the servant Lai Wang, Hsi Men's mistress, who ended her life by hanging. Today by the power and the mercy of the Master I am delivered and born again as a daughter in the house of Chu in the Eastern Capital."

Yet another female specter, pale and emaciated.

"I was born a Lung, with the personal name of Spring Plum, the wife of the Marshal Chow, consumed by wicked lust and brought to death untimely, now by the Master's magic power delivered and awakened to new life as a daughter in the house of Kue in the Eastern Capital."

And again a woman's figure, with a noose about the strangled throat.

"I was born a Sun, and I was Hsi Men's concubine. I died by hanging, but through your magic power I am born again as the daughter of poor folk by the name of Chow outside the Eastern Capital."

And finally, yet another female specter; still young in years, the noose about her throat.

"I am Hsi Men's daughter, the wife of young Chen, and in despair I hanged myself. The Master's magic power has delivered me, and allowed me to live again as a daughter in the house of the barbarian Chung Kwei outside the Eastern Capital."

Little Jewel was shaken by a sudden shuddering, and she awakened from her trance. She rubbed her eyes. The vision had flown. She could see only the mysterious old man, now as before crouching motionless on the prayer bench. The lamp was almost burnt out. She felt afraid; suddenly she hurried back to her cell and crept under the warm blankets.

She had hardly laid herself down when Moon Lady, beside her, woke from sleep with a start, suppressing a shriek. Her body was covered with a cold sweat.

"Horrible! Horrible!" she exclaimed, with panting breath.

"What is it, dear Mistress?" asked Little Jewel.

"I had a terrible vision in a dream. Listen! I dreamed that we had safely arrived in Tsi nan fu, and that we were at first received most courteously and kindly by Yuen Li Shou. Since he is a widower, an elderly lady who lived near by was present at our meeting, in order to keep us women company in the rear apartments. My son and my brother and Tai A he entertained and lodged in the front of the house.

"So all was well, and I had no thought of evil. I told him that we had fled before the Tartars, and that we should wish to live with him for a time, until order and security were restored in the land. I said also that I should like to assist in celebrating in his house the marriage of our two children, who had been betrothed since their earliest childhood, and I gave him, quite unsuspectingly, the golden ring, the hundred pearls, and the handful of jewels which I had brought as a wedding present for his daughter. Then it occurred to me that he had accepted the presents in silence, without saying a word about the marriage.

"That night Neighbor Wang shared my room with me. We chatted together for a while before going to sleep, and then she suddenly began to sound me, as to whether I should be inclined to marry Master Yuen. He had worshiped me for years, and he did not want to go on living the life of a solitary pike. One could then celebrate a double wedding, and after the conclusion of peace we could return together to Tsing ho hsien. Of course, I could see that my person meant less to him than my house and my fortune.

Now, of course, I am quite indifferent to him, and besides, I am not thinking of remarrying. I know what is proper for a respectable widow. I was therefore not a little indignant at the proposal, but I concealed my anger, and was silent. I assumed that Mistress Wang would infer from my silence my aversion to the proposal, and would advise her principal accordingly.

"Next evening he invited me to drink a beaker of wine with him in the women's apartments. I thought, of course, that this was in honor of the children's marriage, and had no scruples as to accepting his invitation. Suddenly, as we were sitting at the table, he began to tell me how he had always been in love with me, and how he desired nothing more ardently than to marry me and celebrate a double wedding. I replied, very angrily, that he concealed the thoughts of a dog beneath his human skin; and I asked him whether this was his loyalty to his friend Hsi Men, who in his lifetime had shown him nothing but kindness. In short, I indignantly rejected his offer.

"Then he laughed insolently, moved up close beside me, embraced me, and began in the most repulsive way to whine that I must listen to him; indeed, he even attempted to force me to drink out of his beaker. In my distress I asked to see my brother, saying that I positively must consult him first.

"Again he gave a vulgar, scornful laugh. 'Your brother, and Tai A too, are already dead. I killed them. You will ask for them in vain,' he said. Then he turned to his servants, and said: 'Hey, just let the lady see the evidence! You know what I mean.'

"Immediately afterwards, to my horror, I was shown a great dish, on which lay the bloody, severed heads of my brother and the faithful Tai A. I shrieked and fell half swooning to the floor. He lifted me up, and said to me: 'Don't take the matter so tragically! What do they matter? Be sensible and become my wife! I have rank and office: am I not worthy of you?'

"In my distress I told myself that I must hold him in play and employ simulation. So I put on an assumed smile, and replied, gently and confidentially: 'Good. I will be yours. But only under one condition.'

" 'Speak. I will fulfill every condition if only you will be mine,' he said.

" 'You must first marry my son to your daughter.'

" 'That's a trifle,' he said, and he sent for the two children. He made them stand facing each other and empty a nuptial goblet; then he declared that they were married and sent them off to the bridal chamber. Of course, I had not imagined that he would do it so quickly, and now, as he tried to drag me to the couch, I resisted with all my might and pushed him away. Then he angrily called me a trollop and a cheat, and shouted that my son should pay for my behavior. He reached under the couch and pulled out a sword. Then he ran into the bridal chamber and returned at once with the head of my son. It was dripping with blood. At this horrible sight I had to shriek aloud, and with that I woke."

She had finished her long narrative.

"Nai nai, just before that I too had a strange vision," said Little Jewel, and now she in her turn told her mistress how she could not sleep, and how she had crept along to the "Hall of Meditation," and there, peeping through the chink of the door, she had listened to the midnight converse of the ancient hermit and the specters.

"Evidently you have seen the dead who lie buried all about here, and haunt the neighborhood at midnight," said Moon Lady.

Outside the dawn was already gray. In the distance the crowing of the first cocks was heard. Moon Lady and Little Jewel hastily rose from their couch, washed themselves, and made themselves ready to continue their journey. But first they wished to burn a little incense in the honor of Buddha. As they entered the "Hall of Meditation," they saw the ancient hermit still crouching on the prayer bench.

"Well, Mistress Wu," he cried to Moon Lady, "did you have a revelation last night? Do you believe now in my magic power?"

Moon Lady humbly knelt before him.

"Venerable Master, pardon your incredulous pupil! Her eyes are earthly substance, and did not realize that you are a venerable Buddha. I have had a revelation in a dream, and now I see."

"If that is so, then you will not go to Tsi nan fu. For disaster awaits you there. If you were to go there all would happen even as I revealed to you in your dream. You would all die, all the five of you. Do you now realize that our meeting was a happy dispensation for you? It was vouchsafed to you because in your life you have performed various good works. And now listen. The accursed soul of your dead husband Hsi Men lives on in your son. If you were to keep him beside you, he would only cause you grief; he would squander your fortune and ruin your household; and when he came to die, you may be sure that his head and his trunk would lie in different places. In order to spare you this grief I have appointed him my assistant. You know the proverb:

"*A son prepared to serve the Buddha to the end*
Will let nine sinful ancestors to Heaven ascend.

"I will deliver his soul if you give me the boy as my assistant. For the time being it is still the tainted soul of his father. Do you not believe me? Come with me! I will give you proof."

Preceding the two women, he entered the cell where the boy was still lying fast asleep. With his magic Khakkharama staff he touched the sleeper's head, and lo! in a moment he was transformed into Hsi Men. He wore a heavy wooden collar about his neck, and iron chains were fastened round his body. Now again the hermit touched him with the staff, and he was once more the peacefully slumbering boy.

"It is really he! My dear, kind Hsi Men!" cried Moon Lady, beside herself with emotion.

The boy opened his eyes.

"Do you really want to follow the Master, have your hair cut off, and renounce the world?" cried the bewildered Moon Lady, tempestuously. "You have just come to the age when you would perpetuate your race! And now the Master wants to run away with you! But I won't let you go!"

861

And she embraced him as though to hold him fast forever.

"You will henceforth bear the temple name of Ming Wu, 'Bright Revelation,'" said the old man calmly to his new assistant. He took him by the hand and turned to go.

"You need not flee any farther," he said, turning to the younger Wu. "Very soon the enemy will turn back; there will be peace, and the 'Middle Plain' will once more have a ruler, or rather two. For the Empire will divide into a Northern and a Southern realm. In ten days' time you may safely return home. Then you will have nothing more to fear."

"Master, tell me at least when I shall see my child again?" pleaded Moon Lady. She still refused to release the boy.

"Silence! There is someone coming!" He pointed over her head. His trick was successful. All turned their heads, and looked behind them; Moon Lady let go of her son's hand. In a moment the old hermit, together with his assistant, had changed into a cloud of blue vapor and had disappeared.

The hermit's prediction was fulfilled. Before ten days had passed the Golden Horde had begun to retreat. Peace was concluded, and the "Middle Plain" was no longer without a ruler. The Northern Empire, with Kai fong fu as its capital, was ruled by Chang Pang Chang as regent. In Hangchow, which became the capital of the Southern Empire, Prince Kang ascended the throne as the Emperor Kao Tsung. The inhabitants returned to their homes and their peaceful avocations.

Moon Lady followed the hermit's advice: with her three companions she remained in the temple of Yung fu se, and was not molested by the enemy. On the tenth day she returned home with her escort. She found her house and all her possessions undamaged. Nothing was missing. As she now had no son, she appointed Tai A her heir, in reward for his faithful service to his employers in good and evil times alike. Moreover, she wished him to continue her husband's line as far as the outer world was concerned, and she therefore gave him the name of Hsi Men An. By the people he was generally known as "the little Hsi Men." He tended Moon Lady to the day of her death as faithfully as a son. She died at the advanced age of seventy years, and had an easy and a beautiful death. This was the blessing vouchsafed her, inasmuch as all her years she had been a good and respectable wife.

> Scan our whole story briefly, asking what it meant:
> Event, we see, is strangely echoed by event.
> A dissolute man of power dies long before his time,
> A bold insidious rogue is snared in his own lime.
> Spring Plum and Lady Ping are each vouchsafed a son,
> But soon, though fortune shines, their earthly race is run.
> Jade Fountain's and Moon Lady's is a brighter page:
> Theirs the reward of virtue—peace, and honored age.
> Gold Lotus? Hers a fate for shuddering and tears!
> But this tale's fragrance will outlast a thousand years.